RHETORICAL ARGUMENTATION
IN PHILO OF ALEXANDRIA

Program in Judaic Studies
Brown University
BROWN JUDAIC STUDIES

Edited by
Shaye J. D. Cohen

Number 322
Studia Philonica Monographs 2
RHETORICAL ARGUMENTATION
IN PHILO OF ALEXANDRIA

by
Manuel Alexandre, Jr.

RHETORICAL ARGUMENTATION
IN PHILO OF ALEXANDRIA

by
Manuel Alexandre, Jr.

With a Foreword by
Burton L. Mack

Scholars Press
Atlanta, Georgia

RHETORICAL ARGUMENTATION IN PHILO OF ALEXANDRIA

by
Manuel Alexandre, Jr.

Copyright © 1999 by Brown University
Copyright © 2007 by the Society of Biblical Literature
Paperback published 2009 by the Society of Biblical Literature

All rights reserved. No part of this work may be reproduced or transmitted in any form or by any means, electronic or mechanical, including photocopying and recording, or by means of any information storage or retrieval system, except as may be expressly permitted by the 1976 Copyright Act or in writing from the Society of Biblical Literature, 825 Houston Mill Road, Atlanta, GA 30329.

Library of Congress Cataloging-in-Publication Data
Alexandre, Manuel, 1936–
 [Argumentação retórica em Fílon de Alexandria. English]
 Rhetorical argumentation in Philo of Alexandria / by Manuel Alexandre, Jr. ; with a foreword by Burton L. Mack.
   p. cm.— (Studia Philonica monographs) (Brown Judaic studies ; no. 322)
 Includes bibliographical references and index.
 ISBN 0-7885-0582-3 (cloth : alk. paper)—ISBN 978-1-58983-440-8 (paper : alk. paper)
 1. Philo, of Alexandria—Language. 2. Rhetoric, Ancient. I. Title. II. Series. III. Series: Brown Judaic studies ; no. 322.
B689.Z7A64 1999
181'.06—dc21   99-41853
                                        CIP

Printed in the United States of America
on acid-free paper

STUDIA PHILONICA MONOGRAPHS

STUDIES IN HELLENISTIC JUDAISM

EDITOR
David M. Hay, *Coe College, Cedar Rapids*

ADVISORY BOARD

Hans Dieter Betz, *University of Chicago*
Ellen Birnbaum, *Harvard University*
Peder Borgen, *University of Trondheim*
Jacques Cazeaux, *CNRS, University of Lyon*
Lester Grabbe, *University of Hull*
Annewies van den Hoek, *Harvard Divinity School*
Pieter W. van der Horst, *Utrecht University*
Jean Laporte, *Paris*
Burton L. Mack, *Claremont Graduate School, Claremont*
Alan Mendelson, *McMaster University*
Birger A. Pearson, *University of California at Santa Barbara*
Robert Radice, *Sacred Heart University, Milan*
Jean Riaud, *Catholic University, Angers*
James R. Royse, *San Francisco*
David T. Runia, *Universities of Leiden and Utrecht*
Dorothy Sly, *University of Windsor*
Gregory E. Sterling, *University of Notre Dame*
Abraham Terian, *St. Nersess Armenian Seminary*
Thomas H. Tobin S. J., *Loyola University, Chicago*
Herold D. Weiss, *St. Mary's College, Notre Dame*
David Winston, *Graduate Theological Union, Berkeley*

Like *The Studia Philonica Annual*, the Studia Philonica Monographs series accepts monographs in the area of Hellenistic Judaism, with special emphasis on Philo and his *Umwelt*. Proposals for books to be published in the Monograph series should be sent to Prof. David M. Hay, Coe College, Cedar Rapids, IA 52402, U.S.A.

Article-length contributions should be sent to the American Editor of *The Studia Philonica Annual,* Prof. Gregory E. Sterling, Department of Theology, University of Notre Dame, Notre Dame, IN 46556, U.S.A. Books for review in the *Annual* should be sent to the Book Review Editor, Prof. Alan Mendelson, Department of Religion, McMaster University, Hamilton, Ontario L8S 4K1, Canada.

CONTENTS

Foreword by Burton L. Mack xi

Preface xiii

Abbreviations
   1. Of writings in the *Corpus Philonicum* xv
   2. Other abbreviations xvi

General Introduction 1
   1. Historical view of Philo's literary personality 3
   2. New directions in Philonic studies 5
   3. A question of method 10
   4. In defense of a rhetorical reading of the Philonic *corpus* 14
   5. Foundation and plan of the present study 17

PART ONE
PHILO OF ALEXANDRIA IN THE CONTEXT OF RHETORICAL ARGUMENTATION

Introduction 23

Chapter One: STRUCTURES OF ARGUMENTATION IN GRECO-ROMAN
    RHETORIC 31
   I   The Platonic Theory of Argumentation 31
   II Formal Structure of an Argument in the Greek Rhetorical
      Tradition 39
      A. The Aristotelian Structure of Rhetorical Argument 39
      B. Categories of Argumentation in Anaximenes' *Rhetorica
         ad Alexandrum* 54
   III Formal Structure of an Argument in the Latin Rhetorical
      Tradition 58
      A. A Complete Argument According to *Rhetorica ad
         Herennium* 58
      B. Theory of Argumentation in Cicero and Quintilian 60
   IV Synoptic Chart of Formal Argumentation Structures 74

Chapter Two: PHILO'S ACCESS TO ARGUMENTATION THEORY 77
   I   The Impact of Rhetorical Argumentation on the Cultural
      Environment of Alexandria 79

II	The Existential Commitment and CulturalTraining of Philo of Alexandria	84
	A. Hellenization of the Jews	84
	B. Philo in the Context of the Hellenistic World	87
III	The Nature of Philonic Discourse and Importance of Rhetorical Argumentation in his Work	92
	A. Exegetical Character of Philo's Treatises	92
	B. Rhetorical Argumentation as an Exegetical Instrument	96

Conclusion 104

PART TWO
ARGUMENTATION STRUCTURES IN PHILO'S WORK

Introduction 107

Chapter Three: FORMAL STRUCTURE OF A DISCOURSE 109
   I   In a Complete Treatise 109
       1. *De Vita Mosis* 109
       2. *Quod Omnis Probus Liber Sit* 114
   II Discourses Embedded in Treatises 132
       1. Judah's Defense (*De Iosepho* 222-231) 132
       2. Discourse on the Search for God (*De Praemiis et Poenis* 24-51) 136
       3. Speech on Virtue (*De Sacrificiis Abelis et Caini* 21-44) 143
       4. Speech on the Drunkenness of the Wise Man (*De Plantatione* 140-177) 153
       5. Letter from King Agrippa to Gaius Caligula (*Legatio ad Gaium* 236-329) 158

Chapter Four: STRUCTURES OF A COMPLETE ARGUMENT 176
   I   In the Argumentation of a Thesis 177
       1. *Legum Allegoriae* II, 1-3 178
       2. *De Opificio Mundi* 7-12 180
       3. *De Fuga et Inventione* 68-70 and *De Opificio Mundi* 134-135 182
       4. *De Iosepho* 28-31 and 125-143 186
       5. *De Sobrietate* 2-16 193
       6. *De Posteritate Caini* 100-111 197
   II In the Elaborate Development of a Theme 204
       1. *Quod Deterius Potiori Insidiari Solet* 34-45 204
       2. *De Migratione Abrahami* 70-82 209

| | CONTENTS | ix |

    3. *De Cherubim* 1-10, 40-52 and 65-83 213
    4. *De Mutatione Nominum* 252-263 223

Chapter Five: RHYTHMIC AND PERIODIC STRUCTURES 234
  I   Introduction 234
  II Examples of Rhythmic and Periodic Structures in Philo 238
    1. *Legatio ad Gaium* 53-56 238
    2. *De Vita Mosis* II, 253-255 240
    3. *In Flaccum* 123-124 243
    4. *De Ebrietate* 157-159 245

CONCLUSION 248
  1. Philosophical Character of his Argumentation 248
  2. Rhetorical Argumentation as a Technique of Argumentation
     and Exposition 250

BIBLIOGRAPHY 251
  I   On Philo of Alexandria 251
  II On Rhetoric: Theory of Argumentation 273
  III Miscellaneous 283

INDICES 285
  I   Index of Passages from Philo 287
  II Index of Authors 291
    1. Index of ancient authors 291
    2. Index of modern authors 292
  III Index of Rhetorical Terms 295
    1. Index of Greek rhetorical terms 295
    2. Index of Latin rhetorical terms 297
    3. Index of English rhetorical terms 299

FOREWORD

by
BURTON L. MACK

This study by Manuel Alexandre, Jr. is a translation from the Portuguese original, *Argumentação Retórica em Fílon de Alexandria*, Biblioteca Euphrosyne 4 (Lisbon: Instituto Nacional de Investigação Cientifica, 1990), with some revisions and additions. It presents the results of a research program undertaken toward the end of the 1970s. About that time a shift in focus for rhetorical studies was clearly under way, from a traditional emphasis upon matters of style and ornamentation to theories of argumentation. Also during the 1970s, a small group of scholars meeting at McCormick Theological Seminary in Chicago and the Institute for Antiquity and Christianity at Claremont had begun to explore the incidence of rhetorical terms, tropes, and patterns of argumentation in the Philonic corpus. Mr. Alexandre joined this group and, intrigued by the question of classical rhetoric in support of the Philonic program of scriptural interpretation, decided to put it to the test.

His study represents a huge undertaking. Not only was it necessary to master the classical rhetorical texts to determine the logic of the various patterns of persuasion they described. An analysis of the entire Philonic corpus was necessary in order to ascertain the incidence and structural significance of rhetorical forms used in its compositions. This was not an easy task. Traditionally, Philo had been viewed as a thinker whose discourse was marked by philosophic and conceptual system building. It was also the case that recent studies had begun to emphasize the exegetical, hermeneutical, and allegorical designs of Philo's commentaries. To pursue the structural significance of rhetorical patterns of argumentation in support of allegorical commentary on the Jewish scriptures was a novel challenge. Alexandre's demonstration of the formal structure of a complete treatise, the rhetorical function of the speeches in a treatise, the use of the complete argument in exegetical *lemmata*, and the effect of periodic structures in smaller units of composition, is a decided advance in our understanding of Philo's cross-cultural program.

Scholars interested in the history of classical rhetoric, and especially its incidence and employment during the early Roman period, will find this study helpful. It demonstrates the vitality and pervasive influence of rhetorical culture during the first century. It also provides a major example of the use of rhetoric in the composition of literary forms not addressed in the handbooks. As for scholars interested in the cross-cultural exchanges during the Greco-Roman period, and especially the phenomenon we call Hellenistic Judaism, this demonstration of the linguistic tools used to argue for cultural translation marks a human endeavor, if not achievement, worthy of much more thought. As it appears, Greek rhetoric was used largely to support a translation designed to emphasize the similarities of two quite difference cultural mentalities. But the "proofs" that counted were not all taken from the Greek traditions of culture. Thus the differences that mattered from a Jewish point of view were also guarded and implicitly infused with conceptual honors and rhetorical status.

I would say that Alexandre's study adds considerable weight to the seriousness with which Philo's allegorical program must have been pursued. And insofar as Philo may be taken as a representative thinker of the phenomenon we call Hellenistic Judaism, the study shows that rhetoric can be used to assess the persuasiveness of its discourse for those engaged in crossing the cultural boundaries of that time. I am pleased to see this book appear and trust that others will find it persuasive.

Claremont, California
March 15, 1998

PREFACE

The origins of this book go back to 1980, when I began reading Philo under the conviction that a rhetorical analysis of his work directed at the theory of argumentation could help us better understand the structure and basic literary motivation of his discourse. Soon I noticed the argumentative character of most of his treatises and discovered that he had mastered the conventions of this art.

Among the scholars who most contributed with their knowledge and scientific experience toward the development of this study I am particularly indebted and especially grateful to two notable Philonists: to Prof. Burton Mack, who gave me the first insights in this direction while I was doing research in Claremont, and proved along those years to be both an inspiring critic and a gracious advisor; and to Prof. Valentin Nikiprowetzky, of blessed memory, for the manner in which he graciously put me in contact with the progressing works of other Philonists, for his scientific rigor in evaluating my work, and for the patience with which he shared his knowledge and directed me to other sources.

Professors Earle Hilgert of the Philo Institute in Chicago, Jacques Cazeaux of Lyon, and David Winston of Berkeley also deserve my appreciation, not only for the helpful support they gave me, but also for the material they granted me and for their expert advice on various occasions. I am grateful to Prof. Edward O'Neil of the University of Southern California and his collaborators in the Hellenistic Text Seminar for allowing me to take part in their fruitful meetings on rhetorical themes and texts over a period of two years, and to Prof. Alain Michel at the Institut des Études Latins, University of Paris, Sorbonne, for sharing his ideas on Philo's culture, the philosophical nature of his argumentation and his affinity to Cicero, thus broadening the scope and range of my own research.

Finally, I cannot but pay well-deserved tribute here to all those who, in some way, helped make this work possible, not forgetting the distinguished colleagues who helped me with the English version. I would like especially to express my gratitude to Prof. David Hay for his patient reading and most helpful comments on the last drafts of this book, and to Arthur Brown and Allan Pallister for their precious help.

The geographical and cultural setting of my work would have been much more limited if I had not received a generous three-year scholarship from the Calouste Gulbenkian Foundation and additional support from other institutions. Their scientific, institutional, affective and financial contributions not only made costly trips possible but also facilitated my research. To them I am very grateful; especially to the Colouste Gulbenkian Foundation for the generous support provided along the years, and the subsidies that made possible this translation, and to the editor for *Studia Philonica*, Dr. Shaye J.D. Cohen, who graciously accepted it for publication in the *Studia Philonica Monograph Series* and contributed toward the cost of producing the camera-ready copy.

I can never adequately acknowledge all my debts to those people in the scholarly community who, through their example of academic excellence and integrity, have taught me, inspired me and helped me to complete this work. My sincere appreciation to all of them is also extended to Mrs. Runia-Deenick for the finished production of this text.

Manuel Alexandre Jr.

ABBREVIATIONS

1. *Of Writings in the Corpus Philonicum*

For the designation of Philo's treatises we have as a rule adopted the abbreviations used in the French Arnaldez-Mondézert-Pouilloux edition, since we find them simpler and more practical. As for the titles of classical works, we have normally chosen to use their complete names, in Latin, following the forms listed in Liddell and Scott-Jones-McKenzie, *A Greek-English Lexicon* (Oxford: Clarendon Press, 1977).

Abr.	*De Abrahamo*
Aet.	*De Aeternitate mundi*
Agric.	*De agricultura*
Alex.	*Alexander*
Anim.	*De animalibus*
Cher.	*De Cherubim*
Confus.	*De confusione linguarum*
Congr.	*De congressu eruditionis gratia*
Contempl.	*De uita contemplatiua*
Decal.	*De decalogo*
Deter.	*Quod deterius potiori insidiari soleat*
Deus	*Quod Deus sit immutabilis*
Ebr.	*De ebrietate*
Flacc.	*In Flaccum*
Fug.	*De fuga et inuentione*
Gig.	*De gigantibus*
Her.	*Quis rerum diuinarum heres sit*
Hypoth.	*Hypothetica (Apologia pro Judaeis)*
Ios.	*De Iosepho*
Legat.	*Legatio ad Gaium*
Leg. I, II, III	*Legum allegoriae I, II, III*
Migr.	*De migratione Abrahami*
Mos. I, II	*De uita Mosis I, II*
Mutat.	*De mutatione nominum*
Opif.	*De opificio mundi*
Plant.	*De plantatione*
Poster.	*De posteritate Caini*
Praem.	*De praemiis et poenis, de exsecrationibus*

Prob.	*Quod omnis probus liber sit*
Prov. I, II	*De Prouidentia I, II*
Quaest. Gen. I, II, III, IV	*Quaestiones et solutiones in Genesim*
Quaest. Ex.	*Quaestiones et solutiones in Exodum*
Sacrif.	*De sacrificiis Abelis et Caini*
Sobr.	*De sobrietate*
Somn. I, II	*De Somniis I, II*
Spec. I, II, III, IV	*De specialibus legibus I, II, III, IV*
Virt.	*De Virtutibus*

2. *Other Abbreviations*

When not cited in their entirety, the titles of periodicals, collections and reference works will be designated by the following abbreviations:

AC	*L'antiquité classique*
A.D.	Anno Domini
AJP	*American Journal of Philology*
AJS	Association for Jewish Studies
AJSL	*American Journal of Semitic Languages*
ALGHJ	*Arbeiten zur Literatur und Geschichte des hellenistischen Judentums.* Leiden: Brill
ANRW	*Aufstieg und Niedergang der römischen Welt*
AP	*L'année philologique*
APA	American Philological Association, Tübingen
B.C.	Before Christ
BGBE	Beiträge zur Geschichte der biblischen Exegese
BGBH	Beiträge zur Geschichte der biblischen Hermeneutik
BGGPR	Beiträge zur Geschichte der griechischen Philosophie
BHT	Beiträge zur historischen Theologie
Bib	*Biblica*
BibOr	*Biblica et Orientalia*
BJRL	*Bulletin of John Rylands Library*
BJS	Brown Judaic Studies
BKP	Beiträge zur klassischen Philologie
BL	*Bibel und Leben*
BR	*Biblical Research,* Journal of the Chicago Society of Biblical Research
CBQ	*Catholic Biblical Quarterly*
CCARJ	*Central Conference American Rabbis Journal*
Cith	*Cithara*

CIG	*Corpus inscriptionum graecarum*
CIJ	*Corpus inscriptionum judaicarum*
CIL	*Corpus inscriptionum latinarum*
CIS	*Corpus inscriptionum semiticarum*
CJ	*Classical Journal*
CP	*Classical Philology*
CPJ	*Corpus papirorum judaicorum*
CQ	*Classical Quarterly*
CRINT	*Compendium rerum judaicarum ad Novum Testamentum*
CS	*Cahiers sioniens*
CSSJ	*Central States Speech Journal*
CTJ	*Calvin Theological Journal*
CW	*Classical World*
DBS	*Dictionnaire de la Bible, Supplement* Paris: Latouzey & Ané, 1966
DELG	*Dictionnaire étymólogique de la langue grecque*. P. Chantraine; Paris: Klincksieck, 1968-1980
Di	*Dionysius*
EJ	*Encyclopaedia Judaica*. Eds. C. Roth and G. Wigoder. Jerusalem: Keter Publishing House, 1971
ETL	*Ephemerides Theologicae Lovanienses*
FRLANT	Forschungen zur Religion und Literatur des Alten und Neuen *Testaments*. Göttingen: Vandenhoeck und Rupprecht
Gl	*Glotta*
GRBS	Greek, Roman and Byzantine Studies
HDR	Harvard Dissertations in Religion
He	*Hermes*. Zeitschrift für klassische Philologie
HNT	*Handbuch zum Neuen Testament*
Ho	*Horeb*
HSCP	*Harvard Studies in Classical Philology*
HTR	*Harvard Theological Review*
HTS	Harvard Theological Studies
HUCA	*Hebrew Union College Annual*
IDB	*Interpreter's Dictionary of the Bible*. Ed. G. A. Buttrick. 4 vols. New York: Abingdon Press, 1962
IL	*L'information littéraire*
JAFA	*Journal of American Forensic Association*
JBL	*Journal of Biblical Literature*
JBR	*Journal of Bible and Religion*
JES	*Journal of Ecumenical Studies*
JHS	*Journal of Hellenistic Studies*
JJS	*Journal of Jewish Studies*

JQR	*Jewish Quarterly Review*
JSJ	*Journal for the Study of Judaism in the Persian, Hellenistic and Roman Period*
JSS	*Journal of Semitic Studies*
JTS	*Journal of Theological Studies*
JU	*Judaica*
KZRT	*Kairos. Zeitschrift für Religionswissenschaft und Theologie*
Lat	*Latomus*
LCL	Loeb Classical Library. Cambridge: Harvard University Press
LCM	*Liverpool Classical Monthly*
LQ	*Lutheran Quarterly*
LSJ	Liddel-Scott-Jones, *Greek-English Lexicon*
LTP	*Laval théologique et philosophique*
LXX	*Septuaginta*. 8th ed. Alfred Rahlfs. Stuttgart, 1965
MGWJ	*Monatsschrift für die Geschichte und Wissenschaft des Judentums*
MnSuppl	*Mnemosyne, Supplements*. Bibliotheca Batava
MSR	Mélanges de science religieuse
NT	*Nouum Testamentum. An International Quarterly for New Testament and Related Studies*
NTS	*New Testament Studies*
NTSuppl	*Nouum Testamentum, Supplements*
PAL	Philon d'Alexandrie, Lyon, September 11-16, 1966, Colloquium. Paris: Édition du Centre Nationale de la Recherche Scientifique, 1967
PCCHS	Protocol of the Colloquy of the Center for Hermeneutical Studies
PCW	*Philo Alexandrinus, Opera edita et versa*. Ed. L. Cohn and P. Wendland, 7 vols. Berlin: W. de Gruyter, 1962
Pho	*Phoenix*
PhRh	*Philosophy and Rhetoric*
PLCL	*Philo, with an English Translation*. Ed. F. H. Colson and G. H. Whitaker. Loeb Classical Library, 12 vols.; Cambridge: Cambridge University Press, 1929-1953
PM	*Les Oeuvres de Philon d'Alexandrie*. Ed. Mondésert *et alii*. Paris: Éditions du Cerf, 1961-1992
Po	*Poétique*
PR	*Philosophical Review*
PSCA	Proceedings of the Summer Conference on Argumentation. Alta: University of Utah, 1980
QJS	*Quarterly Journal of Speech*
RAC	*Reallexikon für Antike und Christentum*. Ed. Theodor Klauser. Stuttgart: Hiersemann, 1950-

RB	*Revue Biblique*
RBib	*Rivista Biblica*
RE	*Realencyclopaedie der klassischen Altertumswissenschaft.* Paulys. Begonnen von G. Wissowa, herausgegeben von W. Kroll und K. Mittelhaus
RESup	Supplement to RE
REG	*Revue des Études Grecques*
REL	*Revue des Études Latines*
RESS	*Revue Européenne de Sciences Sociales*
RFIC	*Rivista di Filologia e di Istruzione Classica*
Rhe	*Rhetorica.* A Journal of the History of Rhetoric
RHPR	*Revue d'Histoire et de Philosophie Religieuses*
RHR	*Revue d'Histoire des Religions*
RIP	*Revue Internationale de Philosophie*
RMM	*Revue de Métaphysique et de Morale*
RP	*Revue de Philologie*
RPFE	*Revue Philosophique de la France et de l'Étranger*
RPL	*Revue Philosophique de Louvain*
RR	*Review of Religion*
RS	*Retorische Studien*
RSPT	*Revue des Sciences Philosophiques et Religieuses*
RSR	Recherches de sciences religieuses
RTP	*Revue de Théologie et de Philosophie*
SBLSP	*Society of Biblical Literature, Seminar Papers*
SBSDS	*Society of Biblical Studies, Dissertation Series*
SCa	*Scuola Cattolica*
SE	*Science et Esprit*
Sem	*Semeia.* An Experimental Journal for Biblical Criticism
Semit	*Semitica*
Ser	*Serafad.* Revista del Instituto Arias Montano de Estudios Hebraicos y Oriente Próximo. Madrid, Barcelona
SH	*Studia Hellenistica*
SJ	*Studia Judaica*
SJLA	*Studies in Judaism in Late Christianity*
SL	*Studia Linguistica*
SM	*Speech Monographs*
SP	*Studia Philonica*
SPhA	*The Studia Philonica Annual*
SSCJ	*Southern Speech Communication Journal*
ST	*Studia Theologica*
SVF	*Stoicorum Veterum Fragmenta.* Ed. H. F. A. von Arnim. Leipzig: Teubner, 1903-1924

TDNT	*Theological Dictionary of the New Testament*. Ed. G. Kittel, G. Friedrich. Grand Rapids: Eerdmans, 1964-1976
TGL	*Thesaurus Graecae Linguae*. Graz: Akademische Druck und Verlagsanstalt, 1954
TS	*Theological Studies*
TU	Texte und Untersuchungen zur Geschichte *der altchristlichen Literatur*. Berlin: Akadamie Verlag
TZ	*Theologische Zeitschrift*
UCPCS	University of California Publications, Classical Studies
UJE	*Universal Jewish Encyclopedia*. 10 vols. New York: Universal Jewish Encyclopedia Inc., 1939-1943
VChr	*Vigiliae Christianae*
Viv	*Vivarium*
VT	*Vetus Testamentum*
WS	*Wiener Studien. Zeitschrift für klassische Philologie*
YCS	*Yale Classical Studies*
YPR	*Yale Publications in Religion*
ZAW	*Zeitschrift für alttestamentliche Wissenschaft*
ZKT	*Zeitschrift für katolische Theologie*
ZNW	*Zeitschrift für neutestamentliche Wissenschaft*

GENERAL INTRODUCTION

In the panorama of Greek Hellenistic literature, Philo of Alexandria emerges as a prolific writer and bold interpreter of Scripture. He was a man of culture without boundaries, an inhabitant of two worlds, firmly committed to the mission of expounding and perpetuating his Hebrew faith in the setting of Hellenistic language and thought.

Coming from one of the most noble and prosperous Jewish families of the Diaspora, Philo was born about two decades before the beginning of our era. There he spent nearly all of his days devoted to study, meditation and contemplation, to intellectual labor and the formal production of a literary *corpus* of considerable density and extension.

We would like to have more precise chronological information about his life. The only dates we have for him are his journey to Rome in 39/40 A.D. as leader of an embassy protesting the atrocities suffered by the Alexandrian Jews and the publication of a historical-theological treatise concerning that journey, one or two years later. The reference made to his advanced age at the beginning of *Legatio ad Gaium,* has led scholars to fix his birth during the last quarter of the first century B.C., and to identify 50 A.D. as the approximate date of his death. The little we know about him has been handed down to us through tradition and acquired from a few autobiographical references.[1]

Nevertheless, the work he left us is an eloquent testimony to the character of this unrivaled figure of Hellenistic Judaism.[2] The forty-nine books that remain to us, representing no more than three-fourths of his total work,[3] are almost entirely a commentary on the Pentateuch. In our opinion these should be divided into the following categories: (1) *Quaestiones et Solutiones in Genesim* and *Quaestiones et Solutiones in Exodum;* (2) an allegorical commentary and exposition of the Law; (3) and works of a general nature.[4]

---

[1] *Spec.* III, 1-6; *Leg.* II, 85; *Migr.* 34-35; *Congr.* 74-76; *Prob.* 26-27, 141; *Prov.* II, 103, 107. Despite the shadow in which the chronology of Philo's life exists, there is a general consensus that he must have been born between 25 and 10 B.C. and died during the decade of 40 A.D. Ronald Williamson however (*Jews in the Hellenistic World: Philo* [Cambridge: Cambridge University Press, 1989], pp. 1-2), places his birth as early as *c.* 30 B.C.
[2] "Le style c'est l'homme." Cf. A. Michel, "Rhétorique, philosophie et esthétique générale," *Revue des Études Latines* (Paris: 1973), p. 302-326.
[3] R. M. Seltzer, *Jewish People, Jewish Thought: The Jewish Experience in History* (New York, London: Macmillan Publishing Co., Inc., 1980), p. 206.
[4] Cf. S. Sandmel, *Philo of Alexandria, an Introduction* (New York, Oxford: Oxford University Press, 1979), p. 29-81. Despite the countless attempts at grouping Philo's works, it has not

His literary personality has progressively drawn more and more attention from specialists in very diverse areas of study and research.[5] In the last fifty

---

yet been possible to reconstruct a chronological order. This is the reason they are usually catalogued according to the alphabetical order of their Latin titles. See also R. Radice, *Filone di Alessandria, "L'Erede delle Cose Divine"* (Milan: Rusconi, 1981), p. 74-75.

Efforts to classify works by Philo, begun in England by T. Mangey (Φίλωνος τοῦ ᾽Ιουδαίου τὰ εὑρισκόμενα ἅπαντα . . . , London, 1742, 2 vols.) and continued in Germany by various scholars up to E. Schürer (*The Jewish People*, trad. [Edinburgh, 1891] part II, vol. III, p. 322-361), were taken up again by M. L. Massebieau ("Le classement des oeuvres de Philon," *Bibliothèque de l'École Pratique des Hautes Études, Sciences Religieuses*, T. I. [Paris, 1889] p. 1-91) and took concrete form in the hands of É. Bréhier ("Essai sur la chronologie de la vie et des oeuvres de Philon,' *Revue de l'histoire des religions*, 53 [1906], p. 25-64, 164-185, 267-289). L. Cohn ("Einteilung und Chronologie der Schriften Philos," *Philologus*, Supl. Bd. VII, III, 1899, p. 431 ff.), inspired by this attempt at systematization, later proposed a classification of the Philonic *corpus* in three groups corresponding to the three periods in Philo's life: (1) treatises of a purely philosophical nature; (2) allegorical commentary, *Quaestiones* and Exposition of the Law; (3) polemic and apologetic writings.

In general, this point of view prevailed, but did not resolve every problem, namely that of the order in which Philo wrote the three great works of his prime, as V. Nikiprowetzky observes (*Le Commentaire de l'Écriture chez Philon d'Alexandrie* [Leiden: Brill, 1977] p. 194). In his historical handling of this problem, this Philonist adds that W. Völker (*Fortschritt und Vollendung bei Philo von Alexandrien* [Leipzig: Hinrich, 1938] p. 16) does not believe in a theological evolution in Philo and refuses to give great importance to the chronology of his writings. In his opinion, nothing prevents us from believing that Philo worked simultaneously on all three commentaries. In principle accepting such a point of view, though subjected to the limits imposed by the facts acquired from the Alexandrian's very work (facts he lists on page 194), Nikiprowetzky, nevertheless, leans towards accepting the traditional order of the edition established by Colson in his translation (Cf. PLCL, VI, p. IX, note a: "In this translation we have followed the traditional arrangement, which is also that adopted by Cohn and Wendland, not perhaps without justification"). Along with Schürer and Siegfried, he feels that Philo, "Having first planned to make the *De opificio mundi* the first of the treatises which he wished to dedicate to the legislative part of the Pentateuch, he would have decided later to transform it into a general preface for the entire commentary, a task for which, as Colson has noted, it is perfectly suited." (Ibid., p. 199).

Furthermore, based on a profuse analysis of the issue, he argues that Philo in fact wrote only two, and not three, commentaries on Scripture: "The series of the *Quaestiones* forms one of these with its own character and particular problems (cf. note 216, p. 231-234); the whole of the *Allegorical Commentary* and the *Exposition of the Law* constitutes the second. " (Ibid., p. 202). In fact, the reading of *Mos.* II, 46-47 and *Praem.* 1-2 gives us, as he opportunely observes, the distinct impression that Philo makes no distinction between these two groups of treatises, apparently referring to them "as organically-connected parts . . . of a larger whole" of one single commentary.

As D. Runia rightly concludes, "the conventional but most informative way of dividing up Philo's writings remains the following double tripartition" (*Philo in Early Christian Literature*, Minneapolis: Fortress Press, 1993, p. 37): (1) the *exegetical* writings: (a) the *Quaestiones in Genesim* and *Quaestiones in Exodum* (6 treatises); (b) the Allegorical Commentary (21 treatises); (c) the Exposition of the Law (12 treatises); (2) five *philosophical* treatises; and (3) four *historical-apologetic* treatises.

[5] Namely, the areas of Jewish and Roman history; Hellenistic culture; classical, rabbinical, biblical and intertestamentary literature; Greek philosophy (Platonism, Pythagoreanism and

years, complete translations of his treatises have appeared in English, French and Spanish. The Loeb English translation was completed, and a new updated edition of C.D. Yonge's complete and unabridged translation has been published. The critical edition of Cohn-Wendland-Reiter has been reprinted in eight volumes. New partial versions in English and Italian have appeared, including translations and commentaries for several treatises previously available only in Latin and Armenian. Thousands monographs and articles devoted to Philo were also produced during this period.

1. *Historical view of Philo's literary personality*

Despite this surge of literature and the fact that he was born about two thousand years ago, *Philo Judaeus* remains a controversial and enigmatic figure.[6] A number of writers have recently pointed out the multiple meanings scholars have detected in his writings.[7] Over the centuries, few works have provoked such divergent analyses as his. Whether dealing with his education and culture, the chronological order of his writings, the dominant orientation of his spirit or the object of his literary efforts, expert readers of Philo continue to differ greatly in their interpretations.

V. Nikiprowetzky feels that, independent of the merit of published works, Philonic studies have not yet developed a consensus "on either the origin and true range of his thought or on the character and value of his work."[8] He even ventures to add that the research which has taken place during the last three centuries, rather than clarifying and resolving contradictory hypotheses and unsettled issues, seems to have contributed to making the horizon of his studies more confusing and the interpretation of his writings more controversial. "It is no exaggeration to say that Philo remains, even today, an author who is fundamentally misunderstood."[9]

Some critics almost venerate Philo, affirming his brilliant nature, praising "the depth and richness of his thought, the sublime and dignified character of his language" and recognizing in him not only a coherent, original

---

Stoicism); Jewish and Christian exegesis and theology; Gnosticism, and Patristicism. Cf. Earle Hilgert, "Central Issues in Contemporary Philo Studies" *Biblical Research* (1979), p. 15. See also A. Terian, *Philonis Alexandrini de Animalibus* (Philadelphia: Scholars Press, 1981), p. IX; and Naomi G. Cohen, *Philo Judaeus: His Universe of Discourse* (Berlin, New York: Peter Lang, 1995, p. xi-xvii, 2-10.

[6] David Winston, *Philo of Alexandria, "Contemplative Life," "The Giants," and Selections* (New York: Paulist Press, 1981), p. 2.
[7] Cf. Nikiprowetzky, *Le Commentaire de l'Écriture*, p. 1-43; and David T. Runia, *Philo of Alexandria and the Timaeus of Plato* (Leiden: Brill, 1986), p. 7-31.
[8] Ibid., p. 1.
[9] "L'Exégèse de Philon d'Alexandrie," RHPR 53 (1973), p. 309.

thinker but also "a great figure in the history of philosophy."[10] Wolfson, for example, argues that Philo was a philosopher of major importance,[11] who perfectly demonstrated his originality in every area of his investigation and critical evaluation, and left us a philosophical system that is "consistent, coherent, and free of contradictions."[12]

Others, by contrast, complain about Philo's lack of originality, the superficiality with which he treats and develops themes, his monotonous verbosity and the constant repetitions in his discourse,[13] maintaining that Philo, at best, was a mediocre imitator of the greatest Greek writers. A.J. Festugière, after synthesizing Philo's ideas, states that one can read his works without finding one simple original thought in them. These do not go beyond the conventions and banalities characterizing a simple handbook[14] and there is nothing in them that cannot also be found in writers from the Hellenistic period.

What can explain this array of contradictory reactions? Could it be that Philo was a man with confused ideas, incapable of expressing himself and logically supporting an argument?[15] Or is it we who are not reading him correctly because of our failure to place ourselves in his *Sitz im Leben,* so as to penetrate his symbolic world and purposes and, once and for all, grasp the nature and method of his discourse?[16]

The history of Philonic studies shows scholars cyclically taking up the same matters, knowing that Philo's place both in the history of Alexandrian Judaism and in the complex syncretism of Hellenistic religions and philosophies has not yet been satisfactorily and definitively determined. Yet, we cannot ignore the influence his works have had on the interpretation of the Bible throughout the centuries, nor the importance and respect he has gained as one of the primary sources most frequently cited in the study of Hellenistic theology and philosophy. His impact on patristic exegesis was so great that Jerome felt compelled to include him among "the ecclesiastical

---

[10] Nikiprowetzky, *Le Commentaire de l'Écriture,* p. 1-2. Cf. R. A. Baer, *Philo's Use of the Categories Male and Female* (Leiden: Brill, 1970), p. 1.
[11] H. A. Wolfson, *Philo. Foundations of Philosophy in Judaism, Christianity and Islam,* 2 vols. (Cambridge, MA: Harvard University Press, 1968), I, p. 114-115.
[12] Ibid., p. 115.
[13] Nikiprowetzky, *Le Commentaire de l'Écriture,* p. 2; Baer, *Philo's Use of the Categories Male and Female,* p. 1-3; T. Tobin, *The Creation of Man: Philo and the History of Interpretation* (CBQMS 14 [Washington, DC: The Catholic Biblical Association of America, 1983]), p. 1-2.
[14] *La Révélation d'Hermès Trismégiste,* Vol. II: *"Le Dieu Cosmique"* (Paris: Gabalda, 1944-1954, 4 Vols., reprinted in 1981), p. 519.
[15] Cf. R. G. Hamerton-Kelly, "Sources and Traditions in Philo Judaeus: prolegomena to an analysis of his writings," SP 1 (Chicago: 1972), p. 3.
[16] Ibid.

writers," and Eusebius to spread the legend of his conversion to Christianity.[17]

T. Tobin observes that these reactions are the result of judging Philo on the basis of whether or not he is capable of expressing a point of view or creating an original and coherent philosophical system.[18] He considers such a judgment unfortunate since such was not Philo's primary intention in any case. The works handed down to us, rather than being philosophical treatises, belong almost entirely to the genre of commentary and should be read as such.[19]

V. Nikiprowetzky's historical review of Philonic studies points out the mistake in unilaterally classifying their subject as either *Philo Alexandrinus* or *Philo Iudaeus*.[20] The Alexandrian side of his personality has led several well-known writers to view him sometimes as a philosopher and sometimes as a mystic. On the other hand, the Jewish side has induced others to connect him with Palestinian Pharisaism and to present him as a rabbi-like preacher from Alexandria or as a long-winded Jewish philosopher.

Would it not be more valid to perceive this Alexandrian as a *sui generis* advocate of Judaic παιδεία of the Diaspora? Does the evidence not suggest that his personality was influenced and molded by a broad range of sources and cultural traditions? B. Mack considers it worthwhile to review and analyse Philonic studies in this light, in the hope of confirming their relationship with exegetical traditions in Alexandria.[21] He argues that Philo's literary personality reflects the power and mixture of Greek literary sources and traditions, of Hellenistic religious sources, and of Judaic sources and Alexandrian traditions of interpretation.[22] All of these are naturally organized and structured upon the foundation of his fundamental spiritual orientation.

2. *New directions in Philonic studies*

Without intending to summarize the history of Philonic scholarship—a task already accomplished by others with marked success—D. Runia[23] focuses

---

[17] Tobin, *Creation of Man*, p. 1. Cf. *De viris illustribus* 11, in reference to Hieronymus including him in the list of Church priests; and *Historia Ecclesiastica* 2, 17, 1, in reference to mention made by Eusebius of a tradition according to which Philo met Peter on a journey to Rome during Claudius' reign.
[18] *Creation of Man*, p. 2.
[19] Ibid.
[20] Cf. *Le Commentaire de l'Écriture*, p. 2; "L'Exégèse de Philon d'Alexandrie," p. 313 ff.
[21] "Philo Judaeus and Exegetical Traditions in Alexandria," ANRW II, 21.1 (Berlin, New York: W. de Gruyter, 1984), p. 229.
[22] Ibid., p. 229-249.
[23] Runia, *Philo of Alexandria and the* Timaeus *of Plato*, p. 7-12. Cf. general bibliographic and critical works on Philo: by H. L. Goodhart and E. R. Goodenough, by L. H. Feldman, by A.

concisely on the various works that have had the greatest influence on studies dedicated to the *Corpus Philonicum* during the last fifty years. He begins by discussing five classics which form a "quintet of dissension". These works were written between 1930 and 1950 and each seeks to present "a 'synthetic' portrait of Philo."[24] (1) I. Heinemann[25] attempts to show the Hellenization of the Alexandrian through his analysis of the Mosaic Law in *De Specialibus Legibus*. (2) E.R. Goodenough[26] considers him a philosopher who was primarily interested in mystical experiences and imbued with eastern elements. (3) W. Völker[27] emphasizes the centrality of his Judaic piety and denounces his constant inconsistencies. (4) H. A. Wolfson[28] claims that he is "a philosopher in the grand manner" who developed his own philosophical system with deep Jewish roots. (5) A. J. Festugière[29] presents him as a perfect example of the educated man produced by Hellenistic schools, but one whose writings are totally unoriginal. None of these five scholars, or any other Philonist of their generation, contributed significantly to a consensus on how Philo should be perceived and evaluated.[30]

Like scholars of previous generations,[31] these five had great difficulty in agreeing with one another, especially in matters such as the degree of Hellenization in Philo, the role of Greek philosophy in his writings, and his attitude toward the Law of Moses.[32]

D. Runia observes that in recent years a new and more promising quintet of studies (or groups of publications) has emerged, and that these have given Philonic scholarship considerable stimulation and forward momentum. He properly identifies (1) studies by M. Harl, with her emphasis on

---

V. Nazzaro and E. Hilgert; also brief references to the development of Philo studies in W. Völker (*Fortschritt und Vollendung*, p. 1-147), R. Arnaldez, (PM, 1, Introduction, p. 17-112), Nikiprowetzky (*Le commentaire de l'Écriture*, and "L'Exégèse de Philon"), and G. Farandos (Kosmos und Logos nach Philon von Alexandria [Amsterdam: Rodopi, 1976], p. 7-149); P. Borgen, "Philo of Alexandria. A Critical and Synthetical Survey of Research since World War II," ANRW II, 21.1, p. 98-154; R. Radice ("Bibliografia generale su Filone di Alessandria negli ultimi quarantacinque anni, I: Fonti bibliografiche, edizioni, traduzioni, commentari e lessici," *Elenchus* III, 1982, p. 109-152).

[24] Runia, *Philo of Alexandria and the* Timaeus *of Plato*, p. 8.
[25] *Philonis griechische und jüdische Bildung* (Breslau, 1932, reprinted by Hildesheim, 1962).
[26] *By Light Light: the Mystic Gospel of Hellenistic Judaism* (New Haven: Yale University Press, 1935).
[27] *Fortschritt und Vollendung*.
[28] Ibid.
[29] Ibid, p. 519-585.
[30] Runia, *Philo of Alexandria and the* Timaeus *of Plato*, p. 6-8.
[31] From 1830 to 1870, the quintet: Gfrörer/Dahne/Ritter/Georgii/Lipsius; and from 1880 to 1920, the quintet: Zeller (Drummond)/Cohn/Schwarz/Bousset/Reitzenstein. Runia, *Philo of Alexandria and the* Timaeus *of Plato*, note 9 to the "Introduction" 2.1.
[32] Ibid., p. 7-8.

Philo's originality and spirituality as the first representative of a new type of *homo religiosus*;[33] (2) those from the Philo Institute established in Chicago by a group of enthusiastic Philonists primarily devoted to the study of traditions in Philo;[34] (3) those by V. Nikiprowetzky, stressing the fact that Philo's exegetical treatises are scriptural commentaries in the technical sense of the term;[35] (4) the work of J. Dillon, who argues that Philo is a middle Platonist;[36] and (5) a book by D. Winston, who views him as a "devoted and ardent Platonist," though one filled with mystical tendencies.[37]

Several of these more recent works have suggested that the centuries-old problem of Philonic studies is largely due to a lack of clarity regarding the form and purpose of his works as exegetical commentaries. V. Nikiprowetzky defends this thesis in his excellent work, *Le Commentaire de l'Écriture chez Philon d'Alexandrie*, where he points out the need for an approach to Philo that seriously considers not only the form of his writings as commentary but also his exegetical intention[38] and the nature of Judaic and Greek elements in his thought.

Nikiprowetzky expressed and supported his conviction that Philo was, above all, an interpreter of the sacred text and that what he wrote was primarily determined by the interpreted text's meaning. This notable Philonist intensified the echo produced decades earlier by the almost muffled voice of W. Völker. In Nikiprowetzky's view, we need only to start from this elementary premise in order to finally overcome the impasse.

> Stemming from the interpretation of scripture as it was practiced in the synagogues of Alexandria, the treatises maintain an exegetical character. Far from being a merely external element, the text of the Bible is the essential pole toward which all Philonic developments are oriented.[39]

---

[33] Ibid., p. 12-14. See M. Harl, PM 15, "Introduction" (Paris: Cerf, 1967); "idem., Cosmologie grecque et representations juives dans l'oeuvre de Philon d'Alexandrie", PAL, p. 189-203.
[34] Runia, *Philo of Alexandria and the* Timaeus *of Plato*, p. 14-17. We will later mention the programmatic essay by R. Hamerton-Kelly, the methodological proposal by Burton Mack and the consequent forming of the Claremont Philo Project. The journal *Studia Philonica* was first published in 1972 with the aim of stimulating, enlivening and disseminating works produced through Philonic research.
[35] Ibid, p. 17-20. Cf. *Le Commentaire de l'Écriture*, and "L'Exégèse de Philon d'Alexandrie"
[36] Runia, *Philo of Alexandria and the* Timaeus *of Plato*, p. 20-22. Cf. J. Dillon, *The Middle Platonists: A Study of Platonism 80 B.C. to A.D. 220* (London, Ithaca NY: Cornell University Press, 1977).
[37] Runia, *Philo of Alexandria and the* Timaeus *of Plato*, p. 22-25. Cf. Winston, *Philo of Alexandria*.
[38] p. 238-239.
[39] *Le Commentaire de l'Écriture*, p. 5. Nikiprowetzky holds credit for reactivating and republishing a fundamental thesis for an understanding of Philo. This thesis has generally been considered of secondary importance, though mentioned by C. Siegfried over 100 years ago in his valuable study, *Philo von Alexandria als Ausleger des Alten Testaments an sich selbst und*

No Philonic scholar should ignore this fundamental motive, despite the need for Philo's writings to be considered from various angles, in order to determine the author's literary stature.[40] As an exegete, Philo presents his own ideas in light of the scriptural text. It is the text that normally mobilizes his thought, and not his thought that mobilizes the text.[41]

Hamerton-Kelly seemed to be in agreement with this idea. In 1971 he presented to the Philo Institute a programmatic essay in which he called for an integrated group effort to investigate sources and traditions behind Philo's works. In his view, in order to overcome the impasse and develop an understanding of Philo, his works should be read not only within the context of the history of Philonic studies but also according to current methods of literary criticism. Each of Philo's treatises should be analysed both as to its purpose and compositional techniques, and the history of traditions and sources it makes use of.[42]

In response to this challenge, B. Mack[43] outlined programmatically some guidelines and methodological principles which an analysis of Philo's *corpus* should follow in order to determine his literary forms and, ultimately, his exegetical traditions.[44] The Claremont Philo Project was the outcome of this proposal, its research group consisting of approximately twenty Philonists.

B. Mack was aware that the history of Philonic studies has been extensively marked by the writing of merely thematic essays and that "the result of this research presents such diverse images of Philo that traditional research methods must be questioned."[45] He proposed to focus on the identification of "the form and function of the various types of interpretation techniques used by Philo of Alexandria," comparing these with rhetorical forms and interpretation methods analogous to what was common usage in the

---

nach seinem geschichtlichen Einfluss betrachtet (Jena: Hermann Drufft, 1875), and more recently by E. Stein (*Die allegorische Exegese des Philo aus Alexandreia*, BZAW 51 [Giessen: Töpelmann, 1912, 1929]), Völker (*Fortschritt und Vollendung*), I. Christiansen (*Die Technik der allegorischen Auslegungswissenschaft bei Philon von Alexandrien*. Beiträge zur Geschichte der biblischen Hermeneutik 7 [Tübingen: J. C. B. Mohr, 1969]), and Jacques Cazeaux ("Aspects de l'exégèse philonienne," RSR 47, 1973, p. 262-269; "Interpréter Philon d"Alexandrie," REG 84, 1972, p. 345-352; "Philon d'Alexandrie exégète," ANRW II, 21.1, 1984, p. 156-226).

[40] R. Arnaldez, PAL, "Introduction," p. 13.
[41] Nikiprowetzky, *Le Commentaire de l'Écriture*, p. 181.
[42] "Sources and Traditions in Philo Judaeus: Prolegomena to an Analysis of his Writings," SP 1 (1972), p. 3-4.
[43] "Exegetical Traditions in Alexandrian Judaism: a program for the analysis of the Philonic Corpus," SP 3 (1974-75), p. 71-112; and "Weisheit und Allegorie bei Philo von Alexandrien," SP 5 (1978), p. 57-105.
[44] As part of the Institute for Antiquity and Christianity, Claremont Graduate School, Claremont, California.
[45] Nikiprowetzky reaches this conclusion in *Le Commentaire de l'Écriture*.

Hellenistic world.[46] He proposed the following steps, to elucidate Philonic hermeneutics: (1) identify the use of Greco-Roman rhetorical techniques, (2) understand how this is used in Philo's interpretation of sacred Judaic literature and, (3) outline the stages of development in each type of exegesis.[47] To this end, he identified and discussed some of Philo's typical exegetical devices: : etymology, anti-anthropomorphic apology, encomium-paraphrase, symbol identification, arithmology, legal exposition, argued allegory and the derivation and development of a theme.

The revitalization of Philonic studies in recent decades has also given rise to research projects at several other universities. These include the Lyon Project, with group collaboration among the most notable French Philonists who, since 1961, have produced a complete translation of Philo,[48] and the Berkeley Philo Project which, being more devoted to commentary on his treatises, has published one on *De Gigantibus* and *Quod Deus*.[49] Also, a project in Italy is involved in translating the *Corpus Philonicum*, and one headed by P. Borgen at the Religionsvitenskapelige Institute of the University of Trondheim, Norway, worked on a concordance of all his works, including the Greek fragments.

Even though in the surge of recent literature there does not exist unanimity among scholars concerning a philosophical or theological system in Philo as a whole, there does seem to be increasing agreement about the profound influence that Plato and Platonism exerted on his ideas.[50] D. Winston presents a convincing argument, one also developed by W. Theiler and J. Dillon, that the philosophical ideas expressed by Philo are Middle Platonic and that many of his apparent inconsistencies are no more than variations allowed by the scholastic tradition of Middle Platonism—a Platonism that included strong Stoic features along with some neo-Pythagorean elements.[51]

---

[46] B. L. Mack, "Interpretation of Sacred Traditions in Philo of Alexandria" (note the original description of the project, IAC, Claremont Graduate School), p. 12.
[47] Ibid., p. 2-4.
[48] "This ambitious project involved the cooperation of about twenty-five scholars," who met in Lyon along with other French Philonists, from September 11 to 15, 1966, for a famous conference "which must be considered a high point in the history of Philonic studies" (Runia, *Philo of Alexandria and the Timaeus of Plato*, p. 9), and whose report was later published in PAL: *Philon d'Alexandrie: Lyon 11-15 September 1966*.
[49] *Two Treatises of Philo of Alexandria. A Commentary on De Gigantibus and Quod Deus Sit Immutabilis*, by David Winston and John Dillon. BJS 25. Chico CA: Scholars Press, 1983. Cf. *Studia Philonica* 5 (1978), p. 137.
[50] B. L. Mack, "Philo Judaeus and Exegetical Traditions in Alexandria," p. 60.
[51] Ibid., p. 3. Cf. W. Theiler, "Philo von Alexandreia und der Beginn des kaiserzeitlichen Platonismus" in his *Untersuchungen zur antiken Literatur* (Berlin: de Gruyter, 1970), p. 170-271, 484-501.

As D. Runia points out, scholars during this recent period also reflect the following areas of potential agreement: (1) a general awareness of the *importance of methodology* in the study of Philo; (2) a growing attempt to consider him *"against the background of his own time";* and (3) a recognition of the *central role exegesis holds* in his work.[52]

Also worth noting is the growing conviction among Philonists that it is necessary "to do Philo justice as a whole."[53] Research should take into consideration the entire *corpus,* interpret it in its broad literary and cultural context, and understand Philo himself in the setting of his work and his world. As E.R. Goodenough well observes, "we shall know Philo only when we accept him as a whole, and in his own terms."[54]

3. *A question of method*

Inspired by Nikiprowetzky's thesis, T. Tobin states that it is essential to analyse the methods Philo used in his interpretations. "Only then can one evaluate fairly the success or failure of his efforts."[55]

Hamerton-Kelly seems to be of the same opinion when he points out, within the scheme of his methodological considerations, three means of access to the compositional history of the Philonic *corpus:* (1) an analysis of its sources, (2) a comparison of genres based on contrasting a text with other cognates, and (3) an analysis of the structure, coherence, wholeness and aim of one single work.

This latter approach has recently received serious attention, especially after George Kennedy's contribution to the practice of rhetorical criticism as applied to the New Testament.[56] Burton Mack observes that «rhetorical criticism may do more than build a bridge across the gap in scholarly interests and methods...»[57]

---

[52] Runia, *Philo of Alexandria and the* Timaeus *of Plato.,* p. 25-27.
[53] A. Terian, *Philonis Alexandrini "De Animalibus"* (Chico, California: Scholars Press, 1981), p. IX.
[54] *An Introduction to Philo Judaeus,* 2nd ed. (Oxford: Basil Blackwell, 1962), p. 19. Among the proposed methods, we point out the following: reading Philo through his language and manner of thought until having a sense of his writings as a whole; penetrating his world of intention and dialoguing with him; carefully observing the context of each passage and the document in which it appears; attempting to understand his language and placing ourselves in his time; trying to hear his voice and realize his interests and motivation (cf. p. 19-29).
[55] Ibid., p. 3.
[56] *New Testament Interpretation through Rhetorical Criticism* (Chapel Hill, NC: University of North Carolina Press, 1984). Kennedy discusses the various stages involved in the practice of rhetorical criticism as applied to the New Testament (pp. 14-15).
[57] *Rhetoric and the New Testament,* Minneapolis: Fortress Press, 1990, p. 93.

Rhetorical criticism...allows a text to be read both ways. It can plunge a writing back into its social setting, not only to be used as a window for viewing other social facets, but as a social factor of significance itself...Rhetorical criticism may be in fact the most promising form of literary criticism for the task of reconstructing Christian origins with social issues in view.[58]

Among the various studies concerned with Philo's methodology, those by Christiansen, Nikiprowetzky and Cazeaux deserve special mention. In her critical study, *Die Technik der allegorischen Auslegungswissenschaft bei Philon von Alexandrien*,[59] I. Christiansen considers Philo a devout Platonist trained and capable of using διαίρεσις as an analysis technique. She also defends the coherence of his methods of interpretation, arguing that these are generally based on a consistent application of the dieretic structuring of reality according to Aristotelian categories.[60] In relation to Philonic allegory, Christiansen shows that Philo, through using this technique, can offer an interpretation of biblical texts that reveals their most profound and universal meaning.[61] But she is not convincing when she states that "dieretic logic is the essential technique by which this interpretation is developed."[62] Also, her argument concerning the meaning of Aristotelian categories is "really very weak",[63] according to B. Mack.

V. Nikiprowetzky, on the other hand, instead of concentrating on a specific method of interpretation, focuses on the major principles governing Philo's methodology. He argues that Philo uses the philosophical language and conceptualization of his time in order to understand and interpret the σοφία expressed in the biblical text. Nikiprowetzky states, however, that Philo uses these to serve his own "system" and that this system, as a general hermeneutic principle, consists of continually recognizing the main theme around which his thought is centered and organized.[64] "The study of Philo is more fruitfully oriented when one realizes that his guiding concern is an exegetical theme more than, properly speaking, a philosophical one." [65] Philo's doctrine seems much more clearly structured when his text involves,

---

[58] Ibid., p. 17.
[59] *Beiträge zur Geschichte der biblischen Hermeneutik* 7 (Tübingen: Mohr-Siebeck, 1969).
[60] Christiansen expresses his opinion briefly at the beginning of each chapter.
[61] Tobin, *The Creation of Man*, p. 4.
[62] See Mack, "Philo Judaeus and Exegetical Traditions in Alexandria" (ANRW II, 21.1, 1984) p. 252. Cf. W. Pöhlman, *Lutheran Monthly* 8 (September, 1969), p. 429-430. According to him, Christiansen's work is filled with false interpretations, deficient in the use of previous studies and faulty in its methodology. Furthermore, she does not adequately understand Philo's terminology and neglects previous studies of Hellenistic-Judaic allegory.
[63] Philo Judaeus and Exegetical Traditions.
[64] "L'Exégèse de Philon d'Alexandrie," *RHPR* 53 (Paris, 1973), p. 326-327.
[65] *Le Commentaire de l'Écriture*, p. 238.

"the study of an exegetical motive through the diverse treatises of the commentary."⁶⁶

J. Cazeaux also perceives a subtle relationship between systematic thought and exegetical method in the treatises of the "Alexandrian sage," affirming the existence of an "implicit system" which controls both his theology and exegesis. He adds, however, that this system includes all available procedures: grammar, simple rhetoric, subtle dialectic and occult philosophy.⁶⁷ In his opinion, Philo always knows where he is headed. He chooses the elements of discourse, the types of proof, the partition of his exegesis and the sequence of arguments according to a specific idea or central point.⁶⁸ Everything takes its meaning from this "focal point": quotations, images, philosophical formulas and even voicelessness.⁶⁹ According to Cazeaux, Philo uses all means available in order to make the profundity of the biblical text perceptible.⁷⁰ He develops a symmetrical structure with a beginning, middle and end in which exegesis of individual passages becomes part of global systems, with the result that a discourse maintains internal coherence. Nevertheless, Cazeaux points out that reading Philo's writings is often considered a difficult and rather unstimulating task—"a real torture," in W. Bousset's opinion.⁷¹ One needs to do a type of "establishment of the text" in terms of a literary analysis beforehand in order to be familiar with the nature of Philo's work, his underlying intention and inspiration and the spiritual horizon toward which his thought moves.⁷²

These literary approaches have the particular merit of emphasizing the capital importance of Philo as an interpreter of the sacred text, an interpreter decisively concerned with that text and its general thematic content, but not necessarily bound to a single method. As a creative expositor of the Judaic Torah, Philo chooses methods suited to the text and its intentions. However, such literary approaches do not actually touch upon whether or not his exegesis has deeper historical roots. They apparently treat Philo's commentaries "as if they were all from the pen of Philo himself".⁷³

---

⁶⁶ Ibid.
⁶⁷ "Philon d'Alexandrie exégète," ANRW II, 21.1, p. 211.
⁶⁸ *La trame et la chaîne. Ou les structures littéraires et l'exégèse dans cinq des traités de Philon d'Alexandrie*, ALGHJ 15 (Leiden: Brill, 1983), p. 506, 517-518.
⁶⁹ "Aspects de l'exégèse philonienne," *Exégèse Biblique et Judaisme*, ed. J. E. Ménard (Strasbourg: Fac. Theologie Catholique, 1973), p. 108.
⁷⁰ *De congressu eruditionis gratia* (an unpublished study, kindly made available by the author), p. 171.
⁷¹ *Die religion des Judentums in späthellenistischen Zeitalter*, 3. verbess. Aufl. hrsgb. von Hugo Gressman (Tübingen, 1926), p. 454.
⁷² Cazeaux, "Aspects de l'éxègese philonienne," p. 114.
⁷³ Tobin, *The Creation of Man*, p. 4. "They tend to treat Philo apart from the exegetical traditions on which he drew," referring especially to Nikiprowetzky's work.

The various methods of interpretation Philo uses are, nevertheless, frequently considered the basis for the identification and definition of sources in his writings, as L. Goppelt points out, emphasizing that "we cannot view Philo as a solitary ingenious exegete."[74] T. Tobin stresses that he "was not only an exegete but also an exegete within a tradition."[75]

Since the publication of H. von Arnim's *Quellenstudien zu Philon von Alexandria*[76] in 1888, only limited attention has been given to Philo as an exegete who followed one tradition and was inspired by that exegetical tradition in writing his commentary. Other than W. Bousset,[77] I. Heinemann[78] and H. Wolfson,[79] few Philonists have taken seriously Philo's use of tradition. Since the early 1970's, thanks to the research work carried out by Hamerton-Kelly and B. Mack, a new awareness has emerged as to the true importance of Philo as an exegete.[80]

According to Mack, the formulation of a typology of exegetical methods and the recognition of a system of interpretation with its historical and

---

[74] L. Goppelt, *Typos* (Grand Rapids: Eerdmans, 1982), p. 43. Cf. Stein, *Die allegorische Exegese*; I. Heinemann, *Philons griechische und jüdische Bildung. Kulturvergleichende Untersuchungen zu Philons Darstellung der jüdischen Gesetze* (Breslau: Marcus, 1932); M. Adler, *Studien zu Philo von Alexandreia* (Breslau: Marcus, 1929).

[75] *Creation of Man*, p. 5.

[76] *Quellenstudien zu Philon von Alexandreia. Philologische Untersuchungen*, ed. A. Kiessling, U. von Wilamowitz-Moellendorff, 11 (Berlin, 1888).

[77] Wilhelm Bousset cites a number of examples in which Philo uses exegetical tradition and transforms it in a few cases, in his study *Jüdische-christlicher Schulbetrieb in Alexandria und Rom. Literarische Untersuchungen zu Philo und Clemens von Alexandria, Justin und Irenäus* (Götingen: Vandenhoeck und Ruprecht, 1915), p. 8-154. Cf. Tobin, *The Creation of Man*, p.7.

[78] Heinemann, *Philons griechische und jüdische Bildung*, p. 137-154.

[79] H. A. Wolfson, *Philo I*, p. 57-73.

[80] Cf. Tobin, *Creation of Man*, p. 7. He points out in reference to this that such an "attempt to understand the exegetical history of Alexandrian Judaism is important, not only for an accurate understanding of Philo, but also an understanding of primitive Christianity and Gnosticism." In fact, this is partly the aim expressed in his thesis: "to examine the exegetical traditions which Philo drew on when he interpreted the Genesis texts dealing with the creation of man . . . and the ways in which he used and, to some extent, transformed those traditions" (Ibid., p. 1).

B. Mack goes further in adding that the ultimate aim of his project on Philo equally entails: contributing to knowledge of the *origins of Western culture*, since "Hellenistic Judaism is a syncretic phenomenon that incorporates an essential form of dialectic in Western culture; . . . providing a basis of comparison for studies in other syncretic cultural developments from the Hellenistic period underlying Western civilization , . . . and the evidence of its literature providing the necessary link between the classical world of Greece and Rome and emerging Western thought." It also entails contributing to an understanding of the *transformation of the cultural phenomenon* itself since, according to him, "Philo's exegesis is characterized by the effort to understand the religious and literary heritage of Judaism in terms of a new cultural situation" ("Interpretation of Sacred Traditions in Philo of Alexandria," Project Description, p. 3-4).

theological interrelationships are both necessary. However, these are not in themselves sufficient for a reconstruction of Alexandria's exegetical history. One must also focus attention on the levels and sequence of these systems in order to have a global and unified view "of what must have been an exceptionally rich history of interpretation in Alexandrian Judaism."[81] B. Mack also argues that Philo appears at the climax of this long and noteworthy tradition as a writer whose coherent and logical mind was dedicated to concrete theological concerns. His writings reflect both a compilation of this traditional exegesis and his personal efforts at systematization.[82] Finally, Mack feels that, if this understanding confirms the suggested correlation, "that would suggest a very profound program indeed and indicate a kind of systematic mind heretofore not imagined for Philo."[83]

In line with the proposal of G. Kennedy for interpreting the New Testament, I agree with F.W. Hughes that "there is no reason to limit the scope of rhetorical criticism (as based on Graeco-Roman rhetorical models) to the New Testament".[84] It is a methodology applicable to the critical analysis of any piece of literature produced by a writer who used rhetoric to shape and compose it. As Jan Botha comments,[85]

> A reading from a rhetorical perspective compels the interpreter to reflect consciously and explicitly on the implications of the *rhetoricity* of the text. It is a way of reading 'between the lines'. It brings to the fore the implicit and unspoken/unwritten values which underpin the argumentation. By bringing this to the surface, the act of interpretation moves beyond a mere linguistic or normal literary analysis of the text.

4. *In defense of a rhetorical reading of the* Philonic *corpus*

The work of M. Adler emerges in the world of Philonic studies as one of the first contributions toward an understanding of composition techniques in Philo and as a good example of analysis touching the field of rhetorical argumentation.[86]

Since Adler's work, other scholarly studies have appeared which, by comparison with his, represent a considerable step forward in an understanding of the architecture of Philo's text. S. Belkin, on the one hand, concentrates

---

[81] "Philo Judaeus and Exegetical Traditions in Alexandria," p. 264.
[82] Ibid., p. 267.
[83] Ibid.
[84] 'New Testament Rhetorical Criticism and its Methodology" (Society of Biblical Literature, Annual Meeting 1990, p. 2, n. 4). Cf. George Aichele, *et al.*, "Rhetorical Criticism" in *The Postmodern Bible* (New Haven and London: Yale University Press, 1995) p. 149–186).
[85] *Subject to Whose Authority? Multiple Readings of Romans 13*, (Atlanta: Scholars Press, 1994) p. 187-188.
[86] *Studien zu Philon von Alexandreia* (Breslau: Marcus, 1929).

on the area of Judaic influence, describing Philo as "a Pharisaic halakist, a Palestinian allegorist and an Alexandrian mystic,"[87] showing in all his works that he "was probably influenced by the traditions and techniques of rabbinical exegesis."[88] On the other hand, Christiansen concentrates on the area of Hellenistic influence by showing, as we have already mentioned, that Philo used the Platonic διαίρεσις system of logic as the basis for the formulation of his allegories.

Attempting to combine these two apparently contradictory ideas, Hamerton-Kelly feels that a simultaneous focusing on the *gezerah shawa*[89] of the rabbinical exegesis and the διαίρεσις can help to significantly illuminate the Philonic method of composition in allegorical commentary. To this effect, he argues that not only did Philo know and use the dieretic method but he also used many of the Palestinian rabbis' hermeneutical techniques, leaving in his treatises sure evidence of the interpenetration of these two areas of influence. A good example of his "transcultural methodology" is *De Agricultura*, a treatise with three dieretic exercises. In two of these, part of his argument is structured by means of a *gezerah shawa* with the apparent aim of ingeniously leading the reader from the literal meaning of the text to the allegorical.[90]

D. Daube,[91] however, seems to go a bit further in his conclusions in arguing that Hillel's exegetic rules were in themselves of Greek origin and were formulated under the influence of Hellenistic rhetoric. So, if transcultural fertilization occurred, it is much more logical to suppose that Philo's hermeneutics was a natural and obvious product of his general studies in Alexandria.

Thus there is a growing agreement that the Judaic and Hellenistic cultures are combined in Philo, not only in terms of ideas but also in methods of

---

[87] *Philo and the Oral Law—The Philonic Interpretation of Biblical Law in Relation to the Palestinian Halakah* (Cambridge: Harvard Semitic Series XI, 1940), p. 27.

[88] R. G. Hamerton-Kelly, "Some Techniques of Composition in Philo's Allegorical Commentary with Special Reference to *De Agricultura*," *Jews, Greeks and Christians* (Leiden: Brill, 1976), p. 46. According to M. Miller ("Targum, Midrash and the use of the Old Testament in the New Testament," *JSJ* II, (1971) p. 79), the work by Belkin "is the most concerted effort to prove the influence of Palestinian Midrash traditions on Philo."

[89] *Gezerah shawa* is one of Hillel's seven hermeneutic rules. They are (1) *Kal wa-homer:* inference *a minore ad maius;* (2) *Gezerah shawa:* influence by analogy; (3) *Binyan ab:* reconstruction of a family based on a passage; (4) *Binyan ab mish shene kethubim:* reconstruction of a family based on two passages; (5) *Kelal u-feret u-feret u-kelal:* the general and the specific viceversa; (6) *Keyose bo bemakom "aher:* explanation by means of another similar case; (7) *Dabar ha-lamed me'inyamo:* deduction through the context (Hamerton-Kelly, "Some Techniques", p. 49-50). See also S. Lieberman, *Hellenism in Jewish Palestine* (New York, 1950), p. 53 ff.

[90] Ibid., p. 52-56.

[91] "Rabbinic Methods of Interpretation and Hellenistic Rhetoric," HUCA 22 (1949), p. 239-264.

argumentation and literary composition. No one seems to doubt that the cultural background of the Alexandrian scholar was extensive enough to include a rhetorical education.

In fact, the development of his exegetical themes seems generally to follow a formal structure that parallels the argumentation laws of rhetorical theory. A critical reading of the actual texts reveals this fact and several recent essays also suggest it, though they focus more on matters of style than of structure.[92] Furthermore, his mastery of the rhetorical code presupposes the existence of a philosophical concept of this art, commends its right use as an art of rational expression and reflects a remarkable creative capacity. The analysis of this matter in several of his treatises shows that such is the case.[93]

Therefore, if "much is known about Philo's ideas but comparatively little about the composition and literary history of his individual treatises;"[94] if, as A. Michel argues, "one cannot identify his philosophy without identifying his rhetoric";[95] if, as C. Perelman states, "the philosophical proof is of a rhetorical nature" and ". . . the rhetorical perspective makes possible a better understanding of the philosophical purpose;"[96] if, as is argued more and more, Philo masters tradition and defines and defends a superior form of rhetoric as the art of expression *par excellence*;[97] then we find it useful and desirable to develop a line of study seriously dedicated to a rhetorical analysis of his *corpus,* giving special attention to the techniques of argumentation he uses in articulating and substantiating his exegetic purpose.[98]

---

[92] T. Conley, "Philo's Rhetoric: Argumentation and Style," ANRW II, 21.1 (Berlin, New York: W. de Gruyter, 1984) 343-371; J. Leopold, "Characteristics of Philo's Style in the *De Gigantibus* and *Quod Deus,*" in *Two Treatises of Philo of Alexandria,* BJS 25, by D. Winston and John Dillon, in collaboration with V. Nikiprowetzky (Chico, CA: Scholars Press, 1983) 141-54.

[93] The studies by A. Michel ("Quelques aspects de la rhétorique chez Philon," PAL, p. 82-103), and Monique Alexandre (PM 16 *De Congressu Eruditionis Gratia,* [Paris: Cerf] p. 27-82; and "La culture profane chez Philon," PAL, p. 105-129) are extremely useful due to their analysis of the main texts in which Philo expresses his ideas on matters of rhetoric and sophism.

[94] Hamerton-Kelly, "Some Techniques", p. 45.

[95] "Quelques aspects", PAL, p. 89.

[96] *The New Rhetoric and the Humanities* (Boston, Dordrecht: D. Reidel Publishing Co., 1979), p. 50, 52.

[97] Cf. Michel, "Quelques aspects", p. 84, 88.

[98] Rhetorical criticism "studies discourse primarily *as argumentation,* as social interaction, and not only as communication, or the transmission of information." (Jan Botha, *Subject to whose Authority?,* p. 186). Cf. R. Dean Anderson Jr., *Ancient Rhetorical Theory and Paul* (Kampen: Pharos, 1996), p. 22-26.

5. Foundation and plan of the present study

How profoundly rhetorical is Philo's exegetical purpose in producing his philosophical commentary? To what extent does he take advantage of these two rival cultures, philosophy and rhetoric, whose opposition produces between them "a creative tension, a reciprocal exhange of influences"? [99] How does he organize his arguments in handling his exegetical themes?

We agree with A. Michel that Philo's thought was both coherent and full of vitality. It was coherent because his rhetoric and philosophy—both in form and content—were connected with the same Middle Platonic teachings. It was full of vitality because Philo was up-to-date and familiar with the latest state of doctrine, and made use of it in an independent, versatile and creative way without subjecting himself to preconceived notions of traditions.[100] As J. Cazeaux adds, Philo never disturbed his own system. He changed styles when he wanted, adjusting them to his motives. His rhetorical code was intelligently placed at the service of scriptural interpretation.[101]

We also agree with T. Conley when he notes that the Alexandrian is a prominent stylist who projects in his work a rhetorical technique that is well developed as an architectonic art,[102] particularly when he suggests that "there is more in store for a student of Philo who is willing to look at his techniques of argumentation and presentation than a mere catalogue of 'unusual expressions.'"[103]

The appearance of these interpretations of Philo as rhetorician, along with a renewed interest in the study of rhetorical criticism,[104] and a revived awareness that in Greek antiquity, particularly in Aristotle, the primary

---

[99] Henri I. Marrou, *Histoire de l'éducation dans l'antiquité* (Paris: Seuil, 1981), p. 313.
[100] Michel, "Quelques aspects", p. 95, 100-101.
[101] Remark made during the annual meeting of the Philo Project in Claremont, November 1-4, 1980.
[102] Ibid.
[103] Thomas M. Conley, *Philo's Rhetoric: Argumentation and Style*, ANRW II, 21.1, p. 369.
[104] Cf. E. Black, *Rhetorical Criticism, a Study in Method* (The University of Wisconsin Press, 1978); W. C. Booth, "The Revival of Rhetoric," *New Rhetorics*, ed. M. Steinman, Jr. (New York: Charles Scribner's Sons, 1967), p. 1-15; T. O. Sloan, "Restoration of Rhetoric to Literary Studies," ST 16 (1967), p. 91-97; W. J. Brandt, *The Rhetoric of Argumentation* (New York: Bobbs-Merrill Co., 1970); P. J. Corbett, *Classical Rhetoric for the Modern Student*, 2nd ed. (New York: Oxford University Press, 1971); *Rhetorical Analysis of Literary Works* (New York: Oxford University Press, 1969); C. Perelman, *Eléments d'une théorie de l'argumentation* (Bruxelles: Presses Universitaires, 1968); *L'empire rhétorique. Rhétorique et argumentation* (Paris: Vrin, 1977); C. Perelman and Olbrechts-Tyteca, *La Nouvelle Rhétorique: Traité de l'argumentation* (Paris: PUF, 1958); Vernon Robbins, *Exploring the Texture of Texts: A Guide to Socio-Rhetorical Interpretation* (Valley Forge, PA: Trinity Press International, 1996), etc.

purpose of rhetoric was the study of argumentation techniques,[105]—all these provide an essential foundation for the present work.

We realize that to attempt to penetrate the dense forest of Philonic studies is not an easy task. Understanding his treatises and the range of their argumentative strategies calls for total immersion in his existential and cultural world. Given, however, the general importance of his works for the history of culture,[106] the present book seeks to contribute to scholarship by offering the fullest investigation ever attempted of Philo's knowledge and use of rhetoric.

Obviously, this is not a topic chosen by chance or taken on lightly. This venture is part of a greater literary project that presently brings together the converging work of a significant number of Philonists, but concentrates more specifically on detecting the presence of a whole rhetorical architecture in Philo's writings and on the critical study of his techniques of argumentation.

I will attempt to demonstrate that Philo assumed the formal methods of argument recommended in Greco-Roman handbooks of rhetoric and used these selectively and creatively in his commentary; that the development of his exegetical themes reflects the formal structure of a complete argument; that there is a great affinity between his argumentation strategy and the philosophical rhetoric defended by Cicero; and that Philo was as eclectic in rhetoric as in philosophy, not tied to a single tradition but freely using the language, methods and concepts which he considered appropriate for exegesis of the sacred text.

Our study begins by placing Philo and his works against the background of an intellectual "empire,"[107] an art once defined as "the old and new queen of the sciences"[108]—in the polychromatic and diachronic light of the theory of persuasive communication. In two stages, seemingly distinct but

---

[105] P. Ricoeur, in his work *La métaphore vive* (Paris: Seuil, 1975), p. 13-14, points out that the rhetoric of Aristotle covers three areas: a theory of argumentation, representing two-thirds of the treatise; a theory of elocution; and a theory of the composition of discourse. E. C. Perelman, stressing the central importance of the theory of argumentation, notes that what the last treatises on rhetoric offer us is, in the appropriate expression by G. Genette, "a limited rhetoric," but limited only in that which concerns one of its parts. He also notes, with great accuracy, that once it lost the link that connected it with philosophy through dialectic, rhetoric had become an erratic and futile discipline (*L'empire rhétorique. Rhétorique et argumentation*, p. 12-13).

Roland Barthes states that in fact it is absurd to limit rhetoric to figures, but the truth is that throughout the centuries the scope of this discipline has become increasingly restricted, such that redirecting it to its whole dimension would be an act of simple justice (Ibid., p. 11).
[106] R. Arnaldez, C. Mondésert and J. Pouilloux, *Philon d'Alexandrie, "De Opificio Mundi"* (Paris: Cerf, 1961), p. 8.
[107] Cf. C. Perelman, *L'empire rhétorique*, p. 168-177.
[108] Ibid., p. 177. W. Jens, *Von deutscher Rede* (München: Pieper, 1969), p. 45.

complementary to our argument, we will move from the general to the specific, from rhetorical theory to the Philonic practice of argumentation, concentrating at length on a systematic analysis of representative passages.

In Part One, we begin by presenting a descriptive analysis of argumentation strategies and structures in classical rhetoric from Plato and Aristotle to Cicero and Quintilian. We then examine the question of Philo's access to this long and complex tradition through a study of its impact on Alexandria's cultural environment and on his intellectual development. Finally, we discuss Philo's general appreciation of a rhetoric guided by philosophy, as opposed to one driven by sophistry.

Part Two is devoted to an analysis of selected Philonic passages. We will demonstrate the presence of rhetorical structures and measure the degree of their conformity to traditional rhetorical theory. We will also examine the variety of rhetorical devices used in his writings as well as the rhythmic constructions which occasionally appear.

PART ONE

PHILO OF ALEXANDRIA IN THE CONTEXT OF RHETORICAL ARGUMENTATION

INTRODUCTION

In recent years, after a long period in which it was regarded as a dead subject, rhetoric has emerged revived "not only as a science of the future, but even more as a relevant science touching the boundaries of structuralism, new criticism and semiology."[1] However, its modern-day revival has occurred not only at the level of language. As R. Barthes pointed out in commenting that "la rhétorique devrá être repensée en termes structuraux"[2] devoting himself to the analysis of Aristotle's *Rhetoric*,[3] this renewal occurred also at the level of ideas, owing primarily to the work of C. Perelman, founder of the so-called "New Rhetoric" and author of *Traité de l'argumentation*, together with Olbrechts-Tyteca.[4]

In his attempt to "bring a glorious and centuries-old tradition back to life,"[5] Perelman brought rhetoric and dialectic together again, as Aristotle had done, and emphasized the study of the structure of argumentation, aware of the interrelationship between such disciplines as grammar, logic, politics, philosophy and dialectic.[6] According to G. Bouchard, Perelman thus

---

[1] J. Dubois, F. Edeline, *et al.*, *Rhétorique Générale* (Paris: Larousse, 1970), p. 8.
[2] Ibid.
[3] "L'Analyse rhétorique," *Littérature et société* (Éditions de l'Institute de Sociologie de l'Université Libre de Bruxelles, 1967), p. 31-35.
[4] The *Traité de l'argumentation. La nouvelle rhétorique* (Paris: P.U.F., 1958) is already in its third edition (in Brussels: Éditions de l'Université de Bruxelles, 1976) and has been translated into English, Italian and German. In C. Perelman's bibliography, the theme of the theory of argumentation takes on a particular importance (Cf. "Bibliographie de C. Perelman" in *Revue Internationale de Philosophie, La Nouvelle Rhétorique* 127-128, 1979, p. 325-342).

Among other works, worth mentioning are: *Eléments d'une théorie de l'argumentation* (Bruxelles: Presses Universitaires, 1968); *Le champ de l'argumentation* (Bruxelles: Presses Universitaires, 1970); *L'empire rhétorique. Rhétorique et argumentation* (Paris: Vrin, 1977); and *The New Rhetoric and the Humanities* (Dordrecht, Boston, London: Reidel Publishing Company, 1979).

[5] *Traité de l'argumentation*, p. 7; *Rhétorique et philosophie, Pour une théorie de l'argumentation en philosophie* (Paris: Presses Universitaires de France, 1952), p. 50. C. Perelman introduced the New Rhetoric to the public for the first time at a conference held in 1949 at the Institut des Hautes Études de Belgique, published in 1950 in the *Revue Philosophique de la France et de l'Etranger*, with the title "Logique et rhétorique," p. 1-35, and later in 1952 printed in *Rhétorique et philosophie*. But it is in this treatise that his thesis is extensively and definitively developed.

[6] C. Perelman, *L'empire rhétorique*, p. 15: "In his memorandum devoted to ancient rhetoric, Roland Barthes rightly observes that 'rhetoric should always be read in the structural game of its neighbours (grammar, logic, poetics, philosophy).' I add for myself that, in order to

carried out the important function of "remembering and discribing the argumentative structure of discourse, and the parts of a speech left to modern logic and semiology."[7]

Perelman's efforts above all others have led to the revival of rhetorical studies at great centers of research, and to the publishing of numerous works on the theory of argumentation.[8] It is primarily as argumentation theory that rhetoric has gained renewed attention, due to an awareness of its close connection with philosophy and to the rediscovery of dialectic and rhetorical techniques recommended by Plato and studied by Aristotle.[9] Rhetorical

---

situate rhetoric properly and define it better, it is also necessary to determine its relations to dialectic."

[7] "Rhétorique des mots, rhétorique des idées," *Laval Théologique et Philosophique*, 35:3 (1979), p. 313.

[8] It is an established fact that studies on rhetoric experienced, particularly following the sixties, "a remarkable increase and a rising fortune" due to the influence of the fundamental work by C. Perelman and his collaborator L. Olbrechts-Tyteca (Cf. Cesare Vasoli, "La 'Nouvelle Rhétorique' di Perelman," in *Attualità della retorica* [Padova: Liviana Editrice, 1975], p. 16-17). As evidence of the interest aroused by his "new rhetoric," we point out by way of example: no. 58 of *Revue Internationale de Philosophie* on "L'argumentation," in 1961; the special issue "Philosophical Argument" in *The Monist*, in 1964; the "Symposium sobre la argumentación filosófica," at the XII Congresso Internazionale di Filosofia, and the collection of articles in *La théorie de l'argumentation*, published by Centre Nationale Belge de Recherches de Logique, in 1963; the volume *Philosophy, Rhetoric and Argumentation*, published by M. Natanson and H. Johnstone, in 1965; the initial publication of the periodical *Philosophy and Rhetoric*, in 1968; the essay by W. J. Brandt, *The Rhetoric of Argumentation*, in which his aim is to propose a new manner of reading literary texts, in 1970; the I Convegno Italo-Tedesco on *Attualità della retorica*, 1973; the work by J. Kopperschmidt, *Allgemeine Rhetorik, Einführung in die Theorie der persuasive Kommunikation*, 1973; the publication of the "Travaux du Centre de Recherches Sémiologiques de l'Université de Neuchâtel, Recherches sur le discours et l'argumentation," in *Revue Européene des Sciences Sociales* 32, under the direction of J. B. Grize, in 1974; the work by George Vignaux on *L'argumentation*, in 1976; numbers 127-128 of *Revue Internationale de Philosophie* on "La nouvelle rhétorique, essais en homage à Chaïm Perelman," in 1979; the International Society for the History of Rhetoric, with its biennial conferences and the publication of *Rhetorica* since 1983; etc.

[9] In his preface to the work *Philosophy, Rhetoric and Argumentation* (ed. by M. Natanson and H. W. Johnstone, Jr., University Park: The Pennsylvania State University Press, 1965), Robert T. Oliver points out that "two thousand years ago the indissoluble nature of the relationship that does and must exist among rhetoric, philosophy, and argumentation was scarcely open to question," stating that "both philosophers and rhetoricians (with students or argumentation included in both groups) have come to insist once again upon the communality of their interests and even, to a significant degree, of their methods and aims," (p. xii, xiii). Such a statement follows C. Perelman's train of thought in asserting, together with Olbrechts-Tyteca, that the renovation of rhetoric corresponds perfectly to the aspirations of our time, since it is a truly human work. "Today, when we have lost the illusions of rationalism and positivism and we perceive the prevalence of confused thought and importance of value-judgments, rhetoric should once again become a living subject, a technique of argumentation in human affairs and a logic of value-judgments." (*Rhétorique et Philosophie*, p. 41).

figures are not mere ornaments; today they are analyzed in the light of their argumentative effectiveness.¹⁰

This neo-Aristotelian approach to rhetoric is inspired by an awareness of the centrality of argumentation and emphasizes that arguments always have structure and that they presuppose the dialogical nature of discourse. Consequently, rhetoric presupposes intellectual contact between an emitter and the receiver and seeks to persuade, convince and provoke agreement with the constant awareness that the λόγος is essentially formal as an apophantic (categorical and declaratory) reality and a coherent expression of thought.¹¹

Defining argumentation and delineating its area of activity has not, however, been an easy task. C. Perelman, in emphasizing his compromise with a logic of argumentation and a pluralistic concept of truth, defines it in the following terms: "Argumentation is generally spoken or written discourse, of varied dimensions, which combines a large number of arguments with the aim of obtaining agreement from an audience on one or more theses."¹² "Its objective is not to deduce the consequences of certain premises, but to provoke or strengthen agreement from an audience on the theses submitted for their approval."¹³

Therefore, any argumentation implies an orator, an audience and a very explicit objective. In proposing to act upon an audience and modify its convictions or dispositions, it does not merely seek pure intellectual agreement. It in fact aims at "quite frequently, inciting to action or, at least, creating a disposition for that action."¹⁴

Though recognizing that this approach has the merit of reviving the idea of a type of "practical reason," G. Vignaux argues that "such a definition tends to reduce argumentation to a set of phenomena of psychosociological nature"¹⁵ and calls attention to the risk of an overly-accentuated conflict between argumentation and demonstration, as well as to the danger of considering it only within the context of this conflict and defining it merely in terms of the audience to which it is directed.¹⁶ According to Vignaux, we do not have to deviate from the essence of Aristotelian doctrine. Argumentation is "a set of clustered reasonings supporting an affirmation or thesis."¹⁷ It

---

[10] See Andreas H. Snyman, *Biblica* 69 (1988), p. 93-107.
[11] Cf. E. Nicol, "Sur la théorie de l'argumentation et le concept de 'pureté'," *La théorie de l'argumentation* (Louvain: Éditions Nauwelaerts, 1963), p. 51-67.
[12] *The New Rhetoric and the Humanities*, p. 24.
[13] *L'Empire rhétorique*, p. 23.
[14] Ibid., p. 25-26.
[15] *L'argumentation* (Genève: Droz, 1976), p. 9.
[16] Ibid., p. 11-25.
[17] Ibid., p. 17.

is a series of arguments directed at the same conclusion, but it is also the manner in which these are prepared and presented.[18] Instead of originating spontaneously or capriciously from the orator, argumentation is, in this light, the visible expression of a set of discursive strategies logically structured and appropriate to dynamic itineraries through which the orator's thoughts flow coherently and the planned objectives are achieved with the audience.[19]

M.-J. Borel, a collaborator of J. B. Grize and G. Vignaux, with whom she is naturally identified in her study and analysis on argumentative phenomena at the Centre de Recherches Sémiologiques de l'Université de Neuchâtel,[20] assesses three other ways of approaching the problem, considering these to be representative of a greater number of attitudes. The three are those by W. J. Brandt, S. Toulmin and G. Kalinowski.[21] The analysis proposed by the first reflects the orientation of traditional rhetoric, though achieved from a descriptive point of view and directed at promoting a specific *reading* of the texts. In his opinion, what distinguishes persuasive discourse from other forms of communication is its rhetorical structure.

In both parts of his essay, Brandt successively deals with structural and textual rhetoric, giving special attention to the parts of an argument, *lato* and *stricto sensu*. He defines argumentation as "the establishment of a convincing connection between two terms"[22] and stresses the importance the form of an enthymeme takes as a simple argument or as the central element of a globalizing structure in giving order to the argumentative *corpus*, without determining its intervening strategies. Thus an argument is "logical in its basic structure," although it does not strictly follow the argumentative sequence of scientific logic, since it normally has to "adapt itself to persuasive strategies."[23] In the *confirmatio* it moves, or seems to move, from a general topic to a conclusion, going through explicative, justificatory or probatory reasoning; or rather, through a "structural enthymeme" which, in turn, can be analyzed in sub-structures of a logical and psychological nature.

---

[18] A. Lalande, *Vocabulaire technique et critique de la philosophie*, 10th edition (Paris: Presses Universitaires de France), p. 1968.
[19] Cf. J. B. Grize, *Travaux du centre de recherches sémiologiques* 7, (Neuchâtel: 1971), p. 3. Also, "Argumentation, schématisation et logique naturelle," in *Revue Européene des Sciences Sociales* 32 (1974), p. 183-199.
[20] Marie-Jeanne Borel, "Raisons et situation d'inter-locution. Introduction à une étude de l'argumentation," RESS 32 (1974), p. 65-93.
[21] Cf., respectively, *The Rhetoric of Argumentation* (New York: The Bobbs-Merrill Co., Inc., 1970); *The Uses of Argument* (Cambridge: Cambridge University Press, 1958); and *La logique des normes* (Paris: P.U.F., 1972), "Le raisonement juridique et la logique déontique," *Logique et analyse* 49-50 (1970), "Le rationnel et l'argumentation," *Revue Philosophique de Louvain* 70, 4th series, number 7 (1972), p. 404-418.
[22] *The Rhetoric of Argumentation*, p. 24.
[23] Ibid., p. 70.

Accentuating further the role of formal logic in the study of argumentation, Toulmin apparently wants to reduce the production of any type of argumentation "to the rigid form of syllogistic deduction,"[24] stating that they should indeed be analysable, but also subject to evaluation in terms of formal coherence and from the point of view of their solidness and effectiveness. He is primarily concerned with the manner in which arguments function, and the accurateness and soundness of the argumentative theses. "In all cases, a thesis is given and the supporting reasons are furnished."[25] The primary function of the argument depends on its formal nature, but this form is unfailingly conditioned by the respective field of argumentation.[26] Based on these premises,

> An argument is like an organism. It has both a gross, anatomical structure and a finer, as-it-were physiological one . . . and this is the structure with which logicians have mainly concerned themselves. It is at this physiological level that the idea of logical form has been introduced, and here that the validity of our arguments has ultimately to be established or refuted.[27]

Micro-arguments should therefore be analyzed and evaluated within the context of the macro-arguments within which they appear.

Finally, Kalinowski, in his logical-rhetorical approach to argumentative texts, proposes a logic "of form" as an alternative to the logic "of field" supported by Toulmin, and contests the conflict Perelman and his collaborator say that exists between *argumentation,* persuasive or convincing, and *demonstration.* According to him, to demonstrate is also to argue and *lato sensu* logic encompasses both "rhetoric and topica".[28]

This brief review of some theoretical discussions of contemporary logic and rhetoric suffices to verify that the Aristotelian tradition has been reactivated. This has inspired new theoretical formulations with effects on rhetorical criticism.

As an element of proof, *argument,* according to its actual meaning, is "reasoning that is meant to prove or refute a given proposition".[29] It is a complete line of reasoning and not just one or the other of its parts. The term is, however, legitimately employed as an equivalent of a rhetorical figure, even when applied to one particular premise.[30] *To argue* is to supply reasons in favor of a thesis, bearing in mind that the power of argumentation

---

[24] M-J. Borel, "Raisons et situation", p. 71.
[25] Ibid., p. 77.
[26] Ibid., p. 78.
[27] S. E. Toulmin, *The Uses of Argument,* p. 94.
[28] "Le rationnel et l'argumentation," RPL 70, 4th series, no. 7 (1972), p. 417.
[29] A. Lalande, *Vocabulaire technique,* cf. C. T. Ernesti, *Lexicon Technologiae Latinorum Rhetoricae* (Hildesheim: G. Olms, 1962).
[30] G. Kalinowski, "Le rationnel et l'argumentation," p. 414.

does not rely on the number or mere accumulation of arguments but on their convergence, validity and effectiveness. In practice, *argumentation* is the action by which a person, through the rational use of his discursive faculties, seeks to cause an audience to agree with the proposed theses, to modify its convictions or beliefs and to actively commit itself to defending the options and values presented. "Etymologically, *argumentatio* means something like 'clarifying the thought' or 'the mind.' Thus arguments are adduced not only to change others' minds, but also to intensify convictions or beliefs already held."[31] In this, as in the fact that all "argumentative discourse has a type of continuity (a taxonomic order) that depends on an element of specific cohesion,"[32] everyone is generally in agreement.

Some, however, interpret argumentation as being essentially an act of communication that is not necessarily logical, placing the function of arguments over and above their form[33] and then describe it as a "benevolent act" distinct from persuasion, even though closely related.[34] Others, more concerned with the reality of a logic of argumentation, insist on the necessity of recognizing the nature and form of arguments used, the logical structures of the reasoning followed, the types of composition and "representation and construction strategies" on which they are based.[35] Still others, such as C. Perelman, consider dangerous any separation between content techniques and form techniques, stressing "the impossibility of separating form from content, or an argument from its context".[36] They prefer to refer to it in terms of "argumentative action." For them argumentation is, first of all, an action—the action of one individual upon another; the orator always tries to change something, to safeguard threatened beliefs—in essence, to transform the listener. It must, however, possess two fundamental qualities: effectiveness and validity. Argumentation is effective if it provokes the listener's agreement and valid if it deserves to do so. Like other writers who have devoted themselves to the theory of rhetoric in modern times, these scholars emphasize above all the concept of audience, since they realize that rhetorical argumentation, in order to be effective, not only implies principles and premises accepted by the listener but must also adapt itself to the

---

[31] T. M. Conley, *Philo's Rhetoric: Studies in Style, Composition and Exegesis* (Urbana: University of Illinois, 1982, draft for discussion), p. 7.
[32] A. Licitra, "Pour une analyse du discours argumentatif" RESS 32 (1974), p. 153.
[33] R. E. Crable, *Argumentation as Communication: Reasoning with Receivers* (Columbus, OH: Bell & Howell Co., 1976).
[34] Cf. D. Ehninger, "Toward a Taxonomy of Prescriptive Discourse," *Rhetoric in Transition: Studies in the Nature and Uses of Rhetoric*, ed. E. E. White (University Park: The Pennsylvania State University Press, 1980), p. 92-95.
[35] G. Vignaux, *L'argumentation*, p. 274-277.
[36] P. Gochet, RIP 127-128 (1979), p. 368.

listener and his already-existing convictions.[37] Argumentation essentially depends on the audience to which it is directed, whether this be universal or private, intentional or empirical.[38]

In general, all of these writers agree with the doctrine that served as the basis for the New Rhetoric, notably expressed in Perelman's treatise. As B. Mack observes,

> 'by emphasizing argumentation, Perelman and Olbrechts-Tyteca revived the ancient classical definition of rhetoric as 'the art of persuasion,' described a logic of communication that could be applied to widely ranging modes of human discourse, and immersed the study of speech events in social situations...They have succeeded in demonstrating the importance of the situation or speech context when calculating the persuasive force of an argumentation...By linking the persuasive power of speech not only to its logic of argumentation, but to the manner in which it addresses the social and cultural history of its audience and speaker'...they have taken 'rhetoric out of the sphere of mere ornamentation and stylistics, embellished literary style, and the extravagances of public oratory, and placed it at the center of a social theory of language.'[39]

In Jan Botha's words, 'Wuellner aptly summarizes what has been said about modern conceptions of rhetoric, by pointing out that four features can be distinguished as the characteristics of modern rhetoric:' (1) the turn toward argumentation; (2) the focus on a text's intentionality or exigency;

---

[37] C. Perelman, *Traité de l'argumentation*, p. 31-34.
[38] Perelman's universal audience is an imaginary construction, the mental structure of an real audience, and at the same time a historically-founded concept "including all men who are rational and competent with respect to the issues that are being debated" (*The New Rhetoric and the Humanities*, p. 48-50). It is that which is ideally envisioned by rhetorical argumentation, but can coincide with a particular audience when we fabricate a human model we try to convince or to change into an elite audience, through the exclusion of those we know from the start will not accept our argumentation and whom we consequently renounce convincing (*Rhétorique et philosophie*, p. 20-22).

The audience "around which the argumentation is centered" is quite variable. It can range from the individual to including all of humanity, "crossing an infinite variety of particular audiences." This is so because "The audience is not necessarily only constituted by those whom the speaker questions directly" (*L'empire rhétorique*, p. 27-28).

Any discourse that is based on universally accepted values, or whose premises and arguments can be universalized, concerns, in effect, a universal audience, and even the people to whom the orator directs himself in the immediate plan are like the incarnation of that audience (Ibid., p. 31). Here he draws a distinction between persuasive discourse and convincing discourse, with everything depending on the orator's intentions. "The discourse addresses itself to a particular audience seeks to persuade, the one that addresses itself to a universal audience seeks to convince" (Ibid.).

Johnstone, Jr., does not necessarily agree, believing that an audience for either a philosophical argument or a rhetorical one should be limited. (*Philosophy, Rhetoric and Argumentation* [University Park: The Pennsylvania State University Press, 1965], p. 128-133; 142-148). See also: C. Perelman, *Le champ de l'argumentation*, p. 24-63; and *Traité de l'argumentation*, p. 17-26.
[39] *Rhetoric and the New Testament*, p.15.

(3) the social, cultural, ideological and values embedded in the argument's premises; (4) emphasis on seeing stylistic techniques as means to an argumentative end and not as merely formal and ornamental features.[40]

These introductory reflections on the pertinence and current nature of the theory of argumentation, on the definition of terms and key concepts within it, and on the problems it raises in terms of a methodology of analysis, justify a detailed study of the Philonic *corpus* within the context of the rhetorical tradition. As a basis of methodological preparation for our rhetorical analysis, we will devote the first part of this work to the study of the formal structures of argumentation, and will examine in the second the sources and trajectories of Philo's rhetorical education as well as the influences that contributed to the use he made of these structures.

---

[40] Jan Botha, *Subject to Whose Authority?*, p 127. Cf. W. Wuellner, 'Rhetorical Criticism and Its Theory in Culture-Critical Perspective: The Narrative Rhetoric of John 11', in Petzer, J.H. and P.J. Hartin (eds.), *A South African Perspective on the New Testament*, (Leiden: Brill, 1991) pp. 171-186.

CHAPTER ONE

STRUCTURES OF ARGUMENTATION IN GRECO-ROMAN RHETORIC

I *The Platonic Theory of Argumentation*

Plato's attitude toward rhetoric has been debated for many centuries. While some writers insist on a distinction between rhetoric and philosophy, and stress only Plato's dislike for the former,[1] others continue to defend the thesis that he drew a distinction between "legal rhetoric" and "factual rhetoric".[2] They fiercely oppose the latter as being sophistic, but with the same vigor argue in favor of an ideal rhetoric which is truly worthy of a philosopher and capable of persuading the very gods.[3]

Scholars such as R. W. Quimby insist on the thesis that Plato's work reflects a sensitive evolution in terms of a maturation of his rhetorical theory.[4] In Quimby's opinion, Plato's thinking about rhetoric is still incomplete in the *Gorgias;* the philosopher only clearly favors it as an art seventeen years later while writing the *Phaedrus.*[5] In fact, it is only here that he reveals "all the elements of a true rhetoric," qualifying it as an art similar to dialectic; such was only possible after having perfected "the dialectical method of collection and division."[6] Instead of merely directing a fierce attack at rhetoric, he finally determines its authentic nature and places it at the service of philosophy and truth.[7]

---

[1] Repeatedly documented in *Euthydemus, Gorgias, Phaedrus, Protagoras,* etc.
[2] L. Robin, *Platon, Oeuvres completes* IV, 3rd part, "Phèdre" (Paris, 1947), p. xxxvii. Cf. B. Cassin, "Bonnes et mauvaises rhétoriques: de Platon à Perelman", in *Figures et Conflits rhétoriques* (Bruxelles: Editions de l'Université de Bruxelles, 1990), p. 17-26.
[3] *Phaedrus,* 273.
[4] "The Growth of Plato's Perception of Rhetoric," article first published in *Philosophy and Rhetoric* 7 (1974), p. 71-79; reprinted in an anthology of significant texts on the Platonic theory of rhetoric, edited by Keith V. Erickson, *Plato: True and Sophistic Rhetoric* (Amsterdam: Rodopi, 1979), p. 21-30. G. Ryle, for example, in reference to this states: "In the *Phaedrus* Plato acknowledges, what he had denied in the *Gorgias,* that there is teachable Art of Rhetoric, but he requires that the student of such must also learn psychology and, more conjecturally, dialectic" ("Dialectic in the Academy," in *New Essays on Plato*), p. 58.
[5] Quimby, "Growth", p. 28.
[6] Ibid., p. 29-30.
[7] Ibid.

E. Black[8] proposes a similar interpretation in stating that Plato was favorable to rhetoric when used with propriety. However, he separates himself from Quimby and from the main commentators on the *Gorgias* and the *Phaedrus* by attempting to resolve conflicting opinions on the unified nature of Plato's rhetorical theory. Based on the observation that these dialogues reflect only an apparent incongruity, Black argues that each is part of a distinct context which aims at a different objective. "The *Gorgias* is a refutative thematic dialogue aimed at refuting Gorgian rhetoric only ..."[9] Furthermore, he points out that Plato's rhetorical doctrine is not exclusively confined to these two texts, and, that nowhere, not even in the *Gorgias*, does he ever attack rhetoric in general. But he did oppose the personal, limited vision defended there by Gorgias, Polus and Calicles as eventual representatives of the sophistic rhetoric of his time. Consequently, there is no contradiction whatsoever between these two treatises. The *Gorgias* is a fundamentally refutative dialogue, while the *Phaedrus* presents itself as its constructive complement.[10] E. Black insists that Plato makes a clear distinction between a "true rhetorical art" that has educational and psychagogic value and the false rhetorical art of sophists which lacks moral effectiveness. According to Black, Plato taught that moral and metaphysical truths "should be rhetorically disseminated."[11]

W. Thompson, following the same train of thought,[12] "examines the rhetorical theory developed in the *Symposium*," pointing out the parallelism between this work and the *Phaedrus* in structure and method. He argues that both dialogues emphasize the importance of recognizing truth, oppose sophistic rhetoric, and offer examples of ideal speech.[13] He also examines the Platonic theory of *dispositio*, comparing the *Symposium* with theoretical aspects of Aristotle's *Rhetorica* regarding epideictic discourse, lines of argumentation, enthymemes, style, qualities of the perfect orator and characteristics of the ideal speech, to show that Plato and Aristotle agree in this area. He ultimately reaches the conclusion that, though there is no evidence of a causal relationship between Plato and Aristotle, the *Symposium* in practice expresses the theories stated in the *Rhetorica*. He further shows that Plato developed with unusual mastery an argumentative strategy perfectly within

---

[8] "Plato's View of Rhetoric," in K. V. Erickson (ed.), *Plato: True and Sophistic Rhetoric* (Amsterdam: Rodopi, 1979), p. 171. Reprinted from *Quarterly Journal of Speech* 44 (1958), p. 361-374.
[9] Ibid., p. 178.
[10] Ibid., p. 179-181.
[11] Ibid., p. 187-191.
[12] "The Symposium: A Neglected Source for Plato's Ideas on Rhetoric," in Erickson, *Plato: True and Sophistic Rhetoric*, p. 325-335. Reprinted from *Southern Speech Communication Journal* (1972), p. 219-232.
[13] *Phaedrus*, 244-257; *Symposium*, 201-222.

the rhetorical tradition of his time and that, in his opinion, the ideal speech "is a combination of rhetoric, dialectic and poetic." Not abstaining from rhetorical techniques, but rather using them to promote truth and not for mere ostentation, Plato introduces in this dialogue a perfect model of the type of rhetoric he approves of: a rhetorical presentation of a dialectical investigation of truth.[14]

G. Morrow reaches the same conclusion[15] when he suggests, in the words of K. Erickson, that "Plato not only distinguished the ideal rhetorician from the sophist, but also advocated the use of his skill in molding human nature."[16] Morrow adds that "Plato's conception is the germ of latter techniques of persuasion. . . ;" that, in sum, the Aristotelian rhetorical treatise exists in embryo in the *Phaedrus*.[17]

E. Hunt had previously defended the same thesis in declaring that Plato "holds an important position in the history of rhetorical theory,"[18] acknowledging that there can be a useful and genuine rhetorical art in *Phaedrus*, and outlining a set of principles which later reappear in Aristotle's *Rhetorica* as clearly developed ideas. In his view, the three books in Aristotle's manual "are virtually an amplified *Phaedrus*,"[19] which, according to Thompson, could very well be considered "a dramatized treatise on rhetoric." The only two differences Hunt sees between these two theoreticians,[20] Plato and Aristotle, have to do with truth and the art of writing. While for Plato it is necessary that the orator recognize the truth of what he will say, Aristotle limits rhetoric to the area of opinion, admitting that most of his premises are mere probabilities. However, Aristotle states that it is not enough to know what to say, but also how to say it. Presumed truth will naturally prevail in the argument since one of the aims of rhetoric is to strengthen it. As Isocrates said in his *Helenae Encomium*, "It is much better to formulate reasonable opinions on useful matters than to have an exact knowledge of useless matters."[21]

In fact, Plato developed a theory of the philosopher-orator, aware that true rhetoric should be based on truth, and that, without this and the

---

[14] Ibid., 337-338.
[15] "Plato's Conception of Persuasion," in Erickson, *Plato: True and Sophistic Rhetoric*, p. 339-354. Reprinted from *Philosophical Review* 62 (1955), p. 234-250.
[16] Ibid., p. 18-19.
[17] Ibid., p. 342.
[18] "Plato on Rhetoric and Rhetoricians," *The Quarterly Journal of Speech* 6 (1920), p. 33.
[19] Ibid., p. 39.
[20] E. L. Hunt opportunely indicates that Plato expresses his ideas on rhetoric through a comparison of the three speeches in *Phaedrus*. As Socrates says in moving to a discussion of oratorical practice, what is wrong is not writing speeches, but writing them badly (Ibid., p. 34-35).
[21] *Hellenae Encomium* 5.

dialectical method, the oratorical art does not exist.²² But, being aware of this fundamental principle, rightly emphasized by a growing number of scholars on such issues related to Plato's theory and rhetorical practice, what does he concretely tell us about argumentation? What argumentative techniques did he use? What formal structures does he recommend?

1. *The formal structure of argumentative discourse*

Comparing discourse to a living being with a head, body and members,²³ Plato argues in the *Phaedrus* in favor of rhetoric with a strong logical element, aiming at achieving persuasion in the listener's soul. Contrary to traditionally accepted interpretations, Floyd Douglas and Ray Anderson defend the thesis that "Plato's 'living creature' analogy alludes to a deeper, philosophical-psychological notion of rhetorical form."²⁴ According to them, Plato's rhetoric demands that the orator be a philosopher and a master of psychology at the same time. The *dispositio* of his discourse necessarily corresponds to the listener's soul and adapts to it. More important than strict submission to an artificial system is a philosophical-psychological awareness of the rhetorical situation and the consequent adaptation of the discourse to the psychic disposition of the listener himself.²⁵

Naturally, if such an image transcends, as they claim, the analogy between the disposition of the physical body and the organization of the speech, it metaphorically represents the analogy between the disposition of the speech

---

²² G. Bouchard, "Rhétorique des mots, rhétorique des idées," *Laval Théologique et Philosophique* 35:3 (1979), p. 306.
²³ Δεῖν πάντα λόγον ὥσπερ ζῷον συνεστάναι σῶμά τι ἔχοντα αὐτὸν αὑτοῦ, ὥστε μήτε ἀκέφαλον εἶναι μήτε ἄπουν, ἀλλὰ μέσα τε ἔχειν καὶ ἄκρα, πρέποντα ἀλλήλοις καὶ τῷ ὅλῳ γεγραμμένα. (*Phaedrus* 264c).
²⁴ "Plato's Conception of *Dispositio*," in Erickson, *Plato: True and Sophistic Rhetoric*, p. 300 (Reprinted from *Southern Speech Journal*, 36, 1971, p. 195-208). According to them, such interpretations which view the image of a living being as a formal schema of *dispositio*, or as a statement in favor of the "organic unity" in rhetorical and literary composition, are essentially wrong and incompatible with the general principles on which Plato's rhetorical philosophy and theory are based (p. 298-301).
²⁵ Ibid., p. 301, 307-308. The structural superiority of Socrates' second speech in *Phaedrus* is derived from his knowledge of philosophy and psychology. "As a philosopher, he has proceeded dialectically to discover the truth about his subject and to make necessary logical distinctions, and has then arranged his arguments in accordance with this knowledge. As a psychologist, he has carefully analysed his audience, in this case the youthful Phaedrus, and has then arranged his materials in the manner most suited to correspond with and thus induce persuasion in Phaedrus' soul. Socrates' speech has a beginning, a middle and an end—'head, body and feet'—but its pattern of arrangement is the result of Socrates' philosophical-psychological understanding of the rhetorical situation, not the result of strict adherence to a formal schema of *dispositio* or of such measured adjustments within the text of his speech so as to give it an internal wholeness and unity."

and the soul of the listener. But does it not actually represent both things simultaneously? We believe so because Plato gives special attention to the notion of a "living creature," stressing the fact that it is the soul that gives life to the body,[26] arguing that "this whole, made of body and soul, is called a living being,"[27] and explicitly declaring that this name is only truly used with propriety "in cases where a harmonious combination of body and soul gives rise to one single form."[28]

F. Douglas and R. Anderson's study has the merit of making us aware of two equally important aspects of Platonic doctrine: that the *dispositio* must be shaped in a way that corresponds to the disposition of the listener's soul in order to persuade him, and that the ideal orator is necessarily a philosopher with great psychological sensibility.[29]

2. *Concrete elements of a global strategy of argumentation*

At any rate, it is more in practice than in theory that Plato has left us evidence of his mastery in the use of a multi-faceted variety of arguments.

W. Thompson analyses the *Symposium* as a neglected source of Plato's ideas on rhetorical theory,[30] stating that the work illustrates argumentation techniques latent in the whole tradition and later dominant in the formal structure of a complete argument. Such is the case of the enthymeme, in perfect consonance with Aristotle's *Rhetorica*.[31] Such is also the case with antithesis, comparison, analogy, and amplification.[32] Example and analogy, for instance, permeate his work.[33]

Among all his strategies, that in which Plato most completely shows his versatile rhetorical-philosophical talent is dialectical investigation,[34] with special emphasis on definition.

By definition, Plato meant the expression of the essential and real meaning of something, having in mind the carrying out of both a logical and

---

[26] *Phaedo* 105c; *Phaedrus* 245e.
[27] *Phaedrus* 246c.
[28] *Epinomis* 981a.
[29] Cf. G. Kennedy, *The Art of Persuasion in Greece* (Princeton: Princeton University Press, 1963), p. 77-79.
[30] Kennedy, *The Art of Persuasion*, p. 332-333.
[31] See 332 of this same study. Thompson includes several examples taken from Plato's *Symposium*.
[32] Ibid., p. 333-335.
[33] Cf. Paul Grenet, *Les origines de l'analogie philosophique dans les dialogues de Platon* (Paris: Éditions Contemporaines, 1948). Cf. also W. K. C. Guthrie, *A History of Greek Philosophy* (Cambridge: Cambridge University Press, 1975), vol. III, p. 425-430.
[34] O. L. Brownstein, "Plato's Phaedrus: Dialectic as a Genuine Art of Speaking," QJS 51 (1965), p. 393.

ontological study. Contrary to Aristotle, who seems to say that it is necessary to move from an affirmation of existence to a definition,[35] to Socrates' disciple the definition of an idea automatically proves its existence as a form of argumentation.[36]

Because a definition is essentially discursive, it is characterized as much by the distinction of its parts as by its intelligible unity.[37] Dieresis as well as the principle of causality come into play here. But the dieretic method is particularly important in Plato as a form of πίστις, though naturally distinct from apodictic syllogism. Aristotle's criticism of the Platonic διαίρεσις, does not deny its proven importance; Aristotle merely points out its range of application. In opposing its claim at demonstrating, he ends up recognizing a much more fundamental value in it as a prerequisite for a syllogism. Though the division does not syllogize, it leads to the construction of the definition and so is inevitably included "among the possible principles in the syllogistic system."[38]

Judging from the doctrine expressed in Plato's last dialogues, "one cannot know without dividing."[39] Although the dieretic method of division is not the only one involved in definition, it is generally indispensable to it. In reference to this, J. Le Blond says in passing that definition is a beginning of argumentation to the extent that it can become the premise of a genuine demonstration.[40] But it is also a probatory argumentation schema, particularly as a logic syllogism of essence, which is based on "an analogy between the dynamic structure of cause and effect, and the intrinsic structure of a

---

[35] J. M. Le Blond, "Aristotle on Definition," in *Article on Aristotle* (London: Duckworth, 1979), p. 77.
[36] R. M. Hare, "Plato and the Mathematicians," in *New Essays on Plato and Aristotle* (London: Routledge & Kegan Paul, 1979), p. 29. "It was therefore natural for Plato to think that, by defining some idea, one had proved that it existed—that by saying *what* it was, one had proved *that* it was" (Ibid.).
[37] Aristotle, *Metaph.* 1034b 20; 1045a 8.
[38] P. Pellegrin, "Division et syllogisme chez Aristote," *Revue Philosophique* 2 (Paris: P. U. F., 1981), p. 187. In his analysis of texts in which Aristotle studies the dieretic method, Pellegrin does not comment on whether it actually has its origin in division or syllogism but points out that the Stagirite recognizes in them a pretentious relationship. Then, even if division does not demonstrate, it shows, thus producing a different type of equally precise knowledge, as an effective method of definition. But Aristotelian division is not the same as Platonic division, "especially because the former divides the genus according to the specific difference" (p. 187). In effect, in Plato's view, what division actually aims at is to demonstrate (p. 168-187).
[39] Ibid., p. 170.
[40] "Aristotle on Definition," in *Articles on Aristotle*, (London: Duckworth, 1979), p. 73. ". . . all demonstration presupposes a definition in its premises" (Ibid.). This same author analyses the nature, method and function of definition in such works by Aristotle as *Metaphysica*, *De Anima* and *Analytica Priora* and *Posteriora*, concluding that it is as much the result as the beginning of scientific work, "science itself, considered as a finished product" (p. 77), though "not completely indubitable" (p. 78).

substance."⁴¹ In *Topica*, for example, Aristotle believes that definition can be proved by syllogism.⁴²

The Platonic διαίρεσις is thus a type of demonstration, which methodically leads to knowledge of the specific differences contained in the *genus*, as a natural complement to the kind of inductive discourse that Socrates used in definition.⁴³ For lack of an actual theory of apodictic syllogism, Plato thus attempted to base his theory of demonstrative reasoning on the dieretic method of definition.⁴⁴ However, this is not the only argumentative technique within the dialectical dimension of his dialogues.

Causal definition and etymology also form a part of his strategic schemes of argumentation. In the *Symposium*, Phaedrus develops as his central argument the idea that Eros causes people to seek virtue and happiness.⁴⁵ An identical argument is present in Eryximachus' speech.⁴⁶ In addition, F. Solmsen points out that one of Plato's main postulates related to a description of rhetoric as a dialectical demonstration and ψυχαγωγία⁴⁷ is the etiological treatment of πάθος, considering that he never comments on the tendency toward a determined emotional state without concomitantly presenting the respective cause (its διὰ τί).⁴⁸ For Socrates, a definition is that which, through clarifying the use of a word, provokes in people a determined moral or esthetic preference and induces them to choose the action which the author considers the right one. Generally understood as a "persuasive definition," it alters "the descriptive meaning of a word without disarming its emotive force."⁴⁹ It should state "not only what we might regard as the essential attributes but also, and primarily, the ἔργον, or the work that the object in question has to perform,"⁵⁰ resulting in a teleological definition.

---

[41] Ibid., p. 75. Cf. Cf. Guthrie, *A History of Greek Philosophy*, (IV, p. 357): "Soul is by definition what gives life to a body. Life *always* accompanies it, is an essential attribute of it. Soul therefore cannot lose, admit its opposite death, and still remain soul. It is essentially deathless. . ." (See also his comment on the *Meno*, p. 245).
[42] *Topica* 153a 6; Cf. *De Anima* I, 1, 402a 11ff.; 402b 19.
[43] It should be noted, however, that ἐπακτικοὶ λόγοι are not the intuitive inductions described in *Analytica Posteriora* II, 2, but conscious inductions—arguments derived from analogy which make possible a knowledge of *genus* or its essence on a growing scale (Aristote, *La métaphysique* II, Paris: Vrin, 1970, p. 735, text and note 1).
[44] Extensively exemplified in *Sophista* and *Politicus* as a "technical elaboration of something with which Plato was familiarized since the beginning" (Guthrie, *History of Greek Philosophy*, V, p. 27).
[45] *Symposium* 178a-180b.
[46] Ibid., 188.
[47] *Phaedrus* 271d-e.
[48] F. Solmsen, "Aristotle and Cicero on the Orator's Playing upon the Feelings," *Classical Philology* 33:4 (1938), p. 404.
[49] Guthrie, *History of Greek Philosophy*, III, p. 437.
[50] Ibid., p. 442.

Understanding the nature of something is, in essence, understanding the service it tries to render. To the Platonic Socrates, everything has its own ἔργον and its consequent ἀρετή which enables it to carry out its specific function[51] in a cause and effect relationship.[52]

As for etymology, the *Cratylus* is eloquent proof of its use. Even if, according to several interpreters, Plato proposes here to correct a false etymological science, he still agrees that "whoever knows names also knows the things" they represent.[53] Words can even communicate the essence of things if that essence is known beforehand. In his commentary on this dialogue, W. Guthrie forthrightly states that "we reach the seriously meant conclusion of the whole dialogue that names offer no help in discovering the essential natures of things, though they serve to communicate those natures when known."[54]

In arguing for a rhetoric worthy of a philosopher, Plato naturally diverges from the rhetoricians of his time. Nevertheless, he does prove himself to be in practice a consummate master of rhetorical art, both in the area of style and in that of formal structure. To him, dialectic is the only valid method in the investigation of truth, definition and division of the genre into the specific differences essentially forming part of it. Genuine rhetoric should use this same method, simply taking into consideration the necessary adjustments for continuous discourse and beginning with the truth to be demonstrated.[55] Otherwise, the difference between dialectic and rhetoric is very small. Both present the same logical structure[56] and both involve a wide variety of argumentation forms, which enriched the whole tradition of philosophical rhetoric that followed, particularly in the writings of Aristotle and Cicero. In essence, the main considerations in the Platonic theory of argumentation are perspective and method. The true orator—the orator-philosopher—is formed by nature, knowledge and practice.[57]

Therefore, Plato's objective was not to destroy rhetoric, but to promote its union with philosophy. He advocated a rhetoric based on truth and designed to promote adherence to authentic theses and not to mere opinions.

---

[51] Ibid., p. 442, n. 1.
[52] Guthrie, *History of Greek Philosophy*, IV, p. 349-364.
[53] *Cratylus*, 435d.
[54] Guthrie, *History of Greek Philosophy*, IV, p. 442.
[55] G. Kennedy, *Classical Rhetoric and its Christian and Secular Tradition from Ancient to Modern Times* (Chapel Hill: The University of North Carolina Press, 1980), p. 64.
[56] Ibid., p. 57.
[57] *Phaedrus* 269d.

II *Formal Structure of an Argument in the Greek Rhetorical Tradition*

A. *The Aristotelian Structure of Rhetorical Argumention*

Aristotle's τέχνη ῥητορική represents for his time a new theory of rhetoric as the overall product of the gathering and critical evaluation of different voices within the tradition, "relishing Platonic tendencies with sophistic-Isocratic doctrines"[58] and developing a model rhetorical system with a long and fertile life. Despite a few problems with internal coherence,[59] this work by the Stagirite has survived and inspired others because it is more than a mere rhetorical manual. In associating this discipline with dialectic right at the beginning,[60] Aristotle emphasizes the logical principles of his τέχνη and introduces a genuinely philosophical rhetoric which aims, not at mere exterior persuasion, but at persuasion by means of the articulation and rational expression of thought through a logical and sound line of argumentation. The purpose of his rhetoric was, in the words of G. Folena, not "the act of persuading, as fatally destined to become an intended instrument of eristic success, but the act of considering the means of persuasion regarding any argument."[61]

One of the most characteristic and original contributions of Aristotelian theory to the rhetorical schema was actually the system of the πίστεις as the means or methods of persuasion.[62] This "proof," or rather probatory reasons,[63] constitutes the conceptual nucleus of the *argumentatio* in a broad sense and is presented in a suggestive way, in binary division, immediately following the definition of rhetoric.[64] There are the πίστεις ἄτεχνοι, extrinsic or non-artificial means of persuasion, and, the πίστεις ἔντεχνοι. The latter, being directly dependent on the orator's reasoning capacity as internal, artificial or artistic means of proof, are derived from the elements that make up the world of oratorical discourse (orator, audience, and subject matter). They develop a triangular structure of argumentation[65] having to do with the orator's ἦθος, the listeners' πάθος and the actual speech's λόγος.

---

[58] B. Riposati, *Introduzione alla filologia classica*. "Problemi di retorica antica" (Milan: C. Marzorati, 1951), p. 662. Cf. B. Cassin, "Bonnes et mauvaises rhétoriques", p. 26-29.
[59] Cf. Kennedy, *Classical Rhetoric*, p. 63-64.
[60] ἡ ῥητορική ἐστιν ἀντίστροφος τῇ διαλεκτικῇ.... (*Rhetorica* I, 1, 1354).
[61] *Attualità della retorica*, atti del I Convegno Italo-Tedesco, Bressanone, 1973 (Padova: Liviana Editrice, 1975), p. 8.
[62] F. Solmsen, "The Aristotelian Tradition in Ancient Rhetoric," *AJP* 62 (1941), p. 36, 39.
[63] Roland Barthes, "A Retórica Antiga" in *Pesquisas de Retórica* (Petrópolis: Editora Vozes, 1975), p. 184.
[64] *Rhetorica* I, 2, 2.
[65] Cf. J. L. Kinneavy, *The Theory of Discourse* (Englewood Cliffs, NJ: Prentice-Hall, 1971), p. 225-226. The author introduces and illustrates here the triangle as the basic structural principle in Aristotle's *Rhetorica*, referring to this same classification tendency in other authors such as, e. g., K. Burke, I. A. Richards and Corbett.

According to Aristotle's rhetorical structure, these three types of intrinsic proof should concur in a harmonious and articulated way in order to provide the speech with force and effectiveness. They are distinct, yet complementary factors in argumentation. The ethical argument, for example, arises from the orator's personal nature and should reflect his good will, common sense, trustworthiness and moral authority in terms of the speech. It therefore constitutes the most powerful proof the orator has.[66] Apparently such was not the opinion of several of Aristotle's contemporary technographers, but his realistic view of human nature and sensibility led him to emphasize this fact since he realized that even the most valid and intelligent appeal to reason "could fall on deaf ears if the audience reacted unfavorably to the orator's moral character."[67] However, it should be pointed out that in Aristotle's view it is the speech itself, in its entirety, that should cause such an impression on the audience and develop the appropriate ethical image of the orator—an image in which φρόνησις, ἀρετή and εὔνοια stand out.[68] In essence, these are "the motives by which orators are themselves the basis of persuasion: prudence, virtue and benevolence."[69]

The pathetic argument is the second persuasion technique mentioned by Aristotle, and one of the most extensively studied and developed in his *Rhetorica*.[70] Whenever it is correctly instigated and directed in the process of argumentation, πάθος appears to be a strategically effective means of proof, particularly when through the arousal of emotions it attempts to act upon the audience together with an appeal to reason with the aim of modifying their convictions or dispositions and leading them to the desired action. Intellectual conviction is not enough. Emotional appeal plays an equally determinant role in the whole process of persuasion.

Yet, if the two πίστεις mentioned are important in the view of the Stagirite, the logical argument is undoubtedly the means of persuasion *par excellence* and the most characteristic of his philosophical rhetoric. We can persuade others through an appeal to our ἦθος and to their πάθος. But, above all, it is through proof that is logically concatenated in the words of the speech, by means of the λόγος itself, as argumentative discourse and rational expression of thought,[71] that we address ourselves to people's

---

[66] *Rhetorica* I, 2, 4.
[67] E. P. J. Corbett, *Classical Rhetoric for the Modern Student* (Oxford: Oxford University Press, 1965; New York: Oxford University Press, 1971), p. 93.
[68] Ibid., p. 93-95. Cf. Kennedy, *Classical Rhetoric*, p. 68.
[69] *Rhetorica* II, 1, 5.
[70] Aristotle devotes sixteen chapters to it in his second book, analyzing some of the more common and important individual emotions in this persuasive process, obviously from his own point of view and within his time.
[71] *Rhetorica* I, 2, 6ff.

minds. Aristotle repeatedly states that the logical aspects of rhetorical theory were not yet duly explored and developed, even though they are the most important.[72] He thus proposes to correct this situation, making available to the orator, in applying logic to rhetoric, the additional resource he lacks in order to better carry out his function.[73] In fact, the philosophical nature of his *Rhetorica* is more evident the deeper we go into a comparative analysis of works such as *Topica* and *De Sophisticis Elenchis*. Both works emphasize the interconnection between logic and rhetoric and offer a coherent philosophical approach to the problems of communication.[74]

If the study of analytical reasoning taken up by Aristotle in the *Analytica Priora* and *Posteriora* gave him the title of "father of formal logic" in the history of philosophy, the study of dialectical reasoning in the three works mentioned above made him, in the words of C. Perelman, the father of argumentation theory.[75] In fact, in setting himself apart from the theoreticians of rhetoric, his predecessors and his contemporaries,[76] Aristotle "does not fail to recognize the role of ἦθος or πάθος in the attempt to persuade, but emphasizes primarily the importance . . . of λόγος,"[77] basing his theory of argumentation on a logical schema identical to that of his dialectic and analysis. However, such argumentation is based on probabilities and not on certainties, having always in mind an audience to which it is directed in the appropriate literary form.[78]

After covering the three πίστεις, Aristotle returns to the treatment of the ἐνθύμημα and the παράδειγμα as basic forms of argumentation and fundamental vehicles of proof. Rhetorical argumentation can be inductive or deductive, just like scientific and dialectical levels of reasoning: inductive, if based on a set of examples that lead to a general conclusion; and deductive if it assumes a form similar to that of a dialectical or demonstrative syllogism. In the former case, there is the paradigm, and in the latter, the enthymeme—both indispensable forms in oratorical discourse since, as the Stagirite argues, they are the only means of persuasion available to the orator.[79]

---

[72] Ibid., I, 1, 3ff; I, 1, 9 and 11-12.
[73] Kennedy, *The Art of Persuasion in Greece*, p. 96.
[74] J. J. Murphy, *Rhetoric in the Middle Ages: A History of Rhetorical Theory from Saint Augustine to the Renaissance* (Berkeley, Los Angeles, London: University of California, 1974), p. 5-7.
[75] *L'empire rhétorique*, p. 15.
[76] *Rhetorica* I, 1, 3.
[77] C. Perelman, *New Rhetoric and the Humanities*, p. 57.
[78] Cf. Solmsen, "The Aristotelian," p. 39; and Kennedy, *The Art of Persuasion in Greece*, p. 84-85. This latter author refers to *Analytica Priora* as the source for the theory of two forms of logical argumentation: the enthymeme and the example.
[79] *Rhetorica* I, 2, 8.

1. The enthymeme

The enthymeme is a rhetorical syllogism, "an adaptation of deductive logic,"[80] "the instrument of deductive reasoning peculiar to rhetorical art,"[81] an argument based on that which is true to the majority of people, generally founded on probabilities and signs.[82] In stating that the enthymeme is "the substance of rhetorical persuasion," Aristotle makes it into a true syllogism. Nevertheless, the conviction it produces is by means of persuasion and not scientific demonstration, even though, judging from the definition in *Analytica Priora*, it should be said that it can be logically valid and produce certain as well as probable knowledge.[83]

Although Aristotle recommends that enthymemes be abbreviated, mentally they are whole syllogisms. They should be abbreviated whenever the listeners are capable of supplying the elements omitted. The definition of such an abbreviated argument that prevailed following Quintilian—that of a fragmented, incomplete or abbreviated syllogism—is perhaps already implicit in Aristotle's τέχνη, when he says that it is made up of few premises, generally fewer than those which constitute a normal syllogism.[84] But this is a practical rule and not actually part of the definition. As R. Barthes states, "if the enthymeme is an imperfect syllogism, this can only be so in terms of language," as an accident or separation from the mental plan.[85] Therefore, the difference between the enthymeme and syllogism is textological and not logical.[86]

For Aristotle, what is unarguable is the idea that, in a rhetorical context, any type of syllogistic argument be called an enthymeme, whether wholly expressed or not, whether derived from premises that are true or merely probable. L. Bitzer reaches this same conclusion defining the enthymeme as

---

[80] D. L. Clark, *Rhetoric in the Greco-Roman Education* (New York: Columbia University Press, 1957), p. 118.
[81] E. P. J. Corbett, *Classical Rhetoric for the Modern Student*, p. 74.
[82] Cf. *Analytica Priora* 2, 27, 70a 10; *Topica* 8, 14, 164a 6; *Rhetorica* I, 2, 4.
[83] *Rhetorica* I, 1, 11-14.
[84] Ibid., I, 2, 13.
[85] Ibid., p. 189. In Kennedy's view, though Aristotle apparently states that premises should not be entirely expressed, what he actually means, judging from the context, is that a rigorously introduced logical argument is not generally effective in rhetoric (*Classical Rhetoric*, p. 71). Just the same, he does emphasize the persuasive importance of arguments lacking a premise. In his explanation of the example he uses, the word πολλάκις is significant. "Aristotle does not define the enthymeme as a fragmented syllogism. But he certainly does point out that arguments have to frequently present this configuration in order to better and more effectively persuade the common man." Cf. E. H. Madden "The Enthymeme: Crossroads of Logic, Rhetoric and Metaphysics," *Philosophical Review* (New York, 1952), p. 373-375.
[86] J. L. Galay, "Le texte et la forme," *Revue Européene de Science Sociales*, 12:32 (1974), p. 61.

"a syllogism based on probabilities, signs and examples, whose function is rhetorical persuasion" and whose construction is successfully achieved through the combined effort of orator and audience.[87] He emphasizes that enthymemes only occur when the audience itself helps to produce the evidence by which it is persuaded.[88] The fact of premises being entirely verbalized or not is of minor importance, since the success of arguments depends generally on the listener's cooperative interaction. He will always end up using them, whether they are implicitly or explicitly stated.[89]

1.1 *Importance of the enthymeme as a method of rhetorical argumentation*
Aristotle's doctrine of the enthymeme is relatively complex but particularly significant. Of the two methods of argumentation studied by him, the enthymeme holds the primary position in his rhetorical theory as a dynamic reality which, when present in a speech, gives it content and form in the nature of the σῶμα τῆς πίστεως.[90]

A current trend among interpreters of his *Rhetorica* is to identify the enthymeme simply with one of the three πίστεις ἔντεχνοι, concretely with the logical method of argumentation. The traditional exegesis of the text interprets these as independent methods of rhetorical demonstration, making a clear distinction between psychological argumentation through the use of ἦθος and πάθος and logical argumentation by means of the enthymeme. Yet Aristotle never calls the enthymeme the third πίστις or suggests its exclusive identification with one. W. Grimaldi[91] is right in arguing that the word ἐνθύμημα "carried with it in the tradition a sense of form and denoted something more than an act of mere reason ...";[92] that "the enthymeme employs both reason, emotion, ethos, and directs itself in its argumentation to the whole man",[93] and that "*reason, ethos* and *pathos* not only permeate the language of discourse but are also unified in its argumentation, particularly in the enthymeme."[94] F. Solmsen[95] had previously expressed the same

---

[87] "Aristotle's Enthymeme Revisited," QJS 45 (1959), p. 408.
[88] Ibid.
[89] A particularly elucidating article on this matter is E. H. Madden's "The Enthymeme: Crossroads of Logic, Rhetoric and Metaphysics," PR (New York, 1952), p. 368-376. See also L. Bitzer, "Aristotle's Enthymeme Revisited," p. 399-408; J. H. McBurney, "The Place of the Enthymeme in Rhetorical Theory," *Speech Monographs* 3 (1936), p. 49-74; and Charles S. Mudd, "The Enthymeme and Logical Validity," QJS 45 (1959), p. 409-414.
[90] *Rhetorica* I, 1, 3.
[91] W. M. A. Grimaldi, "Studies in the Philosophy of Aristotle's Rhetoric," *Hermes*, 25 (1972), p. 65ff.
[92] Ibid., p. 82.
[93] Ibid., p. 144.
[94] Ibid., p. 150. In his acute and convincing analysis and evaluation of traditional exegesis, Grimaldi points out, among others, the following problems it presents: (1) Traditional exegesis assumes a univocal and very limited meaning of the word πίστις, while in *Rhetorica* it

opinion in concluding that Aristotle "rather thinks of the λόγος as a whole and thinks of it as being made πιστός becoming effective by the combined and simultaneous application of three πίστεις . . .";[96] that rhetorical discourse is a unified λόγος, wholly permeated with both psychological and logical arguments, though the beginning and end are more favorable to the former;[97] and that his theory was one of the main sources of inspiration for later technographers.[98]

In Aristotle's view rhetoric should be an integrated process since logical, ethical and pathetic forces interact within it, provoking persuasion and conviction.

More recently, W. Fortenbaugh[99] has dealt with the matter of "Aristotle's Analysis of Emotional Response," studying emotions within the realm of logical argumentation and showing that, "emotional response is intelligent behaviour open to reasoned persuasion"[100] and that "emotions can and should be aroused and allayed throughout an oration by reasoned argumentation."[101] He makes explicit the idea that the deductive analysis of emotion was, for Aristotle, of considerable importance to rhetoric.[102] In fact, emotions are not blind impulses nor should they be confined to the introduction or epilogue, as traditional rhetoric presumed.[103] An emotional appeal within the content and form of logical argumentation can prove to be a profoundly intelligent means of communication and make a discourse more likely to gain its objectives.[104]

---

consists of a wide variety of meanings. (2) It ignores the fact that παράδειγμα is correlative with ἐνθύμημα as a method of demonstration. (3) It contradicts Aristotle himself even in interpreting the enthymeme as a πίστις in contrast with ἦθος and πάθος. (4) It does not give due attention to the Aristotelian theory of the enthymeme, ignoring that the sources from which it derives its premises, εἰκότα, σημεῖα and τεκμήρια, as well as εἴδη, are in turn derived from ἦθος, πάθος and "πρᾶγμα" (p. 65-66).

[95] "Aristotle and Cicero on the Orators Playing upon Feelings," CP 33:4 (1938), p. 390-404.
[96] Ibid., p. 393.
[97] Ibid., p. 400.
[98] Ibid., p. 394.
[99] *Aristotle on Emotion* (London: Duckworth, 1975), p. 9-22; and "Aristotle's Rhetoric on Emotions," in *Articles on Aristotle 4, Psychology and Aesthetics* (London: Duckworth, 1979). p. 133-153.
[100] *Aristotle on Emotion*, p. 17.
[101] Ibid., p. 18.
[102] Ibid., p. 16.
[103] F. Solmsen, *e.g.*, explicitly refers to the fact that in various passages in *Rhetorica ad Alexandrum* precepts related to the arousal of emotions are found, but always in connection with the preface or epilogue ("Aristotle and Cicero," p. 392).
[104] Cf. Fortenbaugh, "Aristotle's Rhetoric on Emotions," p. 146-149.

Aristotle takes a significant step forward in conceiving the enthymeme to be a fundamental instrument of rhetorical argumentation and in consequently recognizing the existence of an epistemology of the probable. Equally significant is his using it to refer to an argument simultaneously incorporating λόγος, ἦθος and πάθος. The Aristotelian enthymeme undoubtedly introduces logic into rhetoric, but ends up transcending it; if communication can be achieved through the mind, it can likewise be achieved through emotions and feelings.[105]

Like Plato, the Stagirite perceives true rhetoric in terms of psychagogy, as an appeal to the whole man. Perhaps this is the reason the enthymeme, in advantageously substituting the dieretic method of definition or eventually being inspired by it as a rhetorical argument *par excellence*, necessarily presupposes resorting to emotions.[106] The language of the enthymeme and its structure must appeal to a listener with intellect, emotions and will.[107]

What can be said of a distinction Aristotle later makes between the enthymeme and the πίστεις?[108] L. Arnhard notes that, in order to understand the relationship between the enthymeme and the three πίστεις, we have to comprehend the different ways in which Aristotle uses the word πίστις.

> The primary meaning of πίστις is "belief," "confidence" or "trust." Aristotle uses the term to refer to any belief that arises either from a syllogism or from induction. But in the *Rhetoric* Aristotle employs πίστις not only in its fundamental meaning of "belief" (*e.g.* 1.2. 1355a6 and 9. 1367b30), but also as referring either to the formal logical process leading to belief (enthymeme or example) (*e.g.* 1.2. 1356b6-8 and 2.20 1393a21-24) or to the material sources of belief (λόγος, ἦθος and πάθος).[109]

In fact, it is important to note the distinction made by the Stagirite between "common proof" and "specific proof" as well as his classification of the enthymeme and example as "common proof."[110] The orator creates πίστις in the listeners' minds "by reasoning with the κοιναὶ πίστεις (enthymeme and example) based upon the ἰδίαι πίστεις (λόγος, ἦθος and πάθος)."[111]

---

[105] Cf. Grimaldi, *Studies in the Philosophy of Aristotle's Rhetoric*, p. 16-17.
[106] Plato emphasized in *Philebus* the existence of a close relationship between cognition and emotion (*Philebus* 17a; 31d; 42d; 46c) and recommended that the λόγος begin with a definition, and that the following argumentative parts of a speech be ordered in accordance with some specific need, keeping in mind the preservation of its coherence, unity and persuasive force (*Phaedrus* 263d-266c). It should be noted that W. Fortenbaugh admits Plato's possible influence on Aristotle concerning the formulation and application of the enthymeme (Cf. "Aristotle's Rhetoric on Emotion," p. 149).
[107] Grimaldi, *Studies*, p. 50.
[108] *Rhetorica* II, 20, 139a 21-24; cf. I, 2, 1381a 1-2.
[109] *Aristotle on Political Reasoning* (DeKalb: Northern Illinois University Press, 1981), p. 38.
[110] *Rhetorica* I, 2, 1381a 1-2. See James L. Kinneavy, *Greek Rhetorical Origins of Christian Faith: An Inquiry*. (New York: Oxford University Press, 1987), p. 33–55.
[111] Cf. Grimaldi, *Studies*, p. 57-67. See also "A Note on the *Pisteis* in Aristotle's *Rhetoric*," AJP

Therefore, it is evident that the enthymeme is not one of the three πίστεις nor is it limited to the πίστις of logical argumentation. Not being explicitly identified with any πίστις in particular, it nevertheless should combine all three and place itself at their service in order to prompt agreement, produce conviction, and lead to action.

1.2 *Sources of enthymematical argumentation*

Aristotle established the distinction among three sources of rhetorical reasoning by saying that the material invested in the enthymeme's premises is basically constituted by probabilities and signs[112] and that these, in turn, are subdivided into two distinct categories, with the following formal classification: (1) Some, σημεῖα ἀναγκαῖα, are specific indications, to which he also gives the name of τεκμήρια; (2) others, σημεῖα ἀνώνυμα, are naturally less specific indications of a more general nature, σημεῖα which are not very distinct from εἰκότα in terms of their degree of probability.[113]

In an interesting and instructive brief study of *Rhetorica*,[114] Grimaldi sums up the Aristotelian doctrine on this issue, giving special attention to the following facts. First, enthymemes are rhetorical syllogisms derived from three distinct categories, σημεῖα, τεκμήρια and εἰκότα.[115] Second, even though there exists no significant difference in meaning between σημεῖον and τεκμήριον, the latter sign is distinct from the former in dealing with a humanly undeniable certainty, while the former is merely a hypothetical and ambiguous indication. Enthymemes developed from εἰκότα and σημεῖα ἀνώνυμα represent the type of argumentative reasoning found in Aristotle's dialectic, while those derived from τεκμήρια are more related to the scientific reasoning studied in his *Analytica*.[116] A third point is that εἰκός and σημεῖον are different types of argumentation, even though no major difference exists between them. Σημεῖα are always indications of a cause-effect relationship,[117] and they are more convincing than εἰκότα. Σημεῖα

---

78 (1957), p. 188-192; G. H. Wikramanayke, "A Note on the *Pisteis* of Aristotle's *Rhetoric*," AJP 82 (1961), p. 193-196; and J. T. Lienhard, "A Note on the Meaning of *Pisteis* in Aristotle's *Rhetoric*," AJP 88 (1966), p. 446-454.

[112] *Rhetorica* I, 2, 14.
[113] *Rhetorica* I, 2, 16.
[114] W. M. A. Grimaldi, "*Semeion, Tekmerion, Eikos* in Aristotle's Rhetoric," *AJP* 101:4 (1980), p. 383-398.
[115] In the texts in which the term τεκμήρια is not referred to, it is presupposed within the classification of σημεῖα, as including necessary and unnecessary signs (*Rhetorica* I, 2, 16). In texts which state that enthymemes are also derived from παράδειγμα (Cf. *Rhetorica* II, 25, 11-13), this should be viewed as a process of induction from which a general principle is obtained; once achieved, it can be used as a premise of deductive reasoning (Cf. *Analytica Priora* 68b 38-69a 19; Grimaldi, *Studies*, p. 104).
[116] Ibid., p. 106, 115.
[117] These are sometimes cause, sometimes effect. Cf. *Rhetorica* I, 9, 14-15; I, 9, 26-27.

possess a greater demonstrative force,[118] since they are mere generalizations, like assertions about universal morality derived from experience. Just the same, the Aristotelian εἰκός "expresses a reasonable and stable aspect of the real order."[119] The knowledge it generates, as a source of the rhetorical enthymeme, is perfectly acceptable and worthy of trust.

Independent of their nature, necessity and level of truth, these three categories, each in its own way, play an essential role in oratory. As sources of premises for enthymemes they support distinct types of argumentation.

Aristotle considers the enthymeme from another angle. He also studies it in terms of its τόποι, deposits of ideas and argumentation formulas, the ultimate sources from which the premises of enthymematical reasoning are developed and upon which that argumentation that aims to ultimately produce πίστις is based.[120]

1.3 The topics of the enthymeme

The Aristotelian system of τόποι is extensively developed in the first two books of his *Rhetorica*. Nevertheless, its classification is neither linearly clear nor has it been interpreted in a coherent, homogenous manner. It consequently poses a few problems.[121]

According to Aristotle, τόποι are principles of a logical or rhetorical nature, being divided into two distinct groups: ἴδιοι τόποι and κοινοὶ τόποι. The former are topics concerning certain arts or sciences and specifically appropriate to each of the three genres of oratorical discourse. Most enthymemes are derived from them. The latter are characteristically rhetorical topics, being more general as principles or logical forms without any specific content and, consequently, they apply to all genres of discourse.[122]

This division needs some clarification. G. Kennedy points out that for Aristotle topics were both material for proof as well as a form of argument.[123] In the material category are the two types dealt with up to the nineteenth chapter of the second book of Aristotle's *Rhetoric*; in the second are the

---

[118] *Analytica Priora* 70a 11 - 70b 6.
[119] Grimaldi, *Studies*, p. 109.
[120] Ibid., p. 115.
[121] In regard to such, see studies and handbooks such as Grimaldi, *Studies*; Y. Pelletier, "Aristote et la découverte oratoire" I, III, in *Laval Théologique et Philosophique* 35:1 (1979), p. 3-20; 36:1 (1980), p. 29-46; 37:1 (1981), p. 45-67; G. Kennedy, *The Art of Persuasion in Greece*, p. 100-101; and *Classical Rhetoric*, p. 70-72; J. L. Kinneavy, *A Theory of Discourse*, p. 245-247; B. Riposati, "Problemi di retorica antica," in *Introduzione alla Filologia Classica*, p. 681-685; J. M. van Ophuijsen, "Where Have the Topics Gone?", in *Peripatetic Rhetoric after Aristotle*, ed. by W.W. Fortenbaugh and D.C. Mirhady (New Brunswick, NJ: Transaction Publishers, 1994), p. 131-173.
[122] B. Riposati, "Problemi di retorica antica," p. 682.
[123] *The Art of Persuasion in Greece*, p. 101.

topics listed after the twenty-third chapter. These are effectively pure lines of argumentation from which two sorts of enthymemes are formed—the demonstrative and the refutative—based on another τρόπος τῆς ἐκλογῆς (method of selection). [124]

Y. Pelletier[125] develops this point a bit further, by drawing a distinction between specific and common oratorical forms and by distinguishing the latter from the topics Aristotle presents at the end of the second book. Pelletier[126] bases his explanation of his topical scheme precisely on εἴδη, the technical term favored by Aristotle to represent the propositions applicable to each genre. In his view, the first book of *Rhetorica* deals with *specific species* particularly applicable to each genre, while most of the second book deals with *common species* pertinent to the three oratorical genres. The aim of the first propositions is to persuade that the action being argued for is useful, just, beautiful, or the opposite. These make up the definitive conclusions of the main arguments. The latter, normally translated as *commonplaces,* make up the preparatory elements of the main argumentation, their aim being to persuade hearers that such action is possible or impossible, real or unreal, having a major or minor level of magnitude.[127]

Even though Aristotle does not normally employ the expression κοινὰ εἴδη, Pelletier justifies his use of the phrase by the following considerations: (1) it is Aristotelian;[128] (2) Aristotle himself says that κοινά may be more specifically adapted to one rhetorical genre than another, though they are exclusive of none;[129] and (3) there is "a certain danger of confusing *common species* and *topics.*"[130] Pelletier calls them *species* because, similar to those which are applicable to each of the three oratorical genres, arguments based on them have one single objective or conclusion. And he calls them *common* because the conclusion aimed at is not an ultimate, definitive one. Still, the audience's acceptance of them will prepare it to accept the conclusion the orator ultimately aims at: τὸ ἀγαθόν, τὸ δίκαιον or τὸ καλόν.

---

[124] *Rhetorica* II, 22, 13-17.

[125] His study is the result of the research carried out by the Groupe Patrimoine Philosophique de la Faculté de Philosophie de l'Université Laval (*Laval Théologique et philosophique* 26:1, 1980), note, p. 29.

[126] *Rhetorica* I, 2, 22. In book I, 3, 7, Aristotle uses the term προτάσεις with the same meaning. However, it should be noted that he also uses the generic term τόποι extensively to designate these types of oratorical arguments. Cf. Pelletier, "Aristote et la découverte oratoire", 25:1 (1979), p. 18.

[127] Pelletier, "Aristote et la découverte oratoire", 26:1 (1980), p. 34-35.

[128] *Rhetorica* I, 9, 40. Cf. I, 2, 22, where Aristotle refers to the fact that most enthymemes originate from proper and particular *species* (εἰδῶν λεγόμενα τῶν κατὰ μέρος καὶ ἰδίων, ἐκ δὲ τῶν κοινῶν ἐλάττω), these being far fewer than those which are derived from common *species* (εἰδῶν ... κοινῶν).

[129] *Rhetorica* I, 9, 40.

[130] Pelletier, "Aristote et la découverte oratoire", p. 35.

After listing the τόποι (specific and common species) "which make up the substance of his method of oratorical discovery,"[131] Aristotle introduces a second classification of topics.[132] One group, that of "material topics," presupposes a knowledge of the types of conclusions to be established. The second, however, is a universal method totally "indifferent to the content of the desired conclusions."[133] Its basis is τόπος as a general strategy of argumentation, "useful for the discovery and construction of a number of different arguments."[134]

These latter τόποι, also called στοιχεῖα, are then lines of argumentation common to all types of conclusions.[135] Obviously, they are no longer the material invested in the premises of enthymemes, but make up the normative basis of arguments and deal with the organization of these premises in a syllogistic manner. In the words of Grimaldi, they are "forms of inference into which syllogistic, or enthymematic reasoning naturally falls . . . independent, in a way, of the subject to which they are applied and may be said to be imposed as forms upon this material."[136] The twenty-eight forms that Aristotle introduces and exemplifies can be classified into three groups: (1) antecedent and consequence or cause and effect,[137] (2) more or less,[138] and (3) some other form of relationship.[139] All take on a form of inference, a movement from the known to the unknown—if this, then that.[140]

In conclusion, we can say that Aristotle distinguished three categories of topics: ἴδια εἴδη, κοινὰ εἴδη, and κοινοὶ τόποι. Ἴδια εἴδη provide premises applicable to each of the three genres of oratorical discourse. Κοινά provide premises not specifically applicable to each of the three genres but applicable to all in general. And κοινοὶ τόποι, also called "enthymematic topics," constitute the formal methods of reasoning "according to which enthymemes can be constructed through the use of the premises provided by the *eide* and *koina*."[141] The topics of the first two categories can also be classified as material since they provide premises for enthymemes; the last type of topics can be classified as formal since they handle the formal structures of

---

[131] εἰς μὲν οὖν τρόπος τῆς ἐκλογῆς πρῶτος οὗτος ὁ τοπικός (*Rhetorica* II, 22, 13).
[132] ἄλλον τρόπον (*Rhetorica* II, 22, 17).
[133] Pelletier, "Aristote et la découverte oratoire", 27:1 (1981), p. 50.
[134] Cf. Pelletier, Ibid., p. 51.
[135] *Rhetorica* I, 2, 22; II, 22, 13; and II, 26, 1.
[136] Grimaldi, *Studies* (Wiesbaden: Steiner, 1972), p. 134.
[137] Numbers 7, 11, 13-14, 17, 19 and 23-24.
[138] Numbers 4-6, 20, 25 and 27.
[139] Numbers 1-3, 8-10, 15-16, 18, 21-22, 26 and 28. Cf. Grimaldi, *Studies*, p. 131; L. Arnhart, *Aristotle on Political Reasoning* (DeKalb: Northern Illinois University Press, 1981), p. 148.
[140] Arnhart, *Aristotle*, p. 148.
[141] Ibid., p. 51.

inference and provide the respective methods of reasoning.[142] However, it is useful to note that the Stagirite normally makes the preposition περί precede the first of these, and ἐκ the latter, in order to avoid the confusion that obviously results from the generalized use of the term τόπος, and to justify his double selection criterion.[143] For example: topics of injustice and topics of the possible and impossible are, respectively, τόποι περὶ ἀδίκου,[144] and τόποι περὶ δυνάτου καὶ ἀδυνάτου,[145] while topics of opposites are τόποι ἐκ τῶν ἐναντίων.[146]

In his treatment of τόποι and πίστεις, Aristotle develops a logical theory of argumentation which is sensibly distinguished from earlier rhetorical tradition. Τόποι are no longer a collection of prefabricated arguments, like "commonplaces," and are transformed into substance and form such as principles, strategies or lines of argumentation, as simple points of departure for the elaboration of arguments. For this reason Grimaldi insists that Aristotle uses the methodology of τόποι not only as logic of invention, but also as logic of inference. These, in fact, involve both the content and form of arguments, providing for some the material through which general or specific propositions are enunciated, and for others the forms of reasoning or means of inference by which enthymematic argumentation is expressed.[147]

Therefore, this new concept of τόπος reveals another capacity for abstraction and offers the orator the necessary resources for an effective argumentation technique, independent even of his having an exhaustive background in the area. The very movement from the specific to the general, present in the organization of the first two books of *Rhetorica,* seems to suggest such a conclusion. First, Aristotle presents specific τόποι (τὰ ἴδια εἴδη) and particular πίστεις (λόγος, ἦθος and πάθος), then, he considers general τόποι (τὰ κοινά), common τόποι and general πίστεις (enthymeme and example),[148] in a coordinated movement from the specific to the general and from the content of enthymemes to their formal structure.

1.4 *The maxim*

Before moving on to an analysis of the example as an inductive form of rhetorical argumentation, we should briefly mention the maxim as an

---

[142] Ibid.
[143] Cf. Pelletier, "Aristote et la découverte oratoire", 27:1, p. 65.
[144] *Rhetorica* II, 22, 16.
[145] Ibid., I, 3, 8; II, 19, 1.
[146] Ibid., II, 23, 1.
[147] Grimaldi, *Studies in the Philosophy of Aristotle's Rhetoric,* p. 118-120.
[148] Arnhart, *Aristotle,* p. 51-52.

elliptical and fragmentary form of the enthymeme, a variant to which Aristotle dedicates chapter 21 of the second book of *Rhetorica*.

A maxim is generally a premise or conclusion of an enthymeme. Aristotle states that its value is based on two facts: it summarizes universal truths based on age-old popular wisdom and it injects in the speech the ethical power necessary for its persuasive effectiveness.[149]

In affirming a general principle of action, the maxim normally presupposes that principle's reason (διὰ τί) and cause (αἰτία). However, the argument is so obvious that the listener dispenses with it, even while grasping the message.[150]

Aristotle considers maxims particularly useful for revealing the orator's moral character or creating an emotional atmosphere, particularly in cases where the enthymeme may not be able to achieve this objective.[151] He actually advises orators to change enthymemes into maxims in order to become more effective in his ethical and emotional argumentation.[152] This is not because enthymematic reasoning does not lend itself to producing ἦθος and πάθος, but because the maxim works better when it is supported by enthymematic inferences too obvious to need explanation. In such circumstances, the enthymemes are implicit in what the orator says; they are just incompletely verbalized, inviting the listener's cooperative interaction. Here Aristotle again repeats a rule he previously presented, that enthymemes should be as brief as possible.[153]

2. The example

Though Aristotle favors the enthymeme and considers it the heart of his rhetoric, he nevertheless stresses the importance and pertinence of this second form of argumentation. We could say that the παράδειγμα is the rhetorical equivalent of logical induction (ἐπαγωγή), just as the ἐνθύμημα is that of deductive reasoning.[154] But in this case the πίστις is separate from the cause, and inferences generally result from verifiable phenomena.

Examples are classified by the Stagirite into two distinct groups: real and fictitious. The former are examples taken from history, the latter are products of human invention and imagination. These are again subdivided into comparisons and fables. Comparisons (παραβολαί) are analogous examples

---

[149] *Rhetorica* II, 21, 15-16.
[150] Cf. Arnhart, *Aristotle*, p. 145-146.
[151] *Rhetorica* II, 21, 18-19; III, 17, 8-21.
[152] Ibid., III, 17, 33-38.
[153] Arnhart, *Aristotle*, p. 181.
[154] *Rhetorica* I, 2, 8; II, 20, 2.

of what could happen in real life; fables are purely imaginary examples. But, among these, by far the most persuasive are historical examples.

Like enthymemes, examples also help establish and strengthen proof. Even though Aristotle recommends the use of the first type, he stresses that use of the example is, in any of its forms, a powerful argumentation strategy. If enthymematic arguments make a stronger impression, those based on examples do not have less ability to persuade,[155] especially in deliberative discourse. This type of discourse is concerned with the future and, in this case, paradigmatic argumentation is the best form of reasoning because a person can infer what will happen based on what has already happened.[156]

Argumentation can in fact be based entirely on a set of examples logically directed toward one conclusion. However, in such a case, reasoning does not move "from a part to the whole, or from the whole to a part, or even from the whole to the whole; but rather from a part to a part, from the similar to the similar."[157] Despite its inductive nature, the example differs not only from deduction, which moves from the whole to a part, but also from induction which, inversely, moves from a part to the whole.[158] While induction directs its reasoning from all details to a generalization, without applying the conclusion to a new detail, paradigmatic reasoning moves from only one or a few well-known details to a generalization, immediately applying this to another lesser-known detail.[159] In the opinion of W. Ross, the real interest of the example in reasoning is precisely found in the movement to a particular conclusion.

Aristotle believes that the paradigmatic argument can also take on a syllogistic form,[160] especially when the example is used as the source of an enthymeme, lending it the universal principle necessary for the formulation of the major premise.[161] In such cases, the example acts as one of the possible types of premise from which enthymemes can be formed, and the resulting argument can be viewed as a form of enthymematic reasoning.[162]

Furthermore, Aristotle seems to favor the use of examples as supplements to enthymemes.[163] When examples are added to these they substantiate the

---

[155] Ibid., I, 2, 10-11.
[156] Arnhart, *Aristotle*, p. 180.
[157] *Rhetorica* I, 2, 27-29.
[158] *Analytica Priora* 69a 14-19.
[159] Arnhart, *Aristotle*, p. 47. Cf. W. D. Ross, *Aristotle's Prior and Posterior Analytics* (Oxford: Oxford University Press, 1949), p. 487-488.
[160] *Analytica Priora* 68b 38 - 69a 19.
[161] For the elaboration of "enthymemes through παράδειγμα" see Grimaldi, "*Semeion, Tekmerion, Eikos*, p. 385.
[162] *Rhetorica* II, 25, 8; cf. Kennedy, *Classical Rhetoric*, p. 70.
[163] J. L. Kinneavy, *Theory of Discourse*, p. 250.

evidence expressed by the enthymemes.¹⁶⁴ All that is needed is one example in the conclusion in order for the argument to be truly effective. However, when they are introduced before the enthymemes, or when they are the only proofs, more of them are needed¹⁶⁵ in order to produce the same effect. In either argumentative schemes, the example plays an important role: in the case of argumentation through the enthymeme, more characteristic of forensic discourse, the enthymeme is or can be followed by a specific example; in the case of paradigmatic argumentation, more applicable to deliberative discourse, as we have already mentioned, all that is needed is a set of examples directed toward one conclusion.¹⁶⁶

Finally, we could say that Aristotle, who is not greatly concerned with the parts of the speech,¹⁶⁷ is primarily interested in the rhetorical system of πίστεις, analysing them in terms of functions and providing with them a more solid basis for argumentation theory. In his *Rhetorica* the logical πίστεις reflect, apart from psychological factors,¹⁶⁸ a structural principle identical to that found in syllogistic reasoning. His analysis of them provided a philosophical argumentative scheme which succeeding systems of rhetorical argumentation would use. S. Toulmin observes that since Aristotle it has been customary, in the analysis of the micro-structure of arguments, to divide them in a very simple way: major premise, minor premise and conclusion.¹⁶⁹ W. Brandt¹⁷⁰ adds that the *confirmatio*, which makes up the backbone of argumentative discourse, would ideally be composed of one simple enthymeme, though this is rarely the case in oratorical practice.

Of the two essential models of argumentation proposed by Aristotle, the enthymeme is the argument appropriate for the orator and his most powerful means of proof. However, the example is not less persuasive, particularly in certain argumentative situations. Either one can function autonomously as an element of proof, but in combination they produce a greater rhetorical effect. Therefore, three types of argumentative structures are useful: the simple enthymeme, the simple enthymeme followed by an example (historical or fictitious), and the set of examples. Within a wider probatory scheme in which both converge, the enthymeme represents, what can be called the

---

¹⁶⁴ F. I. Hill, "The Rhetoric of Aristotle," in *A Synoptic History of Classical Rhetoric* (New York: Random House, 1972), p. 50-51.
¹⁶⁵ *Rhetorica* II, 20, 9.
¹⁶⁶ Ibid., III, 13, 4.
¹⁶⁷ Ibid., I, 9, 40; III, 17, 5.
¹⁶⁸ "Rhetoric, or art of persuasion through discourse—as Aristotle developed it—does not fail to recognize the role of ἦθος and πάθος in an attempt at persuasion, but insists, above all, on the importance of proof, of λόγος. . . ." (C. Perelman, *The New Rhetoric and the Humanities*, p. 57).
¹⁶⁹ S. E. Toulmin, *The Uses of Argument*, p. 96.
¹⁷⁰ W. J. Brandt, *Rhetoric of Argumentation*, p. 67.

essential structure of the argumentative whole, the example functioning as a supporting and substantiating argument for the enthymeme. Thus, παράδειγμα and ἐνθύμημα constitute a coordinated whole, as basic instruments meant for the production of rhetorical demonstration.[171]

In thus applying logic to rhetoric, Aristotle developed a simple and practical schema with numerous applications. This schema would eventually become an embryo-like model for other more ambitious and complex ones, so that the Aristotelian tradition of argumentation theory was influential throughout the Hellenistic period and long afterwards.

B. *Categories of Argumentation in Anaximenes'* Rhetorica ad Alexandrum

As important as Aristotle's highly celebrated and admired rhetorical work, the *Rhetorica ad Alexandrum* (also from the fourth century B.C.E.) is perhaps the most representative expression of ancient rhetorical theory.[172] Its significance is due not so much to its influence on subsequent developments as to the fact that, more than any other work, it represents the sophistic tradition[173] and reflects a structure similar to that of Aristotle's *Rhetorica*.[174]

Although it is not a systematically elaborated work, and the material concerning argumentation is not sufficiently clear, Anaximenes' work[175] deserves serious attention. It represents a first attempt at uniting several topics in an argumentative structure and tries to organize the components that enliven a speech, especially a deliberative speech.

---

[171] Grimaldi, *Studies in the Philosophy of Aristotle's Rhetoric*, p. 104.
[172] Kennedy, *The Art of Persuasion in Greece*, p. 81. Cf. also *Classical Rhetoric*, p. 19, where the same author adds that "the existence of Aristotle's summary seems to have rendered the survival of the original handbooks superfluous. They ceased to be copied and preserved, and save for the work of Anaximenes, which comes at the end of the tradition and was misrepresented by a latter editor as a work of Aristotle, none survives."
[173] Kennedy, *The Art of Persuasion*, p. 115.
[174] Ibid., p. 117-120. B. Riposati concretely points out the influence of the Isocratic doctrine on this handbook, yet also mentions several points of contact with Aristotle: "namely that normative spirit, that equilibrium and practicality of method, the rational and scientific distribution of material, the insistence on three genera (γένη) of eloquence... and also on its seven species (εἴδη) and their factors, as well as the various parts of discourse, to which can be added the topics of argumentation, the kinds and nature of proof, the theory of style and the structure of phraseology." (*Introduzione alla Filologia Classica*, Milan: Marzorati, 1951, p. 662).
[175] Attributed to Anaximenes of Lampsacus (ca. 380-320), based on a text by Quintilian: "Anaximenes recognized two genera only, judicial and public eloquence, but seven species: exhortation, dissuasion, laudation, vituperation, accusation, defence, inquiry, which he called ἐξεταστικόν. The first two belonged to the deliberative genus, the second two to the demonstrative genus, and the three last species are parts of the judicial genus" (III, 4, 9). This attribution is traced back to Victorinus and has been generally well accepted following Wendland, *Anaximenes von Lampsakos* (Berlin, 1905).

After mentioning the three genres of oratorical discourse—perhaps through the direct influence of Aristotelian doctrine[176]—the author of *Rhetorica ad Alexandrum* lists the various species these are subdivided into, namely: exhortation, dissuasion, encomium, vituperation, accusation, defense and investigation.[177] He also points out the lines of argumentation the first two should follow.[178] These abstract rhetorical categories aim at proving the following: in exhortation, that the cause presented is just (δίκαιον), legitimate (νόμιμον), convenient (συμφέρον), noble (καλόν), agreeable (ἡδύ), accessible (ῥᾴδιον), possible (δυνατόν) and necessary (ἀναγκαῖον); and in dissuasion, the opposite.[179]

Aristotle had actually already connected the various genres of discourse with three of the universal values included on the list. For example, forensic discourse is concerned with what is just, deliberative discourse is concerned with what is convenient, and epideictic discourse with what is noble. These categories, like τελικὰ κεφάλαια in oratorical discourse, are normally present in later rhetorical literature in lists which may vary in length but remain very similar to that of Anaximenes.[180] For example, Theon of Alexandria used χρεία as the basis for a significant number of preparatory exercises (προγυμνάσματα), including the commentary, the confirmation and the thesis itself.[181]

---

[176] Quintilian III, 4, 1, in fact, gives evidence that the adoption of this tripartite schema by other theoreticians is largely due to Aristotle's influence. But Solmsen, without contradicting him, states that he arrived at these *tria genera causarum* through deductive reasoning, admitting that it is also possible that the adoption of these three species resulted from the development of rhetorical theory and practice during the fourth century, and that consequently "it may have been his [Aristotle's] authority rather than his originality which determined developments in this phase of the rhetorical system" ("The Aristotelian Tradition in Ancient Rhetoric," *AJP* 62, p. 42-43). Cf. D.C. Mirhady, "Aristotle, the *Rhetorica ad Alexandrum* and the *tria genera causarum*", in *Peripatetic Rhetoric after Aristotle* (New Brunswick, NJ: Transaction Publishers, 1994), p. 54-65.
[177] 1421b 8-11.
[178] This consists of a list of abstract categories, like primary units of argumentation.
[179] 1421b, 21-30.
[180] In reference to this, see "Theon" in E. C. F. Walz, *Rhetores graeci*, (Stuttgartiae et Tubingae, 1832-36), p. 212, 12 - 213, 2; 214, 4 - 216, 1.
[181] In his commentary defending a χρεία, he proposes the use of four categories as an approximate version of the "principal values": true (ἀληθές), noble (καλόν), useful (συμφέρον), and authoritative evidence (ἐκ τῆς τῶν εὐδοκιμῶν μαρτυρίας). In regard to confirming a χρεία, he presents a list of topics as categories of negative value, among which at least two values which correspond to previous ones stand out: "the impossible" (ἀδύνατον), "the inconvenient" (ἀσυμφέρον) and, perhaps in a parallel manner, "the useless" (ἄχρηστον). Finally, in the chapter concerning the thesis, he includes a more complete list of essential rhetorical values (τὰ ἀνωτάτω κεφάλαια), such as: the necessary (ἀναγκαῖον), the noble (καλόν), the convenient (συμφέρον), the agreeable (ἡδύ) and, further ahead, the possible (δυνατόν), the legitimate, etc. (Ibid., I, 244, 13-15; I, 244, 19 - 246, 23).

In Anaximenes' view, the first step to take in the argumentation process is precisely to show that the action at stake manifests or satisfies these values. In order to substantiate these, however, he presents a second list of arguments, first expressed, then illustrated. They are: the analogy (τὸ ὅμοιον), the contrary (τὸ ἐναντίον) and previous judgments (τὰ κεκριμένα).[182] Fundamentally applied to each of the previously presented and defined values or topics, these aim to complement the argument in progress and assure the attainment of those objectives outlined in the primary proof.

The various illustrations used by the author explicitly document his doctrine concerning the combination of both lists into an argumentative whole with a beginning, a middle and an end. The argument appealing to τόπος τὸ ὅμοιον refers to the use of an analogy to illustrate and document each of the eight primary rhetorical values. An argument based on τόπος ἐκ τοῦ ἐναντίου establishes the contrast between two opposing events or statements, using one to prove the other with the aim of confirming, exalting or qualifying it. And κεκριμένα take on the form of quotations, statements or authoritative examples taken from "the gods, men of sound reputation, judges or opponents."[183]

We could therefore say that *Rhetorica ad Alexandrum*, though its theoretical sequential schema is not as clearly and logically elaborated as those later found in rhetorical manuals, does at least offer the elements which constitute the basic structure of argumentation in a purely formal sense: (1) primary proof, (2) analogy, (3) affirmation of the contrary and (4) previous judgments.[184]

In fact, Anaximenes took an important step forward in elaborating a complete argument. In considering the rhetorical values that make up the primary proof as fundamental topics extending to all genres of discourse,[185] he adds new elements to them as supporting arguments. He states, however, that these are especially used by the rhetoric of exhortation. Examples of such are amplification, minimization and πίστεις. The first two are useful for all species, though more effective in encomium and vituperation respectively;[186] the last of these, though equally extensive to all genres, is more useful in processes of accusation and defense.

In the case of the encomium, for example, Anaximenes insists on the need to amplify each of the mentioned topics since, as he explains, "the

---

[182] 1422a, 25 - 1423a, 12.
[183] 1422a, 25.
[184] B. Mack, *The Elaboration of the Chreia*, p. 12 (an essay kindly made available by the author). See R.D. Anderson Jr., *Ancient Rhetorical Theory and Paul* (Kampen: Pharos, 1996), p. 33–34.
[185] 1427b, 39 - 1428a, 1.
[186] 1426b, 18-21.

matters that are worthy of praise are those that are just, legitimate, useful, noble, agreeable and easy to carry out."[187] He goes on to explain that amplification is normally achieved by appealing to complementary arguments, identical to those pointed out earlier, namely those of reciprocity, opposition and previous judgments.[188]

As for πίστεις, these only intervene in the confirmation if the narrated facts do not produce immediate conviction. Generally, it suffices to develop the confirmation based on the rhetorical values making up the primary proof,[189] supporting them with analogies, opposites, previous judgments and examples. But whenever they are used to intervene in the argumentative process as supplementary reinforcing elements, this is done because it is necessary to endow the process with greater persuasive force. But his classification does not correspond to that of Aristotle.[190] Even though the reference to two groups of πίστεις presupposes a distinction between ἄτεχνοι and ἔντεχνοι,[191] Anaximenes lists only seven types without placing them in any kind of classification: εἰκότα, παραδείγματα, τεκμήρια, ἐνθυμήματα, γνῶμαι, σημεῖα and ἔλεγχοι πίστεις.[192]

When they are part of the rhetorical scheme of persuasion, particularly in deliberative discourse, these πίστεις should, however, be submitted to the following formal structure: (1) ἡ δόξα (the orator's opinion), or τὰ τῶν πραγμάτων ἔθη, in order to prove the authenticity of the alleged facts; (2) παραδείγματα and ὁμοιότης τις, in order to support the statements made; (3) γνῶμαι; and (4) conclusions, in the form of enthymemes and maxims (ἐνθυμηματώδεις καὶ γνωμολογικὰς τὰς τελευτάς).[193] In the case of forensic discourse, the line of argumentation followed is basically the same but with the intervention of evidence sufficient to prove it sound: (1) evidence by statements and confessions; (2) confirmation of the evidence through maxims and enthymemes or by resorting to the use of εἰκότα; (3) reconfirmation through παραδείγματα, τεκμήρια, σημεῖα and ἔλεγχα; and (4) a conclusion with maxims and enthymemes.[194]

We have therefore seen, through an analysis of the various texts mentioned, how the author of *Rhetorica ad Alexandrum* generally treats the same subject found in Aristotle's *Rhetorica*. He reveals, however, a less fertile

---

[187] 1425b, 40 - 1426a, 9.
[188] 1426a, 20 - 1426b, 12.
[189] 1439a, 7-11.
[190] Aristotle classifies πίστεις as ἔντεχνοι and ἄτεχνοι, but limits the first of these to two types, ἐνθύμημα and παράδειγμα, connecting the γνώμη to the former and regarding εἰκότα and τεκμήρια as sources of enthymematic reasoning.
[191] 1428a, 16ff.
[192] 1428a, 16-21.
[193] 1438b, 35 - 1439a, 7.
[194] 1442b, 33 - 1443a, 5.

imagination and a weaker capacity to systematize.[195] Nevertheless, his work already reflects a conscious concern with concrete structural elaboration. This is particularly so when he deals with the formulation of argumentative units and composes a list of topics in a more or less logical sequence. Viewed as an integrated system, these elements assume the form of a complete argument, as will be seen later in theoretical elaboration in works like the *Rhetorica ad Herennium*.

III *Formal Structure of an Argument in the Latin Rhetorical Tradition*

A. *A Complete Argument According to* Rhetorica ad Herennium

The rich body of literature on rhetorical theory written during the three centuries from Aristotle to Cicero has been almost entirely lost. Our limited knowledge on the rhetorical evolution of that period comes from evidence by various Greek and Roman writers from later periods who filled their works with references to Hellenistic rhetoricians and their doctrines. Such is the case with Cicero and Quintilian. Even the author of *Rhetorica ad Herennium*, without making any direct reference to them, shows the evolution that took place within that lapse of time.[196]

Rhetorical theory from the Hellenistic period reflects several significant changes from Aristotle's *Rhetorica*. On the one hand, it omitted the concepts of ἦθος and πάθος as forms of persuasion in the argumentative process[197] and did not recognize the basic importance of the enthymeme and example in the πίστις. On the other hand, it increased the number of categories in the process. The number of parts in the τέχνη ῥητορική went from three to five: εὕρεσις, τάξις and λέξις, as well as ὑπόκρισις and μνήμη. The number of parts in a speech also increased from two or four to six:[198] *exordium, narratio, diuisio* or *partitio, confirmatio, confutatio* or *reprehensio* and *peroratio* or *conclusio*. The internal structure of an argument was reformulated and amplified,

---

[195] Kennedy, *The Art of Persuasion*, p. 122-123.
[196] Ibid. Kennedy thinks that this handbook indirectly reflects the traditional system of a Greek source. See G. Kennedy, *A New History of Classical Rhetoric* (Princeton: University Press, 1994), p. 81–101.
[197] Cf. Aristotle, *Rhetorica* II, 1-17.
[198] According to Aristotle's *Rhetorica* III, 13, there are only two, πρόθεσις and πίστις. It is first necessary to state the facts relative to the cause (πρᾶγμα) and then to demonstrate them (ἀπόδειξαι). He nevertheless agrees that in some cases a speech can be divided into four parts: προοίμιον, πρόθεσις, πίστις and ἐπίλογος, even though, in such a case, the preface and the epilogue should merely support the πρόθεσις and πίστις as an aid to memory. But, according to the *auctor ad Herennium* I, 34 and Cicero, *De Inuentione* I, 14, 19, we have: *exordium, narratio, diuisio* or *partitio, confirmatio, confutatio* or *reprehensio* and *peroratio* or *conclusio*.

thinking now in terms of a complete individual argumentation structure and giving special attention to the number of parts in an argument.[199]

The author of *Rhetorica ad Herennium,* for example, treats the issue of an argumentation schema in two steps, presenting in them formal structures distinct from a complete argument.[200] Having little interest in the syllogistic form, in the first text he proposes the elaboration of an argument in five parts: *propositio, ratio, confirmatio, exornatio* and *complexio.* In the *propositio,*[201] a summary exposition of what one intends to prove is made. In the *ratio,* reason is given or cause provided to make the proposition well-grounded and plausible. In the *confirmatio,* additional reasons or arguments are provided which will corroborate the *ratio* and complete the basic structure which makes up the primary proof. The *exornatio* lends to the established proof complementary supporting arguments, and serves to adorn and enrich the whole argumentation schema. Finally, the *complexio* briefly summarizes and concludes the whole developed argument.

Argumentation's central nuclei, which in the *exornatio* corroborate and support the proof, are the following:[202] *simile, exemplum, amplificatio* and *iudicatio.* These are recognized as important elements in the total configuration of the argumentative schema since they grant it the necessary amplitude, soundness and balance. These are not, however, new elements. We have already encountered them in *Rhetorica ad Alexandrum.* But *amplificatio* appears here more clearly defined, like a type of *exornatio* within the *exornatio,* making viable and facilitating the expansion of supporting arguments *ad infinitum.*[203]

The second schema introduced later in the work[204] deals with the *tractatio,* or the development of one theme or thesis into seven parts. If, on the one hand, it constitutes a structural whole relatively close to "the most complete and perfect argument" mentioned earlier,[205] its architecture is much more similar to the elaboration of a χρεία, as later proposed by Hermogenes in his work *Progymnasmata.*[206] Such is a preparatory exercise also viewed as a form of argumentation which we will later define and exemplify.

---

[199] Cf. Kennedy, *The Art of Rhetoric* (Princeton: Princeton University Press, 1972), p. 116; and idem., *The Art of Persuasion in Greece,* p. 266.
[200] *Rhetorica ad Herennium* II, 28-30.
[201] Also called *expositio* in book III, 16.
[202] Ibid., II, 46.
[203] B. Mack, *The Elaboration of the Chreia,* p. 15.
[204] In *Rhetorica ad Herennium* IV, 56.
[205] Ibid., II, 28.
[206] The elaboration model formalized by Hermogenes with the name ἐργασία consists of eight operations in a row, which though not yet wholly confirmed in Aelius Theon, are adopted as a standard scheme by later tradition. These are: ἐγκώμιον or ἔπαινος, παράφρασις τῆς χρείας, αἰτία, κατὰ τὸ ἐναντίον, ἐκ παραβολῆς, ἐκ παραδείγματος, ἐκ κρίσεως and παράκλησις. Similar ἐργασία schemes are present in Aphthonius and Nicolaus' προγυμνάσματα.

Though it can allow for certain variations, the *tractatio* basically adheres to the following plan: (1) *res* - the exposition of the theme; (2) *ratio* - the reason or reasons justifying it; (3) *pronuntiatio* - a reaffirmation of the theme or its expression in a new form, accompanied or not by the respective reasons; (4) *contrarium* - an argument taken from the opposite; (5) *simile* - an analogy; (6) *exemplum* - an illustrative or authoritative example; and (7) the *conclusio*.[207]

The arguments we have just considered thus reveal a very similar organization and internal coherence. In both cases, the first unit of categories establishes and defends the formulated thesis, while the second supports it through a sequential line of arguments. These arguments should not only make clear the importance and credibility of the proposed theme, but also satisfy the principles of congruence and plenitude.[208] Nevertheless, there is a marked difference from the philosophical spirit inherent in Ciceronian rhetorical doctrine.

In fact, the *auctor ad Herennium* reacted strongly to the study of verbal ambiguities, or amphibologies in the exacting manner in which they were taught by the masters of dialectic during his time.[209] Though this author represents the same tradition as Cicero in *De Inuentione*[210] and there exists a certain affinity between them—both in theorization as well as in language and examples[211]—his doctrine concerning the complete argument undoubtedly reflects a more innovative rhetorical trend,[212] even if in principle it is less philosophical.

B. *Theory of Argumentation in Cicero and Quintilian*

Cicero wrote his rhetorical treatises over a relatively long period of his life,[213] but he was always conscious of the need to unite the ideal orator with the eloquent philosopher.[214] His rhetorical and philosophical training had put him in contact with major currents of thought and expression and inspired

---

[207] In terms of the conclusion, the author refers to his reflections in book II, 47ff, where he alludes to its tripartite nature and the extent of its use. However, he does not digress from the rhetorical tradition on the matter, as evidenced by Harry Caplan's note to the text mentioned.
[208] Paul Ricoeur, "Métaphore et le problème central de l'herméneutique," *Revue Philosophique de Louvaine* 70:50 (1972), p. 105.
[209] *Rhetorica ad Herennium* II, p. 16.
[210] Cicero, *De Inuentione* II, 8, points out that the schools of Aristotle and Isocrates which existed in the 4th century merged progressively into one single tradition. Cf. F. Solmsen, "The Aristotelian Tradition in Ancient Rhetoric," *AJP* 62 (1941), p. 46ff.
[211] Kennedy, *The Art of Rhetoric*, p. 126.
[212] J. Murphy, *Rhetoric in the Middle Ages*, p. 19.
[213] Approximately fifty years.
[214] Kennedy, *Classical Rhetoric*, p. 89.

in him a continuous effort to harmonize the various tendencies.[215] In a self-conscious testimony to the eclectic nature of his oratorical theory and practice, Cicero in one of his letters[216] states that he tried to summarize the rhetorical doctrine of Isocrates and Aristotle. Actually, he had previously admitted this in *De Inuentione*[217] when he declared that, just as Zeuxis had painted his famous Helena by using the five most beautiful young girls in Crotona as models, he too had adopted the theories of rhetoricians preceding him.

In Cicero's time, the Aristotelian and Isocratic schools of rhetoric had already become united into one single tradition.[218] But the Platonic issue about the relationship between this literary τέχνη and philosophy was far from being resolved. It was Cicero who attempted to interpret the deep meaning of rhetoric, clarifying its true nature and training himself in it. Just as for Plato "true philosophy is rhetoric, and true rhetoric is philosophy,"[219] for Cicero, too, eloquence implies philosophy,[220] from which necessarily follows the integration of philosophical thought in rhetorical schemes.

It is no accident that his model is Pericles, the *princeps* who led "the citizens of a democratic city solely by the authority of his eloquence and disinterestedness."[221]

1. The philosophical nature of a Ciceronian argument

H. Marrou states that rhetoric and philosophy are two rival cultures whose opposition generates between them "a creative tension, a reciprocal exchange of influences."[222] This tension and interpenetration permeate the whole Ciceronian theory and practice of argumentation, both in its philosophical conception of oratory and its deliberate use of philosophy. Cicero never tires of insinuating or even emphasizing the need for an orator's training to be simultaneously philosophical and rhetorical.[223]

---

215 "It is well known that Cicero derived from Aristotle and from the later Peripatetic school many precepts" (Lucia C. Montefusco, "Aristotle and Cicero on the *officia oratoris*", in *Peripatetic Rhetoric after Aristotle* [New Brunswick, NJ: Transaction Publishers, 1994], p. 68).
216 *Ad Familiares* I, 9, 23.
217 *De Inuentione* II, 1-4.
218 Ibid., II, 8. Cf. Kennedy, *The Art of Rhetoric*, p. 137, note; *Classical Rhetoric*, p. 95.
219 E. Grassi, *Rhetoric as Philosophy* (University Park: The Pennsylvania State University Press, 1980), p. 32.
220 A. Michel, *Rhétorique et philosophie chez Cicéron; essay sur les fondements philosophiques de l'art de persuader* (Paris: P. U. F., 1960), p. 84.
221 A. Michel, "La théorie de la rhétorique chez Cicéron," *Le Classicisme à Rome XXV de Entretiens sur l'antiquité classique*. (Genève: Vandoeuvres, 1978), p. 117. Cf. *De Oratore* I, 216.
222 *Histoire de l'education dans l'antiquité* (Paris: Seuil, 6th ed.), p. 313.
223 The dialogue *De Partitione Oratoria* is evidence of this fact, as D. J. Ochs indicates in "Cicero's Rhetorical Theory," *A Synoptic History of Classical Rhetoric*, ed. James E. Murphy

In *De Oratore*, for example,[224] he says that Socrates capriciously put an end to the previous unity between these two disciplines—a separation which Cicero considers "truly absurd, useless and condemnable,"[225] with tragic consequences for both. In *Orator*, he argues the same thesis, pointing out that philosophy is an indispensable component in the education of the ideal orator and that the schism between these two areas of study explains the scarcity of truly eloquent orators.[226]

Cicero therefore does not cling to any school in particular, nor adhere to a rhetorical theory which emphasizes purely technical and exterior persuasion. What he does reveal are various equally balanced trends, without losing sight of their basis.

The general techniques of argument did not experience great changes from Aristotle to Cicero. The form of the argument is still deduction or induction.[227] But the Roman orator generalizes the thought of Aristotle and produces a synthesis which appears virtually complete in his *Topica*.

This brief and informal treatise, remotely based on Aristotle's Τοπικά, is a description of the main topics of argumentation and reflects a clear dependence on Stoic logic, though written from an Academic point of view.[228] J. Dillon argues, the logical theory taken up here by Cicero "is basically the same professed by Antiochus" of Ascalon as Academic-Peripatetic logic.[229] It is, however, bolder. In A. Michel's view, we only need to compare the theory of definition in *Academica* and *Topica* with the definition theory offered by Cicero in his major oratorical treatises to realize that he attempted to go beyond the disputes among the philosophers of his time and regain what was common among them, that is, the teachings of Plato.[230]

His terminology is evidently influenced by Stoicism or Aristotelianism, but "if we study the different types of arguments referred by the author we notice

---

(New York: Random House, 1972), p. 143, when comparing this treatise with *De Inuentione*.
[224] *De Oratore* III, 56-95.
[225] Ibid., III, 60-61.
[226] *Orator* 11-19. Cf. D. J. Ochs, "Cicero's Rhetorical Theory," p. 136-137. See A. Michel, "Rhétorique et Philosophie dans les traités de Cicéron," ANRW I.3 (1973), p. 142; "One could say in short that philosophy too is language and that, as we are relearning at present, there is no language without rhetoric."
[227] *De Inuentione* I, 51.
[228] Cf. Michel, *Rhétorique et philosophie chez Cicéron*, p. 87: "The methods of thought used are philosophical. We have seen that they derive from Aristotle, the Stoics, the Academy."
[229] *The Middle Platonists* (Ithaca, NY: Cornell University Press, 1977), p. 50, 103-104. In regard to this, John Dillon states that Antiochus, like Philo of Larissa, "seems to have been an advocate of a reconciliation between philosophy and oratory . . . insisting that the good orator must also be a philosopher" (p. 104-105). Cicero's doctrine was most influenced by these masters.
[230] *Rhétorique et philosophie chez Cicéron*, p. 196.

that they have a more ancient origin" and that "as a whole, he tries to follow Plato adjusting him to his own time."[231] We have mentioned before that Cicero himself confesses that at the start of his career he had been sensitive to various forms of rhetorical doctrine and that he had used the most varied sources to produce his first *ars rhetorica*.[232] However, as the years began to weigh upon him and his ideas matured through constant study and prolific oratorical activity, a philosophical spirit began to pervade his doctrine. Though Cicero wanted to remain faithful to Aristotle's rhetorical tradition, he creatively interpreted and adapted it according to the spirit of the Academy.[233] In his noteworthy analysis of the Ciceronian theory of argumentation, A. Michel points out that Cicero's doctrine ends up being coherent in its complexity and that it evolves toward simplicity in its profound unity.[234]

2. Argumentation theory in Cicero

Cicero's argumentative strategy normally reveals a certain tendency toward systematization and formalism, already evident in *Rhetorica ad Herennium*.

In his theory of *argumentatio*, dealt with in *De Inuentione*, Cicero classifies arguments as probable and necessary, or irrefutable. Necessary arguments generally take on the form of dilemma (*complexio*), of enumeration (*enumeratio*), or of a simple conclusion or inference (*simplex conclusio*). Probable arguments are signs, probabilities, judgments of opinion or comparisons, and preferably take on the form of an epichirema.

Though he accepts and recommends a certain variety in the presentation of arguments, he gives special attention to their elaboration and disposition, since he considers this extremely useful and necessary. He laments the fact that this subject was largely neglected by rhetoricians preceding him.[235]

2.1 *Ratiocinatio*

The two formal structures recognized by Cicero basically correspond to Aristotle's rhetorical induction and deduction.[236] By *inductio*, however, he

---

[231] Ibid., p. 188, 193.
[232] *De Inuentione* II, 4.
[233] *Rhétorique et philosophie chez Cicéron*, p. 231-232. "K. Barwick has emphasized Cicero's originality on this score. The entire structure of books I and III of *De oratore* depend on the dialogue with Plato, who opposes rhetoric to philosophy, with Isocrates, who affirms the political role of speech, and with Aristotle, who shows that such politics are philosophical and so brings about a synthesis of the two preceding inclinations," *Le classicisme à Rome*, vol. XXV de *Entretiens sur l'antiquité classique* [Genève: Vandoeuvres, 1978], p. 117).
[234] Ibid., p. 229-231.
[235] *De Inuentione* I, 50.
[236] Ibid., I, 51. Quintilian gives appropriate evidence of the Ciceronian division of all arguments into classes, *inductio* and *ratiocinatio*, like most Greeks who divide them into παραδείγματα and ἐπιχειρήματα (*Institutio Oratoria* V, 11, 2-3).

means more specifically argument through analogy; and to represent the rhetorical syllogism, he prefers the term *ratiocinatio*.[237]

"Induction is an argument which procures assent to certain undisputed facts on the part of the person with whom the argument commenced."[238] Technically, it is divided into three parts: the first includes one or more analogies; the second consists of the point we wished to accept, and in favor of which the analogies were cited; and the third provides the conclusion which can either confirm the previous concession or reveal the resulting consequences. Nevertheless, he admits that an example can be added for greater demonstrative clarity.[239]

Ratiocinatio, the name Cicero gives to the *epichirema*, "Deductive reasoning is an argument which elicits a probable conclusion from the matter under discussion itself, which when expounded and recognized by itself proves itself by its own force and reasoning."[240] It is a type of deductive syllogism like the Aristotelian enthymeme; it is simply more complete—even more complete than the epichirema proposed by Quintilian.[241] This form of argumentation is a reasoning process, which causes its premises to accompany their respective secondary proofs, as justification and confirmation of the truth expressed in them.

Ratiocinatio thus has five parts: *propositio, propositionis approbatio, assumptio, assumptionis approbatio* and *complexio*.[242] The *propositio* briefly explains the principle from which the whole power of meaning in syllogistic reasoning arises; it is the underlying affirmation which is accepted or "assumed" in the *assumptio*. The *assumptio* establishes as a premise the point which, based on the *propositio*, is pertinent to proving the case. The *complexio* expresses the logical consequence resulting from the encounter between both premises mentioned. And the *rationes* prove what would otherwise be obscure or dubious.

Cicero defends this division as being the most precise and complete in the

---

[237] Cicero is normally careful to find in his own language the appropriate term corresponding to the Greek concept, avoiding whenever possible, its transliteration. The Greek terms συλλογισμός in the field of philosophy (Aristotle, *Rhetorica* I, 2, 13), and ἐνθύμημα (Ibid., I, 2, 13) and ἐπιχείρημα in the field of rhetoric (Quintilian V, 10, 1) essentially correspond to the term *ratiocinatio*. Cf. H. Lausberg, *Manual de Retórica Literaria. Fundamentos de una ciencia de la literatura* (Madrid: Editorial Gredos, 1975), p. 309-312, 371-372.
[238] *De Inuentione* I, 51.
[239] Ibid., I, 54-55.
[240] Ibid., I, 57.
[241] Quintilian, who claims to represent most authors, merely recognizes three parts in it—major premise, minor premise and conclusion. He states that "But the epichirema in no way differs from the syllogisms, except that they have various species and draw true conclusions from true premises, whereas the use of the epichirema is more frequent in relation to matters that are credible" (V, 14, 5-14). However, he accepts a schema similar to his, though arguing the thesis that every premise, even in this case, makes up only one part together with its reason or proof (V, 14, 5-14; Cf. *De Inuentione* I, 60).
[242] *De Inuentione* I, 67.

art of rhetoric, though realizing that there are cases where proof is unnecessary due to the evidence and the effectiveness of the truth expressed in the premises. He thus admits the possibility of reducing a logical argument from five to four parts, or even to three. For such, we merely need to omit the proof of one or both propositions.

According to some, the conclusion itself can be dispensed with, whenever obvious. Cicero feels it is preferable to keep it, though directing it in such a way that it does not become mere repetition.[243] However, epichiremas consisting of fewer than five parts are generally interpreted as unusual.[244]

What Cicero considers important is the manner in which thought is developed within the argumentation process. More than the simple joining of five affirmations with bizarre names, *ratiocinatio* is logical and coherent reasoning. The function of this reasoning is to introduce the order of reflection within the apparent disorder of discussion.[245] For reasons of elegance and strategy, the orator should be able to vary the order of the intervening parts. The arguments he uses should be clear and distinct, and his language appropriate and fairly ornate. Undoubtedly, as he states, the word *argumentatio* has two complementary meanings: it designates both the reasons which make something probable and necessary, as well as the art of expressing these in an ornate and artistic manner.[246]

Consequently, the orator should lend life to the *argumentatio*. He should be able to give it variety and exuberance, through using the most expressive figures as well as different types of arguments, developing these according to the most convenient and appropriate order.[247]

Partitiones Oratoriae briefly reproduces the same argumentation schema, equally emphasizing the idea that it should be varied in its disposition of arguments.[248] Not only do individual arguments found in the argumentative process of a work obey this formal structure of thought, but the entire speech itself can be based on a fundamental logical structure, a basic argument, to which all partial reasonings contained within it refer. A. Michel reaches this conclusion in his analysis of *Pro Milone*. The partial arguments contained within it only acquire their full meaning by their connection to the central schema, which, in a certain way, animates the speech. The whole logical plan is an epichirema.[249]

Thus, *ratiocinatio* provides argumentation with its spirit, its method and its

---

[243] Ibid., I, 70-74.
[244] F. Solmsen, "Aristotelian and Cicero," p. 169.
[245] Michel, *Rhétorique et philosophie chez Cicéron*, p. 177.
[246] *De Inuentione* I, 74: "Et inuentum aliquam in rem probabile aut necessarium uocatur, et eius inuenti artificiosa expolitio."
[247] *De Inuentione* I, 74-76; Cf. Quintilian V, 14, 31-33.
[248] *De Partitione Oratoria* 46-47. A similar reference is made by Cicero in *De Oratore* II, 177.
[249] *Rhétorique et philosophie chez Cicéron*, p. 180-181.

general structure.²⁵⁰ More than a rhetorical argument in five parts, it is philosophically "a dialectical syllogism."²⁵¹ This means that it involves the application of the rules of logic to orators' debates,²⁵² having experienced "in its form the Stoic influence which Cicero uses in an Academic spirit."²⁵³

Although Cicero manifests a strong preference for Peripatetic rhetoric and states that he is indebted to Aristotle for many of his ideas,²⁵⁴ he nevertheless expressly recommends for his son an Academic education in dialectic, considering the indirect benefits this can have for oratory.²⁵⁵ Remaining firm in his refusal to link himself with any rigid system of doctrine, Cicero repeatedly points out the need for philosophical training for an orator, insisting on the value of a science which teaches him to define terms, to draw a distinction between a genus and a species, to enumerate the parts of a whole, and to relate them to each other.²⁵⁶

Together with the *ratiocinatio* or epichirema, which is presumably the natural extension of the Aristotelian enthymeme, Cicero points out equally important forms of argumentation in which Platonic influence is more directly felt.

2.2 *Ciceronian theory of definition*

The number of times Cicero refers to definition in his final treatises is significant, as well as the context in which he does so. The amount of text he dedicates to it in *Topica* and *Academica* is no less symptomatic. Among the different types of intrinsic arguments he enumerates in *Topica*, definition stands out from the rest due to its variety of methods and applications.²⁵⁷ According to the doctrine here expressed, we can essentially form a definition in two ways: by enumerating its parts and by dividing or indicating the genre and its species. But *diuisio* and *partitio* are not the only methods of definition. There exist others which the author does not explicitly identify.²⁵⁸

Definition through reference to etymology is one of these. However, Cicero prefers to call it *notatio*, because words are distinct signs (*notae*) for

---

[250] Ibid.
[251] Aristotle, *Topica* VIII, 11, 162a15: ἔστι δὲ φιλοσόφημα μὲν συλλογισμὸς ἀποδεικτικός, ἐπιχείρημα δὲ συλλογισμὸς διαλεκτικός.
[252] A. Michel, "Un type d'argumentation philosophique (l'ἐπιχείρημα) dans les discours de Cicéron," *Revue des Études Latines*, 35 (1957), p. 47. Michel mentions here (briefly) the fact that Kroll had merely recognized the rhetorical aspect of the epichirema, purely and simply ignoring its important philosophical significance.
[253] Michel, *Rhétorique et philosophie chez Cicéron*, p. 187.
[254] *Topica* II, 6.
[255] *De Partitione Oratoria* 40, 139.
[256] *Orator* 4, 16.
[257] *Topica* II, 8-10; XXII, 83.
[258] Ibid., VI, 28.

things, and definition is normally only used "cum ex ui nominis argumentum elicitur."²⁵⁹

In *Academica*,²⁶⁰ letting Varro have his say, he briefly states the doctrine of the Old Academy pointing out the following elements from the system inherited from Plato: approval of the method of definition and its application to all the themes in discussion; approval of the intelligible explanation of words through use of their etymology; and use of complementary arguments, as elements of conclusion and proof.

The phenomenon of the identification of etymology with definition is also present in *De Oratore*²⁶¹ and *Partitiones Oratoriae*.²⁶² In these latter treatises, Cicero adds that once a definition is given, based on a word's common meaning and real value as much as possible, it should be supported and consolidated through the use of analogy and example.

Another possible method of definition he treats in *Topica* is *descriptio*.²⁶³ After discussing in a detailed manner each of the *Topica* Cicero takes up the theme of definition once again, adding to his two essential methods this other less exact variant, though not less significant. In a vivid and penetrating manner, he points out the distinctive signs, the most characteristically defining features of a person, his virtues, vices and passions.

As we have just observed, for Cicero definition "is not only an abstract method of classification based on the syllogism. It is also sometimes an art of analysing and describing the concrete."²⁶⁴

Whether periphrastic, dieretic, etymological or descriptive, Ciceronian definition reveals a relatively profound Academic influence. This is particularly so in what concerns the logical theory of a definition, since this has to do with the defense of authentic true doctrines, or those taken as such.²⁶⁵ Though Cicero considers himself merely a *magnus opinator* and not a *sapiens*,²⁶⁶ he causes two distinct attitudes to converge within the art of definition, certainty and doubt, in an attempt to adapt Plato to his period. We see in him a clear approximation to the Platonic scheme of philosophical argumentation²⁶⁷ in describing, through the words of Varro, the logic and

---

[259] Ibid., VIII, 35.
[260] *Academica* I, 8, 30-33.
[261] *De Oratore* II, 39, 162-165.
[262] *De Partitione Oratoria* 36, 123-128.
[263] *Topica* XXII, 83-84. Cf. *De Partitione Oratoria* 22, 41.
[264] Michel, *Rhétorique et philosophie chez Cicéron*, p. 191.
[265] *Academica* II, 8, 43.
[266] Ibid., II, 20, 60.
[267] His essential argumentative elements were the ὅρος or ὁρισμός, the διαίρεσις, the ἐτυμολογία and the αἰτίαι. In *Analytica Posteriora*, in agreement with the Platonic doctrine, Aristotle extensively analyzes the nature of the syllogism and demonstration, referring to the elements which intervene in the basic definition and concretely pointing out the import-

argumentative techniques which appear in his dialogues and in pointing out the importance of topics such as definition and etymology.[268]

2.3 The thesis theory in Cicero

While Cicero imbued his τέχνη with philosophical content and became uninterested in traditional rhetorical methods, he was at the same time very aware of the overall importance of the thesis in raising issues.[269]

It is perhaps in this area that his originality becomes most apparent. Being heir to a long tradition in which the controversy between philosophers and rhetoricians evolved from a series of isolated conflicts toward an eclectic solution, Cicero, on Roman soil, searches for a final word on numerous open-ended issues. Having mastered ancient culture as a whole and being inspired by the doctrine of the most famous masters of his time (Philo of Larissa and Antiochus of Ascalon, among others), Cicero commits himself to giving form and content to his rhetorical-philosophical ideal. He thus represents the most refined synthesis of Platonic, Aristotelian and Stoic trends which in his time were in the final phase of their conciliation.[270]

The coherence and unity of his work are closely connected with his use of the thesis in generalizing his own thoughts. Moving toward "a perfect rhetoric whose ways are progressively mixed with philosophy,"[271] Cicero gives special attention to this important rhetorical element, drawing a distinction between two kinds of issues: the *quaestio infinita*, also called *propositum* or simply *quaestio*, and the *quaestio finita* or *causa*.[272] The first of these deals with general important issues or theses of a primarily philosophical nature; the second addresses particular issues or causes of a purely rhetorical nature, which are distributed among the three genres of oratorical discourse.[273] They correspond, respectively, to the Greek notions of θέσις and ὑπόθεσις, already present in Aristotle[274] and Hermagoras.[275]

Even though Cicero, in his first rhetorical treatise, says that the *quaestio*

---

ance of the διαίρεσις and the αἰτία.
[268] *Academica* I, 32.
[269] S. F. Bonner, *Education in Ancient Rome* (London: Methuen & Co., Ltd., 1977), p. 82-83. See H. Lausberg, *Manual de Retórica Literaria* (Madrid: Gredos, 1976), § 1134-1138.
[270] *Academica* II, 5, 15. Cf. B. Riposati, p. 678-679.
[271] Michel, *Rhétorique et philosophie chez Cicéron*, p. 218.
[272] *De Inuentione* I, 8; *De Oratore* III, 109; *Topica* XXI, 79; *De Partitione Oratoria* 61.
[273] The *genus iudiciale*, the *genus demonstratiuum* and the *genus deliberatiuum*.
[274] *Rhetorica* II, 18, 1; III, 2, 3; *Analytica Posteriora* I, 2, 72a15; *Topica* I, 11, 104b, 19-36.
[275] *De Inuentione* I, 8. Cf. translator's note on the LCL page. In M. L. Clarke's view, Hermagoras was the first rhetorician to state that theses are also connected with the rhetorical field of argumentation ("The Thesis in the Roman Rhetorical Schools of the Republic," *Classical Quarterly* 45, 1951), p. 161. Cf. Hermogenes, *L'art rhétorique: Exercices préparatoires, Etats de cause, Invention Catégories stylistiques, Méthode de l'habileté*, trad. by Michel Patillon (Paris: L'Age d'Homme, 1997), p. 149–150.

is outside the realm of the orator, he is nevertheless already aware of its existence and important destiny as a universal philosophical matter. However, he departs from his initial position[276] when he later argues not only that general issues are within the orator's realm but also that all causes can and should be connected with them.[277] He makes it evident, at any rate, that the schools of rhetoric of his time were not concerned with this matter, adding that it was considered the sole property of Academics and Peripatetics.[278] This reality did not keep him from openly and decisively stating that the *orator excellens* "a propriis personis et temporibus semper, si potest, auocat controuersiam," and that the general issue resulting from this is called θέσις, best translated as *propositum,* as a *genus universum* of argumentation.[279]

Cicero's theory of general issues therefore has a philosophical origin. But, independent of its heritage, it eventually reveals itself as one of Cicero's most important contributions to the development of rhetoric. Despite having been introduced by masters such as Antiochus of Ascalon, Cicero claims that his style is unique within the genre and that no one before him had been able to go from a particular issue to a more general one.[280] By introducing the θέσις into the rhetorical system with its full philosophical meaning and recommending its practice to orators, Cicero himself could very well have been the ultimate author of this thesis theory.[281] More than a mere argumentative exercise in the style of rhetoricians,[282] the thesis should constitute the first term and the real basis of a *ratiocinatio,* epichirema or syllogism; it can be developed "as the treatment of a general proposition by the method of *in utramque partem,*" having a tripartite structure of *proemium,* arguments for and against.[283]

---

[276] A natural reflection of the doctrine he had received from his masters of rhetoric, Quintilian states that Cicero, in *De Inuentione,* merely repeated what he had learned, and its contemporary *Rhetorica ad Herennium* does not even mention the θέσις.
[277] *De Oratore* II, 133-136.
[278] Ibid., 106-107.
[279] *Orator* 45-46, 126-127.
[280] M. L. Clarke, "The Thesis in the Roman Rhetorical Schools", p. 163.
[281] *Brutus* 322. Cf. A. Michel, *Rhétorique et philosophie chez Cicéron,* p. 218-219. H. Throm, in his important study on "Die Thesis im rhetorischen System," mentions Cicero's originality, who gives the word θέσις its full philosophical meaning (*Die Thesis. Ein Breitrag zu ihrer Entstehung und Geschichte, Rhetorische Studien XVII.* Paderborn, 1932), chap. 2, p. 89-155. And D. Runia argues that the thesis was used "as a pedagogic method in both the philosophical and rhetorical schools of Philo's day" ("Philo's De Aeternitate Mundi: The Problem of its Interpretation," VChr 35, p. 117).
[282] Quintilian (II, 4, 24-25) refers to theses as important themes in oratorical exercises. Later, Theon of Alexandria, Hermogenes and Aphthonius consider the thesis one of the most important προγυμνάσματα.
[283] D. T. Runia, "Philo's De Aeternitate Mundi: The Problem of its Interpretation," p. 116. As Runia asserts, "The essential feature of the genre is its disputatory character, finding expression most often in the practice of the *pro et contra dicere* or *in utramque partem tractare,*

2.4 *Thesis and* loci communes *in Ciceronian argumentation*

Considering Cicero's doctrine as a whole, we can ignore neither the connection between the thesis and commonplaces nor the complexity of their different classifications. However, we are interested in analysing the doctrine expressed in *De Oratore* since this is considered his most complete work and seems to represent the final form of his thought.[284]

A. Michel's interpretation helps us to establish a link among its elements and to recognize the logical coherence of Ciceronian exposition.[285] In his classification of *loci*, Cicero draws a distinction between those that make up the formal argumentation schema and those that give specific content to arguments. Somewhat like Aristotle in *Rhetorica*, Antonius introduces a list of τόποι, reducing his whole argumentation to its most general forms, as *sedes argumentorum*. Crassus studies εἴδη, composing a list of universal issues which he calls theses.[286]

In the dialogical exposition in *De Oratore*, what might appear to be the individual thoughts of different theoreticians is combined in *Topica* as a unified body of doctrine. In the first part, Cicero presents the *loci* or *maximae propositiones*,[287] while in the second he introduces, as we mentioned, a classification of the theses, showing how the actual *loci* can be used in such general issues.[288]

In sum, without separating himself significantly from the general method of argumentation in Peripatetic rhetoric, Cicero clearly enriches his τέχνη by drawing on the entire Greek rhetorical tradition and lending it as a philosopher a markedly original form, content and style—in accord with his goal of harmonizing philosophy and rhetoric. The rhetoric he represents is, in fact, a philosophical rhetoric; it is a rhetoric that inspires him, both in theory and practice, to generalize his thought and appeal to universal reason.[289] Ciceronian rhetoric influences Philo of Alexandria, both in his philosophical and exegetical treatises.

3. Theory of argumentation in Quintilian

Quintilian's rhetorical doctrine does not diverge from the trajectory represented by Cicero within the long Aristotelian tradition, being a reflection of the synthesis produced in the setting of Middle Platonism. Though it does

---

as Cicero repeats on numerous occasions" (Ibid., p. 117).

[284] *De Oratore* I, 5. Cf. J. Murphy, *Rhetoric in the Middle Ages*, p. 17.

[285] *Rhétorique et philosophie chez Cicéron*, p. 220-223. Cf. D. L. Clark, *Rhetoric in Greco-Roman Education* (New York: Columbia University Press, 1957), p. 75-78.

[286] *De Oratore* II, 162-173. Cf. *De Partitione Oratoria* 2, 7.

[287] *Topica* II, 8-20, 78.

[288] Ibid., XXI, 81f.

[289] Cf. A. Michel, "Quelques aspects de la rhétorique chez Philon," p. 100-101.

not follow any specific rhetorical school or tendency, there is no doubt that Cicero's influence is strongly felt.[290] Many considered him a mere echo of Cicero, despite their different attitudes toward the nature and function of rhetoric, and their different concepts of the ideal orator.[291]

Although Quintilian's work is later than Philo,[292] we still find it important to refer to him since his writings summarize rhetorical theories formed throughout the Hellenistic period. He enriched his summaries with comments reflecting his own extensive oratorical experience.[293]

The theories summarized are eminently practical. By defining rhetoric as "*ars bene dicendi*,"[294] he in effect defines a good rhetoric—ethically, structurally and artistically. He seems to follow the Stoics Cleanthes and Chrysippus, who conceive it as "the art of speaking correctly."[295]

Like Cicero, he follows the Aristotelian theory of argumentation in dividing proofs into artificial and non-artificial[296] and considering the rational argument of primary interest.[297] However, he relegates ethical and pathetic proof to a lesser or purely ornamental plane. He nevertheless classifies these into three groups: those based on signs,[298] arguments[299] and examples.[300]

The *signa, indicia* or *uestigia*[301]—Aristotelian σημεῖα—are processes of proof which allow a relatively safe deduction of what is signified. Following this, an Aristotelian distinction should be drawn between the *signum necessarium* (τεκμήριον) and the *non necessarium*.[302]

Argumenta are rational and deductive proofs based on facts about the case.[303] They correspond formally to Cicero's *ratiocinatio* and consequently,

---

[290] Cf. G. Kennedy, *Quintilian* (New York: Twayne, 1969), p. 55; and "Peripatetic Rhetoric as it Appears (and Disappears) in Quintilian", in *Peripatetic Rhetoric after Aristotle* (New Brunswick, NJ: Transaction Publishers, 1994), p 174-182. "Quintilian had some knowledge of Aristotle's *Rhetoric*, but it is not directly a major source for him" (p. 182).
[291] While Cicero's is critical-philosophical, Quintilian's is more pragmatic and scholastic. See A. Gonzalez, "Cicéron y Quintiliano ante la retórica," *Helmantica* 34 (1983), p. 251-266.
[292] Quintilian was born in the final period of Philo's life, around 40 AD. Cf. Kennedy, *Quintilian*, p. 15.
[293] Cf. Kennedy, *Quintilian*, p. 11.
[294] *Institutio Oratoria* II, 4, 34.
[295] Kennedy, *Quintilian*, p. 58. Cf. E. Z. Rowell, "Prolegomena to Argumentation," *QJS* 18 (1932), p. 231.
[296] *Institutio Oratoria* V, 1, 1.
[297] Ibid., V, 8, 2-3.
[298] Ibid., V, 9.
[299] Ibid., V, 10.
[300] Ibid., V, 11.
[301] Ibid., V, 9, 9.
[302] Ibid., V, 9, 3-8.
[303] Ibid., V, 10, 11.

to the concepts expressed in Greek by the terms συλλογισμός,[304] ἐνθύμημα[305] and ἐπιχείρημα.[306] However, Quintilian considers the συλλογισμός their most perfect form and the ἐνθύμημα their least perfect, reserving for the ἐπιχείρημα the status of complete rhetorical syllogism, in contrast to the philosophical syllogism.[307] He identifies this latter syllogism with the Ciceronian *ratiocinatio*,[308] despite the apparent fluctuation in terminology. In his view, the *argumentum*, rhetorical syllogism or *epichirema*, is made up of only three parts: major premise, minor premise and conclusion. He nevertheless admits that the first two parts should be accompanied by respective reasons, resembling Cicero once again in his division of an argument into five parts.[309]

Finally, *exempla* are inductive proofs exterior to the cause. Corresponding to Aristotelian παραδείγματα, they similarly are divided into historical and poetic examples, *poetica fabula* and *fabellae,* and are able to adopt two literary forms: that of a brief intersected allusion and that of the *narratio*.[310] In this case, the *exemplum* is a *digressio* within the *argumentatio*.[311]

The *similitudo* and *auctoritas* are also linked to the *exemplum*. The first assumes the same literary form and the same levels of likeness—*simile, dissimile* and *contrarium*,[312] and both have a similar probatory function and identical persuasive force.[313]

In his treatment of *loci* in arguments, Quintilian also seems connected with Ciceronian theory. To formal topics, among which we point out, by way of example, arguments of comparison which prove the major starting from the minor and vice-versa, he adds a long list of material topics which he

---

[304] Ibid., V, 14, 24.
[305] Ibid., V, 10, 4.
[306] Ibid., V, 10, 1 and 4; V, 14, 14.
[307] Ibid., V, 10, 1; V, 14, 14.
[308] Cf. J. Cousin, *Études sur Quintilien,* I (Amsterdam: Schippers, 1967), p. 272-273. To Cicero, *ratiocinatio* corresponds to ἐπιχείρημα; and Quintilian, in translating συλλογισμός as *ratiocinatiuus,* invokes the affinity that exists between the syllogism and epichirema. Cf. *Institutio Oratoria* V, 10, 6: "Quidam epichirema appellarunt, Cicero melius, ratiocinationem, quanquam et ille nomen hoc duxisse magis a syllogismo videtur: nam et statum syllogisticum ratiocinatiuum appelat;" V, 14, 14: "epichirema autem nullo differt a syllogismis, nisi quod illi et plures habent species et uera colligunt ueris epichirematis frequentior circa credibilia est usus."
[309] 310. Ibid., V, 10, 122-125; V, 14, 15ff.
[310] Ibid., V, 11, 6 and 15.
[311] Cf. Lausberg, *Manual de Retórica,* I, § 415.
[312] *Institutio Oratoria* V, 11, 30-31. Cf. V, 11, 5 and 17. The *exemplum simile* can emerge as: *exemplum totum simile,* when of equal intensity; and *exemplum impar,* when the similarity is of unequal intensity (*exemplum ex maiore ad minus ductum,* and *exemplum ex minore ad maius ductum*). The *exemplum contrarium* is different from the *dissimile* primarily in the contraposition of the main verbs (Lausberg, *Manual de Retórica,* I, § 420).
[313] Ibid., V, 11, 36-39.

divides into *loci a persona* and *loci a re*.[314] Personal arguments can be derived from one's birth, sex, age, country, education, etc.; material arguments, much more numerous, arise from a consideration of cause, time, place, means, circumstances, definition, etc. However, he does not seem satisfied with *loci* as proofs, since he believes that each case has its particular characteristics that suggest an appropriate line of argumentation, and that proof requires much broader knowledge and practical experience than that provided by a simple argument handbook or a list of *loci* as *sedes argumentorum*.[315]

In terms of the use of arguments and their order of distribution, Quintilian compares the orator to a musician, insisting that arguments "should spontaneously follow the orator's thoughts,"[316] using only those considered convenient and necessary. In addition, they should not be mechanically limited to consequential and incompatible premises and conclusions.[317] Contrary to Greeks who, in his view, failed in their excessive concern with linking their thoughts through an inflexible chain of argumentation, he insists on the need for an orator to breathe life into schemas and to lend variety, diversity and exuberance to their development. Arguments should be clear and distinct, expressed in appropriate and relatively ornate language. Their formal structure is important. More important still, is the way speakers use them, separating the strongest ones and joining the weakest in such a way that their number also produces an effect. Although he is not as explicit as Cicero and proclaims a natural or rational order of preference, he does not seem to diverge from him in terms of his preference for the Nestorian order of arguments in discourse.

Giving us a global vision of the rhetorical conventions of his time, Quintilian laments the decline of true eloquence, disassociating it from sophistry and considering it an integral part of creative and constructive human activity.[318] He insists that an orator needs a good philosophical education.

Though rejecting sophistic and formalistic rhetoric, he nevertheless recognizes, from a Stoic perspective, the intrinsic value of this science, declaring its pragmatic, realistic and human character "comme un apologiste du bon sens, de la mesure et de l'équilibre."[319] In his view, the ideal orator is a man who is honorable, gifted with great natural talent, educated in all the technical knowledge outlined in the *Institutio* and able to use it in his oratorical practice.[320] Even though Quintilian's only remaining work is

---

[314] Ibid., V, 10, 20-23.
[315] Ibid., V, 10, 119-123. Cf. Kennedy, *Quintilian*, p. 69-70.
[316] Ibid., V, 10, 122-125.
[317] Ibid., V, 14, 31-33.
[318] Cousin, *Études sur Quintilien*, p. 733.
[319] Cousin, *Études sur Quintilien*, p. 798.
[320] *Institutio Oratoria* XII, 1, 1-13.

primarily a treatise on rhetorical technique, modern scholars judge that he is among those who contributed most to the restoration of philosophical rhetoric.³²¹ This is particularly true because of his consistent assertion of the vital importance of philosophy in oratorical theory and practice.

IV *Synoptic Chart of Formal Structures of Argumentation*

A synoptic view of the basic argumentation structures proposed by the handbooks on rhetorical theory following Aristotle seems to be a necessary first step in considering the range of influences which could have affected a cultured individual with a good rhetorical-philosophical education—Philo of Alexandria. It is useful to end this chapter with a summary chart in which the various structures taught are compared with one another in an overview, correlated with the basic structure of a speech as well as with the development of a theme and the elaboration of a χρεία.³²²

We are aware of the period of time separating Philo from Hermogenes.³²³ However, we feel it is useful to refer at least to one structure of argumentation considered in his *Progymnasmata:* the elaboration of a χρεία.³²⁴ In the first place, because the affinity of this rhetorical exercise with the amplification of a theme in *Rhetorica ad Herennium* is evident. In the second place, because a growing tendency is apparent among rhetoricians in the Hellenistic period toward the formalization of a "complete argument." And in the third place, because of the attention being given by scholars of the new rhetorical criticism «to blocks or units of material rather than to occasional instances of figures, tropes, ideas, or themes».³²⁵ Such formalization consists of the following sequential movement: proposition, primary reasoning and proof, supporting arguments, and conclusion.³²⁶

In practice, the argumentative sequence can vary, even substantially, both in terms of the order and disposition of the arguments, and of their number, variety and need for expansion.³²⁷ But its basic structure remains relatively

---

³²¹ In J. Cousin's view, "He merits a place to which Cicero cannot make a claim, despite those celebrated developments of the *De oratore*, namely as the reviver of philosophical rhetoric" (Cousin, *Études sur Quintilien*, p. 770).
³²² According to Theon of Alexandria, χρεία is a concise affirmation or a subtle action attributed to a specific person or to something analogous to a person.
³²³ Approximately two centuries.
³²⁴ See M. Alexandre, Jr., "The *Chreia* in Greco-Roman Education", *Ktema* 14 (1989), p 161-68.
³²⁵ Burton L. Mack, *Rhetoric and the New Testament,* pp. 20-21. "One of the lasting contributions of form criticism, for instance, was to draw scholarly attention to the importance of smaller literary units for larger literary compositions in late antiquity" (ibid.). See Vernon K. Robbins, "Using Rhetorical Discussions of the Chreia to Interpret Pronouncement Stories", *Semeia* 64 (1994), p. vii-xvi; and *Exploring the Texture of Texts*, p. 52-58.
³²⁶ Cf. Mack, *The Elaboration of the Chreia*, p. 23.
³²⁷ Cf. Cicero, *De Partitione Oratoria* 46; Quintilian V, 14, 31-33. Perelman, basing himself on

constant. Argumentative figures[328] and topics constitute a wide variety of resources of which an able and intelligent orator makes use to lend rhythm, effectiveness and persuasive energy to his speech. The basic structure is logical and coherent, gradually tested and improved on as a standard schema to be followed. In this model, we can diachronically recognize the two essential forms of rhetorical argumentation: deduction and induction—or rather, the rhetorical syllogism which, according to Aristotle, also functioned with analogies, and the example.

Summarizing the results of our analysis, we would say that an argument follows a relatively complex strategic operation in its external configuration. The thesis or *propositio* is first established with proofs or universal rhetorical values, and then supported through the use of supplementary proofs, until it is finally justified. We need, however, to draw a clear distinction between two types of rhetorical argumentation. One, which is purely technical, is defended and adhered to by rhetoricians who are connected with the Sophistic tradition. Originally outlined in Anaximenes' *Rhetorica*, it becomes prominent primarily in the Second Sophistic, though already studied in *Rhetorica ad Herennium*. The second type, based on a philosophical rhetoric with an Aristotelian background, is energetically defended and demonstrated in Cicero's work.

Structurally presented as a micro-model of the rhetorical discourse itself, the complete argument can inclusively constitute its essential framework. At the core of an *oratio* there should exist a fundamental line of reasoning, a basic argument, on which the whole speech is founded and to which every detailed argument is linked.[329]

Having become aware of this common vision—a vision which the following chart synthesizes and illustrates—I read Philo again and was encouraged to study his use of rhetoric. Questions concerning his knowledge and use of the rhetorical conventions gradually disappeared as his texts were analysed. We now turn to an examination of Philo's knowledge of rhetorical theory and, thereafter, to the ways in which he applied that knowledge.

---

these and other similar texts, points out the importance of the Nestorian order of arguments within a general argumentative schema. That is, one begins and ends preferentially with the strongest arguments (*L'empire rhétorique*, p. 163).

[328] Such as analogy, the *contrarium*, rhetorical issue and definition. W. J. Brandt includes the enthymeme, *ratiocinatio*, *sententia* and *exemplum* (*The Rhetoric of Argumentation*, p. 120-135). C. Perelman goes even further in pointing out the double action of figures: "We regard a figure as *argumentative* if it entails a change of perspective and its use seems normal in relation to the new suggested situation. If, by way of contrast, the discourse does not entail the adherence of the listener to this argumentative form, the figure will be perceived as an ornament, i.e. a figure of *style* (*L'empire rhétorique*, p. 13. Cf. C. Perelman and Olbrechts-Tyteca, *La nouvelle rhétorique, Traité de l'argumentation*, 3rd ed., p. 229).

[329] A. Michel, *Rhétorique et philosophie chez Cicéron*, p. 179.

SYNOPTIC CHART

2. FORMAL STRUCTURE OF AN ARGUMENT

FORMAL STRUCTURE OF A SPEECH	Aristotle's *Rhetorica*	*Rhetorica ad Alexandrum*	*Rhetorica ad Herennium*		Cicero	Quintilian	Aelius Theon	Hermogenes	
			complete argument	amplification of a theme	*ratiocinatio*	*epichirema*	argumentation of a thesis	elaboration of an argument	elaboration of a *chreia*
1. προοίμιον (Ar. Rhet. *Exordium* (Her., Cic., Quint.)							1. προοίμιον	1. προοίμιον	1. προοίμιον encomium/ praise
2. πρόθεσις, διήγησις *narratio* 3. *divisio = partitio*			1. *propositio*	1. *res*	1. *propositio*	1. *propositio* major premise	2. χρεία	2. proposed theme	2. χρεία paraphrase
4. πίστις *argumentatio probatio* 5. *refutatio confutatio = reprehensio*	1. ἐνθύμημα enthymeme 2. παράδειγμα example(s)	1. primary proof (list of 8 topics) 2. supporting arguments 2.1 similar 2.2 contrary 2.3 judgements	2. *ratio* 3. *confirmatio* 4. *exornatio* 4.1 *simile* 4.2 *exemplum* 4.3 *amplificatio* 4.4 *iudicatio*	2. *ratio* 3. *pronuntiatio* 4. *contrarium* 5. *simile* 6. *exemplum*	2. *propositionis approbatio* 3. *assumptio* 4. *assumptionis approbatio*	2. *assumptio* minor premise	3. primary proof confirmation / refutation (12 topics) 4. supporting arguments (11 topics) 4.1 consequences 4.2 example 4.3 minor/major 4.4 part/whole 4.5 similar/contrary 4.6 judgement	3. primary proof reason / confirmation (6 topics) 4. supporting arguments 4.1 analogy 4.2 example 4.3 minor/major 4.4 similar/contrary	3. αἰτίαι 4. ἐναντίον 5. παραβολή 6. παράδειγμα 7. κρίσις or μαρτυρίαι
6. ἐπίλογος *peroratio conclusio*			5. *complexio*	7. *conclusio*	5. *complexio/conclusio*	3. *conclusio*	5. summary/ conclusion		8. παράκλησις

CHAPTER TWO

PHILO'S ACCESS TO ARGUMENTATION THEORY

A contemporary of Jesus and Paul, as well as of several celebrated figures of Palestinian rabbinic Judaism (such as Hillel, Shammai and Gamaliel), Philo lived in Alexandria during a time when this city was known in the Roman world as a principal center of research and cultural activity. If his own work is ample, no less is the scholarly literature devoted to his person, work and ideas.[1] Nevertheless, the important problem of his Hellenization remains unresolved, in spite of the efforts of recent decades to clarify and reduce the areas of controversy.[2]

It is not his loyalty to Judaism that is in doubt,[3] nor the fact that he became Hellenized as a consequence of a long process of acculturation. These are facts generally recognized by those who study his works. But the issue is the degree of this Hellenization and its impact on him as a thinker and interpreter of Scripture.

---

[1] In less than fifty years there have already been, in whole or in part, more than one thousand monographs and articles dedicated to him. Cf. Earle Hilgert, "Central Issues in Contemporary Philo Studies," *Biblical Research* (1979), p. 15; "Bibliographia Philoniana 1935-1981," in *Aufstieg und Niedergang der römischen Welt*, II, 21.1, ed. Hildegard Temporini, Wolfgang Haase (Berlin: de Gruyter, 1984), p. 47-97; "Bibliography of Philo Studies, 1976-1977," *Studia Philonica* 5 (1978), p. 113-120; "A Bibliography of Philo Studies, 1977-1978," *Studia Philonica* 6 (1979-1980), p. 197-200; R. Radice, "Bibliografia generale su Filone di Alessandria negli ultimi quarantacinque anni, I: Fonti bibliografiche, edizioni, traduzioni, commentari e lessici." *Elenchus* III, 1982, p. 109-152; R. Radice and D. Runia, in *Philo of Alexandria: an Annotated Bibliography 1937-1986* (Leiden: Brill, 1988); D.T. Runia, R. Radice and D. Satran, "A Bibliography of Philonic Studies 1981-1986", *The Studia Philonica Annual* 1 (1989), p. 95-123; D.T. Runia, R. Radice and P.A. Cathey, "Philo of Alexandria: an Annotated Bibliography 1987-88", and "A Provisional Bibliography 1989-91", *SPhA* 3 (1991) p. 347-374; D.T. Runia, R. Radice and D. Satran, "Philo of Alexandria: an Annotated Bibliography 1988-89", and "A provisional Bibliography 1990-92", *SPhA* 4 (1992), p. 97-124; D.T. Runia and R. Radice, "Philo of Alexandria: an Annotated Bibliography 1990", and "A Provisional Bibligraphy 1991-1993", *SPhA* 5 (1993), p. 180-208; D.T. Runia, *et al.*, "Philo of Alexandria: an Annotated Bibliography" 1991, and "A Provisional Bibliography 1992–94", *SPhA* 6 (1994), p. 111–170; idem, *SPhA* 7 (1995), p. 186–222; *SPhA* 8 (1996), p. 122–154; *SPhA* 9 (1997), p. 332–366.

[2] Samuel Sandmel, *Philo's Place in Judaism* (New York: Ktav Pub. House, Inc., 1971), p. 1.

[3] Ibid., p. 6. Cf. É. Bréhier, *Les Idées Philosophiques et Religieuses de Philon d'Alexandrie* (Paris: Vrin, 1950, 3rd ed.), p. 3; R. Williamson, *Jews in the Hellenistic World: Philo*, p. 2-18.

Concerning the indications of Greek and Jewish influences in Philo's treatises, V. Nikiprowetzky points out that Philonic criticism has never been able to free itself of this problem, which was already emphasized by Mosheim and Ritter in the last two centuries.[4] It is not because Nikiprowetzky does not question the existence of either of these two sides of Philo's literary personality, but he tenaciously presses the classic question whether Philo is more Greek or Jewish, perhaps without giving due attention to the fact "that he is both at the same time, always in a unique way which constitutes his own originality."[5]

The most casual reading of the writings of Philo immediately gives one the impression of a vast Greek and Hellenic culture permeating his ideological world and conditioning the expression of his thoughts. The text flows more or less naturally in a provocatively impeccable κοινή—,[6] using a copious and appropriate vocabulary. His manifest knowledge of the most varied genres of

---

[4] *Le Commentaire de l'Écriture*, p. 11.
[5] Ibid., p. 241. In the first two chapters of his important dissertation, Nikiprowetzky proceeds to a critical evaluation of the most representative theses of two distinct lines of interpretation. Among the authors for whom Philo is essentially a *Philo Alexandrinus* are, beginning with A. F. Dähne (*Geschichtliche Darstellung der jüdische-alexandrinischen Religions-Philosophie*, 2 vols. [Halle, 1834]) and A. H. Ritter (*Geschichte der Philosophie alter Zeit* [Hamburg, 1834]); also E. Zeller (*Die Philosophie der Griechen* 4 [Leipzig, 1923], III, 2, p. 385-467), J. Drummond (*Philo Judaeus* [London, 1888]), M. Heinze (*Die Lehre von Logos in der griechischen Philosophie* [Oldenburg, 1872]) and É. Bréhier (*Les idées philosophiques et religieuses de Philon d'Alexandrie*. For these, Philo's principal source is Greek philosophy. Other authors in agreement are W. Bousset (*Jüdisch-christlicher Schulbetrieb in Alexandria und Rom. Literarische Untersuchungen zu Philo und Clemens von Alexandria*; R. Reitzenstein (*Die hellenistischen Mysterienreligionen* [Leipzig, 1927]); J. Pascher ('Η βασιλικὴ 'Οδός. *Der Königsweg zu Wiedergeburt und Vergottung bei Philo von Alexandreia* [Paderborn, 1931]); H. Leisegang (*Der Heilige Geist. Das Wesen und Werden der mystisch-intuitiven Erkenntnis in der Philosophie und Religion der Griechen* [Leipzig-Berlin, 1919]; and his article "Philon" in RE, IV, 2) and more recently E. R. Goodenough, for whom, Philo's source is "an oriental religious doctrine or the piety of mystery religions" (Nikiprowetzky, *Le Commentaire de l'Écriture*, p. 14) involving a mix of "Persian, Isiac, Platonic and Pythagorean influences" (Ibid., p. 15). Among the authors for whom he is essentially *Philo Judaeus*, are particularly included I. Heinemann (*Philonis griechische und jüdische Bildung*, W. Völker (*Fortschritt und Vollendung bei Philon von Alexandrien*, S. Belkin (*Philo and the Oral Law* and H. A. Wolfson (*Philo, Foundations of Religious Philosophy in Judaism, Christianity and Islam*, 2 vols. This last representative of the Jewish pole of interpretation even considers, just like Belkin, that Philo knew Hebrew well, affirming that we find in him "a Hellenization in language only, not in religious belief or cult" (*Philo*, I, p. 13) and that he was a religious philosopher, "the first who tried to reduce the narratives and laws and exhortations of Scripture to a coherent and closely knit system of thought and thereby produced what may be called scriptural philosophy in contradistinction to pagan Greek philosophy" ("The Philonic God of Revelation and his Latterday Deniers," *HTR* 53:2, 1960, p. 101).
[6] David Winston, *Philo of Alexandria, "The Contemplative Life," "The Giants," and Selections.*

Greek literature is remarkable for a Jew; according to S. Sandmel, he cites fifty-four different classical authors.[7]

His writings are highly influenced in their form and function by the rhetorical theory of argumentation,[8] and the themes developed are often elaborated with "a wide variety of rhetorical techniques."[9] Besides all this, there is the enormous variety of his thought, so singularly expressed "in the form of a detailed philosophical exegesis of the Pentateuch,"[10] and the vast knowledge of Hellenistic culture which informs his work to the extent that some consider him Stoic, others Platonic, Aristotelic, neo-Pythagorean, or simply an eclectic due possibly to the influence of Antiochus of Ascalon.[11] According to D. Winston, for instance, "he must be regarded . . . as a highly competent student of the entire range of the Greek philosophical tradition available to his generation, fully acquainted with the texts at first hand. . . ."[12] According to D. Runia, he "is primarily a philosophically oriented exegete of scripture"[13] who "strove to produce a 'synthesis' between his Judaism and Greek culture."[14] We ask ourselves, however: what about the Greco-Roman rhetorical tradition? Could the same be true of Philo's knowledge of that tradition? The cultural environment of Alexandria would suggest it; Philo's education and the literary structure of his works bear witness to it and confirm it.

I *The Impact of Rhetorical Argumentation on the Cultural Environment of Alexandria*

Alexandria, almost since its founding, was known as a great intellectual metropolis, a magnet for the most erudite *intellegentia*, and a generative and dynamic center of culture in the most expressive and universal sense of the term. According to the testimony of H. Marrou, the *curriculum* supporting the intense cultural activity of that cosmopolitan city during the Hellenistic period was composed of the two forms of higher education of classical culture—philosophy and rhetoric—and of all other branches of know-

---

[7] *Philo of Alexandria, an Introduction* (New York: Oxford University Press, 1979), p. 15.
[8] See M. Alexandre, Jr., "Some Reflections on Philo's Concept and Use of Rhetoric", *Euphrosyne* 19 (1991), p. 281-290.
[9] D. Winston, *Philo of Alexandria*, p. 1.
[10] Ibid., p. 2.
[11] Cf. R. Arnaldez, PM 1, "Introduction General" (Paris: Cerf, 1961), p. 70-83.
[12] "Introduction General", p. 3.
[13] *Philo of Alexandria and the* Timaeus *of Plato*, p. 545.
[14] Ibid., p. 543. "I am persuaded", he says, "that it is in the triangular reciprocation between loyalty to his Judaic heritage (the Law), love for the Greek *paideia* (philosophy), and concern for his people's welfare (apologetics), that Philo's literary career finds its *raison d'être* (ibid.).

ledge.[15] For centuries the large public library and the museum attracted masters and specialists in literary criticism, who developed one of the great centers of systematized knowledge in existence anywhere.

The manuscripts contained in the library were, for example, classified according to the eight categories of Callimachus: oratory, rhetoric, poetry, law, philosophy, history and miscellany.[16] Although there is no evidence that any of its masters produced a significant work in the field of rhetoric, "their interest in digesting, analyzing and editing the work of others gives us a good illustration of the intellectual tone of the period immediately following Aristotle."[17] As witness to this fact we have the example of the establishment of the canon of the Greek orators.

In fact, the cultural connection between Athens and Alexandria is a phenomenon that is traceable to the first decades of the city. Ptolemy Soter himself, aware of what Aristotle meant to Alexander the Great, desired to surround himself with some of his closest and best qualified disciples. In vain he invited Theophrastus and Menander to reside in Alexandria. For a little while he retained Straton to teach his son Philadelphus. He warmly received Demetrius of Phalerum, an Athenian statesman, "a man of great talent and eloquence",[18] who remained there as a political refugee, encouraging him to found the royal library. In spite of our limited knowledge, at least we have evidence that this distinguished disciple of Theophrastus gave new impulse to the educational project of Alexandria previously begun by Philitas and Zenodotus, impregnating it with Aristotelian doctrine and leaving the visible marks of this inescapable influence throughout the length of the Hellenistic period.[19]

Since Demetrius was an orator and theoretician of rhetoric,[20] naturally he

---

[15] *Histoire de l'éducation dans l'antiquité* (Paris: Seuil, 1981), p. 262, 292, 318-319.
[16] R. W. Smith, *The Art of Rhetoric in Alexandria* (The Hague: Martinus Nijhoff, 1974), p. 12.
[17] J. J. Murphy, ed., *A Synoptic History of Classical Rhetoric* (New York: Random House, 1972), p. 77-78.
[18] Quintilian X, 1, 80.
[19] Cf. J. E. Sandys, *A History of Classical Scholarship*, I (New York: Hofner Pub. Co., 1964), p. 105; R. Pfeiffer, *History of Classical Scholarship*, I (Oxford: Clarendon Press, 1968), p. 95-96, 99. According to Pfeiffer (p. 104), the disciples of Aristotle represent in Alexandria the second phase of a cultural process begun by Philitas, Zenodotus and Callimachus. They "were able to bring priceless help to the ποιητικοὶ καὶ κριτικοί who already existed in Alexandria; they transferred collections of learned material from their Athenian home to them, they instigated further antiquarian research, they stimulated new literary criticism, often opposed to their master's views, and they taught them to organize institutions for the promotion of scholarship" (p. 95). The latter, in turn, acquiesced to the impact of the new tradition, thus opening the way to a fertile and explosive intellectual experience that through the centuries would produce delicious fruits.
[20] The treatise Περὶ Ἑρμηνείας is generally attributed to him (Smith, *The Art of Rhetoric*, p. 11), although W. R. Roberts believes this work is of uncertain authorship, and prefers to

must have contributed to energizing its studies, strengthening the foundations of this noble tradition just as his master Aristotle would have desired. There is clear evidence of the influence that the rhetorical treatises of the Stagirite and the *ad Alexandrum*, as well as some of Isocrates' works, exerted upon the educated class of Alexandria,[21] an influence so deep and enduring that "under Augustus and his immediate successors, Alexandria became for a time the chief seat of polite learning in the Empire, as rhetoric combined with philology and literary criticism."[22]

The study of rhetoric, which progressively infiltrated the city, flourished in singular fashion in the first century B.C.. The rhetorical models and voluminous number of papyri found in Egypt bear witness of this fact, as do the influence and popularity of masters such as Philo of Larissa, Antiochus of Ascalon, Eudorus of Alexandria and the writings of Aelius Theon, a no less worthy son of this important cultural center.

R. Smith refers to these models in general, and to the groups of papyri in particular, stressing the importance of the works of certain Greek rhetoricians and orators as a basic element of consultation and study: Aristotle's *Rhetorica*, the *Rhetorica ad Alexandrum* and certain of Isocrates' discourses.[23] He notes that, alongside the presence of Greek rhetoric in the educational system of Alexandria, the influence of Latin rhetoric was also felt. However, the latter was hidden in the instructional activity of the Alexandrian masters, dressed in Greek clothing,[24] since we have no certain evidence that any Latin rhetorical author was widely studied there, in contrast to other parts of the empire.

According to existing evidence, Cicero is virtually the only ancient Roman orator that stands out in this cultural context.[25] Nevertheless, it is significant that in Alexandria there were Peripatetic and Academic masters whose education was similar to his.[26] These masters received their inspiration from the doctrine of Philo of Larissa[27] and Antiochus of Ascalon.[28]

---

identify it with Demetrius of Tarsus, at a much later date (50-100 A.D.). Cf. *Demetrius, on Style*, LCL (Cambridge: Harvard University Press, 1973).

[21] Smith, *The Art of Rhetoric*, p. 63, 113.

[22] Ibid., p. 112. R. Smith adds that "in accordance with the demands of the age, rhetoric and philosophy, which had previously been of minor consequence, became the chief subjects of study, and with the coming of large numbers of students from over the seas she developed into a large center of instruction".

[23] Ibid., p. 63, 111, 126.

[24] Ibid., p. 113.

[25] Ibid., p. 126.

[26] A. Michel, "Quelques aspects de la rhétorique chez Philon," 1966, p. 82.

[27] Perhaps Eudorus of Alexandria, among others. Cf. V. Brochard, *Les sceptiques grecs* (Paris: Vrin, 1969), p. 221-222. Harold Tarrant opines that "Though his school did not endure, his brand of Academicism was still to be found in Cicero, in anon. *In Tht.*, probably in Eudorus, ... often in Philo of Alexandria, often in Ammonius and Plutarch" ("Agreement and the

Philo of Larissa, a disciple of Clitomachus and spiritual heir of Carneades in the defense of the New Academy, was accustomed to teaching rhetoric along with philosophy, and by preference dedicated himself to the treatment of general themes.[29] According to V. Brochard, it was under him that the New Academy reached its apogee[30] and it was with him that Cicero identified,[31] particularly regarding his probabilism.

Antiochus, who at first was part of the school of Philo of Larissa ended up going his own way, taking some ideas from the Old Academy and causing the eclectic dogmatism of the Stoics to triumph. According to Cicero's testimony, he was in Alexandria, together with Lucullus,[32] around the year 84 or 87 B.C.[33] and there had his first contact with two books of Philo of Larissa, previously published and distributed in Rome. These books provoked in him no small indignation and quick response. Antiochus and Philo of Larissa both insist, nevertheless, that a good orator should be equally a philosopher, effecting a reconciliation between philosophy and oratory.[34]

All historians agree that "the fundamental trait of intellectual education in Alexandria . . . is its scholarly nature."[35] R. Arnaldez observes that "the grammatical and philological, the rhetorical and philosophical studies, responded to precise programs for which there existed manuals, anthologies and doxographies." And he deliberately adds that during Philo of Alexandria's time there developed a rhetorical logic and a judicial logic, "à base de grammaire."[36]

The *curriculum* of the grammatical schools, followed in model fashion in Alexandria, besides including exercises in morphology, the study of literature and theoretical grammar, also included a series of rhetorical exercises

---

Self-Evident in Philo of Larissa," *Dionysius* 5 [Halifax, Canada, 1981], p. 97). He also maintains that "Eudorus is a potent influence on Philo Judaeus and Plutarch," since both show more respect for a light academic Platonism than for an Antiochan Platonism (Ibid., p. 68, note 8). This is not a difficult trajectory to accept, especially since one of the disciples of Philo of Larissa—Heraclitus of Tyre—is found in Alexandria in 79 B.C. (Cicero, *Academica* I, 11. Cf. J. Dillon, "The Academy in the Middle Platonic Period," *Di* 3 [1979], p. 65).

[28] Michel, "Quelques aspects," p. 82.
[29] Brochard, *Les sceptiques grecs*, p. 191, 204. Cf. Cicero, *Tusculanae Disputationes* II, 8-11; *De Oratore* III, 110. Plutarch refers to the great eloquence with which he presented his lessons (*Cic.* 4; J. Dillon, "The Academy in the Middle Platonic Period,"p. 65).
[30] Dillon, "The Academy in the Middle Platonic Period,"p. 208.
[31] Cf. *Ad Familiares* IX, 1; *Academica* II, 12.
[32] *Academica* II, 11.
[33] Cf. Brochard, *Les sceptiques grecs*, p. 210.
[34] J. Dillon, *The Middle Platonists*, p. 104-105.
[35] R. Arnaldez, PM 1, "Introduction generale," p. 95. Cf. W. Bousset, *Jüdische-christlicher Schulbetrieb in Alexandria und Rom*.
[36] Ibid.

of literary composition called προγυμνάσματα.[37] The work of Aelius Theon, probably a contemporary of Quintilian,[38] precisely reflects this reality. His *Progymnasmata*, the oldest existing collection of elementary exercises, and the most important manual of rhetoric of Alexandrian origin known, provided students, professors and other intellectuals with a unified system of instruction as a preparatory base for the higher studies of rhetoric. These exercises gradually accustomed the student to the intelligent and structured use of words, to the analysis of model discourses and to the consequent composition of their own discourses, beginning with the development and elaboration of simple topics.[39]

Theon, closely connected to the Alexandrian rhetorical tradition, wrote several other treatises—all of them, as far as we know, strictly of a rhetorical nature. But none of them survived. We merely know that among them were found writings on argumentation and oratorical structure, besides a few commentaries.[40]

The impact of the theory of argumentation on the cultural environment of Alexandria was felt progressively, and came to penetrate the works of educators of persuasive discourse in the early centuries, before and after the beginning of the common era. Rhetoric not only influenced the decisions of judges, but even the very manner in which they gave form and expression to those decisions.[41] It influenced and deepened all genres of discourse as orators presented their evidence, structured their arguments and defended their theses,[42] at a time when conference rooms and theaters overflowed almost daily with those listening to orations on virtue and similar themes.[43]

Actually, it is difficult to exaggerate the importance given to rhetoric in the Greco-Roman world, beginning with the monumental works of Cicero. From the tribunal judge to the itinerant cynic preacher and the occasional orator in every type of assembly, "the art of speaking was perhaps the highest art to be mastered for a man of action."[44] This was true specially in

---

[37] H. I. Marrou, *Histoire de l'éducation dans l'antiquité*, I, *Le Monde Grec*, p. 257-258.
[38] W. Stegemann ("Theon," RE V, 2 [1934], p. 2037-2054), after carefully analyzing the various proposals, decides upon 50-100 A.D., a position that has been generally followed since that time. See, for example, A. Lesky, *Historia de la Literatura Griega* (Madrid: Gredos, 1968), p. 875; G. A. Kennedy, *The Art of Rhetoric in the Roman World*, p. 616; R. W. Smith, *The Art of Rhetoric in Alexandria*, p. 133.
[39] Smith, *The Art of Rhetoric*, p. 113-114.
[40] Cf. *Suda*, Wulfins' Latin version (Basileia, 1581), p. 435; Smith, *The Art of Rhetoric*, p. 137.
[41] Smith, *The Art of Rhetoric*, p. 71.
[42] Ibid.
[43] Ibid., p. 130.
[44] R. Scroggs, "Paul as Rhetorician: Two Homilies in Romans," in *Jews, Greeks and Christians* (Leiden: Brill, 1976), p. 274.

Alexandria, that commercial crossroads and cultural center *par excellence*, where the most privileged classes could avail themselves of an extraordinary rhetorical and philosophical education.[45]

II *The Existential Commitment and Cultural Training of Philo of Alexandria*

In spite of the many studies devoted to determining "the place of Philo in Judaism," this issue has not been settled definitively. We have had occasion to mention that, while some consider him almost a Palestinian Pharisee, recognizing in his work mere traces of a superficial Hellenization, and others insist that he passed through a deep Hellenization, still others see in him a combination of dual existential and historical-cultural realities: loyalty to his Jewish origins and creative immersion in the life of the great pluralistic metropolis of Alexandria.[46]

A. *Hellenization of the Jews*

Philo's Hellenization appears within the context of a greater phenomenon of acculturation on the part of a people of common blood, tradition and faith. Whether in or out of Palestine, particularly in the privileged environment of Alexandria, the accommodation of the Jews to the influx of Greek culture is a generally accepted fact. M. Hengel, in his stimulating and enlightening historical study of the first centuries of the Hellenistic period, entitled *Judentum und Hellenismus*,[47] defends the proposition that after the conquest of Judea by Alexander, Hellenization to a certain extent permeated all Jewish culture. According to him, *stricto sensu*, all Judaism should be considered Hellenistic from about the middle of the third century B.C.,[48] even Palestinian Judaism.[49]

---

[45] On the abundance of sophists and sophist's schools in Alexandria, see Bruce W. Winter, *Philo and Paul among the Sophists* (Cambridge: University Press, 1997), p. 5–39.
[46] Samuel Sandel summarizes and answers these two opposing lines of interpretation, more recently represented by E. Goodenough and H. Wolfson, and comes to identify himself with the defenders of the third, adding that he has no reason "to deny Lauterbach's assertion of cross fertilization." Cf. *Philo's Place in Judaism*, p. 1-25; and "Palestinian and Hellenistic Judaism and Christianity: The Question of the Comfortable Theory," in HUCA 50 (Cincinnati, 1979), p. 137-140.
[47] *Judentum und Hellenismus: Studien zur ihren Begegnung unter besonderer Berücksichtigung bis zur Mitte des 2 Jr. v. Chr.*, Vol. I (Tübingen: Mohr, 1973). English translation: *Judaism and Hellenism. Studies in the Encounter in Palestine during the Early Hellenistic Period* (Philadelphia: Fortress Press, 1974).
[48] Ibid. (English version), p. 104, 310.
[49] "Its boundaries towards the Diaspora were fluid, and no straight lines can be drawn.... In Hellenistic-Roman times Jerusalem was an international city in which representatives of the Diaspora throughout the world met together" (Ibid., p. 254).

The influence of Hellenistic civilization in Palestine was so great and deep that in 175 B.C. a gymnasium for ephebes was established in Jerusalem—an unthinkable fact if Greek language and literature had not previously been promulgated, at least among the more favored classes.[50]

The Hasmonean nationalist resistance finally gave in to the irreversible process of Hellenization.[51] Even the Essenes, who at first vigorously opposed Hellenistic civilization, acknowledged the evidences of that same influence, to the point that their teaching was "especially suitable for a philosophical and apologetic *interpretatio graeca*."[52] All social strata were more or less affected, especially the aristocracy, which showed itself more susceptible to the winds of change and, obviously, more receptive to new subjects and forms of education.[53]

Hengel notes that Alexandria was the chief cultural space in which "the Jewish Diaspora developed an extraordinarily lively spiritual life. At least the upper classes acquired an often astonishing rhetorical and philosophical education."[54] There, in fact, was developed the most authentic experience of Jewish-Hellenist syncretism. The *Septuaginta* was completed, all of it perhaps by Jews from Jerusalem, showing themselves to be retainers of a quite complete Hellenistic culture and manifesting a well-developed knowledge of the Greek language. The texts which remain of the Jewish literature produced there reflect an even higher grade of Hellenization of its authors "and the fusion of Greek and Jewish thought."[55] All of its literary forms are pregnant with a poetic, rhetorical and philosophical influence markedly Hellenistic. In truth, on a par with the traditional literature of edification, one may observe the "tendency toward the glorification of the Jewish people, of its divinely guided history, of its truly philosophical Law and religion," expressed in a rich variety of literary forms of Hellenic background.[56]

---

[50] M. Hengel, *Juden, Griechen und Barbaren. Aspeckte der Hellenisierung des Judentums in worchristlicher Zeit* (Stuttgart: Verlag Katholisches Bibelwerk, 1976). English version: *Jews, Greeks and Barbarians* (Philadelphia: Fortress Press, 1980), p. 170-171.

[51] The attempt at Hellenistic reform failed, but "the collective trauma" suffered in spite of the victory had a decisive influence in the later course of Jewish history, argues Hengel. "Zeal for the law" revived, including the spiritual awakening and extreme sensibility of Palestinian Judaism in the defense of its spiritual values and the fortifying of its national conscience, but the influence of Hellenistic culture did not fail to be progressively felt (*Judaism and Hellenism*, p. 255ff).

[52] Ibid., p. 124. Cf. M. Hengel, "Qumran und der Hellenismus," in *Qumrân. Sa piété, sa théologie et son milieu* (Paris e Louvain: M. Delcor, 1978), p. 333-373.

[53] Ibid., p. 125-126.

[54] Ibid., p. 100-101. "That means that they gained access to the educational institutions of the Greek world, the Greek school, the gymnasium and advanced study in rhetoric and philosophy" (Ibid.).

[55] Ibid., p. 97.

[56] Ibid., p. 100.

Hellenism's penetration into Judaism was a fact already demonstrated by W. D. Davies when he affirmed the existence of "a Greco-Judaic atmosphere even in Jerusalem."[57] This fact was recently reaffirmed by E. P. Sanders, who says that Jewish influences existed in Hellenism and Hellenistic influences in Palestinian Judaism; he defends the thesis that there are no "watertight compartments" in the trajectory of their mutual relationship.[58] D. Daube claims that "the rabbinic methods of interpretation are derived from Hellenistic rhetoric."[59] According to him, the teachers of Hillel were either natives of Alexandria or had studied and taught there long enough to assimilate and set in motion the principles that gave rise to his seven hermeneutical rules.[60] Though bold, this idea is also taken up by H. Fischel, who admits, as have several others who preceded him, that there are many types of interrelationship between Talmudic-Midrashic exegesis and corresponding Hellenistic sources, probably based on a popularized form of rhetoric "in its oral crystallization" rather than on consultation of difficult works of rhetorical art.[61]

In fact, all branches and forms of Judaism were affected, to a greater or lesser degree, as much by spiritual considerations and social pressures as by the dominant language and culture. But the greatest influence was felt by the Jews of the Mediterranean Diaspora, particularly in the Ptolemaic capital.[62] Considered the metropolis of Judaism,[63] Alexandria offered to the Jews of the time of Philo not only an economic and cultural framework but also social conditions favorable to "a harmonious symbiosis" of Jewish and pagan cultures.[64]

---

[57] *Paul and Rabbinic Judaism,* 2nd ed. (London: SPCK, 1958), p. 8.
[58] E. P. Sanders, "The Covenant as a Soteriological Category and the Nature of Salvation in Palestinian and Hellenistic Judaism," in *Jews, Greeks and Christians* (Leiden: Brill, 1976), p. 11.
[59] "Rabbinic Methods of Interpretation and Hellenistic Rhetoric," *Hebrew Union College Annual,* 22 (Cincinnati, 1949). p. 240. From the same author: *The New Testament and Rabbinic Judaism* (London: Athlone, 1956); "Alexandrian Methods of Interpretation and the Rabbis," *Festschrift Hans Lewald* (Basel: 1953), p. 21-44.
[60] D. Daube, "Alexandrian Methods," p. 40-41. M. Hengel arrives at the same conclusion, when he says that "even rabbinic Judaism is an end result of Hellenization." But S. Sandmel (in survey of his book *Judaism and Hellenism,* in the *Journal of Biblical Studies,* 11:4, 1974) considers this thesis hardly defensible, and L. H. Feldman firmly refutes it (in "Hengel's Judaism and Hellenism, in Retrospect," *Journal of Biblical Literature* 96, Philadelphia, 1977).
[61] "Story and History: Observations on Greco-Roman Rhetoric and Phariseeism," in *Essays in Greco-Roman and Related Talmudic Literature* (New York: Ktav Pub. House, Inc., 1977), p. 65.
[62] R. M. Seltzer, *Jewish People, Jewish Thought: Jewish Experience in History,* p. 200.
[63] Marcel Simon, "Situation du Judaïsme alexandrin dans la diaspora," PAL (Paris: CNRS, 1967), p. 18-19.
[64] Ibid., p. 21-22.

B. *Philo in the Context of the Hellenistic World*

The figure of Philo of Alexandria is so complex and rich in intellectual and human content that it has been practically impossible to include in just one study all the facets of his personality and thought. In the opinion of R. Arnaldez he was "the principal artisan of that gigantic development from which all western civilization proceeded: the merging of Judaism and Hellenism."[65] In fact, he not only Hellenized Judaism; he also Judaized Greek ideas, adapting them to the structures of his own religious thought, born of the sacred text.

In carrying out this double process of adoption and adaptation of language, schemes and concepts, Philo reflects, as much in content as in form, the depth of Hellenization.[66] No other Jew exceeded Philo "in loyalty to Judaism," writes S. Sandmel.[67] But few can have assimilated Greek literature so well and have become immersed so deeply and penetratingly in Hellenistic culture. He is, consequently, the one well-known trustworthy representative of "a direct and permanent contact between Judaism and the Greco-Roman culture."[68]

How did Philo acquire his education, and what place did studies of rhetoric occupy in his academic *curriculum*? We agree with J. Dillon that "the question of Philo of Alexandria's educational background is certainly of the greatest importance in order to understand his work."[69] Nevertheless, in this educational background we must include, not only his environment and cultural formation, but also his spiritual roots and his existential commitment, as a disciple of Moses.

We may not ignore the two sides of his literary personality. These are facts fully recognized by those who have dedicated themselves to the study of Philo and his literary *corpus*.[70]

Monique Alexandre[71] provided us a very useful and opportune analysis of the principal texts that testify to the encyclopedic familiarity of this Jewish

---

[65] "Introduction," p. 14.
[66] S. Sandmel, *Philo of Alexandria. An Introduction* (New York: Oxford University Press, 1979), p. 122.
[67] Ibid., p. 134.
[68] Simon, "Situation du Judaisme", p. 21.
[69] In answer to Thomas Conley, in *Protocol of the 15th Colloquy of the Center for Hermeneutical Studies*, "General Education in Philo of Alexandria" (Berkeley: The Center for Hermeneutical Studies, 1975), p. 12.
[70] According to Dorothy Sly, 'Philo is a genuine son of Alexandria. He is a multidimensional man' (*Philo's Alexandria*, London & New York: Routledge, 1996, p. 18), a man 'deeply involved with civic affairs, yet at heart a contemplative man' (p. 10), 'a man set apart, not only by religion, but also by money, education and prestige.' (p. 9).
[71] At the Colloquium of Lyon on *Philon d'Alexandrie*, in September of 1966: "La culture profane chez Philon," *PAL* (Paris:CNRS), p. 105-129.

thinker with Greek culture, at the same time highlighting the fact of his participation in it as an already traditional inheritance. The educated man was, according to her view, as much the one who followed the ἐγκύκλιος παιδεία[72] as he who possessed an insatiable desire for education.[73] This cycle of studies was considered an indispensable phase in the preparation of the student for access to higher education.[74] As T. Conley observes in his suggestive study on this theme, for Philo ἡ ἐγκύκλιος παιδεία should theoretically continue the teaching administered in the home and function as προπαιδεία or μέση παιδεία.[75]

For confirmation we have the testimony of his personal experience, when he tells us that he began by studying grammar, as a preparation for philosophy.[76] This training included exercises in reading and writing, as well as literary study of the poets and prose writers.[77] Writing and reading were included in a program of elementary grammar, conducted by the γραμματιστής; the study of literature came at a higher level of grammar, directed by the γραμματικός,[78] in accordance with the *curriculum* of the "encyclical culture" appropriately so-called.[79] Certainly beginning with studies of elementary grammar, he passed through the cycle of propaedeutic studies which constituted the normal education of the Hellenistic man, that is to say, the ἐγκύκλιος παιδεία,[80] and entered the realm of

---

[72] *Congr.* 72, 121; *Leg.* III, 244; *Cher.* 6; *Agric.* 18; *Somn.* I, 240; *Mos.* I, 23; *Spec.* I, 336. General education, or cycle of studies, also referred to by him as: ἐγκύκλιος μουσική (cf. e.g., *Congr.* 9, 23; *Agric.* 9, 18; *Ebr.* 49; *Migr.* 72; *Her.* 274; *Mutat.* 229; *Cher.* 93); αἱ ἐγκύκλιοι ἐπιστῆμαι (*Congr.* 14); αἱ ἐγκύκλιοι θεωρίαι (*Congr.* 20); ἐγκύκλια προπαιδεύματα (*Congr.* 35; *Cher.* 102; *Sacrif.* 43; *Fug.* 183, 213; *Poster.* 137); or simply: τὰ ἐγκύκλια (*Congr.* 10, 19; *Leg.* III, 167; *Cher.* 3, 105; *Sacrif.* 44; *Ebr.* 49; *Sobr.* 9; *Gig.* 60; *Prob.* 160; *Legat.* 166, 168); προπαιδεύματα (*Leg.* III, 167; *Cher.* 8, 10; *Sacr.* 38, 43; *Agr.* 9; *Congr.* 9, 24, etc.).
[73] The ἵμερος παιδείας described in *Spec.* III, 1-7. Cf. Alexandre, "Some Reflections", p. 106-107.
[74] *Congr.* 24.
[75] "General Education in Philo of Alexandria," PCCHS 15, 1975, p. 2. Cf. *Congr.* 2, 14, 145; *Cher.* 3, 6; *Fug.* 183-188, etc.
[76] *Congr.* 74.
[77] This first phase of philosophy is later referred to as being divided into two successive parts or levels: elementary grammar and higher grammar. One, the γραμματιστική, consisted of reading and writing; the other, properly called γραμματική, consisted of literary study of the poets and "historians" (or writers of prose in general). *Congr.* 148; Cf. 15.
[78] *Congr.* 148.
[79] "Normal education of the Hellenistic man." Cf. M. Alexandre, PM 16, p. 41. The same author highlights that this cycle of studies is that which even Philo "pursued in his youth," not casting doubts on the *personal* character of *De Congressu* 73ff as Wolfson had previously done (*Philo* I [Cambridge: Harvard University Press, 1948], p. 8).
[80] A κύκλος, that is, a certain totality that involves the seventh of the liberal arts. According to H. Marrou (*Histoire de l'éducation dans l'antiquité*, I, p. 265), the seven liberal arts, "finally and definitively formulated in the middle of the first century B.C.," include the three literary arts that constitute the Carolingian *Trivium* (grammar, rhetoric and dialectic) and the four

philosophy[81] on his way to authentic wisdom as a supreme hierarchical value of his complete παιδεία.

But how, where, and under what circumstances did the Alexandrian acquire his literary education? Personal references to his dialogue with Hellenistic masters and his participation in cultural manifestations do not seem to hold any importance for authors who, like H. Wolfson, insist on the purely Jewish character of his training "under the auspices of Jewish professors in a school belonging to the synagogue."[82] For others, nevertheless, these references are the natural expressions of the beneficiary of a long, mature and well-founded scholarly education.[83]

The Philonic concept of ἐγκύκλιος παιδεία, though accommodated to his own religious philosophy, evidently conforms to the doctrine of the Greek and Roman authors of the period. "His basic comprehension of this notion is virtually identical to that which he found in various Stoic writings," affirms D. Winston,[84] adding that, when defining philosophy as "the study of wisdom," and wisdom as "the knowledge of divine and human things and their causes,"[85] Philo is merely following common Stoic practice.[86]

We know that the Hellenistic system of education generally adopted in the first century B.C. was divided into three levels—primary, secondary and higher education—and had the following plan of study: primary instruction consisted of elementary grammatical studies (reading and writing); secondary education, administered in the grammar schools, included in its program the seven liberal arts, with particular emphasis on the study of grammar, rhetoric and dialectic; higher education, as a rule administered in the schools of rhetoric, was also primarily dedicated to the language sciences, but in them, as in later phases of specialization, the study of rhetoric and philosophy particularly stood out.[87]

Hellenistic education was, therefore, almost exclusively literary and rhetorical.[88] From the earliest point at which a student was placed in direct

---

mathematical disciplines of the *Quadrivium* (geometry, arithmetic, astronomy and music theory).
[81] *Congr.* 73, 79: ὥσπερ ἡ ἐγκύκλιος μουσικὴ φιλοσοφίας, οὕτω καὶ φιλοσοφία δούλη σοφίας.
[82] H. A. Wolfson, *Philo* I, p. 78-85.
[83] Cf. M. Alexandre, "La culture profane chez Philon," PAL, p. 123.
[84] In answer to T. Conley, "General Education in Philo of Alexandria," PCCHS 15, p. 20.
[85] *Congr.* 79.
[86] Cf. Seneca, *Ep.* 89, 4; Cicero, *De Off.* 2, 5.
[87] Cf. D. L. Clark, *Rhetoric in Greco-Roman Education*, p. 59-66; M. L. Clarke, *Higher Education in the Ancient World*, p. 2-5; G. A. Kennedy, *Classical Rhetoric and its Christian and Secular Tradition from Ancient to Modern Times*, p. 34-35; H. I. Marrou, *Histoire de l'éducation dans l'antiquité* I, p. 227-320.
[88] Clark, *Rhetoric in Greco-Roman Education*, p. 64-65; G. A. Kennedy, *Classical Rhetoric*, p. 35.

contact with even a very simple text, such as for example a maxim or a χρεία, he was obliged to follow a whole series of exercises of literary composition called προγυμνάσματα.[89] These "preparatory exercises," done first under the guidance of the γραμματικός and then of the ῥήτωρ, taught him to compose the most varied types of discourse, until he attained a full mastery of the written and spoken word.

To what degree is Philo's education, such as reflected in his writings, the product of a system of this nature? J. Dillon wonders about Philo's cultural roots during the most formative years of his life, while affirming that he developed intellectually in the cultural environment of Hellenism, having no doubt been educated by teachers with a Greek mentality and having gone through the *curriculum* of studies represented by the ἐγκύκλιος παιδεία.[90]

This thesis had already been defended by M. Massebieau, as he argued that "his teachers of grammar and, in general, of Greek courses, were not hellenized Jews but Greeks."[91] In fact, as M. Alexandre clearly shows, Wolfson's opinion [92] is without foundation. "Nothing in Philo supports such an affirmation"[93] that the schools where he was educated must have had good roots in the Alexandrian Judaic tradition. Without direct evidence, Wolfson rests on mere inferences and invokes texts which, while describing the synagogues as places of learning, "clearly show what that learning consisted of: readings and commentaries on the Bible on the Sabbath day."

Moreover, the evidence shows that, contrary to what Wolfson maintains, the γυμνάσια of Alexandria were a familiar reality to Philo as centers of physical and cultural education.[94] Along with a deep knowledge of Palestinian rabbinic tradition, reflecting his existential commitment to the Jewish faith and people, Philo had Greek culture deep in his soul, and he could not have acquired this except in two ways: through tutors in Greek culture and/or by frequent attendance at the γυμνάσιον. Bearing witness to this are his explicit cultural ideal, the manner in which he refers to the totality of the encyclical culture, the liberty with which in eleven of his treatises he refers to all the disciplines that constitute the seven liberal arts, and the propaedeutic

---

[89] Marrou, *Histoire de l'éducation*, p. 257-258.
[90] T. Conley, "General Education," p. 30. Cf. *The Middle Platonists*, p. 140.
[91] L. Massebieau-É. Bréhier, "Essai sur la chronologie de la vie et des oeuvres de Philon," RHR 53 (1906), p. 7.
[92] *Philo* I, p. 79-81.
[93] PM 16, p. 45-46.
[94] *Spec.* II, 229-230. H. A. Wolfson says that, since gymnasiums and ephebes were Greek institutions of a religious nature, they excluded Egyptians and Jews (*Philo* I, p. 79). Tcherikover disagrees, and points to numerous enlightening references from Philo to the γυμνάσια and demonstrates that they were of relatively easy access to the Jews, only being effectively forbidden to them after 40 A.D. (V. Tcherikover-A. Fuks, *Corpus Papyrorum Judaicarum* [Harvard, 1957, I], p. 39, note 99). Cf. M. Alexandre, PM 16, p. 45-46.

value he attributes to the ἐγκύκλιος παιδεία as a μέσος or stage halfway to perfection. Also bearing witness, finally, is his more ample notion of παιδεία, as he includes in it not only the προπαιδεύματα,[95] but also traditional philosophy itself,[96] interpreted as the servant of knowledge and as an indispensable stage in the soul's journey toward the light of virtue and divine wisdom.

Since Philo is one of the most notable products of the παιδεία of his time and lived in the bosom of Alexandrian Judaism, he admirably unites Jewish faith and Hellenistic culture. His objective was not, however, to promote a change in his religion, or to harmonize the Mosaic Law with Greek philosophy, as if he were the architect and builder of a higher synthesis; it was rather the comprehension of his spiritual heritage in the light of his new intellectual horizons, and the preservation, if not the very recovery, of those spiritual and human values that the Jewish community seemed destined to lose[97] in an ever more rapid process of assimilation. The apologetic tone of his work "gives evidence of a deep religious universalism and missionary sense"[98] and the language he employs, not only at the level of vocabulary, categories and concepts, but also at the level of schemes and figures of argumentation, is appropriate for his project.[99]

There remains no doubt that his work reflects a solid education in the encyclical studies. It also reflects the manner in which he used the language of reason to expound the contents of the Scriptures.[100]

---

[95] The term προπαιδεύματα occurs in Philo 19 times, always in connection with ἐγκύκλιος παιδεία, as a copy of the προπαιδεία that Plato speaks of in *Respublica* VII, 536d (prerequisite study of the future philosopher). Cf. M. Alexandre, PM 16, p. 125.

[96] We say "traditional philosophy" because Philo distinguishes between φιλοσοφία in the purely technical sense of "Greek philosophy," φιλοσοφία as "wisdom" or a uniting of knowledge and arts that make up the παιδεία, φιλοσοφία as practice or study of Mosaic legislation, and authentic φιλοσοφία as the Word revealed to Moses, the contemplation of the universe; in a word, true wisdom. Cf. Nikiprowetzky, *Le Commentaire de l'Écriture*, p. 97-108. Above and beyond the level of the liberal arts and Greek philosophy there is a third level of knowledge and life, which Philo develops in passing into the concept of "authentic philosophy," or "consummate philosophy" (D. Winston, PCCHS 15, p. 19), identifying it with the Law of Moses, as an incarnation of wisdom itself. *Congr.* 79; *Poster.* 101-102.

[97] S. Sandmel, *The First Christian Century in Judaism and Christianity and Uncertainties* (New York, 1969), p. 123.

[98] Jean Daniélou, *Philon d'Alexandrie* (Paris: Fayard, 1958), p. 24.

[99] Cf. Nikiprowetzky, *Le Commentaire de l'Écriture*, p. 191-192; R. Arnaldez, PM 1, p. 94-96.

[100] Cf. Nikiprowetzky, *Le Commentaire de l'Écriture*, p. 183.

III *The Nature of Philonic Discourse and Importance of Rhetorical Argumentation in His Work*

A. *Exegetical Character of Philo's Treatises*

Philo's works have been evaluated by modern scholars in very different ways. Some categorically affirm that he "does not know how to compose" and spend little time on questions of logic, method and rigor in the exposition of his commentaries; they also castigate his style as bombastic, inclined toward an excess of rhetorical symmetries and a profusion of images, too parenthetical and complicated, at times painfully pedantic.[101] Others, on the contrary, argue that few men have surpassed him in the art of composition, praising the logical division, clarity and architectonic harmony of his works,[102] and affirming his unity, symmetry and internal coherence.[103] Still others, more moderate, comment on the richness of his vocabulary and stylistic versatility,[104] the wide variety of his rhetorical composition techniques, and finally the fact that "the language of Philo remains faithful to the usages of the Greek literary discourse of his time."[105] Such is the case with É. Bréhier, who highlights the fact that Philo knew and practiced the rules of rhetoric artfully.[106]

If his work were understood, in almost its totality, not as the development of a philosophical system, but "*essentially* and in the technical sense of the

---

[101] Ibid., p. 170-171. Here, Nikiprowetzky makes specific reference to: E. Herriet (*Philon le juif. Essai sur l'école juive d'Alexandrie* [Paris, 1898], p. 144); J. Martin (*Philon* [Paris, 1907], p. 13); G. Trotti (*Filone Alessandrino* [Rome, 1932], p. 10); and Völker (*Fortschritt und Vollendung*, p. 5-6). He considers their evaluations to be excessively severe, particularly those of the first three, reflecting "insufficient critical penetration." Cf. F. H. Colson and G. H. Whitaker, PLCL I, p. xxii.
[102] This is the case with L. Massebieau ("Le classement des oeuvres de Philon," whose position Nikiprowetzky (Ibid.) also considers extreme.
[103] J. Cazeaux, "Philon d'Alexandrie exégète," ANRW II, 21.1; *Philon d'Alexandrie, "De Migratione Abrahami"* (Paris: Cerf, 1965), p. 15-23; "Système implicite dans l'exégèse de Philon. Un exemple: le 'De Praemiis,'" SP 6 (1979-80), p. 3-5.
[104] J. Leopold, "Philo's Vocabulary and Word Choice," and "Characteristics of Philo's Style in the *De Gigantibus* and *Quod Deus*" in *Two Treatises of Philo of Alexandria*, BJS, 25, by D. Winston and J. Dillon (Chico, CA: Scholars Press, 1983), p. 137-154.
[105] Nikiprowetzky, "Στεῖρα, στέρρα, πολλή et l'exégèse de I Sam. 2, 5 chez Philon d'Alexandrie," *Sileno* 3:2-4 (1977), p. 185. D. Winston, *Philo of Alexandria: "The Contemplative Life," "The Giants," and Selections*, p. 1.
[106] "Many passages, when one looks at the care with which they have been composed and the precautions that the author takes to remind us of their divisions, resemble those exercises in which rhetors develop commonplaces... Often these logoi can be discerned through a very brief outline which makes one think of a rhetorical manual" (*Les idées philosophiques et religieuses de Philon d'Alexandrie*, p. 285).

term, as a commentary,"[107] then certain misunderstandings regarding his composition techniques would vanish and its real value would be recognized. V. Nikiprowetzky's dissertation on the theme rightly insists in the "intrinsically exegetical nature of Philo's commentary on the Pentateuch,"[108] and underscores the necessity of never losing sight of the exegetical character of his discourse in order to correctly read and interpret it.[109]

É. Bréhier had already appropriately mentioned that "the works of Philo are not simply dissertations and are presented above all as works of exegesis,"[110] and argues that it is important to study them for the commentaries which they are.[111] Several others have noted this as well.[112] But the truth is, that, as Nikiprowetzky observes, scholars have not known how to derive "the necessary practical consequences from such a conclusion."[113] Thus the persistence of statements that his work is an original and notably coherent "philosophical system,"[114] the construct of an eclectic synthesis of all Greek philosophy,[115] or the introduction of a "Judaic mystery" by the "elaborate

---

[107] Nikiprowetzky, *Le Commentaire de l'Écriture,*, p. 192.
[108] Ibid., p. 236.
[109] Ibid. Other basic works dedicated to interpreting Philo as an exegete are those of S. Siegfried (*Philo von Alexandria als Ausleger des alten Testaments* [Iena: Dufft, 1875; reprinted Amsterdam: Aalen, 1970]); E. M. Stein (*Die allegorische Exegese des Philos aus Alexandreia*, Beihefte zur ZAW 51); I. Christiansen (*Die Technik der allegorischen Auslegungswissenschaft bei Philon von Alexandrien*, BBH 7); J. Cazeaux ("Aspects de l'exégèse philonienne," RSR 47 [1973], p. 262-269; reprinted in *Exégèse biblique et Judaisme*, ed. Jacques-Ménard [Strasbourg, 1973], p. 108-115); "Interpreter Philon d'Alexandrie"; "Philon d'Alexandrie exégète".
[110] *Les idées philosophiques*, p. 179.
[111] Cf. "Philo Judaeus," in *Études de philosophie antique* (Paris:, 1955), p. 209; Nikiprowetzky, *Le Commentaire de l'Écriture*, p. 243, note 1.
[112] H. A. Wolfson (*Philo* I, p. 95-96) asserts that "the external form given by Philo to his writings is a purely Jewish form of literary exposition;" that his style is predominantly that of the synagogue preacher and scriptural commentator. J. Daniélou (*Philon d'Alexandrie*, p. 85) asserts that Philo's work is essentially composed of Biblical interpretation. J. Cazeaux likewise departs from the presupposition that the Philonic treatise is an allegorical commentary, dependent on the sacred and teleologic text, for the typical structural analysis of some of his writings (*La trame et la chaîne. Structures littéraires et l'exégèse dans cinq traités de Philon d'Alexandrie*, p. 1-5, 27-33). Finally, S. Sandmel takes up Nikiprowetzky's thesis in stating that, although Philo frequently avails himself of his vast knowledge of Greek philosophy, it is always the explanation of Scripture that controls and determines the philosophy he uses, and not the other way around; for, "it is Scripture that is sacred for Philo, not Greek philosophy" (*Philo of Alexandria. An Introduction*, p. 123).
[113] Nikiprowetzky, *Le Commentaire de l'Écriture*, p. 236.
[114] H. A. Wolfson, *Philo* I, p. 114-115.
[115] W. Theiler, *Die Vorbereitung des Neuplatonismus* (Berlin: Weidmann, 1930), p. 37. Cf. W. Völker, *Fortschritt und Vollendung*, p. 31; R. Arnaldez, PM 1, p. 79-83.

transformation of Judaism within a mystic philosophy".[116] Some scholars have drawn mistaken inferences on the issue of coherence and the alleged lack of a coordinating center of his thought based on the supposition that he is above all a philosopher.

One must, in fact, realize that Philo's work "is not generally an organized exposition of doctrine," but rather a commentary functionally oriented to the text of Scripture. If certain inconsistencies appear, they "are the product of his different reactions to different texts."[117] The Alexandrian is not concerned with creating a new philosophy. Rather, he intends "to present Biblical truth in terms of the best philosophical thought of his time,"[118] employing it as a useful instrument for his interpretation, but subordinating it to the theology which flows from the interpreted text.

By the same token, we agree with V. Nikiprowetzky that, taking it together, the intimate unity of Philo's thought leaves intact the problem of its coherence at the level of detail. *"Exegetical constraints* ... lead Philo to formulate contradictory statements."[119] This fact caused Völker to assert that not everything is the expression of his own thinking,[120] finding that he lacked a center of attraction around which his thought could organize itself. But this center of general articulation exists as a constant theme infused in all his works.[121] It is the theme of the migration of the soul, undoubtedly inspired by Plato's *Theaetetus*.[122] It is a theme which flows and permeates the whole work as a subterranean structure and implicit system, animating and inspiring the sentiment expressed in his explicit enunciated ideas. It is a dominant exegetical theme around which all of Philo's thought revolves. It is, according to Nikiprowetzky, a theme which rather resides "at the foundation of the texts and behind the symbols of Scripture": the theme of the spiritual itinerary

> which leads the soul of the individual sage or the consecrated people as a whole from flesh to spirit, from the material world, with its darknesses and its passions, to the light of the intelligible world, from the slavery in Egypt to the liberty in Canaan, land of virtue or city of God.[123]

---

[116] E. R. Goodenough, *By Light, Light*, p. 261-263. Later, he alters his position in his book *An Introduction to Philo Judaeus*, 2nd ed., p. 154-155, when he affirms that "if mystic Judaism made use of rites, it would have used Jewish rites, suffused, indeed transformed, with pagan ideology, but externally as unchanged as Philo's Pentateuch," afterward concluding that "there is no evidence whatever to support a view that mystic Jews had distinct rites of their own."
[117] Dillon, *The Middle Platonists*, p. 144.
[118] R. A. Baer, Jr., *Philo's Use of the Categories Male and Female*, p. 5.
[119] *Le Commentaire de l'Écriture*, p. 239.
[120] Ibid. Cf. Völker, *Fortschritt und Vollendung*, p. 9.
[121] Nikiprowetzky, *Le Commentaire de l'Écriture*, p. 239; "L'exégèse de Philon d'Alexandrie," p. 326-327.
[122] Cf., e.g., *Theaetetus* 176 a-b.
[123] Nikiprowetzky, *Le Commentaire de l'Écriture*, p. 239.

The deep convictions which guide Philo's thought can be identified, according to G. Reale, as four fundamental ideas: (1) the idea of the fundamental transcendence and absolute omnipotence of God; (2) the idea of the creation as divine *gift* and *grace;* (3) the idea of the fundamental helplessness and structural impotence of man; and (4) the conviction of the impossibility of man's knowing God and truth, or of saving himself, through his own efforts.[124] In his view, Philo sees Abraham as a paradigmatic model of the journey toward God, and describes in him the theme of migration, conscious that, with divine help, it "transcends the story of the Hebrew people and is valid for *every soul* which wants to depart to God" to an encounter with the Absolute.[125]

Therefore, if we wish to really understand Philo's thinking, we have to read his commentary in the context of the spiritual journey. This is so because, "his text is not a conglomeration of heterogeneous elements, which we can trace to different sources and which simply reflect his dual cultural heritage (Greek and Jewish), lacking any integration."[126] M. Harl shows that, on the contrary, his treatises possess a deep religious inspiration and philosophy, to which he related his faith in the God of his fathers and the philosophical tradition of Middle Platonism.[127]

Once the exegetic *Leitmotif* of Philonic thought is recognized, and the intrinsic unity of his commentary discovered, it becomes much easier to comprehend the meaning of the language he employs and his techniques of composition. As Nikiprowetzky fittingly emphasizes, "it is the general sense of the Biblical text, a certain philological touch and a philosophical inspiration that determine in each case the precise meaning that Philo gives to a symbol, or even to a type."[128] But the text is normally the nucleus around which gravitate all the resources of philosophy and rhetorical technology, mobilized by exegesis to illuminate, explain or apply the fundamental theological affirmation put in motion by it.

---

[124] *Filone di Alessandria, "L'Erede delle cose divine"* (Milano: Ruscone, 1981), p. 9-13.
[125] Ibid., p. 15. M. Harl, in reference to *Migr.* 20, points to the theme of migration in the life of Abraham, calling him "The first 'Hebrew', the first 'migrant', the first 'seer', the first of an entire people of philosophers, who have received the revelation from the true God" (*Philon d'Alexandrie, Quis Rerum Divinarum Heres Sit* [Paris: Cerf, 1966], p. 47).
[126] Ibid., p. 20.
[127] Ibid. M. Harl refers specifically to the treatise she introduces and translates, *Quis Rerum Divinarum Heres Sit,* but her affirmation seems to us to apply to all the rest of the Philonic commentary. Cf. W. Theiler (*Untersuchungen zur antiken Literatur,* p. 484-501), and more recently J. Dillon (*The Middle Platonists,* p. 138-183) who clearly demonstrate, according to D. Winston's testimony, that Philo's philosophical ideas are "Middle-Platonic, that is, a highly Stoicized form of Platonism, laced with neo-Pythagorean preoccupations" (*Philo of Alexandria,* p. 3).
[128] "L'exégèse de Philon d'Alexandrie,", p. 328.

B. Rhetorical Argumentation as an Exegetical Instrument

There has been a long debate on the issue of whether Philonic exegesis was mainly shaped by classical and Hellenistic models,[129] or molded in the matrix of Palestinian traditions of Halakic and Midrashic interpretations.[130] Despite having been a highly competent student of all branches of παιδεία accessible to his generation[131] and exhibiting a singular erudition throughout all his work, Philo is extremely reticent about indicating his sources.

Philo's text speaks for itself, however, and testifies to the unmistakable fact that the Alexandrian exegete made use of a prodigious wealth of means to bring out the depths of the Biblical text. His exegesis at times proceeds from the simple to the more complex; at other times it seems to follow the reverse order or to linger on an intermediate theme or observation. Philo writes as one who speaks, but nothing is produced by chance in his discourse. According to J. Cazeaux, his tactic is inspired by a global project in which an obsession for unity, totality and harmony is manifest.[132] Cazeaux speaks of

---

[129] Isaak Heinemann (*Philone griechische und jüdische Bildung*) busied himself primarily with the issue of the exact nature of the mixture of Jewish and Greek elements in Philo: the degree of influence received from each of the sources and the meaning of that combination, thus arriving at certain curious conclusions—that Philo was debtor to the Jewish traditions of Alexandria and not to pre-rabbinic oral traditions; that he did not know Hebrew; that he was limited to adopting the teaching of the Pentateuch and the Jewish practices of his community; that the influence of Greek philosophical tradition was deeply felt in his interpretation. Considered by Goodenough as a mine of information and a prime work of synthesis, this important study on the *Exposition of the Law* systematically focuses on the problem of the relationships in Philo between his Greek education and his Jewish education, demonstrating that he uses the material of Greek background only to confirm his national heritage (Ibid., p. 557-578. Cf. Nikiprowetzky, *Le Commentaire de l'Écriture*, p. 40). It does not, however, represent an important advance in the identification of the sources. W. Bousset had already argued, in a no less important work (*Jüdischchristlicher Schulbetrieb in Alexandria und Rom. Literarische Untersuchungen zu Philo und Clemens von Alexandria, Justin und Irenäus*) about Alexandrian scholarly activity, that Philo appropriated traditional material from the Jewish schools of Alexandria and incorporated it in his work. See also E. R. Goodenough (*By Light, Light: The Mystic Gospel of Hellenistic Judaism; An Introduction to Philo Judaeus*); and S. Sandmel (*Philo's Place in Judaism: A Study of Conceptions of Abraham in Jewish Literature; Philo of Alexandria. An Introduction*).

[130] Theses principally defended and developed by H. A. Wolfson (*Philo* I, II) and S. Belkin (*Philo and the Oral Law*).

[131] Cf. Winston, *Philo of Alexandria*, p. 3.

[132] "The principle of 'totality', as necessity of allegory and literary structure", p. 1. Cf. *La trame et la chaîne*, p. 506,558-559. In the words of D. Runia, the main thesis of his book *La trame et la chaîne* can be summed up in a small phrase: "A careful analysis of Philo's exegesis reveals beyond all doubts the *total coherence* of the literary composition and structure of his treatises" ("The Structure of Philo's Allegorical Treatises," VChr 38 [1984], p. 211).

Philo as practising *teleological* or finalistic exegesis, aware that Philo believes in and uses an inspired rhetoric as much at the level of overall form as at that of the very argumentative figures.[133] He does it, overall, with the liberty of an artist and the memory of one who continuously has in mind the details of his discourse, carefully connecting the end to the beginning in symmetric, chiastic or dialectic structure.

The rhetorical nature of Philo's exegetical activity is also emphasized by T. Conley[134] when he asserts that the Alexandrian pursued his work of interpretation in the context of a tradition which was not only religious but also profoundly rhetorical.[135] Conley asks whether Philonic exegesis might not be "little more than a Greek rhetoric, perhaps a rhetoric of amplification like an interpretation adapted to a non-Greek situation",[136] since, as he tries to show, Philo's work is replete with typically rhetorical terminology, concepts and forms. In fact, according to him, the rhetorical strategy of Philo transcends the concept of style and composition as mere vestments of thought. His "sensibility toward a rhetorical 'form' that is dynamic, progressive, climactic and symmetrical" is too evident to be ignored.[137] The form-content relationship is unavoidable. The very style acts as an agent of persuasion and conviction, being normally governed by argumentative needs and intentions[138] integrated in the context of a comprehensive strategy in which, in the treatment of each exegetical theme, the end is progressively and gradually hinted at from the beginning.[139]

---

[133] *La trame et la chaîne: ou les structures littéraires et l'exégèse dans cinq des traités de Philon d'Alexandrie*, p. 518, 532.
[134] Cf. "Philo's Rhetoric: Argumentation and Style,". D. Daube had already proved that a clear and active presence of Greco-Roman rhetorical influence in his writings is undeniable, when he defended his thesis that the very rabbinic methods of interpretation are derived from them. In his view, Philonic as well as Palestinian rabbinic hermeneutics benefited from the same common Hellenistic origin ("Rabbinic Methods of Interpretation and Hellenistic Rhetoric,", p. 251-257).
[135] "Philo's Rhetoric: Composition and Hermeneutic," p. 53; "Further Investigation," p. 5. Conley,s contributions to the study of Philo's rhetoric are in fact worth noting. He centers his attention on the aesthetic side of it and the argumentative nature of figures, basically trying to prove the hermeneutical character of his rhetoric. Our thesis, however, aims to prove that Philo's use of rhetoric has basically to do with formal structures of argumentation, those clearly defined by the conventions of the centuries-old tradition that preceded him.
[136] "Philo's Rhetoric: Composition and Hermeneutic," p. 62-64. It is his conviction that later studies on the rhetoric of Philo and the benefit that should come from that, will demonstrate precisely that "Philo's rhetoric is the essence of his hermeneutic and that his hermeneutic was Jewish both in its inspiration and in its intention" (Ibid., p. 165). See his "Philo of Alexandria" (in *Handbook of Classical Rhetoric in the Hellenistic Period 330 B.C. –A.D. 400*, edited by Stanley E. Porter, Leiden: Brill, 1997) p. 695–713.
[137] "Further Investigations," p. 2.
[138] "Philo's Rhetoric: Argumentation and Style," p. 345.
[139] Ibid., p. 351.

J. Cazeaux expresses a similar opinion when he says that the Alexandrian avails himself of a great variety of rhetorical processes of exposition to make the depth of the Biblical text meaningful.[140] And he contends that the simple processes of grammar and rhetoric, as well as those of subtle dialectic and hidden philosophy, are technical means of argumentation in a global exegetical process with pedagogic intentions, and not purely decorative or elegant elements providing the coherence and grace in the discourse.[141] Like T. Conley, Cazeaux has not paid enough attention to the argumentative character of Philo's rhetorical devices and his consistent use of formal structures of argumentation. If his work helps us better to understand Philo's strategy of composition, he fails in my opinion to pay adequate attention to Philo's rhetoric of argumentation, and especially to the rhetorical way he structures his commentary units, argues his theses and develops his exegetical themes.

Conscious of the sequential relationship between reading, comprehending, and interpreting, Philo in fact makes the text come alive and explains it by simultaneous recourse to a philosophical conceptualization and an aesthetic and structurally rhetorical exposition. His knowledge of rhetorical theory is directly or indirectly expressed, sometimes in his use of accurate technical vocabulary and his many observations on the genres of persuasive discourse, sometimes in critical digressions on issues relating to the value of a healthy rhetoric and to the danger of sophistic perversion.[142] Philo defines the discipline several times, enumerates its fundamental operations,[143] mentions the various types of oratorical discourse,[144] and refers to its parts.[145] He likewise makes use of the Aristotelian language and rules of εὕρεσις. The terms σημεῖον, εἰκός and τεκμήριον, τόπος, ἐνθύμημα, παράδειγμα and παραβολή are common in his writings. The πίστεις (D. Hay rightly shows that "more than half of all Philo's uses of *pistis* give it the sense of 'evidence'")[146] are classified according to their traditional division into ἔντεχνοι and ἄτεχνοι ἀποδείξεις.[147] The innumerable τόποι are referred to in order to reflect, by

---

[140] *La trame et la chaîne*, p. 517-543.
[141] "Philon d'Alexandrie, exégète," p. 211, 224.
[142] Leopold, "Philo's Knowledge of Rhetorical Theory," 129-131.
[143] Εὕρεσις, φράσις, τάξις, οἰκονομία, μνήμη, ὑπόκρισις (*Somn.* I, 205).
[144] *Plant.* 130-131. É. Bréhier appropriately highlights that "nous trouvons tous les genres de discours" in his work: "les discours de conseil, de blâme, d'éloge, particulièrement les discours de consolation" (*Les idées philosophiques*, p. 285-286. Cf. note 7 for references).
[145] προοίμιον, διήγησις, πίστεις or ἀποδείξεις, and ἐπίλογος (*Plant.* 128, 173-174; *Mos.* II, 51; *et al.*).
[146] "*Pistis* as 'Ground for Faith' in Hellenized Judaism and Paul", *JBL* 108 (1989), p. 461-476, esp. 464-465.
[147] *Plant.* 173-174.

their usage, an optimal preparation in the strategy of rhetorical and philosophical argumentation.¹⁴⁸ As for his stylistic vocabulary, it is so rich and varied that we need not dwell on it. As J. Leopold avers,¹⁴⁹ the grammatical and stylistic erudition displayed by Philo "belongs to Hellenistic tradition specialized in the matter," making it impossible that he should have followed only one manual or that he allied himself to any specific rhetorical tendency. "His acquaintance with the tradition was rich enough that he could be somewhat eclectic in his use of it."¹⁵⁰

The little that Philo circumstantially writes on rhetorical theory is not only in tune with his concept of παιδεία but also illuminates its role as a structural foundation of his exegetical hermeneutic. Like Plato, he explicitly makes a distinction between a "true" and a "false" rhetoric; between a sophistic rhetoric, almost always with a negative connotation, and a philosophical rhetoric of recognized propaedeutic value, integrated as a τέχνη with other encyclical disciplines and considered indispensable to a complete education.¹⁵¹

It is not, therefore, the τέχνη itself which is bad. Its formative character is recognized and safeguarded. Although in a cultural context marked by great sophistic influence Philo is a bit reserved in praising this art, he does not hesitate to recommend its good use. "Far from condemning it, he sees in it a technique in the Aristotelian sense of the term,"¹⁵² a useful and necessary method with which to correctly express ideas. In *De Congressu Quaerandae Eruditiones Gratia* he declares, for example, that rhetoric awakens the mind to the discovery and contemplation of facts and defines it as the art of rational expression, underlining the fact that it is destined for the development of the human faculties of language.¹⁵³ What he deplores is its wrong use, especially in a veiled attack on the sophists.¹⁵⁴

Undoubtedly inspired by the Isocratic concept of λόγος as a distinctive human trait and humanity's supreme natural gift,¹⁵⁵ Philo understands that perfect communication depends on both parts of this very λόγος and not

---

¹⁴⁸ *E.g.*, definition (*Plant.* 154-155; *Deus* 83, 86), etymology (*Plant.* 165; *Deus* 42, *et al.*), cause-effect (*Deus* 77-79 *et al.*), dieresis (genus-species, *Deus* 95, 117-119), things contrary (*Agr.* 118; *Heres* 242; *Somn.* II, 134), *a maiore ad minus* (*Deus* 26, 78), *a minore ad maius* (*Probus* 40, *et al.*).
¹⁴⁹ Leopold, "Philo's Knowledge", p. 132-133.
¹⁵⁰ Ibid.
¹⁵¹ *Congr.* 74; *Quaest. Gen.* III, 20.
¹⁵² A. Michel, "Quelques aspects de la rhétorique chez Philon," p. 83.
¹⁵³ ῥητορικὴ δὲ καὶ τὸν νοῦν πρὸς θεωρίαν ἀκονησαμένη καὶ πρὸς ἑρμηνείαν γυμνάσασα τὸν λόγον καὶ συγκροτήσασα λογικὸν ὄντως ἀποδείξει τὸν ἄνθρωπον ἐπιμεληθεῖσα τοῦ ἰδίου καὶ ἐξαιρέτου, ὃ μηδενὶ τῶν ἄλλων ζῴων ἡ φύσις δεδώρηται. (§ 17).
¹⁵⁴ The most casual reading of his work immediately gives us the impression that Philo, far from identifying himself with them, criticizes their purely technical rhetorical education, teaching and methods.
¹⁵⁵ *Antidosis* 253-257; Cicero, *De Oratore* I, 8, 32ff.

simply on one of them—on reasoning that suggests ideas and on discourse that gives them expression. While some reason well but express themselves poorly for lack of an adequate rhetorical education, others, the so-called sophists, show great ability in the development and exposition of their themes, although they are empty of content.[156] In his commentary he interprets Abel and Cain as symbols of thought and word, complementary aspects of the more excellent λόγος. Regarding the composition of the word εὐλογήσω, which he deliberately translates as "I will give you an excellent λόγος," he changes to speaking of the blessing or excellence of the λόγος, dieretically divided into reason and elocution, and introduces the idea of the wise man's need to master language so that he may triumph over the ingenious assaults of the so-called sophists.

There are, in effect, two λόγοι ἀδελφοί, one mental and the other verbal, the latter acting as ἑρμηνεύς for the former.[157] Eloquence is an indispensable weapon, even for the wisest, as an instrument of defense, detection and refutation of the specious arguments of the sophists, and for the transmission of truth.[158]

But, as he adds, rhetoric is not valuable merely for the services it provides. It is good in itself. This is not true of sophistic rhetoric, as is obvious. This latter is generally false and condemnable,[159] based on fallacious argumentation, persuasively ornate and structured only to distract and detour the hearer from those values and principles which in all circumstances should occupy his mind.[160] But there is a higher form of rhetoric, perfectly conscious of the truth that it transmits as its ἄριστος ἑρμηνεύς.[161] It is a rhetoric that Philo laudably models in Moses and Aaron, by the uniting of the mind with the word and the consequent passing from λόγος ἐνδιάθετος to λόγος προφορικός. In this other allegorical *digressio* those thoughts generated in the mind of the wise man are transmitted by the word, in logical and articulate form, only after an exhaustive training in the art of communication. Aaron, symbol of the expressed word and, as such, brother of the mind, receives from the πάνσοφος Moses the deposit of divine thoughts and transmits them to the people after their illumination by prophetic eloquence.[162]

---

[156] *Migr.* 71-78.
[157] *Migr.* 78.
[158] *Deter.* 35-45. Cf. *Agric.* 159-165; *Confus.* 34-39; *Her.* 125. In this last reference, rhetoric is conceived as a means of defense for the innocent, and therefore a safeguard against injustice. Thus, it presupposes a false rhetoric that produces sophistry.
[159] *Deter.* 130-131.
[160] Concretely τοῦ θεοῦ τιμῆς (*Conf.* 129), τῶν ἀληθῶν πίστεως (*Her.* 305), ἀληθείας (*Leg.* III, 233).
[161] *Deter.* 129.
[162] *Deter.* 38-40; 126-128.

In contrast to those who have applied themselves to practical wisdom while neglecting the art of speaking, and also to those who have studied the techniques of discourse without retaining in the soul the noble teachings that they received,[163] the authentic rhetorician is the incarnation of "a species of 'perfect synthesis' of wisdom and eloquence."[164] It is, in effect, in the encounter of the τέλειος Ἀαρών with the thoughts (τοῖς ἐνθυμήμασιν) of the τελειώτατος Μωυσῆς that true discourse occurs.[165]

Like Plato, Philo compares discourse to a living being,[166] to a harmonious whole with head, body and members,[167] but logical, rational, alive and eloquent.[168] The λόγος contained in the mind of the wise man is incarnate in the orator's discourse, so that he can effectively communicate truth, availing himself of the mechanisms of argumentation and demonstration appropriate to each situation.

Now this need of the orator to express the truth contained in his mind and to put the logic of his thought into words, is more than sufficient reason for the Alexandrian to insist on the obligation to gain a perfect command of rhetorical τέχνη.[169]

Although Philo confronts conventional rhetoric with a certain reserve and suspicion, especially the eloquence of the falsely-called sophistry, he does not distance himself from the concept developed by Cicero in the definition of the *orator excellens*. This is especially the case when he attempts to reconcile the teachings of Aristotle with Isocratic tradition and affirms that there is no true philosophy without eloquence. It should be noted in passing that this eloquence appears to both of them as the perfect expression of perfect thought.[170]

According to A. Michel, "it is not possible to identify his philosophy without identifying his rhetoric," for even the latter has a philosophical nature.[171] As he attempts to situate in time the elaboration of Philonic thought, this distinguished French Latinist concludes: first, that Philo reflects the philosophical debates which occurred after Philo of Larissa and Antiochus of Ascalon and adopts, along with his contemporaries, a certain

---

[163] *Deter.* 43. Cicero, in *De Oratore* III, 141-143, develops exactly the same reasoning.
[164] Conley, "General Education," p. 8-9.
[165] *Deter.* 132-133.
[166] *Sacr.* 85.
[167] *Sacr.* 82-83.
[168] *Deter.* 130-131.
[169] *Migr.* 82.
[170] Michel, "Quelques aspects," p. 83. Cf. Cicero, *De Oratore* III, 141-142.
[171] Ibid., p. 89. Cf. R. M. Berchman, *From Philo to Origen. Middle Platonism in Transition*, BJS 69 (Chico, CA: Scholars Press, 1984), p. 215: "In these circles philosophical issues were debated publicly, and the method of debate was rhetorical. . . . The union of philosophy and rhetoric is evident in all the eminent minds of this period."

eclecticism which distances him from Antiochus; secondly, that his thought is simultaneously coherent and alive: "coherent, because his rhetoric and his philosophy, in form and content, are connected with the same Neoplatonic teaching; alive, because Philo is up-to-date, because he knows that doctrine in its latest form;" and thirdly, that his rhetoric is clearly akin to that of Cicero and, that, just like him, he learned to generalize and express his thought in a universal language founded upon reason.[172]

Similar to the Roman jurist, Philo in effect seems to speak the very tongue of the rhetoricians and to derive from them, at least in part, their language and exegetical method.[173] His manner of approaching and rhetorically treating the most varied philosophical themes identifies him with the Academic and Peripatetic schools, and brings him close to Ciceronian tradition. P. Boyancé, aware of this at the beginning of the decade of the sixties, underscored his interest in comparing the works of Philo with those of Cicero.[174] A. Michel, as we said, took a first step in this direction by defending, in "Quelques aspects de la rhétorique chez Philon," the thesis that the two men derived their thought from the same sources and formulated it in accordance with the same rhetorical-philosophical canons.[175] R. Smith specifically asserts that there are quotations and texts in Philo's writings, especially in *De Specialibus Legibus,* that indicate his probable knowledge of Cicero and suggest the hypothesis of a direct contact with his theory of argumentation.[176] And R. Horsley offers a similar opinion in his essay "The Law of Nature in Philo and Cicero,"[177] affirming that there are many

---

[172] Ibid., p. 99-101.
[173] J. Leopold, "Rhetoric and Allegory," in *Two Treatises of Philo of Alexandria,* p. 155-156. Cf. Berchman, *From Philo to Origen,* p. 215: "Thinkers in the New and Middle Academies such as Cicero, Seneca, Philo, Clement, and Origen argued ideas rhetorically." And he adds: "If we are to properly understand the philosophical context of Philo's thought we have to examine his theoretic within the parameters of the early Middle Platonisms of Antiochus of Ascalon, Archytas, and Eudorus of Alexandria" (Ibid., p. 23).
[174] "Études philoniennes," REG, 76 (Paris, 1963), p. 64-110.
[175] *PAL,* p. 99-101.
[176] R. W. Smith, *The Art of Persuasion in Alexandria,* p. 52.
[177] "The Law of Nature in Philo and Cicero," *HTR* (71:1-2, 1978), p. 35-79. Among these parallelisms: Cicero, *Respublica* 3, 33 and Philo, *Jos.* 29-31; Cicero, *Academica* I, 24 and Philo, *Opif.* 8-9. Horsley effectively shows that there exists "clear and complete evidence that the eclectic philosophy of Antiochus of Ascalon lies behind both Philo's and Cicero's argument for the law of nature and closely related ideas" (p. 50). Horsley further argues that Antiochus was the real synthesizer of Academic, Peripatetic and Stoic thought and that he claimed that Plato, Aristotle and Zeno proposed essentially the same doctrines; that it was he who exercised direct influence over both Cicero and Arius Didymus; and that he must have been one of the elements through whom Plato's ideas came to Alexandria and Philo, as he was his contemporary there (p. 43). If, as he avers, Antiochus was his common source, since Cicero expressly indicates such and Philo follows the same formulas (cf. p. 49), then there can be no doubt that Philo experienced the same eclectic revival of Platonism and was

parallels between Cicero and the treatises of Philo and suggesting that both authors were allied to a wider movement of eclectic philosophy marked by a revival of Platonism.

Although a certain distrust of eloquence is present in Philo, similar to that expressed by Socrates in his *Apologia*,[178] his discourse overall is profoundly rhetorical. In simple terms, rhetoric was for him an intellectual art closer to logic than to eloquence, and its objective was more theological-philosophical than literary. The τέχνη Philo used as an exegetical instrument is obviously rhetorical, an art that stimulates the mind as a function of the εὕρεσις and trains it (γυμνάσασα) for hermeneutic expression (ἑρμηνεία)[179] of thought, disciplining (συγκροτήσασα) its verbal communication.[180]

---

stimulated by the same doctrines that guided the Roman orator-philosopher.

[178] Socrates was proud of the fact that he was not eloquent (cf. *Apologia* 17bd); Moses confesses that he does not have the gift of words (*Deter.* 38); and the "therapist" interprets the Scripture without any pretension of oratorical brilliance (*Contempl.* 75).

[179] The term ἑρμηνεία in Philo generally describes an activity of communication and not of interpretation. Actually, that was the normal meaning of the word in ancient times. Jean Pepin underscores that fact when he says that the original meaning of ἑρμηνεία is that of "discourse," "expression," "elocution," "communication." In the preface of his article "Hermeneutique ancienne," T. Todorov says that he had the merit to remember that "le verbe ἑρμηνεύειν désigne autant, sinon plus, l'activité de production du discours que celle de leur compréhension" (*Poétique* VI [Paris, 1975], p. 289). Thus the relationship between rhetoric and hermeneutics (Cf. *Her.* 22, 108; *Cherub.* 32, 113; *Migr.* 13, 14, 71-73, 78; *Deter.* 12, 40). The form ἑρμηνεία, that occurs in Philo thirty times, as well as the major portion of his compositions and derivations refer to "articulation of thought or meaning in intelligible discourse," observes A. C. Thiselton ("The 'Interpretation' of Tongues: A New Suggestion in the Light of Greek Usage in Philo and Josephus," *JTS* 30 (1979), p. 15-35), sustaining that "the ἑρμηνεύω form can refer only to the production of articulate speech," in clear sense, and articulated in a rhetorical context (p. 18-21). Philonic comparisons of ἑρμηνεία springing from a fountain and to a μαίευσις are significant (*Deter.* 126-127).

[180] *Congr.* 17. Cf. T. Conley, "Philo's Rhetoric: Composition and Hermeneutic," p. 61. "The importance of a living and personal rhetoric in Philo's mode of thought is effectively demonstrated by the example of two series of images...," in the study by R. Arnaldez, "Les images du sceau et de la lumière dans la pensée de Philon d'Alexandrie," *L'information littéraire* 15 (1963), p. 62-72. (Cf. A. V. Nazzaro, *Reccenti studi filoniani* [Napoli: Loffredo Editore, 1975], p. 32).

CONCLUSION

Up to this point we have confined ourselves to the analysis of the various rhetorical traditions that, directly or indirectly, could have influenced Philo of Alexandria. We have especially dwelt on issues relating to the theory of argumentation in the most representative extant manuals. We gave consideration to Alexandria as a cultural center and to the importance given there to the study of rhetoric and philosophy. We beheld Philo in his time and in his world, and lingered over the question of his access to Hellenistic culture in the context of his spiritual heritage. We asked ourselves about the nature of his discourse and the importance of rhetorical argumentation in his work, as an exegetical and technical instrument of interpretation. Finally, we considered the trajectories that he might have followed, in his education as well as in the maturation and application of his τέχνη to the sacred text.

The general information gathered already suggests the direction in which the analysis of Philonic texts will lead us. When we read Philo we seem to stand, in fact, before an original creative process. The argumentative nature of his discourse is obvious to one who is at all sensitive to this issue. His exegetical commentary is couched in formal mechanisms of well-founded rhetorical argumentation. We immediately become conscious that he thoroughly knows the different rhetorical traditions in all their variations, without slavishly subjecting himself to any of them. He eclectically appropriates their strategies and formal structures, and then uses them autonomously as the text demands and inspiration attends him. It even seems to us that he at times surpasses the text itself, as by it he tries to penetrate the mind of the author, recreating the material it contains and making it intelligible to the audience of his generation.

It is left to us to ask: What is the formal structure of his argumentation? What patterns of rhetorical argumentation does he use for interpretation? Is his argumentation rigorous, leading to demonstration, or merely persuasive and parenthetic? When he takes a text of Scripture, how does he arrive at the truth, transform it into a thesis and sustain it?

We will now finally attempt to give answer to these and other questions by means of a critical analysis of some passages that seem to us most representative of Philonic rhetorical technique.

PART TWO

ARGUMENTATION STRUCTURES IN PHILO'S WORK

INTRODUCTION

As we read Philo we are not immediately captivated by any aesthetic beauty, semantic transparency or architectonical simplicity. Nevertheless each one of his treatises, as J. Cazeaux says, "offers the unity, art and mastery of a tapestry,"[1] subtly woven and fitted into a wider general scheme. Each one is a mental or moral journey, made up of different stages, through the course of which the reader makes contact with an integrated group of Biblical references and at the same time can see one prevalent "idea," which is equally complete and structured.[2]

The Alexandrian commentator was well aware that, to pay "homage to the natural harmony of Scripture", he would have to structure his discourse and adorn it in accordance with the "inspired" nature of the Biblical text, understood as "true discourse."[3] When Philo remarks that Abel perished because he was defeated by the artifices of false rhetoric and because he lacked the weapons of true eloquence, we can see in this a defense of the methodology which Philo himself adopts.[4] Without these weapons he says that the righteousness and natural wisdom of Cain's brother could never come to be manifested victoriously. In the same way, without these methods all of Philo's interpretative discourse would also fail.

The aim of the second part of our book is to demonstrate this fact. It will be evident that we cannot apply this rhetorical perspective to all of Philo's numerous texts. What we aim to do is to examine samples of his techniques of argumentation, which we hope will be sufficiently revealing. The plan we aim to pursue is as follows: After analysing and commenting on some of his treatises, we will identify the rigorous rhetorical structures which some of the treatises manifest. Then, we will offer a critical evaluation of Philo's argumentation structures. In this section of our study, we will select material according to themes and will pay attention especially to the formal schemes which he uses at the level of macro- and micro-arguments. In this way we will be able to view a representative spectrum of some of the basic ideas which

---

[1] *La trame et la chaîne, II: Le cycle de Noé dans Philon d'Alexandrie* (Leiden: Brill, 1989), p. 275.
[2] "The principle of 'totality', as necessity of allegory and literary structure", p. 1. Cf. "Philon d'Alexandrie exégète," ANRW II, 21.1, p. 169; *La Trame et la chaîne* (Leiden: Brill, 1984), p. 506-511.
[3] *Mos.* II, 35, 188, etc.
[4] *Deter.* 37-45. Cf. J. Cazeaux, "Philon d'Alexandrie exégète," p. 169.

make up his literary personality. Finally, we will show the rhythmic and periodic structures which are present throughout and the way these fit into his scheme of rhetorical argumentation.

CHAPTER THREE

FORMAL STRUCTURE OF A DISCOURSE

I *In a Complete Treatise*

The argumentative character of Philo's treatises can be seen especially in their micro-structure, in harmony with their specific motivation and exegetical intention. However it can also be seen sometimes in their overall macro-structures. As evidence of this fact, we will begin by analysing the "organic structure" of two treatises: *De Vita Mosis* and *Quod Omnis Probus Liber Sit*. In the first case, we will examine very briefly the rhetorical configuration of the treatise. In the second, we will comment on his rhetoric in more detail.

Several other treatises, such as *De Opificio Mundi, Quis Rerum Diuinarum Heres, De Vita Contemplatiua, De Virtutibus,* or *De Aeternitate Mundi,* could be cited to a greater or lesser extent as evidence of this same rhetorical structure. But the two treatises already mentioned will be sufficient to prove the point.

1. *De Vita Mosis*

Considered by most Philonists as a missionary document written for Gentile readers,[5] *De Vita Mosis* is a closely argued biographical narrative. Philo presents Moses as the model of the ideal man.[6] Such force and rhetorical clarity can be felt in this balanced and simple narrative that it has been considered one of his best apologetic works.[7]

This treatise reflects an unusual familiarity with the literary models of the period, especially models of eulogistic prose, which are part of a tradition apparently dating back to Isocrates. The method he applies, especially in *Euagoras,* inspires the enthusiasm of several later writers.[8] The rhetorical

---

[5] *Mos.* II, 44. Cf. E. R. Goodenough, "Philo's Exposition of the Law and his *De Vita Mosis,*" *HTR,* 26:2 (1933), p. 113, 124-125; F. H. Colson, PLCL, VI, p. xi, note a; and S. Sandmel, *Philo of Alexandria. An Introduction,* p. 47, 52.
[6] Cf. R. Arnaldez, C. Mondésert, *et alii,* PM 22, p. 13; E. R. Goodenough, *An Introduction to Philo Judaeus,* 2nd ed., p. 145-148.
[7] Cf. F. H. Colson, PLCL, VI, p. xvi; B. Botte, "La vie de Moïse par Philon," *Cahiers Sioniens,* 8 (1954), p. 60.
[8] Isocrates is said to have been the first to attempt a eulogy in prose (*Euagoras* 8-11). Cf. É. Brémond, *Isocrate, Discours,* II (Paris: "Les Belles Lettres," 1961), p. 142.

eulogy even permeates literary works of the historical and biographical genre.[9] It should be no surprise, therefore, that the structure of Philo's treatise, despite its essentially narrative character, bears the characteristic marks of epideictic discourse.

Just like a Greek orator, Philo gives life to Moses' biography and interprets it in ethical terms through the juxtaposition of the events and the fundamental aspects of Moses character. On a superficial level, *De Vita Mosis* appears to be a simple historical account, especially in the first part. But behind the exterior of Philo's description of the events, his deeper and truer intentions can be detected, complex but nevertheless perfectly clear, within the total argumentative structure he develops. The Alexandrian not only transmits information about the life of a hero; he also meditates on it and derives inspiration from it to support his mission to persuade, convince and move to action.

This treatise has the characteristics of a rhetorical discourse belonging to the epideictic genre.[10] The two natural divisions of the discourse, book I and book II, are structured sequentially in five parts: *exordium* (I, 1-4), *narratio* (I, 5-333), *transitio* (I, 334-II, 7), *confirmatio* (II, 8-287) and *peroratio* (II, 288-291).

The structure of *exordium* obeys quite clearly and concisely the doctrine of the πρέπον.[11] Receptivity is ensured by the definition, exposition and summary clarification of the *causa* (§1-3); attention, by the importance and unusual nature of the subject matter, and by the justification of the theme (§3); and benevolence, by the ethical nature of the subject, as well as by the authority of the sources upon which Philo's thesis is based (§4). Contrary to normal practice, Philo considers the study of the lives of virtuous men indispensable and sets out to treat Moses' life as that of the perfect man.

The *narratio* (I, 5-333) is little more than a straightforward and detailed exposition of the Biblical narrative with some significant omissions and additions which are no doubt the result of his underlying exegetical purpose. However, as a *narratio continua*, it contains *argumenta* interwoven into it,[12] as a result of which Philo's threefold objective is achieved: *docere*, *delectare* and *mouere*:[13]

(1) The birth, early childhood and education of Moses, including a *digressio* on his moral and intellectual training, without any direct basis in Scriptural narrative (§§5-33).

---

[9] Xenophon's *Anabasis* and the *Cyropaedia;* Plutarch's "Parallel Lives."
[10] On epideictic rhetoric, particularly the encomium, see L. Pernot, *La rhétorique de l'éloge dans le monde gréco-romain*, 2 vols. (Paris: Institut d'Études Augustiniennes, 1993), esp. p. 117-127.
[11] Cf. Lausberg, *Manual de Retórica Literaria*, §264 ff.
[12] Ibid., §290, 324.
[13] Ibid., §293, 325.

(2) The humiliating situation of extreme poverty and slavery suffered by the Jews in Egypt, and Moses' effort to ease their sufferings (§§34-46).

(3) Moses' flight into the Arabian desert, his marriage and preparation as shepherd of Jethro's flocks, in order to become the shepherd and liberator of his own people (§§47-70).

(4) Moses' call by God, his return to Egypt, the confirmation of his vocation and the triumphant liberation of the people (§§71-147).

(5) Moses' election as a sovereign ruler, argued and substantiated on the basis of the virtue and nobility of his character, his humility and wisdom, and above all on the ground that he is a νόμος ἔμψυχος τε καὶ λογικός,[14] a philosopher-king in the Platonic sense of the term (§§148-162).

(6) Forty years of adventure in the wilderness, from which the Mount Sinai episode appears to have been deliberately omitted, in order to be considered later in the second book. Here are to be found also persuasively argued additional points, especially Phineas' noble example of zeal and courage, in defense of the moral and spiritual values of the elect nation (§§163-318).

(7) The request made by the two tribes, Moses' "nouthetic" discourse, and the preliminary distribution of East Jordan (§319-333).

The *transitio* (I, 334-II, 7) appears in line with the rhetorical recommendation to avoid an abrupt transition between the end of the narrative and the beginning of the argument. In this way a rational and effective setting is provided for the *probatio*, coinciding with the division between the first and second books. In it Philo, like a highly qualified orator, summarises the *narratio* and introduces the points that make up the *argumentatio* (I, 334-II, 1-2). He then justifies them (II, 3-6), arguing in the first place on the basis of syllogistic (τὸν μὲν βασιλέα νόμον ἔμψυχον, τὸν δε νόμον βασιλέα δίκαιον[15]) and enthymematic reasoning, saying that the king must be the first among the *priests*, in order to be able to intercede for the people (§5) and, by *prophetic* illumination, to assure them true guidance (§6). He finds in Moses the beautiful and harmonious union of the four faculties that make up the ideal ruler.[16]

---

[14] Cf. *Mos.* I, 162; II, 2.
[15] §4. The idea that "the king is a living law" seems to have its roots in the current thought of the Hellenistic world. See examples in the article by E. R. Goodenough, "The Political Philosophy of Hellenistic Kingship," YCS I (1928), p. 56-101.
[16] According to the assertions of J. Laporte, we find in the portrait of Moses "a complete summary of the true Hellenistic doctrine, just as it is defined in the neo-Pythagorean treatises" (PM, 21, p. 32). Even more than Joseph, he embodies also "an essential element of Homeric royalty, such as described by Aristotle. As high priest... in possession of the four titles of king, legislator, priest and prophet (*Mos.* II, 3–15), he is the sole leader who is complete and perfectly equipped" (Ibid.).

After the narrative exposition of the main facts of the life of Moses as ideal king, which is already a *probatio* in narrative form,[17] Philo demonstrates in the *confirmatio* (II, 8-287) his basic character traits in terms of legislative, priestly and prophetic functions. Here the logical order of events must take precedence over the natural order, and the *argumentatio* takes the form of a further confirmation of the *narratio*, situating itself conceptually as the center of the discourse.

The character of Moses is next defined as being the union of these four faculties, though the three last ones are basically extensions of the first,[18] and, with it, make up the main divisions of the *confirmatio*.

(1) Moses as legislator (II, 8-65)

After the definition and idealized characterization of a legislator in general (§§8-11), the Alexandrian commentator argues the genius and the glory of Moses as the νομοθετῶν ἄριστος τῶν πανταχοῦ πάντων, the permanence of his laws (§§12-16) and the respect they inspired amongst other nations (§§17-24). He sustains these πίστεις with the historical example of the Greek translation of the Law, at the initiative of Ptolemy Philadelphus (§§25-41) and the annual commemoration of this event on the Island of Pharos, where at least the Pentateuch had been translated by the Seventy (§§41-44).[19] This argument, is then extended [20] by a laudatory reference to the greatness and originality of the Mosaic legislation (§§45-52) and by an account of the punishments prescribed for transgressors and the rewards promised to the virtuous (§§53-65), all of which are illustrated in the historical section of the Pentateuch.

(2) Moses as high priest (§§66-186)

This second part of the *probatio* is introduced by a description of the ideal priest that the Hebrew legislator embodies (§§66-69). It includes the Sinai episode, although it essentially limits itself to giving examples of the priestly ministry which was begun there (§§70ff).

Included in this context is a long, detailed description of the tabernacle and its accessories, as well as of the priestly vestments with all their heavily symbolic meanings (§§66-140). Associated with this description is also a narrative section, including argumentation, relating the election of the priests and levites, and the appointment of the latter to punish idolaters

---

[17] Cf. Lausberg, *Manual de Retórica Literaria*, §348.
[18] Cf. F. H. Colson, PLCL, VI, p. 274.
[19] Cf. Sandmel, *Philo of Alexandria*, p. 51; R. Arnaldez, PM 22, p. 206, n. 2, and p. 208, n. 1.
[20] Cf. Lausberg, *Manual de Retórica Literaria*, §400.

(§§141-173). The superiority of the priests is also defended, with reference to the episode where the temple servers defy them (§§174-186), as proof that Moses is singularly qualified for the ministry to which he was called.[21] The priestly phase of his career, begun at Sinai, is in this way used as an example to prove the thesis[22] that he was not only naturally gifted for this task but that he also in practice became a model of piety, which is the "supreme and most essential quality".[23]

(3) Moses as prophet (§§187-287)

This final section of the *confirmatio* represents, in our opinion, the most beautiful and effective of all. Here, the eulogy of the "philosopher-king" reaches its acme as Philo proves that Moses was not only the best of kings, legislators and high-priests, but also the most illustrious of prophets; and that, "as prophet, he declares under divine inspiration that which cannot be known by reason" (§§187).

Organising his arguments in Nestorian order,[24] Philo applies in this last section a τέχνη which is effective both in logical and in aesthetic terms. After a brief general reference to the three types of oracles interpreted and pronounced by Moses (§§188-190),[25] the Alexandrian justifies his *praeteritio* of the first one (§191) and goes on immediately to praise the last two.

Each of these two arguments, which serve as proofs of the prophetic capacity of the legislator, is confirmed by four examples. The first, which is that his pronouncements arise from oracles given in answer to questions, is paradigmatically confirmed by the punishment of the Egyptian's son for blasphemy and wickedness (§§192-208), the sanctions for Sabbath profanation (§§209-220), the special rules for Passover celebrations (§§221-232) and the inheritance laws (§§233-245). The second, which is that they arise from his own prophetic inspiration in a state of divine rapture, is illustrated by the destruction of the Egyptians at the crossing of the Red Sea (§§246-257), the provision of manna in the desert (§§258-269), the punishment of the worshippers of the golden calf (§§2+70-274) and the destruction of Korah and his companions (§§275-287).

---

[21] Cf. *Mos.* II, 187.
[22] As. Lausberg observes, "the principal contents of the (extensive) digressions are epideictic description . . . and particular *narratio*" (§342), in which the narration of examples enters (§290, 292). In fact, the literary form of the *exemplum* can take the form of the *narratio*, in this case constituting a *digressio* within the *argumentatio* (§415).
[23] Cf. *Mos.* II, 66.
[24] C. Perelman, *L'empire rhétorique*, p. 163.
[25] (1) Oracles proceeding directly from the mouth of God and interpreted by his prophet; (2) oracles resulting from the dialogic process of the divine answer to his questions; (3) oracles coming directly from Moses under prophetic inspiration.

The conclusion of the discourse (II, 288-291) makes reference to Moses' prophetic prediction of his own death and in this way summarizes the sublime capacity with which he was invested as the man chosen for the functions of legislator and liberating guide of the Jewish nation.

As Philo emphasizes Moses' migration from earth to heaven, the strange liberation from his mortal condition by the metamorphosis of his dual nature and its fusion into a simple spiritual union, as luminous as the Sun, he seems to be saying that "Only at the end of his life did Moses enjoy the condition of the ideal man."[26]

This epilogue, brief but made more pleasant, both literarily and ideologically, by the *ornatus*, comes to us, therefore, as a highly expressive psychological climax as it exalts the life and work of the one who of all men is considered the πάνσοφος,[27] ἱερώτατος[28] and a real κοσμοπολίτης.[29]

2. Quod Omnis Probus Liber Sit: *Discourse on the "liberty of the wise"*

Generally considered a treatise written during Philo's youth, *Quod Omnis Probus* argues the truth expressed in the Stoic "paradox", that only the wise man is truly free. Though the characteristics that distinguish this work from the others have led some scholars (including Z. Fraenkel,[30] R. Ausfeld,[31] H. Graetz[32] and A. Hilgenfeld),[33] to deny or cast doubt on its authenticity, Philo's authorship was proved by P. Wendland.[34] His thesis, that there is not the least basis for doubt about the authenticity of this treatise, was later defended by highly qualified scholars like L. Massebieau,[35] E. Schürer,[36] L. Cohn[37] and É. Bréhier,[38] who settled the matter once and for all.[39]

---

[26] Arnaldez, *et alii*, PM 22, p. 318.
[27] *Migr.* 76.
[28] *Leg.* III, 185, etc.
[29] *Mos.* I, 157.
[30] *Über palaestinische und alexandrinische Schriftforschung* (Programm, Breslau, 1854).
[31] *De libro* περὶ τοῦ πάντα σπουδαῖον εἶναι ἐλεύθερον *qui inter Philonis Alexandrini opera fertur* (Diss. Göttingen, 1887).
[32] *Geschichte der Juden* (Leipzig, 1863), vol. III, p. 463-471.
[33] "Die Essäer Philos," in *Zeitschrift für wissenschaftliche Theologie*, XXV (1888), p. 49-71.
[34] "Philo's Schrift περὶ τοῦ πάντα σπουδαῖον εἶναι ἐλεύθερον" in *Archiv für Geschichte der Philosophie*, I (1888), p. 509-517; and "Die Essäer bei Philo," in *Jahrbücher für protestantische Theologie*, XIV (1888), p. 100-105.
[35] "Le classement des oeuvres de Philon," p. 79-87.
[36] *Geschichte des jüdischen Volkes im Zeitalter Jesu Christi*, III (Leipzig, 1901; anastatic ed., Hildesheim: Olms, 1964), p. 676.
[37] "The Latest Researches in Philo of Alexandria," *JQR* V (1893), p. 24-50.
[38] *Les idées philosophiques et religieuses de Philon d'Alexandrie*, p. 255, note 5.
[39] Cf. the historical review of Madeleine Petit on the issue of the authenticity of the *Probus*, in PM 28, p. 20-25.

These distinctive characteristics reveal rather, in an ampler and more complete form, the other aspect of his literary personality which is generally hidden in his exegetical discourse and which is seen clearly only when its deeper structure comes to the surface and is contemplated in the paradigmatic harmony of the text.

The rhetorical character of this treatise has often been noted. But the tendency is always to identify it with the genre of the diatribe. Ever since the work of P. Wendland, *Philo und die kynisch-stoische Diatribe*,[40] emphasis has been given to the question of the diatribe in Philo, maintaining that it is precisely in this treatise that all the characteristic elements of the genre are found.[41] In fact, in this book as well as in another, published twelve years later,[42] Wendland emphasized the twofold origin and nature of the diatribe, especially the fact that its specific nature as a genre is the result of the fusion of the cynic style of exhortation and the methods of Hellenistic rhetoric.[43] He ended by classifying it as a *Literaturgattung* of predominantly didactic and formative influence.[44] In his view, *Probus* is a typical example of the use to which the Alexandrian puts the diatribe genre.[45] Since Wendland's studies there has been a widespread agreement that "Philo's works reflect the influence of the diatribe."[46]

But the matter becomes more complex, if we take account of more recent research. G. L. Kustas observes, for example, that "no one in antiquity ever spoke of the diatribe as a γένος,"[47] always preferring to speak of it as a "tactic of genre"[48] and a type of amplification[49] integrated within the rhetorical discourse, especially when this is of a judicial nature. Far from being (with reference to Hermogenes' definition) "the transcendent objective of human

---

[40] *Beiträge zur Geschichte der griechischen Philosophie und Religion:* Fest. Hermann Diels (Berlin: G. Reimer, 1895).
[41] Cf. M. Petit, PM 28, p. 40.
[42] *Die hellenistische-römische Kultur in ihren Beziehungen zu Judentum und Christentum.* Handbuch zum NT, I (Tübingen: J. C. B. Mohr, 1907; 2nd ed., 1912).
[43] "Philo und die kynisch-stoische Diatribe," in *Beiträge zur Geschichte der griechischen Philosophie und Religion:* Fest. Hermann Diels (Berlin: George Reimer, 1895), p. 3: "Ein äusserst lebendiger, oft durch Einführung fingierter Gegner oder Personifikationen dialogisch gestalteter Vortrag, eine vorwiegend polemische Tendenz, ein überreicher Schmuck von Versen der Lieblingsdichter, ein ebenso reichlicher Gebrauch von Apophthegmen und Anedokten, eine Vorliebe für witzige Pointen und Antithesen, für stets treffende, nicht immer gewählte Vergleiche...."
[44] Ibid., p. 3-5.
[45] Cf. S. K. Stowers, *The Diatribe and Paul's Letter to the Romans*, SBL, Dissertation Series (Philadelphia: Scholars Press, 1981), p. 69.
[46] Ibid.
[47] "Diatribe in Ancient Rhetorical Theory," PCCBS 22 (Berkeley, 1976), p. 3.
[48] Ibid., p. 5.
[49] Ibid., p. 11.

thought", the diabribe becomes reduced to an instrument of the discourse,"⁵⁰ to a rhetorical strategy of amplification with the principal aim of stirring up emotions.⁵¹

B. P. Wallach takes the position that diatribe is no more than a hybrid or mixed genre, which owes as much to the rhetorical-philosophical θέσις as to the last dialogues of Plato.⁵² She adds that a distinction must be made between the cynic-stoic diatribe genre of Bion, Teles, Musonius, Epictetus, and a merely diatribic style, to be found, for example, in Lucretius, which is similar to true diatribe and influenced by it but is clearly different in important respects. This term has, therefore, more than one connotation in ancient literature. In Hermogenes it is a figure of discourse identifiable with the *expositio*, and is defined by Ernesti as *commemoratio* and *excursio*.⁵³

Wallach takes a position opposed to that of Kustas, defending forcefully the thesis that "diatribe" was a purely epideictic form,⁵⁴ and affirming that Kustas confuses διατριβή as a figure (Hermogenes) or rhetorical strategy (Aristotle) with the "diatribe" as a form or literary genre.⁵⁵

In view of this, it is easy to understand why A. Michel refuses to describe Philo's works as diatribes,⁵⁶ considering Wendland's position to be mistaken. Moreover, as S. Stowers repeatedly points out, the Alexandrian philosopher is among the sources available for the study of the characteristic features of diatribe, the only "possible exception"⁵⁷ because the usual dialogical style of this form is not found in his work, except in a very limited and accidental way.

Philo certainly was influenced by the "bionian diatribe" as well as by the calmer and more didactic style of the later stage.⁵⁸ Signs of this phenomenon

---

⁵⁰ Ibid., p. 12.
⁵¹ Ibid., p. 10, 15.
⁵² According to her, "The best definition is given by Hermann Throm, who says that diatribes are 'nicht anderes als ethische, besonders paränetische Thesis'" (*Die Thesis, Rhetorische Studien* 17 [Paderborn, 1932], p. 191). But to Throm's description should be added Eduard Norden's declaration (*Die Antike Kunstprosa*, I, 2nd ed. [Leipzig: Weidmann, 1909], p. 129) that diatribe is a dialogue in the form of a recitation, as diatribe seems to have assumed the function of the interlocutor of philosophical dialogue, reducing it to an impersonal figure, and the resulting genre is a lecture or θέσις in which the dialogue can be introduced by means of the assumption of an adversary or interlocutor (identified merely by φησι) to whom the orator responds" ("Lucretius and the Diatribe," *De Rerum Natura* III), p. 6-7.
⁵³ B. P. Wallach, in reply to G. L. Kustas, *Diatribe in Ancient Rhetorical Theory*, PCCHS 22 (Berkeley, 1976), p. 30.
⁵⁴ *A History of the Diatribe from its Origin up to the First Century B.C. and a Study of the Influence of the Genre upon Lucretius* (Dissertation, University of Illinois, Urbana, 1974; Ann Arbor: University Microfilms, 1976), p. 234ff.
⁵⁵ In *Diatribe in Ancient Rhetorical Theory*, p. 31-32.
⁵⁶ "Quelques Aspects," PAL, p. 81-101.
⁵⁷ "Quelques Aspects," p. 76.
⁵⁸ P. Wendland, "Philo und die kynisch-stoische Diatribe," p. 4-5. Cf. *Die hellenistisch-römische*

exist in his work, possibly more visible in this treatise than in any of his others. However, *Probus* is not a simple diatribe. As "the type of discourse employed in the philosophical school . . . the form of the diatribe and the way it functions presupposes a student-teacher relationship," and the dialogical style is indispensable to it; this is not the case in this treatise.[59]

The undoubted similarity between the *Probus* of Philo and the *Paradoxa Stoicorum* and *Tusculanae Disputationes* of Cicero has, on the other hand, led some specialists to emphasize the influence of the latter on the former.[60] The same hesitations have occurred to commentators concerning the diatribic character of these two works of the Roman orator. But both conclusions, that of C. Fohlen on the *Tusculanae* and that of J. Molanger on the *Paradoxa*, seem to me to apply in just the same way to the *Probus* of Philo. According to the first, "we discover in the five lectures a rhetorical unity, we find there an ingenious design consistent at every point with the technique of Cicero the lawyer."[61] The second conclusion is that Cicero uses some of the techniques employed by diatribists and sophists in a way that reflects "a necessary adjustment to the average audience, which would be incapable of classifying this work as a diabribe."[62]

For these reasons we are inclined to classify the *Probus* as a rhetorical discourse of a genre in which the "diatribe", as a "purely epideictic form,"[63] played a significant part. A problem arises, however, regarding its internal coherence.

In her brilliant introduction to this work, M. Petit, after listing in summary fashion the various criticisms that have been made of the organisation of the text, and the consequent attemps to reconstruct it on the basis of a logically acceptable and coherent plan, points out explicitly that the formal structure of *Probus* seems to obey "a deliberate plan of the author."[64] How seriously should we take all these attempts to reconstruct the text, when "the most ancient complete manuscripts (AMP) present the treatise as we know it, and

---

Kultur in ihren Beziehungen zu Judentum und Christentum, p. 43: "Philo und Musonius in seinen von Lucius aufgezeichneten Gesprächen vertreten zuerst einen neuen Typus des populären Traktates, der sich trotz aller Abhängigkeit von der älteren Entwickelung stilistisch scharf von der alten Diatribe scheidet. Übersichtliche Disposition, systematische Ordnung der Gedanken, breite und doktrinäre Darlegung gerundeter Periodenbau, Entfernung oder Melderung jener grellen Lichter und starken Effekte, Zurücktreten des dialogischen Elementes sind die unterscheidenden Markmale."
[59] S. K. Stowers, *The Diatribe*, p. 175.
[60] Petit, PM 28, p. 42-43.
[61] *Cicero: Tusculanes* (Paris: "Les Belles Lettres," 1964), p. vi. Cf. observations of Petit, PM 28, p. 41, 41 and notes.
[62] *Cicero: Les Paradoxes des Stoiciens* (Paris: "Les Belles Lettres," 1971), p. 67.
[63] Cf. B. P. Wallach, in *Diatribe in the Ancient Rhetorical Theory*, PCCHS, p. 31.
[64] Wallach, *Diatribe in the Ancient*, p. 38.

none of the known manuscripts presents its contents in a different order?"[65] We consider that the rhetorical analysis of the treatise will help us to answer this question of organization, if we take into account the strategies sanctioned by Hellenistic theorizers and the liberties considered acceptable to the orator in delivering his discourses.

We are not ignoring the apologetic and hortatory functions of this discourse, but there can be no doubt that Philo's primary objective is to point out and praise the virtue the wise man embodies and which makes him truly free.[66] We do not hesitate, therefore, to classify this discourse as epideictic, this genre being confirmed moreover by the dominant role played here by diatribe. In fact, in any of the genres of discourse "the goal of an argument" is "to stimulate or to increase the adherence of an audience to the theses being presented for its assent."[67] But, as C. Perelman insists, the epideictic genre plays a central part in the intensification of "adherence to those values without which the speeches designed to inspire action could not find the lever needed to touch and move their listeners."[68] Rather than bringing about immediate action, epideictic discourse aims overall to create pedagogically an inclination to act, emphasizing "a shared commitment to certain values that we try to implement. . . ."[69]

The discourse which Philo addresses to Theodotus[70] is not in effect, an invitation to pass judgment on the past or to make a decision as to any future action, but rather an affirmation and exaltation of present values which

---

[65] Ibid., p. 37. Petit accepts "The refusal, as formulated by A. Michel, to call the works of Philo diatribes as applied to the entirety of his œuvre", but believes that "here, in this youthful treatise which is dependent on school exercises in the philosophical-literary fashion of the time, it cannot be doubted that the diatribe genre has influenced the author" (*PM* 28, p. 41).

[66] As Lausberg observes, each one of the three *species* of rhetoric can naturally contain elements of the other two (Lausberg, *Manual de Retórica Literaria*, §65).

[67] C. Perelman, *L'empire rhétorique*, p. 23.

[68] Ibid., p. 33.

[69] Ibid. See L. Pernot, *La rhétorique de l'éloge dans le monde gréco-romain* (Paris, 1993), p. 591-600.

[70] "The *Probus* and the *De Providentia* are the only works of Philo where he uses the classic method of addressing an interlocutor in order to enliven the treatise" (Petit, PM 28, p. 36). Whether the name belongs to a particular individual and/or representative of a universal audience we do not know (Cf. Ibid., on attempts to identify Theodotus). What we do know is that "the audience is not necessarily made up of those whom the orator expressly interpellates" and that, in terms of argumentative discourse, "one has to regard it as *the sum of those whom the author wishes to influence through his argumentation*" (C. Perelman, *L'empire Rhétorique*, p. 27). And in this light, we find it pertinent to here refer to the observation of S. W. Baron (*Histoire d'Israel*, Paris, 1956, trad. V. Nikiprowetzky, I, p. 520) that "hellenized Jews seemed have had a preference for names such as Theodoros, Theophilos, Theodotos, Dositheos and other similar names" (Cf. Petit, PM 28, p. 136, note 2). In the New Testament Luke and Acts are, e.g., dedicated to "Theophilus", perhaps to be considered as a universal addressee.

both should be interested in cultivating, preserving, and passing on to others.

Made up of four parts, *exordium* (§§1-15), *propositio* (§§16-20), *probatio* (§§21-151) and *conclusio* (§§152-160),[71] this treatise reflects the art of an orator who, as he composes his work, knows how to subordinate form to content and, for this reason insists on the configuration of the values defined in the theme. He submits these unhesitatingly to the order of the arguments, while at the same time managing to preserve the overall logic and aesthetics of the discourse.

In order to understand this better, we consider it best to proceed with a paradigmatic analysis, considering first the parts in which the psychological appeal is predominant and afterwards those in which logical reasoning prevails.

(1) *Exordium* (§§1-15) and *conclusio* (§§152-160)

To satisfy the basic prerequisites of the *exordium*, Philo establishes in it a kind of ethical presence, and points out his qualifications for this through a presentation and definition of the problem he aims to deal with. Having affirmed the strict affinity between this treatise and the previous one, he announces his firm intention to demonstrate ὅτι πᾶς ὁ ἀστεῖος ἐλεύθερος (§1), and offers high praise of wisdom, exhorting young people especially to acquire it.

Next comes a contrasting of wisdom and ignorance based on an argument from authority. According to the doctrine of the Pythagoreans the paths of philosophy are the royal highway which leads to virtue (§2); these paths are inaccessible to the ignorant, the uneducated multitudes (§3); for these have not tasted philosophical doctrines, or have received them in a distorted form, and transform the extraordinary beauty of wisdom into the abominable figure of sophistry. Unable to discern the light of philosophical concepts, they dwell in the dark, and do not believe in those who enjoy it (§§4-5).[72]

Afterwards, taking advantage of the "genre" of the diatribe, Philo paints a telling and colorful picture of the way the ignorant react to the paradoxes which assert that the wise and the foolish are, respectively, citizen and exile (§§6-7), rich and poor (§§8-9), freeman and slave (§10), independent of their social status. Using here the "diatribe style", Philo allows to speak, parenthetically, the "inhabitants of the shadows"; "slaves of opinion" who,

---

[71] The structural parts of the speech as identified by Petit in the section related to genre (p. 39) do not agree with her own analytical plan, and the *exemplum, testimonium* and *contrarium* should rightly be taken as parts of *probatio*.
[72] Allusion to Platonic allegory of the cavern.

because of their ignorance or unphilosophical attitude to life, are unable to understand statements like these, considering them absurd and paradoxical.

Next he draws an analogy between the doctor and the wise man. In the same way that the sick crowd to the doctor to cure their physical ills, the ignorant should place themselves under the direction and care of the wise in order to be healed from the illnesses of their souls and to acquire true knowledge. The Alexandrian exalts wisdom as the most divine, generous, welcoming and intoxicating good, and exhorts all men to consecrate to culture the firstfruits of their youth (§11-14).

Finally he confirms the excellence of wisdom through yet another interesting analogical argument, apparently from a Stoic source.[73] Just as new glasses maintain the odour of the first liquids poured into them, so the souls of young people take the indelible impressions from the first ideas they assimilate, preserving their original form (§15).

The conclusion of the treatise recapitulates the main themes of the introduction and at the same time underlines its three rhetorical functions. It does this, however, through an exposition in reverse order,[74] delimiting the discourse chiastically, and linking the end to the beginning by the *inclusio*.

In the *enumeratio* (§§152-155), a section which certifies the credibility of the matter in hand, Philo briefly refreshes the memory of the reader, reaffirming the sovereignty of the wise man attained through his total submission to virtue and the consequent mastery of his passions. To do this, he draws on enthymemes, maxims and especially ancient authorities, in agreement with the doctrine defended by the *Rhetorica ad Alexandrum*;[75] namely that of a tragic poet,[76] the lyrical Theognis[77] and a humorous formula from Bias of Priene, who reinforces enthymematically the thesis he is recapitulating through a *locus a contrario*.

τὸ γὰρ πλάγιον καὶ ποικίλον καὶ ἀπατηλὸν ἦθος ἀγενέστατον, ὥσπερ εὐγενὲς τὸ εὐθὺ καὶ ἄπλαστον καὶ ἀνύπουλον, λόγων βουλεύμασι καὶ βουλευμάτων λόγοις συναιδόντων.

---

[73] Cf. F. H. Colson, PLCL, p. 511, note to §15. It is important to highlight the fact that "In its entirety *Probus*—the choice of subject, the manner in which it is dealt with, the vocabulary used, the book's conclusion (τὸ ἀκολούθως τῇ φύσει ζῆν)—reveals a dominant Stoic coloring" (Petit, PM 28, p. 75). Equally evident is the superabundance of the Hellenistic topic and the frequent quoting of Greek writers, especially Homer and the Tragedians. Also it is interesting to note direct and indirect references to Pythagoras, Plato and the Stoics in this simple proem.
[74] Cf. the observation of Petit, PM 28, p. 37.
[75] *Ad Alexandrum* 1439a 3ff; 1442b 33ff.
[76] Euripides, in the understanding of Nauck, Frg. trag. adesp. 327.
[77] *El.* 535-536.

For the crooked, artificial, deceitful character is utterly ignoble, while the straight, simple and ingenuous, in which thoughts agree with words and words with thoughts, is noble. [Colson-Whitaker translation used throughout]

In the *amplificatio* (§§156-157), he considers first the ridiculous situation of those who ignorantly imagine themselves to be free, just because they have gained legal emancipation, whereas in fact they end up becoming more completely enslaved to their vices and fleshly passions. He confirms this later through a χρεία from Diogenes,[78] which he goes on to explain through an analogy expressed in three terms.[79]

In the *conquestio* (§§158-160), the "orator" seeks openly to arouse the emotions of his "audience." Having convinced it intellectually, he now has only to elicit its sympathy for the cause he defends and stimulate it to action through an intensive use of a pathetic appeal. But, as W. Brandt points out, the traditional πάθος is merely a variety of ἦθος,[80] and, ethically, Philo speaks in the first person. Following the example of the wise man, who is free because he exercises dominion over his passions, people should set their souls free from real slavery through the study of philosophy. To do this, an individual will have to set himself free once and for all from δόξα, in any of its manifestations, and cling to the ἀλήθεια—"the most sacred of all virtues"—scrutinizing "the nature of the soul" alone. For,

εἰ μὲν γὰρ πρὸς ἐπιθυμίας ἐλαύνεται ἢ ὑφ' ἡδονῆς δελεάζεται ἢ φόβῳ ἐκκλίνει ἢ λύπῃ στέλλεται ἢ ὑπ' ὀργῆς τραχηλίζεται, δουλοῖ μὲν αὐτήν, δοῦλον δὲ καὶ τὸν ἔχοντα μυρίων δεσποτῶν ἀπεργάζεται· εἰ δὲ φρονήσει μὲν ἀμαθίαν, σωφροσύνη δ' ἀκολασίαν, δειλίαν δὲ ἀνδρείᾳ καὶ πλεονεξίαν δικαιοσύνῃ κατηγωνίσατο, τῷ ἀδουλώτῳ καὶ τὸ ἀρχικὸν προσείληφεν.

if the soul is driven by desire, or enticed by pleasure, or diverted from its course by fear, or shrunken by grief, or helpless in the grip of anger, it enslaves itself and makes him whose soul it is a slave to a host of masters. But if it vanquishes ignorance with good sense, incontinence with self-control, cowardice with courage and covetousness with justice, it gains not only freedom from salvery but the gift of ruling as well (§159).

A dual rhetorical syllogism full of manifest psychological insight, this defines the intermediate situation of those souls who still have not turned in the direction of slavery nor of freedom. They are virgins like the newborn, and need to be cared for and fed at the right moment; in the first place through the sweet and rational milk of their early studies and afterwards

---

[78] Χρεία is the brief exposition of that which a person said or did, with the object of edification, sometimes confused with ἀπόφθεγμα, ἀπομνημόνευμα and παράδειγμα.
[79] Cf. C. Perelman, *L'empire Rhétorique*, p. 129.
[80] *Rhetoric of Argumentation*, p. 224: "The speaker steps forward in a role that is ordinarily a modification of the one assumed to that point, and takes for himself a stance toward the subject which his audience will presumably assume with him."

through the solid food which philosophy produces,[81] in the direction of complete wisdom, for a life in harmony with their real nature.

The relationship between peroration and exordium are based on the double common objective:[82] (1) affirmation of the *status causae* in the beginning and its reaffirmation at the end; (2) an emotional appeal, which in the beginning aims to establish contact between the emitter and the receiver, but which in the end aims to consolidate the effects achieved in the process of argumentation.[83] As W. Wuellner correctly observes, an emotional appeal of this kind should adapt itself to the nature of the problem being introduced, argued and later recapitulated[84]. The persuasive power of the

---

[81] Cf. *Congr.* 19: "οὐχ ὁρᾷς, ὅτι καὶ τὸ σῶμα ἡμῶν οὐ πρότερον πεπηγυίαις καὶ πολυτελέσι χρῆται τροφαῖς, πρὶν ἢ ταῖς ἀποικίλοις καὶ γαλακτώδεσιν ἐν ἡλικίᾳ τῇ βρεφώδει; τὸν αὐτὸν δὴ τρόπον καὶ τῇ ψυχῇ παιδικὰς μὲν νόμισον εὐτρεπίσθαι τροφὰς τὰ ἐγκύκλια καὶ τὰ καθ' ἕκαστον αὐτῶν θεωρήματα, τελειοτέρας δὲ καὶ πρεπούσας ἀνδράσιν ὡς ἀληθῶς τὰς ἀρετάς." Monique Alexandre in passing mentions that "the theme of degrees of knowledge is expressed in Philo by the opposition between baby (βρέφος), infant (νήπιος; cf. Congr. 154; παῖς) and adult (...). The formation of the soul consists in cultivating the plants of the ἐγκύκλιος παιδεία during infancy, and later those of virtue" (M. Alexandre, PM 16, p. 70, note 4). Colson and Whitaker also observe that "underlying Philo's philosophy is the conviction of the value of general education as a stepping-stone to higher things. He accepts without question the ordinary course of education of his time, commonly called the Encyclia, consisting of literature, rhetoric, mathematics, music and logic. He enlarges several times on its value as a mental training. The Encyclia are the ornaments of the soul conceived of as the house which is being fitted to receive the Divine Lodger, the saplings which must be planted in young minds, the milk which must precede the meat, the source of that spiritual strength, the 'much substance' which Israel must take for its sustenance, as it journeys out of the spiritual Egypt. But above all the Encyclia are symbolized by Hagar, for as Abraham, when Sarah bore him no child, took the handmaiden, so the young soul as yet unable to mate with philosophy must have union with the school subjects, the lower or secular education. True, this is only useful as a stepping-stone to philosophy. If it is persisted in too long or misused, as it well may be, particularly the rhetorical branch, it breeds the sophist Ishmael and must be cast out, as he and his mother were. But in its proper place it is valuable, and Philo's insistence on this makes him one of our chief authorities on the educational ideas of his time" (PLCL, I, p. xvi-xvii). According to Wolfson, "Philo compares the relation of philosophy, in the sense of Greek philosophy, to 'wisdom,' in the sense of the revealed Law, to the relation of the 'encyclical studies' to philosophy, for, he says, 'just as the encyclical culture is the bondwoman of philosophy, so also is philosophy the bondwoman of wisdom' (*Congr.* 79).... This subservience which he says that 'philosophy teaches the control of the belly and the control of the parts below the belly and the control also of the tongue,' but while all these qualities are 'desirable in themselves,' still 'they will assume a grander and loftier aspect if practised for the honor and service of God;' for the service and worship, as we have seen, constitutes wisdom, and wisdom is the revealed Law embodied in Scripture. When, therefore, Philo speaks of philosophy as being bondwoman or handmaid of wisdom, he means thereby that it is the bondwoman or handmaid of Scripture." (H. Wolfson, *Philo* I [Cambridge: Harvard University Press, 1968], p. 149-150).

[82] Lausberg, *Manual de Retórica Literaria*, §432.

[83] Ibid., §436-437. Cf. C. Perelman and Olbrechts-Tyteca, *New Rhetoric*, p. 44, 54.

[84] W. Wuellner, "Paul's Rhetoric of Argumentation in Romans," *CBQ*, 38:3 (1976), p. 339.

discourse is enhanced by this means, and it is reinforced by the style, by the chiasm and by the *inclusio* mentioned above. Having begun the discourse with a reference to the τῶν πυθαγορείων ἱερώτατον θίασον and to one of its numerous "divine principles,"⁸⁵ as a precept-symbol of the "royal highway" to virtue,⁸⁶ Philo ends symmetrically with an allusion to the Pythic oracle of a blessed consummation.

(2) *Transitio* (§§16-20) and *probatio* (§§21-151)

The rhetorical function of the *transitio*, in this treatise, is to mark the end of the *exordium* and to prepare the audience for the *argumentatio*. The "argumentative situation"⁸⁷ which has just been introduced is explicity stated:

Ἅλις μὲν δὴ τούτων. ἀκριβωτέον δὲ τὸ ζητούμενον, ἵνα μὴ τῇ τῶν ὀνομάτων ἀσαφείᾳ παραγόμενοι πλαζώμεθα, καταλαβόντες δὲ περὶ οὗ ὁ λόγος τὰς ἀποδείξεις εὐσκόπως ἐφαρμόττωμεν.

So much for these matters. Let us proceed to the subject of our discourse and give it careful consideration, that we may not go astray, misled by the vagueness in the terms employed, but apprehend what we are talking about, adjust our arguments to it, and so prove our point (§16).

The antithetical formulation which follows defines dieretically the subject of the treatise:

δουλεία τοίνυν ἡ μὲν ψυχῶν, ἡ δὲ σωμάτων λέγεται· δεσπόται δὲ τῶν μὲν σωμάτων ἄνθρωποι, ψυχῶν δὲ κακίαι καὶ πάθη. κατὰ ταὐτὰ δὲ καὶ ἐλευθερία· ἡ μὲν γὰρ ἄδειαν σωμάτων ἀπ' ἀνθρώπων δυνατωτέρων, ἡ δὲ διανοίας ἐκεχειρίαν ἀπὸ τῆς τῶν παθῶν δυναστείας ἐργάζεται.

Slavery then is applied in one sense to bodies, in another to souls; bodies have men for their masters, souls their vices and passions. The same is true of freedom; one freedom produces security of the body from men of superior strength, the other sets the mind at liberty from the domination of the passions (§17).

The emphasis on the καλόν/αἰσχρόν alternative, with reference to the epideictic genre,⁸⁸ announces the author's intention to postpone consideration of the slavery or liberty of the body and concentrate only on spiritual liberty. Meanwhile he justifies enthymematically its *praeteritio* by affirming the nobility of the theme he intends to deal with and by declaring paraenetically that true freedom, like true sovereignty, consists in serving God in exclusive

---

⁸⁵ θεσμός (§3), "divine principle" or institution established by God. Cf. *Opif.* 143 (θεσμός, νόμος θεῖος ὤν); *Probus* 79 (θεσμὸν φύσεως = the law of nature). Those who break it are considered wicked. Cf. Petit, PM 28, p. 138, note 1.
⁸⁶ Ibid., p. 137, note 5.
⁸⁷ Cf. C. Perelman and Olbrechts-Tyteca, *New Rhetoric*, p. 491.
⁸⁸ Lausberg, *Manual de Retórica Literaria*, §278.

submission. He confirms this by quoting a line from Sophocles, attributing to it the *auctoritas* of the Delphic oracles.[89]

The general line of argument which he so clearly and consciously proposes to expound is clearly defined, in fact, in the *probatio*. But here a problem arises as to the treatise's unity and internal coherence, a problem raised especially by L. Massebieau,[90] E. Krell and B. Motzo,[91] but partially justified and resolved by M. Petit,[92] who prefers to consider the plan of the existing text as "un dessein délibéré de l'auteur," and considers "la notice sur les Esséniens" as "le pivot réel du traité."

To what extent does analysis of the nature and function of the argumentation in this treatise help us to overcome the problem? The creative liberties Philo takes, especially in the paradigmatic section, are rhetorically acceptable, and the treatise actually reveals great argumentative coherence. The order is not necessarily rigorously logical; but it is natural and determined more by rhetorical than scientific considerations. It is adapted to a specific argumentative context which aims above all to produce the best possible pratical effect on the audience.[93]

The *probatio* is divided into two distinct parts. The first deals logically with the proofs of the liberty of the wise man (§§21-61); the second deals with examples which confirm this same liberty (§§62-135) and is followed by a brief digression on the nobility of liberty and the ignominy of slavery (§§136-143). It constitutes, therefore, a homogeneous whole with a unity made clear by the statement of the central theme at the beginning (§§21-22) and its reaffirmation at the end (§§144-151). It is a kind of circular structure in which, through the use of a *locus a contrario*, true freedom, seen as the mastery of the passions, is contrasted with subjection to these same passions.

The syntagmatic analysis of the πίστεις reveals the following overall argumentative structure:

2.1 *Arguments which constitute "apodeictic" reasoning (§§21-61)*[94]

2.1.1 *The argument from sovereignty (§§21-31)*

In this first part, the structural enthymeme—the wise man is free because he exercises sovereignty over his passions—is developed micro-structurally according to the model of argumentation defended by the *auctor ad Herennium*,

---

[89] Fragment 688, 3 of Sophocles, cited by Aristotle in *Ethica Eudemia*, VII, 10, 1242a 37.
[90] Massebieau, "Essai sur la chronologie de la vie et des oeuvres de Philon," p. 82f.
[91] E. Krell, *Philo*, περὶ τοῦ πάντα σπουδαῖον εἶναι ἐλεύθερον, *die Echtheitfrage* (Augsburg, 1896), p. 24-29; B. Motzo, "Per i testo del *Quod omnis probus liber* di Filone," in *Atti della Reale Accademia delle Scienza di Torino*, XLVII (1911-1912), p. 172-178.
[92] PM 28, p. 37-39.
[93] Cf. Perelman, *L'empire rhétorique*, p. 162-167.
[94] Term used by Philo in §62 to classify this section: Ἐπεὶ δέ τινες τῶν ἥκιστα κεχορευκότων Μούσαις λόγων ἀποδεικτικῶν οὐ συνιέντες.

in five parts: *propositio* (§21)—the wise man is free from all passions and fears, through his αὐτοπραγία; *ratio* (§22)—so, inspired by his desire and thirst for liberty, he learns to resist all sorts of intimidation against his soul, including even the fear of death; *confirmatio*, through additional arguments (§§23-25)—the man who doesn't allow himself to be intimidated by death and also resists stoically all other evil circumstances is free indeed; *exornatio*, the argument is supported and enriched by the *simile* comparing the wise man to an athlete (§§26-27),[95] the apothegmatic *exemplum* of Antisthenes (§28) and the *res iudicata* of the Jewish law-maker (§29);[96] and *complexio* (§§30-31). In this final part, Philo summarizes the argument about the sovereignty of the wise man, reformulating his initial thesis and developing at the same time a complete *argumentatio per ratiocinationem*.[97] This argument includes the Platonic analogy of the shepherd and the leader in the *propositionis approbatio* and the Homeric metaphor of kings as shepherds of the people. In this way he confirms, through a *locus a contrario*, the superiority of wise men as true kings, as opposed to kings of peoples who are in fact slaves of their passions.

2.1.2 *A digression argued and illustrated (§§32-40)*

Here Philo describes the inconsistency of some popular concepts of slavery and liberty, in their attempt to define the quality of the slave and the free man. Such concepts fail a series of tests. The test of ὑπηρεσία: war and poverty force free men to do servile work, and slaves to occupy positions of leadership and administration (§§32-35). The test of obedience: children and pupils obey without being slaves (§36). The test of purchase and ranson: captives are sold or ransomed without being slaves, and slaves often exercise sovereignty over their masters (§§37-39), just like lions who intimidate their owners (§40).

All the examples given here show that the mere appearance of slavery or liberty does not make anyone a slave or free man. The final illustration of the lions brings the Alexandrian back to the central theme, through a *locus a minore ad maius* inserted into an *interrogatio*, which confirms once again the liberty and invulnerability of the wise man.[98]

---

[95] Commonplace particularly utilized by Philo who, according to the observation of Petit, makes Jacob the archetype of the athlete of virtue (PM 28, p. 156, note 3) and purposely underlines the correspondence of the terms ἀθλητής and ἀσκητής in Philo, both reflecting the vocabulary of sports (Ibid., p. 170, note 1).

[96] In this first reference to Moses, in which he is curiously designated by his function and not by his name, Philo adapts the text of Exodus 17:12, instead of quoting it. Cf. Petit, Ibid., p. 159, notes 6-7.

[97] Cicero, *De Inuentione* I, 37, 67.

[98] If "the lions are not slaves of those who feed them, but those who feed them are slaves of the lions" (expression attributed to Diogenes the Cynic), it becomes even more impossible

2.1.3 *Arguments from quality (§§41-47)*

The structural enthymeme,[99] that the wise man is free because he possesses the qualities of the free men, is developed through the following simple arguments: (1) The wise man is free because he is happy (§41). A *ratiocinatio* in four parts (*propositio, propositionis approbatio, assumptio* and *complexio*).[100] (2) The wise man is free because, like Moses, he is a friend of God (§§42-44), possessed by divine love and exclusively dedicated to His service. An argument structured as a *locus a contrario* and confirmed by the epithets attributed to a God who protects and honours the rights of friendship: ὁ ὑπέρμαχος θεὸς ἑταιρεῖος, ἔφορος (τὰ κατὰ τοὺς ἑταίρους ἐφόρων). (3) The wise man is free because he obeys the law of pure reason (§§45-47) and lives in conformity with it.[101] This argument is developed in two ways: through an analogy in symmetrical parallelism, which casts light on the previous argument, at the same time it proves and adorns this one, thus bringing together the two forms in which it is presented: *similitudo per contrarium* and *per conlationem*;[102] and through a rhetorical syllogism which, based on a *locus a minore ad maius*, confirms it by showing the superiority of the ὀρθὸς λόγος as the true source of all other laws. In a word, if these qualities of the wise man are proved to be the qualities of a free man, then a wise man is truly free.

2.1.4 *The argument from "ἰσηγορία" (§§48-57)*

This complex argument on the right of wise men to speak on equal terms to each other (§§48-50), a right which is not shared by the ignorant (§§51-52),[103] is proved in the first place by two analogical arguments in identical terms, showing the freedom of the former and the slavery of the latter, respectively *per conlationem* and *per negationem*. After this, it is confirmed by an aphorism from Zeno, which Philo interprets and applies (§§53-56),

---

to reduce a wise man to servitude, "for fear is the mark of the slave and wild animals are feared by men" (Cf. Diogenes of Laertius VI, 7).

[99] As W. Brandt explains, the enthymeme is often the backbone of a line of argumentation, in whose basic structure various simple enthymemes are situated. These can be organized in series, or chained to each other. But they usually support a single conclusion (Brandt, *Rhetoric of Argumentation*, p. 61-63).

[100] Petit points out that "in this paragraph ... it seems that Philo summarizes a school argument which was far too well-known and had already been analysed far too often (see for example Book V of Cicero's *Tusculan Dialogues*)" (PM 28, p. 168, n. 3).

[101] The νόμος is here ὁ ὀρθὸς λόγος, the "perfect or imperishable law" as an expression of the ἀθάνατος φύσις.

[102] Cf. *Rhetorica ad Herennium* IV, 59-60.

[103] The Socratic concept of ignorance is expressed in §55-56 and is implicit in the terms φαῦλος (§51, 57) and ἄφρων (§52). Dementia (*de-mentiam*) is, effectively, the affection of the soul that consists in the absence of the light of intelligence (*mentis*), affirms Cicero in the *Tusculanae* III, 10, adding that "all the unwise are foolish (*non sanos*)" (Cf. Petit, PM 28, p. 180, n. 2).

supposing it to have been derived from the Mosaic account of Isaac condemning Esau to be a slave of Jacob (§57).[104]

Overall, it reflects the complete formal structure of a Ciceronian *ratiocinatio*, with its premises justified.[105] (1) *Propositio:* the fact that wise men speak on equal terms to each other is a proof of the freedom of the wise man (§48); (2) *approbatio:* the knowledge of a science confers this right on all those who specialize in it (§49); (3) *assumptio:* the wise man possesses the science of the realities of life and, as some wise men are free, all of them must in reality be free, because they are all equal (§50). On the other hand, all bad men are slaves (§§51-52), and are necessarily subject to wise men (§§53-54); (4) *assumptionis approbatio:* This is true because, through their ignorance, they are also subject to the vices that affect the soul (§§55-56); (5) partial *complexio:* for this reason slavery is the supreme good of the foolish man (§57).

2.1.5 Arguments from virtue (§§58-61)
Philo now makes a brief reference to the desirability of presenting various arguments, with an analogical reference to the clinical habit of treating illnesses with a variety of remedies. In this way he justifies the need to supply various supplementary proofs, when theses are being defended that are new and seem paradoxical (§58), and goes on immediately to develop these. His statements constitute the following structural enthymeme: "The wise man is free because he voluntarily does good, cannot be compelled to do evil, and treats disdainful things indifferently" (§§59-61).[106] Taken individually, they are as follows: The first argument, beginning with a *gradatio*, goes on gradually towards a climax which is presented to us in an enthymematic form, and to its appropriate conclusion: only the virtuous man is free, because he does all things wisely (§59). The second is proved syllogistically and afterwards is amplified with recourse to a *locus a contrario:* if the virtuous man cannot be constrained or impeded, he certainly is not a slave (§60). The third, referring one by one to the actions which proceed from virtue and vice, as well as to indifferent actions, confirms enthymematically the sovereign will and the balanced disposition of the good man who is superior to all forms of intimidation and for that reason is free.

The argumentative structure of Philo in this first part of his *probatio* reflects a twofold concern: to be complete, if not exhaustive, in his apodictic reasoning, and to be as varied as possible in the selection and formulation of

---

[104] Philo, more discreetly here than in *Her.* 214, "subordinates Greek philosophy to Jewish revelation" (Petit, PM 28, p. 180, n. 2).
[105] Cf. Petit, Ibid., p. 31.
[106] Cf. F. H. Colson, PLCL IX, p. 7.

his arguments. It also reflects a rich and natural application of the Hellenistic theory of argumentation, implicitly sanctioning its correct use, as an important and valid expression of the intimate relation between the soul and wisdom.[107] The result is a logical sequence which is to be pleasing and persuasive.

Aware, however, that not everyone will be mentally equipped for this kind of reasoning, because the audience he has in mind is vast and varied, Philo sets out to confirm his thesis through a series of examples.

2.2 Corroborative examples (§§62-135)

The examples of the freedom of the wise man are introduced by an extensive discussion explaining, on the one hand, the scarcity of such people (§§62-63 and 71-72),[108] and, on the other hand, the need to seek their company (§§63-67) and to cultivate the virtues which they embody and inspire (§§69-70). They are expounded, however, in terms of a criterion of transcultural selection. Though they are rare, virtuous men still exist, in Greece as well as elsewhere.

2.2.1 Examples in hierarchical perspective and with chiastic structures

This section begins with examples of groups who demonstrate sovereignty and freedom: (1) the seven wise men of Greece (§73), the Magi from Persia (§74a) and the Gymnosophists from India (§74b) illustrate, on an ascending scale, the superiority of wise men; (2) the Essenes represent, at the top of the pyramid, the culmination of virtue and wisdom (§§75-91). Owing to the Essenes' climactic excellence, Philo attributes to them a lengthy *digressio* in the form of descriptive narrative[109] emphasizing their sanctity as ministers of God (§75), the simplicity and innocence of their occupations (§§76-78), their rejection of slave labor (§79), their dedicated study of the Law (§§80-82), their love for God, virtue and humanity (§§83-84a), their mutual sharing (§§84b-87), the respect which the excellence of their ascetic way of life has inspired even in tyrants and oppressors (§§88-90) who have been finally overcome by the virtue of these wise men (§91).

To these Philo adds individual examples, representing, in ascending scale, the freedom of the wise man in any situation of life (§§92-109): (1) the

---

[107] In *Migr.* 168-170, discourse accompanies the wise man, and according to *Her.* 14, those who confide in the divine love of wisdom should employ "bold discourse" (παρρησία).
[108] The theme of the reduced number of wise men is a Biblical as well as Stoical common place (Cf. Petit, PM 28, p. 186, n. 2). This is a theme introduced in §63 and taken up circularly by the *inclusio* in §72.
[109] Cf. Lausberg, *Manual de Retórica Literaria*, §415: "Concerning *narratio*, the *exemplum* is a *digressio* within the *argumentatio*." Cf. Ibid., §290.

heroic resistance of Calanus[110] who, forced to accompany Alexander from Macedonia to Greece, pointed out by letter that a wise man cannot be constrained (§§93-97); (2) the supreme audaciousness of Heracles who, bought by Silenus, treated his master as if he were a slave (§§98-104); (3) the Stoic courage, prudence and nobility of character of the philosophers Zeno and Anaxarchus who, in the hands of cruel tyrants, endured torture and death anticipating the migration of their souls from their bodies to take refuge in wisdom and the other virtues (§§105-109).

In these two series of examples Philo certainly has in mind the exaltation of the Essene community as a paradigm of genuine wisdom. The parallelism of the scheme is not totally complete, its symmetry being imperfect in the second term of the scale. But, if we understand the correspondence between the Magi and Heracles in terms of their function and not their origin, this dissymmetry is at least attenuated. In fact, the Magi are as remarkable as Heracles, not only because of their knowledge and perfect liberty, but also because of their spirituality.[111] In terms of its internal dynamic Philo's construction is as follows:

```
                    The Essenes
                    (§§75-91)
                        D

   The Gymnosophists – C           C' – Calanus (§§93-98)
   of India (§74b)

   The Magi of Persia – B           B' – Heracles
   (§74a)                           (§§99-104)

   The Seven Wise – A               A' – Anaxarchus and
   Greeks (§73)                     Zeno of Elea (§§105-109)
```

2.2.2 *Examples amplified by the* incrementum *(§§110-143)*
The courage of the wise man, which the last three examples testify to in such an expressive way, is now cast into strategic relief by means of a new series of examples grouped together in the following *gradatio* of intensification,[112] proving an unassailable superiority.

---

[110] A gymnosophist who, according to Strabo, consumed himself by fire in Alexander's presence (Str. XV, 1, 69).
[111] The wisdom of the Magi is "a visionary knowledge," and is seen in the apprehension of truth through scrutinizing the works of nature. It is as seers that "they receive and transmit the revelation of the divine virtues" (§74). Some indirectly attribute to them a spiritual affiliation with the Jews (Cf. Petit, PM 28, p. 101). As for Heracles, Philo is equally conscious of the growing spiritualization of which he was the object, to the point of being considered as the savior of men and the purifier of evil (Cf. Petit, PM 28, p. 71).
[112] Cf. Lausberg, *Manual de Retórica Literaria*, §401-403.

(A) The courage of those who prefer death to a life without glory and liberty:
1) Two athletes (§§110-113).
2) Adolescents and women (§§114-117).
  – A young Laconian in captivity, who preferred death to submission to servile labour (§114).
  – The Dardanian women prisoners of the Macedonians, who preferred to kill their sons rather than see them become slaves (§115).
  – Polyxena who, according to Euripides, chose to die free (§116).
3) An entire people like the Xanthians who, because of their love of freedom, chose glorious death over slavery (§§118-120).

(B) The courage of those who face up to adverse life situations, boldly and positively, taking refuge in the superiority of their spirit (§§121-130):
1) Anecdotes about Diogenes, the Cynic: characteristics which denote the supreme liberty of his spirit (§§121-124).
2) Other cases of courageous replies:
  – Chaereas of Alexandria and the nobility of his παρρησία in the face of Ptolemy's irritation (§§125-126).
  – Theodorus and the explanation of his exile from Athens, showing the superiority of his spirit as a citizen of the world (§§127-130).

(C) The courage of those who defy death itself (§§131-135); illustrated by fighting cocks, whose combat may be taken as a model and source of inspiration for men in their resistance to slavery.

2.2.3 *Digression on the nobility of freedom and the ignominy of slavery* (§§136-143), in the form of an argument of Aristotelian structure.

Aware that the enthymeme and the example are the fundamental vehicles of the πίστις, Philo here uses both, placing the examples after the enthymeme, as evidence to confirm the truth stated.[113]

(A) Enthymeme (§136)—it is the character and not the name that makes the slave.

> Καὶ μὴν οὐδ' ἐκεῖνό τις τῶν ἐπὶ βραχὺ παιδείας ἀψαμένων ἀγνοεῖ, ὅτι καλὸν μὲν πρᾶγμα ἐλευθερία, αἰσχρὸν δὲ δουλεία, καὶ ὅτι τὰ μὲν καλὰ πρόσεστι τοῖς ἀγαθοῖς, τὰ δ' αἰσχρὰ τοῖς φαύλοις· ἐξ ὧν ἐναργέστατα παρίσταται τὸ μήτε τινὰ τῶν σπουδαίων δοῦλον εἶναι, κἂν μυρίοι τὰ δεσποτῶν σύμβολα προφέροντες ἐπανατείνωνται, μήτε τῶν ἀφρόνων ἐλεύθερον, κἂν Κροῖσος ἢ Μίδας ἢ ὁ μέγας βασιλεὺς ὢν τυγχάνῃ.

> Certainly, no one who received the smallest amount of education will be unaware that freedom is a beautiful thing and slavery is unworthy; that beautiful things belong to good

---

[113] Cf. Aristotle, *Rhetorica* II, 20, 1394a 9-18.

men, and unworthy things to the bad. From this it is clearly to be concluded that no good man is a slave, even when threatened by innumerable masters who display their deeds of ownership, and that no foolish man is free, even though he be a Croesus, a Midas, or even the great king.

(B) Examples in confirmation (§§137-143):
– On the blessing of political freedom, defended in the council and assembly as on the battlefield (§§137-139).
– On the curse of slavery, hated by all. Amongst Greeks, the exclusion of slaves from some festivals (§§140-141); amongst the Argonauts, their exclusion from all types of service (§§142-143).

2.2.4 *Return to the main theme*, to affirm for the last time the enslaving nature of the passions and the dominion of the wise man over them, in the form of a structural enthymeme (§§144-151): the wise man repudiates every sort of threat to his sovereign liberty and gives it an adequate response (§§144-147), because he finds his virtue to be a protection and security superior to that which a conventional slave finds in a place of refuge (§148-151).

(3) Conclusion

Our rhetorical analysis of the *Probus* has demonstrated that it is an epideictic discourse, not only coherent with the *status* of its *causa*, but also in terms of its overall architecture.

The arguments are surprisingly varied and at the same time harmoniously woven together. The examples themselves are presented, in most cases so as to cover the most varied aspects of the question; and the order of their presentation adds to their persuasive force.

The audience Philo has in view, seems to include Gentiles as well as Jews. He does not seek only to intensify adhesion to the values he extols. The argumentative nature of the epideictic oratory is pedagogical in its inspiration and in its intention. In it, the speaker plays the part of a teacher.[114] His main theme is the love of virtue and the freedom of the wise man, supremely embodied in the Essene community. The fact that Philo quotes only five biblical texts, as opposed to the superabundance of themes, quotations, allusions and examples gathered from the culture of the Hellenistic world, together with his apologetic eulogy of the Judaic faith and the consequent exhortation to young people from all countries to embrace this 'philosophy,' bear witness to an "intended audience" of ecumenical dimensions. The "maximum effort" he spends in argumentation, as well as

---

[114] Cf. C. Perelman and Olbrechts-Tyteca, *New Rhetoric*, p. 51-54.

his philosophical foundation, seem to support this intention. As C. Perelman observes, "the audience is not necessarily constituted by those whom the orator explicitly addresses". It must be understood as "all those whom the orator wishes to influence by means of his argument;"[115] and this number may include the whole of humankind, which he qualifies as "a universal audience, comprising an infinite variety of particular audiences."[116]

Philo knew very well how to "adapt the weapons of his rhetoric to the public he wished to convince,"[117] inspire or inform didactically—in this case not only his fellow citizens in the diaspora, but also other strata of Greco-Roman society.

II *Discourses embedded in Treatises*

1. *Defense of Judah (*De Iosepho *222-231)*

The *De Iosepho* is basically a historical commentary on the life of Joseph, depicting him above all as the ideal statesman. The treatise has a narrative character and for this reason is full of brief discourses, typical of historians of the period,[118] as vectors of dramatic animation.[119]

Amongst them, we consider to be representative Judah's brief speech, in defense of his brother Benjamin. When Joseph's brothers were falsely and strategically accused of having stolen the silver vessel of the governor of Egypt, they were brought back into his presence and subjected to the shock of seeing their youngest brother sentenced to slavery. This was Benjamin, the favorite son of his ageing father (§224), the one for whose life and return the oldest brother had sworn to sacrifice his two sons (§188). What could they do to appeal the sentence, since they themselves had just invoked the death sentence on the one who was found guilty (§216) and they had no way of proving his innocence?

It is in this tense setting that the fourth oldest of the brothers, "the most courageous of all, gifted with the temperament of leadership and of great eloquence" (§189), boldly offers a passionate discourse of great vigor and oratorical balance, structured in four parts.

Given the straightforwardness of the cause, he limits himself to gaining the attention of the judge and appealing to his benevolent sensibility by

---

[115] *L'empire rhétorique*, p. 207.
[116] Ibid., p. 27-28. Cf. *Rhétorique et philosophie*, p. 20-21, 50-51.
[117] Arnaldez, *et alii*, PM 22, p. 21.
[118] Cf. F. H. Colson, PLCL VI, p. 138.
[119] The censure and lamentation of Reuben (§17-21), lamentations of Jacob (§23-27), Joseph's virtuous protest (§42-48), challenge of the "popular passion" of the political man (§64-66 [allegory of Potiphar's wife and Joseph]), courageous answer of the political man (§67-78), Judah's speech in defense of Benjamin (§222-231).

means of a very brief proem (§222). In it he asserts that the judge should be serene and upright and that he, to safeguard his personal honor, will not pronounce sentence precipitously before hearing the defence. The brevity of the discourse does not lessen its force. The emphasis given to one of the major motivating causes[120] in a context of injustice, that is θυμός as an expression of ὀργή, makes a lively appeal to the noble sentiments of the human heart and displays oratorical balance.

The *narratio* (§§223-225), which addresses the intelligence of the judge, purely and simply ignores the issue at stake, and diverts attention to the father, describing Jacob's character, giving examples of his feelings and relationship with his youngest son. Recalling the judge's previous expressions of interest in obtaining information about the father and Benjamin, perhaps in hope of stirring up some feeling of empathy, Judah reinforces his diegetic argument *a persona* by referring not only to the *educatio, disciplina* and *fortuna*[121] of Jacob, but also to the way these factors have contributed to his premature ageing:

> πατὴρ μέν ἐστι πρεσβύτης, οὐ χρόνῳ μᾶλλον γεγηρακὼς ἢ ταῖς ἐπαλλήλοις δυστυχίαις, ὑφ' ὧν γυμναζόμενος ἀθλητοῦ τρόπον ἐν πόνοις καὶ δυσκαρτερήτοις κακοπαθείαις διετέλεσεν·
>
> Our father is an old man, aged not so much by years as by repeated misfortunes, whereby as in a training-school he has been continually exercised amid labours and sufferings which have tried him sore (§223b).

Judah also alludes to the *aetas* of Jacob and Benjamin, apologetically stressing the latter's inexperience, so as to implicitly diminish the extent of his responsibility:

> μόλις πείθεται τοῦτον συνεκπέμψαι μυρία μὲν αἰτιώμενος, ὅτι ἀδελφὸν ἄλλον ἔχειν ὡμολογήσαμεν, μυρία δ' οἰκτιζόμενος, εἰ μελλήσει διαζεύγνυσθαι· νήπιος γάρ ἐστι καὶ πραγμάτων ἄπειρος, οὐ μόνον τῶν κατὰ τὴν ἀλλοδαπήν, ἀλλὰ καὶ τῶν κατὰ τὴν πόλιν.
>
> Many a time did he blame us for admitting that we had another brother. Many a time did he pity himself for the coming separation from the boy, for he is but a child and without experience, not only of life in a foreign land, but of city life in general (§225b).

As Quintilian points out, the only difference between proof and narration is that narration is an exposition relating to that which one wishes to prove, and proof is the verification of that which has just been declared.[122] Now it is precisely this relationship that "Judah" establishes, interpreting it first and then arguing it. His *confirmatio* (§§226-230) is an appeal articulated along the lines developed in the *narratio*, where attention is again centered on the

---

[120] Aristotle, *Rhetorica* I, 10 1369a 32 - 1369b 17.
[121] Cf. Lausberg, *Manual de Retórica Literaria*, §376.
[122] *Institutio Oratoria* IV, 2, 79.

figure of the father. Allying closely reasoned argument to more direct passionate involvement, the argument in linear terms presents the following structure:

(1) A dual introductory *interrogatio* (§226a):

πρὸς οὖν οὕτω διακείμενον τὸν πατέρα πῶς ἂν ἀφικοίμεθα; τίσι δ' ὀφθαλμοῖς αὐτὸν θεάσασθαι δίχα τούτου δυνησόμεθα;

Then, since such are our father's feelings, how can we return to him? How can we look him in the face without the boy?

(2) An anticipated *commiseratio* (§226b-227a),[123] organized in *gradatio* and including the *ratio* of its final portion:

τελευτὴν οἰκτίστην ὑπομενεῖ μόνον ἀκούσας, ὡς οὐκ ἐπανελήλυθεν· εἶθ' ἡμᾶς ἀνδροφόνους καὶ πατροκτόνους ἕκαστος ἐρεῖ τῶν φιλαπεχθημόνων καὶ ἐπὶ ταῖς τοιαύταις συμφοραῖς ἐθελοκακούντων. τὸ δὲ πλεῖστον τῆς κατηγορίας ῥυήσεται κατ' ἐμοῦ· πολλὰ γὰρ ὑπεσχόμην τῷ πατρὶ προέσθαι παρακαταθήκην λαμβάνειν ὁμολογῶν, ἣν ἀποδώσειν, ὅταν ἀπαιτηθῶ.

He will suffer the saddest of deaths on merely hearing that he has not returned, and we shall be called murderers and parricides by all the spiteful people who gloat over such misfortunes. And the chief stream of obloquy will be directed against me, for I pledged myself with many forfeits to my father, and declared that I received the boy as a deposit which I would restore when it was demanded from me.

(3) A new *interrogatio* as a reinforcement (§§226b-227a), to end this *gradatio* and to introduce the central argument, in the form of a hypothetical sentence in the potential mood (§227b):

πῶς δ' ἄν, εἰ μὴ ἐξευμενισθείης αὐτός, ἀποδοῦναι δυναίμην;

But how can I restore it, unless you yourself are propitiated?

(4) Finally, the persistent *deprecatio* (§§227c-230), in which he attempts, on the one hand, to conciliate and encourage the Egyptian governor, in order to assure his favour through the use of the *loci* of humanity, piety and pardon,[124] and, on the other hand, to highlight the dignity, virtue, honour and nobility of character of the one who will in the end either be the great victim or the great beneficiary of his final verdict. In the first place, Judah makes an appeal for mercy on behalf of an aged Jacob unable to suffer such a blow. Then, in case this should fail, he offers himself as a substitutionary ransom on his brother's behalf. Finally, he expresses hope in the judge's goodness, sensitivity, and empathy:

---

[123] *Rhetorica ad Herennium* II, 47.
[124] Ibid. II, 25.

οἶκτον δέομαι τοῦ πρεσβύτου λαβεῖν καὶ εἰς ἔννοιαν ἐλθεῖν τῶν κακῶν οἷσπερ ἀνιαθήσεται μὴ κομισάμενος ὃν ἀβουλῶν ἐνεχείρισεν. ἀλλὰ σὺ μὲν ὑπὲρ ὧν ἔδοξας ἠδικῆσθαι δίκας λάμβανε. δώσω δ᾽ ἐθελοντὴς ἐγώ· δοῦλον ἀπὸ ταύτης ἀνάγραφε τῆς ἡμέρας, ἄσμενος ὑπομενῶ τὰ τῶν νεωνήτων, ἐὰν τὸ παιδίον ἐθελήσῃς ἐᾶσαι. λήψεται δ᾽ οὐκ αὐτὸς τὴν χάριν, ἐὰν ἄρα διδῷς, ἀλλ᾽ ὁ μὴ παρὼν ἐπικουφισθεὶς τῶν φροντίδων, ὁ τῶν τοσούτων πατὴρ ἱκετῶν ἁπάντων· ἱκέται γάρ ἐσμεν καταπεφευγότες ἐπὶ τὴν σὴν ἱερωτάτην δεξιάν, ἧς μηδέποτε διαμάρτοιμεν. ἔλεος οὖν εἰσελθέτω σε γήρως ἀνδρὸς τοὺς ἀρετῆς ἄθλους κατὰ πᾶσαν ἡλικίαν διαπονήσαντος·

I pray you to take pity on the old man, and realize the miseries which he will suffer if he does not recover him who he unwillingly entrusted to my hand. But do you exact the penalty for the wrongs which you believe yourself to have received. I will willingly pay it. Write me down your slave from this day onwards. I will gladly endure what the newly-bought endure if you will spare the child. This boon, if indeed you grant it, will be a boon not to the boy himself but to one who is not here present, whom you will relieve of his cares, the father of all these many suppliants. For suppliants we are who have fled for refuge to your most august right hand, which we pray may never fail us. Take pity, then, on the old age of one who spent all his years labouring in the arena of virtue.

The grammatical structure of the hypothetical sentences in the subjective mood is significant. Judah's reference to the rights of supplicants and their situation as refugees is telling,[125] as is the trusting reference to Joseph's "august right hand," the symbol of the saving and protecting power of a divinity.[126]

The argument from Jacob's age and his virtue won in the arena of life is supported by the paradigmatic allusion to the welcome and esteem he received from people with very different customs, because of the honesty, nobility and consistency of his life.

The *peroratio* (§231), no longer than the *exordium*, limits itself to a *conquestio* of enthymematic structure, which aims to move the judge's mercy to action,[127] by focussing on the unlimited gratitude he will receive, corresponding to the size of the favor which is being asked. "A merciful sentence is awarded by the glory of *clementia* (a virtue that makes mortals like gods)."[128] The final reason given takes the form of an *interrogatio*, whose function is beyond any doubt that of an argument *a fortiori* (§231b).

---

[125] According to *Mos.* I, 34, foreigners are supplicants aspiring to the rights of citizenship; according to *Legat.* 1-7, the Jewish people are a race of supplicants who make intercessory prayer to their God in favor of those who welcome them, and who call down vengeance on those who oppress them (cf. Jean Laporte, PM 21, p. 136, n. 1).
[126] J. Laporte, PM 21, p. 136, n. 2. Cf. the reference to E. M. Smallwood, *Philonis Alexandrini, Legatio ad Gaium* (Leiden: Brill, 1961), p. 201.
[127] In such at case this is, according to Cicero, the only *locus communis* recommendable is 'that in which the audience is entreated with a humble and suppliant language, so that they will have mercy' (*De Inuentione* I, 109).
[128] Lausberg, *Manual de Retórica Literaria*, §194. Cf. Quintilian VII, 4, 19.

τοιαύτην μέλλεις κατατίθεσθαι χάριν, ἧς οὐκ ἂν δύναιτό τις μείζονα λαβεῖν· τίς γὰρ ἂν γένοιτο πατρὶ δωρεὰ μείζων ἢ υἱὸν ἀπογνωσθέντα κομίσασθαι;

> Such is the gratitude which you will earn, and what greater could be earned? For what greater boon could a father have than the recovery of a son of whose safety he has despaired?

Considered as a whole, this speech is an extended structural enthymeme,[129] in which logical and psychological proof go together, and whose essential *Leitmotif* is the principle of contradiction. Beginning with the assumption that Jacob inspires pity, the rhetorical macro-syllogism takes the following form: If "Joseph" has pity on Jacob (§§227, 230), and the absolving of Benjamin is the supreme proof of that pity (§229), then Joseph should absolve Benjamin.

2. *Discourse on the Search for God* (De Praemiis et Poenis 24-51)

A discourse on the Abraham-Isaac-Jacob triad "forms a systematic whole"[130] in the heart of a less homogeneous treatise. In it the exposition of Philo's thought on Jewish morality and spirituality, in synthetic form, comes to its conclusion. In contrast with the previous triad—Enos, Enoch and Noah—which exemplifies the particular virtues of hope, repentance and justice together with their specific fruits, this triad symbolizes virtue, piety and wisdom, as a threefold expression of "generic virtue," and Philo extends his discussion by describing three paths for the journey towards God and the respective reward for each.[131]

The architecture of the passage and its style,[132] have an oratorical character. It contains the fundamental parts of a rhetorical discourse: *exordium* (§24-27a), *diuisio* (§27b), *probatio* (§28-48) and *peroratio* (§49-51). The *narratio*, as we know, is dispensable in epideictic and symbouletic discourse, and here we find all the characteristics of the former, eulogizing as it does the virtues embodied in the three patriarchs.

W. Brandt points out that one of the greatest needs to be satisfied in the introduction of an argument is the definition of the matter or issue to be considered.[133] The Alexandrian fulfills this task in a masterly way in this

---

[129] Brandt, *Rhetoric of Argumentation*, p. 60-63.
[130] A. Beckaert, PM 27, p. 13.
[131] *Leg.* I, 64. Cf. Beckaert, PM 27, p. 20, who observes in a note that the three patriarchal virtues in *Abr.* 54 are compared to the three Graces of fable. It should be stressed that these "three types do not represent a gradation: beginning, progress, end. They are three attitudes, three ways of doing, which are united together (Ibid., p. 37).
[132] Cf. Ibid., p. 14.
[133] Brandt, *Rhetoric of Argumentation*, p. 51, 72.

interesting proem, developing at the same time the ἦθος necessary to capture and hold the attention of the audience.

The indisputable nobility of the cause requires a direct opening,[134] and for this reason Philo makes his introduction according to the following sequence:

(1) Introduction of the patriarchal triad, whom he describes as "most holy and most beloved of God" (§24a).

(2) Epideictic definition of the triad[135]: a father, son and grandson who all pursued arduously the same ideal in life (§24b).

(3) Its concrete expression in the *descriptio*: the ideal of pleasing the Creator and Father of all things, despising the values that the multitudes admire—glory, riches and pleasure—and scorning deceitful and false vanity (§24c).

(4) Circumlocution to define and describe vanity: vanity is the impostor that deifies inanimate objects; great engine of aggression; a power zealous to capture young souls through specious maneuvres and sophistry; the one that finds a place in the souls of all persons except those enlightened by the truth (§25a).

(5) Antithetic confrontation of vanity (τῦφος) with the truth (§25b).

(6) Redefinition of the triad, as a paradigm of those who despise vanity, by antithesis, dieresis and structural *distributio*.[136] These argumentative figures reveal syntagmatically the qualitative superiority[137] of those who renounce vanity and cling to the truth, their passage from the world of the senses to the world of ideas in their intense aspiration to contemplate the divine and the resulting abandonment of the irrational part of the soul as they cling to what they call νοῦς καὶ λογισμός (§26).

(7) Enumeration of the members of the triad, in their passage from vanity to truth,[138] by applying to the three patriarchs the formula "nature, instruction and practice," characteristic of classical literature on education, from Plato and Aristotle to Cicero and Quintilian.[139] The first—Abraham—reaches

---

[134] *Rhetorica ad Herennium* I, 6.

[135] Lausberg observes that "exists a close relationship between the *demonstratiuum* and the *status finitionis*," and that "it is known in the proemium" (§250-251).

[136] Although related to the dieretic definition and similar to the antithesis, the *distributio* is distinguished by the argumentative force which accrues to it from the distribution of the divided concept, proportionally attributing the parts to each one of the actors. Brandt calls it *"structural distributio"* (Brandt, *Rhetoric of Argumentation*, p. 133-134).

[137] It should be underscored that the *status qualitatis* is the nuclear *status* of the *genus demonstratiuum* (Quintilian III, 7, 28), the *status quantitatis* being included in it (Quintilian VII, 4, 15-16) which Aristotle (*Rhetorica* III, 17 1417b 25) "studies on an equal footing" (Lausberg, *Manual de Retórica Literaria*, §128).

[138] It is curious to note that the contrast between τῦπος and ἀλήθεια corresponds to the contrast between αἴσθησις and νοῦς καὶ λογισμός.

[139] Cf. PLCL VIII, p. 453.

perfection through "didactic" virtue, and receives faith as his reward. The second—Isaac—reaches it through "autodidactic" virtue, and receives happiness as his prize. The third—Jacob—reaches it through "ascetic" practice, and is crowned with a vision of God.

Curiously, along with these structural traits which characterize an argumentative proem, there can be discerned at the same time stylistic traits from the domain of textual rhetoric, which was recognized by the ancients as "a crucial element in persuasion."[140] The argumentative structure of the proem constitutes rhythmically an *inclusio* in chiastic order, and this is conveyed symmetrically by "a dynamic element, able to provide the necessary movement" to the transition from the fight against vanity to the final victory.[141]

A – *The patriarchal trinity*, its identification.
    B – Their struggle against *vanity*,
        C – This is the very enemy of the *truth* that the patriarchs seek.
            D – The qualitatively superior strength of those who despise vanity and love truth.
        C' – The search for *truth*, in the journey from the material world to the world of ideas.
    B' – The escape from and final victory over *vanity*.
A' – The *patriarchal trinity*, their final victory and their rewards.

The *exordium* ends with an erotema, used strategically as an *a fortiori* argument, to repeat and emphasize the excellence of the rewards granted, and to begin the *transitus* to the *argumentatio*, completed in the *propositio* as is expressed in the beginning of the following paragraph (§28a).[142]

> τοῦ δὲ πιστεύειν θεῷ καὶ διὰ παντὸς τοῦ βίου χαίρειν καὶ ὁρᾶν ἀεὶ τὸ ὂν τί ἂν ὠφελιμώτερον ἢ σεμνότερον ἐπινοήσειέ τις; Ἐπαυγασώμεθα δ' αὐτῶν ἕκαστον ἀκριβέστερον, μὴ τοῖς ὀνόμασι παραχθέντες, ἀλλὰ διακύψαντες εἴσω καὶ ταῖς διανοίαις ἐμβαθύναντες.

> Belief in God, life-long joy, the perpetual vision of the Existent—what can anyone conceive more profitable or more august than these? But let us look into each of them more carefully and not be led away by mere names but with a peering eye explore the inwardness of their full meaning (§27b-28a).

The conceptual nucleus of the *probatio* is made up of three arguments, each one of them appropriate to one of the three types of perfection and

---

[140] Brandt, *Rhetoric of Argumentation*, p. 19.
[141] Cf. J. Cazeaux, "Philon d'Alexandrie Exégète," p. 198.
[142] Cf. Quintilian IV, 4, 1: "The proposition is the beginning of every proof, which is used no only in order to demonstrate the principal question, but sometimes also in particular arguments, especially those which are called *epichiremata*."

their respective rewards, and each one technically organized in accordance with the rhetorical conventions of the Hellenistic period.

We will limit ourselves to observing the logical sequence of their internal structure. But we must point out, in the first place, the fact that the Alexandrian commentator makes use of a dual formal argumentation structure: the Ciceronian *ratiocinatio* in the first two arguments, and the *absolutissima et perfectissima argumentatio* of the *auctor ad Herennium* in the last.[143]

The first argument (§§28-30), on the education of Abraham, has the following formal content: (1) *Propositio:* He who has confidence in God learns to lose confidence in all that is perishable, beginning with his λογισμός and αἴσθησις. (2) *Approbatio:* To each one of these faculties was assigned the role of studying, respectively, the domain of ideas and the domain of the senses, with the objective of distinguishing the truth from human opinions. (3) *Assumptio* and *assumptionis approbatio:* Now these values are unstable and uncertain: opinion, because it is based on appearances and probabilities, and falsifies and betrays the original; and reason, because, although it exercises dominion over the senses and believes itself to be responsible for the judgment of intelligible things, it is like an athlete who is forced to give up when defeated by a superior power. (4) *Complexio:* Thanks to his firm reasoning and unshakable faith, it was granted to Abraham to rise above material things and even immaterial things. Because he took God as his only foundation and support, he was truly happy and blessed.

The second section (§§31-35), on Isaac's auto-didacticism, is also presented with an epichirematic structure. (1) *Propositio* (§31a): The prize for the one who acquired virtue naturally and without effort is happiness (χαρά). (2) *Approbatio* by means of the etymological argument (§31b): Its name—γέλως—is a visible physical sign of invisible noetic joy. (3) *Assumptio* (§32): Now χαρά is the noblest and most beautiful of the higher emotions. (4) *Assumptionis approbatio* (§§33-34): Because by it the soul is filled with satisfaction, rejoicing in the Creator of all things and in the perfect work of His hands. He always exercises providential care of His universe, notwithstanding the accidents permitted in His divine economy for the well-being and final security of the κόσμος.

The reasoning is confirmed by two analogies—that of the doctor and that of the pilot—and is reinforced by an *a contrario* argument. The doctor sometimes amputates members of the body in order to assure health. The pilot sometimes throws the cargo into the sea to provide security for the passengers. Now, just as they are praised and not criticized when they are led to prefer utility to pleasure, so it is important to admire and revere universal nature in its sovereign government of the κόσμος. For, like "a city blessed

---

[143] *Rhetorica ad Herennium* II, 28.

with good laws," universal security is more important than individual hedonism which endangers that same security. (5) *Complexio* (§35): Thus, Isaac is blessed, no less than Abraham. This conclusion is supported by an interesting enthymeme:

> μακάριος οὖν καὶ οὗτος οὐχ ἧττον τοῦ προτέρου, συννοίας καὶ κατηφείας ἀμέτοχος ὤν, ἄλυπόν τε καὶ ἄφοβον ζωὴν καρπούμενος, αὐστηροῦ καὶ αὐχμηροῦ βίου μηδ' ὄναρ προσαψάμενος διὰ τὸ πάντα τόπον τῆς ψυχῆς αὐτοῦ χαρᾷ προκατέχεσθαι.

> So he too is blessed no less than the first named. He never knows gloom and depression; his days are passed in happy freedom from fears and grief; the hardships and squalor of life never touch him even in his dreams, because every spot in his soul is already tenanted by joy (§35).

The final argument (§§36-48), on the asceticism of Jacob, is presented on a different model of argumentation, to which we have already referred; a phenomenon which is very typical of the Alexandrian exegete who, in his thirst for originality and demonstrative versatility, constantly uses new approaches.[144]

(1) *Propositio* (§36a): Jacob receives, as a result of his ascetic practice, the special reward of a vision of God.

(2) *Ratio* (§§36b-37a): His eyes were progressively opened to the visual apprehension of the divine existence. In the first stage, when his eyes were still closed, he struggled to discern the truth, but only discovered deep darkness in the mortal realm. In the second, the eyes of his soul began to open little by little through diligent and unceasing struggle, so that he eventually became free of that deep darkness in which he was immersed so as to gain a vision of reality.

(3) *Confirmatio* (§37b-40): The *ratio* is here corroborated by two additional arguments added in sequence, and they themselves are supported by enthymematic digressions, to define the nature of the vision and its limits. For, first of all, thanks to an incorporeal ray of light purer than ether, Jacob was able to contemplate the world of ideas governed by its sovereign Controller, though he was unable to discern His form because of the dense and impenetrable band of light that surrounded Him. Afterwards, thanks to his persistent and sincere longing for exhaustive contemplation, his capacity for vision was intensified by the πατὴρ καὶ σωτήρ who conceded to him as complete a contemplation of His person as is possible for a mortal.

> ἐκεῖνο μὲν γάρ, ὃ καὶ ἀγαθοῦ κρεῖττον καὶ μονάδος πρεσβύτερον καὶ ἑνὸς εἰλικρινέστερον, ἀμήχανον ὑφ' ἑτέρου θεωρεῖσθαί τινος, διότι μόνῳ θέμις αὐτῷ ὑφ' ἑαυτοῦ καταλαμβάνεσθαι.

---

[144] Cf. J. Pouilloux, PM 10, p. 17.

FORMAL STRUCTURE OF A DISCOURSE 141

For this which is better than the good, more venerable than the monad, purer than the unit, cannot be discerned by anyone else; to God alone is it permitted to apprehend God (§40).

(4) *Exornatio* (§§41-46): This is a lengthy digression on the nature of the divine revelation οὐχι τῆς ὅ ἐστιν ἐμφαινούσης, ἀλλὰ τῆς ὅτι ἔστιν: (Vision did not show *what* He is, but *that* He is [§39]). It effectively enriches the argument by making use of an *amplificatio*, a piece of analogical reasoning and a *sententia*. The amplification by the *incrementum*[145] concentrates on the problem of the knowledge of God, in the framework of a philosophical dissertation, and highlights the various degrees of apprehension and awareness of the divinity, by describing different attitudes towards it. Some deny it, pure and simply; others drift and persist in doubt; still others, more given to tradition than to reason, think that they are exercising themselves in wholesome piety, but in fact disfigure it through superstition; yet others, stimulated by reasoning and reflection, behold the world in its beauty, balance and harmony and rising, as if by a heavenly stairway, infer the architect and creator of the universe as well as His providence; others, finally, are enabled to apprehend divinity by divinity without recourse to reasoning. These last are persons who ἐν ὁσίοις καὶ γνησίοις θεραπευταῖς καὶ θεοφιλέσιν ὡς ἀληθῶς ἀναγραφέσθωσαν (should be remembered as saints and genuine worshippers, true friends of God(§43b)); among them Israel is numbered, as occupying the highest position on this scale. In substantiating this, Philo adds the following arguments: an etymological[146] one based on alliteration,[147] and the *a contrario*.

The way in which the revelation of the divine person took shape on the level of human perception is, first of all, illustrated by the εἰκών[148] of the sun, the other stars and light in general, all of which are seen, thanks to their own light. This is afterwards confirmed by the *sententia* ἀλήθειαν δὲ μετίασιν οἱ

---

[145] One of the four *genera amplificationis* (Quintilian VIII, 4, 3).
[146] Although the etymological topic is not currently appreciated by the critics, because it seems to them to lack the logical force recognized in others, "it was common in Philo's time, however, highly regarded, and very important to Philo himself" (T. Conley, *Philo's Rhetoric: Studies in Style, Composition and Exegesis*, p. 104).
[147] Cf. A. Beckaert, PM 27, p. 64, n. 1.
[148] The two essential terms used by Aristotle for "comparison" are παραβολή and εἰκών. Παραβολή normally carries the sense of "illustrative comparison" or "analogy." Εἰκών, here used by Philo, is *stricto sensu* a *simile* (*Rhetorica* III, 4, 20-26) but, in a latent sense, comprehends all the types of stylistic comparison (Cf. M. H. McCall, Jr., *Ancient Rhetorical Theories*, p. 24-32, 53). They are terms which, together with παράδειγμα, are applied more or less indiscriminately by the ancient critics, McCall observes (Ibid., p. 258), although Aristotle normally takes this as a generic term and relates it dieretically with the others. I believe, therefore, that here we can consider the εἰκών, or *imago*, as a type of example (*Rhetorica* II, 20) analogically developed and structured.

τὸν θεὸν θεῷ φαντασιωθέντες (the seekers for truth are those who envisage God through God (§46b)).

(5) *Complexio* (§§47-48): Again taking up the beginning of the argument, the *complexio* concentrates especially on the symbolic sense of the name given to the prize awarded and moves on from there to describe the full expansion of the best part of the soul, through the exhaustion and paralysis of the passions, summarizing at the same time the essence of its propositionally argued content.

The *peroratio* (§§49-51) of the discourse limits itself, as is fitting to the epideictic genre, to enumerating and amplifying the various parts. This amplification satisfies at the same time the remaining essential functions of the epilogue[149] and demonstrates, through a triple enthymematic structure, the appropriateness of the reward given to each one of the patriarchs.

> Προσεξεταστέον δὲ ὅτι καὶ οἰκειότατον ἑκάστῳ τῶν τριῶν ἀπενεμήθη τὸ ἆθλον. τῷ μὲν γὰρ ἐκ διδασκαλίας τελειωθέντι πίστις, ἐπειδὴ τὸν μανθάνοντα πιστεῦσαι δεῖ τῷ διδάσκοντι περὶ ὧν ὑφηγεῖται· δύσκολον γάρ, μᾶλλον δ' ἀδύνατον ἀπιστοῦντα παιδεύεσθαι. τῷ δὲ κατ' εὐμοιρίαν φύσεως ἐπ' ἀρετὴν φθάσαντι χαρά· χαρτὸν γὰρ ἡ εὐφυΐα καὶ τὰ φύσεως δῶρα. τῆς διανοίας εὐθιξίαις καὶ εὐσκόποις ἐπιβολαῖς προσγανουμένης, ἐν αἷς ἀπόνως εὑρίσκει τὰ ζητούμενα, καθάπερ ὑποβολέως ἔνδοθεν ὑπηχοῦντος· ἡ γὰρ σύντομος τῶν ἀπορουμένων εὕρεσις χαρτόν. τῷ δὲ δι' ἀσκήσεως περιποιησαμένῳ φρόνησιν ὅρασις· μετὰ γὰρ τὸν ἐν νεότητι πρακτικὸν βίον ὁ ἐν γήρᾳ θεωρητικὸς βίος ἄριστος καὶ ἱερώτατος, ὃν οἷα κυβερνήτην παραπέμψας ἐπὶ πρύμναν ὁ θεὸς ἐνεχείρισε τοὺς οἴακας ὡς ἱκανῷ πηδαλιουχεῖν τὰ ἐπίγεια· χωρὶς γὰρ θεωρίας ἐπιστημονικῆς οὐδὲν τῶν πραττομένων καλόν.

> A further question for consideration is the special suitability of the reward assigned to each of the three. Faith for him who was perfected through teaching, since the learner must believe the instructions of his teacher: to educate a disbeliever is difficult or rather impossible.
> Joy for him who through the happiness of his natural endowments arrives at virtue. For good abilities and natural gifts are a matter for rejoicing. The mind exults in the facility of its apprehension and the felicity of the processes by which it discovers what it seeks without labour, as though dictated by an inward prompter. For to find the solution of difficulties quickly must bring joy.
> Vision for him who attains wisdom through practice. For after the active life of youth the contemplative life of old age is the best and most sacred—, that life which God sends to the stern like a helmsman and entrusts the rudder into its hands as well fitted to steer the course of earthly things. For without contemplation and the knowledge which it gives no activity attains excellence (§49-51).

In an apparently original application[150] of the formula "nature, teaching and practice" to spiritual experience, Philo here develops, in a very explicit

---

[149] Cf. Lausberg, *Manual de Retórica Literaria*, §431-439. "The theory of amplification was primarily formed for the epideictic," observes Harry Caplan (*Cicero, Rhetorica ad Herennium* [Cambridge: Cambridge University Press, 1977], p. 146, note b), purposely adding that "Gorgias, Tisias (Plato, *Phaedrus* 267a) and Isocrates gave it preeminence." And as we know, it is in peroration that it mostly finds a place (cf. Cicero, *De Partitione Oratoria* 15, 22) as a more impressive affirmation of the theme, in order to excite the emotions of the audience.
[150] Cf. F. H. Colson, PLCL VI, p. xi.

fashion, one of his dominant ideas in the context of his central theme—the migration of the soul of the wise man. As in an educational system, these three elements are all necessary, though in different degrees.[151] It is a discourse with a beginning, a middle and an end, which justifies the "rewards" alloted to the virtues embodied in the patriarchal figures, Abraham-Isaac-Jacob, and develops a system in which, in contrast with mere linear enumeration, the moral and spiritual values they represent are considered in their inwardness and in ever-increasing depth.

3. *Speech on Virtue* (De Sacrificiis Abelis et Caini *21-44*)

In his exegetical commentary on Genesis 4:2-4 Philo establishes the ethical contrast between Cain and Abel as representatives of vice and virtue. First he demonstrates the primacy of the last born, arguing this from their experience of life (§15), by the example of Jacob and Esau (§§17-18), and by the witness of the Law itself—in Deuteronomy 21:15-17—which functions here as a *gezerah shawa* (§19)[152] conveying the underlying sense of the text. Then he develops an expressive and elaborate allegory.

In open dialogue with his soul (§20),[153] the exegete begins by interpreting the Deuteronomy passage, identifying the beloved woman as ἡδονή and the hated woman as ἀρετή, and maintaining that these two women exist within each one of us. It is a relatively simple and brief proem, but it is adequate to the genre of epideictic discourse.[154]

The *narratio* which follows (§§21-28), of a predominantly descriptive character, establishes a vivid contrast between passion[155] and virtue, completing its definition in this epideictic *descriptio*,[156] and then complementing this with an extensive affective *digressio*, preparing the way for the central argument.[157]

---

[151] Cf. *Abr.* 53.
[152] Philo's methodological versatility is verified *pari passu* in the natural way he makes use of the current rhetorical practice of the Hellenistic world as well as the subtlest rabbinical hermeneutic, which according to D. Daube itself originates from that culture ("Rabbinic Methods of Interpretation and Hellenistic Rhetoric,"). In this case, the Alexandrian moves from "Abel and Cain" (textual inversion of the order of names, that justifies the commentary [§11]) to the concept of virtue and vice, in order to confirm the precedence of virtue in the hierarchy of moral values and the primacy of all those sons who seek it, independently of the chronological order of their births.
[153] "That part of us which is gifted by reason: the νοῦς" (A. Méasson, PM 4, p. 40). Cf. *Sacr.* 45: Ταῦτα ἀκούσας ὁ νοῦς ἀποστρέφεται μὲν ἡδονήν, ἁρμόζεται δὲ ἀρετή.
[154] As Lausberg refers, this can even be dispensed with, or as seems to us to be the case, especially make use of the *beneuolentia* (Lausberg, *Manual de Retórica Literaria*, §286).
[155] Along with Méasson, we prefer to translate ἡδονή as "passion" and not "pleasure," to designate a feminine allegorical personage.
[156] Cf. the treatment of the *status finitionis* and *status qualitatis* in their application to the ἐπιδεικτικὸν γένος in Lausberg, *Manual de Retórica Literaria*, §250-252.
[157] Ibid., §345.

Each one of these allegorical figures directs its diegetical-persuasive *argumentum* to the νοῦς.[158] But Philo lets each one of them speak only after having described them sufficiently.

Inspired by the famous apologue of Prodicus, mentioned by Socrates in the *Memorabilia* of Xenophon,[159] Philo contrasts Virtue (ἡ ἀρετή) with Passion (ἡ ἡδονή) and not with Vice (ἡ κακία), preferring to attack the root cause.[160] In fact, as Méasson points out, pleasure in Philo is the serpent of Genesis,[161] the false friend who wrongs his friends and helps his enemies,[162] the treacherous harlot[163] or Potiphar's wife who tries to seduce Joseph.[164] This is the reason why Philo uses the most expressive images to impress the mind with the description of her lascivious character (§21), depicting her completely surrounded by vices, her closest friends, and confidently promising to open up the treasures of delight, to provide all the joys of human pleasure to those who seek her company.

Virtue, on the other hand, anxious lest the νοῦς be captivated by τοσαύταις δωρεαῖς καὶ ὑποσχέσεσιν (26b), overcomes her natural modesty and shows herself in all the glory of her magnificent figure, escorted by an innumerable multitude of specific virtues.[165] But, before he refers to some of

---

[158] We do not ignore that the *narratio*, as an integrating part of persuasive discourse and foundation of the *argumentatio* itself, equally must have the virtue of *persuadere* and consequently lend itself to the triple objective of *delectare, mouere* and *docere* (Quintilian IV, 2, 31, 46 and 111), although its more specific, indispensable and central end is really *docere* (Quintilian IV, 9, 35; cf. Lausberg, *Manual de Retórica Literaria*, §293). The genus of literary narration admits the *argumentum* as a sub-species of the "narration of things and processes" (Cf. Lausberg, *Manual de Retórica Literaria*, §290), and consequently the Philonic technique of inserting in it the λόγος of the ἡδονή, as well as the first part of the ἀρετή, seems to us legitimized by rhetorical tradition, in this case to develop the role of a new *exordium* before the properly-called *argumentatio* (Lausberg, *Manual de Retórica Literaria*, §345-346).
[159] *Mem.* II, 1, 21-34. In the illustration of his own thought Philo closely follows this model, but distances himself sufficiently from it so as not to compromise his fundamental exegetic motivation.
[160] Cf. Méasson, PM 4, p. 30-31.
[161] *Opif.* 160-162; *Leg.* II, 73-75; *Agric.* 97-98.
[162] *Gig.* 43.
[163] *Sacr.* 21.
[164] *Leg.* III, 236-237.
[165] Just as the ἡδονή is the deeper cause of the κακία and the general representative of all the vices, so the ἀρετή is the representative of a genus that is broken down into its specific virtues (§84).

τὸ γὰρ ὅλον καὶ ἐν γένει ἡ ἀρετή, ἡ κατὰ εἴδη τὰ προσεχῆ τέμνεται, φρόνησιν καὶ σωφροσύνην καὶ ἀνδρείαν καὶ δικαιοσύνην, ἵνα τὰς καθ᾽ ἕκαστον εἰδότες διαφορὰς ἑκούσιον ὑπομένωμεν λατρείαν καὶ καθ᾽ ὅλα καὶ κατὰ μέρη.

"Philo speaks at length about 'generic and fertile virtue', ἡ γενικὴ ἀρετή or ἡ γενικωτάτη, symbolized by the mighty stream that flows from Eden..." (A. Méasson, PM 4, p. 33).

those virtues, Philo describes the most visible traits of her character, finally allowing her to speak, giving full expression to her argument.

According to Aristotle, the *narratio* should be effectively presented in such a way as to integrate and exhibit ἦθος[166] and πάθος[167] since, as Quintilian says, its specific aim is not only *docere*, but also *delectare* and *mouere*.[168] The Alexandrian commentator achieves this aim like a true orator. But, in contrast to that of passion, the λόγος of virtue is above all based on the appeal to reason and emerges, in the economy of Philo's discourse, as a true oratorical gem with crystalline and penetrating rhetorical effect.

First, Philo alerts the mind in the *confirmatio* (§§29-41) to the risk of heeding promises that are no more than the product of a fabulous imagination. Then, he goes on to reveal the whole truth about pleasure's true character, ingeniously disguised and covered with the seductive mask of sophisticated external appearance.[169] This is, in synthesis, the architecture of his argument, which he brings to a climax with an inpassioned eulogy of hard work.

After a brief proem (§29), which serves as a *transitio* to the true *confirmatio*,[170] in which the delight which comes from ἡδονή is denounced as external and false, ἀρετή affirms her twofold purpose of reducing ἡδονή's image to its true insignificance and describing the traits that really characterize it.

Continuing to base her argumentative structure on the strategic recourse to the dialectic topic *a contrario*, she (virtue) develops a *ratiocinatio* in which both of the elements of the topic are supported and clarified by reasons which derive their persuasive force from the combination of an aesthetic parallelism and the ethical appeal of the *locus a minore ad maius* (§30):

> ἐγὼ δὲ καὶ ταῦτα ἀπαμφιάσασα ἀναδείξω καὶ οὐ μιμήσομαι τρόπους ἡδονῆς, ὡς ὅσα μὲν ἐπαγωγά ἐστιν ἐν ἐμοὶ μόνα ἐπιδείξασθαι, τὰ δὲ ἔχοντα δυσκολίαν συσκιάσαι καὶ περιστεῖλαι, ἀλλὰ τοὐναντίον τὰ μὲν τέρψιν ἐξ ἑαυτῶν καὶ χαρὰν ἐνδιδόντα ἡσυχάσω, εἰδυῖα ὅτι φωνὴν ῥήξει τὴν δι' ἔργων, τὰ δ' ἐπαχθῆ καὶ δυσυπομόνητα κυρίως ἑρμηνεύσω τοῖς ὀνόμασι γυμνοῖς κἂν μέσῳ τιθεῖσα αὐτά, ὡς ἔκδηλον τὴν ἑκάστου φύσιν καὶ τοῖς ἀμυδρῶς ὁρῶσι προφαίνεσθαι· τῶν γὰρ ἡδονῆς μεγίστων ἀγαθῶν τὰ παρ' ἐμοὶ μέγιστα δοκοῦντα εἶναι κακὰ καλλίω καὶ τιμιώτερα τοῖς χρωμένοις ἐξελεγχθήσεται.

---

[166] *Rhetorica* III, 16, 1417a 16-35.
[167] Ibid. III, 16, 1417a 36 - 1417b 7.
[168] *Institutio Oratoria* IV, 9, 35. Cf. Cicero, *De Partitione Oratoria* 9, 31.
[169] For Philo, as for Aristotle, the knowledge of the natural man does not transcend the level of appearance and of the probable. Nevertheless, it remains imprisoned by skeptic philosophy, assuming that the man of God, and only he, has access to truth. Thus there is constant disagreement between δόξα and ἀλήθεια, and between τὸ ἀληθές and τὰ εἰκότα (*Sacr.* 11, 12, 13, 81, 136; *Opif.* 45; *Leg.* III, 231-233; *Ebr.* 34-39; *Virt.* 64). Only virtue and wisdom are thus enabled to utter true discourse.
[170] "The arts of transition should be applied to all the parts of the discourse" (Lausberg, *Manual de Retórica Literaria*, §288), comments Lausberg, adding that if "other parts of the discourse can contain introductions properly belonging to the exordium" (cf. Quintilian IV, 1, 74), "the favored place for a second exordium is in the *argumentatio*" (Ibid., §287).

But these too I will strip bare and set before you, and will not follow Pleasure's way, to lay before you only what in me is attractive, and slur over and conceal what involves discomfort. Rather all such things as of themselves offer joy and delight I will pass in silence, for I know that they will speak for themselves in the language of facts, but all that spells pain and hardship I will set out in plain terms, without figure of speech, and show them openly, so that the nature of each may be clearly visible, even to those who see but dimly. For what of mine seems most to partake of ill shall be found by those who make trial thereof to be more beautiful and precious than the greatest goods which Pleasure has to give.

In elaborating on what ἡδονή did not say in her exuberant and deceptive speech, ἀρετή refers to the same topic and presents a long and impressive catalogue of her actual bad qualities.[171] These are introduced dramatically by a rhetorical syllogism of the ἐάν ... οὖν structure, discreetly veiled in the expression ἴσθι οὖν, ὦ οὗτος ὅτι γενόμενος φιλήδονος πάντ' ἔσει ταῦτα (know then, my friend, that if you become a pleasure-lover you will be all these things (§32a)).[172] Moreover this catalogue is contrasted with the immeasurable and unsurpassed wealth of the good things virtue stores up. Here the *interrogatio* produces the effect of an *a fortiori* argument, justifying this option by the *praeteritio*[173] and with the following to reinforce it (§33):

τῶν δὲ παρ' ἐμοὶ θησαυριζομένων ἀγαθῶν τὸ πλῆθος ἢ μέγεθος τίς ἂν ἀξίως εἰπεῖν δυνηθείη;

But the riches of goodness that I have stored in my treasuries are such in number and greatness that none can tell of them as is their due (§33).

In fact, Philo's use here of the *praeteritio* gives weight to and enlivens the ethical argument which is present, as it reflects his consciousness of the psychagogical function of the discourse. If he passes over them silently, this

---

[171] "Probably the most formidable catalogue of bad qualities ever drawn up" (F. H. Colson, PLCL II, p. 89)—an apparently insipid catalogue (cf. Méasson, PM 4, p. 34), but a process familiar to the rhetoricians of Philo's era and not entirely improper: "It might, however, be thought that Philo is being excessive here. Ought one to see here the indignation of a virtuous soul, whose holy wrath continued for the full length of 146 adjectives, without any other guide than that associations of ideas and sometimes only the associations of words? Or, what is more likely, die Philo wish to show that the lover of pleasure is fatally inclined to search for every form of pleasure, that such a search can only exasperate him, make him irascible, egotistical and anti-social? Philo believes that a vice does not remain alone in the soul but summons up others (he thinks in fact that the same applies to virtue)" (É. Bréhier, *Les idées philosophiques*, p. 265-266).
[172] Cf. Brandt, *Rhetoric of Argumentation*, p. 33.
[173] This argumentative figure normally produces a great rhetorical effect since, without isolating the introduced material from the argumentative structure, as occurs in the case of the παράλειψις (cf. Brandt, *Rhetoric of Argumentation*, p. 167), instead of interrupting that sequence, it saves time by honoring the *breuitas* and holding the attention of the audience with more sympathy.

is because he knows that φωνὴν ῥήξει τὴν δι' ἔργων (they will speak for themselves [§30]), that they are already known by those that have experienced them, and that in due course they will be experienced by those who are in natural harmony with them (§§33-34a). He further supports this argument by formulating and defending an analogy, the overall structure of which ends up taking the form of an epichirema (§34):

> διὰ μὲν δὴ ταῦτα καὶ τὸ πάλαι λεχθέν, ὅτι πέφυκεν ἐξ ἑαυτῶν φωνὴν ἀφιέναι, κἂν ἡσυχάζηται, τὰ ὅσια ἅτε ὄντως ἀγαθά, τὸν περὶ αὐτῶν λόγον ἐῶ· οὐδὲ γὰρ ἥλιος ἢ σελήνη χρῄζουσιν ἑρμηνέως, ὅτι τὸν σύμπαντα κόσμον, ὁ μὲν ἡμέρας, ἡ δὲ νυκτὸς ἀνασχόντες, φωτὸς ἐμπιπλᾶσιν· ἀλλ' ἔστιν αὐτοῖς ἡ ἐπίλαμψις ἀμάρτυρος πίστις ὀφθαλμοῖς ὤτων ἐναργεστέρῳ κριτηρίῳ βεβαιουμένη.

> For this cause and because, as I said before, things holy in virtue of their essential goodness cannot but through their very nature have speech for us, though we pass them by in silence, I say no more about them. For neither do sun and moon need an interpreter, because their rising by day or night fills the whole world with light. Their shining is a proof that needs no further witness, established by the evidence of the eyes, an evidence clearer than the ears can give.

By postponing reference to that which is attractive in itself, he follows the opposite method to ἡδονή, choosing instead the road of frankness and transparency, expressing his preference for dealing openly with a theme which it would apparently be better to hide, and transforming it into his main argument.[174]

Philo's impassioned eulogy of the πόνος is in effect a πίστις full of great persuasive power, and discreetly brings together the logical and psychological appeal into a homogeneous whole, organizing this according to a profoundly human dialectic and not on the basis of a mere association of ideas. Perhaps this is why he follows the model of the complete argument just as he was taught by the *auctor ad Herennium,* and not the simple and more logical structure of the Ciceronian *ratiocinatio* (§§35-40a).

(1) *Propositio* (§35a):

> τὸ δὲ δοκοῦν τῶν παρ' ἐμοὶ μάλιστα δυσκολίαν ἔχειν καὶ χαλεπότητα οὐδὲν ὑποστειλαμένη μετὰ παρρησίας λέξω· ... ἔστι δὲ ὁ ῥᾳστώνης ἐχθρὸς πόνος, πρῶτον καὶ μέγιστον ἀγαθόν, προσφερόμενος τὸν ἀκήρυκτον πρὸς ἡδονὴν πόλεμον·

> But in my store there is one thing which seems especially to involve hardship and discomfort, and this I will tell you frankly without concealment; ... this thing is toil, the first and greatest of blessings, the enemy of ease, waging war to the death against pleasure (§35c).

---

[174] Also here the basic chiastic structure is curious: The ἡδονή reveals what the ἀρετή hides, and hides what the latter reveals.

(2) *Ratio* (§35b):

καὶ γὰρ τοῦτό που φαντασίᾳ μὲν κατὰ τὴν πρόχειρον ἔντευξιν ἀργαλέον εἶναι δοκεῖ, μελέτῃ δὲ ἥδιστον καὶ ἐξ ἐπιλογισμοῦ συμφέρον.

For though at the first encounter it seems on the surface painful to the imagination, practice makes it sweet and reflection shows it to be profitable (§35b).

(3) *Confirmatio* (§35c):

ἀρχὴν γάρ, εἰ δεῖ τἀληθὲς εἰπεῖν, παντὸς ἀγαθοῦ καὶ ἀρετῆς ἁπάσης ὁ θεὸς ἀνέδειξεν ἀνθρώποις πόνον, οὗ χωρὶς τῶν καλῶν παρὰ τῷ θνητῷ γένει συνιστάμενον οὐδὲν εὑρήσεις.

For in very truth, God has appointed toil as the beginning of all goodness and true worth to men, and without it you shall find that nothing excellent takes shape amongst mortal men (§35d).

(4) *Exornatio* composed of two analogies, an amplification and two examples, which substantiate and adorn the reasoning formulated in the previous arguments: (4.1) The first *simile* (§36), which shows that, just as physical sight requires light in order to behold the colours of the world of the senses, so the soul's sight requires the cooperation of hard work in order to discern the works of virtue.[175] (4.2) The *amplificatio* (§37), which shows once again by analogical reasoning that intense and arduous toil is the true source of all good things: both of piety and holiness, which are only acquired by serving God, as well as particular virtues themselves,[176] which are only received as a result of constant effort. After this, Philo compares the soul to a musical instrument, and virtue to the harmony that results from the strong tension applied to the strings, in order to confirm the amount of effort which needs to be dedicated to it.[177]

ὁποῖον γὰρ ἂν ἐθέλῃς ἑλοῦ τῶν ἀγαθῶν, καὶ τοῦθ' εὑρήσεις πόνῳ περιγινόμενόν τε καὶ βεβαιούμενον· εὐσέβεια καὶ ὁσιότης ἀγαθά, ἀλλ' οὐκ ἄνευ θεραπείας θεοῦ τυχεῖν αὐτῶν δυνάμεθα, θεραπεία δὲ ταῖς ἐν πόνοις φιλοτιμίαις συνέζευκται· φρόνησις καὶ ἀνδρεία καὶ δικαιοσύνη καλαὶ πᾶσαι καὶ τέλεια ἀγαθά, ἀλλ' οὐ τῇ ῥᾳστώνῃ ταῦτα ληπτά, ἀγαπητὸν δέ,

---

[175] In the *Opif.* 53, Philo speaks of light as "the best of creatures," and of sight as "the best of the senses," making of the former the image of the science ἐπιστήμη, and of the latter an instrument, in its acquisition seeming to imitate Plato, who refers to light and sight as representations of "science" and "truth," in his analogy with the sun, itself the image of Good (*Respublica* VI, 507d-508. Cf. Méasson, PM 4, p. 99, n. 4). The affirmation of the superiority of sight over the rest of the senses was during its time "a school topos" (Ibid., p. 198).

[176] Here prudence, courage and justice are referred to, when he usually cites four: φρόνησις, ἀνδρεία, δικαιοσύνη, and also σωφροσύνη (cf. §27; *Leg.* I, 63).

[177] Arnaldez believes that Philo is inspired by the doctrine of soul-harmony of the Pythagoreans (PM 18, p. 72, note 1); and F. Colson says that this comparison is no more than an adaptation of the Platonic idea of virtue as a harmony of the soul, in conjunction with the Stoic point of view that "moral evil is the loosening of its πόνος (tension, muscular vigor)" (PLCL II, p. 490).

εἰ συνεχέσι ταῖς ἐπιμελείαις ἐξευμενισθήσονται· τὴν πρὸς θεὸν καὶ ἀρετὴν ἀρέσκειαν ὥσπερ τινὰ ἔντονον καὶ σφοδρὰν ἁρμονίαν οὐ δυνηθὲν τὸ πάσης ψυχῆς ὄργανον ἐνεγκεῖν ἀνείθη καὶ ἐχαλάσθη πολλάκις, ὡς ἀπὸ τῶν ἄκρων ἐπὶ τὰς μέσας καταβῆναι τέχνας·

Choose any good thing whatsoever, and you will find that it results from and is established through toil. Piety and holiness are good, but we cannot attain to them save through the service of God, and service calls for earnest toil as its yoke-fellow. Prudence, courage, justice, all these are noble and excellent and perfectly good, yet we cannot acquire them by self-indulgent ease. It is much indeed if by constant care and practice there arise a kindliness between us and them. Service pleasing to God and to virtue is like an intense and severe harmony, and in no soul is there an instrument capable of sustaining it, without such frequent relaxation and unstringing of the chords that it descends from the higher forms of art to the lower (§37).

(4.3) The *exempla* (§38), which confirm the true and necessary universality of that constant and absorbing toil:

ἀλλ' ὅμως κἂν ταῖς μέσαις πολὺς ὁ κάματος· ἴδε τοὺς τῶν ἐγκυκλίων καὶ τῶν λεγομένων προπαιδευμάτων ἀσκητὰς ἅπαντας· ἴδε τοὺς γεωπόνους καὶ ὅσοι τὸν βίον ἔκ τινων ἐπιτηδεύσεων πορίζουσιν· οὗτοι τῶν φροντίδων οὐ μεθ' ἡμέραν οὐ νύκτωρ ἀφίστανται, ἀλλ' ἀεὶ καὶ πανταχοῦ τὸ λεγόμενον δὴ τοῦτο χειρὶ καὶ ποδὶ καὶ πάσῃ δυνάμει κακοπαθοῦντες οὐ παύονται, ὡς καὶ θάνατον ἀντικαταλλάττεσθαι πολλάκις.

Yet even these lower forms demand much toil. Consider all who practise the school-learning, the so-called preparatory culture. Consider the labourers on the soil and all who get their living by some trade or profession. Neither by day nor night do they cast their cares aside, but always and everywhere they cease not to bear affliction, as the saying goes, in hand and foot and every faculty, so that often they choose death in its stead (§38).

(4.4) and a final comparison (§39), which elaborately emphasizes, in chiastic parallelism with the first, the indispensable value of toil, for the soul as well as for the body:

ἀλλ' ὥσπερ τοῖς ψυχὴν τὴν ἑαυτῶν ἵλεων σπουδάζουσι λαβεῖν θεραπευτέον ἐξ ἀνάγκης τὰς ψυχῆς ἀρετάς, οὕτως καὶ τοῖς ἵλεων τὸ σῶμα ἔχειν προαιρουμένοις θεραπευτέον ὑγίειαν καὶ τὰς συγγενεῖς αὐτῇ δυνάμεις, καὶ δῆτα θεραπεύουσι μετ' ἀνηνύτων καὶ ἀπαύστων πόνων οἷς φροντὶς εἰσέρχεται τῶν ἐν αὑτοῖς δυνάμεων, ἐξ ὧν συνεκρίθησαν.

But just as those who desire to have their soul attuned and favourable must needs cultivate the virtues of the soul, so those who purpose to gain the same qualities for their body must cultivate health and the powers that accompany health; and indeed all who take thought for the faculties within them, which combine to make them what they are, do so cultivate them with constant and unremitting toil (§39).

(5) *Complexio* (§40a), with an exhortation to persistent toil. However, Philo expands this conclusion of the discourse of ἀρετή, reaffirming vigorously the theme of πόνος as the source of all good, by means of a brief *tractatio* (§§40-41).[178]

---

[178] Cf. *Rhetorica ad Herennium* IV, 54: "Refinement occurs when we remain on the same

This is in synthesis its development:

(1) *Res* and *ratio* (§40a) - a *sententia* followed by an exhortation and sustained by a *subiectione rationis:*[179]

πάντ' οὖν ὁρᾷς τὰ ἀγαθὰ ἐκ πόνου καθάπερ ἐκ ῥίζης μιᾶς ἐκπεφυκότα καὶ βλαστάνοντα· ὃν μήποτε ὑπομείνῃς μεθέσθαι, λήσῃ γὰρ ἅμ' αὐτῷ καὶ σωρὸν ἀθρόον ἀγαθῶν μεθέμενος.

You see then how good things spring and grow from toil as from a single root. Never therefore suffer yourself to lose your hold of toil, for with it will be lost, though you little know it, a vast heap of blessings (§40a).

(2) *Pronuntiatio* and *contrarium* (§40b)—the expression of the theme in another form, with reasons and counter-arguments:

ὁ μὲν γὰρ τοῦ σύμπαντος ἡγεμὼν οὐρανοῦ τε καὶ κόσμου καὶ ἔχει καὶ παρέχει οἷς ἂν ἐθέλῃ τὰ ἀγαθὰ μετὰ πάσης εὐμαρείας, ἐπεὶ καὶ τὸν τοσοῦτον κόσμον ἄνευ πόνων πάλαι μὲν εἰργάζετο, νυνὶ δὲ καὶ εἰσαεὶ συνέχων οὐδέποτε λήγει - θεῷ γὰρ τὸ ἀκάματον ἁρμοδιώτατον-, θνητῷ δὲ οὐδενὶ κτῆσιν ἀγαθοῦ δίχα πόνων ἡ φύσις δεδώρηται, ἵνα καὶ ταύτῃ τὸ μακάριον ἐν τοῖς οὖσι μόνον ὁ θεὸς εὐδαιμονίζηται.

The Ruler indeed of all heaven and the world possesses and provides to whom He wills good things in ease absolute. Without toil He made this vast universe long ages ago, and now without toil He holds it in perpetual existence, for to know no weariness is an attribute most fitting to God. But it is not so with mortals. To them Nature has given no good thing to be acquired without toil, that here too God may alone be accounted happy—the one and only blessed being (§40b).

(3) *Simile* and *exemplum* (§41a)—Beginning with the paradigmatic figure of food as indispensable to life, he establishes, in its relation to toil, a double justified analogy in a chiasm, giving us in a few lines an illuminating image of the creative originality with which the logic and aesthetics of discourse are harmonized, making them converge to produce a delightful pathetic effect. The *simile:*

δοκεῖ γάρ μοι πόνος τὴν αὐτὴν προσφέρεσθαι δύναμιν τροφῇ·

Toil, it seems to me, assumes a function similar to that of food (§41a).

The *similitudo:*[180]

---

theme and appear to say things that are ever different." A species of χρεία, or generally ethical thought developed in detailed manner in accordance with the rules formulated for this type of προγύμνασμα, first elaborated by the *auctor ad Herennium* in his treatment of a theme, and structured in seven parts: *res, ratio, pronuntiatio, contrarium, simile, exemplum* and *conclusio* (IV, 56; cf. the *tractatio* in Hermogenes, *Progymnasmata* III [ed. Rabe, p. 6-8]).

[179] *Rhetorica ad Herennium* IV, 24: "Simple maxims are not to be rejected, because a brief exposition, if there is no need for an explanation, has great charm."

[180] As Lausberg says, the *exemplum*, according to its content, is a special case of the general *similitudo*, or παραβολή (Lausberg, *Manual de Retórica Literaria*, §422-425. Cf. Quintilian V,

AB - καθάπερ (τροφή) γοῦν αὕτη τὸ ζῆν ἐξήρτηκεν ἑαυτῆς συναρτήσασα καὶ τὰ ἐν τῷ ζῆν ἅπαντα ἔργα τε καὶ πάθη,

CD - οὕτως καὶ πόνος ἐκκεκρέμακεν ἑαυτοῦ τὰ ἀγαθά.

BA - ὥσπερ οὖν τοῦ ζῆν τοῖς γλιχομένοις τροφῆς οὐκ ἀμελητέον,

DC - οὕτως τοῖς τῶν ἀγαθῶν κτήσεως ἐφιεμένοις πόνου προνοητέον·

AB - As food has made itself a necessity to life and has joined in the same connexion with itself all the conditions active or passive that are involved in life,

CD - so toil has made all good things dependent on itself.

BA - And therefore just as those who seek to live must not neglect food,

DC - so those who desire the acquisition of the good must make provision for toil (§41b),

The *ratio*, which serves as the mediating center of this double analogy:

BA - ὃ γὰρ πρὸς τὸ ζῆν τροφή,

DC - τοῦτο πρὸς τὸ καλὸν πόνος·

for it bears to the noble and excellent the same relation as food does to life (§41c).

(4) *Conclusio* (§41b) - Return in full circle to the exhortation based on the theme and the promise of the good things already articulated:

ἑνὸς οὖν ὄντος αὐτοῦ μηδέποτε ὀλιγωρήσῃς, ἵνα τὰ πάντα ἀγαθὰ ἀθρόα καρπώσῃ.

Never then despise toil, that from the one you may reap a multitude, even the harvest of every good thing (§41d).

Once the eulogy of toil is finished, and with it the main argumentative section of the discourse, Philo returns in the *peroratio* (§§42-44) to the thesis he initially formulated on the basis of the Biblical text, and takes as fully established the identification of ἀρετή with Abel and that of ἡδονή with Cain. The long oratorical digression and even the exegetical question which he brought up, about the younger son being mentioned first, have not made him lose sight of the basic theme of his commentary.[181] Rather it has served to illuminate and explain the primacy of moral and spiritual values. It should be stated in passing that this inversion is in harmony with the concepts and philosophical preoccupations of the age. For, as A. Méasson observes: "the image of fighting against the passions is habitually used by Cynic philosophers... ."[182] And, according to É. Bréhier, "to see in pleasure the foundation

---

11, 5-6), being permissible to speak of analogic example, as is the case here.
[181] Méasson, PM 4, p. 104, n. 4.
[182] Ibid., p. 78, n. 2. The four basic virtues—ἀνδρεία, φιλανθρωπία, μετάνοια and εὐγένεια

of evil and vice and to see in temperance the chief good, which enables us to resist the seductions of pleasure, these are the two essential marks of Cynic morality."[183]

Beginning with a brief *enumeratio* (§42a), Philo goes on directly to the *conquestio*, as is appropriate in epideictic discourse, in order to complete the rhetorical effort he invested in the defense of hard work and to create in the mind of the reader-listener a willingness to accept the thesis defended and the action which will result from it. To do this he makes use of moral exhortation,[184] having recourse to the *locus a minore ad maius* in enthymematic structure, going on naturally to the exemplum of Jacob, as a τύπος of man in progress towards a more excellent good.[185] This example presupposes those of Abraham and his son Isaac as heir and transmitter of all his father's goods, *i. e.*, the perfect virtues.[186]

Philo is aware that, along with life in the spirit, there exists another level of life in the body.[187] For this reason he adds the allegorical examples of Hagar and Keturah, and identifies with these "the imperfect," those who only attained to the cycle of studies represented by Hagar—τῶν ἐγκυκλίων προπαιδευμάτων—that is, the basic level of secular studies and not true wisdom. While, on the one hand, Philo contrasts life as a pilgrimage with settled residence in the homeland of σοφία, he at the same time points out that the person who situates himself permanently outside the frontiers of wisdom may only inhale her perfume but will never acquire the rights of citizens.[188]

—after Plato were the object of moral reflection among the Greeks (R. Arnaldez, PM 26, p. 12).

[183] É. Bréhier, *Les idées philosophiques*, p. 261.

[184] More characteristic of philosophical literature, especially of the diatribes of the Hellenistic period (cf. A. Oltramare, *Les origines de la diatribe romaine* [Lausanne, Genève, Neuchâtel, 1926]; W. Capelle and H. I. Marrou, "Diatribe," RAC 3, p. 990-1009), but also referred to in the manuals of ancient rhetoric (Quintilian III, 6, 47; IX, 2, 103; Aristotle, *Rhetorica* I, 3, 3 1358b).

[185] Cf. *Somn.* I, 170. The βελτιούμενοι are the progressionists in the sense of virtue (*Fug.* 166; *Mutat.* 19, 23, 88).

[186] "The perfect and legitimate son" of Abraham and the heir "of the perfect virtues," which are transferred to Jacob as the spiritual firstborn.

[187] Méasson, PM 4, p. 107, n. 5.

[188] Méasson synthesizes Philo's thought on the theme as he inclines toward this curious definition of the imperfect: "For Philo perfect virtue is situated at the end of two paths which happen to flow together either simultaneously or in succession (cf. *Agric.* 18): the one is of an intellectual kind (this is especially the journey of Abraham, who goes from Hagar to Sarah); the other is of the moral kind (this is the one that Jacob follows). Those who have reached the goal are the 'perfect' and those who are still en route are the 'imperfect'. But in opposition to the 'perfect' are those who have not even commenced on the quest of virtue. These should not be confused with the involuntary ignorant, concerning which he says in §48 that instruction is their remedy. The wicked are therefore the voluntary ignorant. Philo

He ends with an increasing *gradatio* exalting virtue and wisdom, urging that the latter be pursued to its final stage and distinguishing, in relation to it, three types of persons:[189] (1) those who are satisfied merely with τοῖς ἐγκυκλίοις and do not know the way of wisdom and so settle in a strange land; (2) those who pass through secular education unconscious of the way of wisdom, but who pursue their pilgrimage and end up tasting her and coming to dwell in her company; (3) and those who naturally inhabit the homeland of wisdom and there enjoy the service of others.

4. *Speech on the drunkenness of the wise man* (De Plantatione *140-177*)

We share F. Colson and G. Whitaker's opinion that this discourse has come to us in an incomplete form having lost "not only the end of the supporter's speech, but also the whole of the opponent's answer."[190] We consider, however, that we should include it all the same in our analysis of internal discourses for the simple reason that it provides further evidence of Philo's knowledge and deliberate use of hellenistic rhetoric.[191]

It is, in effect, an interesting epideictic discourse[192] in which Philo, inspired by the Stoic maxim that the wise man will freely drink and not become drunk, proposes "to demonstrate the coherence and relevance of

---

in fact makes a neat distinction between the three categories. In Gig. 60–61 he presents in succession: those who 'belong to the earth' because they seek after the pleasures of the body, those who 'belong to the heaven', i.e. the artists, scientists and scholars, and finally 'the men of God'" (Ibid., p. 198-199, note to §43).

[189] This is one of Philo's favorite themes. Of the two triads of Biblical personalities that he uses to signal the stages of this journey, he refers at this point to the most important: Abraham, Isaac and Jacob, who represent three "attitudes of the soul" (τρόποι ψυχῆς, *Abr.* 52) toward God, the three roads to perfection through the experience of virtue. Abraham is the figure of διδασκαλία, Jacob that of ἄσκησις, and Isaac that of φύσις. It is an allegory even more significant in the context of a rhetorical reading of Philo as it is true that "Socrates presents as a perfect orator him to whose natural gifts are added knowledge and practice" (*Phaedrus* 269d. Cf. Méasson, PM 4, p. 22), reuniting the distinctive factors that Aristotle relates with the process of education (cf. *Ethica ad Nicomachum* I, 9; II, 1; VI, 13; X, 9). That the requisites necessary to a complete education are represented in the trilogy *nature, teaching* and *practice* is a common place in ancient scholastic literature, but Philo is the first to apply such a formula to spiritual life (cf. F. H. Colson, PLCL VI, p. x).

[190] PLCL III, p. 211. Although it is the general opinion that a complete discourse does not end this way, some Philonists believe that the Alexandrian exegete limited himself to treating the thesis that "the wise man can become drunk", only the final part of the arguments in his defense having been lost; others, that the treatise *De Ebrietate* is a direct result of this one, his personal opinion being effectively developed there (cf. Jean Pouilloux, PM 10, p. 106-107).

[191] Especially in §149-150a and 173, which use terms like σκέψεως, λόγον, κατασκευάζοντα, αἱ πίστεις, ἐντέχνοις and ἀτέχνοις ἀποδείξεσιν, μαρτυρίαν, μαρτυριῶν.

[192] A thesis sustained by I. Heinemann, and highlighted by F. Colson-G. Whitaker, PLCL III, p. 209.

the words of Moses and to intensify his audience's commitment to them and therefore to the Law itself."[193] This discourse apparently seeks to contribute towards the exegetical clarification of a text which either raised an ethical problem for his contemporaries or had been the object of criticism on the part of detractors of the Jewish faith (§141):

> ἤρξατο Νῶε ἄνθρωπος εἶναι γεωργὸς γῆς· καὶ ἐφύτευσεν ἀμπελῶνα, καὶ ἔπιε τοῦ οἴνου, καὶ ἐμεθύσθη [Gen. 9:20-21].
>
> Noah began to be a husbandman, a tiller of the soil: and he planted a vineyard and drank of the wine, and became drunk (§140b).

Calling attention to the drunkenness τοῦ δικαίου Νῶε and formulating two contrasting theses—ὁ σοφὸς μεθυσθήσεται; (ὁ σοφός) ... οὐ μεθυσθήσεται—, the Alexandrian exegete certainly has in mind a specific audience and problem.[194]

The rhetorical nature and function of this literary unit is revealed not only by its structure and argumentative sequence. It is also manifest in Philo's explanation of apparent ambiguities. In fact, what T. Conley finds particularly noteworthy in this passage "is the similarity between Philo's way of dealing with what he sees as a difficult passage and Cicero's discussion in the *De Inuentione* of the standard ways of arguing when an ambiguity in a written document is at issue."[195] There seems to be no doubt that Philo follows the lead of the Roman orator, who suggests that, whenever an author's intentions are questioned, "primum, si fieri poterit, demonstrandum est non esse ambigue scriptum."[196] Certain that the sacred writer left out nothing that is "honestum aut utile aut necessarium,"[197] Philo only attempts to demonstrate the semantic exactness of his words although, like Cicero, he is aware that one should bear in mind the period and the circumstances in which the document was written.[198]

It is true that the form of the remaining text comes only with προοίμιον (§§140-148), πρόθεσις (§149) and part of the πίστεις.[199] The original, to judge from Philo's information, must certainly have contained the remaining arguments of the contrary thesis and an ἐπίλογος. Of the latter, however, the text only contains Zeno's first argument,[200] and along with it the corre-

---

[193] T. Conley, *Philo's Rhetoric: Studies in Style, Composition and Exegesis*, p. 113.
[194] Conley in this regard weaves in some interesting and suggestive considerations (Ibid., p. 173, note 44).
[195] Ibid., p. 100. Cf. Cicero, *De Inuentione* II, 40, 116ff.
[196] *De Inuentione* II, 40, 116: "In the first place it should be shown if possible, that there is no ambiguity in the statement".
[197] Ibid. II, 40, 119.
[198] Ibid. II, 40, 121.
[199] As Colson-Whitaker suggest, in PLCL III, p. 211 and 199 (note to §176-177).
[200] Seneca, *Epistolae Morales* 83, gives evidence of this origin, refuting it in exactly the same

sponding refutation (§§175-177). However, we will devote our analysis to the parts of the text which have been preserved intact.

After a preliminary explanation of the text (§140) and having announced the theme (§141), the Alexandrian commentator reviews the various opinions on the question raised, εἰ μεθυσθήσεται ὁ σοφός (§§142-148), and explicitly declares the proem to be complete (§149a), going on through the πρόθεσις (§149) to the πίστεις.[201]

Suitably brief and clear, the πρόθεσις limits itself to expounding the issue in a resumed form by introducing the theses relevant to its double argument: (1) ὅτι ὁ σοφὸς μεθυσθήσεται (§§150-174); (2) ὅτι (ὁ σοφὸς) οὐ μεθυσθήσεται (§§175-177).

The πίστεις that sustain the first thesis consist of five arguments grouped in a natural increasing order,[202] in accordance with Aristotelian theory. The truth expressed in the first four, of a syllogistic nature, is confirmed by the evidence contained in the final paradigm.[203]

The first argument (§§150-155) establishes that the terms μέθυ and οἶνος are synonyms and infers, on this basis, that the derivatives μεθύειν and οἰνοῦσθαι are also synonyms:
(1) Some names are synonyms and others are homonyms.
– Homonym and synonym are opposites: a name applied to many things *uersus* many names applied to the same thing.
– Amplified exemplification of these two categories.
– The argument from authority: the ancients used these terms as synonyms.
(2) Now if οἶνος and μέθυ are synonyms, their derivatives τὸ οἰνοῦσθαι and τὸ μεθύειν are also synonyms.
(3) So, if the wise man drinks in excess he will also become drunk.

The second argument (§§156-164), based on the philosophical-literary commonplace[204] of the decadence of the race, in words as well as in deeds, maintains that there is no incompatibility between τὸ μεθύειν and moral excellence. Here is the logical structure:
(1) Contemporary humanity as a rule differs from the ancients, in language as well as in actions (§§156-159).
– Descriptive exemplification of the contrast and its real consequences: Then, poets and prose-writers flourished; now, specialists in culinary, pastry and cosmetic arts flourish.

---

way as Philo. Cf. Colson-Whitaker, PLCL III, p. 499.
[201] Called ἀποδείξεις in §156, the arguments or proofs.
[202] Cf. C. Perelman, *L'empire rhétorique*, p. 163-164.
[203] Aristotle, *Rhetorica* II, 20, 1394a 9-18.
[204] Cf. Conley, *Philo's Rhetoric*, p. 109.

(2) The current manner of drinking differs substantially from that of the ancients (§§161-162) who only became drunk after religious sacrifices.

– Contrast between contemporary indulgence and vice, and the sobriety and temperance of the forefathers (§160).

– Amplification (§§161-162) of the theme by the *comparatio*.[205]

– Justification of the current meaning of μεθύειν, based on the common habit of the forefathers of regulated and religious excess only "after the sacrifices," which practice brought about the word μεθύειν as a derivative of μετὰ τὸ θύειν (§163a).[206]

(3) If μεθύειν is used in this sense, that practice is altogether appropriate for the wise man, *because* it is the character of the wise man that adjusts itself best to the sacrificial act and only good men carry it out (§§163b-164).

The third argument (§§165-171), based on a different form of etymological topic and developed from it,[207] demonstrates that regulated drunkenness benefits the character of the wise man because it relieves tension and reinforces the natural qualities.

(1) The etymological topic (§165): μέθη derives its name not only from μετὰ θυσίας but also from μέθεσις, because it is μεθέσεως ψυχῆς αἰτία.

(2) The *ratio* (§166): The wise man becomes more genial when, under the influence of alcohol, he is happy and his spirit is free from stress.

(3) The *confirmatio* (§167), by the *locus a contrario*.

(4) The *exornatio*: To the primary proof of this argument from etymology, Philo adds in the *exornatio* several other supporting arguments:

– *Exempla* of Moses (§168), Isaac and Rebeccah (§169a).
– *Contrarium* (§169b).
– *Interrogatio* (§170).
– *Similitudo* (§171): Like money and fame, strong wine can intensify either vice or virtue.

(5) The *complexio* (§171b): By means of drink, the man that cultivates the εὐπάθεια becomes more benevolent and amiable, but he who gives himself over to passions becomes even more subject to them.

A fourth argument (§172) attempts to show that ὁ ἀστεῖος (the morally sound individual) may become drunk without losing any of his virtues. This

---

[205] Quintilian VIII, 4, 9. The *comparatio* corresponds to the *locus a minore ad maius* and lends itself especially to the epideictic *genus*, Lausberg observes (Lausberg, *Manual de Retórica Literaria*, §404).

[206] This etymology perhaps has its origin in Aristotle, for according to Athenaeus (*Epit.* II, 40c) he would have been its creator (cf. J. Pouilloux, PM 10, p. 100, n. 1).

[207] Cf. Cicero, *Topica* VIII, 36: "In debate many arguments are elicited from a word through etymology." Also cf. Colson-Whitaker (PLCL III, p. 299, note b) for a version of the text in reference to the third argument: "based on another and different form of the argument from etymology."

takes the form of an argument suggested by analogical reasoning and based on the following *locus a contrario:* whenever one of two contrary notions is applicable to different types of people, the other of necessity also is.[208]

> οἷον λευκοῦ καὶ μέλανος ἐναντίων ὄντων, εἰ τὸ λευκὸν ἀστείοις τε καὶ φαύλοις, καὶ τὸ μέλαν ἐξ ἴσου δήπουθεν ἀμφοτέροις, οὐχὶ μόνοις προσέσται τοῖς ἑτέροις. καὶ μὴν τό γε νήφειν καὶ τὸ μεθύειν ἐναντία, μετέχουσι δὲ τοῦ νήφειν, ὡς ὁ τῶν προτέρων λόγος, ἀγαθοί τε καὶ φαῦλοι· ὥστε καὶ τὸ μεθύειν ἑκατέρῳ τῶν εἰδῶν ἐφαρμόττει. μεθυσθήσεται τοιγάρτοι καὶ ὁ ἀστεῖος μηδὲν τῆς ἀρετῆς ἀποβαλών.
>
> For instance, black and white are opposites. If white is predicable of bad and good, black too will of course be equally so of both, not only of one of the two sets. So too soberness and drunkenness are opposites, and both bad and good men, so our forefathers said, partake of soberness. It follows that drunkenness also is predicable of both sorts. Accordingly the man of moral worth will get drunk as well as other people without losing any of his virtue (§172).

And as if these four ἔντεχνοι ἀποδείξεις (artificial proofs) were not enough, Philo deems it well to add to them one of the ἄτεχνοι λεγόμεναι, in the usual manner of what is done ἐν δικαστηρίῳ. That is to say, he briefly refers to the documented testimony of many physicians and philosophers, who confirm in their writings the correctness of this thesis.[209] By this argument (§§173-174) he shows that those writers identified μεθύειν with οἰνοῦσθαι without associating μέθη (drinking to excess) with λῆρος (intemperance).

Through this dense forest of argumentation Philo gradually and intelligently advances toward the full demonstration of his thesis that οὐ τοίνυν διαμαρτησόμεθα λέγοντες ὅτι (ὁ σοφὸς) μεθυσθήσεται ("we shall not be wrong, then, in saying that he will get drunk"). The arguments that he uses are methods of proof that enjoy the approval both of philosophy and of rhetoric.[210] More than merely an exhibition of culture, they reflect Philo's exegetical commitment to clarifying the text and gaining the adherence of the reader to the principles with which it is impregnated. Its rhetorical structure reveals the conscious concern of the author to capture, retain and direct the reader's attention by the creation of an atmosphere of expectancy and the gratification which results from this.[211] To this end Philo uses an

---

[208] Pouilloux observes that "The use of this reasoning on contraries and incompatibles goes back to Plato, *Phédon* 105b f." (Cf. PM 10, p. 104, n. 1).
[209] The pistic or apodeictic use of texts in the form of quotations or authorized maxims was recommended and frequent in orators (cf. Cicero, *Topica* 19, 73; and *De Oratore* I, 46, 201). The Roman orator says in the first text: "This form of argumentation, which is said to be devoid of art, depends of testimony. Testimony we define as everything which is taken from some external matter in order to bring about conviction. But not every kind of person has a weighty testimony. In order to bring about conviction authority is sought after. Authority is furnished either by one's nature or one's circumstances. In the case of nature the greatest authority is found in virtue..."
[210] Cf. F. Colson-G. Whitaker, PLCL III, p. 498, note to §615.
[211] Cf. Conley, *Philo's Rhetoric*, p. 112.

argumentative strategy which is at the same time logical and psychological, presenting a series of arguments successively developed from the topics "of definition"[212] and "etymology,"[213] as well as the dialectical topic of "things contrary".[214] Finally, he presents the authoritative words of the ancients, delighting the audience at the same time he instructs it.

5. *Letter from King Agrippa to Gaius Caligula* (Legatio ad Gaium *236-329*)

As we move now from Philo's exegetical commentary to another category of his writings, normally called "historical,"[215] we note that he not only makes use of rhetoric to interpret the sacred text and to organize a commentary. He also uses it as he develops the argumentative structure of his thoughts, documenting and enlivening his texts by the insertion of discursive and epistolary material.

The letter of Agrippa to Gaius Caligula, due to its apologetic-argumentative character, is a fascinating example to prove this point. It must be underlined that this example is rooted in and inspired by a tradition that goes back to the fourth century B.C. According to A. Momigliano,[216] the nature of the "apologetic letter," created by the Socratics and illustrated by the *Epistolae* 7 of Plato,[217] in fact presupposes "not only the existence of the epistolary form, but also the genres of autobiography and apologetic discourse."[218]

It may be claimed that this letter is a reproduction *ipsissimis uerbis* of that of Agrippa. But in light of Josephus' testimony, who gives a totally different version of the episode,[219] and from the evidence furnished by the best historiography accessible to Philo and frequently referred to in the *corpus*,[220]

---

[212] Cf. Cicero, *Topica* IV, 26-27.
[213] Ibid. IV, 35-36; *Academica* I, 32.
[214] Cicero, *Topica* IV, 47-49.
[215] More strictly historical-theological, or simply "non-Biblical" (cf. S. Sandmel, *Philo of Alexandria. An Introduction*, p. 30-31).
[216] *The Development of Greek Biography* (Cambridge: Harvard University Press, 1971), pp. 60-62.
[217] The authenticity of the Platonic letters is currently a matter of scholarly debate, a detail which, for the genus itself, is of little importance. Cf. H. D. Betz, *Galatians: A Commentary on Paul's Letter to the Churches in Galatia* (Philadelphia: Fortress Press, 1979), p. 14-15.
[218] Ibid. See also, from the same author, *Der Apostel Paulus und die sokratische Tradition. Beiträge zur historischen Theologie* 45 (Tübingen: Mohr, Siebeck, 1972), chap. 2.
[219] Josephus gives a romanticized version of the reasons that led Gaius to renounce his project (*Antiquitates Judaicae* XVIII, 289-301). According to him, Agrippa offered to the emperor, in Rome, a magnificent banquet that so impressed him that he volunteered to satisfy his fondest wish; afterward, a prisoner of his promise, he consented to desist from consecrating the statue that he had ordered erected in the temple of Jerusalem (cf. A. Pelletier, PM 32, p. 345-346).
[220] See "Index to Notes, "PLCL *Philo* X, for Thucydides, Herodotus and Xenophon.

such a hypothesis is dubious. As A. Pelletier points out, E. Smallwood prefers to believe that Philo may have participated directly in the preparation of this letter,

> for the evidence used in paragraphs 291-320, on the respect of preceding emperors for everything that regards the Temple of Jerusalem, and especially the philosophical or ritual considerations which follow them, are well adjusted to the environment of Alexandrian Jews, wishing to be honored by the Romans as they had been by the Ptolemies.

If it is not the product of Philo's collaboration with Agrippa, then it is a creation wholly his own, or a literary amplification of the original document.

Working with the presupposition that this epistle is the direct product of Philo's pen, we will now go on to analyse it rhetorically.

Agrippa visits Gaius Caligula at an extremely critical moment for the Jews. In response to his self-divinization,[221] the worship of the emperor becomes generalized, provoking Jewish resistance. The synagogues of Alexandria are desecrated. Petronius receives orders to introduce in the sanctuary at Jerusalem a colossal statue of the autocrat under the name of Zeus (§188). Following his failure to pacify the Jewish authorities, Petronius is persuaded by the poignant appeal of the multitudes to send a diplomatic letter to Gaius to justify the delay in carrying out his orders.

Arriving in Rome at the climax of these events, Herod Agrippa is ungraciously received by the emperor, who brings him up-to-date on the latest happenings relating to his people and the exchange of correspondence with Petronius. Agrippa's spirit is shocked by the determined attitude of the Emperor even more than by his own cool reception. Only days later does he find enough courage to send Caligula an intercessory letter. It is a long apologetic document displaying consummate rhetorical energy and argumentative efficacy.

Its structure, although not altogether outside the conventions of contemporary epistolography,[222] reveals above all the defining traits of deliberative discourse. As we know, the object of deliberative rhetoric is to exhort or

---

[221] "The worship of the emperor in the early empire was more like a civil ceremony than a religious event..." Gaius is the emperor "who seems most sincerely to have believed himself to have been a god". (Stevan L. Davies, *The New Testament: A Contemporary Introduction*, San Francisco: Harper & Row, 1988, p. 28).

[222] The composition of an epistle obeys the following basic schematic sequence, in accordance with the conventions of the time: (1) *prescriptum*, with its *superscriptio, adscriptio* and *salutatio;* (2) the body of the letter; (3) and a *postscriptum*, normally autobiographical (cf. R. Hercher, ed., *Epistolographi Graeci* (Paris, 1873); F. H. Reuters, *Die Briefs des Anacharsis griechisch und deutsch* (Berlin, 1963); J. Strugnell and H. Attridge, "The Epistles of Heraclitus and the Jewish Pseudepigrapha: A Warning," HTR 1:14 (1971), p. 411-413; J. L. White, *The Body of the Greek Letter*, SBL Dissertation Series 2 (Missoula, MT: Scholars Press, 1972).

persuade, while that of forensic rhetoric is to accuse or defend and that of the epideictic is to praise or to censure. In practice, any of them can take on the functions represented by the other forms, as long as these are reinforced and conducive to the primary argumentative end.[223]

So it is with this epistolary discourse. The appeal of the Jewish sovereign seeks to dissuade Gaius Caligula from his sacrilegious intention respecting the Jewish temple. But Agrippa also feels the need to defend and exalt his own people.

In terms of rhetorical structure, the epistle presents the following internal organization: *exordium* (§§276-278), *propositio* (§279a), *confirmatio* (§§279b-320) and *peroratio* (§§321-329), enclosing in the *confirmatio* argumentation in favor of the nation, the city and the temple. The absence of a *narratio* fits this form of discourse[224] because it does not presuppose or require any exposition of facts. Only forensic discourse requires a recital of the *causa* as a foundation for the *argumentatio*.[225]

(1) *Exordium*:

Conscious that the success of his petition depends on its two fundamental motives—*honestas* and *utilitas*[226]—Agrippa immediately introduces them with a simultaneous appeal to emotions and reason. He confronts, in effect, a case that the ancients would call "difficult," "a quo est alienatus animus eorum qui audiri sunt,"[227] although the receiver need not be completely hostile to the transmitter. Thus he decides on a simple proem or *principium*,[228] in his proleptic attempt to make Caligula *beniuolum, docilem* and *attentum*. As Quintilian says, "the only purpose of the *exordium* is to prepare our audience in a way that it is disposed to give the deserved attention to the rest of our discourse,"[229] and a speaker should offer "a courteous and natural opening."[230] This "Agrippa" achieves with uncommon tact and prudence.

He begins by assuring the *beneuolentia* of the autocrat by recurring to three possible topics.[231] His modesty, no less than the virtue of his character, is

---

[223] Cf. Aristotle, *Rhetorica* I, 3, 1358b 4 - 1359a 5.
[224] *Rhetorica ad Herennium* III, 4, 7.
[225] Aristotle, *Rhetorica* III, 16, 11; Cicero, *De Partitione Oratoria* 9, 31; Quintilian IV, 2, 1.
[226] Aristotle, *Rhetorica* I, 3, 4-6; Cicero, *De Inuentione* II, 82, 334; *Rhetorica ad Herennium* III, 2, 3; Quintilian III, 8, 1.
[227] Cicero, *De Inuentione* I, 15, 20: "one which has alienated the sympathy of those who are about to listen to the speech".
[228] Ibid. I, 15, 21.
[229] Quintilian IV, 1, 41.
[230] Ibid. III, 8, 59.
[231] "Goodwill is obtained from four places: from our own person, from that of one's adversaries, from that of the judges, and from the case itself" (Cicero, *De Inuentione* I, 16, 22). But here the opponent and the judge are embodied in one and the same person, so it is

reflected in the deference and reverence that explain Agrippa's renouncing of the opportunity to intercede face to face, and his choice of written communication. It is also reflected in the way he directs the petition to him, presenting the letter as one who extends an olive branch, to indicate metaphorically the gesture of a supplicant.[232] The character of the Emperor is eulogized when Agrippa affirms the greatness of his majesty and uses the appropriate title of αὐτοκράτωρ.[233] The importance of Agrippa's cause is made clear by means of an argument that dramatically evolves from the general to the specific and tries to simultaneously capture Caligula's attention and receptivity. The subject dealt with is important because it concerns all humanity and every individual. Even the Emperor may testify to it, should he so desire.[234] It concerns moreover the sacred temple and the worship of the most high God.

πᾶσιν ἀνθρώποις, αὐτοκράτορ, ἐμπέφυκεν ἔρως μὲν τῆς πατρίδος, τῶν δὲ οἰκείων νόμων ἀποδοχή· καὶ περὶ τούτων οὐδεμιᾶς ἐστί σοι χρεία διδασκαλίας, ἐκθύμως μὲν στέργοντι τὴν πατρίδα, ἐκθύμως δὲ τὰ πάτρια τιμῶντι. καλὰ δὲ ἑκάστοις, εἰ καὶ μὴ πρὸς ἀλήθειάν ἐστι, διαφαίνεται τὰ οἰκεῖα· κρίνουσι γὰρ αὐτὰ οὐ λογισμῷ μᾶλλον ἢ τῷ τῆς εὐνοίας πάθει. γεγέννημαι μέν, ὡς οἶδας, Ἰουδαῖος· ἔστι δέ μοι Ἱεροσόλυμα πατρίς, ἐν ᾗ ὁ τοῦ ὑψίστου θεοῦ νεὼς ἅγιος ἵδρυται· πάππων δὲ καὶ προγόνων βασιλέων ἔλαχον, ὧν οἱ πλείους ἐλέγοντο ἀρχιερεῖς, τὴν βασιλείαν τῆς ἱερωσύνης ἐν δευτέρᾳ τάξει τιθέμενοι καὶ νομίζοντες, ὅσῳ θεὸς ἀνθρώπων διαφέρει κατὰ τὸ κρεῖττον, τοσούτῳ καὶ βασιλείας ἀρχιερωσύνην· τὴν μὲν γὰρ εἶναι θεοῦ θεραπείαν, τὴν δὲ ἐπιμέλειαν ἀνθρώπων.

All men, my emperor, have planted in them a passionate love of their native land and a high esteem for their own laws; and on this there is no need to instruct you, who love your native city as ardently as you honour your own customs. Every people is convinced of the excellence of its own institutions, even if they are not really excellent, for they judge them not so much by their reasoning as by the affection which they feel for them. I as you know am by birth a Jew, and my native city is Jerusalem in which is situated the sacred shrine of the most high God. It fell to me to have for my grandparents and ancestors kings, most of whom had the title of high priest, who considered their kingship inferior to the priesthood, holding that the office of high priest is as superior in excellence to that of king as God surpasses men. For the office of one is to worship God, of the other to have charge of men (§§277-278).

These two paragraphs offer an argument that is both psychological and logical. Logically, we have the formal structure of an epichirema: (1) All men have implanted in the depths of their soul a passionate love of their homeland and a great esteem for its laws; (2) Gaius needs no instruction on the matter, as he himself loves his native land with his heart and honors its customs; (3) everyone is convinced of the excellency of his own institutions,

---

strategically reasonable to choose that which pertains to the judge.
[232] Concerning the δέησις and προτείνω, cf. Pelletier, PM 32, p. 258-259, n. 2.
[233] On the use and sense of this title of honor, cf. Pelletier, PM 32, p. 259, n. 3.
[234] Cf. Cicero, *De Inuentione* I, 16, 23; Quintilian X, 1, 41.

even if they are not excellent; (4) they judge them, not only by reason but especially by the affection that they feel for them; and (5) Agrippa and his people also have this right. Psychologically we have the ethical portrait of Agrippa in this courageous and venturesome identification with his people.

Here, paraphrastically, is his testimony:[235] Ὡς οἶδας, (as you know) I am a Jew by birth, Jerusalem is my native city, and it is there that the holy temple of the Most High God is located. I am honored to have had kings as grandfathers and forefathers, most of them high priests, who preferred the sacerdotal office, believing that the high priest is as superior in excellence to that of a king as God is greater in majesty than men."

To the sequence: *all, each one, I,* follows the other sequence: *my homeland, city, temple;* moving from the topic of quantity to that of quality and affirming in it the excellence of his faith. The suggestion, implicit and veiled, is that to honor institutions is above all to honor the temple and safeguard its inviolability.

In order to reach his ultimate objective of dissuading the Emperor from sacrilege, it is also necessary to induce him to show himself *docilem* and *attentum* by the "aperte et breuiter" exposition of the essence of the cause, in the *propositio*. To do this, Agrippa introduces here the structural elements of the *confirmatio* and proleptically announces the points he goes on to discuss in ascending order as he unfolds his argument:[236]

ἔθνει δὴ τοιούτῳ προσκεκληρωμένος καὶ πατρίδι καὶ ἱερῷ δέομαι ὑπὲρ ἁπάντων·

As my lot is cast in such a nation, city and temple I beseech you for them all (§279a).

(2) *Confirmatio*:

In the coherent progression of his thought "Agrippa" does not limit himself to expounding his petition linearly. He develops it by means of a line of argumentation structurally and functionally suitable to the conventional canons of deliberative rhetoric.

(2.1) *Agrippa's petition on behalf of the nation* (§§279b-280) is epichirematically based on a *locus honestatis*.[237]

– His people have from the beginning shown the greatest piety and most perfect loyalty toward Caesar's household.

– The proof of their unsurpassing piety is their prayers and votive

---

[235] "At times, the attorney can personally assume the role of strict intimacy with his client, as Cicero does in *Pro Milone* [where he himself] assumed the role of the supplicant" (Quintilian VI, 1, 24-25).
[236] Precisely three, in harmony with the ideal proposed by rhetorical technique.
[237] Cf. *Rhetorica ad Herennium* I, 3.

offerings on behalf of the Emperor, as well as the number of victims sacrificed in the festive solemnities and in the daily sacrifices.[238]

– This piety is real and not fictitious.

– For it is seen less by the tongue than by the intentions of their invisible souls, as they are not satisfied merely to declare themselves friends of Caesar, but truly are his friends.

– It is just, then, to honor him in accordance with his rightful reputation.

(2.2) *Agrippa's petition on behalf of the holy city* (§§281-289) is equally a deductive argument, but it begins from the definition of the ἱερόπολις, his native land.

In the *propositio* (§281a) he maintains that this μητρόπολις is the capital of a territory that transcends Judea and includes Jewish communities in the Diaspora. In the *ratio* or *approbatio* (§§281b-282) he supports the *propositio* by listing the regions of the empire, extending in all directions from Judea, where the Jewish colonies have been established. In the *assumptio* (§283) he declares that the demonstration of benevolence on the part of the Emperor toward his πατρίς represents the concession of that benefit, not only to a city, but its extension to thousands of others scattered in all regions of the inhabited earth. For—*assumptionis approbatio* (§284)—it befits the greatness of his brilliant destiny that, by extending benefits to a city, he benefits thousands of others, so that his glory will be celebrated in all parts of the Roman territory.

From this point the argument is enriched by the introduction of an *exornatio* (§§285-289)[239] in which the *exemplum*, the *amplificatio* and the *simile* play important roles. The paradigmatic reference to the honor conceded to the homelands of some of his friends with the rights of Roman citizenship, transforming slaves into lords, is used to signal the happiness and contagious gratitude of all the recipients of that gracious act, but especially to highlight his personal position of advantage in relation to the rest of his companions, in dignity as well as in loyalty. In a tone of oratorical amplification, "Agrippa" makes use of the *locus a contrario* to contrast his discretion and personal modesty with the opportunism of others, for never did he dare request such favors for his people, not even the remission of taxes. He develops an internal argument in four parts, strategically structured around a nuclear *interrogatio* and distributed by two collateral enthymemes (§§287-288).

---

[238] Cf. Pelletier, PM 32, p. 261, note 6.
[239] Although the formal structure of this argument does not strictly correspond to the model of the *absolutissima et perfectissima argumentatio*, instructed and illustrated by the *auctor ad Herennium*, and conforms more to the Ciceronian *ratiocinatio*, it represents here a strategy of compromise, not entirely original, for Quintilian is acquainted with the practice of the *exornatio* as a part of the epichireme, and considers it acceptable (*Institutio Oratoria* V, 14, 6).

– A much more modest act of benevolence is requested, because this favor will cost the Emperor nothing but will benefit his homeland greatly.

– For, what greater good could his subjects receive than the benevolence of their lord?

– It was in Jerusalem that Caligula's long-hoped-for succession to the empire was first announced. It was also from the Holy City that this news was spread to two continents. For these reasons its citizens deserve to receive at least equal favors.

The final analogy (§289) confirms the reasoning developed in the *amplificatio*, but serves equally as a conclusion to the central argument:

> καθάπερ γὰρ ἐν ταῖς συγγενείαις οἱ πρεσβύτατοι παῖδες τυγχάνουσι πρεσβείων, ὅτι πρῶτοι τὸ πατρὸς καὶ τὸ μητρὸς ὄνομα τοῖς γονεῦσιν ἐφήμισαν, τὸν αὐτὸν τρόπον, ἐπειδὴ τῶν ἀνατολικῶν πρώτη πόλις αὕτη σε προσεῖπεν αὐτοκράτορα, δικαία τυγχάνειν πλειόνων ἐστὶν ἀγαθῶν, εἰ δὲ μή, τῶν γοῦν ἴσων.

> For just as in families the oldest children hold the primacy because they have been the first to give the name of father and mother to their parents, so too this city since it was the first of eastern cities to address you as emperor deserves to receive greater boons than they or at least no less (§289).

Both its parts are symmetrically organized so as to capture the attention of the receiver psychologically and to predispose him to be favorable.

(2.3) *The petition for the temple* (§§290-320):
The ascending argument begun and developed in the first two parts of the discourse here reaches its culmination. After a brief *transitio*,[240] "Agrippa" unfolds a double deductive scheme of argumentation based on the inviolability of the temple and arguing in favor of it. In this scheme the end of the first argument serves as a point of departure for the elaboration of the second (§§290b-292a and 292b-293):

> τοσαῦτα δικαιολογηθεὶς καὶ δεηθεὶς ἅμα περὶ τῆς πατρίδος εἶμι τὸ τελευταῖον ἐπὶ τὴν περὶ τοῦ ἱεροῦ δέησιν. τοῦτο, Γάιε δέσποτα, τὸ ἱερὸν χειρόκμητον οὐδεμίαν ἐξ ἀρχῆς μορφὴν παρεδέξατο διὰ τὸ ἔδος τοῦ ἀληθοῦς εἶναι θεοῦ· γραφέων μὲν γὰρ καὶ πλαστῶν ἔργα μιμήματα τῶν αἰσθητῶν θεῶν εἰσιν· τὸν δὲ ἀόρατον εἰκονογραφεῖν ἢ διαπλάττειν οὐχ ὅσιον ἐνομίσθη τοῖς ἡμετέροις προγόνοις. Ἀγρίππας ἐτίμησε τὸ ἱερὸν ἐλθών, ὁ πάππος σου, καὶ ὁ Σεβαστὸς διὰ τοῦ κελεῦσαι τὰς πανταχόθεν ἀπαρχὰς ἐπιστολαῖς πέμπειν ἐκεῖσε καὶ διὰ τῆς ἐντελεχοῦς θυσίας· καὶ ἡ προμάμμη σου *** ὅθεν οὐδείς, οὐχ Ἕλλην, οὐ βάρβαρος, οὐ σατράπης, οὐ βασιλεύς, οὐκ ἐχθρὸς ἄσπονδος, οὐ στάσις, οὐ πόλεμος, οὐχ ἅλωσις, οὐ πόρθησις, οὐκ ἄλλο τι τῶν ὄντων οὐδὲν ἐνεωτέρισέ ποτε οὕτως εἰς τὸν νεών, ὡς ἄγαλμα ἢ ξόανον ἤ τι τῶν χειροκμήτων ἱδρύσασθαι. καὶ γὰρ εἰ τοῖς οἰκήτορσι τῆς χώρας ἀπήχθοντο δυσμενεῖς ὄντες, ἀλλ' αἰδώς γέ τις ἢ φόβος εἰσῄει παραλῦσαί τι τῶν ἐξ ἀρχῆς νενομισμένων ἐπὶ τιμῇ τοῦ ποιητοῦ τῶν ὅλων καὶ πατρός· ᾔδεσαν γὰρ ἐκ τούτων καὶ τῶν ὁμοιοτρόπων τὰς τῶν θηλάτων κακῶν φυομένας ἀνηκέστους συμφοράς. ἧς χάριν αἰτίας ἀσεβὲς σπέρμα

---

[240] *Rhetorica ad Herennium* IV, 26, 35: "Transition is the name given to the figure which briefly points out what has been said and in the same way briefly puts forward what is to follow."

σπείρειν εὐλαβοῦντο δεδιότες, μὴ θερίζειν ἀναγκασθῶσι τοὺς ἐπ' ὀλέθρῳ παντελεῖ καρπούς.

Having said thus much as a claimant for justice and as a suppliant also on behalf of my native place I come finally to my supplication for the temple. This temple, my Lord Gaius, has never from the first admitted any figure wrought by men's hands, because it is the sanctuary of the true God. For the works of painters and modellers are representations of gods perceived by sense but to paint or mould a likeness of the invisible was held by our ancestors to be against their religion.

Your grandfather Agrippa visited and paid honour to the temple, and so did Augustus by the letters in which he ordered the first fruits to be sent from every quarter and by instituting the perpetual sacrifice. Your great-grandmother too . . . Thus no one, Greek or non-Greek, no satrap, no king, no mortal enemy, no faction, no war, no storming or sacking of the city, nor any existing thing ever brought about so great a violation of the temple as the setting up in it of an image or statue or any hand-wrought object for worship. For even if they were ill-disposed and hostile to the inhabitants of the land yet an instinct of reverence or fear warned them against breaking down any of the customs observed from the first in honour of the Maker and Father of all, for they knew that it was from these and like actions that the irreparable calamities of divine visitations spring.

Therefore they took good care not to sow the seed of impiety, lest they should be compelled to reap its fruits which bring utter destruction (§290b-293).

The doctrine expressed in this passage is supported by a series of examples directly connected to the Emperor's family. This strategy of persuasion is apparently inspired by Aristotle, who prefers paradigmatic argumentation in a deliberative discourse and favors its general use to confirm and substantiate the evidence expressed by the enthymematic argumentation.[241]

The first example is that of Marcus Agrippa, Caligula's maternal grandfather. As soon as he had arrived in Judea[242] he made a point of visiting the capital, and once there he was touched by the enthusiastic welcome of the multitude and profoundly amazed by the dignity of the temple ritual and the worship offered by the native population. He was so impressed that in communications to his friends he praised everything that his eyes had seen, and he himself offered sacrifices to God[243] and bestowed favors on the city's inhabitants.[244]

In this example as in the others, Philo adopts the wider literary form of the *narratio*, as an affective *digressio* within the *argumentatio*,[245] which seeks to produce gradually the atmosphere favorable to the cause.[246] In an expressive

---

[241] *Rhetorica* I, 9, 40; II, 20, 9.
[242] In the autumn of 15 B.C., upon the invitation of Herod the Great (cf. Josephus, *Antiquitates Judaicae* XII, 12, 55-56).
[243] According to Josephus, Marcus Agrippa offered a hecatomb to God and a banquet to the people (cf. *Antiquitates Judaicae* XII, 55-56).
[244] E. M. Smallwood sees here an allusion to the banquet offered to all the Jews in Jerusalem (cf. Josephus, *Antiquitates Judaicae* XIV, 14).
[245] Quintilian V, 11, 151; IV, 3, 15-17; Cicero, *Pro Milone* 4, 9. Cf. Lausberg, *Manual de Retórica Literaria*, I, §415.
[246] Ibid., §345.

climactic finale he makes reference by the *a contrario* argument to the response of the entire nation which accompanies him in procession to the port, captivated and impressed by his piety.

The second example cited is that of Caligula's other grandfather, Tiberius Caesar (§§298-308), the emperor who during the twenty-three years of his reign followed the same policy, leaving the Jewish ceremonies intact and safeguarding them from any violation. His φιλοτιμία is curiously illustrated by the quick solution to the case of the scandal provoked among the Jews by the golden shields that Pilate introduced in Jerusalem.

The Judean governor figures in this example as an anti-model and point of departure for a long *a contrario* argument. His dedication of the shields in Herod's palace was intended not so much to honor Tiberius as to vex the people. They apparently were objects without any figurative engraving, but their consecration by pagan rites was undoubtedly understood as a profaning sacrilege.[247] They therefore were objects that should have been withdrawn, because they disturbed the people and threatened the peace.

However, the subversive nature of Pilate's measure is psychologically highlighted by the amplified narration of a successful process of dissuasion and intimidation, that culminated in a direct appeal to Tiberius; this gives more persuasiveness to the second part of the paradigm (§§304-305).

> ὁ δὲ διαναγνοὺς οἷα μὲν εἶπε Πιλᾶτον, οἷα δὲ ἠπείλησεν· ὡς δὲ ὠργίσθη, καίτοι οὐκ εὐληπτος ὢν ὀργῇ, περιττόν ἐστι διηγεῖσθαι, τοῦ πράγματος ἐξ αὐτοῦ φωνὴν ἀφιέντος. εὐθέως γὰρ οὐδὲ εἰς τὴν ὑστεραίαν ὑπερθέμενος ἐπιστέλλει, μυρία μὲν τοῦ καινουργηθέντος τολμήματος ὀνειδίζων καὶ ἐπιπλήττων, κελεύων δὲ αὐτίκα καθελεῖν τὰς ἀσπίδας καὶ μετακομισθῆναι ἐκ τῆς μητροπόλεως εἰς τὴν ἐπὶ θαλάττῃ Καισάρειαν, ἐπώνυμον τοῦ προπάππου Σεβαστήν, ἵνα ἀνατεθεῖεν ἐν τῷ Σεβαστείῳ· καὶ ἀνετέθησαν. οὕτως ἀμφότερα ἐφυλάχθη, καὶ ἡ τιμὴ τοῦ αὐτοκράτορος, καὶ ἡ περὶ τὴν πόλιν ἀρχαία συνήθεια.

> When he had read them through what language he used about Pilate, what threats he made! The violence of his anger, though he was not easily roused to anger, it is needless to describe since the facts speak for themselves. For at once without even postponing it to the morrow he wrote to Pilate with a host of reproaches and rebukes for his audacious violation of precedent and bade him at once take down the shields and have them transferred from the capital to Caesarea on the coast surnamed Augusta after your great-grandfather, to be set up in the temple of Augustus, and so they were.
>
> So both objects were safeguarded, the honour paid to the emperor and the policy observed from of old in dealing with the city (§§304-305).

In contrast to Pilate, Tiberius is here presented as a model to be imitated by Gaius Caligula, in the firmness and urgency with which he lamented and repudiated the fearful violation, ordering that Pilate move the shields from the capital to Caesarea and there dedicate them in the temple of Augustus

---

[247] Pelletier, PM 32, p. 375.

(§305). Agrippa proceeds to note a crucial difference between Pilate's shields and Gaius' statue. Recurring to the topic of past-present tense and to the argument *a minore ad maius*, he highlights the transcendent gravity of this worsening situation (§306):

τότε μὲν οὖν ἀσπίδες ἦσαν, αἷς οὐδὲν ἀνεζωγράφητο μίμημα· νυνὶ δὲ κολοσσιαῖος ἀνδριάς. καὶ τότε μὲν ἡ ἀνάθεσις ἐν οἰκίᾳ τῶν ἐπιτρόπων ἦν· τὴν δὲ μέλλουσάν φασιν ἐσωτάτω τοῦ ἱεροῦ κατ' αὐτὰ τὰ ἄδυτα γίνεσθαι, εἰς ἃ ἅπαξ τοῦ ἐνιαυτοῦ ὁ μέγας ἱερεὺς εἰσέρχεται τῇ νηστείᾳ λεγομένῃ μόνον ἐπιθυμιάσων καὶ κατὰ τὰ πάτρια εὐξόμενος φορὰν ἀγαθῶν εὐετηρίαν τε καὶ εἰρήνην ἅπασιν ἀνθρώποις.

Now at that time it was shields on which no likeness had been painted; now it is a colossal statue. Then too the installation was in the house of the governors; now they say it is to be in the inmost part of the temple in the special sanctuary itself, in which the Grand Priest enters once a year only on the Fast as it is called, to offer incense and to pray according to ancestral practice for a full supply of blessings and prosperity and peace for all mankind (§306).

"Agrippa" concludes his paradigmatic argument with a double enthymeme, in the manner of Philo's exegetical-persuasive style, symmetrically organized in the chiastic structure of ABCB'A', connecting the eventual mode of the hypothetic period in the first case with the potential in the second (§§307-308).

A – κἂν ἄρα τίς που, οὐ λέγω τῶν ἄλλων Ἰουδαίων, ἀλλὰ καὶ τῶν ἱερέων, οὐχὶ τῶν ὑστάτων, ἀλλὰ τῶν τὴν εὐθὺς μετὰ τὸν πρῶτον τάξιν εἰληχότων, ἢ καθ' αὐτὸν ἢ καὶ μετ' ἐκείνου συνεισέλθῃ, μᾶλλον δὲ κἂν αὐτὸς ὁ ἀρχιερεὺς δυσὶν ἡμέραις τοῦ ἔτους ἢ καὶ τῇ αὐτῇ τρὶς ἢ καὶ τετράκις εἰσφοιτήσῃ,

B – θάνατον ἀπαραίτητον ὑπομένει.

C – τοσαύτη τίς ἐστιν ἡ περὶ τὰ ἄδυτα φυλακὴ τοῦ νομοθέτου μόνα ἐκ πάντων ἄβατα καὶ ἄψαυστα βουληθέντος αὐτὰ διατηρεῖσθαι.

B' – πόσους ἂν οὖν οἴει θανάτους ἑκουσίως ὑπομένειν τοὺς περὶ ταῦτα ὡσιωμένους,

A' – εἰ θεάσαιντο τὸν ἀνδριάντα εἰσκομιζόμενον; ἐμοὶ μὲν δοκοῦσι γενεὰς ὅλας αὐταῖς γυναιξὶ καὶ τέκνοις ἀποσφάξαντες ἐπὶ τοῖς τῶν οἰκείων πτώμασιν ἑαυτοὺς τελευταῖον καθιερεύσειν. ταῦτα μὲν Τιβέριος ἔγνω.

And if any priest, to say nothing of the other Jews, and not merely one of the lowest priests but of those who are ranked directly below the chief, goes in either by himself or with the High Priest, and further even if the High Priest enters on two days in the year or thrice or four times on the same day death without appeal is his doom. So greatly careful was the law-giver to guard the inmost sanctuary, the one and only place which he wished to keep preserved untrodden and untouched. How many deaths think you would those who have been trained to holiness in these matters willingly endure if they should see the statue imported thither? I believe that they would slaughter their whole families, women and children alike, and finally immolate themselves upon the corpses of their kin. This Tiberius knew (§307-308).

Then "Agrippa" turns to speak of Gaius' great-grandfather, (§§309-318) describing him as the best of the emperors. He is introduced by a double erotema to emphasize his piety and religious circumspection as well as his first-rate theoretical-practical education in each of the branches of philosophy (§§309-310),[248]

> τί δὲ ὁ σὸς πρόπαππος, ὁ τῶν πώποτε γενομένων αὐτοκρατόρων ἄριστος, ὁ πρῶτος ἀρετῆς ἕνεκα καὶ τύχης Σεβαστὸς ὀνομασθείς, ὁ τὴν εἰρήνην διαχέας πάντη διὰ γῆς καὶ θαλάττης ἄχρι τῶν τοῦ κόσμου περάτων; οὐκ ἀκοῇ πυνθανόμενος τὰ περὶ τὸ ἱερὸν καὶ ὅτι οὐδέν ἐστιν ἀφίδρυμα ἐν αὐτῷ χειρόκμητον, ὁρατὸν ἀοράτου μίμημα φύσεως, ἐθαύμαζε καὶ προσεκύνει, φιλοσοφίας οὐκ ἄκροις χείλεσι γευσάμενος ἀλλ' ἐπὶ πλέον ἑστιαθεὶς καὶ σχεδόν τι καθ' ἑκάστην ἡμέραν ἑστιώμενος, τὰ μὲν μνήμαις ὧν ἡ διάνοια προμαθοῦσα τὰ φιλοσοφίας ἀνεπόλει, τὰ δὲ καὶ ταῖς τῶν συνόντων ἀεὶ λογίων συνδιαιτήσεσι· κατὰ γὰρ τὰς ἐν δείπνῳ συνουσίας ὁ πλεῖστος χρόνος ἀπενέμετο τοῖς ἀπὸ παιδείας, ἵνα μὴ τὸ σῶμα μόνον ἀλλὰ καὶ ἡ ψυχὴ τοῖς οἰκείοις ἀνατρέφοιτο.

> But what of your greatgrandfather the best of the emperors that ever were to this day, he who first received the title of Augustus for his virtue and good fortune, who disseminated peace everywhere over sea and land to the ends of the world? Did he not, hearing by report the story of the temple and that it had no work of man's hands, a visible effigy of an invisible being, erected in it, marvel and pay it honour? For he had not taken a mere sip of philosophy but had feasted on it liberally and continued so to feast almost every day, partly by the memories of the lessons which his mind had conned from its earlier instruction in philosophy, partly by intercourse with the learned who from time to time were in his company. For in the gatherings at his table most of the time was assigned to listening to men of culture so that not only the body but also the soul might be nourished by the food proper to each (§§309-310).

This example is expanded by a rhetorical allusion to the abundance of testimonies he possesses to the aims of Augustus, followed by a detailed discussion of two particularly instructive and revealing pieces of evidence: (1) a letter sent to the governors of the provinces of Asia to correct a flagrant case of disrespect and religious discrimination,[249] assuring the Jews the right to meet in their synagogues (as well as full freedom to collect their annual tithes and to send delegates to Jerusalem according to their ancestral

---

[248] The text highlights the fact that Augustus was accustomed to seat educated men at his table, allowing the philosophers and rhetoricians of the time to speak freely (cf. Pelletier, PM 32, p. 282, n. 4), so that both the body and the spirit should receive the proper nutrition.

[249] Josephus testifies that the Jews of Asia Minor and those of Libya were mistreated, and that the Greeks unjustly persecuted them to the point of spoiling them of the "sacred money" (*Antiquitates Judaicae* XVI, 160-173). The treatment ordered by Augustus constituted an exception to the general interdiction of the *collegia*, as Suetonius (*Caes.* 42, 4) asserts that "Caesar caused all associations to dissolve, except the most ancient ones": "cuncta collegia, praeter antiquitus constituta distraxit" (A. Pelletier, PM 32, p. 283, n. 9). And Augustus did the same by means of a *lex Iulia de collegiis* ("collegia praeter antiqua et legitima dissoluit") with the purpose of neutralizing "certain groups suspected of fomenting political agitation" (Ibid.).

practice); and (2) the decision that sacrifices be offered daily, at their expense, in perpetual holocaust to the Most High God (§311-317).

Two πίστεις of great persuasive effectiveness thus reveal Augustus's reasoning:

> ὅτι ἀναγκαῖόν ἐστιν ἐν τοῖς περιγείοις ἐξαίρετον ἀπονενεμῆσθαι τόπον ἱερὸν τῷ ἀοράτῳ θεῷ μηδὲν ὁρατὸν ἀπεικόνισμα περιέξοντα πρὸς μετουσίαν ἐλπίδων χρηστῶν καὶ ἀπόλαυσιν ἀγαθῶν τελείων.

> that within the precincts of earth there must needs be a special place assigned as sacred to the invisible God which would contain no visible image, a place to give us participation in good hopes and enjoyment of perfect blessings (§318).

In the first, he observed that there was no place in Jewish synagogues for drunkenness and orgies that would incite conspiracies and disturb the peace, since they were schools of temperance and justice for persons who exercise virtue. The second, used to show the indisputable superiority of Augustus as sovereign and the uniqueness of his clear reasoning as a philosopher, consists in his recognizing the need for a special place of worship consecrated to the invisible God and free of any visual representation—a πίστις that acts terminally as an *inclusio,* to connect the end to the beginning, in this integrated paradigmatic scheme.

As the final dissuading example (§§319-320), "Agrippa" makes a brief reference to Julia Augusta who, instructed in and inspired by the piety of Augustus, never tired of adorning and enriching the temple with the most valuable offerings. It is the climax of a consecutive argumentative *gradatio*, reinforced[250] by a simple *interrogatio* that obviously seeks to lead Caligula to the only possible response (§319).

> τί παθοῦσα καὶ αὕτη, μηδενὸς ἔνδον ὄντος ἀφιδρύματος;

> What made her to do this, as there was no image there (§319)?

It was certainly not feminine sensibility that awakened in her such a gesture of religious piety, argues the writer of the letter, but her virile and clear-sighted intelligence, that resulted from a perfect education in which φύσις, παιδεία and μελέτη were combined in orderly fashion,[251] that discerns the things of the mind even better than the things of the senses.

(3) *Peroratio* (§321-329)

"It is in peroration," writes Quintilian, "that we should give free expression to the exuberant flowing of our eloquence. For, if we speak well in the rest of

---

[250] *Rhetorica ad Herennium* IV, 15, 22.
[251] Variation of the classical educational triad of Plato and Aristotle to Cicero and Quintilian: διδασκαλία, φύσις, ἄσκησις.

the discourse, we should now have the judges on our side".[252] As H. Lausberg observes, in harmony with the Latin master, *peroratio* has a twofold objective: to refresh the memory and to influence the affections.[253] Some rhetoricians may divide it into three parts and others into four.[254] But the result is the same, because both *amplificatio* and *conquestio* answer to the *ratio posita in affectibus*.[255]

And Philo develops it in model fashion, satisfying with effectiveness and theoretical rigor each one of its fundamental requirements. As is appropriate to deliberative discourse, "Agrippa" progressively creates in the conclusion of his letter the psychological ambience suited to the desperately needed decision. In the *enumeratio* (§§321-322) he repeats logically and psychologically his appeal,[256] urging Gaius to follow the example of his progenitors (§321):

ἔχων οὖν, δέσποτα, τῆς ἡμερωτέρας προαιρέσεως τοιαῦτα παραδείγματα, πάντα οἰκειότατα καὶ συγγενέστατα ἀφ' ὧν ἐσπάρης καὶ ἀνέβλαστες καὶ τοσοῦτον ηὐξήθης, διατήρησον ἃ κἀκείνων ἕκαστος.

So then, my lord, having such patterns of the gentler line of treatment, patterns so closely connected by kinship to yourself, the seed-bed from which you sprang and grew up and rose to such greatness, maintain what each of them also maintained (§321).

Their ethical sense is expressively interpreted by the following affective *gradatio* (§322a):

παρακλητεύουσι τοῖς νόμοις αὐτοκράτορες πρὸς αὐτοκράτορα, Σεβαστοὶ πρὸς Σεβαστόν, πάπποι καὶ πρόγονοι πρὸς ἔκγονον, πλείους πρὸς ἕνα, μονονουχὶ φάσκοντες·

The cause of the laws is pleaded by emperors to emperor, by Augusti to an Augustus, by grandparents and ancestors to their descendant, by several to one, and you may almost hear them say (§322a),

After all, it is not only the Jewish sovereign that makes moving appeals to persuade the Emperor. It is the superior intercessory and prophetic

---

[252] *Institutio Oratoria* VI, 1, 52.
[253] Lausberg, *Manual de Retórica Literaria*, §431.
[254] Aristotle (*Rhetorica* III, 19, 1) divides the conclusion into four parts: (1) ἔκ τε τοῦ πρὸς ἑαυτὸν κατασκευάσαι εὖ τὸν ἀκροατὴν καὶ τὸν ἐναντίον φαύλως, καὶ (2) ἐκ τοῦ αὐξῆσαι καὶ ταπεινῶσαι, καὶ (3) ἐκ τοῦ εἰς τὰ πάθη τὸν ἀκροατὴν καταστῆσαι, καὶ (4) ἐξ ἀναμνήσεως. The *auctor ad Herennium* and Cicero, *De Inuentione*, divide them into three: *enumeratio, amplificatio* and *commiseratio*, according to the first (*Her.* II, 30, 47); or *enumeratio, indignatio* and *conquestio*, according to the second (*De Inu.* I, 52, 98), the *conquestio* corresponding to the *commiseratio*, the *indignatio* generally to the purpose of the *amplificatio*, and the *enumeratio* to the *recapitulatio* or *repetitio* (Quintilian VI, 1, 1).
[255] For this reason, Cicero reduces the *peroratio* to two divisions (in *De Partitione Oratoria* 15, 52 ff): *amplificatio* and *enumeratio*, subordinating the *indignatio* as well as the *conquestio* to the former.
[256] This part can also be developed into the form of a recommendation (cf. *Rhetorica ad Alexandrum* 20).

exhortation of august emperors to an august emperor, of progenitors to their descendant, whom we can almost hear saying (§322b):

ἐν ταῖς ἡμετέραις βουλήσεσιν ἃ μέχρι καὶ τήμερον ἐφυλάχθη νόμιμα μὴ καθέλῃς· καὶ γὰρ εἰ μηδὲν ἐκ τῆς καταλύσεως αὐτῶν ἀπαντηθείη παλίμφημον, ἀλλ' ἥ γε τοῦ μέλλοντος ἀδηλότης καὶ τοῖς θαρραλεωτάτοις, εἰ μὴ καταφρονηταὶ τῶν θείων εἰσίν, οὐ παντελῶς ἐστιν ἄφοβος.

Do not destroy the institutions which under the shelter of our wills were safeguarded to this day, for even if no sinister result were encountered through their overthrow, still the uncertainty of the future cannot entirely fail to strike fear into the most courageous unless he holds things divine in contempt (§322b).

In the *amplificatio* (§§323-325) the argument is expanded by two rhetorically powerful effective devices, the *praeteritio* and the *gradatio*, which in turn antecipate the pathetic tone of the *conquestio*.[257] The first (§323), points to the many past favors "Agrippa" has received from Gaius; τίς οὐκ οἶδεν; ("Who does not know it?"). They are so many and so evident that they speak eloquently by themselves. The second, (§§324-326) asks the Emperor to act once again in conformity with the generosity he manifested later.

The mention of these benefits, in gradual ascending order, corresponds symmetrically to the progressive intensification of his appeal. It is a complex and dense argumentation, but one intelligible, alive, effective and pregnant with penetrating dramatic tension. The *locus a contrario* appears dialectically articulated in the chiastic parallelism of an ABA' structure and becomes especially manifest in the order of the parts of affirmation-negation:

A - ἔλυσάς με σιδήρῳ δεδεμένον· τίς οὐκ οἶδεν; ἀλλὰ μὴ χαλεπωτέροις δεσμοῖς, αὐτοκράτωρ, ἐπισφίγξῃς· οἱ μὲν γὰρ λυθέντες μέρει περιβέβληντο τοῦ σώματος, οἱ δὲ νῦν προσδοκώμενοι ψυχῆς εἰσιν, ὅλην αὐτὴν δι' ὅλων μέλλοντες πιέζειν.

B - τὸν ἐπικρεμάμενον ἀεὶ τοῦ θανάτου φόβον ἀπώσω καὶ τεθνεῶτα τῷ δέει ζωπυρήσας καθάπερ ἐκ παλιγγενεσίας ἀνήγειρας· διατήρησον τὴν χάριν, αὐτοκράτωρ, ἵνα μὴ ὁ σὸς Ἀγρίππας ἀποτάξηται τῷ βίῳ· δόξω γὰρ οὐ τοῦ σωθῆναι χάριν ἀφεῖσθαι μᾶλλον ἢ τοῦ βαρυτέρας ἐνδεξάμενος συμφορὰς ἐπισημότερον τελευτῆσαι.

A' - τὸν μέγιστον καὶ εὐτυχέστατον ἐν ἀνθρώποις κλῆρον ἐχαρίσω μοι, βασιλείαν, πάλαι μὲν μιᾶς χώρας, αὖθις δὲ καὶ ἑτέρας μείζονος, τὴν Τραχωνῖτιν λεγομένην καὶ τὴν Γαλιλαίαν συνάψας· μὴ τὰ πρὸς περιουσίαν μοι χαρισάμενος, ὦ δέσποτα, τὰ ἀναγκαῖα ἀφέλῃς μηδὲ εἰς φῶς ἀναγαγὼν τηλαυγέστατον ἐξ ὑπαρχῆς εἰς βαθύτατον σκότος ῥίψῃς.

A - You released me bound fast in iron fetters, who does not know it? but do not clamp me, my emperor, with still more grievous fetters, for those which were then unbound encompassed but a part of my body, those which I see before me are of the soul and must press hard on every part of its whole being. (§324)

B - You thrust away the ever imminent terror of death, you kindled fresh life in me when dead with fear, you awakened me as though I were born anew. Maintain your

---

[257] Cf. *Rhetorica ad Herennium* III, 24.

bounty, my emperor, that your Agrippa may not bid farewell to life, for it will seem as though my release was not given to save me but that a victim to heavier misfortunes I should come to a more notorious end. (§325)

A' - The greatest gift of fortune that man can possess you granted to me, a kingdom, in the past of one country, later of another and a greater when you added Trachonitis as it is called and Galilee. Do not after granting me favours in super-abundance take from me bare necessities, and after restoring me to light of fullest radiance cast me anew into deepest darkness. (§326)

Paragraph 326b climactically reconnects the several parts of the *gradatio*, suggesting in synthesis the structural elements of a chiastic symmetry, mediated dialectically:[258]

A – Gaius restored "Agrippa" to liberty and to life as in a new birth (§§324-325).

  B – He gave him the greatest gift to which a mortal can aspire (§326a).

    C – Favors received are superfluous, if one is deprived of the essential good (§326b).

  B' – Let him not take away—but rather give a new—that supreme good (§326b).

A' – Let him not cast him into even deeper darkness (§326c).

By this argumentative figure the autocrat is confronted with the dilemma of either annulling with his decision all the benefits he has previously conferred, or confirming them by the conceding of this most excellent gift. This passage shows him the road from the good to the better, grounded in the transcendent reality that only he can safeguard.

This *tour de force* is then formalized in the *conquaestio* (§§327-329), an appeal in which the πάθος reaches its maximum persuasive force:

ἐξίσταμαι τῶν λαμπρῶν ἐκείνων, τὴν πρὸ μικροῦ τύχην οὐ παραιτοῦμαι, πάντα ὑπαλλάττομαι ἑνός, τοῦ μὴ κινηθῆναι τὰ πάτρια. τίς γὰρ ἄν μου γένοιτο λόγος ἢ παρὰ τοῖς ὁμοφύλοις ἢ παρὰ τοῖς ἄλλοις ἅπασιν ἀνθρώποις; ἀνάγκη γὰρ δυοῖν θάτερον ἢ προδότην τῶν ἰδίων ἢ σοὶ μηκέτι ὁμοίως φίλον νομισθῆναι· ὧν τί ἂν εἴη μεῖζον κακόν; εἰ μὲν γὰρ ἐν τῇ τάξει τῶν ἑταίρων ἔτι καταριθμοῦμαι, προδοσίας ἐξοίσομαι δόξαν, ἐὰν μήτε ἡ πατρὶς ἀπαθὴς παντὸς κακοῦ διαφυλαχθῇ μήτε τὸ ἱερὸν ἄψαυστον· τὰ γὰρ τῶν ἑταίρων καὶ προσπεφευγότων ταῖς αὐτοκρατορικαῖς ἐπιφανείαις ὑμεῖς οἱ μεγάλοι διασῴζετε. εἰ δὲ ὑποικουρεῖ τί σου τὴν διάνοιαν ἔχθος, μὴ δήσῃς ὡς Τιβέριος, ἀλλὰ καὶ τὴν τοῦ δεθῆναί ποτε αὖθις ἐλπίδα συνανελὼν κέλευσον ἐκποδὼν αὐτίκα γενέσθαι· τί γὰρ ἐμοὶ ζῆν καλόν, ᾧ μία σωτηρίας ἐλπὶς ἦν τὸ σὸν εὐμενές;

---

[258] Jacques Cazeaux, in an effort to reconstruct the "noetic plan" of the Philonic treatises, carried out a remarkably stimulating and original analysis, by means of which he sustains the predominance of the law of symmetry in regulating the formal architecture of Philo's thought. Cazeaux also maintains that the symmetrical structure is often developed dialectically, presenting in the middle an important element of mediation, whose function is necessarily that of transferring the first idea to the last, or simply transforming one into the other.

> I renounce all that brilliance, I do not beg to keep my shortlived good fortune. I exchange all for one thing only, that the ancestral institutions be not disturbed. For what would be my reputation among either my compatriots or all other men? Either I must seem a traitor to my people or no longer be counted your friend as I have been; there is no other alternative, and what greater ill could befall me than these? For if I still keep my place in the list of your companions I shall lie under an imputation of treachery, unless my homeland is guarded unscathed from every kind of mischief and the temple is untouched. For you great potentates safeguard the interests of your companions and those who take refuge with you by manifestations of your absolute power. But if your mind harbor any hostility to me, do not imprison me as Tiberius did, rather do away with any idea of future imprisonment and at the same time bid me take myself out of the way forthwith. For of what value would life be to me whose one hope of salvation lay in your goodwill (§§327-329)?

It is presupposed that intellectual conviction has been achieved. The emotions have just been stimulated by the grateful recalling of benefits and friendship. And as if those arguments were not enough, "Agrippa" finally develops the theme of "sympathy" as a conceptual topic indispensable to the whole pathetic appeal.

Quintilian writes that when we direct our appeal to a judge who is prejudiced against the cause we are defending, although it may be hard to persuade him, we should courageously affirm our confidence in his integrity and in the justice of our cause.[259] "Agrippa's" strategy accords with this recommendation. Conscious that sympathy is conquered primarily by the use of *loci communes*,[260] he saturates this whole section with those most appropriate to his cause,[261] beginning with the use of a delightful and impressive *gradatio* in order to highlight the supremacy of the ancestral institutions in his scale of values.

> ἐξίσταμαι τῶν λαμπρῶν ἐκείνων, τὴν πρὸ μικροῦ τύχην οὐ παραιτοῦμαι, πάντα ὑπαλλάττομαι ἑνός, τοῦ μὴ κινηθῆναι τὰ πάτρια.

> I renounce all that brilliance, I do not beg to keep my shortlived good fortune. I exchange all for one thing only, that the ancestral institutions be not disturbed (§327a).

Then, he proceeds to the use of the *ratiocinatio* as an argumentative figure perfectly adapted to the oral style, just as defined by the *auctor ad Herennium*.[262] And he ends with a decisive syllogistic reasoning (§329), reinforced and majestically finalized by an *interrogatio*.[263]

---

[259] *Institutio Oratoria* II, 1, 75.
[260] Cf. Cicero, *De Inuentione* I, 55, 106.
[261] Ibid. I, 107-109.
[262] *Rhetorica ad Herennium* IV, 16, 23. An author progressively moves toward his conclusion by means of a series of arguments in the form of questions and answers. He captivates and assures the attention of the reader-listener, as much by the anticipation of the reasoning, as by his stylistic grace.
[263] *Rhetorica ad Herennium* IV, 15, 22.

εἰ δὲ ὑποικουρεῖ τί σου τὴν διάνοιαν ἔχθος, μὴ δήσῃς ὡς Τιβέριος, ἀλλὰ καὶ τὴν τοῦ δεθῆναί ποτε αὖθις ἐλπίδα συνανελὼν κέλευσον ἐκποδὼν αὐτίκα γενέσθαι· τί γὰρ ἐμοὶ ζῆν καλόν, ᾧ μία σωτηρίας ἐλπὶς ἦν τὸ σὸν εὐμενές;

> But if your mind harbour any hostility to me, do not imprison me as Tiberius did, rather do away with any idea of future imprisonment and at the same time bid me take myself out of the way forthwith. For of what value would life be to me whose one hope of salvation lay in your goodwill (§329)?

Protection of the temple and his homeland is more important to him than his own life.

What happier way could there be to end the oratorical *peroratio* than that in which the *breuitas* is discreetly sweetened by the *ornatus* and the argumentative tension keeps in balance ἦθος, πάθος and λόγος?[264]

Taken together, this discourse is essentially based on the double rhetorical syllogism, which constitutes the touchstone and backbone of the whole argument. W. Brandt calls this argumentation scheme that of basic enthymematical structure, admitting at the same time the integrated concurrence of several other enthymemes, both simple and structural. At first glance, we distinguish the following syllogistic structure:

– If all people passionately love their laws and customs, and Gaius is an eloquent witness of that fact;
– If the ancestral customs of the Jews were always honored by their progenitors;
– Then it is important that these institutions also be honored by him and that the temple not be profaned.

Taking another look, we can detect a second logical structure, no less essential:

– If the Jewish nation has always demonstrated, as no other, the greatest piety and the most perfect loyalty toward the house of the Emperor, and was generously treated by his forefathers in the defense and honor of its institutions;
– If the benefits given to their temple and city are extended to the entire world, because of the worldwide expansion of the Jewish people, and those benefits lead to a universal glorification of the very Emperor;
– Then it is only to Gaius' advantage to honor those institutions, desisting from his destructive and sacrilegious intention.

This dual argumentative macro-structure is developed in an ascending movement in which the more important micro-arguments are reserved for the final phase. We must, however, note two essential factors in this strategic progression, one of structure and the other of intention. Brandt points out that, while logical in its basic structure, an argument does not always proceed

---

[264] Cf. Lausberg, *Manual de Retórica Literaria*, §440; Cicero, *De Inuentione* I, 109.

logically from the premise to the conclusion, mostly for reasons of function and strategic persuasion.²⁶⁵ This is so because effective rhetoric combines psychological subtlety with logical clarity. Hence the relative complexity of the structure of this discourse, which is the result not of its basic logic but of the intention that shapes and gives it life.²⁶⁶

Profound in its unity and in its balance of logic and πάθος, this "letter of Agrippa" is in fact a demonstration of Philo's remarkable rhetorical expertise.

---

²⁶⁵ Cf. Brandt, *Rhetoric of Argumentation*, p. 70.
²⁶⁶ Ibid., p. 92.

CHAPTER FOUR

STRUCTURES OF A COMPLETE ARGUMENT

The argumentative tone of rhetorical discourse is a constantly perceptible phenomenon in the Philo's commentaries on scripture. It can be seen not only in the general rhetorical structure of some of his treatises and certain speeches they contain, but also, with surprising regularity, in his treatment of exegetical issues.

In its dynamic relationship to the suggested philosophical-theological theme, the rhetorical system affords the commentator an appropriate strategy for reading, interpretation and exposition. It is a system that, far from being a mere ornamental artifice, is the basis of his fundamental hermeneutics. Bearing witness to this is the way Philo generally develops his commentary on a text, acceding to the message expressed in it or allegorically imposed on it, and transforming that message into a thesis, which in turn is supported with arguments suitable to his basic exegetical motivation.

Yet, if the Alexandrian commentator employed παιδεία "to express and understand human origins, experiences, communities, and destinies;"[1] if the composition of his commentaries reflects a structural rhetoric appropriate to the explanation and defense of the principles upon which his faith, spiritual horizon, and hope are based,[2] then to what extent and in what form does the theory of assimilated argumentation determine his methodological strategy?

Although our analysis will treat only a limited number of Philonic texts, we will try to produce as clear an image as possible of the ways in which the Alexandrian constructs an argument. The passages selected illustrate some of the important themes expressed in his *corpus*, and provide a dual vision of it—revealing both ideas that configure his literary personality and the forms of argumentation that he uses to communicate them.

The simple exegesis of a text, the logical argument of a thesis, or the elaborate development of a theme show the rhetorical creativity with which Philo structures and animates a discourse even down to small details.

---

[1] W. H. Wagner, "Philo and Paideia," *Cithara* X (1975), p. 62.
[2] See M. Alexandre, Jr., "Rhetorical Argumentation as an Exegetical Technique in Philo of Alexandria", in *Hellenica et Judaica* (Leuven, Paris: Peeters, 1986), p. 13-27; "Some Reflections on Philo's Concept and Use of Rhetoric", *Euphrosyne* 19 (1991), p. 281-290.

Through rhetorical study we can discover, behind the apparent density and complexity of a treatise, its harmonious coherence.

I. *In the Argumentation of a Thesis*

The adoption and strategic adaptation of the conventions of Hellenistic rhetoric is evident in Philo's treatises, even at the level of the simplest and most direct exegesis of a text.

At times, the spiritual subject of a scriptural text is identified and demonstrated merely by the elaboration of an analogy, perhaps in combination with dieretic or etymological definition. In *De Fuga* 183, for example, the Alexandrian commentator explains analogically the propaedeutic character of the encyclical studies: [3]

εἰσὶ δὲ καὶ τῆς παιδείας πολύτροποι πηγαί, αἷς ὀρθοὶ καὶ τροφιμώτατοι λόγοι, καθάπερ στελέχη φοινίκων, παρανέβλαστον. "ἦλθον" γάρ φησιν "εἰς Αἰλίμ, καὶ ἐν Αἰλὶμ ἦσαν

---

[3] The outside door of a house is one of the many figures provoking analogies that Philo uses to illustrate the inescapable importance of encyclical education, in the career that leads to virtue and wisdom. Cf. *Congr.* 10. Among others, refer especially to these illustrations: of the vassal (*Congr.* 18), of the rational milk (*Congr.* 19), of the earthly and Egyptian body (*Congr.* 20) and of the resident foreigner (*Congr.* 22-23); also the illustration of the younger sister, Rachel (*Ebr.* 47-51), and especially that of the servant Hagar (*Congr.* 23). Seen from the elevated and sublime point of view of the σοφία, the encyclical paideia is for Philo "the ἀρχή of philosophy-ἀρετή and the προπαιδεία of the σοφία" (Wagner, "Philo and Paideia," p. 55-56).

In *De Posteritate Caini* 22, Philo interprets the "Naid" or Nod = σάλος segment of the basic text, decoding it by comparing the foolish man represented by Cain, impotent, unable to direct the course of his life and two steps from the abyss, to a ship lost in the middle of a swollen sea, lost and ready to perish.

Ἄξιον δὲ σκέψασθαι καὶ τὴν χώραν, εἰς ἣν ἐκ προσώπου γενόμενος θεοῦ στέλλεται· ἔστι δὲ ἣ καλεῖται σάλος, δηλοῦντος τοῦ νομοθέτου ὅτι ὁ ἄφρων ἀστάτοις καὶ ἀνιδρύτοις ὁρμαῖς κεχρημένος σάλον καὶ κλόνον, οἷα κυμαῖνον πέλαγος πρὸς ἐναντίων πνευμάτων χειμῶνος ὥρᾳ, ὑπομένει, γαλήνης δὲ ἢ νηνεμίας ἀλλ' οὐδ' ὄναρ ἐπῄσθηται. ὥσπερ δ'ὅταν ναῦς σαλεύῃ θαλαττεύουσα, τότ' οὔτε πλεῖν οὔτε ὁρμεῖν ἐστιν ἱκανή, διαφερομένη δὲ ὧδε κἀκεῖσε πρὸς ἑκάτερον τοῖχον ἀποκλίνει καὶ ταλαντεύουσα ἀντιρρέπει, οὕτως ὁ φαῦλος παραφόρῳ καὶ χειμαινούσῃ διανοίᾳ κεχρημένος εὐθύνειν τὸν ἑαυτοῦ πλοῦν ἀπταίστως ἀδυνατῶν αἰεὶ σαλεύει βίου μελετῶν ἀνατροπήν.

"It is worth while to notice the country also into which he betakes himself when he has left the presence of God; it is the country called 'Tossing.' In this way the lawgiver indicates that the foolish man, being a creature of wavering and unsettled impulses, is subject to tossing and tumult, like the sea lashed by contrary winds when a storm is raging, and has never even in fancy had experience of quietness and calm. And as at a time when a ship is tossing at the mercy of the sea, it is capable neither of sailing nor of riding at anchor, but pitched about this way and that it rolls in turn to either side and moves uncertainly swaying to and fro; even so the worthless man, with a mind reeling and storm-driven, powerless to direct his course with any steadiness, is always tossing, ready to make shipwreck of his life." (See *Heres* 263-265; *Post.* 124-125.)

δώδεκα πηγαὶ ὑδάτων καὶ ἑβδομήκοντα στελέχη φοινίκων· παρενέβαλον δὲ ἐκεῖ παρὰ τὰ ὕδατα". Αἰλὶμ πυλῶνες ἑρμηνεύονται, εἰσόδου τῆς πρὸς ἀρετὴν σύμβολον· ὥσπερ γὰρ οἰκίας ἀρχαὶ πυλῶνες, καὶ ἀρετῆς τὰ ἐγκύκλια προπαιδεύματα.

There are also a variety of springs of education, by the side of which there grow up, like stems of palm-trees, upright forms of reason rich in nourishing food. For we read that "they came to Elim, and in Elim there were twelve springs of water, and seventy stems of palm-trees; and they encamped there by the waters" [Ex. 15:27]. "Elim" means "gateways," a figure of the entrance to virtue; for just as gateways are the beginnings of a house, so are the preliminary exercises of the schools the beginning of virtue (§183).

At other times, an interpretation is articulated and set in motion by a *locus a contrario*, and in the same way this may or may not be combined with a definition.[4] At still other times exegesis is made dynamic and sustained by a rhetorical syllogism, which may or may not be followed in Aristotelian fashion, by an example. But in the majority of cases, a text's ideas are exhaustively dissected and its thought systems architectonically fortified and vitalized as much as possible so that they agree with the argumentation structures sanctioned in the oratorical canons.

We will first of all observe how the unified argument of a thesis is developed in his treatises.

1. *Legum Allegoriae II, 1-3*

The word μόνον, from Genesis 2:18, suggests to Philo the enunciation of a thesis on the unity and simplicity of the divine nature, which he argues in a way influenced by the Ciceronian *ratiocinatio*. Ably conceived and mediated by the *locus a contrario*, the *propositio* (§1) is sustained by the same *locus* in a chiastic conjunctural structure:

διὰ τί τὸν ἄνθρωπον, ὦ προφῆτα, οὐκ ἔστι καλὸν εἶναι μόνον; ὅτι, φησί, καλόν ἐστι τὸν μόνον εἶναι μόνον· μόνος δὲ καὶ καθ' αὐτὸν εἷς ὢν ὁ θεός, οὐδὲν δὲ ὅμοιον θεῷ· ὥστ' ἐπεὶ τὸ

---

[4] Cf. *Legum Allegoriae* I, 36-37a: "ἐνεφύσησεν."
Definition – ἴσον ἐστὶ τῷ ἐνέπνευσεν ἢ ἐψύχωσε τὰ ἄψυχα·
Thesis – μὴ γὰρ τοσαύτης ἀτοπίας ἀναπλησθείημεν, ὥστε νομίσαι θεὸν στόματος ἢ μυκτήρων ὀργάνοις χρῆσθαι πρὸς τὸ ἐμφυσῆσαι·
Reason and confirmation – ἄποιος γὰρ ὁ θεός, οὐ μόνον οὐκ ἀνθρωπόμορφος. ἐμφαίνει δὲ τι καὶ φυσικώτερον ἡ προφορά. τρία γὰρ εἶναι δεῖ, τὸ ἐμπνέον, τὸ δεχόμενον, τὸ ἐμπνευόμενον· τὸ μὲν οὖν ἐμπνέον ἐστὶν ὁ θεός, τὸ δὲ δεχόμενον ὁ νοῦς, τὸ δὲ ἐμπνευόμενον τὸ πνεῦμα.
"'Breathed into,' we note, is equivalent to 'inspired' or 'be-souled' the soul-less; for God forbid that we should be infected with such monstrous folly as to think that God employs for inbreathing organs such as mouth or nostrils; for God is not only not in the form of man, but belongs to no class or kind. Yet the expression clearly brings out something that accords with nature. For it implies of necessity three things, that which inbreathes, that which receives, that which is inbreathed; that which inbreathes is God, that which receives is the mind, that which is inbreathed is the spirit or breath." (See also *Her.* 52, 67, 78-79, 81; *Congr.* 71-72.)

μόνον εἶναι τὸν ὄντα καλόν ἐστι —καὶ γὰρ περὶ μόνον αὐτὸν τὸ καλόν—, οὐκ ἂν εἴη καλὸν τὸ εἶναι τὸν ἄνθρωπον μόνον.

Why, O prophet, is it not good that the man should be alone? Because, he says, it is good that the Alone should be alone: but God, being One, is alone and unique, and like God there is nothing. Hence, since it is good that He Who is should be alone—for indeed with regard to Him alone can the statement "it is good" be made—it follows that it would not be good that the man should be alone (§1).

The *assumptio* (§2) makes viable the proof of the thesis by providing those elements pertinent to its demonstration and by the consequent explanation of the deciphered term. Significantly, however, its paradigmatic foundation is again articulated antithetically, based on an AB B'A' structure.

τὸ δὲ μόνον εἶναι τὸν θεὸν ἔστι μὲν ἐκδέξασθαι καὶ οὕτως, ὅτι οὔτε πρὸ γενέσεως ἦν τι σὺν τῷ θεῷ οὔτε κόσμου γενομένου συντάττεταί τι αὐτῷ· χρῄζει γὰρ οὐδενὸς τὸ παράπαν. ἀμείνων δὲ ἥδε ἡ ἐκδοχή· ὁ θεὸς μόνος ἐστὶ καὶ ἕν, οὐ σύγκριμα, φύσις ἁπλῆ, ἡμῶν δ' ἕκαστος καὶ τῶν ἄλλων ὅσα γέγονε πολλά· οἷον ἐγὼ πολλά εἰμι, ψυχὴ σῶμα, καὶ ψυχῆς ἄλογον λογικόν, πάλιν σώματος θερμὸν ψυχρὸν βαρὺ κοῦφον ξηρὸν ὑγρόν· ὁ δὲ θεὸς οὐ σύγκριμα οὐδὲ ἐκ πολλῶν συνεστώς, ἀλλ' ἀμιγὴς ἄλλῳ·

There is another way in which we may understand the statement that God is alone. It may mean that neither before creation was there anything with God, nor, when the universe had come into being, does anything take its place with Him; for there is absolutely nothing which He needs. A yet better interpretation is the following. God is alone, a Unity, in the sense that His nature is simple not composite, whereas each one of us and of all other created beings is made up of many things. I, for example, am many things in one. I am soul and body. To soul belong rational and irrational parts, and to body, again, different properties, warm and cold, heavy and light, dry and moist. But God is not a composite Being, consisting of many parts, nor is He mixed with aught else (§2).

No less lacking in persuasive force, the proof of the minor premise is syllogistically organized in conjunction with the *complexio* (§3), which simultaneously provides its conclusion and closes the argument which has just been proven by deduction.

ὃ γὰρ ἂν προσκριθῇ θεῷ, ἢ κρεῖσσόν ἐστιν αὐτοῦ ἢ ἔλασσον ἢ ἴσον αὐτῷ· οὔτε δὲ ἴσον οὔτε κρεῖσσόν ἐστι θεοῦ, ἔλασσόν γε μὴν οὐδὲν αὐτῷ προσκρίνεται· εἰ δὲ μή, καὶ αὐτὸς ἐλαττωθήσεται· εἰ δὲ τοῦτο, καὶ φθαρτὸς ἔσται, ὅπερ οὐδὲ θέμις νοῆσαι. τέτακται οὖν ὁ θεὸς κατὰ τὸ ἓν καὶ τὴν μονάδα, μᾶλλον δὲ ἡ μονὰς κατὰ τὸν ἕνα θεόν· πᾶς γὰρ ἀριθμὸς νεώτερος κόσμου, ὡς καὶ χρόνος, ὁ δὲ θεὸς πρεσβύτερος κόσμου καὶ δημιουργός.

For whatever is added to God, is either superior or inferior or equal to Him. But there is nothing equal or superior to God. And no lesser thing is resolved into Him. If He do so assimilate any lesser thing, He also will be lessened. And if He can be made less, He will also be capable of corruption; and even to imagine this were blasphemous. The "one" and the "monad" are, therefore, the only standard for determining the category to which God belongs. Rather should we say, the One God is the sole standard for the "monad." For, like time, all number is subsequent to the universe; and God is prior to the universe, and is its Maker (§3).

2. De Opificio Mundi 7-12

In *De Opificio Mundi* 7-12 Philo exegetically reproduces the same argumentative scheme of the *ratiocinatio*, as he makes a pronouncement on the creation of the world in the context of divine providence. However, the cause here is only demonstrated after having been conveniently informed and founded by a brief *narratio* (§§7-9a), in which first of all the Aristotelian theory of the eternity of the world is rejected.[5]

Perhaps inspired by the Stoic argument regarding providence,[6] Philo accomplishes its transformation in order to base his creation argument on divine providence. The *propositio* (§9b) affirms the existence of the world as a product of the creative and preserving work of God.[7]

> ὃν οἱ φάσκοντες ὡς ἔστιν ἀγένητος λελήθασι τὸ ὠφελιμώτατον καὶ ἀναγκαιότατον τῶν εἰς εὐσέβειαν ὑποτεμνόμενοι τὴν πρόνοιαν.
>
> Those who assert that this world is unoriginate unconsciously eliminate that which of all incentives to piety is the most beneficial and the most indispensable, namely providence (§9b).

---

[5] Cf. *Phys.* VIII, 4, 254b 27-33 and 255a 12-15; *Metaph.* XII, 7, 1072a 25ff.

[6] Cf. H. A. Wolfson, Philo I, p. 297-298: "Those who grant that the gods exist must acknowledge that they perform some action (*aliquid agere*), and that action an exalted one. But there is nothing more exalted than the administration of the world. Consequently the world is administered by the divine forethought."

[7] Although Philo limits himself in this first treatise to touching on the theme of creation to prove that this world is not eternal, without making an explicit pronouncement on its origin, a synoptically-oriented reading of the various affirmations made on the theme in the whole of the *corpus* is enlightening. His apparent vacillation between a creation of the world beginning with preexisting matter and a *creatio ex nihilo* has lead some renowned Philonists to different conclusions. But the fact is, as G. Reale demonstrates (*Filone di Alessandria, "L'erede delle cose divine"* [Milano: Rusconi, 1981], p. 65-66; cf. his "Filone di Alessandria e la prima elaborazione filosofica della dottrina della creazione," in *Paradoxos Politeia* [Milano: Vita e Pensiero, 1979], p. 247-287), "for Philo it is in fact not a matter of either-or, but rather of and-and; God for him is both Creator (out of nothing) and Demiurge." The creation scheme adopted by him contemplates two phases: "'in a first moment God creates the Logos and the Ideas, as well as the unformed matter in the quantity required for constructing the universe. In a second moment God forms and orders unformed matter, through the mediation of the Logos and in conformity with the ideas, and so produces the cosmos. In the 'first moment' the activity of God is that of the κτίστης, of κτίζειν, i.e. producing *ex nihilo*; in the 'second moment' the activity of God is that of the Demiurge, or of δημιουργεῖν, i.e. forming, informing or giving form to what is unformed." Sometimes they can naturally be distinguished logically and ideally, but not chronologically, for "time comes into being only together with the cosmos." Thus there is no doubt that Philo clearly asserts the creation of matter, underlines G. Reale, also affirming that "the great innovation of Philo lies precisely in this. Plato had introduced the celebrated 'three principles' for explaining the world: the Demiurge, the Ideas and the χώρα or matter, and he had conceived them as coeternal. Philo transformed the Demiurge into the omnipotent God of the Bible, and made him *creator of the other two principles*, which he makes use of in order to create the physical world" (Ibid.).

The *approbatio* (§10) supports the validity of the formulated thesis by proving that belief in divine providence logically presupposes the creation, first by the argument from analogy and then by its opposite.

> τοῦ μὲν γὰρ γεγονότος ἐπιμελεῖσθαι τὸν πατέρα καὶ ποιητὴν αἱρεῖ λόγος· καὶ γὰρ πατὴρ ἐκγόνων καὶ δημιουργὸς τῶν δημιουργηθέντων στοχάζεται τῆς διαμονῆς καὶ ὅσα μὲν ἐπιζήμια καὶ βλαβερὰ μηχανῇ πάσῃ διωθεῖται, τὰ δὲ ὅσα ὠφέλιμα καὶ λυσιτελῆ κατὰ πάντα τρόπον ἐκπορίζειν ἐπιποθεῖ· πρὸς δὲ τὸ μὴ γεγονὸς οἰκείωσις οὐδεμία τῷ μὴ πεποιηκότι.

> For it stands to reason that what has been brought into existence should be cared for by its Father and Maker. For, as we know, it is a father's aim in regard of his offspring and an artificer's in regard of his handiwork to preserve them, and by every means to fend off from them aught that may entail loss or harm. He keenly desires to provide for them in every way all that is beneficial and to their advantage: but between that which has never been brought into being and one who is not its Maker no such tie is formed (§10).

The *assumptio* (§11) confirms by contrast the undeniable reality of providence as an authentic guarantee of the order and balance of the universe and demonstrates in the argumentative sequence of its *approbatio* (§12a) the inconsistency of those who believe in the eternity of the world, gradually and naturally opening the way for the *complexio* (§12b).

> ἀπερίμαχητον δὲ δόγμα καὶ ἀνωφελὲς ἀναρχίαν ὡς ἐν πόλει κατασκευάζον τῷδε τῷ κόσμῳ τὸν ἔφορον ἢ βραβευτὴν ἢ δικαστὴν οὐκ ἔχοντι, ὑφ' οὗ πάντ' οἰκονομεῖσθαι καὶ πρυτανεύεσθαι θέμις. ἀλλ' ὅ γε μέγας Μωυσῆς ἀλλοτριώτατον τοῦ ὁρατοῦ νομίσας εἶναι τὸ ἀγένητον—πᾶν γὰρ τὸ αἰσθητὸν ἐν γενέσει καὶ μεταβολαῖς οὐδέποτε κατὰ ταὐτὰ ὄν—τῷ μὲν ἀοράτῳ καὶ νοητῷ προσένειμεν ὡς ἀδελφὸν καὶ συγγενὲς ἀιδιότητα, τῷ δ' αἰσθητῷ γένεσιν οἰκεῖον ὄνομα ἐπεφήμισεν. ἐπεὶ οὖν ὁρατός τε καὶ αἰσθητὸς ὅδε ὁ κόσμος, ἀναγκαίως ἂν εἴη καὶ γενητός· ὅθεν οὐκ ἀπὸ σκοποῦ καὶ τὴν γένεσιν ἀνέγραψεν αὐτοῦ μάλα σεμνῶς θεολογήσας.

> It is a worthless and baleful doctrine, setting up anarchy in the well-ordered realm of the world, leaving it without protector, arbitrator, or judge, without anyone whose office it is to administer and direct all its affairs.
>
> Not so Moses. That great master, holding the unoriginate to be of a different order from that which is visible, since everything that is an object of sensible perception is subject to becoming and to constant change, never abiding in the same state, assigned to that which is invisible and an object of intellectual apprehension the infinite and undefinable as united with it by closest tie; but on that which is an object of the senses he bestowed "genesis," "becoming," as its appropriate name. Seeing then that this world is both visible and perceived by the senses, it follows that it must also have had an origin. Whence it was entirely to the point that he put on record that origin, setting forth in its true grandeur the work of God (§11-12).

In summary, the syllogistic rationale employed here presents the following structure: (1) Those who maintain that this world had no beginning unconsciously eliminate providence, for the divine fatherhood is indispensable to its preservation. (2) Now a doctrine that presupposes the elimination of providence is unsustainable and pernicious for it establishes anarchy in the world, like a city where there is no guarantee of good government and administration. It follows that the theory of the eternity of the world is also unsustainable for, since every tangible object is temporal and subject to constant change, Moses—to cite the testimony of authority—attributes eternity to the invisible and intelligible, giving to the tangible the name γένεσις. And (3) therefore the world must have had an origin, because it belongs to the realm of the visible and tangible.

3. De Fuga et Inuentione 68-70 *and* De Opificio Mundi 134-135

Philo's exegetical treatment of these two narratives of the creation of man reflect the same epichirematic scheme of argumentation.

In the introduction to his treatise on the creation of the world, when he affirms that the κόσμος was conceived and formed in harmony with the Law of God (§3), that its Father and Creator is the perfect νοῦς of the universe, superior to all virtue and science, superior even to the Good and the Beautiful (§8), and that He cares for the world because of His goodness (§21), Philo asserts that the νοητὸς κόσμος is the λόγος of God, the image and archetypal seal by which man was created (§§24-25).[8] According to him, the αἰσθητὸς κόσμος is a μίμημα of the εἰκών, "the image of an image." For, just as God is the archetype of the λόγος/ἄνθρωπος/νοητὸς κόσμος, He is also the archetype of the tangible world.[9] Therefore, man is the product of a dual divine operation, first as γένος and then as empirical man.

In *De Opificio* 75-76, and in a more developed way in *De Fuga* 68-70, the Alexandrian interprets Genesis 1:26, suggesting in the γένος the creative act of God in collaboration with his powers.[10] Both passages logically argue the

---

[8] Although Philo's God is that of the Bible, his commentary on the cosmology of Genesis 1-3 is obviously impregnated with the language and doctrine of Plato, especially as expressed in the *Timaeus*. Cf. É. Bréhier, *Les idées philosophiques*, p. 78-79. But, as T. Tobin observes, "the interpretation of the creation of the world through the use of the Platonic distinction between paradigm and copy is not the only model of creation, not even the only Platonic model, found in Philo" (*The Creation of Man*, p. 60). See his list of the concepts and vocabulary about the creation of man in Philo (Ibid., p. 62ff). Cf. D.T. Runia, *Philo of Alexandria and the Timaeus of Plato*, p. 433–446.

[9] B. Pearson, "Philo and the Gnostics on Man and Salvation," PCCBS 29 (Berkeley, 1977), p. 2. Cf. J. Martín, *Filón de Alejandría y la génesis de la cultura occidental* (Buenos Aires: Depalma, 1986), p. 98-101. As he asserts, "in Philo and other Jewish texts of the time the philosophical path towards the concept of creatio ex nihilo commences. God the creator not only gives the form (or the 'light'), but also the existence (the 'being')".

[10] As Pearson trenchantly observes, "the inspiration for this explanation of Gen. 1:26 is, of course, Plato's *Timaeus* 41A-42B. Plato has his Creator (the 'Demiurge') fashion with his own hands the immortal part of man, but relegates to the lesser gods man's mortal nature, his body and lower soul. Plato's 'gods' become Philo's 'powers' or 'angels,' and the immortal part of man is equated (at least in some texts) with the εἰκών of God and ... with the divine inbreathing of Gen. 2:7" ("Philo and the Gnostics", p. 3).

same proposition: that man was the only being formed by God with the help of collaborators. But the second is completely developed in epichirematical structure, even revealing who these collaborators were (ταῖς ἑαυτοῦ δυνάμεσιν) and which part of man the Father of all things created by direct intervention (the νοῦς, that is, the rational part of our soul).[11]

(1) *Propositio:*

διὰ τοῦτ', οἶμαι, καὶ ἡνίκα τὰ τῆς κοσμοποιίας ἐφιλοσόφει, πάντα τἆλλα εἰπὼν ὑπὸ θεοῦ γενέσθαι μόνον τὸν ἄνθρωπον ὡς ἂν μετὰ συνεργῶν ἑτέρων ἐδήλωσε διαπλασθέντα.

It is for this reason, I imagine, that Moses, when treating in his lessons of wisdom of the Creation of the world, after having said of all other things that they were made by God, described man alone as having been fashioned with the co-operation of others (*Fug.* 68α).

(2) *Approbatio:*

"εἶπε" γάρ φησιν "ὁ θεός· ποιήσωμεν ἄνθρωπον κατ' εἰκόνα ἡμετέραν", πλήθους διὰ τοῦ "ποιήσωμεν" ἐμφαινομένου.

His words are: "God said, let us make man after our image" [Gen. 1:26], "let us make" indicating more than one (§68b).

(3) *Assumptio:*

διαλέγεται μὲν οὖν ὁ τῶν ὅλων πατὴρ ταῖς ἑαυτοῦ δυνάμεσιν, αἷς τὸ θνητὸν ἡμῶν τῆς ψυχῆς μέρος ἔδωκε διαπλάττειν μιμουμέναις τὴν αὐτοῦ τέχνην, ἡνίκα τὸ λογικὸν ἐν ἡμῖν ἐμόρφου,

So the Father of all things is holding parley with His powers, whom He allowed to fashion the mortal portion of our soul by imitating the skill shewn by Him when He was forming that in us which is rational (§69a),

(4) *Assumptionis approbatio:*

δικαιῶν ὑπὸ μὲν ἡγεμόνος τὸ ἡγεμονεῦον ἐν ψυχῇ, τὸ δ' ὑπήκοον πρὸς ὑπηκόων δημιουργεῖσθαι. κατεχρήσατο ⟨δὲ⟩ καὶ ταῖς μεθ' ἑαυτοῦ δυνάμεσιν οὐ διὰ τὸ λεχθὲν μόνον, ἀλλ' ὅτι ἔμελλεν ἡ ἀνθρώπου ψυχὴ μόνη κακῶν καὶ ἀγαθῶν ἐννοίας λαμβάνειν καὶ χρῆσθαι ταῖς ἑτέραις, εἰ μὴ δυνατὸν ἀμφοτέραις.

since He deemed it right that by the Sovereign should be wrought the sovereign faculty in the soul, the subject part being wrought by subjects. And He employed the powers that are associated with Him not only for the reason mentioned, but because, alone among created beings, the soul of man was to be susceptible of conceptions of evil things and good things, and to use one sort or the other, since it is impossible for him to use both (§§69b-70a).

---

[11] It is noteworthy that "Philo does not attribute the forming of the *body* of man to the 'powers,' only the mortal part of the soul," here again marking out the Platonic formulation in order to remain faithful to the meaning of the following text, Gen. 2:7 (Ibid., p. 3-4).

(5) *Complexio:*

ἀναγκαῖον οὖν ἡγήσατο τὴν κακῶν γένεσιν ἑτέροις ἀπονεῖμαι δημιουργοῖς, τὴν δὲ τῶν ἀγαθῶν ἑαυτῷ μόνῳ.

Therefore God deemed it necessary to assign the creation of evil things to other makers, reserving that of good things to Himself alone (§70b).

In *De Opificio* 134-135 he concentrates on the second narrative of creation in Genesis 2:7, in order to prove that there is a world of difference between the man formed from the dust of the earth—pneumatically made alive by the breath of the Creator—and the ideal type of man previously created in the image of God; and to show, consequently, that individual and tangible man is the product of a combination of earthly substance with the divine breath.

By means of a structure of dynamic and coherent argumentation Philo illuminates and sustains the major premise by the *a contrario* explanation of the fact that the man thus formed is distinguished from the ideal type created in God's image.

ὁ μὲν γὰρ διαπλασθεὶς αἰσθητὸς ἤδη μετέχων ποιότητος, ἐκ σώματος καὶ ψυχῆς συνεστώς, ἀνὴρ ἢ γυνή, φύσει θνητός· ὁ δὲ κατὰ τὴν εἰκόνα ἰδέα τις ἢ γένος ἢ σφραγίς, νοητός, ἀσώματος, οὔτ' ἄρρεν οὔτε θῆλυ, ἄφθαρτος φύσει.

for the man so formed is an object of sense-perception, partaking already of such or such quality, consisting of body and soul, man or woman, by nature mortal; while he that was after the [Divine] image was an idea or type or seal, an object of thought [only], incorporeal, neither male or female, by nature incorruptible (§134b).

Then he bases the minor premise on the exegetical commentary of the text itself, opposing the origin of the body to that of the soul and explaining its nature based on the same topic.[12]

τοῦ δ' αἰσθητοῦ καὶ ἐπὶ μέρους ἀνθρώπου τὴν κατασκευὴν σύνθετον εἶναί φησιν ἔκ τε γεώδους οὐσίας καὶ πνεύματος θείου· γεγενῆσθαι γὰρ τὸ μὲν σῶμα, χοῦν τοῦ τεχνίτου λαβόντος καὶ μορφὴν ἀνθρωπίνην ἐξ αὐτοῦ διαπλάσαντος, τὴν δὲ ψυχὴν ἀπ' οὐδενὸς γενητοῦ τὸ παράπαν, ἀλλ' ἐκ τοῦ πατρὸς καὶ ἡγεμόνος τῶν πάντων· ὃ γὰρ ἐνεφύσησεν, οὐδὲν ἦν ἕτερον ἢ πνεῦμα θεῖον ἀπὸ τῆς μακαρίας καὶ εὐδαίμονος φύσεως ἐκείνης ἀποικίαν τὴν ἐνθάδε στειλάμενον ἐπ' ὠφελείᾳ τοῦ γένους ἡμῶν, ἵν' εἰ καὶ θνητόν ἐστι κατὰ τὴν ὁρατὴν μερίδα, κατὰ γοῦν τὴν ἀόρατον ἀθανατίζηται.

It says, however, that the formation of the individual man, the object of sense, is a composite one made up of earthly substance and of Divine breath: for it says that the body was made through the Artificer taking clay and moulding out of it a human form, but that the soul was originated from nothing created whatever, but from the Father and Ruler of all: for that which He breathed in was nothing else than a Divine breath that

---

[12] It is affirmed in the text, in the commentary on Gen. 48:15, that God takes the most important things under His care, those things having to do with the soul's nourishment, giving the less important things to the care of His minister.

migrated hither from that blissful and happy existence for the benefit of our race, to the end that, even if it is mortal in respect of its visible part, it may in respect of the part that is invisible be rendered immortal (§135).

Once the distinctive character and composite nature of empirical man are demonstrated, Philo concludes his argument without repeating himself, transcending the deduction that obviously results from the combining of the two premises[13] and declaring that "man stands on the border between the mortal nature and the immortal, to the extent that he needfully participates in both and in which he was created simultaneously mortal and immortal, θνητὸν μὲν κατὰ τὸ σῶμα, κατὰ δὲ τὴν διάνοιαν ἀθάνατον."

The impact of the encyclical and philosophical culture on the works of the Alexandrian, is very apparent here. Moreover, he does not limit himself to slavishly reproducing a specific body of doctrine, nor does he propose to create a philosophical system with a Jewish flavor. His deeper concern is rather to provide an exegesis that honors the truth expressed in the biblical text within its context and its spiritual horizon. To that end he does not hesitate to make use of all the available resources of the period, whether "the best philosophical thought"[14] or methods of reasoning and rhetorical argumentation, modifying them and adapting them to his pedagogic and apologetic project of exposition.

Similar results would be obtained from examining other Philonic discussions of the origin, nature and destiny of man. Literary units like, *Quis Rerum Diuinarum Heres* 230-236 and *Legum Allegoriae* I, 105-108 also illustrate his characteristic way of argumentatively interpreting and commenting on a text. In the first passage Philo seeks to prove the dual nature of man and the indivisibility of the rational soul by means of its analogical confrontation with heaven[15] and the divine λόγος. In the second passage he attempts to epichirematically demonstrate human destiny, based on the dieretic classification of two kinds of death and their resulting antithetical characterization.[16]

---

[13] Cf. Cicero, *De Inuentione* I, 34, 59.
[14] R. Melnick, "On the Philonic Conception of the Whole Man," JSJ XI:1 (1980), p. 14-15.
[15] ὁ γάρ, οἶμαι, ἐν ἀνθρώπῳ ψυχή, τοῦτο οὐρανὸς ἐν κόσμῳ.
"In fact I regard the soul as being in man what the heaven is in the universe."
[16] (1) ὅτι διττός ἐστι θάνατος, ὁ μὲν ἀνθρώπου, ὁ δὲ ψυχῆς ἴδιος· ὁ μὲν οὖν ἀνθρώπου χωρισμός ἐστι ψυχῆς ἀπὸ σώματος, ὁ δὲ ψυχῆς θάνατος ἀρετῆς μὲν φθορά ἐστι, κακίας δὲ ἀνάληψις.
(2) παρὸ καί φησιν οὐκ ἀποθανεῖν αὐτὸ μόνον ἀλλὰ "θανάτῳ ἀποθανεῖν", δηλῶν οὐ τὸν κοινὸν ἀλλὰ τὸν ἴδιον καὶ κατ' ἐξοχὴν θάνατον, ὅς ἐστι ψυχῆς ἐντυμβευομένης πάθεσι καὶ κακίαις ἁπάσαις.
(3) καὶ σχεδὸν οὗτος ὁ θάνατος μάχεται ἐκείνῳ·
(4) ἐκεῖνος μὲν γὰρ διάκρισίς ἐστι τῶν συγκριθέντων σώματός τε καὶ ψυχῆς, οὗτος δὲ τοὐναντίον σύνοδος ἀμφοῖν, κρατοῦντος μὲν τοῦ χείρονος σώματος, κρατουμένου δὲ τοῦ κρείττονος ψυχῆς. ὅπου δ' ἂν λέγῃ "θανάτῳ ἀποθανεῖν", παρατήρει ὅτι θάνατον τὸν ἐπὶ τιμωρίᾳ παραλαμβάνει, οὐ τὸν φύσει γινόμενον·
(5) φύσει μὲν οὖν ἐστι, καθ' ὃν χωρίζεται ψυχὴ ἀπὸ σώματος, ὁ δὲ ἐπὶ τιμωρίᾳ συνίσταται,

However, we will finish our study of the main structures Philo uses by considering his treatment of certain other themes.

4. De Iosepho 28-31 and 125-143

To the treatises that deal with the lives of the "wise men" of Israel who represent the three ways of perfection, Philo adds *De Iosepho*, dedicated to the study of the life of the political man (§1).

Apparently inspired by the Hellenistic doctrine of the ideal king, the Alexandrian sets forth in this document the distinctive traits of Joseph as a statesman:[17] the excellence of his birth and his superior intelligence (§4), his vocational education as a pastor of people (§3), his initiation in governmental practice as Potiphar's steward (§38) and his own rule (§§54-58), the recognition of his majesty by his own brothers (§165), his authority demonstrated as much by the rectitude and equity of his judgments as by the persuasive force of his eloquence (§269), and the universal recognition of his kindness (§267), philanthropy (§240) and moderation (§§26,166,246-250).[18]

ὅταν ἡ ψυχὴ τὸν ἀρετῆς βίον θνήσκῃ, τὸν δὲ κακίας ζῇ μόνον. εὖ καὶ ὁ Ἡράκλειτος κατὰ τοῦτο Μωυσέως ἀκολουθήσας τῷ δόγματι, φησὶ γάρ· "Ζῶμεν τὸν ἐκείνων θάνατον, τεθνήκαμεν δὲ τὸν ἐκείνων βίον," ὡς νῦν μέν, ὅτε ζῶμεν, τεθνηκυίας τῆς ψυχῆς καὶ ὡς ἂν ἐν σήματι τῷ σώματι ἐντετυμβευμένης, εἰ δὲ ἀποθάνοιμεν, τῆς ψυχῆς ζώσης τὸν ἴδιον βίον καὶ ἀπηλλαγμένης κακοῦ καὶ νεκροῦ συνδέτου τοῦ σώματος.

"That death is of two kinds, one that of the man in general, the other that of the soul in particular. The death of the man is the separation of the soul from the body, but the death of the soul is the decay of virtue and the bringing in of wickedness. It is for this reason that God says not only 'die' but 'die the death,' indicating not the death common to us all, but that special death properly so called, which is that of the soul becoming entombed in passions and wickedness of all kinds. And this death is practically the antithesis of the death which awaits us all. The latter is a separation of combatants that had been pitted against one another, body and soul, to wit. The former, on the other hand, is a meeting of the two in conflict. And in this conflict the worse, the body, overcomes, and the better, the soul, is overcome. But observe that wherever Moses speaks of 'dying the death,' he means the penalty-death, not that which takes place in the course of nature. That one is in the course of nature in which soul is parted from body; but the penalty-death takes place when the soul dies to the life of virtue, and is alive only to that of wickedness. That is an excellent saying of Heracleitus, who on this point followed Moses' teaching, 'We live,' he says, 'their death, and are dead to their life.' He means that now, when we are living, the soul is dead and has been entombed in the body as in a sepulchre; whereas, should we die, the soul lives forthwith its own proper life, and is released from the body, the baneful corpse to which it was tied."

[17] J. Laporte, PM 21, p. 30-31. Cf. E. Goodenough, *The Politics of Philo Judaeus, Practice and Theory* (New Haven: Yale University Press, 1938), p. 42-63.

[18] Μετριοπάθεια (moderation of the passions), greatness of soul and firmness of character. See also *Virt.* 195. The Stoics emphasized the ideal of ἀπάθεια (see *Stoicorum Veterum Fragmenta* III, 443ff.). But, according to Diogenes Laertius V, 31, Aristotle ἔφη τὸν σοφὸν ἀπαθῆ μὲν μὴ εἶναι μετριοπαθῆ δὲ (F. H. Colson and G. H. Whitaker, PLCL I, p. 483, note on *Leg.* III, 129).

The narrative commentary is interrupted by three distinct units of allegorical exegesis,[19] and two of them are worth mentioning on account of their argumentation structures.

In *De Iosepho* 28-31 Philo produces an argument on the law of nature, conceptually identical to that of Cicero in his *De Republica* III, 33,[20] but different both in basic motivation and in structure. According to his argument the universe is an immense megalopolis ruled by a single constitution[21] which, as reason or natural law, is called ὀρθὸς λόγος/*recta ratio*, or νόμος θεῖος.[22]

Philo's point of departure is his etymology[23] of the name "Joseph"—"addition of a lord"—which, in the context of the Greek philosophical tradition suggests the addition of political science to wisdom.[24] His thesis (based on this concept of the political man as an addition to him who lives according to nature) is argued along the lines of the formal structure defended by the *auctor ad Herennium* (not that of the *absolutissima et perfectissima argumentatio*, but that which obviously dispenses the *exornatio*).[25] In linear sequence the interpretation of the political practice of the people, as an addition to the sovereign and universal law of nature, is first demonstrated antithetically in the *ratio* (§29) and then substantiated by arguments organized in chiastic structure (§30).

---

[19] "The first of these units (28–37) interprets the symbolism of the multicolored coat, the sale of Joseph and his purported death through mauling by beasts; the second (58–80) sees in the temptation of Joseph by Potiphar's wife and his imprisonment the fat of the man of politics who refuses to please the crowd; the third finally (125–157) explains in what sense Joseph, who represents the man of politics, can be called an interpreter of dreams" (Laporte, PM 21, p. 12).

[20] Cf. R. Horsley, "The Law of Nature in Philo and Cicero," HTR 71:1-2 (1978), p. 37.

[21] An argument quite probably of Stoic origin, according to the opinion of R. Horsley, based on observing its explicit or implicit presence in authors such as Arius Didymus and Dio Chrysostomus, sustaining that "there was a well-established common tradition concerning the Law of nature upon which both Cicero and Philo ... depend" (Ibid., p. 38-40). But for Philo that constitution is literally concretized in the Law of Moses, "which is distinguished from all conventional laws by its universality, its definitive character and its eternal nature" (Nikiprowetzky, *Le Commentaire de l'Écriture*, p. 122). As suggested in the note, see *Mos.* II, 12-41). It is a copy of the cosmic law, and perfect image of the ὀρθὸς λόγος as some assert; but it is also legitimately and indisputably the Law of nature and the Law of God, by virtue of the fact that God was its author (Ibid., p. 126-131).

[22] Cicero, *De Legibus* I, 23; *De Republica* 3, 33. Philo, *Opif.* 143. Also in Philo: ὁ τῆς φύσεως ὀρθὸς λόγος (Ibid.), ὁ τῆς φύσεως νόμος (*Mos.* II, 48).

[23] Philo's etymologies are not necessarily scientific nor do they presuppose a good knowledge of the Hebrew language. Rather they are the result of consulting documents available at the time, relating to the etymology of proper names (Cf. Arnaldez, PM 1, p. 48; Nikiprowetzky, *Le Commentaire de l'Écriture*, p. 52).

[24] Cf. Laporte, PM 21, p. 12.

[25] Cf. *Rhetorica ad Herennium* II, 30.

ἡ μὲν γὰρ μεγαλόπολις ὅδε ὁ κόσμος ἐστὶ καὶ μιᾷ χρῆται πολιτείᾳ καὶ νόμῳ ἑνί· λόγος δέ ἐστι φύσεως προστακτικὸς μὲν ὧν πρακτέον, ἀπαγορευτικὸς δὲ ὧν οὐ ποιητέον· αἱ δὲ κατὰ τόπους αὗται πόλεις ἀπερίγραφοί τέ εἰσιν ἀριθμῷ καὶ πολιτείαις χρῶνται διαφερούσαις καὶ νόμοις οὐχὶ τοῖς αὐτοῖς, ἄλλα γὰρ παρ' ἄλλοις ἔθη καὶ νόμιμα παρεξευρημένα καὶ προστεθειμένα. αἴτιον δὲ τὸ ἄμικτον καὶ ἀκοινώνητον οὐ μόνον Ἑλλήνων πρὸς βαρβάρους ἢ βαρβάρων πρὸς Ἕλληνας, ἀλλὰ καὶ τὸ ἑκατέρου γένους ἰδίᾳ πρὸς τὸ ὁμόφυλον· εἶθ' ὡς ἔοικε τὰ ἀναίτια αἰτιώμενοι, καιροὺς ἀβουλήτους, ἀγονίαν καρπῶν, τὸ λυπρόγεων, τὴν θέσιν ὅτι παράλιος ἢ μεσόγειος ἢ κατὰ νῆσον ἢ κατὰ ἤπειρον ἢ ὅσα τούτοις ὁμοιότροπα, τἀληθὲς ἡσυχάζουσιν· ἔστι δ' ἡ πλεονεξία καὶ ἡ πρὸς ἀλλήλους ἀπιστία, δι' ἃς οὐκ ἀρκεσθέντες τοῖς τῆς φύσεως θεσμοῖς τὰ δόξαντα συμφέρειν κοινῇ τοῖς ὁμογνώμοσιν ὁμίλοις ταῦτα νόμους ἐπεφήμισαν.

> For this world is the Megalopolis or "great city," and it has a single polity and a single law, and this is the word or reason of nature, commanding what should be done and forbidding what should not be done. But the local cities which we see are unlimited in number and subject to diverse polities and laws by no means identical, for different peoples have different customs and regulations which are extra inventions and additions.
> The cause of this is the reluctance to combine or have fellowship with each other, shewn not only by Greeks to barbarians and barbarians to Greeks, but also within each of them separately in dealing with their own kin. And then we find them alleging causes for this which are no real causes, such as unfavourable seasons, want of fertility, poverty of soil or how the state is situated, whether it is maritime or inland or whether it is on an island or on the mainland and the like.
> The true cause they never mention, and that is their covetousness and mutual mistrusts, which keep them from being satisfied with the ordinances of nature, and lead them to give the name of laws to whatever approves itself as advantageous to the communities which hold the same views (§29-30).

Finally, the *complexio* (§31) is enthymematically articulated, bringing together the parts of the developed argument and establishing the probatory force of the sustained proposition.

ὥστε εἰκότως προσθῆκαι μᾶλλον αἱ κατὰ μέρος πολιτεῖαι μιᾶς τῆς κατὰ τὴν φύσιν· προσθῆκαι μὲν γὰρ οἱ κατὰ πόλεις νόμοι τοῦ τῆς φύσεως ὀρθοῦ λόγου, προσθήκη δέ ἐστι πολιτικὸς ἀνὴρ τοῦ βιοῦντος κατὰ φύσιν.

> Thus naturally particular polities are rather an addition to the single polity of nature, for the laws of the different states are additions to the right reason of nature, and the politician is an addition to the man whose life accords with nature (§31).

Faithful to the same argumentative model that appears in the *Rhetorica ad Herennium*, the commentator from Alexandria develops in *De Iosepho* 125-147 a rhetorical structure which is extremely persuasive and architectonically elaborated in order to prove that "the statesman is surely an interpreter of dreams." This argument reflects the skeptic tradition in its critique of tangible knowledge,[26] especially regarding the use of images and commonplaces. Yet it finally departs from that course when it opposes, by a radical pessimism, the vision of the statesman who embodies the mission of an

---

[26] Cf. Laporte, PM 21, p. 33-34.

authentic prophet of the true, as an interpreter of the "common dream that is the life of society,"[27] and as a parenetic guide of the man who, in search of the truth, is able to glimpse beyond τύχη the sovereign hand of divine providence.

This rich and suggestive literary unit is organized around the following basic structural enthymeme: that the statesman is an interpreter of dreams, because society's life is no more than a dream. Human life is unstable, the future always uncertain and the present full of confusion (§§127-142). For this reason the clear diagnosis of the statesman becomes necessary (§§143-147). Each part of the argumentative structure is integrated into the whole and logically subordinated to it, in order to progressively enliven and make homogeneous the total message. Each of the individual arguments helps establish the formulated principle and thereby influences the audience, both awakening and guiding its convictions and dispositions.

The *propositio* (§125), ὅτι ὁ πολιτικὸς πάντως ὀνειροκριτικός ἐστιν, presupposes not only a theory of the interpretation of dreams, already expressed in *De Somniis* I, 89 and II, 1-3,[28] but also the conviction that the political man is here understood as the wise man, capable of discerning the truth about things by the light of reason inspired by divine illumination (§110) and not by means of any other form of divination. Philo defines the true statesman as a man used to analyzing with exactness the great common and public dream of humanity—whether asleep or awake—in contrast to charlatans, and sophists, as condemnable for their inability to correctly interpret dreams as for their motives.[29]

However, if in this argumentative sequence the *propositio* is defined and explained by the *locus a contrario,* the *ratio* finds in analogical reasoning the formula best suited to its clarification and foundation.

ἐγὼ δ' ἐρῶ μηδὲν ὑποστειλάμενος, ὅτι ὁ πολιτικὸς πάντως ὀνειροκριτικός ἐστιν, οὐχὶ τῶν βωμολόχων οὐδὲ τῶν ἐναδολεσχούντων καὶ ἐνσοφιστευόντων ἐπὶ μισθῷ καὶ τὴν τῶν καθ' ὕπνον φαντασιῶν διάκρισιν ἀργυρισμοῦ πρόβλημα πεποιημένων, ἀλλὰ τὸν κοινὸν καὶ πάνδημον καὶ μέγαν ὄνειρον οὐ κοιμωμένων μόνον ἀλλὰ καὶ ἐγρηγορότων εἰωθὼς ἀκριβοῦν. ὁ δὲ ὄνειρος οὗτος, ὡς ἀψευδέστατα φάναι, ὁ τῶν ἀνθρώπων ἐστὶ βίος· ὡς γὰρ ἐν ταῖς καθ' ὕπνον φαντασίαις βλέποντες οὐ βλέπομεν καὶ ἀκούοντες οὐκ ἀκούομεν καὶ γευόμενοι ἢ ἁπτόμενοι οὔτε γευόμεθα οὔτε ἁπτόμεθα λέγοντές τε οὐ λέγομεν καὶ περιπατοῦντες οὐ περιπατοῦμεν καὶ ταῖς ἄλλαις κινήσεσι καὶ σχέσεσι χρῆσθαι δοκοῦντες

---

[27] Ibid., p. 37-38.
[28] "In which he adopts the classification of Posidonius," distinguishing "dreams where the interpreter enters in direct contact with the divinity, other where he only communicates with the universe or with the angels, and others which he decodes with the light of his reason only" (Laporte, PM 21, p. 37. Cf. Cicero, *De Diuinatione* I, 30, 64).
[29] Cf. *Ios.* 103-106; *Mos.* I, 92. Philo sometimes confuses Manticism with Sophisticism, describing the magical and divining processes both in terms of ἔντεχνος μαντική and μαγικὴ σοφιστεία (*Deter.* 38. Cf. É. Bréhier, *Les idées philosophiques,* p. 180-182).

190   CHAPTER FOUR

οὐδεμιᾷ τὸ παράπαν χρώμεθα—κεναὶ δ' εἰσὶ τῆς διανοίας πρὸς οὐδὲν ὑποκείμενον ἀληθείᾳ μόνον ἀναζωγραφούσης καὶ ἀνειδωλοποιούσης τὰ μὴ ὄντα ὡς ὄντα—, οὕτω καὶ τῶν παρ' ἡμῖν ἐγρηγορότων αἱ φαντασίαι τοῖς ἐνυπνίοις ἐοίκασιν· ἦλθον, ἀπῆλθον, ἐφάνησαν, ἀπεπήδησαν, πρὶν καταληφθῆναι βεβαίως ἀπέπτησαν.

But I will say quite plainly that the statesman is most certainly an interpreter of dreams, not one of the parasites, nor one of the praters who shew off their cleverness for hire and use their art of interpreting the visions given in sleep as a pretext for making money; but one who is accustomed to judge with exactness that great general universal dream which is dreamt not only by the sleeping but also by the waking.

This dream in veriest truth is human life: for, just as in the visions of sleep, seeing we see not, hearing we hear not, tasting and touching we neither taste nor touch, speaking we speak not, walking we walk not, and the other motions which we make or postures we adopt we do not make or adopt at all, but they are empty creations of the mind which without any basis of reality produces pictures and images of things which are not, as though they were, so, too, the visions and imaginations of our waking hours resemble dreams. They come; they go; they appear; they speed away; they fly off before we can securely grasp them (§§125b-126);

This rationale is immediately corroborated by an argument from experience in the *confirmatio* (§§127-129), to complete the basic structure that constitutes, so to speak, the primary proof of the whole *argumentatio*.

ἐρευνησάτω δ' ἕκαστος αὐτὸν καὶ τὸν ἔλεγχον οἴκοθεν ἄνευ τῶν παρ' ἐμοῦ πίστεων εἴσεται, καὶ μάλιστ' εἴ τις πρεσβύτερος ἤδη γεγονὼς τυγχάνοι· οὗτος ἦν ὁ ποτὲ βρέφος καὶ μετὰ ταῦτα παῖς, εἶτ' ἔφηβος, εἶτα μειράκιον, καὶ νεανίας αὖθις, εἶτ' ἀνήρ, καὶ γέρων ὕστατον. ἀλλὰ ποῦ πάντ' ἐκεῖνα; οὐκ ἐν μὲν παιδὶ τὸ βρέφος ὑπεξῆλθεν, ὁ δὲ παῖς ἐν παρήβῳ, ὁ δ' ἔφηβος ἐν μειρακίῳ, τὸ δὲ μειράκιον ἐν νεανίᾳ, ἐν ἀνδρὶ δ' ὁ νεανίας, ἀνὴρ δ' ἐν γέροντι, γήρᾳ δ' ἕπεται τελευτή; τάχα μέντοι τάχα καὶ τῶν ἡλικιῶν ἑκάστη παραχωροῦσα τοῦ κράτους τῇ μεθ' ἑαυτὴν προαποθνήσκει, τῆς φύσεως ἡμᾶς ἀναδιδασκούσης ἡσυχῇ μὴ δεδιέναι τὸν ἐπὶ πᾶσι θάνατον, ἐπειδὴ τοὺς προτέρους εὐμαρῶς ἠνέγκαμεν, τὸν βρέφους, τὸν παιδός, τὸν ἐφήβου, τὸν μειρακίου, τὸν νεανίου, τὸν ἀνδρός, ὧν οὐδεὶς ἔτ' ἐστὶ γήρως ἐπιστάντος.

Let every man search into his own heart and he will test the truth of this at first hand, with no need of proof from me, especially if he is now advanced in years. This is he who was once a babe, after this a boy, then a lad, then a stripling, then a young man, then a grown man and last an old man. But where are all these gone? Has not the baby vanished in the boy, the boy in the lad, the lad in the stripling, the stripling in the youth, the youth in the man, the man in the old man, while on old age follows death?

Perhaps, indeed, each of the stages, as it resigns its rule to its successor, dies an anticipatory death, nature thus silently teaching us not to fear the death which ends all, since we have borne so easily the earlier deaths:—that of the babe, of the boy, of the lad, of the stripling, of the man, who are all no more when old age has come (§§127-129).

Undoubtedly conscious of the fact that the nature and relevance of the theme suggests a more solid and effective substantiation, in the *exornatio* (§§130-142) Philo prolongs this fundamental nucleus of argumentation with the evident purpose of conferring on it the amplitude, foundation and balance necessary to a consequent, finished and incontrovertible demonstration. This is not merely to adorn the presentation, but especially to enrich it by means of additional arguments that work harmoniously, unite logical and psychological appeal, and promote its dynamic as well as its persuasive efficacy.

By means of a consistent and homogeneous progression of argumentation, the *exornatio* reconsiders in the *simile* (§§130-131) the analogical reasoning first considered in the *ratio*, and confirmatorially supports it in the *exemplum* (§§132-133), *sententia* (§134) and *amplificatio* (§§135-142). The comparison of physical and material goods to a dream calls attention to the ephemeral character of beauty, the fragility of health, the inconstancy of strength and the unreliability of the senses, as well as the uncertainty and instability of riches, honor and power. The stories of Dionysius of Corinth and Croesus of Lydia are presented as illustrations of the state of uncertainty and insecurity of human life in general. The *sententia* perfectly summarizes the theme in focus, sustaining the truth expressed with the authority of popular wisdom, and climactically closing the generalization begun by the specific examples.[30] This also suggests a new chain of *testimonia* in the *amplificatio*, which attest not only the inconsistency of the human τύχη but also the contrast between the disorder of earthly things and the order and stability of the heavenly (§145).[31] First, Philo mentions the cases of Egypt and Macedonia, by the *locus a contrario* (§135). Then, he cites those of Ptolemies and the successors of Alexander, of independent cities and nations, of vassals, of Persians and Parthians, by the *interrogatio* (§136). Finally, in the *a contrario* argument (§§137-139) he speaks of persons who expect radiant futures but instead reap misfortunes and calamities, or vice-versa; of athletes who suffer defeat when they are confident of winning, and of those who are surprised by victory when they expect to lose; of travelers who shipwreck in summer but arrive at their destination safely in winter; and of merchants who at times full of confidence hasten into ruinous business deals, and of others, who, without reason for hope, achieve great gain.

The argumentative structure reaches a climax in a series of metaphors for the uncertainty and fleetingness of life. Philo offers two pairs of analogies symmetrically related to this dual dialectic reality: images of a scale with unequal weights and of deep sleep (§140), followed by images of a procession and the impetuous torrent of winter rains (§141).

---

[30] The *sententia* is currently viewed with suspicion, but in the classical and Hellenistic period it was a powerful method of argumentation (cf. W. J. Brandt, *The Rhetoric of Argumentation* [Indianapolis: Bobbs-Merrill, 1970], p. 125).

[31] All of the literary themes considered here—vanity and the uncertainty of human things, the inconstancy of the ψυχή, the confusion, insecurity and disorder of the world—are Hellenistic commonplaces that according to the observation of R. P. Festugière go back to the fourth century B.C. and are directly or indirectly linked to Aristotle's *Protrepticus* (*Frag.* 59R).

As an affective phenomenon involving intensification and probatory consolidation, the *amplificatio* gradually and cumulatively enables the reader/listener to grasp intellectually and accept emotionally the essence of Philo's message. He is maintaining that we live as in a dream, ignorant of reality, deceived by confidence in the infallibility of our reason, and seduced by senses that not only mislead the intelligence but also confuse and impede the soul from walking upright in the full exercise of its faculties (§142).

In keeping with this, the *complexio* (§143) summarizes the main thesis, explaining not only the true statesman's need to diagnose the dreams and visions of his subjects but also his need to demonstrate persuasively the truth pertinent to each case:

> ὅτι τοῦτο καλόν, ἐκεῖνο αἰσχρόν, τοῦτο ἀγαθόν, κακὸν ἐκεῖνο, τουτὶ δίκαιον, ἄδικον τοὐναντίον, καὶ τἄλλα ταύτῃ, τὸ φρόνιμον, τὸ ἀνδρεῖον, τὸ εὐσεβές, τὸ ὅσιον, τὸ συμφέρον, τὸ ὠφέλιμον, καὶ πάλιν τὸ ἀνωφελές, τὸ ἀλόγιστον, τὸ ἀγεννές, τὸ ἀσεβές, τὸ ἀνόσιον, τὸ ἀσύμφορον, τὸ βλαβερόν, τὸ φίλαυτον
>
> that this is beautiful, that ugly, this just, that unjust, and so with all the rest; what is prudent, courageous, pious, religious, beneficial, profitable, and conversely what is unprofitable, unreasonable, ignoble, impious, irreligious, deleterious, harmful, selfish (§143b).[32]

The passage ends with a *conquestio* (§§144-147) marked by a hortatory tone and syllogistic reasoning, which sets forth the fundamentals of Philo's political thinking. By contrasting a dream with reality, αἴσθησις to ἐπιστήμη and δόξα to ἀλήθεια, the exegete of Alexandria expresses his confidence that behind the game of the τύχη one can glimpse the hand of providence in the governing of the world.[33] For if in human affairs, as well as in the universe generally, things governed by the canons of truth move in perfectly harmonious and symphonic order, while things darkened and ruled by false opinions lead to a lethargic and erratic sleepwalking, then the common man needs the oneirocritical intervention of the political man to move from one plane of existence to the other.

---

[32] Both the integration of the universal categories—τελικὰ κεφάλαια—of oratorical discourse in these two lists of values (cf. *Rhetorica ad Alexandrum* 1421b, 8-11; Theon, in E. C. F. Walz, *Rhetores Graeci* I, p. 212-216, 244-246) and the previous allusion to εἰκόσι στοχασμοῖς καὶ εὐλόγοις πιθανότησι suggest circularly the function of the political man, in contrast to that of the sophist mentioned in the beginning, as a wisely enabled philosopher-orator, whether in intellectually discerning the truth of things, or whether interpreting them and expounding them psychagogically. It is a doctrine certainly inspired by the real Hellenistic ideal "prefigured in the portrait of the good tyrant and in the platonic conception of the king who possesses a superior nature and achieves a joyful obedience on the part of his subjects through persuasion" (J. Laporte, PM 21, p. 30).

[33] *Deus* 173-177. Cf. Laporte, PM 21, p. 35.

5. *De Sobrietate* 2-16

This section is one more example of the diverse ways in which Philo avails himself of rhetorical τέχνη to give consistency and direction to his exegetical writings. The text suggests the theme, and the theme gives birth to a thesis, always, however, in the context of a system of convictions or concerns and generally in harmony with a formal principle of organization.

The basic text (Genesis 9:24) is rhetorically decoded and interpreted in relation to two distinctive themes: that of sobriety and that of "youth" (allegorically understood in the order of moral values). The first is achieved by formulating two interrelated but brief arguments on the extreme usefulness of sobriety as much for the body as for the soul. One, enthymematically structured (§2), is complemented by the *locus a contrario* to prove that sobriety is the best thing for the body since it assures health and a clear perception of material realities. The other, articulated in the form of a *ratiocinatio* (§3-5) inspired by the *locus a minore ad maius*, is psychologically animated by the *interrogatio* in each of its premises, and closes with an analogy that, once enunciated, is equally structured and explained syllogistically. Philo proceeds to demonstrate the transcendent value of the sobriety of the soul, which assures "a lucid spirit, clear thoughts and an exact sense of duty."[34]

The second theme (§§6-16) is treated by the amplified argumentation of the topic that the word νεώτερον suggests here the disposition of a character which is unstable and ready to rebel,[35] regardless of the age or physical vigor of the person. Curiously, however, its probatory structure is now framed within the plane of the *absolutissima argumentatio* of the *auctor ad Herennium*.

The truth of the *propositio* is strategically tested and sustained in the *ratio* by combining two figures of particular argumentative force: the *interrogatio* and the enthymeme. Actually the correct Aristotelian form of the latter only becomes apparent in the extended question (§6b):

ἐπεὶ πῶς ἂν ἢ τὰ ἀθέατα κατιδεῖν παρὰ νόμον καὶ δίκην ἐβιάσατο ἢ ἐκλαλῆσαι τὰ ὀφείλοντα ἡσυχάζεσθαι ἢ εἰς τοὐμφανὲς προενεγκεῖν τὰ δυνάμενα οἴκοι συσκιάζεσθαι καὶ τοὺς ψυχῆς ὅρους μὴ ὑπερβαίνειν, εἰ μὴ νεωτέρων πραγμάτων ἥπτετο γελῶν τὰ ἑτέροις συμπίπτοντα, δέον ἐπιστένειν καὶ μὴ χλευάζειν ἐφ' οἷς εἰκὸς ἦν καὶ εὐλαβούμενον τὸ μέλλον σκυθρωπάζειν;

For how could Ham thus roughly defying custom and right have looked where he should not look, or how could he loudly proclaim what ought to be passed in silence, or expose to public view what might well be hidden in the secrecy of the home and never pass the boundaries of his inward thoughts, if he had not set his hand to deeds of defiance, if he

---

[34] J. Gorez, PM 11-12, p. 123.
[35] Νεωτεροποιία δὲ ἀγαπῶντος ἐμφαίνει τρόπου διάθεσιν.
 "but suggests the tendency of the temperament which loves rebelliousness and defiance."

had not mocked at the troubles of another, when he should rather bewail, instead of jeering at sights which call for the gloomy face that dreads the worse to come (§6b)?

Ham is a "νεώτερος" because his behavior is the "sign of a spirit of juvenile revolt."[36]

Such an interpretation is further confirmed by the fact that Moses was accustomed to calling immature persons of advanced age "νέοι," and to calling "πρεσβύτεροι" mature individuals who were physically young.

οὐκ εἰς πολυετίαν ἀφορῶν ἢ βραχὺν καὶ μήκιστον χρόνον, ἀλλ' εἰς ψυχῆς δυνάμεις κινουμένης εὖ τε καὶ χεῖρον·

for he does not consider whether the years of men are many or few, or whether a period of time is short or long, but he looks to the faculties of the soul whether its movements are good or ill (§7b).

The arguments that follow in the *exornatio*, to support and substantiate the truth expressed in these first elements of proof, are predominantly made up of examples taken from the epic history of the origins of the Israelite people. It could almost be said that the two central units of this complex *argumentatio* correspond, in their grand structural lines, to one of the most eloquent and effective schemes of probatory reasoning proposed and defended by Aristotle—that in which the ἐνθύμημα and the παράδειγμα converge as elements which produce an elaborate and developed rhetorical demonstration.[37]

Although one example is generally sufficient, it does not surprise us that in this case Philo uses a series of them. Multiple examples are not, in fact, uncommon in Hellenistic literature. Whenever the several paradigms are logically integrated into a line of argumentation and add to the development of the theme, they are rhetorically acceptable and even desirable.[38] In this case the examples not only satisfy those conditions but also are contextually justified. They lead into arguments contained in the *exornatio* of the argumentative structure, as conceived and set forth by the *auctor ad Herennium*.

Curiously, also, each of the examples is related to its opposite,[39] in order to reveal in direct progression the defining character traits of the νεώτερος as opposed to the πρεσβύτερος.

---

[36] Gorez, PM 11-12, p. 123.

[37] *Rhetorica* II, 20, 1394a 9-18. Aristotle concludes his treatment of the "example" counselling that whenever the orator makes use of enthymemes and examples he should place his examples after the enthymemes, so that the latter provide the evidence for the truth expressed and defended in the former.

[38] Cf. B. L. Mack, "Decoding the Scripture: Philo and the Rules of Rhetoric," essay presented at the first *Seminar on Philo, Society of New Testament Studies* (Canterbury, England, August, 1983), p. 34.

[39] Cf. Lausberg, *Manual de Retórica Literaria*, §395-397 and 420, 2-3.

In his first example (§7-9), adopting the literary form of a *narratio*,[40] Philo explains that Ishmael is called παιδίον at twenty years of age because, by comparison with his much younger brother (τὸν ἐν ἀρεταῖς τέλειον Ἰσαάκ) he was only a sophist.

> ἀλλ' ὅμως παιδίον νεανίας ὢν ἤδη καλεῖται ὁ σοφιστὴς ἀντεξεταζόμενος σοφῷ·
>
> Still all the same, grown up as he was, he is called a child, thus marking the contrast between the sophist and the sage (§9a).

In addition, Philo confirms this exegetical inference by means of the elaboration of a fairly suggestive and revealing *simile per contrarium* (§9b):

> σοφίαν μὲν γὰρ Ἰσαάκ, σοφιστείαν δὲ Ἰσμαὴλ κεκλήρωται, ὡς, ἐπειδὰν ἑκάτερον χαρακτηρίζωμεν, ἐν τοῖς ἰδίᾳ λόγοις ἐπιδείκνυμεν. ὃν γὰρ ἔχει λόγον κομιδῇ νήπιον παιδίον πρὸς ἄνδρα τέλειον, τοῦτον καὶ σοφιστὴς πρὸς σοφὸν καὶ τὰ ἐγκύκλια τῶν μαθημάτων πρὸς τὰς ἐν ἀρεταῖς ἐπιστήμας.
>
> For wisdom is Isaac's inheritance and sophistry Ishmael's, as we propose to shew in the special treatise, when we deal with the characteristics of the two. For the mere infant bears the same relation to the full-grown man as the sophist does to the sage, or the school subjects to the sciences which deal with virtues (§9b).

Based directly on the authority of the "great canticle,"[41] the second example (§§10-11) has the force of a κρίσις, μαρτυρία or *res iudicata*,[42] indicating that such terms do not apply just to isolated individuals. All Israelites are called τέκνα when, in revolt against God, they tread the road of insanity and perversity, exhibiting infantile behavior (§11).

> οὐκοῦν τέκνα ἐναργῶς ὠνόμακε τοὺς μώμους ἔχοντας ἄνδρας ἐν ψυχῇ καὶ μωρίᾳ καὶ ἀνοίᾳ τὰ πολλὰ σφαλλομένους ἐν ταῖς κατὰ τὸν ὀρθὸν βίον πράξεσιν, οὐκ εἰς τὰς ἐν παισὶ σώματος ἡλικίας ἀπιδών, ἀλλ' εἰς τὸ τῆς διανοίας ἀλόγιστον καὶ πρὸς ἀλήθειαν βρεφῶδες.
>
> We see clearly that he has given the name of "bairns" or "children" to men within whose souls are grounds for blame, men who so often fall through folly and senselessness and fail to do what the upright life requires. And in this he had no thought of literal age in the sense in which we use it of the bodies of the young, but of their truly infantine lack of a reasonable understanding (§11).

---

[40] Ibid., §415.

[41] Ὠδὴ μείζων is here the designation of the "major song" of Moses (Deut. 32) in contrast with his "minor song" (Ex. 15).

[42] "In a forensic case the citation of authorities functioned as precedent judgments or decisions. In the speech in support of a thesis the citations were still called 'judgments' (κρίσις) or 'witnesses' (μαρτυρία), but the authorities were taken from the canons of literature and philosophy, not law" (Mack, "Decoding the Scripture," p. 19). As B. Mack adds, "the purpose of the citation was to confirm the truth of the developed proposition by showing that recognized authorities had said much the same thing." And no literary or philosophical authority could be compared, in Philo's view, to the inspired authority of the πάνσοφος (*Cher.* 121; *Deter.* 126, etc.) and ἱερώτατος (*Leg.* II, 185; *Cher.* 45, etc.) Μωυσῆς.

In the third example (§12a), Philo takes the fact that Rachel was considered "younger" than Leah as additional evidence to prove the thesis that the νεώτερος also means to be inferior in perfection. In effect, Rachel is physical beauty, perishable and bound to the reality of the senses, while Leah is the immortal beauty of the soul.

This point is further substantiated by the example of Joseph (§12b-15), always called νέος and νεώτατος because he remained attached to the faculties of the body[43] and not having fully reached the perfect good of an adult soul (§13a).

οὗτος δέ ἐστιν ὁ τῆς περὶ τὸ σῶμα ἁπάσης ὑπέρμαχος δυνάμεως καὶ ὁ τῆς τῶν ἐκτὸς ἀφθονίας ἀκολάκευτος ἑταῖρος, ὁ τῆς πρεσβυτέρας ψυχῆς πρεσβύτερον καὶ τιμιώτερον ἀγαθὸν μήπω τέλειον εὑρημένος. εἰ γὰρ εὕρητο, κἂν ὅλην Αἴγυπτον ἀμεταστρεπτὶ φεύγων ᾤχετο·

Now Joseph is the champion of bodily ability of every kind, and the staunch and sincere henchman of abundance in external things, but the treasure which ranks in value and seniority above these, the seniority of the soul, he has never yet gained in its fullness. For if he had gained it, he would have fled quite away from the length and breadth of Egypt, and never turned to look back (§13a).

In the amplification of this final paradigmatic argument (§§14-15), the Alexandrian describes the character of Joseph by degrees based on the two levels of behavior suggested by the terms νέος and νεώτερος. He observes that in it are concentrated the defects of the three former ones, but then in a hortatory way visualizes its return to a more adult way of thinking, to moral beauty and to the disinterested love of virtue.

νέος μὲν οὖν τρόπος ὁ μήπω δυνάμενος μετὰ τῶν γνησίων ἀδελφῶν ποιμαίνειν, τὸ δ' ἐστὶ τῆς κατὰ ψυχὴν ἀλόγου φύσεως ἄρχειν τε καὶ ἐπιτροπεύειν, ἀλλ' ἔτι μετὰ τῶν νόθων, (οἷς τῶν ἀγαθῶν) τὰ δοκήσει πρὸ τῶν γνησίων καὶ τῷ εἶναι παραριθμουμένων τετίμηται. νεώτατος δέ, κἂν ἐπίδοσιν καὶ αὔξησιν πρὸς τὸ ἄμεινον λάβῃ, παρὰ τῷ τελείῳ νενόμισται μόνον ἀγαθὸν ἡγουμένῳ τὸ καλόν· οὗ χάριν προτρέπων φησί· "πρὸς μὲ ἀνάστρεψον," ἴσον τῷ πρεσβυτέρας γνώμης ὀρέχθητι, μὴ πάντα νεωτέριζε, ἤδη ποτὲ τὴν ἀρετὴν δι' αὑτὴν μόνην στέρξον, μὴ καθάπερ παῖς ἀφρων τῇ τῶν τυχηρῶν λαμπρότητι περιαυγαζόμενος ἀπάτης καὶ ψευδοῦς δόξης ἀναπίμπλασο.

The "young" disposition, then, is one which cannot as yet play the part of shepherd with its true-born brothers, that is, rule and keep guard over the unreasoning element in the soul, but still consorts with the base-born, who honour as goods such things as are good in appearance rather than the genuine goods which are reckoned as belonging to true existence.

---

[43] Setting aside *De Iosepho* Philo, perhaps constrained by his own allegorical schema, does not seem to give to the figure of Joseph the treatment that the book of Genesis inspires. Joseph is generally the politician who, moving in ambiguity, attempts to reconcile two worlds (*Migr.* 158-162), accommodating himself to both and suffering the influence of human ambition (*Migr.* 163). Living in Egypt, a type of the body and its passions, and not desirous of leaving it, he becomes easy prey of passion and pleasure (*Deus* 111). Cf. J. W. Earp, "Index of Names," *Philo*, PLCL, X, p. 351-356.

And "youngest" too this youth is held to be, even though he has received improvement and growth to something better, when compared with the perfect or full-grown mind which holds moral beauty to be the only good. And therefore Jacob uses words of exhortation: "return to me," he says, that is, desire the older way of thinking. Let not your spirit in all things be the spirit of restless youth. The time is come that you should love virtue for its own sake only. Do not like a foolish boy be dazzled by the brightness of fortune's gifts and fill yourself with deceit and false opinion (§14-15).

Philo's *complexio* concludes this rhetorical unit, synthesizing it and pointing out its ethical implications (§16a).

ὡς μὲν τοίνυν πολλαχοῦ νέον οὐκ εἰς τὴν σώματος ἀκμήν, ἀλλ' εἰς τὴν ψυχῆς νεωτεροποιίαν ἀφορῶν εἴωθε καλεῖν, ἐπιδέδεικται.

We have shown, then, that it is Moses' wont in many places to call a person young, thinking not of his bodily vigour, but only of his soul, and the spirit of rebelliousness which it displays.

Since the beginning and the end correspond as much by thematic vocabulary as by antithetical structures, the *inclusio* of paragraphs 6 and 16 is here more than a merely decorative figure.[44] It captures and pedagogically excites the attention of the reader, while at the same time animating and completing the argumentative circuit.

6. *De Posteritate Caini 100-111*

Rhetoric, sophistry, philosophy and wisdom are themes that permeate Philo's works. They are micro-themes that reflect a culture, a rhetorical-philosophical problem and a single exegetical intention. All of them are framed in or inspired by a wider basic ideological structure, and they are coherently organized around the predominant thematic of his commentary —that of a spiritual journey, the migration from the tangible to the intelligible, from the material to the spiritual, from the human to the divine.[45] Each one of them, however, assumes distinct textual or contextual configurations when observed from different visual angles or oriented to illuminate some special exegetical motive, although each is persistently faithful to that implicit system.[46]

In this, our final example of argumentation in support of a thesis, Philo touches on precisely four questions which have been raised, semantically linking them with the royal road to the divine. Genuine and true philosophy is here the discourse and word of God—θεοῦ ῥῆμα καὶ λόγον. This discourse

---

[44] On the use of this figure in Philo, see J. Cazeaux, *De Congressu*, p. 191.
[45] Cf. Nikiprowetzky, *Le Commentaire de l'Écriture*, p. 238-239.
[46] Cf. J. Cazeaux, "Système implicite dans l'exégèse de Philon, un exemple: le *De Praemiis*," *Studia Philonica* 6 (1979-1980), p. 3, see note, p. 34.

is set in contrast, not to a valid rhetoric, but to its corrupt and sophistic falsification that, emphasizing outward appearance, neglects the deep truth of things and seeks its audience's adherence to mere opinions. It is consequently a philosophy identical to rhetoric, understood as a technical basis for divine oratory itself, because the text of the θεοῦ ῥῆμα is a text in which God speaks eloquently and persuasively. If to Plato the rhetoric worthy of the philosopher is that which can persuade even the gods, seeking the acceptance of true theses and not merely opinions,[47] then to Philo that rhetoric is divine philosophy itself embodied in words, the contemplation of the realities of nature, by means of inspired discourse.[48]

The basic biblical text is progressively elucidated by means of the formulation of four distinct arguments. The first three, briefer, interdependent and arranged in an orderly sequence, determine the theme suggested by the etymology of the name "Jubal"[49] and define it by demonstrating the nature of the "royal road," not only as authentic philosophy but also as the very word of God. The last argument is amply developed, through a logical and persuasively concatenated series of reflections on music and the human

---

[47] *Phaedrus* 273.
[48] Without disparaging Greek philosophy, Philo considers that "the *true* or *authentic philosophy*" is contained in the writings of Moses (Nikiprowetzky, *Le Commentaire de l'Écriture*, p.101).
[49] Arnaldez highlights that "the *De posteritate* is essentially based on the etymology of proper names." This is a process of analysis predominant in all of Philo's works, but "it is perhaps here that it has the most importance, for it appears to be the chief driving force of the exposition of ideas" (PM 6, p. 19). Biblical names are interpreted in his exegesis as aspects of human personality. S. Sandmel observes, in fact ("Philo's Knowledge of Hebrew: The Present State of the Problem," SP 5, 1978, p. 107), that "the personality, trait or quality ascribed to the person or the place is reached through the supposed meaning and etymology of the Hebrew name."

Faithful to contemporary practice, the Alexandrian commentator uses the etymologies that best serve his exegetical purposes. But this does not mean that they are necessarily of his authorship. Independent of the long-debated question of his degree of knowledge of the Hebrew language (cf. S. Sandmel, "Philo's Knowledge of Hebrew", p. 109; *Philo of Alexandria. An Introduction* [New York: Oxford University Press, 1979], p. 131-134), J. Kahn divided Philo's etymologies in seven distinct categories (PM 13, p. 19-20). A. Hanson, in a later study, ended up reducing them to three: (1) those clearly derived from Hebrew, (2) those tortuously derived from Hebrew, (3) and those so remotely derived from it that they hardly suggest some knowledge of the language, attributing to him only the final category, and proposing other sources for the first two ("Philo's Etymologies," *JTS* 18, 1967, p. 128-139). This opinion seems to be shared not only by J. Kahn and S. Sandmel ("Philo's Knowledge of Hebrew," SP 5, 1978, p. 109-110), but also by R. Cadiou who explicitly allows that Philo used a *notarikon* (*Dictionnaire de la Bible*, Suplement VII [Paris: Letouzey & Ané, 1966], p. 1290-1299), and R. Arnaldez. The latter equally underscores that as a rule the same arbitrarities are verified in them, "the same scorning of the demands of the language, the same liberty in the treatment of the words" that was noted among the Jews or Greeks of his time; and that "in order to defend Philo, scholars have often made reference to the disconcerting etymologies of the Cratylus, without taking into account those of the Alexandrian interpreters and glossators of Homer and Hesiod" (PM 1, p. 20).

voice, which are designed to prove conclusively the nature, importance and risks of rhetoric itself.

In the first argument (§100), we have the enthymematic explanation of the meaning of the name "Jubal," previously etymologically explained as "he who inclines toward different sides" and symbolically interpreted as ὁ κατὰ προφορὰν λόγος, who is by nature brother of the mind.[50]

> τὸν δὲ τοῦ μεταποιοῦντος νοῦ τὰ πράγματα λόγον μετακλίνοντα σφόδρα δεόντως ὠνόμασε· συμβαίνει γὰρ τρόπον τινὰ καὶ ἐπαμφοτερίζειν καθάπερ ἐπὶ πλάστιγγος ἀντιρρέπον ἢ ὥσπερ θαλαττεῦον σκάφος ὑπὸ πολλοῦ κλύδωνος πρὸς ἑκάτερον τοῖχον ἀποκλῖνον· βέβαιον γὰρ ἢ σταθηρὸν οὐδὲν ὁ ἄφρων λέγειν ἔμαθε.

It is a most appropriate name for the utterance of a mind that alters the make of things, for its way is to halt between two courses, swaying up and down as if on a pair of scales, or like a boat at sea, struck by huge waves and rolling towards either side. For the foolish man has never learned to say anything sure or well-grounded (§100).

Therefore Jubal is the figure of the language of the mind who modifies the nature of things, because, due to his lack of firmness and balance, he is accustomed to vacillating and hesitating between two tendencies or extremes. This picture is illustrated in the minor premise by analogical reasoning, by evoking the images of scales and a ship on a tempestuous sea.

In the second argument (§§101-102a), we have the parenetic demonstration of its opposite by the *ratiocinatio*. It is an epichirematic scheme of argumentation in which both premises are antithetically structured and the *approbatio* of the first is itself presented as justified by the enthymeme. It is also significant that the *assumptio* is organized in a chiasm of AB B'A' structure, to animate both style and meaning and to create the psychological atmosphere appropriate to the proof.

> Μωυσῆς δὲ οὔτ' εἰς δεξιὰ οὔτ' εἰς ἀριστερὰ οὐδ' ὅλως εἰς μέρη τοῦ γηίνου Ἐδὼμ ἀποκλίνειν οἴεται δεῖν, τῇ δὲ μέσῃ ὁδῷ παρέρχεσθαι, ἣν κυριώτατα καλεῖ βασιλικήν ... ἐπειδὴ γὰρ πρῶτος καὶ μόνος τῶν ὅλων βασιλεὺς ὁ θεός ἐστι, καὶ ἡ πρὸς αὐτὸν ἄγουσα ὁδὸς ἅτε βασιλέως οὖσα εἰκότως ὠνόμασται βασιλική.

---

[50] Λόγος προφορικός, as we have already noted, is a notion of Stoic influence (cf. *Deter.* 126-127), a notion according to which the thoughts and emotions originating in the νοῦς or the ψυχή by the λόγος ἐνδιάθετος are verbally expressed by means of the λόγος προφορικός.
Robert Sonkowsky purposefully observes that "the Stoics defined the λόγος προφορικός as φωνὴ διὰ γλώττης σημαντικὴ τῶν ἔνδον καὶ κατὰ ψυχὴν παθῶν (Porphyr., *De Abstin.* 3, 3);" that "it is possible to consider this conception as the background against which a shift of emphasis in rhetorical studies took place;" that "Plato and Aristotle emphasized 'psychology,' but Aristotle prepared the way to the study of the outward expressions of the ψυχή by briefly incorporating delivery into rhetoric. Theophrastus expanded delivery, and the Stoics followed him by including delivery in their rhetorical scheme" ("An Aspect of Delivery in Ancient Rhetorical Theory," in *Aristotle: The Classical Heritage of Rhetoric*, ed. K. V. Erickson [Metuchen, NJ: Scarecrow Press, 1974], p. 259).

A - ταύτην δ' ἡγοῦ φιλοσοφίαν,

B - οὐχ ἣν μέτεισιν ὁ νῦν ἀνθρώπων σοφιστικὸς ὅμιλος

B' - λόγων γὰρ οὗτοι τέχνας μελετήσαντες κατὰ τῆς ἀληθείας τὴν πανουργίαν σοφίαν ἐκάλεσαν ἔργῳ μοχθηρῷ θεῖον ἐπιφημίσαντες ὄνομα

A' - ἀλλ' ἣν ὁ ἀρχαῖος ἀσκητῶν θίασος διῆθλει, τὰς τιθασοὺς τῆς ἡδονῆς γοητείας ἀποστρεφόμενος, ἀστείως καὶ αὐστηρῶς χρώμενος τῇ τοῦ καλοῦ μελέτῃ.

Moses thinks that none ought to turn away either to the right or to the left or to the parts of the earthly Edom at all, but to go by along the central road, to which he gives the most proper title of the king's highway or royal road; for since God is the first and sole King of the universe, the road leading to Him, being a King's road, is also naturally called royal. This road you must take to be philosophy, not the philosophy which is pursued by the sophistic group of present-day people, who, having practised arts of speech to use against the truth, have given the name of wisdom to their rascality, conferring on a sorry work a divine title. No, the philosophy which the ancient band of aspirants pursued in hard-fought contest, eschewing the soft enchantments of pleasure, engaged with a fine severity in the study of what is good and fair (§101).

The real and authentic φιλοσοφία presented in this unit is the βασιλικὴ ὁδός, the middle road,[51] the certain and direct way,[52] the avenue of the king of the universe that leads to Him. It is not an intermediate road, as "a stage to be followed between a beginning point and an arrival point, perfection," but a just mean, understood in the Aristotelian sense of the term, "situé entre un excès et un défaut," as a standard to be constantly followed.[53]

The third argument (§102), which arises directly from the conclusion of the previous one and presupposes the first in the scriptural proof of authority, is likewise an enthymeme.

<u>τὴν βασιλικὴν γοῦν ταύτην ὁδόν</u>, ἣν ἀληθῆ καὶ γνήσιον ἔφαμεν εἶναι φιλοσοφίαν, ὁ νόμος καλεῖ θεοῦ ῥῆμα καὶ λόγον. γέγραπται γάρ· "οὐκ ἐκκλινεῖς ἀπὸ τοῦ ῥήματος οὗ ἐγὼ ἐντέλλομαί σοι σήμερον δεξιὰ οὐδὲ ἀριστερά" (Deut. 28:14). <u>ὥστε</u> ἐμφανῶς ἐπιδεδεῖχθαι ὅτι ταὐτόν ἐστι τῇ βασιλικῇ ὁδῷ τὸ θεοῦ ῥῆμα, εἴγε προτρέπει μήτ' ἀπὸ τῆς βασιλικῆς ὁδοῦ μήτ' ἀπὸ τοῦ ῥήματος, ὡς συνωνύμων ὄντων, ἀποκλίνοντας ὀρθῇ διανοίᾳ τὴν ἐπ' εὐθείας ἄγουσαν ἀτραπὸν μέσην τε καὶ λεωφόρον βαδίζειν.

This royal road then, which we have just said to be true and genuine philosophy, is called in the Law the utterance and word of God. For it is written "Thou shalt not swerve aside from the word which I command thee this day to the right hand nor to the left hand" (Deut. 28:14). Thus it is clearly proved that the word of God is identical with the royal road. He treats the two as synonymous, and bids us decline from neither, but with upright mind tread the track that leads straight on, a central highway (§102).

---

[51] Cf. *Deus* 159-165; *Migr.* 146.
[52] *Gig.* 64.
[53] Arnaldez, PM 6, p. 103, n. 4. Cf. A. Mosès, PM 8, p. 142-143, n. 2.

This first section or sequence of argumentation offers a probatory *gradatio* that leads into the following exegetical unit and in it reaches its climax. In effect, once the relationship of identity is confirmed between the βασιλικὴ ὁδός, the ἀληθὴς καὶ γνήσιος φιλοσοφία and the θεοῦ ῥῆμα καὶ λόγος, a relationship that in Philo seems to have an interior and spiritual meaning,[54] the Alexandrian returns to the basic text to decode allegorically its semantic nucleus.

Philo contrasts the divine word, supposedly equivalent to the inner λόγος of man (λόγος ἐνδιάθετος),[55] with the outer λόγος (προφορικός), represented by Jubal as the creator of musical instruments. It is a discourse articulated in words, and consequently inferior to the first; for just as the divine λόγος is, as "sacred discourse," but a shadow of God Himself, and as such, a formula inferior to God, so human discourse is no more than a corruptible imitation of the original model, born and preserved in the mind.[56] But it is nonetheless useful and necessary as long as it is consistent with the truth and honestly conforms to thought in the interpretation and sending forth of the message.

In this final *argumentatio* (§§103-111), when he proposes to justify the propriety of the title "father of music and of all musical instruments," attributed to the "uttered discourse" (τὸν γεγωνὸν λόγον), Philo effectively stresses the vulnerability of the rhetorical discipline. For this reason he presents that art in the *ratio* (§103b) as a simple imitation of the organs of sound created in animals by nature, and illustrates it in the *confirmatio* (§104) by analogical reasoning, describing the structure of the ear as a model for the construction of theaters in thriving cities; and he concludes that this same nature, in forming its living beings, sets a pattern for all musical instruments, which for that very reason are inferior to it.

The arguments that form the *exornatio* (§§105-111a) are thus an expansion and probatory enrichment of the first three. But this one likewise has the virtue of gradually highlighting the value and usefulness of well-articulated discourse. Here also, exalting analogical reasoning as a fundamental technique of persuasion, the commentator from Alexandria returns to the *locus a minore ad maius* to underscore comparatively the qualitative difference between the sound produced by wind and stringed instruments

---

[54] According to Bréhier, the λόγος is for the Alexandrian both "the power that directs the world (logos in the Stoic sense), as well as the divine word of revelation... this interior revealed speech that the pious person hears in the hidden depths of his soul and constitutes the instruction on divine matters, i.e. worship and philosophy'" (*Les idées philosophiques*, p. 101).

[55] "That interior word is identical to the divine λόγος revealed to the Wise," for intelligence, "en tant qu'intelligence du sage est gardienne 'des dogmes de la vertu' et des 'paroles de Dieu'" (Ibid., p. 103).

[56] §105. Cf. Bréhier, *Les idées philosophiques*, p. 102-104.

and the songs of nightingales and swans. He demonstrates in logical order, enthymematically through a lovely *simile per contrarium*, the superior excellence of the music produced by the human voice (§§105-106). Its power of harmonious articulation is manifest both in song and speech, attracting by its melody not only the ear but also the mind.

> ὅσα γοῦν αὐλοὶ καὶ λύραι καὶ τὰ παραπλήσια μελῳδοῦσι, τῆς ἀηδόνων ἢ κύκνων μουσικῆς τοσοῦτον ἀπολείπεται, ὅσον ἀπεικόνισμα καὶ μίμημα ἀρχετύπου παραδείγματος, φθαρτὸν εἶδος ἀφθάρτου γένους. τὴν μὲν γὰρ ἀνθρώπων μουσικὴν οὐδενὶ τῶν ἄλλων συγκρίνειν ἄξιον ἔχουσαν γέρας ἐξαίρετον, ᾧ τετίμηται, τὴν ἔναρθρον σαφήνειαν. τὰ μὲν γὰρ ἄλλα τῇ περὶ τὴν φωνὴν κλάσει χρώμενα καὶ ταῖς ἐπαλλήλοις τῶν τόνων μεταβολαῖς ἀκοὰς αὐτὸ μόνον ἡδύνει, ὁ δ' ἄνθρωπος, ὥσπερ πρὸς τὸ λέγειν, οὕτως καὶ πρὸς τὸ ᾄδειν ἀρθρωθεὶς ὑπὸ φύσεως ἑκάτερον, ἀκοήν τε καὶ νοῦν, ἐπάγεται, τὴν μὲν τῷ μέλει κηλῶν, τὸν δὲ τοῖς νοήμασιν ἐπιστρέφων.

> To show how true this is, I may mention that all the melodious sounds produced by wind- and stringed-instruments fall as far short of the music that comes from nightingales and swans, as a copy and imitation falls short of an original, or a perishable species of an imperishable genus. For we cannot compare the music produced by the human voice with that produced in any other way, since it has the pre-eminent gift of articulation, for which it is prized. For whereas the other kinds by use of the modulation of the voice and the successive changes of the notes can do no more than produce sound pleasing to the ear, man, having been endowed by nature with articulate utterance equally for speaking and for singing, attracts alike both ear and mind, charming the one by the tune, and gaining the attention of the other by the thoughts expressed (§§105-106).

The following analogy (§107) is strategically submitted to a careful symmetrical elaboration, in order to provide the definitive transition to the level of rhetorical discourse, and to sensitize the mind of the reader to the necessity of making the proper distinction between the sophist and the rhetorician-philosopher.[57] For, as he says, just as a musical instrument is tuneless in the hands of a person that does not understand music but, in the hands of a musician, produces the most beautiful harmonies, so the word is discordant when spoken by a perverse spirit but perfectly harmonious when uttered by a virtuous man. This idea is developed by the illustration of the lyre and similar instruments (§108a); but it is put in perspective by a final analogy which highlights the manifold ability of interpretive articulation[58] of the oratorical discipline (§108b).

---

[57] In fact, Philo seems to have in mind here the group of contemporary Sophists that he refers to in §101, individuals that exercised themselves in the arts of discourse in order to combat the truth, and that τὴν πανουργίαν σοφίαν ἐκάλεσαν ἔργῳ μοχθηρῷ θεῖον ἐπιφημίσαντες ὄνομα; this group is opposed, as is obvious, to the rhetorician-philosopher, "virtuously and austerely occupied with the study of that which is good, proportionate and beautiful."

[58] On the normal meaning of ἑρμηνεύς, ἑρμηνεύειν in Philo, see A. C. Thiselton ("The 'Interpretation' of Tongues: A New Suggestion in the Light of Greek Usage in Philo and Josephus," *JTS* 30, 1979, p. 18-24).

καὶ μὴν ὥσπερ ὄργανα κατὰ τὰς τοῦ μέλους ἀπείρους ὅσας κράσεις μεθαρμόττεται, οὕτως καὶ ὁ λόγος συνῳδός τις ἑρμηνεὺς πραγμάτων γινόμενος ἀμυθήτους λαμβάνει μεταβολάς.

Moreover, just as instruments are tuned to vary in accordance with the infinite number of combinations of the music which they have to give forth, so speech proves itself an harmonious interpreter of the matters dealt with and admits of endless variations (§108b).[59]

If analogical argumentation prevailed in the previous passages of the *exornatio*, in the *amplificatio* (§§109-111a) rhetorical interrogation predominates. However, it is always articulated and prolonged, descriptively or explanatorily, in antithetic structure, in order to allude, with evident persuasive force, to the fundamental qualities of style and to the various *loci*, whether *a persona* or *a re*, required by circumstances.[60]

τίς γὰρ ἂν ὁμοίως γονεῦσι καὶ τέκνοις διαλεχθείη, τῶν μὲν φύσει δοῦλος, τῶν δὲ γένει δεσπότης ὤν; τίς δ' ἂν ἀδελφοῖς καὶ ἀνεψιοῖς ἢ συνόλως τοῖς ἐγγὺς γένους καὶ μακρὰν οὖσιν; τίς δ' ἂν οἰκείοις καὶ ἀλλοτρίοις, ἢ πολίταις καὶ ξένοις, οὐ μικρὰς οὐδὲ τὰς τυχούσας ἢ φύσεως ἢ ἡλικίας ἔχουσι διαφοράς; πρεσβύτῃ γὰρ ἑτέρως ὁμιλητέον καὶ νέῳ, καὶ πάλιν ἐνδόξῳ καὶ ταπεινῷ, καὶ πλουσίῳ καὶ πένητι, καὶ ἄρχοντι καὶ ἰδιώτῃ, καὶ θεράποντι καὶ δεσπότῃ, γυναικί τε αὖ καὶ ἀνδρί, καὶ ἀτέχνῳ καὶ τεχνίτῃ. καὶ τί δεῖ τὰς τῶν προσώπων ἀμυθήτους ἰδέας καταλέγεσθαι, πρὸς ἃς ὁ λόγος τρεπόμενος ἄλλοτε ἀλλοῖα λαμβάνει σχήματα; καὶ γὰρ αἱ τῶν πραγμάτων ἰδιότητες τυποῦσιν αὐτὸν κατὰ τοὺς ἰδίους χαρακτῆρας· μεγάλα γὰρ καὶ μικρὰ ἢ πολλὰ ἢ ὀλίγα ἢ ἰδιωτικὰ ἢ δημόσια ἢ ἱερὰ καὶ βέβηλα ἢ ἀρχαῖα καὶ νέα οὐ τὸν αὐτὸν ἂν ἑρμηνεῦσαι τρόπον, ἀλλὰ τὸν ἑκάστοις ἐφαρμόζοντα τῷ πλήθει καὶ ἀξιώματι καὶ μεγέθει, τοτὲ μὲν ὑψηλὸν ἢ ἀρχαῖα καὶ νέα οὐ τὸν αὐτὸν ἂν ἑρμηνεῦσαι τρόπον, ἀλλὰ τὸν ἑκάστοις ἐφαρμόζοντα τῷ πλήθει καὶ ἀξιώματι καὶ μεγέθει, τοτὲ μὲν ὑψηλὸν αἴρων ἑαυτόν, τοτὲ δ' ἔμπαλιν συνάγων τε καὶ συστέλλων. παρέχουσι δ' ὥσπερ τὰ πράγματα καὶ τὰ πρόσωπα τῷ λόγῳ μεταβολάς, οὕτως καὶ αἱ τῶν γινομένων αἰτίαι καὶ οἱ τρόποι καθ' οὓς γίνεται, προσέτι μέντοι καὶ τὰ ὧν οὐκ ἄνευ πάντα, χρόνοι καὶ τόποι.

For who would talk in the same way to parents and children, being slave of the former by nature, and master of the latter in virtue of the same cause? Who would speak in the same way to brothers, cousins, near relatives generally, and to those only distantly connected with him? to those associated with him, and to those with whom he has nothing to do; to fellow-citizens and foreigners; to people differing in no slight or ordinary degree in nature or age? For we have to talk in one way to an old man, in another to a young one, and again in one way to a man of importance and in another to an insignificant person, and so with rich and poor, official and non-official, servant and master, woman and man, skilled and unskilled. What need to make a list of the innumerable sorts of persons, in our conversation with whom our talk varies, taking one

---

[59] F. H. Colson points out that in this section to the following Philo applies the rhetorical notion of the περιστάσεις (*circumstantiae*), which determines "the nature of language required in each occasion" (PLCL II, p. 388-389 and note, p. 500).

[60] Cf. Lausberg, *Manual de Retórica Literaria*, §376-399. As R. Arnaldez indicates (PM 6, p. 110, n. 1), F. Colson summarily refers to the stylistic qualities of πλῆθος, ἀξίωμα and μέγεθος. He also explicitly enumerates the six fundamental περιστάσεις ("ἀμυθέτους ... μεταβολάς"), technically represented in Latin rhetoric by questions such as *quis, quid, cur, quomodo, quando, ubi*, from which result the *loci a persona, a materia, a causa, a modo, a tempore, a loco*, etc. (PLCL II, p. 500, note to §108. Cf. Lausberg, *Manual de Retórica Literaria*, §377).

shape at one time, another at another? For indeed the same thing is true of subjects of thought. Their several peculiarities mould our language in conformity with their characteristic aspects; for it would not set forth great things and little, many and few, private and public, sacred and profane, ancient and modern, in the same style, but in the style suited to their respective number or importance or greatnesss; at one time rising to a lofty tone, at another restraining and holding itself in. Nor is it only persons and matters dealt with that occasion our speech to vary its form, but the causes too of the things that happen, and the ways in which they happen, and besides these, times and places which enter into all things (§§109-111a).

Once more inspired by the pattern of enunciation, substantiation and conclusion defended by the *auctor ad Herennium*, Philo inventively varies his micro-arguments and the way he presents them. He adapts them to the nature of the theme and the complexity of the material, but the basic structure prevails untouched.[61] The *complexio* (§111b), while announcing the closure of the argumentative unit by the *inclusio*, considers as demonstrated the thesis allegorically suggested by the basic text (Gen 4:21).

By means of a variety of argumentative structures—enthymeme, *ratiocinatio*, enthymeme and *argumentatio*[62]—the exegete from Alexandria finally seems to want to say, in the contextual environment of the doctrine expressed in his *corpus*, that the word of God is a consummate and authentic "philosophy," offering a wisdom that transcends even Greek philosophy,[63] one which constitutes the Royal Road which leads to the divine. As revelation, its language should rigorously agree with the linguistic articulation of thought.[64] Human rhetoric is a replica and imitation of the original model, a corruptible species of an incorruptible genre, susceptible to detours, but useful and necessary for the harmonious "interpretation" of the reality of things.

II. *In the Elaborate Development of a Theme*

1. *Quod Deterius Potiori Insidiari Solet 34-45*

The discipline of rhetoric is so important to Philo that, in keeping with his constant use of it as a valid technique of expression and exegesis, he devotes significant space to theorizing about it directly. In commending a rhetoric worthy of a philosopher, which as an instrument of thought and not a

---

[61] Cf. *De Inuentione* I, 34, 58ff. on the liberties granted to the orator.
[62] The *absolutissima et perfectissima argumentatio* of *Rhetorica ad Herennium*.
[63] Cf. D. Winston in his answer to T. Conley, "General Education in Philo of Alexandria." PCCHS 15 (1975), p. 19.
[64] Cf. Klaus Otte, *Das Sprachverständnis bei Philo von Alexandrien: Sprache als Mittel der Hermeneutik* (Tübingen: Mohr, 1968); É. Bréhier, *Les idées philosophiques*, p. 103-107. Language is generally understood by Philo as the outward expression of rational ideas, presupposing a dualism between thought and language (Thiselton, "The 'Interpretation' of Tongues", p. 23-24).

substitute for thinking[65] will make a man a perfect master in the verbalization of the sublimest ideas,[66] he must dieretically oppose the ill-conceived rhetoric of the sophists.[67]

One of the best treatments of this theme is developed in *Quod Deterius* 34-45. It is a structurally complete unit in which the Alexandrian not only argues the need for a sound rhetorical education but also recommends the right use of the assimilated τέχνη. Inspired by the *tractatio* model recommended by the *auctor ad Herennium,* Philo describes the difficult situation in which good persons may find themselves when they lack the rhetorical art which is indispensable in the battle against the sophists.[68]

After having shown the symbolic sense of the controversy between Cain and Abel, as well as that of the challenge Abel inadvertently faced (§32), Philo focuses his attention on the theme of rhetoric, indicating its vital importance by indirectly arguing the thesis that every virtuous person who is gifted with wisdom also needs a solid education in that τέχνη. He notes that Cain represents the category of those who love themselves, who are talented in the formulation of specious arguments and always pursue their own interests. Abel, on the contrary, represents that less fortunate class of lovers of virtue who devote themselves only to the practice of the good, without ever having had a solid preparation in the τέχνας ... λόγων (§37).

In Philo's presentation, the *res,* the *ratio* and the *pronuntiatio* constitute the basic probatory unit. The *exemplum,* the *contrarium* and the *simile* furnish supporting arguments that enrich the demonstration of the thesis, which is summarized in circular form in the *conclusio* and there given a final substantiation in the suggestive example of Rebekah.

The *res* (§37a) enthymematically affirms that a better attitude on Abel's part would have led him to decline the challenge to a debate based on πιθανοῖς σοφίσμασιν (§1).[69]

---

[65] Cf. Bréhier, *Les idées philosophiques,* p. 289.
[66] *Congr.* 17.
[67] "It should be borne in mind that every praise of rhetoric is accompanied by a note of caution" (M. Alexandre, PM 16, p. 37). Cf. *Migr.* 72: πολλοὶ γὰρ λογίζονται μὲν τὰ βέλτιστα, ὑπὸ δὲ ἑρμηνέως κακοῦ προὐδόθησαν, λόγου, μουσικὴν τὴν ἐγκύκλιον οὐκ ἐκπονήσαντες· οἱ δὲ ἔμπαλιν ἑρμηνεῦσαι μὲν ἐγένοντο δυνατώτατοι, βουλεύσασθαι δὲ φαυλότατοι, καθάπερ οἱ λεγόμενοι σοφισταί·
'For many reason excellently, but find speech a bad interpreter of thought and are by it betrayed, through not having had a thorough grounding in the ordinary subjects of culture. Others, again, have shewn great ability in expounding themes, and yet been most evil thinkers, such as the so-called sophists'.
[68] Cf. *Deter.* 1-2. Cain, who challenges Abel, and the sophists, whom Moses fought in Egypt, certainly represent the many Alexandrian sophists, contemporaries of Philo, whom it was also important to denounce (*Deter.* 41).
[69] In his defense of an allegorical reading of Gen. 4:8a, Philo explains the assassination of Abel in terms of defeat in a test of eristic ability.

ὁ τοίνυν Ἄβελ τέχνας μὲν λόγων οὐκ ἔμαθε, διανοίᾳ δὲ μόνῃ τὸ καλὸν οἶδεν· οὗ χάριν τὴν εἰς τὸ πεδίον ἄφιξιν ἐχρῆν παραιτήσασθαι καὶ τῆς τοῦ δυσμενοῦς προκλήσεως ἀλογῆσαι·

Now Abel has never learned arts of speech, and knows the beautiful and noble with his mind only. For this reason he should have declined the meeting on the plain, and have paid no regard to the challenge of the man of ill-will (§37a).

The *ratio* (§37b) justifies the *res* by the *locus a minore ad maius* and the *pronuntiatio* (§37c) reaffirms the *res*, simultaneously confirming the *ratio* by the same topic.

ἥττης γὰρ πᾶς ὄκνος ἀμείνων· τὸν δὲ ὄκνον τοῦτον οἱ μὲν ἐχθροὶ δειλίαν, ἀσφάλειαν δ' οἱ φίλοι προσαγορεύουσι· φίλοις δὲ πρὸ δυσμενῶν ἅτε ἀψευδοῦσι πιστευτέον.

for any shrinking back as this, though our enemies call it cowardice, is called caution by our friends; and since they are free from falsehood, we should believe friends in preference to men who have ill-will towards us (§37b).

In a second phase, the example of Moses testifies not only to the prudence that should characterize virtuous persons who are not trained in oratory, but also to the urgency with which this training should be pursued. The spoken word is important as the sister of the mind and faithful "interpreter" of the message generated in it. An *a contrario* argument confirms the legitimate use of rhetoric, structuring in chiastic symmetry the principles illustrated in the example. In this double march from the specific to the general and back (Μωυσῆς ... τις ... Ἄβελ), Philo also argues that the rhetorical art is indispensable to the virtuous man as he faces the onslaughts of the sophists. But, as A. Mendelson observes, his primary objective is not to commend a superficial technique. It is rather to assure virtuous persons a correct "interpretation" of thought.[70]

A – οὐχ ὁρᾷς ὅτι <u>Μωυσῆς</u> τοὺς ἐν Αἰγύπτῳ τῷ σώματι σοφιστάς, οὓς φαρμακέας ὀνομάζει, παραιτεῖται—<u>σοφισμάτων γὰρ τέχναις</u> καὶ ἀπάταις ἤδη χρηστὰ τρόπον τινὰ φαρμακεύεται καὶ διαφθείρεται— φάσκων μὴ εἶναι "εὔλογος" (Exod. 4:10), <u>ἴσον τῷ μὴ πεφυκέναι πρὸς τὴν τῶν εὐλόγων καὶ πιθανῶν εἰκαστικὴν ῥητορείαν</u>, ἔπειθ' ἑξῆς διαβεβαιούμενος, ὅτι οὐ μόνον οὐκ εὔλογος ἀλλὰ καὶ παντελῶς "ἄλογός" ἐστιν (Exod. 6:12); ἄλογος δέ, οὐχ ὡς φαμεν τὰ μὴ λογικὰ τῶν ζῴων, ἀλλ' ὁ μὴ δικαιῶν τῷ διὰ τοῦ φωνητηρίου ὀργάνου γεγωνῷ λόγῳ χρῆσθαι, μόνῃ δὲ σημειούμενος καὶ ἐνσφραγιζόμενος διανοίᾳ τὰ τῆς ἀληθοῦς σοφίας, ἥτις ἀντίθετός ἐστι ψευδεῖ σοφιστείᾳ, θεωρήματα.

B – καὶ οὐ βαδιεῖται πρότερον εἰς Αἴγυπτον οὐδ' εἰς ἅμιλλαν ἀφίξεται τοῖς αὐτῆς σοφισταῖς, <u>πρὶν ἢ τὸν προφορικὸν ἄκρως ἀσκηθῆναι λόγον</u>, τὰς πρὸς ἑρμηνείαν ἁπάσας ἰδέας ἀναδείξαντος καὶ τελειώσαντος θεοῦ διὰ τῆς Ἀαρὼν χειροτονίας, ὃν ἀδελφὸν Μωυσέως ὄντα "στόμα" καὶ ἑρμηνέα καὶ "προφήτην" εἴωθε καλεῖν·

C – πάντα γὰρ ταῦτα <u>τῷ λόγῳ</u> συμβέβηκεν, ὃς ἀδελφός ἐστι <u>διανοίας·</u> πηγὴ γὰρ <u>λόγων διάνοια</u> καὶ στόμιον αὐτῆς <u>λόγος</u>, ὅτι τὰ ἐνθυμήματα πάντα διὰ

---

[70] *Secular Education in Philo of Alexandria* (Cincinnati: Hebrew Union College Press, 1982), p. 8.

τούτου καθάπερ νάματα ἀπὸ πηγῆς εἰς τοὐμφανὲς ἐπιρρέοντα ἀναχεῖται· καὶ ἑρμηνεύς ἐστιν ὧν ἐν τῷ ἑαυτῆς βουλευτηρίῳ βεβούλευκεν· ἔτι μέντοι καὶ προφήτης καὶ θεοπρόπος ὢν ἐξ ἀδύτων καὶ ἀοράτων χρησμῳδοῦσα οὐ παύεται.

Β' – Τοῦτον μὲν οὖν τὸν τρόπον ἐναντιοῦσθαι τοῖς περὶ τὰ δόγματα ἐριστικοῖς χρήσιμον· <u>γεγυμνασμένοι γὰρ περὶ τὰς τῶν λόγων ἰδέας οὐκέτ' ἀπειρίᾳ σοφιστικῶν παλαισμάτων ὀκλάσομεν</u>, ἐξαναστάντες δὲ καὶ διερεισάμενοι τὰς ἐντέχνους αὐτῶν περιπλοκὰς εὐμαρῶς ἐκδυσόμεθα. οἱ δ' ἅπαξ εὑρεθέντες σκιαμάχων ἀλλ' οὐκ ἀγωνιστῶν ἐπιδείκνυσθαι δόξουσι δύναμιν· καὶ γὰρ ἐκεῖνοι καθ' ἑαυτοὺς μὲν χειρονομοῦντες εὐδοκιμοῦσι, πρὸς δ' ἅμιλλαν ἐλθόντες οὐ μετρίως ἀδοξοῦσιν.

Α' – εἰ δέ τις τὴν μὲν ψυχὴν ἀρεταῖς ἁπάσαις κεκόσμηται, <u>τέχνας δὲ λόγων οὐκ ἐμελέτησεν</u>, ἡσυχίᾳ χρώμενος ἀσφάλειαν γέρας ἀκίνδυνον εὑρήσεται, παρελθὼν δ' ὡς <u>"Ἀβελ εἰς σοφιστικὸν ἀγῶνα</u> πρὶν διερηρεῖσθαι πεσεῖται.

A - Do you not see that Moses fights shy of the sophists in "Egypt," that is, in the body? He calls them "magicians" because good morals are spoiled by the tricks and deceptions of sophistry acting on them like the enchantments of magic. Moses' plea is that he is not "eloquent" [Exod. 4:10], which is equivalent to saying that he has no gift for the oratory which is but specious guesswork at what seems probable. Afterwards he follows this up by emphatically stating that he is not merely not eloquent but absolutely "speechless" [Exod. 6:12]. He calls himself "speechless," not in the sense in which we use the word of animals without reason, but of him who fails to find a fitting instrument in the language uttered by the organs of speech, and prints and impresses on his understanding the lessons of true wisdom, the direct opposite of false sophistry (§38).

B - And he will not go to Egypt nor engage in conflict with its sophists, until he has been fully trained in the word of utterance, God having shown and perfected all the qualities which are essential to expression of thought by the election of Aaron who is Moses' brother, and of whom he is wont to speak as his "mouth" and "spokesman" and "prophet" [Exod. 4:16; 7:1] (§39);

C - for all these titles belong to Speech or Word, which is brother of Mind. For mind is the fountain of words and speech is its outlet. For all the thoughts of the heart, like streams from a spring, well up and flow forth into the open through speech; and Speech is the expounder of the plans which Understanding has formed in its own council-chamber. Speech, moreover, is the spokesman and prophet of the oracles which the understanding never ceases to utter from depths unseen and unapproachable (§40).

B' - It will be well for us to counter in this manner those who are pugnacious over the tenets which they maintain; for when we have been exercised in the forms which words take, we shall no more sink to the ground through inexperience of the tricks of the sophistic wrestling, but we shall spring up and carry on the struggle and disentangle ourselves with ease from the grips which their art has taught them. And when we have once found them out, they will be seen to be exhibiting the prowess of men sparring for practice, not that of men engaged in a real combat. For they are boxers who win admiration in a mock encounter among themselves and are thought very little of when they engage in a match (§41).

A' - But if a man, though equipped in soul with all the virtues, has had no practice in rhetoric, so long as he keeps quiet he will win safety, a prize that entails no risk, but, when like Abel he steps out for a contest of wits, he will fall before he has obtained a firm footing (§42).

Rhetoric is in fact a valid study of persuasive communication. Each one of Philo's previous arguments leads to the same conclusion. His reader must be already convinced that, however wise and virtuous a person may be, he will inevitably fail if he lacks solid rhetorical education. But Philo is concerned to make this idea even more limpid and unmistakable. For this he uses an argument by analogy (§§43-44) soberly amplified, in order to highlight the pertinence of the former arguments and confirm the thesis they support.

<u>καθάπερ γὰρ ἐν ἰατρικῇ τινες</u> μὲν θεραπεύειν εἰδότες πάντα σχεδὸν πάθη καὶ νοσήματα καὶ ἀρρωστήματα λόγον οὐδενὸς αὐτῶν οὔτε ἀληθῆ οὔτ' εἰκότα ἀποδοῦναι δύνανται, <u>οἱ δ'</u> ἔμπαλιν τὰ μὲν περὶ λόγους εἰσὶ δεινοί, σημείων καὶ αἰτιῶν καὶ θεραπείας, ἐξ ὧν ἡ τέχνη συνέστηκεν, ἑρμηνεῖς ἄριστοι, τὰ δὲ πρὸς καμνόντων ἐπιμέλειαν σωμάτων φαυλότατοι, τῶν εἰς ἴασιν ἀλλ' οὐδὲ τὸ μικρότατον παρασχεῖν ἱκανοί, <u>τὸν αὐτὸν τρόπον</u> οἱ μὲν τῆς δι' ἔργων ἀσκηταὶ σοφίας πολλάκις λόγων ἠμέλησαν, <u>οἱ δὲ</u> τὰς ἐν λόγῳ τέχνας ἀναδιδαχθέντες οὐδὲν ἐν ψυχῇ παίδευμα καλὸν ἐθησαυρίσαντο. <u>τούτους μὲν οὖν</u> ἀχαλίνῳ κεχρημένους γλώττῃ μετ' αὐθαδείας θρασύνεσθαι παράδοξον οὐδέν, ἀπόνοιαν γὰρ ἦν ἐξ ἀρχῆς ἐμελέτησαν ἐπιδείκνυνται· <u>ἐκείνοις δ' ὥσπερ ἰατροῖς</u> τὸ ὑγιάζον τὰς ψυχῆς νόσους τε καὶ κῆρας ἀναδιδαχθεῖσι μέρος ἐπέχειν ἀναγκαῖον, μέχρις ἂν ὁ θεὸς καὶ τὸν ἄριστον ἑρμηνέα κατασκευάσῃ τὰς τοῦ λέγειν πηγὰς ἀνομβρήσας καὶ ἀναδείξας αὐτῷ.

For, just as in medicine there are some practitioners who know how to treat almost all afflictions and illnesses and cases of impaired health, and yet are unable to render any scientific account either true or plausible of any one of them; and some, on the other hand, who are brilliant as far as theories go, admirable exponents of symptoms and causes and treatment, the subject matter of the science, but no good whatever for the relief of suffering bodies, incapable of making even the smallest contribution to their cure: in just the same way, those who have given themselves to the pursuit of the wisdom that comes through practice and comes out in practice have often neglected expression, while those who have been thoroughly instructed in the arts that deal with speech have failed to store up in soul any grand lesson which they have learned. It is in no way surprising that these latter should discover an arrogant audacity in the unbridled use of their tongue. They are only displaying the senselessness which has all along been their study. Those others, having been taught, as doctors would be, that part of the art which brings health to the sicknesses and plagues of the soul, must be content to wait, until God shall have equipped in addition the most perfect interpreter, pouring out and making manifest to him the fountains of utterance (§§43-44).

The architectonic balance of this rich argumentative figure functions literarily to make his thesis more alive and convincing, aesthetically producing in the audience the greatest possible psychological impression and consequently making it more receptive to his message. In comparing rhetoric to medicine, and concomitantly making the distinction between practical and theoretical medicine, the Alexandrian commentator has no other objective than that of clarifying the relationship between wisdom and eloquence. Rhetorical argumentation is as necessary to logic as is clinical practice to medical theory. For it is by the discipline of language that thought is expressed and the mind is able to mold into intelligible form its most beautiful ideas. Without it, the philosopher would lose himself in a logomachy of abstract terms "that befog the masses and hide the truth under their fictions" (*Opif.* 1)."[71]

In the conclusion (§45), Philo finally returns to the particular case treated in the beginning. The thesis is demonstrated not only by the convergence of the arguments already presented; now it is concluded with an *inclusio,* and reinforced by the example of Rebekah.

> Σύμφορον οὖν ἦν εὐλαβείᾳ σωτηρίῳ ἀρετῇ χρησάμενον τὸν "Αβελ οἴκοι καταμεῖναι τῆς εἰς τὸν ἐριστικὸν καὶ φιλόνεικον ἀγῶνα προκλήσεως ἀλογήσαντα, μιμησάμενον 'Ρεβέκκαν τὴν ὑπομονήν, ἥτις ἀπειλοῦντος Ἡσαῦ τοῦ κακίας θιασώτου τὸν ἀρετῆς ἀσκητὴν Ἰακὼβ ἀποκτενεῖν ἀναχωρῆσαι τῷ μέλλοντι ἐπιβουλεύεσθαι παραγγέλλει, μέχρις ἂν ἐκεῖνος τῆς ἐπ' αὐτῷ σχετλίου λύττης ἀνῇ.

> It would have been well, then, for Abel to have exercised the saving virtue of caution, and to have stayed at home taking no notice of the challenge to the contest in wrangling. He should have imitated Rebecca, who represents patient waiting. When Esau, the votary of wickedness, threatens to murder Jacob, the devotee of virtue, she charges him against whom the plot was being hatched to go away, until Esau's cruel madness against him be allayed (§45).

2. *De Migratione Abrahami 70-82*

Dedicated to the same theme, this other passage recommends, in an even more incisive way, the cultivation of sound rhetoric, highlighting its philosophical character.

Within the account of the "gifts" bestowed on Abraham, eloquence is linked here, together with reason, with the fulfillment of the third divine promise: "καὶ εὐλογήσω σε." This exegetical derivation is possible only after a dual operation that involves the allegorical interpretation of the text as well as the etymological and dieretic clarification of the theme. Once the semantic transformation of the word εὐλογία is realized, based on the etymological topic,[72] the Alexandrian commentator divides the generic λόγος into its two species. Underlining its excellence (εὖ + λόγος) both in mental conceptualization and adequate linguistic verbalization, he begins as follows:

> λόγος δὲ ὁ μὲν πηγῇ ἔοικεν, ὁ δὲ ἀπορροῇ, πηγῇ μὲν ὁ ἐν διανοίᾳ, προφορὰ δὲ ἡ διὰ στόματος καὶ γλώττης ἀπορροῇ. ἑκάτερον δὲ εἶδος λόγου βελτιωθῆναι πολὺς πλοῦτος, διάνοιαν μὲν εὐλογιστίᾳ πρὸς πάντα μικρὰ καὶ μείζω χρωμένην, προφορὰν δὲ ὑπὸ παιδείας ὀρθῆς ἡνιοχουμένην.

> "Logos" has two aspects, one resembling a spring, the other its outflow; "logos" in the understanding resembles a spring, and is called "reason," while utterance by mouth and

---

[71] Cf. R. Arnaldez, "Les images du sceau et de la lumière dans la pensée de Philon d'Alexandrie," *L'Information Littéraire* XV (1963), p. 71. *Opif.* 1.

[72] The use of this topic is frequent in Philo, with the purpose of generating themes for exegetic and argumentative amplification.

tongue is like its outflow, and is called "speech." That each species of logos should be improved is vast wealth, the understanding having good reasoning at its command for all things great and small, and utterance being under the guidance of right training (§71).

The thesis enunciated in paragraph 71 affirms the necessity of these two species of λόγος perfecting themselves, each in its own way. This thesis is then argued in the *ratio* (§72) by the *locus a contrario* and confirmed in the *pronuntiatio* (§73) by exposure to the rhetorical values that constitute, according to Anaximenes,[73] the ethical foundation of all persuasive discourse. These are, namely, the topics founded universally in the categories of τὸ δίκαιον and of τὸ ἀναγκαῖον.

πολλοὶ γὰρ λογίζονται μὲν τὰ βέλτιστα, ὑπὸ δὲ ἑρμηνέως κακοῦ προὐδόθησαν, λόγου, μουσικὴν τὴν ἐγκύκλιον οὐκ ἐκπονήσαντες· οἱ δὲ ἔμπαλιν ἑρμηνεῦσαι μὲν ἐγένοντο δυνατώτατοι, βουλεύσασθαι δὲ φαυλότατοι, καθάπερ οἱ λεγόμενοι σοφισταί· τούτων γὰρ ἀχόρευτος μὲν καὶ ἄμουσος ἡ διάνοια, πάμμουσοι δὲ αἱ διὰ τῶν φωνητηρίων ὀργάνων διέξοδοι. χαρίζεται δὲ ὁ θεὸς τοῖς ὑπηκόοις ἀτελὲς οὐδέν, πλήρη δὲ καὶ τέλεια πάντα· διὸ καὶ νῦν τὴν εὐλογίαν οὐχ ἑνὶ λόγου τμήματι, τοῖς δὲ μέρεσιν ἀμφοτέροις ἐπιπέμπει δικαιῶν τὸν εὐεργετούμενον καὶ ἐνθυμεῖσθαι τὰ βέλτιστα καὶ ἐξαγγέλλειν τὰ νοηθέντα δυνατῶς· ἡ γὰρ τελειότης δι' ἀμφοῖν, ὡς ἔοικε, τοῦ τε ὑποβάλλοντος τὰ ἐνθυμήματα καθαρῶς καὶ τοῦ διερμηνεύοντος αὐτὰ ἀπταίστως.

For many reason excellently, but find speech a bad interpreter of thought and are by it betrayed, through not having had a thorough grounding in the ordinary subjects of culture. Others, again, have shewn great ability in expounding themes, and yet been most evil thinkers, such as the so-called sophists; for the understanding of these men is wholly untrained by the Muses, whose united voice is heard in the output of the vocal organs.

But God bestows on those who obey Him no imperfect boon. All His gifts are full and complete. And so, in this case, also, He does not send the blessing or "logos-excellence" in one division of logos, but in both its parts, for He holds it just that the recipient of His bounty should both conceive the noblest conceptions and give masterly expression to his ideas. For perfection depends, as we know, on both divisions of logos, the reason which suggests the ideas with clearness, and the speech which gives unfailing expression to them (§§72-73).

Like the previous thematic elaboration, this one appears to be inspired by the *tractatio* of the *auctor ad Herennium*, adding to the former proof the same categories of argumentative figures. The only difference worthy of note is the use of two examples and the way that the other arguments are inserted and structured in them.

The example of Abel (§§74-75) acts as an anti-model in the context of the thesis defended. Moses (§§76-81) is presented, in contrast, as a model of a wise person. Both examples are structured enthymematically, serving as a point of departure for a new *a contrario* argument. The first of these (§75)

---

[73] *Rhetorica ad Alexandrum* 1421b 21-30.

highlights the imprudence of Abel in accepting a debate for which he was not prepared.

> τῶν γὰρ ἀγροικοσόφων οἱ τὰ πολιτικὰ κεκομψευμένοι μάλιστά πως εἰώθασι περιεῖναι.

> for village sages usually get the worst of it when they encounter those who have acquired the cleverness of the town (§75b).

The second example shows that rhetorical education is especially appropriate for the treatment of questions κατὰ αἴσθησιν ἢ πάθος ἢ σῶμα. In these cases both a perfect theoretical mastery of the techniques of argumentation and oratorical practice are essential.

> ὅταν μὲν οὖν τοῖς τοῦ πανηγεμόνος ἐμπεριπατῇ πράγμασιν ὁ νοῦς, οὐδενὸς ἑτέρου προσδεῖται πρὸς τὴν θεωρίαν, ἐπειδὴ τῶν νοητῶν μόνη διάνοια ὀφθαλμὸς ὀξυωπέστατος· ὅταν δὲ καὶ τοῖς κατὰ αἴσθησιν ἢ πάθος ἢ σῶμα, ὧν ἐστιν ἡ Αἰγύπτου χώρα σύμβολον, δεήσεται καὶ τῆς περὶ λόγους τέχνης ὁμοῦ καὶ δυνάμεως.

> Yes, whensoever the mind is moving amid matters concerned with the Ruler of all, it needs no extraneous help in its study, inasmuch as for objects of intellectual apprehension unaided mind is an eye of keenest sight: but when it is occupied besides with matters affected by sense-perception or passion or the body, of which the land of Egypt is a symbol, it will need alike the art of speaking and ability in exercising it (§77).

A rhetorical pun, based on the words ἄσημος and ἐπίσημος, suggests to Philo a comparison of the ideas conceived in the mind and then verbalized with a coin and its coinage.

> ἐπειδὴ τῷ ὄντι ὁ λόγος τοῖς ἐνθυμήμασιν ὑπαντῶν, ῥήματα καὶ ὀνόματα προστιθεὶς χαράττει τὰ ἄσημα, ὡς ἐπίσημα ποιεῖν.

> for it is indeed a fact that speech meeting the mind's conceptions, and wedding the parts of speech to them, mints them like uncoined gold, and gives the stamp of expression to what was unstamped and unexpressed before (§79b).

The strict and clear *expression* of the ideas *impressed* on the mind requires, therefore, the existence of a "mold" that will make them dynamic, intelligible and ἐμφαντικώτατα (§81).

> γήθει γὰρ ὁ λόγος καὶ εὐφραίνεται, ὅταν μὴ ἀμυδρὸν ᾖ τὸ ἐνθύμημα, διότι τηλαυγοῦς ὄντος ἀπταίστῳ καὶ εὐτρόχῳ διερμηνεύσει χρῆται κυρίων καὶ εὐθυβόλων καὶ γεμόντων πολλῆς ἐμφάσεως εὐπορῶν ὀνομάτων·

> for speech does exult and is glad, when the conception is not indistinct, because it finds that the wording which issues from its rich store of terms apt and expressive and full of vividness is fluent and unhalting when the thought is luminous (§79c).

Although the conclusion (§§82-85) is rather long and complex, it suits the purpose of the author. In this thematic unit his line of argumentation is pedagogical. Philo is as keenly determined to enlighten the reader on the intrinsic value of rhetoric as he is to awaken in him the consciousness of the need for a solid technical preparation in that art. Consequently he closes his argument with a vigorous exhortation to its study, stressing that rhetoric is more than an instrument of defense for the wise man. It serves equally well as an arm of attack, demonstrating unequivocally its superiority, both theoretical and practical, in the combat against the λεγόμενοι σοφισταί (§82).

> ἀναγκαῖον οὖν ἐστι τῷ μέλλοντι πρὸς ἀγῶνα σοφιστικὸν ἀπαντᾶν ἐπιμεμελῆσθαι λόγων ἐρρωμένως οὕτως, ὡς μὴ μόνον ἐκφεύγειν τὰ παλαίσματα, ἀλλὰ καὶ ἀντεπιτιθέμενον ἀμφοτέροις, τέχνῃ τε καὶ δυνάμει, περιεῖναι.
>
> It is a vital matter, then, for one about to face a contest with sophists to have paid attention to words with such thoroughness as not only to elude the grips of his adversary but to take the offensive in his turn and prove himself superior both in skill and strength (§82).

The exhortation is prolonged in a double *interrogatio* (§§83-84), elucidated and shielded by the authorized testimony of the divine oracles (§85).

Conscious that an epilogue permits recapitulation as well as psychological appeal and exhortation, Philo knows how and when to effectively avail himself of these functions to produce the desired effect on the reader. He begins by adopting the Stoic position that the λόγος can be divided into two parts: "reasoning that suggests the ideas with clarity, and discourse that expresses them with truth and rigor" (§73).[74] He affirms without ambiguity the supreme importance of both in the life of the πάνσοφος. He then goes on to defend the encyclical discipline of rhetoric, which as a neutral technique of argumentation, can and should legitimately be placed at the service of truth. He encourages its good usage, especially in denouncing and dismantling deceitful arguments of the sophists who distort doctrine and improperly use its methods to combat truth itself.[75] By means of a coherently structured proof, he argues both the existence and the efficacy of that which could be called "a superior form of rhetoric,"[76] demonstrating it to be that which makes genuinely possible the movement from the λόγος ἐνδιάθετος to the λόγος προφορικός.[77] Finally, based on the accumulated evidence, he asserts the perfect harmony of the whole: Ὦ ἀκολουθίας ἐναρμονίου! For, as he underscores, "it is evident that sophistic reasoning is always defeated by wisdom whenever these two values come together in it." Πρὸς οὓς πῶς ἐνῆν ἀπαντῆσαι μὴ τὸν ἑρμηνέα διανοίας λόγον ... ἑτοιμασάμενον; ("How would it

---

[74] The Stoics strongly emphasized the distinction between the λόγος προφορικός (discourse) and the λόγος ἐνδιάθετος (thought). Cf. PLCL II, p. 503, note to §52.
[75] Cf. *Leg.* III, 36.
[76] Michel, "Quelques aspects," p. 88.
[77] *Migr.* 78; *Abr.* 83. Cf. A. Mendelson, *Secular Education in Philo of Alexandria*, p. 8.

have been possible for Moses to encounter these men, had he not had in readiness speech the interpreter of thought...?"(§84)

3. De Cherubim *1-10, 40-52 and 65-83*

Considered one of Philo's most perfect treatises,[78] *De Cherubim* in exemplary fashion comments on Genesis 3:24 and 4:1 in two relatively distinct but complementary parts. As J. Cazeaux rightly observes, "everything occurs ... as if Philo discovers in the text the 'ground' of the first," and "as if the *De Cherubim* leads us back from effect to cause, from exile to fault."[79] In fact, the Philonic strategy of persuasion is here structured in such a way as to demonstrate that "the name Cain, translated as *possession,* justifies the definitive punishment imposed on Adam."[80]

In this twofold analysis of the same fundamental truth, Philo is led to define Adam as νοῦς ἄλογος, because he made himself possessor of himself and opposed the ὀρθὸς λόγος, understood in this text as recognition of the divine cause[81] and submission to its eternal sovereignty. His interpretation of the verb contained in the expression καὶ (ὁ θεός) ἐξέβαλε τὸν Ἀδάμ methodically follows the rhetorical structure of Ciceronian *ratiocinatio,* explaining the definitive exile of Adam from Paradise beginning with the explicit meaning of "ἐξέβαλε" by semantic differentiation from "ἐξαπέστειλεν" in the previous verse.[82] The sequential order of the argument is as follows:

(1) *Propositio* (§2a)

ὁ μὲν οὖν ἀποστελλόμενος ἐπανόδου τυχεῖν οὐ κεκώλυται, ὁ δ' ἐκβληθεὶς ὑπὸ θεοῦ τὴν ἀίδιον φυγὴν ὑπομένει·

He who is sent forth is not thereby prevented from returning. He who is cast forth by God is subject to eternal banishment.

(2) *Propositionis approbatio* (§2b)

τῷ μὲν γὰρ μήπω κραταιῶς ὑπὸ κακίας καταληφθέντι δέδοται μετανοήσαντι καθάπερ εἰς πατρίδα τὴν ἀρετὴν ἀφ' ἧς ἐξέπεσε κατελθεῖν, τὸν δὲ πιεσθέντα καὶ ὑποβεβλημένον σφοδρᾷ καὶ ἀνιάτῳ νόσῳ φέρειν ἀνάγκη τὰ δεινὰ μέχρι τοῦ παντὸς αἰῶνος ἀθάνατα σκορακισθέντα εἰς ἀσεβῶν χῶρον, ἵν' ἄκρατον καὶ συνεχῆ βαρυδαιμονίαν ὑπομένῃ·

For to him who is not as yet firmly in the grip of wickedness it is open to repent and return to the virtue from which he was driven, as an exile returns to his fatherland. But

---

[78] J. Cazeaux, *De la grammaire à la sagesse: Le traité "De Cherubim"* (Lyon, 1978), p. 1.
[79] Ibid.
[80] Ibid.
[81] Ibid., p. 1-2.
[82] The first verb presupposes a definitive expulsion, while the second admits the possibility of a return.

to him that is weighed down and enslaved by that fierce and incurable malady, the horrors of the future must needs be undying and eternal: he is thrust forth to the place of the impious, there to endure misery continuous and unrelieved.

(3) *Assumptio* (§3)

Philo proceeds to make a comparison with the two times that Hagar left the house of her masters—the first was a voluntary departure, the second was a definitive expulsion.

(4) *Assumptionis approbatio* (§4-9)

The basis of the minor premise is provided by the change of names of Abraham and Sarah and the semantic implications that their symbolic values have. As a μέση καὶ ἐγκύκλιος παιδεία, Hagar has some affinity with Ἀβραάμ and Σάρα before their names are changed—when Abram resembled a philosopher who relies on the astronomy of the Chaldeans and Sara, a queen who rests on her personal authority but still moves within the sphere of the perishable. After her masters left that stage of life behind and received new names, they entered the dominion of the imperishable, of σοφία and γενικὴ ἀρετή, finally abandoning the sophistic culture and casting out Hagar and Ishmael, its representatives.

(5) *Complexio* (§10)

> τί οὖν θαυμάζομεν, εἰ καὶ Ἀδὰμ τὸν νοῦν ἀφροσύνην ἀνίατον νόσον κτησάμενον ἐκβέβληκεν εἰσάπαν ὁ θεὸς ἐκ τοῦ τῶν ἀρετῶν χωρίου μὴ ἐπιτρέψας ἔτι κατελθεῖν αὐτῷ; ὁπότε καὶ ⟨κατὰ⟩ πάντα σοφιστὴν καὶ μητέρα αὐτοῦ, τὴν τῶν προπαιδευμάτων διδασκαλίαν, ἐλαύνει καὶ φυγαδεύει ἀπὸ σοφίας καὶ σοφοῦ, ὧν ὀνόματα Ἀβραάμ τε καὶ Σάρραν καλεῖ.

> Since then the sophist, who is ever sophist, and his mother, the instruction in the preliminary learning, are expelled and banished by God from the presence of wisdom and the wise, on whom he confers the titles of Sarah and Abraham, can we wonder that he has cast forth Adam, that is the mind, which is sick with the incurable sickness of folly, from the dwelling-place of virtue for ever and permits him not to return?

The conclusion of the argument is marked and its integrity assured by an *inclusio*. It is a very curious rhetorical structure, for it not only encloses the argument by connecting the end to the beginning (ἀνιάτῳ νόσῳ [§2], and ἀνίατον νόσον [§10]) but also acts within it as a means of persuasion by highlighting the fact that Adam allowed himself to be overtaken irremediably and definitively by the incurable sickness of ἀφροσύνη. However, in the course of exegesis a strategic detour worthy of note is at work. As Philo passes from the literal level of reading to the allegorical, he orients us first toward the divine λόγος, the source of all virtue and wisdom, pointing out indirectly the deeper cause of the Adamic exile. While Abraham and Sarah participated in the λόγος, Adam—τὸν νοῦν ἀφροσύνην ἀνίατον νόσον κτησάμενον—remains forever enslaved to himself because of his willful independence of the divine sovereignty.

> Avec les §2-10, le crime supposé d'Adam se déplace déjà vers la figure intellectualisée qui sert de parabole à la religion dans Philon, des rapports du νοῦς au λόγος. . . . La spécification regrettable du premier nom de Sara, "*autorité de moi*" annonce sans doute l'abusive "possession" de *soi* dont Caïn reste l'occasion pour Adam.[83]

In §§11-20, Philo determines the positive and correct meaning of ἀντικρύ by the *expeditio*,[84] developing from there the theme of intimate communion with God in contrast to the hostility shown by Adam, Hagar and Cain in placing themselves on the way of false knowledge ἥτις λυμαίνεται ψυχήν – "which destroys the soul" (§9). Then he examines the symbolic meanings of the *Cherubim* (§§21-39) and the flaming sword by the same rhetorical process of elimination, finally adopting and promoting the interpretation according to which they represent the two principal "powers" of God—ἀγαθότης and ἐξουσία—and the latter represents the λόγος as its unifying and dynamizing power: the Reason through which God created and governs all things.

If in this first part of his treatise Philo describes the intimate relationship that exists between true knowledge (§§1-10), communion with God (§§11-20) and the correct use of reason, acquired as a fountain of happiness (§§21-39), in the second section he definitively takes up again the theme of possession, misused and consequently taken away from Adam. An expression related to the birth of Cain bears witness to his insanity (§§40-52). The way Adam refers to his son's name confirms his presumption (§§53-130).

Taking Philo's interpretation as a whole, the story of Cain manifests and extends that of Adam, so that the truth first expressed summarily (§2) is taken up again and progressively explained in concentric circles.[85]

Paragraphs 40 to 52 reproduce the argumentative pattern of the first ten paragraphs, mentioning Adam only at the beginning and at the end, but freshly developing, antithetically, the theme of the knowledge that emanates from the λόγος. But now its formal elaboration follows the structure recommended by the *auctor ad Herennium* regarding the varied treatment of a theme already argued.[86]

Without betraying the grammatical order of the basic text, Philo organizes his commentary in relation to this specific form of argumentation, combining exegetical sequence with the logical development of the theme in order to more persuasively illumine his ideas:

---

[83] Cazeaux, *De la grammaire*, p. 4.
[84] *Rhetorica ad Herennium* IV, 40-41.
[85] Cf. Cazeaux, *De la grammaire*, p. 88.
[86] A typical case of *expolitio* (refinement) which according to him 'occurs when we remain on the same theme and appear to say things that are ever different'" (IV, 54).

–Ἀδὰμ δὲ ἔγνω τὴν γυναῖκα αὐτοῦ (§§40b-41)—Adam knew his wife;
–καὶ συνέλαβε καὶ ἔτεκε... (§§42-52a)—she conceived and gave birth;
–τὸν Κάϊν (§52b)—Cain.

The first part of this text is commented on in the three initial passages of the *tractatio: res, ratio* and *pronuntiatio;* the second part is more amply developed in the three following arguments: *contrarium, simile* and *exemplum;* and the third, in the *conclusio.*

Let us consider the details.

(1) In the *res* (§40), the theme of knowledge suggested by the text is enunciated in the form of a thesis, with an allusion to the *a contrario* argument.

"'Ἀδὰμ δὲ ἔγνω τὴν γυναῖκα αὐτοῦ· καὶ συνέλαβε καὶ ἔτεκε τὸν Κάϊν, καὶ εἶπεν Ἐκτησάμην ἄνθρωπον διὰ τοῦ θεοῦ. καὶ προσέθηκε τεκεῖν τὸν ἀδελφὸν αὐτοῦ τὸν "Ἀβελ". οἷς ἀρετὴν μεμαρτύρηκεν ὁ νομοθέτης, τούτους γνωρίζοντας γυναῖκας οὐκ εἰσάγει, τὸν Ἀβραάμ, τὸν Ἰσαάκ, τὸν Ἰακώβ, τὸν Μωυσῆν, καὶ εἴ τις αὐτοῖς ὁμόζηλος·

"And Adam knew his wife and she conceived and bare Cain, and he said, 'I have gotten a man through God,' and He added to this that she bore his brother Abel" [Gen. 4:1-2]. The persons to whose virtue the lawgiver has testified, such as Abraham, Isaac, Jacob and Moses, and others of the same spirit, are not represented by him as knowing women (§40).

(2) In the *ratio* (§41a), the thesis is proved by the symbolic definition of the woman as αἴσθησις.

ἐπειδὴ γὰρ φαμεν εἶναι γυναῖκα τροπικῶς αἴσθησιν, ἀλλοτριώσει δ' αἰσθήσεως καὶ σώματος ἐπιστήμη συνίσταται, τοὺς σοφίας ἐραστὰς αἴσθησιν ἀποδοκιμάζοντας μᾶλλον ἢ αἱρουμένους ἐπιδείξεται·

For since we hold that woman signifies in a figure sense-perception, and that knowledge comes into being through estrangement from sense and body, it will follow that the lovers of wisdom reject rather than choose sense (§41a).

(3) In the *pronuntiatio* (§41b), the theme is implicitly reaffirmed and justified.

καὶ μήποτ' εἰκότως· αἱ γὰρ τούτοις συνοικοῦσαι λόγῳ μέν εἰσι γυναῖκες, ἔργῳ δὲ ἀρεταί, Σάρρα μὲν ἄρχουσα καὶ ἡγεμονίς, Ῥεβέκκα δὲ ἐπιμονὴ τῶν καλῶν, Λεία δὲ ἀνανενευμένη καὶ κοπιῶσα ἐπὶ τῇ συνεχείᾳ τῆς ἀσκήσεως, ἣν ἐκνένευκε καὶ ἀποστρέφεται πᾶς ἄφρων ἀρνούμενος, Σεπφώρα δὲ ἡ Μωυσέως ἀπὸ γῆς εἰς οὐρανὸν ἀνατρέχουσα καὶ τὰς ἐκεῖ θείας καὶ εὐδαίμονας φύσεις κατανοοῦσα, καλεῖται δὲ ὀρνίθιον.

And surely this is natural. For the helpmeets of these men are called women, but are in reality virtues. Sarah "sovereign and leader," Rebecca "steadfastness in excellence," Leah "rejected and faint" through the unbroken discipline, which every fool rejects and turns from with words of denial, Zipporah, the mate of Moses, whose name is "bird," speeding upwards from earth to heaven and contemplating there the nature of things divine and blessed (§41b).

Once the theme is defined and the formulated thesis confirmed, the latter is sustained by a series of complementary arguments, which simultaneously constitute the commentary on the central part of the Biblical text.

(4) *Contrarium* (§§42-43)—The divine mystery of the virtues that conceive and give birth to sons is only revealed to those initiated into the practice of authentic piety, and not to the "superstitious," who oppose virtue and piety[87] by their lack of religious intelligence.[88] This contrast is repeated in the comparison of the woman who is naturally inseminated by her husband and the virtues which are not inseminated by mortals.

(5) *Simile* (§44)—Like a human female, virtue needs to be inseminated in order to conceive and bear fruit. But the good seed that inseminates it is a gift of God and not of man. This argument is implicitly embellished and illuminated by the *similitudo*.

(6) *Exemplum* (§§45-47)—The fact that Philo here uses a series of examples does not surprise us for such a phenomenon is not uncommon in Hellenistic literature. The wives of the patriarchs and of Moses are presented as models of highest virtue, made fruitful by God for the benefit of their husbands. They are four exemplary personalities, previously mentioned in chronological order (§41) but now progressively organized "around a complete moral system"[89] to demonstrate that lovers of wisdom reject αἴσθησις. Adam admits to having "known" his wife, but none of these heroes is represented as having known their wives (*i. e.*, αἴσθησις).

In providing us this suggestive exegetical progression, in a context emphasizing the movement of the initiate toward the sacred mysteries, the Alexandrian certainly wishes to have us notice the spiritual steps one must climb. He expands the paradigmatic argument by referring to his own vision and understanding of the divine oracle, directed to the εἰρηνικοτάτην ἀρετήν by the prophetic ministry of Jeremiah.

Introduced by an exhortation to those initiated into the mysteries concerning knowledge of the Cause and of Virtue, as well as of the fruit they bear, his testimony leads to an epichirematically argued interpretation of the "oracle" referred to (§§49b-51), which not only illuminates the history of the

---

[87] Cf. *Deter.* 18 and 24; *Spec.* IV, 147.
[88] Cazeaux understands here "as 'superstitious' those spirits weighed down by mythology and divine love affairs,' adding that 'certain texts allow us to understand that superstitious makes the knowledge of God go astray though the influence of customs and traditions, of which teachers, nannies and education are the unreasoning vehicles. This may be concluded if one adds *Praem.* 40 to *Sacr.* 15 and joins them up with *Virt.* 178. According to him 'there is a possibility that our passage of *Cher.* 42 leads in this direction: as soon as there is question of mortal women entering in union with God, Philo fears that the association is unwise: the person who is culturally polished or is simply a witness to cultic worship and popular stories could find himself tempted to operate between the surrounding mythology and the Bible. We have a very clear confirmation of this anxiety in *Mut.* 137–140." (*De la grammaire*, p. 39).
[89] Ibid., p. 33.

patriarchs but also explains the paradoxical "mystery" of the sublimated "virginity" of their "women." God, the incorporeal habitation of ideas and first cause of all things, is also the "husband of wisdom." This sowing of the soul with the seed of pure and immortal virtues causes it to finally abandon the passions and transforms into a virgin her who previously was simply a 'woman'.

(7) *Conclusio* (§52)—Once the central thematic development is concluded, contrasting the positive patriarchal marriages with the negative one of Adam and Eve, Philo brings us back, by "symmetrical conversion,"[90] to the basic issue initially proposed.

The nuclear vocabulary around which the exegesis of the text is structured and advanced (ἐπιστήμη/αἴσθησις, γυνή/παρθένος/παρθενία, κύησις/ὠδίς, ἀρετή/σοφία, γινώσκειν/οὐ γνωρίζειν) explicitly or implicitly concentrates on this parenetic discussion of the soul, so as to intensify even further the contrast between the state of Adam and that of Abraham. The soul which does not cling to Abraham, who moves from Evil to Good by his union with the woman-virtue transformed by God into a virgin, inevitably clings to Adam, who walks in the opposite direction for pretending to "know" God by the ways of perishable feelings, thus producing the fratricidal and accursed Cain as a "possession unworthy of acquisition."

Paragraphs 65 and 83 in this treatise constitute another literary unit no less significant from the rhetorical point of view. Taking again the name of Cain and the theme of dispossessed possession linked to it (§52), Philo elaborates an argument structurally identical to the previous one but more developed in terms of the types of proof adopted, and a little more liberal in the selection and confection of the various ingredients of the proof.

The introduction to this argumentative unit (§§63-64) already suggests the form of treatment that the Alexandrian will choose, illustrating the irrational pride of the νοῦς with the arrogant and pretentious claim of Alexander of Macedonia: καὶ τὰ τῇδε καὶ τὰ τῇδε ἐμά. This affirmation arose in a specific historical context, and consequently it satisfies the essential requirements for a χρεία, as those were later defined by Theon of Alexandria: σύντομος ἀπόφασις ἢ πρᾶξις μετ' εὐστοχίας ἀναφερομένη εἴς τι ὡρισμένων πρόσωπον ἢ ἀναλογοῦν προσώπῳ –"a concise statement or action which is attributed with aptness to some specified character or to something analogous to a character".[91]

It is on this basis that the antithesis formulated in paragraph 64 again denounces the negative figure of the abusive possessor, embodied in Adam

---

[90] Ibid., p. 27.
[91] E. Christian Walz, *Rhetores Graeci*, "Progymnasmata" of Aelius Theon (Stuttgart and Tübingen: J. G. Cotta, 1854), I, p. 201.

and perpetuated in the race by Cain, for believing that "all things are their property," suggesting at the same time the thematic development to come and seeming somehow to explain its architecture.[92]

Although not explicitly pointed out in the discussion of the boastful νοῦς and Alexander, the theme of knowledge here returns, not as a mere redundancy but as part of a coherent exegetical discourse. Now it is not a syntagmatically dominating and absorbing theme. Instead it is paradigmatically inserted into the discussion of the alleged possessions of the mind. To summarize, we find here this rhetorical structure:

(1) *Res* (§65a)—The mind that bases its knowledge on the faculty of the senses is insane and impiously believes that all things are its property.[93]

(2) *Ratio* (§§65b-66)—It thinks itself an owner of that which is divine property, while it does not even exercise dominion over, or have knowledge of, its own self.

(3) *Exemplum* (§§67-70,72-74a,74b-76)—Philo presents the examples of three persons who are condemned for their uncontrolled assertions of possession because they pronounced, each one in his way and in different circumstances, the decisive word "mine," claiming sovereignty over that which in reality belongs only to God. Laban, "symbol of manifold sensations,"[94] declares himself absolute sovereign of all his goods, including the family members that no longer belong to him, in total abandonment of sound knowledge.[95] The slave rejects the liberty that is rightfully his in the sabbatical year, equally rejecting virtue by showing excessive affection for the senses as his possession and supreme good. Pharaoh, lover of the body and

---

[92] We have here present the elaboration of a χρεία in Hermogenes, Aphthonius and Libanius. On the existence of the προγυμνάσματα in the first century B.C., and the specific use of this type of amplified exercise (ἐργασία, *expolitio*) from earliest times by Greek and Roman theoreticians, see S. F. Bonner, *Education in Ancient Rome* (Berkeley: University of California, 1977), p. 250-251 and 259.

[93] Notice the coincidence between the conclusion of the previous argument and the thesis of the current one: §52b - τοιγάρτοι γέννημα πάμφυρτον καὶ πανώλεθρον ἀποτέξῃ τὸν ἀδελφοκτόνον καὶ ἐπάρατον Κάιν, κτῆσιν οὐ κτητήν· λέγεται γὰρ ὁ Κάιν κτῆσις.

For this thou shalt bring forth that thing of ruin and confusion, Cain, the fratricide, the accursed, the possession which is no possession. For the meaning of Cain is "possession."

§65a - Οὗτος ἐστιν ὃν χαρακτηρίσας Μωυσῆς τρόπον ἐν ἡμῖν ἐπεφήμισε Κάιν, ἑρμηνευόμενον κτῆσιν, εὐηθείας μᾶλλον δὲ ἀσεβείας μεστὸν ὄντα·

It is this feeling in us which Moses expresses under the name of Cain, by interpretation Possession, a feeling foolish to the core or rather impious.

[94] Cf. Cazeaux, *De la grammaire*, p. 57.

[95] His name means λευκασμός (*Agr.* 42), λευκός (*Fug.* 44), symbolically representing the man that embodies the senses and is slave to the passions (*Leg.* III, 15-22), by abandoning sound knowledge (*Cher.* 67-71). Cf. F. H. Colson and J. W. Earp, PLCL X, p. 360-362.

fleshly passion,[96] fails for thinking to persecute when he is the one persecuted and to dominate when he is the one dominated, an enemy of reason and even of nature itself.

(4) *Testimonium* (77a)—The fact that he is that enemy is confirmed by the authoritative testimony of Moses. This argument is reinforced by the following *interrogatio*, confirming the fact that in effect there is no more lethal enemy of the soul than he who in his pride claims for himself that which pertains to God.

(5) *Contrarium* (§§77b-78)—The problem of activity which is opposed to passion (§76) is explained by a well-elaborated and suggestively-illustrated antithesis, which is prolonged in the following paragraphs.

ἴδιον μὲν δὴ θεοῦ τὸ ποιεῖν, ὃ οὐ θέμις ἐπιγράψασθαι γενητῷ, ἴδιον δὲ γενητοῦ τὸ πάσχειν. ὁ προλαβὼν μέν τις ὡς οἰκεῖον καὶ ἀναγκαῖόν ἐστι, ῥᾳδίως οἴσει τὰ προσπίπτοντα, κἂν ᾖ βαρύτατα, νομίσας δὲ ἀλλότριον ἀνηνύτῳ πιεζόμενος ἄχθει Σισύφειον τιμωρίαν ἀναδέξεται, μηδ᾽ ὅσον ἀνακῦψαι δυνάμενος, ἀλλὰ πᾶσι τοῖς ἐπιτρέχουσι καὶ τραχηλίζουσι δεινοῖς ὑποβεβλημένος καὶ προστιθεὶς ἑκάστῳ τὸ ὑπεῖκον καὶ εὐένδοτον, ἀγεννοῦς καὶ ἀνάνδρου ψυχῆς πάθη·

> For it belongs to God to act, and this we may not ascribe to any created being. What belongs to the created is to suffer, and he who accepts this from the first, as a necessity inseparable from his lot, will bear with patience what befalls him, however grievous it may be. He who thinks it a strange and alien thing will incur the penalty of Sisyphus, crushed by a vast and hopeless burden, unable even to lift his head, overwhelmed by all the terrors which beset and prostrate him, and increasing each misery by that abject spirit of surrender, which belongs to the degenerate and unmanly soul (§§77b-78).

(6) *Similitudo* (§§79-81)—Introduced by a *distributio* enumerating the types of passivity, this analogy antithetically compares inert, submissive and enslaving passivity to resistant passivity which is simultaneously accommodated to contrary action,[97] contrasting the images of the sheep before the shearer and the slave with those of the man at the barber's shop and the boxer in the combat arena.

---

[96] Φιλήδων (*Leg.* III, 212), φίλαυτος (*Cher.* 74), φιλοσώματος (*Abr.* 103), φιλοπαθής (*Ebr.* 208 f.).

[97] Philo often divides his demonstrative reasoning into direct proofs and *a contrario* proofs. As Cazeaux observes: "Individual exegeses enter into systems or structures which a compact dialectic orders in symmetrical constructions. The memory of the reader is invited to project the entire reasoning in a vision: the reasoning becomes imagination. The universal law of symmetry gives suitable expression to the eternal 'division': a given element always catches sight of its brother, contrary or parent, on the other side of an imaginary line. This is the implication of the visible procedures and hidden devices of Philo's discourse" (*Philon: "De congressu eruditionis gratia" – Les ressorts de l'exégèse*, p. 188).

(7) Conclusio (§§82-83)—The argument is concluded with an exhortation to renounce the first type of passivity in favor of the second, with the reaffirmation of the theme of the absolute sovereignty of God.

Naturally Philo does not reduce his elaborations to mere rhetorical exercises, rigidly formed around one predetermined model or another. The choice of the themes, the enunciation of the theses, the nature, content, form and order of the arguments, the ebb and flow of the ideas and their condensation or amplification doubtless are in accord with a well established rhetorical tradition. Yet they are the product of Philo's own *inuentio* and *dispositio*. The exegetical and thematic presentation we have examined, its internal coherence, the convergence of the arguments employed and the relative novelty of its organization, bear witness to Philo's flexible rhetorical expertise.[98]

Even when he seems to wander from the original thesis, he keeps in view its complete elucidation. This is what occurs in the passage just cited. After the treatment of the insanity of the soul that leans toward the senses and arrogantly believes itself sovereign over that which is not its property, the second part of the argument confirms the thesis by means of a triangular exemplification in which the secondary theme of activity/passivity emerges psychologically. The immobility of the slave, voluntarily remaining a servant in the house of his lord (the middle example) is contrasted with the mobility of Laban and Pharaoh.

Seemingly unnecessary, this theme nevertheless proves useful in the development of the main argument, when finally Philo reveals, by a semantic conversion, the alternative to impious claims of possession. The negative burden of the senses linked to the terms "activity/passivity" emerges subtly explained by the symbolic identification of the examples which they represent, but it is openly neutralized and corrected by their juxtaposition. For that, it is enough to contrast the "passive" person who abandons himself to the "passive" individual who "reacts" and resists the contrary action,[99] thereby developing an *active passivity*. "Passivity" thus is transformed into "passion" (§§76-77), and he who accepts it as a natural and necessary reality will bear with patience the vicissitudes and misfortunes of day-to-day life. Sisyphus, who succumbs to the weight of his evils because he resisted the divine sovereignty, is contrasted with an anti-Sisyphus, who is strong enough to mitigate and bear them.

---

[98] This passage in *De Cherubim* should be compared with formal structures of the *tractatio* in the *auctor ad Herennium*, the χρεία in Theon, and the ἐργασία in Hermogenes (respectively: *Rhetorica ad Herennium* IV, 56-58; C. Walz, *Rhetores Graeci* I, p. 216; H. Rabe, *Hermogenis Opera* [Stuttgart: Teubner, 1969], p. 7-8).

[99] Cf. Cazeaux, *De la grammaire*, p. 61.

> τοῦτο μὲν οὖν τὸ πάθος μήτε σώματι μήτε πολὺ μᾶλλον ψυχῇ δεξώμεθά ποτε, τὸ δ' ἀντιπεπονθὸς ἐκεῖνο—ἐπειδὴ πάσχειν ἀνάγκη τὸ θνητόν—, ἵνα μὴ καθάπερ οἱ θηλυδρίαι κεκλασμένοι καὶ παρειμένοι καὶ προαναπίπτοντες μετ' ἐκλύσεως ψυχικῶν δυνάμεων ἐξασθενῶμεν, ἀλλ' ἐρρωμένοι τοῖς διανοίας τόνοις ἐπελαφρίζειν κἀπικουφίζειν ἰσχύωμεν τὴν φορὰν τῶν ἐπαρτωμένων δεινῶν.

> This is a condition we should never admit into our bodies, much less into our souls. As mortals we must suffer, but let our suffering be that other kind which is the reaction of our own activity. Let us not like womanish folk, nerveless and unstrung, flagging ere the struggle begin, with all our spiritual forces relaxed, sink into utter prostration. Rather let the tension of our minds be firm and braced, that so we may be strong to relieve and lighten the force and onset of the misfortunes which menace us (§82).

Thus the sub-theme of action/passion is inserted into the development of the fundamental theme of "my/mine". To act belongs to God, and only suffering passivity (active or reactive passivity) belongs to man.

The coherence of the treatise is shown in the combination of its themes and not in its isolated parts. The beginning and the end meet, the latter being announced beforehand and then progressively developed, until we arrive at the final demonstration of the dominant thesis. God is the creative cause of all things and their absolute owner (§§84,124). Everything that humans seem to possess are gifts from God (§123), for human life is no more than a pilgrimage (§120). Only the wise individual, who submits to God's sovereignty and rejoices in it (§§106-107) and does so with true insight (active passivity) is happy (§130). The thesis enunciated at the beginning (§§1-2) is gradually manifested and explained in concentric circles until in the end each one of its parts is recognized to be not only justified but also necessary to the whole to satisfy the underlying exegetical purpose.

The backbone of this long argumentative sequence is finally presented to us with a structural enthymeme which regulates each one of its parts. The reasoning that sustains the conclusion is implicit in the thesis. The individual arguments (we have analysed only three of the most representative ones) are presented to give it support. But it is that enthymematic contribution that gives the individual arguments a dynamic unity and logical coherence. The secondary premises support the same conclusion. As J. Cazeaux observes,

> The *De Cherubim* demonstrates first of all that chapter 3 of Genesis says the same thing, in reverse, as chapters 12-14, presenting the story of Abraham. Abraham and Adam are the two *first men*, but they are antithetical and thus each one is the inverted reflection of the other. Abraham has Lot and Ishmael as opponents, just as Adam has Eve and Cain, signifying sense perception and sophistical rhetoric. Abraham connects the idea of 'creation' with that of Cause, while Adam comes from the hands of the Potter.[100]

Adam is permanently cast out of paradise *because* he commits the mistake of claiming to possess that which belongs only to God. Abraham is saved and

---

[100] Ibid., p. 88.

brought to the promised land *because* he allies himself to the sovereign Cause of all things, responding submissively and positively (active passivity) to the offer of friendship and communion with his Creator (§§20,106-107,130).

4. De Mutatione Nominum *252-263: The gift of wisdom*

We conclude the present chapter with the analysis of a double exegetical periphrasis whose argumentative structure, even more than that of the previous example, is like the ἐργασία (elaboration) later presented in the manuals of rhetoric as the elaboration of a χρεία. Nevertheless, its study reminds us of some previous considerations. The first pertains to the evolution and final form of this new argumentative structure. The second has to do with the reasons for its integration into the Alexandrian's hermeneutical practice.

Besides the techniques of persuasion and argumentation developed and taught by rhetoricians who preceded Philo, others were certainly taking shape in schools of his day. They were techniques that an experienced and up-to-date writer could not fail to test and adapt. If the text Philo interprets is for him a unified and sublime document of sacred rhetoric,[101] only a master skilled in rhetorical τέχνη would venture to make manifest its intentions.[102]

Bearing witness to a dynamic evolution in the theory of argumentation, S. Bonner correctly observes that the exercises registered in the *Progymnasmata* of Theon of Alexandria, and later formalized in the writings of Hermogenes, represent a pedagogical practice widely known in Greek and Roman circles from the beginnings of the first century B.C.[103] First, there appear very simple variations of literary units connected with their adaptation to argumentative contexts.[104] Such, for example, is the case in narrative expansion,[105] or *aetiologia* (a particular form of exercise whose basic affirmation is accompanied by its αἰτία, closely related with the enthymeme).[106] Later these become starting points for the making of short discourses, molded in accordance with actual rhetorical structures. In such cases, the χρεία was used as a thesis and its validity was supported by means of encomium,

---

[101] Cf. *Mos.* II, 45-52.
[102] Burton Mack, "Decoding the Scripture: Philo and the Rules of Rhetoric", in *Nourished with Peace: Studies in Hellenistic Judaism in Memory of Samuel Sandmel* (Chico, CA: Scholars Press, 1984), p. 112-115.
[103] *Education in Ancient Rome* (Berkeley: University of California Press, 1977), p. 250-259.
[104] Cf. V. K. Robbins, "Pronouncement Stories and Jesus' Blessing of Children: A Rhetorical Approach," *SBLSP*, 21 (1982), p. 409. See also "The Rhetoric of Pronouncement", *Semeia* 64 (1993), p. XII–XIV.
[105] Cf. Theon, "Progymnasmata," in Walz, *Rhetores Graeci* I, p. 213-214.
[106] Bonner, *Education in Ancient Rome*, p. 258.

paraphrase, arguments by analogy and contrast, example and exhortation.[107]

These χρεῖαι are defined by Theon as brief affirmations or actions properly attributed to a specific person.[108] They are distinguished from maxims by their reference to concrete figures in a context, so that in their structure *who* and *why* are actually more important than *what* is said or done.[109] Although they may serve either for instruction or edification, they are not at first bound to either of those functions. But in subsequent rhetorical practice they are primarily placed at the service of education.

The lists of arguments suggested by Aelius Theon for their development at first give us the impression that they are limited to providing to the student an introduction to the principal elements of proof and the way to use them. But at the end of his exposition on the χρεῖαι he explicitly states that a χρεία can be the thesis of an argument which then can be developed in conformity with the theme dealt with and the context in which it is inserted.[110] His long list of twenty-three probatory topics, however, is no more than "an ordered set of arguments presented as possible and necessary ingredients for a complete and coherent demonstration."[111] In fact, Theon has no intention of imposing a prefabricated scheme of composition on the student or the orator. But while seeming to respect and promote the creative liberty of the latter, he declares that every χρεία used as a thesis should present not only an introduction but also select and conveniently arrange its arguments.[112]

Now, between this basic development and the ἐργασία of Hermogenes the distance is short. Rather than a flexible scheme of probatory articulation, he simply prefers a form which experience has proved to provide a normative logical sequence and an inspiring model for the persuasive elaboration of a theme. Beginning with an affirmation of Isocrates about the importance of the παιδεία—"Isocrates said that education's root is bitter, but its fruit is sweet"—Hermogenes illustrates the elaboration of a χρεία, dividing it into eight parts: (1) author's encomium (ἐγκώμιον), lightly amplified; (2) a paraphrase of the χρεία, transformed into the thesis of the argument; (3) reason or reasons (αἰτία) that affirm and sustain the validity of the thesis,

---

[107] Cf. James R. Butts, "Jesus and the Fox: Paradigm for Pronouncement(s) of Jesus" (New Testament Seminar, CGS, 1983), p. 24-25. Also V.K. Robbins, *Semeia* 64 (1993), p. XIV–XVI.
[108] σύντομος ἀπόφασις ἢ πρᾶξις μετ' εὐστοχίας ἀναφερομένη εἴς τι ὡρισμένον πρόσωπον ἢ ἀναλογοῦν προσώπῳ – "A chreia is a concise statement or action which is attributed with aptness to some specified character or to something analogous to a character". See James R. Butts, *The Progymnasmata of Theon: A New Text with Translation and Commentary*. Dissertation, Claremont Graduate School, 1987, p. 186.
[109] Butts, "Jesus and the Fox", p. 25.
[110] Walz, *Rhetores Graeci* I, p. 216.
[111] Mack, "Decoding the Scripture," p. 90.91.
[112] Walz, *Rhetores Graeci* I, p. 216. Cf. Mack, "Decoding the Scripture," p. 11-12.

continuously confirmed by a series of supporting arguments; (4) an *a contrario* argument (ἐναντίον), to test the validity of the reasons set forth; (5) an argument by analogy (παραβολή), to confirm the validity of the principle formulated; (6) an argument by example (παράδειγμα), to substantiate that validity by reference to previous cases in which it has been carried out; (7) κρίσις or μαρτυρία, the possible quoting of a qualified authority, to establish the truth initially expressed; and (8) a final exhortation (παράκλησις) to apply the proven thesis.[113]

When Philo says that rhetoric "will make of man a true master of words and thoughts"[114] and argues that his primary objective is to provide discourse with the mechanisms indispensable to an effective ἑρμηνεία of ideas,[115] when he understands the λόγος as a distinctive trait of man and adopts the Stoic position that it is both reason that suggests ideas and discourse that correctly expresses them,[116] there is no doubt that he esteems this discipline as a most precious cultural acquisition. He regards rhetoric not, obviously, as a substitute for thought, but as one of the most valid and effective instruments of articulation and communication.[117]

The plurality of techniques for expression described up to this point should not surprise us, nor should the fact that Philo develops the homily of *De Mutatione Nominum* 252-263 according to this recently-expanded model of elaboration. As we have already said, although Hermogenes was a rhetorician of the third century A.D., this pattern of thematic development has deep roots in the rhetorical tradition. Its conception and the first phase of its formation go back at least to the first century B.C.

B. Mack arrives at the same conclusion when he analyzes *De Sacrificiis* 1-10. According to him, the Hermogenian expansion of a χρεία "is the pattern of elaboration which gives structure and movement to section after section of his commentaries."[118]

---

[113] H. Rabe, *Hermogenis Opera*, p. 7-8.
[114] *De Congressu* 17. M. Alexandre comments that "rhetoric makes the person doubly λογικός, forming at the same time λόγος ἐνδιάθετος and λόγος προφορικός" (PM 16, p. 116, n. 3).
[115] Cf. *Congr.* 33; *Migr.* 73.
[116] *Migr.* 73; cf. *Deter.* 127-129.
[117] Cf. Alan Mendelson, *Secular Education in Philo of Alexandria*, p. 8-10.
[118] "Decoding the Scripture: Philo and the Rules of Rhetoric," in *Nourished with Peace: Studies in Hellenistic Judaism in Memory of Samuel Sandmel*, p. 99. See also *Rhetoric and the New Testament*, p. 43–47; and Vernon K. Robbins, *Exploring the Texture of Texts* (Valley Forge, Pennsylvania: Trinity Press, 1996), p. 52–58.

Thematic Development of De Mutatione 252-263

In looking at this Philonic treatise as a literary whole, we perceive two curious facts: first, that it is composed of a series of apparently autonomous exegetical units, each with its own argumentative structure; second, that those units are combined around one common theme, giving coherence to the commentary as a whole and causing its thought to advance progressively.

If, as we believe, this section of his commentary employs the χρεία elaboration technique, Philo not only uncovered the main theme in the scriptural text and enunciated it in the form of a thesis, he also articulated his proofs in logical form. Let us analyse it, giving special attention to its literary architecture.

The theme that emerges in the preface is formally enunciated in the thesis and augmented in the elaboration. The elaboration follows the pattern defended by Hermogenes.

(1) Word of praise (§253a)

After a brief *transitio* from the previous section (§252), Philo makes reference to the goodness and generosity of God, author of the *lemma* upon which his exegetical elaboration is founded.

> τί οὖν ὁ χρηστὸς θεός; ἓν αἰτησαμένῳ δύο δίδωσι καὶ τὸ ἔλαττον εὐξαμένῳ χαρίζεται τὸ μεῖζον

What then does God in his kindness do? Abraham had asked for one thing, God gives him two. He had prayed for the less, God grants him the greater (§253a).

(2) "Χρεία" (§§253b-255a)

The way the text is cited satisfies the essential two attributes of a χρεία, for we are simultaneously in the presence of an action and a personal declaration. The speaker is identified: ὁ χρηστὸς θεός ... εἶπε. The divine action and revelation are specified:

> ἓν αἰτησαμένῳ δύο δίδωσι καὶ τὸ ἔλαττον εὐξαμένῳ χαρίζεται τὸ μεῖζον. "εἶπε" γάρ φησι "τῷ Ἀβραάμ· ναί, ἰδοὺ Σάρρα ἡ γυνή σου τέξεταί σοι υἱόν"

Abraham had asked for one thing, God gives him two. He prayed for the less, God grants him the greater. He said to him, we read, "Yes, Sarah thy wife shall bear a son" [Gen. 17:19] (§253a).

Its very grammatical structure confirms it: a participial construction followed by a declarative verb.[119] Besides that, the allegorical interpretation that follows in the later stages (§§255-262) makes manifest its ethical content, pedagogic function and parenetic intention:

---

[119] In fact, the form of a χρεία presupposes this construction, as we can verify by observing the following example from Theon: Ἐπαμεινώνδας, ἄτεκνος ἀποθνῄσκων, ἔλεγε τοῖς φίλοις, δύο θυγατέρας ἀπέλιπον, τήν τε περὶ Λεύκτραν νίκην, καὶ τὴν περὶ Μαντίνειαν·

Μάθε οὖν, ὦ ψυχή, ὅτι καὶ "Σάρρα", ἡ ἀρετή, "τέξεταί σοι υἱόν", οὐ μόνον "Ἀγαρ, ἡ μέση παιδεία·

Learn then, soul of man, that Sarah also, that is virtue, shall bear thee a son, as well as Hagar, the lower instruction (§255b).

Τέξεται οὖν σοι ἡ ἀρετὴ υἱὸν γενναῖον ἄρρενα παντὸς ἀπηλλαγμένον θήλεος πάθους,

Virtue then shall bear thee a true-born, male child, one free from all womanish feelings (§261a),

Philo amplifies the quotation, along the lines recommended by Hermogenes.[120]

Even more significant, from a rhetorical point of view, is the fact that this expansion satisfies the precepts established by Theon for the commentary on a χρεία. That is, it lucidly makes use of the categories that according to him define the ultimate objectives of a discourse—τὸ ἀληθές, τὸ καλόν and τὸ συμφέρον—conferring on it the function of ἦθος in preparation for the main argument, and announcing its theme.[121]

εὐθυβόλος γε ἡ συμβολικὴ ἀπόκρισις ἡ ναί. τί γὰρ ἐμπρεπέστερον ἢ τἀγαθὰ ἐπινεύειν θεῷ καὶ ταχέως ὁμολογεῖν; ἀλλ' οἷς ἐπινεύει τὸ θεῖον, ἅπας ἄφρων ἀνανένευκε. τὴν γοῦν Λείαν μισουμένην εἰσάγουσιν οἱ χρησμοί· διὸ καὶ τοιαύτης ἔτυχε προσρήσεως· ἑρμηνευθεῖσα γάρ ἐστιν ἀνανευομένη καὶ κοπιῶσα διὰ τὸ πάντας ἡμᾶς ἀρετὴν ἀποστρέφεσθαι καὶ κοπώδη νομίζειν ἐπιτάγματα οὐχ ἡδέα πολλάκις ἐπιτάττουσαν. ἀλλὰ τοσαύτης ἀποδοχῆς ἠξίωται παρὰ τοῦ πανηγεμόνος, ὥστε τὴν μήτραν ὑπ' αὐτοῦ διοιχθεῖσαν σπορὰν θείας γονῆς παραδέξασθαι πρὸς τὴν τῶν καλῶν ἐπιτηδευμάτων καὶ πράξεων γένεσιν.

How significant is that answer "Yes," fraught as it is with inner meaning. For what can be more befitting to God than to grant and promise His blessings in a moment and with a sign of assent? Yet those who receive a sign of assent from God are refused assent by every fool. Thus the oracles represent Leah as hated and for this reason she received such a name. For by interpretation it means "rejected and weary," because we all turn away from virtue and think her wearisome, so little to our taste are the commands she often lays upon us. But from the Ruler of all she was awarded such acceptance that her womb which He opened received the seed of divine impregnation [Gen. 29:31], whence should come the birth of noble practices and deeds (§§253b-255a).

(3) Rationale and basic reason (§255b)

This is the reproduction of the χρεία in the form of an argumentative thesis and its primary defense. Through allegorical interpretation the theme of *virtue* is explicitly manifested as a basis for the following argumentation.

μάθε οὖν, ὦ ψυχή, ὅτι καὶ "Σάρρα", ἡ ἀρετή, "τέξεταί σοι υἱόν", οὐ μόνον "Ἀγαρ, ἡ μέση παιδεία· ἐκείνης μὲν γὰρ τὸ ἔγγονον διδακτόν, ταύτης δὲ πάντως αὐτομαθές ἐστι.

---

[120] H. Rabe, *Hermogenis Opera*, p. 7-8.
[121] C. Walz, *Rhetores Graeci* I, p. 212. His substitution of the Aristotelian category of τὸ δίκαιον (*Rhetorica* I, 3, 5) for that of τὸ ἀληθές possibly reflects the fact that the χρεία is treated as a maxim in a philosophical context rather than a forensic one (B. Mack, "Decoding the Scripture," p. 9-10).

Learn then, soul of man, that Sarah also, that is virtue, shall bear thee a son, as well as Hagar, the lower instruction. For Hagar's offspring is the creature of teaching, But Sarah's learns from none other at all than itself (§255b).

(4) Opposite (§256a)

Having just introduced the *locus a contrario* in the *ratio*, and returning to it consistently throughout his argumentative process, the Alexandrian here underscores the contrast between earthly virtues and heavenly virtue.

μὴ θαυμάσῃς ⟨δ'⟩, εἰ πάντα φέρων σπουδαῖα ὁ θεὸς ἤνεγκε καὶ τοῦτο τὸ γένος, σπάνιον μὲν ἐπὶ γῆς, πάμπολυ δ' ἐν οὐρανῷ.

And wonder not that God, who brings about all good things, has brought into being this kind also, and though there be few such upon earth, in Heaven vast is their number (§256a).

The simple contrast between earth and heaven, allied to the *locus a minore ad maius*, is used to test the validity of the formulated argument. But its force results from the connection with the following ones. The concept of οὐρανός accompanies that of ἀρετή and philosophical σοφία, that of autodidacticism and that of the spontaneous production of fruit in the sabbatical year. The concept of γῆ is linked to those of the encyclical studies, the "teaching" set forth by the masters, and agriculture. Nevertheless, as P. Borgen asserts, contrary to the views defended by Windisch, Pascher, Goodenough, Leisegang and Jonas, this contrast does not mean that Philo develops in the homily a cosmic and anthropologic dualism of the "not earthly, but heavenly" type, as occurs in the *Leg.* III, 162-168.

> Although the homily of *Mut.* 253-263 makes a clear distinction between heaven and earth, the philosophy for the souls and encyclia, it concludes by assigning a positive "virtue" to each, although earth and encyclia represent, of course, a weaker one.[122]

The way the contrast, first formulated in paragraph 255b, is progressively explained in §§258-259 and §263 is significant. For Philo two distinct categories of "virtues" exist: an inferior category produced by the encyclical studies, and a superior one produced in the soul by philosophy. Yet the contrast is not as radical as the Cynics, the Epicureans or even some Stoics define it.[123] The comparison of education with agriculture indicates that, while the ἐγκύκλια produce knowledge through learning, philosophy manifests the intuitive wisdom of nature. Thus, the dual relationship of Abraham with Sarah and Hagar not only allegorically expresses the clear distinction

---

[122] *Bread from Heaven. An Exegetical Study of the Concept of Manna in the Gospel of John and the Writings of Philo.* Supplements to Novum Testamentum (Leiden: Brill, 1965), p. 118.

[123] Borgen, "Philo of Alexandria", p. 102-103. Cf. F. H. Colson, "Philo on Education," JTS, 18 (1917), p. 153; H. J. Mette, "'Εγκύκλιος παιδεία" *Gymnasium* 67 (1960), p. 304; H. A. Wolfson, *Philo* I, p. 145.

between the knowledge transmitted by the masters and the knowledge acquired by divine revelation. It also justifies the apologetic reinterpretation of the Jewish faith in the light of Greek cultural tradition.[124] Nevertheless, it is only the transformation effected in paragraph 259 that helps us understand the extent of the contrast initially formulated:

> ταῖς μὲν οὖν ἀπὸ γῆς καὶ ἄνθρωποι γεωπόνοι συνεργοῦσι, τὰς δ' ἀπ' οὐρανοῦ νίφει χωρὶς συμπράξεως ἑτέρων ὁ μόνος αὐτουργὸς θεός. καὶ μὴν λέγεται· "ἰδοὺ ὕω ὑμῖν ἄρτους ἀπ' οὐρανοῦ". τίνα οὖν ἀπ' ⟨οὐρανοῦ⟩ τροφὴν ἐνδίκως ὕεσθαι λέγει, ὅτι μὴ τὴν οὐράνιον σοφίαν;

> The earthly food is produced with the cooperation of husbandmen, but the heavenly is sent like the snow by God the solely self-acting, with none to share His work. And indeed it says "Behold I rain upon you bread from heaven [Exod. 16:4]. Of what food can he rightly say that it is rained from heaven, save of heavenly wisdom (§259)?

In the "agricultural" activity of divinity, therefore, two forms of labor stand out: one direct and the other indirect. The heavenly bread (αὐτομαθὴς σοφία) is directly sent by God to the earth in the form of αὐτουργός. That is, virtue and philosophical wisdom, the "authentic philosophy,"[125] is a gift given by nature itself and implanted directly in the soul. The earthly bread (ἐγκύκλιος παιδεία) is equally produced by it, but with the collaboration of γεωπόνοι.

(5) Analogy (§§256b-258a;259b-260;262)

Like the *a contrario* argument, the *similitudo* also permeates the central development of this elaboration. The first structure confirms the validity of the principle enunciated by demonstrating the existence of autodidactic virtue and its divine origin, giving rise to the process of thematic specification by elucidating the formulated contrast and promoting its illustration by recourse to the *locus a minore ad maius*.

> μάθοις δ' ἂν ἀπὸ τῶν ἄλλων, ἐξ ὧν συνέστηκεν ἄνθρωπος. ἆρά γε οἱ ὀφθαλμοὶ διδαχθέντες ὁρῶσι; τί δ'; οἱ μυκτῆρες ὀσφραίνονται μαθήσει; ἅπτονται δ' αἱ χεῖρες ἢ οἱ πόδες προΐασι κατ' ἐπιτάγματα ἢ παραινέσεις ὑφηγητῶν; αἱ δ' ὁρμαὶ καὶ φαντασίαι—πρῶται δ' εἰσὶν αὗται κινήσεις καὶ σχέσεις ψυχῆς—διδασκαλίᾳ συνέστησαν; παρὰ δὲ σοφιστὴν φοιτήσας ὁ νοῦς ἡμῶν νοεῖν καὶ καταλαμβάνειν ἔμαθε; πάντα ταῦτ' ἀφειμένα διδασκαλίας ἀπαυτοματιζούσῃ φύσει χρῆται πρὸς τὰς οἰκείας ἐνεργείας. τί οὖν ἔτι θαυμάζεις, εἰ καὶ

---

[124] Cf. Borgen, "Philo of Alexandria", p. 109-110. "Abraham, representing the Jewish nation, receives education from two schools: the encyclical education is the bastard school which the Jews have in common with the pagan surroundings: the other school is the genuine, Jewish philosophy." So that, according to Borgen, Philo "places encyclical education on the borderline between Judaism and paganism, as an adiaforon which in itself is neither good or bad;" it is a neutral ἐγκύκλιος in contrast to the Jewish philosophy contained in the laws of Moses and studied on the Sabbath in the synagogues (Ibid., p. 109, 113).

[125] τὴν πάτριον φιλοσοφίαν (*Mos.* II, 216) contained in the writings of Moses. For a definition of φιλοσοφία in Philo, consult Nikiprowetzky, *Le commentaire de l'Écriture*, p. 97-108.

ἀρετὴν ἄπονον καὶ ἀταλαίπωρον ὁ θεὸς ὀμβρήσει μηδεμιᾶς δεομένην ἐπιστασίας, ἀλλ' ἐξ ἀρχῆς ὁλόκληρον καὶ παντελῆ;

You may learn this truth from the other elements, out of which man is constituted. Have the eyes been taught to see, do the nostrils learn to smell, do the hands touch or the feet advance in obedience to the orders or exhortations of instructors? As for our impulses and mental pictures, which are the primal conditions of the soul, according as it is in motion or at rest, are they made what they are by teaching? Does our mind attend the school of the professor of wisdom and there learn to think and to apprehend? All these exempt from teaching make use of self-worked independent nature for their respective activities. Why then need you still wonder that God showers virtue without toil or trouble, needing no controlling hand but perfect and complete from the very first (§§256b-258a)?

Commenting on this passage, R. Arnaldez observes that "sensitive intuition is the sign that enables to grasp the possibility of a mental intuition of illuminative virtue."[126] Consequently, if God is the author of all those physical gifts listed, only He can be the source of perfect virtue.

In the second passage (§§259b-260), the comparison of education with agriculture is developed, already initially referred to in the suggestive expression ἀρετὴν ἄπονον καὶ ἀταλαίπωρον ὁ θεὸς ὀμβρήσει, in paragraph 258a. The heavenly bread, here analogically interpreted as "virtue" and divine "wisdom" poured out on the soul, is spontaneously engendered and automatically gathered as the perfect "manna" of abundant philosophy,[127] because by nature it is associated with the αὐτομαθής.[128]

τίνα οὖν ἀπ' (οὐρανοῦ) τροφὴν ἐνδίκως ὕεσθαι λέγει, ὅτι μὴ τὴν οὐράνιον σοφίαν; ἣν ἄνωθεν ἐπιπέμπει ταῖς ἵμερον ἀρετῆς ἐχούσαις ψυχαῖς ὁ φρονήσεως εὐθηνίαν καὶ εὐετηρίαν ἔχων καὶ τὰ ὅλα ἄρδων καὶ μάλιστα ἐν ἱερᾷ ἑβδόμῃ, ἣν σάββατον καλεῖ (Exod. 16:23ff.). τότε γὰρ τὴν τῶν αὐτομάτων ἀγαθῶν φορὰν ἔσεσθαί φησιν, οὐκ ἐξ ὕλης τέχνης ἀνατελλόντων, ἀλλ' αὐτογενεῖ καὶ αὐτοτελεῖ φύσει βλαστανόντων καὶ τοὺς οἰκείους φερόντων καρπούς.

Of what food can he rightly say that it is rained from heaven, save of heavenly wisdom which is sent from above on souls which yearn for virtue by Him who sheds the gift of prudence in rich abundance, whose grace waters the universe, and chiefly so in the holy seventh (year) which he calls the Sabbath? For then he says there will be a plentiful supply of good things spontaneous and self-grown, which even all the art in the world

---

[126] PM 18, p. 152, n. 1.

[127] Cf. §256a.

[128] It is significant to note in this homily the rhetorical usage of αὐτός in the composition of words: αὐτομαθές (§255); ἀπαυτοματιξούσῃ φύσει (§257); αὐτουργὸς θεός (§259); αὐτομάτων or αὐτομαθῶν ἀγαθῶν; αὐτογενεῖ καὶ αὐτοτελεῖ (§260); and αὐτομαθοῦς (§263). P. Borgen observes that τὸ αὐτομαθές and τὸ αὐτόματον are interchangeable as descriptions of the sabbatical year (cf. Fug. 170), and that both ideas are explicitly represented in the text. The interpretation of automatic growth in §257 (αὐτοματιξούσῃ) is developed in §260 where, according to this authoritative Philonist, one should contrast the reading τῶν αὐτομαθῶν ἀγαθῶν to that of τῶν αὐτομάτων ἀγαθῶν, suggested by Mangey and adopted by P. Wendland and F. H. Colson (PLCL II, p. 106).

could never raise, but springing up and bearing their proper fruit through self-originated, self-consummated nature (§§259b-260).

A third analogy (§262) confirms the thesis.

καθάπερ λύπη καὶ φόβος ἰδίας ἀναφθέγξεις ἔχουσιν, ἃς ἂν τὸ βιασάμενον καὶ κρατῆσαν ὀνοματοποιήσῃ πάθος, οὕτως εὐβουλίαι καὶ εὐφροσύναι φυσικαῖς ἐκφωνήσεσιν ἀναγκάζουσι χρῆσθαι, ὧν οὐκ ἂν εὕροι τις κυριωτέρας καὶ εὐθυβολωτέρας κλήσεις, κἂν τυγχάνῃ περὶ τὰς κλήσεις σοφός.

Just as fear and grief have their own special ejaculations, which the overpowering force of emotion coins, so moods of happy planning or of gladness compel us to break out into natural utterances, as aptly and exactly expressing our meaning as any which an adept in the study of names could devise (§262).

(6) Example (§§258-259)

Moses and his word here function as authoritative example and testimony to substantiate the validity of the argument, affirming that "τοῖς μὲν ἄλλοις ἀνθρώποις ἀπὸ γῆς εἶναι τὰς τροφάς, μόνῳ δὲ ἀπ' οὐρανοῦ τῷ ὁρατικῷ."[129] This shows that "ταῖς μὲν οὖν ἀπὸ γῆς καὶ ἀνθρώπῳ γεωπόνοι συνεργοῦσι, τὰς δ' ἀπ' οὐρανοῦ νίφει χωρὶς συμπράξεως ἑτέρων ὁ μόνος αὐτουργὸς θεός."[130] That is, heavenly wisdom – "τὴν οὐράνιον σοφίαν."

(7) The oracular testimony of God Himself (§263a), interpreted by the Alexandrian exegete in his decoding of the text, provides the logically necessary conclusion to the thematic development.

διό φησιν· "εὐλόγηκα αὐτόν, αὐξήσω αὐτόν, πληθυνῶ, δώδεκα ἔθνη γεννήσει", τὸν κύκλον καὶ τὸν χορὸν ἅπαντα τῶν σοφιστικῶν προπαιδευμάτων. "τὴν δὲ διαθήκην μου στήσω πρὸς Ἰσαάκ"

Therefore he says: "I have blessed him, I will increase and multiply him: he shall beget twelve nations (that is, the whole round and train of the early branches of the professional schools), but my covenant I will establish with Isaac" [Gen. 17:20ff] (§263a).[131]

(8) Epilogue (§263)

Having begun the argument with Hagar and Sarah (§§255b-260), Philo ends it with Isaac and Ishmael (§§261-263) to demonstrate that there are two forms of virtue:

ἵν' ἑκατέρας ἀρετῆς τὸ ἀνθρώπων μεταποιῆται γένος, διδακτῆς τε καὶ αὐτομαθοῦς, τὸ μὲν ἀσθενέστερον διδασκομένης, ἑτοίμης δὲ τὸ ἐρρωμένον.

---

[129] "While other men receive their food from earth, the nation of vision alone has it from heaven".
[130] "The earthly food is produced with the cooperation of husbandmen, but the heavenly is sent like the snow by God the solely self-acting ..."
[131] Cf. Genesis 17:20-21.

> Thus both forms of virtue, one where the teacher and learner are the same, will be open to human kind. And where man is weak he will claim the former, where he is strong the latter which comes ready to his hands (§263b).

One type results from the teaching of others, and the other is manifest in oneself as natural talent or direct insemination from God; the two types correspond to the encyclical studies and Jewish philosophy. The former is represented by Hagar and Ishmael; the latter, by Sarah and Isaac. Both, however, were received and appropriated by Abraham.[132] Although Philo's objective is to "encourage the Jews to place the divine virtue of Jewish philosophy at the center," they should still not altogether reject the ἐγκύκλια.[133]

The parenetic intention of this passage, appropriately stressed by H. Hegermann,[134] is especially visible beginning with §255b; and the hortatory character of the epilogue is particularly evident when we compare it with the thesis enunciated there.

> μάθε οὖν, ὦ ψυχή, ὅτι καὶ "Σάρρα", ἡ ἀρετή, "τέξεταί σοι υἱόν", οὐ μόνον "Αγαρ, ἡ μέση παιδεία· ἐκείνης μὲν γὰρ τὸ ἔγγονον διδακτόν, ταύτης δὲ πάντως αὐτομαθές ἐστι.

> Learn then, soul of man, that Sarah also, that is virtue, shall bear thee a son, as well as Hagar, the lower instruction. For Hagar's offspring is the creature of teaching, but Sarah's learns from none other at all than itself (§255b).

> ἵν' ἑκατέρας ἀρετῆς τὸ ἀνθρώπων μεταποιῆται γένος, διδακτῆς τε καὶ αὐτομαθοῦς, κτλ

> Thus both forms of virtue, one where the teacher is another, one where the teacher and learner are the same, will be open to humankind (§263b).

The fundamental terms of the main argument are repeated according with the technique of ring-composition, connecting the end to the beginning. Thus the thematic presentation is concluded, the thesis appropriately expanded and the *lemma* of Scripture exegetically treated. It is worth noting that there is a sequential interpretation of ἀρετή, as an allegorical designation of "Sarah," to ἀρετή as a designation equally applied to the fruit of "Hagar's" womb, through the following intermediate developments of clarification and specification: διδακτόν/αὐτομαθές; γῆ/οὐρανός; πάντα σπουδαῖα/τοῦτο τὸ γένος; τροφὴ ἀπὸ γῆς/ἄρτος (τροφή) ἀπ' οὐρανοῦ; ἐγκύκλιος παιδεία/οὐράνιος σοφία; ἀρετὴ διδακτή/ἀρετὴ αὐτομαθής. In expanding concentric movements, the exegetical discussion continually returns to the initially formulated thesis, in its progression articulating the

---

[132] Cf. *Congr.* 35.
[133] Borgen, "Philo of Alexandria", p. 121.
[134] "Philo und seine Kreis," in *Die Vorstellung vom Schöpfungsmittler im hellenistischen Judentum und Urchristentum*. Texte und Untersuchungen zur Geschichte der altchristlichen Literatur 82 (Berlin: Akademie-Verlag, 1961), p. 18.

material gathered in the *inuentio* in order to confer substance and organic consistency to the argument.

The complete and finished elucidation of the text thus involves all the steps of an elaboration. Exegesis and thematic development go hand in hand; as the text of the *lemma* is being decoded, the thesis is progressively confirmed until it is totally clarified and substantiated.

There can be no doubt that Philo consciously and persistently employed rhetorical techniques both for the development of his exegetical analyses and for the formulation and defense of the principles of his theological-philosophical system. The passages that we have analyzed reveal not only his comprehensive knowledge of the many devices of Greco-Roman rhetoric but also his ability to transform, adapt and apply them.

While exhibiting in practice the ideas later expressed by Quintilian, Philo seems to resist a rigid adherence to the various traditional topics when constructing arguments.[135] As the Roman educator urges, Philo usually develops a line of argumentation freely and creatively, exploring possible types of proof, choosing those most pertinent and arranging them hierarchically in terms of teleological convergence and persuasive efficacy. While basing his compositional strategy on the taxonomy defended by the rhetoricians, Philo knows when and how to adapt it to his audience and the goals of an exegetical discourse. The Alexandrian sometimes reproduces Greco-Roman rhetorical norms faithfully, but never does so in servile imitation. The structures are adapted to concrete argumentative situations and always in conformity with Philo's overall purpose.

---

[135] Quintilian V, 10, 122-125; V, 14, 31-33.

CHAPTER FIVE

RHYTHMIC AND PERIODIC STRUCTURES

I. *Introduction*

In the previous two chapters we showed that the essential principles of rhetorical structure, in their argumentative dimension, are positively and consistently employed in Philo's literary work. The influence of Hellenistic rhetoric is noticeable both at the level of an entire treatise as well as at that of its individual thematic and exegetical arguments. There is no doubt that the Alexandrian exegete easily and effectively employed many different devices widely representative of the rhetorical tradition.

Our study would be incomplete however, if we did not also consider the advantages Philo knows how to gain from rhythmic and periodic style,[1] —especially since some of the criticisms leveled at him by modern scholars emphasize the superficiality, lengthiness, monotony and lack of logical rigor of his compositions.

As we have already observed, many such criticisms are based on inaccurate understanding of our author.[2] It is true that, like those of Isocrates, Demosthenes, and even Thucydides, Philo's periods are generally long and apparently complex.[3] But it is no less true that, like these Attic models, he knows when it is convenient to use a periodic structure of technically correct length in keeping with respiratory capacity. Even his longest sentences comply with acceptable standards, making more sense when heard than when read in silence.[4] As Cicero maintains,[5] periodic style should be used

---

[1] See Manuel Alexandre, Jr. "The Art of Periodic Composition in Philo of Alexandria", in *The Studia Philonica Annual: Studies in Hellenistic Judaism* 3 (1991), p. 335-350.
[2] On this basic issue, see especially the study by Nikiprowetzky, *Le commentaire de l'Écriture*.
[3] Cf. A. W. DeGroot, *Handbook of Antique Prose Rhythm* (Groningen, 1919); and Andrew Q. Norton and James McHeman, *Paul, the Man and the Myth. A Study in the Authorship of Greek Prose* (New York: Harper & Row, 1966). These books offer some statistics relative to Philo's periodic style: the first, on his *clausulae* (p. 178-197); and the second, on the extension of his phrases (compare Table 6, on "Sentence length distributions - Philo," Table 5, 9 and 10 on "Sentence length distributions - Thucydides, Demosthenes and Isocrates," respectively).
[4] T. Conley, *Philo's Rhetoric: Studies in Style, Composition and Exegesis* (Urbana: University of Illinois, 1982. Draft for discussion), p. 59.
[5] *Orator*, 205.

with moderation so as not to become artificial. This opinion is also shared by the two masters of Greek oratory previously mentioned.[6]

In fact, Philo is able to keep the argumentative structure of his literary text in balance, tactfully and strategically composing oratorical periods in line with the canons, especially when it is necessary to speak with pugnacity and energy,[7] to amplify important facts through narrative[8] or to condense central principles of his exegetical message. We will demonstrate this through the analysis of a few brief passages. First, however, it is appropriate to give some attention to the principles which shape the doctrine norms of periodic style in the Hellenistic period. Aristotle says that it is very advantageous for rhetorical prose to be rhythmical. Rhythmic discourse, he explains, far from interfering with rhetorical reasoning, has the virtue of being not only more pleasant but also more intelligible to the listener.[9] Likewise he maintains that periodic style, organized as a structural whole with clear indications of beginning and end,[10] offers the discourse the same properties as rhythm and is even more effective when it is structured antithetically.[11] In two of his examples, both taken from Isocrates' *Panegyricus*, Aristotle calls the attention of the reader to models of textual structure in which the divisions of rhythm and thought coincide. This confirms the thesis that a periodic text is of necessity rhythmic.[12] He also refers to the structure of the two cola period, that it is divided rhythmically into two parts, and that the rhythmic division corresponds to a logical division.[13]

Demetrius[14] devotes the first thirty-five paragraphs of his treatise *De*

---

[6] Cf. Isocrates, *Paneg.* 4-10; Demosthenes, *De Corona* 320-321.
[7] Cf. Quintilian IX, 4, 126.
[8] Ibid. IX, 4, 127.
[9] *Rhetorica* III, 8, 1408b 22-29.
[10] Ibid. III, 9, 1409a 35 - 1409b 6. Cf. *Poetica* 1451a 2-6, 1459a 30-35. Aristotle explains in identical fashion the structure of a piece.
[11] *Rhetorica* III, 9, 1410a 19-23.
[12] See T. Adamik, "Aristotle's Theory of the Period," *Philologus* 128:2 (1984), p. 186-187. "In the question of the relationship between rhythm and period I agree with these authors who interpret these two as belonging together: J. Zehetmeier, "Die Periodenlehre des Aristoteles," *Philologue* 85 (1930), p. 261-264; D. M. Schenkeveld, *Studies in Demetrius on Style* (Amsterdam, 1964), p. 28-29" (Ibid.).
[13] Ibid., p. 187. Cf. *Rhet.* 1409b 13ff.
[14] *De Elocutione* 1-35. The question of the authorship of this work has not yet been settled. W. R. Roberts, *Demetrius on Style* (Cambridge: Cambridge University Press, 1902; Hildesheim: Georg Holms, 1969) p. 49-64, defends the thesis that its author lived very probably at the beginning of the Christian era, putting aside the hypothesis of Demetrius Phalereus being its author. But G. M. A. Grube, (*A Greek Critic: Demetrius on Style* Toronto: University of Toronto, 1961, p. 39-56) supports the traditional opinion that Demetrius lived in the third century B.C.E., and that he could reasonably be the author. In response D.M. Schenkeveld has argued (*Studies in Demetrius on Style* diss. Amsterdam 1964, p. 147) that Demetrius probably wrote in the first century c.e., but used materials dating from the late 2nd or early 1st

Elocutione to the systematic exposition of this theme, taking Aristotelian doctrine for his starting point. Cicero and Quintilian, aware of the importance that this can assume in rhetorical discourse, follow an identical path, carefully applying the same principles to Latin literature.

To summarize, the oratorical period[15] is formed by a varied but coherent number of κῶλα, each of them approximately as long as a dactylic hexameter.[16] Although Aristotle preferred a period with two κῶλα, Demetrius notes that the most significant detail is his distinction between a simple and a compound period.[17] Ideally, he adds, the period will have between two and four "members."[18] Even more important is the harmonic and homogeneous balance of its form,[19] adding attractiveness to the content.[20]

Cicero asserts that a complete period has approximately four κῶλα, each one of them about twelve to seventeen syllables. This does not mean that they should not vary according to the circumstances, both in the number of syllables within each member and in the number of members within the period.[21] What is indispensable is that the thought expressed be completed in a clear and intelligible manner, without jeopardizing the memory.[22] It is said that "the natural pattern for the period is the number of words that a person can produce during one simple respiratory exhalation." Artistic oratory, however, creates cadence patterns of various lengths so as to produce the maximum pleasure in communicating the message.[23] According to T. Adamik, when Aristotle affirms that the period is εὐανάπνευστος (an adjective that occurs only with him and is generally translated "easily spoken in one breath"), he is saying that it is "easily utterable with regard to breath, from the point of view of breathing"; signifying by this expression "that the period is naturally divided into units in both rhythmical and logical terms;

---

century B.C.E. According to George Kennedy "a possible conclusion is that it was written in the early first century B.C." (*A New History of Classical Rhetoric*, p. 88–89.

[15] Demetrius establishes the difference between historical, dialogical and rhetorical periods, referring to the latter as the most compact and elaborated (I, 19-21). See Doreen C. Innes, "Period and Colon: Theory and Example in Demetrius and Longinus", in W.W. Fortenbaugh and D.C. Mirhady (eds.), *Peripatetic Rhetoric after Aristotle* (New Brunswick, NJ: Transaction Publishers, 1994) p. 36-53.

[16] Demetrius I, 3. Compare Cicero, *Orator*, 65, 221-222; Quintilian IX, 4, 125-126.

[17] *De Elocutione* I, 35-36.

[18] Ibid. I, 16.

[19] Ibid. I, 13-15, 20.

[20] Ibid. I, 28.

[21] *Orator* 65, 220-222.

[22] Cf. Quintilian IX, 4, 125-126.

[23] D. J. Ochs, "Cicero's Rhetorical Theory," in *A Synoptical History of Classical Rhetoric* (ed. J. J. Murphy [New York: Random House, 1972], p. 124), in his commentary-synthesis on Cicero, *De Oratore* III, 181-186, and *Orator* 190.

[that] these units of rhythm and thought coincide, and thus, one can take breath comfortably at the end of each kolon."[24]

Regarding the principles of periodic style, one must take into consideration that often a phrase cannot be expressed in a single breath. Demetrius[25] affirms that in Isocrates' discourses "the periods follow one another with a regularity in no way inferior to the hexameters in Homeric poetry." The opening of *Panegyricus*, with two periods that take up no less than twenty-five lines, is typical in the work of this master of periodic style. Of course, the longest expressions are divided into smaller units, constituting the periods or their equivalents.[26]

In fact, the composite period is a phenomenon common in Greek and Latin literature of the Hellenistic period. C. Robbins cites and comments on, as a typical illustration of the compound period, the introductory sentence of Cicero's third oration against Catilina;[27] it is a sentence composed of two units of four κῶλα each, separated by the emphatic κόμμα *hodierno die*.

The Roman orator considers that periodic style is essential in historiography and in epideictic discourse, but less common and necessary in the other genres. He also believes that in all cases it should be used with naturalness and moderation.[28] Quintilian also underlines that, although more appropriate to *exordium* and peroration, it is suitable for all genres of amplification[29] which affect each of the parts of the discourse, especially the *argumentatio*.[30]

---

[24] Adamik, "Aristotle's Theory", p. 187-188.
[25] *De Elocutione* I, 12.
[26] Cf. C. J. Robbins, "Rhetorical Structure of Philippians 2:6-11," CBQ 42 (1980), p. 77.
[27] *Rem publicam, Quirites, uitamque omnium uestrum*
   bona, fortunas, coniuges, liberosque uestros
   atque hoc domicilium clarissimi imperi
   fortunatissimam pulcherrimamque urbem
   hodierno die
   deorum immortalium summo erga uos amore,
   laboribus, consiliis, periculis meis
   et flamma atque ferro ac paene ex faucibus fati
   ereptam et uobis conseruatam ac restitutam uidetis.

"At the end of the first unit, the reader will pause for breath. A definite unit of thought has been given, a whole series of ideas in the objective case. They are merely listed here, and only in the second unit or period do we have a prediction concerning them" (p. 77-78).

[28] *Orator* 205.
[29] *Institutio Oratoria* IX, 4, 128-130.
[30] Lausberg, *Manual de Retórica Literaria*, §400.

II. Examples of Rhythmic and Periodic Structures in Philo

1. Legatio ad Gaium 53-56

Curiously one of the best examples of this style in Philo is found in the answer of the emperor Gaius Caligula to Macro, set in the context of one of his bursts of insane and homicidal fury.

Inserted in the narrative of the assassination of three important political figures, in a *gradatio* of rhetorical motivation,[31] this *amplificatio per ratiocinationem*[32] is formed by four sections in chiastic structural order. The first is devoted to an ironic definition of Macro's character; the second, to Caligula's self-glorification and personal exaltation; and the third, by returning to the original issue, is devoted to the exaltation of his own person and to the consequent denigration of Macro, thus confirming by analogy the previous argument and determining the content of the fourth.

[53] πάρεστιν ὁ διδάσκαλος τοῦ μηκέτι μανθάνειν ὀφείλοντος,
ὁ παιδαγωγὸς τοῦ μηκέτι παιδὸς ὄντος,
ὁ νουθετητὴς τοῦ φρονιμωτέρου,
ὁ τὸν αὐτοκράτορα τῷ ὑπηκόῳ πειθαρχεῖν ἀξιῶν,[33]
    ἐθάδα τῆς ἡγεμονικῆς ἐπιστήμης
    καὶ παιδευτὴν ἑαυτὸν γράφει
    παρὰ τίνι μαθὼν τὰ ἀρχικὰ ἔγωγε οὐκ οἶδα.

[54] ἐμοὶ μὲν γὰρ ἐξ ἔτι σπαργάνων μυρίοι διδάσκαλοι γεγόνασι,
πατέρες, ἀδελφοί, θεῖοι, ἀνεψιοί, πάπποι,
πρόγονοι μέχρι τῶν ἀρχηγετῶν,
οἱ ἀφ' αἵματος πάντες καθ' ἑκάτερον γένος.
    τό τε πατρῷον καὶ μητρῷον,
    αὐτοκρατεῖς ἐξουσίας περιποιησάμενοι,
    χωρὶς τοῦ κἂν ταῖς πρώταις τῶν σπερμάτων καταβολαῖς εἶναί
    τινας δυνάμεις βασιλικὰς τῶν ἡγεμονικῶν.

[55] ὡς γὰρ αἱ τοῦ σώματος καὶ τῆς ψυχῆς ὁμοιότητες
κατά τε τὴν μορφὴν καὶ σχέσεις καὶ κινήσεις βουλάς
τε καὶ πράξεις ἐν τοῖς σπερματικοῖς σῴζονται λόγοις,
    οὕτως εἰκὸς ἐν τοῖς αὐτοῖς ὑπογράφεσθαι τυπωδέστερον
    καὶ τὴν πρὸς ἡγεμονίαν ἐμφέρειαν.

[56] εἶτα ἐμὲ τὸν καὶ πρὸ τῆς γενέσεως
ἔτι κατὰ γαστρὸς ἐν τῷ τῆς φύσεως ἐργαστηρίῳ
διαπλασθέντα αὐτοκράτορα τολμᾷ τις διδάσκειν,
ἀνεπιστήμων ἐπιστήμονα;

---

[31] On the chronological order of the death of Gemellus, Silanus and Macro, and possible rhetorical justification for the order adopted by Philo, consult A. Pelletier, PM 32, p. 22.
[32] Quintilian VIII, 4, 15.
[33] Note that, according to Aristotle, the end of the rhetorical period should be clearly delineated, not necessarily by a punctuation mark, but by the rhythm itself (*Rhet.* 1409a 6; 1409b 4).

ποῦ γὰρ τοῖς ἰδιώταις πρὸ μικροῦ θέμις
εἰς ἡγεμονικῆς ψυχῆς παρακύψαι βουλεύματα;
τολμῶσι δὲ ὑπ' ἀναισχύντου θράσους ἱεροφαντεῖν
καὶ τελεῖν τὰ ἡγεμονικὰ μόλις ἂν ἐν μύσταις ἀναγραφέντες.

Here comes the teacher of one who no longer needs to learn, the tutor of one who is no longer in tutelage, the censor of his superior in wisdom, who holds that an emperor should obey his subjects, who rates himself as versed in the art of government and an instructor therein, though in what school he has learnt its principles I do not know.

For I from the cradle have had a host of teachers, father, brothers, uncles, cousins, grandparents, ancestors, right up to the founders of the House, all my kinsmen by blood on both the maternal and paternal sides, who attained to offices of independent authority, apart from the fact that in the original seeds of their begetting kinglike potentialities for government were contained.

For just as the seminal forces preserve similarities of the body in form and carriage and gait, and of the soul in projects and actions, so we may suppose that to the governing faculty they contain a resemblance in outline.

And then does anyone dare to teach me, who even while in the womb, that workshop of nature, was modelled as an emperor, ignorance dare to instruct knowledge? How can they who were but now common citizens have a right to peer into the counsels of an imperial soul? yet in their shameless effrontery they who would hardly be admitted to rank as learners dare to act as masters who initiate others into the mysteries of government.

The periodic style of this mini-discourse is antithetically structured in a way that causes it to resemble a rhetorical syllogism.[34] Each one of its four sections is divided into two periodic units, with those of four κῶλα predominating.

The units that make up the first section cast doubt on Macro's pretended function as master, teacher, counselor and lord of one who surpasses him in everything, in wisdom and maturity, political knowledge and sovereignty. The four κῶλα of the first period are gradually followed by the verbal association of key terms that reveal the false and dangerous position in which Macro places himself. The three κῶλα of the second section limit themselves to inversely confirming the contradiction of such behavior. Taken together, they produce a symmetrical rise and fall of rhythm, in language as well as in thought developing a species of cadence very characteristic of oratorical discourse.

The second section is similarly formed by two periods of four cola, both concentrated on the Emperor's ego. The first, structured in two complementary parts, highlights his innate vocation and learning, founded and

---

[34] "For Aristotle, who emphasized the importance of logical argumentation, the period was important from two points of view. On the one hand its structure is similar to that of the syllogism, therefore it expresses the logical content convincingly, and at the same time also pleasantly (1401a 19ff.).... On the other hand it helps us realize the general principle of splitting up the text into natural unities according to the rhythm of thought and so making it easily performable and comprehensible" (Adamik, "Aristotle's Theory", p. 193). Cf. Aristotle, *Rhetorica* III, 9.

deeply rooted in a long imperial ascendancy. The chiastic alliteration of the second κῶλα is especially noteworthy: πατέρες, ἀδελφοί, θεῖοι, ἀνεψιοί πάπποι. The second section expands and explains the same thesis.

The analogy by which the third section is structured substantiates Caligula's hereditary and natural aptitude, at the same time philosophically[35] justifying the argument begun in the fourth. Again there are two periods of four κῶλα, in which a double *interrogatio* predominates.

Considered as a whole, these compound periods form a chiasm of A B C B' A' structure. This is a rhetorical figure in which verbal and conceptual antitheses are central and also one in which concepts of teaching, learning and nature play a fundamental role.

    A - Macro intends to teach Gaius (§53).
        B - Gaius learned since the cradle (§54).
            C - The natural gift of authority (§55).
        B' - Gaius was formed as emperor from his mother's womb, nature's workshop (§56a).
    A' - Who is (Macro) to dare to teach him? (§56b).

Without doubt this passage reveals a coherent and logical structure, visibly shaped in accordance with the principles of periodic style. The harmonious arrangement of words and sounds in its cola reaffirm this fact. The rhythm is fast and most of the feet are short, as they should be in *contentiones*. The words that compose the rhythmic structure of the *clausulae* obey the rule of variety in order to avoid the accumulation of isosyllabic, isochronic or isotonic sequences in their musical, rhythmic and metrical movement.[36] The features of conscious literary composition are apparent in the circular argumentative sequence which makes a powerful appeal ethically, logically and emotionally.

2. De Vita Mosis *II, 253-255*

Another instance of a continuous rhythmic and periodic structure is the vivid description of the Hebrew people crossing the Red Sea. Philo inserts the passage in his discourse in order to demonstrate Moses' prophetic inspiration.[37]

---

[35] The expression ἐν τοῖς σπερματικοῖς ... λόγοις ("principles," or "seminal reasons") is, according to A. Pelletier, an "image souvent exploitée dans la conception stoïcienne de l'action divine immanente au monde" (PM 32, p. 102, n. 1).
[36] See M. Patillon, *La théorie du discours chez Hermogène le Rhéteur. Essai sur la structure de la rhétorique ancienne* (Paris, 1988) p. 202-203.
[37] A literary form of the *exemplum* which Quintilian seems to understand under the collective name, though imprecise, of *commemoratio* (V, 11, 6. Cf. Lausberg, *Manual de Retórica Literaria*, §415).

RHYTHMIC AND PERIODIC STRUCTURES 241

[253] ῥῆξις θαλάττης, ἀναχώρησις ἑκατέρου τμήματος,
πῆξις τῶν κατὰ τὸ ῥαγὲν μέρος
διὰ παντὸς τοῦ βάθους κυμάτων
ἵν' ἀντὶ τειχῶν ᾖ κραταιοτάτων,
    εὐθυτενὴς ἀνατομὴ τῆς μεγαλουργηθείσης ὁδοῦ,
    ἣ τῶν κρυσταλλωθέντων μεθόριος ἦν,

[254] ὁδοιπορία τοῦ ἔθνους ἀκινδύνως πεζεύοντος διὰ θαλάττης
ὡς ἐπὶ ξηρᾶς ἀτραποῦ καὶ λιθώδους ἐδάφους
    —ἐκραυρώθη γὰρ ἡ ψάμμος
    καὶ ἡ σποράς αὐτῆς οὐσία συμφῦσα ἡνώθη—,
ἐχθρῶν ἀπνευστὶ διωκόντων ἐφόρμησις
σπευδόντων ἐπ' οἰκεῖον ὄλεθρον,
νεφέλης ὀπισθοφυλακούσης ἡνιόχησις
ἐν ᾗ θεία τις ὄψις πυρὸς αὐγὴν ἀπαστράπτουσα ἦν.

πελαγῶν ἃ τέως ἀνακοπέντα διειστήκει παλίρροια,
τοῦ διακοπέντος καὶ ἀναξηρανθέντος μέρους αἰφνίδιος θαλάττωσις,
    [255]πολεμίων φθορά,
οὓς τά τε κρυσταλλωθέντα τείχη καὶ ἀνατραπέντα κατεύνασε
καὶ αἱ πλήμμυραι τοῦ πελάγους,
ὥσπερ εἰς φάραγγα τὴν ὁδὸν ἐπενεχθεῖσαι κατέκλυσαν,
ἐπίδειξις τῆς φθορᾶς διὰ τῶν ἐπαναπλευσάντων σωμάτων,
ἃ τὴν ἐπιφάνειαν τοῦ πελάγους κατεστόρεσε,

καὶ σφοδρὰ κυμάτωσις,
ὑφ' ἧς ἅπαντες οἱ νεκροὶ σωρηδὸν ἀπεβράσθησαν εἰς τοὺς ἀντιπέραν αἰγιαλούς,
    ἀναγκαία θέα γενησόμενοι τοῖς διασωθεῖσιν,
    οἷς ἐξεγένετο μὴ μόνον τοὺς κινδύνους διαφυγεῖν
    ἀλλὰ καὶ ἐπιδεῖν τοὺς ἐχθροὺς
οὐκ ἀνθρωπίναις ἀλλὰ θείαις δυνάμεσι παντὸς λόγου μεῖζον κολασθέντας.

    The sea breaks in two, and each section retires. The parts around the break, through the whole depth of their waters, congeal to serve as walls of vast strength: a path is drawn straight, a road of miracle between the frozen walls on either side:
    The nation makes its passage, marching safely through the sea, as on a dry path or a stone-paved causeway; for the sand is crisped, and its scattered particles grow together into a unity: the enemy advance in unresting pursuit, hastening to their own destruction: the cloud goes behind the travellers' rear to guide them on their way, and within is the vision of the Godhead, flashing rays of fire. Then the waters which had been stayed from their course and parted for a while return to their place: the dried-up cleft between the walls suddenly becomes a sea again:
    The enemy meet their doom, sent to their last sleep by the fall of the frozen walls, and overwhelmed by the tides, as they rush down upon their path as into a ravine! that doom is evidenced by the corpses which are floated to the top and strew the surface of the sea: last comes a mighty rushing wave, which flings the corpses in heaps upon the opposite shore, a sight inevitably to be seen by the saved, thus permitted not only to escape their dangers, but also to behold their enemies fallen under a chastisement which no words can express, through the power of God and not of man.

    The theme is introduced in §253 by a simple yet lively and energetic description, in an appropriate rhythmic structure in which verbal forms are not abundant.[38] By this structure Philo creates tension and expectancy in the reader, which only begins to be relieved with the fifth κῶλον of the first section.

In §§254-255 the Alexandrian colorfully describes the episode within a subtle system of anticipation and resolution in which normally one leaves to the end of the section or period the elements indispensable to its progression and full comprehension. This is the case with the main verb, which nearly always takes the last position in the κῶλα. This is also the case with the rhetorical signals of progression in the exposition of the facts (e. g., μὴ μόνον presupposes the addition of ἀλλὰ καί, and οὐκ antithetically presupposes ἀλλά in the last period). However, the former is not a rigid principle of periodic style. Demetrius did not consider as periods only those expressions which completely suspend the meaning until the end; otherwise, he would not have considered as a period the following example from Plato's *Respublica*:

κατέβην χθὲς εἰς Πειραιᾶ μετὰ Γλαύκωνος τοῦ Ἀρίστωνος
προσευχόμενός τε τῷ θεῷ
καὶ ἅμα τὴν ἑορτὴν βουλόμενος θεάσασθαι
τίνα τρόπον ποιήσουσιν ἅτε νῦν πρῶτον ἄγοντες

I went down yesterday to the Peiraeus with Glaucon, the son of Ariston, to pay my devotions to the Goddess, and also because I wished to see how they would conduct the festival since this was its inauguration.

The tendency is seen less in Greek than in Latin writing. Yet Cicero himself insists that what is important in the rhythmic structure of prose, especially oratory, is that the language not be diffuse, that its parts be distinct and the periods complete.[39] What is necessary, he adds in another passage from *De Oratore*, is that there be a natural, harmonious and agreeable flow of the language.[40]

The symmetrical structure of Philo's text reflects not only balance in the order of the parts but also a variety of stylistic techniques. A chiastic composition is discernible *in toto* in the content as well as in the form. Antithesis is a pervasive presence (τοῦ ἔθνους/ἐχθρῶν; νεφέλης/ἐν ᾗ ... πυρὸς αὐγὴν; ἀνακοπέντα/τοῦ διακοπέντος; τά τε κρυσταλωθέντα τείχη/αἱ πλήμμυραι τοῦ πελάγους, etc.). The *similitudo* and the probatory *ratio* here play an implicit and explicitly important role in terms of syntactic structure (ὡς, ὥσπερ; γὰρ, ἐπίδειξις).

---

[38] Cf. Quintilian IX, 4, 126: "Ubicumque acriter erit, instanter, pugnaciter dicendum, membratim caesimque dicemus, nam hoc in oratione plurimum valet; adeoque rebus accommodanda compositio, ut asperis asperos etiam numeros adhiberi oporteat et cum dicente aeque audientem inhorrescere."

[39] *De Oratore* III, 190.

[40] Ibid. III, 173.

At the beginning of their crossing, the Jews go forward *without danger* and the Egyptians pursue them into the sea, accelerating their own destruction. In the end, the Jews are *free of danger;* and their enemies, punished by divine intervention, lie unburied on the opposite shore before the astonished eyes of the Jews. Thus we have two external periods of six κῶλα each, divided in units of four plus two, and two plus four κῶλα, respectively.

These periodic nuclei internally touch two pairs of members, somehow interrelated (the protective νεφέλη, that separates the enemy, in the first; the κυμάτωσις, that casts him lifeless on the opposite shore and isolates him forever, in the second). The cloud referred in the middle develops its centrifugal movement toward the shores: the Jews, being guided in one direction safe and sound; the Egyptians, being violently thrown in the other, dead. A phenomenon that is highlighted by a central nucleus of three periods (two, plus four, plus two κῶλα) of A B A' structure (πελάγου ... + πολεμίων ... + τοῦ πελάγους), in which the drama of the adversaries is described, at last drowned and dead.

The observation of H. Gotoff that "when they were at their best, the Greek orators often produced rhythmical prose either by accident of their genius or because of the very nature of their sentence structure,"[41] and his assessment of the Ciceronian periodic style as functionally rhetorical and not merely ornamental also apply to Philo.[42] His characteristic use of parallelism in antithesis and chiasm, giving his writings dynamic energy as well as structure,[43] supports this conclusion.

3. In Flaccum *123-124*

Another good illustration of prose rhythm in Philo's literary work is the brief song of thanksgiving sung by the Alexandrian Jews, when they learned of the arrest and punishment of Flaccus, the governor who was largely responsible for the persecutions from which they had recently suffered.

[123] γῆν καὶ θάλατταν, ἀέρα τε καὶ οὐρανόν,
τὰ μέρη τοῦ παντὸς καὶ σύμπαντα τὸν κόσμον,
ὦ μέγιστε βασιλεῦ θνητῶν καὶ ἀθανάτων,
παρακαλέσοντες εἰς εὐχαριστίαν τὴν σὴν ἥκομεν,
  οἷς μόνοις ἐνδιαιτώμεθα,
  τῶν ἄλλων ὅσα δημιουργεῖται πρὸς ἀνθρώπων ἐληλαμένοι
  καὶ στερόμενοι πόλεως καὶ τῶν ἐν πόλει δημοσίων καὶ ἰδιωτικῶν περιβόλων,
  ἀπόλιδες καὶ ἀνέστιοι μόνοι τῶν ὑφ'ἥλιον ἐξ ἐπιβουλῆς ἄρχοντος γενόμενοι.

---

[41] *Cicero's Elegant Style: An Analysis of the "Pro Archia"* (Urbana, Chicago, London: University of Illinois Press, 1979), p. 63.
[42] Ibid., p. 63-65.
[43] Cf. T. Conley, *Philo's Rhetoric: Studies in Style, Composition and Exegesis*, p. 258, note 7 to chap. II.

[124] χρηστὰς ὑπογράφεις ἡμῖν ἐλπίδας
καὶ περὶ τῆς τῶν λειπομένων ἐπανορθώσεως,
ἤδη ταῖς ἡμετέραις λιταῖς ἀρξάμενος συνεπινεύειν.

εἴ γε τὸν κοινὸν ἐχθρὸν τοῦ ἔθνους
καὶ τῶν ἐπ' αὐτῷ συμφορῶν ὑφηγητὴν
καὶ διδάσκαλον μέγα πνέοντα καὶ οἰηθέντα
διὰ ταῦτα εὐδοκιμήσειν ἐξαίφνης καθεῖλες.

οὐ πορρωτάτω γενόμενον,
ἵν' αἰσθόμενοι δι' ἀκοῆς οἱ κακῶς πεπονθότες ἀμβλύτερον ἡσθῶσιν,
ἀλλ' ἐγγὺς οὑτωσί, μόνον οὐκ ἐν ὄψει τῶν ἠδικημένων,
πρὸς τρανοτέραν φαντασίαν τῆς ἐν βραχεῖ καὶ παρ' ἐλπίδας ἐπεξόδου.

> Most Mighty King of mortals and immortals, we have come here to call on earth and sea, and air and heaven, into which the universe is partitioned, and on the whole world, to give Thee thanks. They are our only habitation, expelled as we are from all that men have wrought, robbed of our city and the buildings within its walls, public and private, alone of all men under the sun bereft of home and country through the malignancy of a governor.
>
> Thou givest also a glimpse of cheering hopes that Thou wilt amend what remains for amendment, in that Thou hast already begun to assent to our prayers. For the common enemy of the nation, under whose leadership and by whose instruction these misfortunes have befallen it, who in his windy pride thought that they would promote him to honour, Thou hast suddenly brought low; and that not when he was afar off, so that they whom he ill-treated would hear it by report and have less keen pleasure, but just here close at hand almost before the eyes of the wronged to give them a clearer picture of the swift and unhoped-for visitation.

Inserted in the heart of the treatise as an aretalogy,[44] this hymn contains three essential themes. The first unit sounds the theme of the fierce persecution which fell upon the Jews; the second, the divine intervention as an answer to their prayers; and the third, the clear evidence of that intervention in Flaccus's sudden fall from power.

Regarded as a whole, this hymn has a coherent periodic structure in which both the first and the last units are divided into two tetracola, while the central unit takes the form of a tricolon. The tension initially produced by the syntactic suspension of the verb until the end of first period, and dramatically intensified in the second, is alleviated in the central period by a subtle reference to signs of a well-grounded hope. But it is only at the end of the penultimate period that such tension is completely resolved.

In the movement from evil to good, the middle period reverses the situation by evoking a transcendent being who not only encourages hope but also finally satisfies it. To confirm this, at the end Philo elaborates a beautiful symmetrical period of AB A'B' structure in which the first pair of members is

---

[44] Cf. A. Pelletier, PM 31, p. 16.

antithetically contrasted to the last (οὐ πορρωτάτω ... + αἰσθόμενοι ... ≠ ἀλλ' ἐγγὺς ... + πρὸς τρανοτέραν ...). This is a method of raising and then satisfying expectations which apparently Philo greatly appreciated. More than mere stylistic figures, parallelism and antithesis are means by which Philo enlivens and advances his thought rhetorically.

4. De Ebrietate *157-159*

The fundamental traits of periodic style appear crystal-clear in the syntactic and argumentative structure of the following text:

[157] τὸ παραπλήσιον οὖν ἐν ψυχῇ πάντως ἄγνοια ἐργάζεται
τὰ βλέποντα καὶ ἀκούοντα αὐτῆς λυμαινομένη
καὶ μήτε φῶς μήτε λόγον παρεισελθεῖν ἐῶσα,
τὸν μέν, ἵνα μὴ διδάξῃ, τὸ δέ, ἵνα μὴ δείξῃ τὰ ὄντα,
βαθὺ δὲ σκότος καὶ πολλὴν ἀλογίαν καταχέασα
κωφὴν λίθον τὸ περικαλλέστατον εἶδος ψυχῆς εἰργάσατο.

[158] καὶ γὰρ τῇ ἀγνοίᾳ τὸ ἐναντίον, ἡ ἐπιστήμη,
τρόπον τινὰ ψυχῆς καὶ ὀφθαλμοὶ καὶ ὦτά ἐστι·
καὶ γὰρ τοῖς λεγομένοις προσέχει τὸν νοῦν
καὶ καταθεᾶται τὰ ὄντα
καὶ οὐδὲν οὔτε παρορᾶν οὔτε παρακούειν ὑπομένει,
πάντα δ' ὅσα ἀκοῆς καὶ θέας ἄξια περισκοπεῖ καὶ περιβλέπεται,
κἂν εἰ πεζεύειν καὶ πλεῖν δεῖ,
γῆς καὶ θαλάττης ἄχρι τῶν περάτων ἀφικνεῖται,
ἵνα ἴδῃ τι πλέον ἢ ἀκούσῃ καινότερον.

[159] ἀοκνότατον γὰρ ὁ ἐπιστήμης ἔρως,
ἐχθρὸς μὲν ὕπνου, φίλος δὲ ἐγρηγόρσεως·
διανιστὰς οὖν καὶ ἀνεγείρων καὶ παραθήγων ἀεὶ διάνοιαν
πανταχόσε περιφοιτᾶν ἀναγκάζει λίχνον ἀκοῆς ἐργαζόμενος
καὶ μαθήσεως δίψαν ἄληκτον ἐντήκων.

An exactly similar result in the soul is produced by ignorance, which destroys its powers of seeing and hearing, and suffers neither light, which might shew it realities, nor reason, which might be its teacher, to find their way in; but sheds about it profound darkness and a flood of unreason, and turns the soul's fair and lovely form into a senseless block of stone.

Similarly knowledge, the opposite of ignorance, may be called the eyes and the ears of the soul. For it fixes the attention on what is said and contemplates what is, and allows no mis-seeing or mis-hearing, but surveys and observes all that is worthy to be heard and seen. And if it be necessary to travel or take ship, it makes its way to the ends of the earth or ocean, to see something more or hear something new.

For nothing is so active as the passion for knowledge; it hates sleep and loves wakefulness. So it ever arouses and excites and sharpens the intellect, and compelling it to range in every direction makes it greedy to hear, and instils an incessant thirst for learning.

After concluding his detailed exposition on drunkenness, as a spiritual insanity produced by the ἀπαιδευσία (§§11-153),[45] Philo proceeds to treat the second reality that, in Moses' view, is symbolized by wine (§§154-205): ἀναισθησία or "insensibility" and its causes. If ἀναισθησία is produced in the body by wine, in the soul it is produced by ignorance. This is a theme which, because of its importance, will merit some philosophical consideration.

Inserted in this argumentative *digressio* (§§154-161), the passage cited is significant not only for its periodic style but also for the way its structure affects and enhances its meaning. The two fundamental units, each composed of two periods, find their fulcrum and transition in a central double period framed in a complex antithetic structure. The first of these rhetorical units is an *inclusio* (ἐν ψυχῇ πάντως ἄγνοια ἐργάζεται, in the first member; εἶδος ψυχῆς εἰργάσατο, in the last) which, in its circularity, seems to suggest the situation in which the soul finds itself when it is a prisoner of the ἄγνοια - alienated, destroyed, petrified. However, several other "patterns" are combined in a complete and coherent intellectual system. Divided in two parts, the initial period compares the effect of ignorance on the soul to that produced by wine on the body in the first. This is chiastically defined in the second.

> A - μήτε φῶς;
> B - μήτε λόγον;
> B'- τὸν μέν (λόγον), ἵνα μὴ διδάξῃ;
> A'- τὸ δέ (φῶς), ἵνα μὴ δείξῃ τὰ ὄντα.

An identical rhythmical balance is also developed in the antithetic connection between this second part of the first period and the two cola that make up the following period (φῶς + λόγον ≠ σκότος + ἀλογίαν).

---

[45] The treatise *De Ebrietate* is another interesting example of the influence that the structure of persuasive discourse exercised on Philo. As an exegetical commentary on Genesis 9:20-29, especially its final part—"And [Noah] drank wine and became drunk"—this treatise continues, so to speak, the discussion started in the final part of *De Plantatione*. Philo here contrasts Mosaic doctrine with the many philosophical opinions touched on therein concerning drunkenness. In the προοίμιον (1-10) Philo affirms that the Jewish legislator uses wine as a symbol of five things and introduces in summary fashion each one of them, pointing to their respective causes: (1) τοῦ ληρεῖν καὶ παραπαίνειν; (2) ἀναισθησίας παντελοῦς; (3) ἀπληστίας ἀκορέστου καὶ δυσαρέστου; (4) εὐθυμίας καὶ εὐφροσύνης; (5) γυμνότητος. In the ἀπόδειξις (here I use the terms used by Philo in his division of the treatise [cf. §11]) he makes the detailed exposition of the first three things introduced in the proem, while the part relating to the treatment of the last two seems to have been lost (see F. H. Colson and G. H. Whitaker, PLCL III, p. 309). In the ἐπίλογος (§224), if it is the final conclusion of the discourse, he directs an invitation to prayer that God might destroy ἀγρίαν ἄμπελον and assure to His people the good fruits that feed the practice of good and the full exercise of virtue.

The middle period antithetically introduces a new element (τῇ ἀγνοίᾳ τὸ ἐναντίον, ἡ ἐπιστήμη) which not only points toward the following unit but also permits a dialectical progression of thought. In its ethical and mental dimensions, knowledge is the eyes and ears of the soul, the opposite of ignorance, which corresponds to bodily blindness and deafness.

Just as the rhythmic balance is antithetically established between the first two periods, that balance is also apparent in the chiastic connection of the latter with the first two cola unit of the following (ὀφθαλμοὶ + καὶ ὦτα : τοῖς λεγομένοις + τὰ ὄντα). And it is indirectly projected in the symmetric connection of the latter with the second (οὔτε παρορᾶν + οὔτε παρακούειν = ἀκοῆς + θέας), simultaneously inserted and articulated in an antithesis of chiastic structure (καὶ οὐδὲν οὔτε παρορᾶν + οὔτε παρακούειν : πάντα δ' ὅσα ἀκοῆς + καὶ θέας).

An identical strategy is observed in the final tricolon of this unit in conjunction with the following one, as they highlight and substantiate the dynamic force and energizing passion that characterize ἐπιστήμη and stimulate the διάνοια.

In his spiritual journey, the reader is induced to follow a course that leads away from ignorance and toward knowledge, from evil to good, from vice to virtue (§160). However, this is true not only aesthetically. By means of periodic composition, elements of expectation and consumation are realized. The meaning of the cola and the periods is normally concealed until the end by suspending the main verb, thus assuring them a circular movement. Yet the periodic style is not merely a whim of the author. At the same time that it delights, it also impresses, instructs and motivates the reader.[46]

The words of W. R. Johnson, "prose style means not merely the ability but almost the necessity to shape thoughts and feelings, which were otherwise hidden (because unexpressed) into significant, *i. e.,* intelligible, patterns,"[47] are fulfilled in exemplary fashion in Philo's writings. They suggest the freedom and naturalness with which he employed conceptual and formal structures. Although his stylistic devices may escape us at first reading, they give strength and life to his message.

---

[46] As A. D. Leeman observes, although the rhythmic and periodic structure of a phrase is essentially an aesthetic element that above all tries to *delectare,* it is far from being merely an element of weakness. "Not only the aesthetic requirements of the *genus medium,* but also the pathetic qualities of the *genus uehemens* may involve a periodic treatment, namely in the peroration, when the audience already hangs on the speaker's lips and is no longer suspicious and skeptical towards his artifices. Rhythm is so far from being an instrument of weakness that it may even be an instrument of force!" (*Orationes Ratio* I [Amsterdam: Hakkert, 1963], p. 151-152).

[47] *Luxuriance and Economy: Cicero and the Alien Style,* UCPCS, V (Berkeley: University of California Press, 1971), p. 6-7.

CONCLUSION

We have enunciated and defended the thesis that Philo benefited from an excellent rhetorical education, and that he not only mastered this branch of knowledge but also used the most diverse structures of argumentation.

The fact that Philo was chosen to lead the embassy of the Alexandrian Jews to Rome in one of the most critical moments of persecution in their history indicates that he must have been considered a very capable speaker by his fellow citizens. In his writings we are directly confronted with the exuberant evidence of his rhetorical competence.

His exegetical treatises are filled with references to rhetoric as well as discussions of the validity, importance and risks of a discipline that throughout the centuries was the object of animated and heated philosophical debates. In addition, Philo used time-tested rhetorical strategies and techniques in designing these treatises.

We have confirmation of that fact in the two levels of analysis used here: (a) the diachronic examination of the theory of argumentation in the Hellenistic period and (b) delineation of the most salient characteristics of Philo's exegetical-narrative methodology. Rhetorical τέχνη permeates all his treatises. In the commentaries it functions as a means of reading, interpretation, organization and persuasive exposition.

Rhetorical conventions usually impose their space, movement and architecture on Philo's text. Each phrase, image, figure or argument is shaped in conformity with those conventions, and is invested with a dynamic persuasive power. In the universe of his discourse the argumentative units are organized around primary affirmations. The organic structure of the whole makes all the parts fit together coherently, illuminates the deeper truth of the main thesis, and makes a persuasive appeal to the reader.

There is no need here to enumerate the detailed conclusions presented in the preceding chapters. We will, however, underscore two major literary features of Philo's work.

1. *Philosophical Character of his Argumentation*

Philo knew how to give a careful rhetorical treatment to the *lemmata* of Scripture and to the themes that emanate from them. He even knew how to adapt the weapons of his rhetoric to the public he sought to teach, convince or inspire. The argumentative tone of oratorical discourse impregnates his commentary. Bearing witness to this, as we have seen, are not only the rhetorical structures of his treatises and some speeches they contain, but also their development, natural though self-conscious, of the exegetical issues that the scriptural text suggests. Also bearing witness to this is the way he causes the commentary to progress, decoding the text, drawing a theme from it, enunciating and supporting a thesis with appropriate arguments. This is always accomplished, however, in accord with Philo's basic exegetical intention.

In the logical argumentation of a thesis, as in the elaborate development of a theme, there is apparently no model or structure sanctioned by the rhetorical conventions that Philo did not make use of or strategically adapt to his literary project. The plurality of sources which inspired him as well as the variety of rhetorical structures he employed, the diversity of the philosophical themes he argued, and his use of a wealth of dialectical or formal topics, —all these link him with the Aristotelian tradition in ancient rhetoric. But his preoccupation with religious and moral truth, the Jewish character of his main theses, the versatility and originality with which he structures and animates his commentaries, harmoniously combining all their parts, set him apart from other writers.

Philo is, in fact, an exceptional figure of his time. More than just an eclectic, he effects a synthesis of the entire Hellenistic rhetorical tradition, but sets it in philosophical perspective. He consistently rejects a purely sophistic rhetoric and a conventional theory which is limited to elaborating formally valid arguments which begin with probable premises. As V. Nikiprowetzky says, Philo's exegetical themes "combine philosophical ideas and scriptural symbols in a new creation."[1] The symbols generate ideas, the ideas suggest themes and those themes are argued as theses, thanks to comprehensive view of language and structure that facilitates both exegesis of texts and the writing of elaborate commentaries.

Convinced that rhetoric should be based on the truth, or be used to promote adherence to true theses and not mere opinions, Philo encourages the union of rhetoric with philosophy. In this Philo resembles Cicero, whose rhetorical theory and practice combine Platonic, Aristotelian and Stoic ideas. Philosophical themes receive a rhetorical treatment and ideas are clothed in effective discourse, i. e., the λόγος ἐνδιάθετος in the λόγος προφορικός.

---

[1] V. Nikiprowetzky, "L'exégèse de Philon d'Alexandrie dans le *De Gigantibus* et le *Quod Deus*," in David Winston and John Dillon (eds.), *Two Treatises of Philo of Alexandria* (BJS 25; Chico, CA: Scholars Press, 1983), p. 58.

2. Rhetorical Argumentation as an Exegetical Technique of Exposition

Despite his negative judgments regarding conventional rhetoric, Philo uses not only its basic technical terminology but also its figures and forms of argumentation. If he rejects sophistic rhetoric, it is not from disdain of the technical resources it affords but because of its intentions. Like Cicero he filters out what he considers the best in the rhetorical tradition and gives it the imprint of his own thought and style.

If Philo makes use of a wide range of rhetorical devices, it is to revive an awareness of the depth of the biblical text in his generation. He seeks to make the message of Scripture intelligible and appealing, especially for Diaspora Jews. The biblical text is sovereign. Philo identifies the Mosaic legislation with the law of nature, divine wisdom, and perfect philosophy. He makes regular use of rhetoric as the means he deems essential for adequate expression of biblical ideas. Far from being merely an artifice of argumentation or ornament, rhetoric underlies his hermeneutic.

Philo generally makes use of rhetorical structures both in the development of his exegetical analyses as well as in the affirmation and defense of the principles of his theological-philosophical system. He illuminates and explains each biblical *lemma* in terms of a basic hermeneutical principle, that of the soul's migration from the material realm to God.

Committed to a biblical text that he considers normative in every detail, the Alexandrian exegete avails himself of all the resources provided by ancient rhetoric. To examine all aspects of a thesis, he sometimes combines differing patterns of argumentation into a single exegetical discussion, amplifying it and digressively chaining together parallel elements of clarification. It is difficult to comprehend any part of his discourse without first having a clear idea of the argumentative whole. The explicit formulas of his discourse are intimately linked to the implicit system that animates and justifies them. Behind each formal structure there is a message that ultimately has its deeper roots, as we have emphasized, in the theme of migration.

A man of culture, well read and familiar with Greco-Roman concepts of παιδεία in its most developed form, sophisticated in his mastery of communication devices, Philo surely did not intend to produce a monument to his own literary and rhetorical skills. Instead he sought to explain and defend Judaism and the Jewish Bible, a work he read in Greek as a literary document and sought to explain and defend as the perfect expression of sacred rhetoric. As a result of his rhetorical reading of Moses, perhaps inspired after a long period of reflection on the spiritual problems of his age, he set out his conclusions in a series of writings in which the great cultural streams of Western civilization meet.

BIBLIOGRAPHY

I. ON PHILO OF ALEXANDRIA

A. *Editions, Translations, Bibliographies and Indexes*

Arnaldez, R., Pouilloux J., Mondésert, C. *Les oeuvres de Philon d'Alexandrie*, publiées sous le patronage de l'Université de Lyon, par R. Arnaldez, J. Pouilloux, C. Mondésert. 36 vols. Paris: Édition du Cerf, 1961.
Ballino, Giulio *Vita de Moisè*, a cura di Giulio Ballino. Ancona, 1857.
Calvetti, Gianmaria (trad.). *Filone di Alessandria: La Creazione del Mondo*. Prefazione, traduzione e note di Gianmaria Calvetti; *Le Allegorie delle Leggi*. Prefazione, traduzione e note di Renata Bigatti. Milano: Rusconi, 1978.
Cohn, L., Heinemann, I., and Adler, M. *Philo von Alexandria, die Werke in deutscher Uebersertzung*. 6 vols.; Breslau: H. Marcus, 1909-1938; 2nd edition: W. Theiler, Berlin: Walter de Gruyter, 1962-1964 with the addition of *Sachweister zu Philo*, Vol. VII.
Cohn, Leopoldus, Wendland, Paulus and Reiter, S. *Philonis Alexandrini Opera quae Supersunt*. 6 vols. Berlin: Walter de Gruyter & Co., 1896-1915 (reprinted 1962). An *editio minor* exists, without *Prolegomena* or critical apparatus, in eight volumes.
Colson, F.H., and Whitaker, G.H. (trads.) *Philo in Ten Volumes* (and *Two Supplementary Volumes*). London: Heinemann; Cambridge, MA: Harvard University Press, 1929-1962. The two supplementary volumes contain the translation, by R. Marcus, of the works contained in the Armenian language version.
Delling, Gerhard. *Bibliographie zur jüdisch-hellenistischen und intertestamentarischen Literatur 1900-1970*. TU 106:2; Berlin: Akademie Verlag, 1975, p. 56-80.
Earp, J. W. *Indices to Volumes I-X* of *Philo in Ten Volumes* (and *Two Supplementary Volumes*). Edition in Colson-Whitaker; London: Heinemann, 1971, vol. X, p. 189-268. This volume equally contains a final *Index of Names*, p. 269-433.
Feldman, Louis. *Scholarship on Philo and Josephus* (1937-1962). *Studies in Judaica*. New York: Yeshiva University, no date (1963?). Classified and annotated critical bibliography.
Goodenough, E.R. and Goodhart, H.L. "A General Bibliography of Philo". In E.R. Goodenough, *The Politicis of Philo Judaeus*. New Haven: Yale University Press, 1938; reprinted Hildesheim, 1967, p. 128-348.
Haussleiter, J. "Nacharistotelische Philosophen 1931-1936." *Jahresbericht über die Fortschritte der klassischen Altertumswissenschaft* (1943), p. 107-116. (A critical bibliography on Philo with very valuable summaries. Cover the period 1926-1936.)
Kraus, C. *Flaco; L'ambasceria a Gaio* (incomplete), supplement to the work of C. Kraus, *Filone Alessandrino e un'ora tragica della storia ebraica*. Napoli, 1967, p. 165-254.
Kraus, R.C. *De Opificio Mundi, De Abrahamo, De Iosepho*, analisi crit., testi trad. e comm. a cura di Kraus Reggiani C.: Bibl. Athena XXIII. Roma: Ed. dell'Ateneo, 1979.
Hilgert, Earle. "A Bibliography of Philo Studies in 1971 with Additions for 1965-70." *Studia Philonica* 1 (1972), p. 57-71.

—— "A Bibliography of Philo Studies in 1971 with Additions for 1965-70." *Studia Philonica* 2 (1973), p. 51-54.
—— "A Bibliography of Philo Studies, 1972-1973." *Studia Philonica* 3 (1974-1975), p. 117-125.
—— "A Bibliography of Philo Studies, 1974-1975." *Studia Philonica* 4 (1976-1977), p. 79-85.
—— "A Bibliography of Philo Studies, 1976-1977." *Studia Philonica* 5 (1978), p. 113-120.
—— "A Bibliography of Philo Studies, 1977-1978." *Studia Philonica* 6 (1979-1980), p. 197-200.
—— "Bibliographia Philoniana 1935-1981." ANRW II, 21.1. Berlin: W. de Gruyter, 1984, p. 47-97.
Leisegang, I. *Indices ad Philonis Alexandrini Opera*. Berlin: Walter de Gruyter, 1926-1930. This index constitutes Vol. VII of the Cohn-Wendland-Reiter edition.
Mangey, T. *Philonis Judaei Opera quae reperiri potuerunt omnia*. 2 vols. London, 1742.
Marcus, R. "Recent Literature on Philo (1924-1934)." In *Jewish Studies in Memory of George A. Kohut*. New York, 1935, p. 463-491.
Marcus, Ralph. "Selected Bibliography (1920-1945) of the Jews in the Hellenistic-Roman Period." *Proceedings of the American Academy for Jewish Research* 16 (1946-1947), p. 97-181.
Mayer, Günter. *Index Philoneus*. Berlin: Walter de Gruyter, 1974.
Mazzarelli, C. (trad.). *Filone di Alessandria: Le origini del male. I Cherubini, I sacrifici di Abele e di Caini, Il malvagio tende sopraffare il bouno, La posterità di Caino, I Giganti, L'immutabilità di Dio*. Introduzione, prefazioni, note e apparati di R. Radice; Milano: Rusconi, 1984.
Nazzaro, Antonio V. *Recenti studi filoniani (1963-1970)*. Napoli: Loffredo Editore, 1973.
Radice, Roberto. "Bibliografia generale su Filone di Alessandria negli ultimi quarantacinque anni, I: Fonte bibliografiche, edizioni, traduzioni, commentari e lessici." *Elenchus* III, 1982, p. 109-152.
—— (trad.). *Filone di Alessandria: L'erede delle cose divine*. Prefazione, traduzione e note di Roberto Radice; introduzione di Giovanni Reale. Milano: Rusconi, 1994.
—— *Filone di Alessandria, La migrazione verso l'eterno: L'agricoltura, La piantagione di Noè, L'ebrietà, La sobrietà, La confusione delle lingue, La migrazione di Abramo*, Saggio introduttivo, note e apparati di R. Radice. Presentazione di G. Reale, I Classici del Pensiero, Sezione di filosofia classica e tardo-antica. Milano: Rusconi, 1988.
—— *Filone di Alessandria: Tutti I tratati del Commentario Allegorico alla Bibbia*, edited by R. Radice. Presentazione di G. Reale, I Classici del Pensiero: sezione I Filosofia classica e tardo-antica. Milano: Rusconi, 1994.
Radice, R. and Runia, D.T., with R.A. Bitter, N.G. Cohen, M. Mach, A.P. Runia, D. Satran, D.R. Schwartz. *Philo of Alexandria: An Annotated Bibliography 1937-1986*. Supplements to Vigiliae Christianae. Leiden: Brill, 1988.
Reggiani, Kraus (trad.). *Filone di Alessandria: L'uomo e Dio. Il connubio con gli studi preliminari, La fuga e il ritrovamento, Il mutamento dei nomi, I sogni sono mandati da Dio*. Introduzione, traduzione, prefazioni, note e apparati di Kraus Reggiani, presentazione di G. Reale. Milano: Rusconi, 1986.
Reggiani, Kraus, and Radice, R. (trads.). *Filone di Alessandria: la filosofia Mosaica. La creazione del mondo secondo Moisè*, traduzione di Kraus Reggiani, *Le allegorie delle Leggi*, traduzione di R. Radice. Prefazione, apparati e commentari di R. Radice, monografia introduttiva di G. Reale and R. Radice. Milano: Rusconi, 1987.

Runia, D.T., Radice, R. and Satran, D. "A Bibliography of Philonic Studies 1981-1986". *The Studia Philonica Annual: Studies in Hellenistic Judaism*, vol. 1, 1989. Edited by D.T. Runia. Brown Judaic Studias 185. Atlanta: Scholars Press, 1989, p. 91-123.
Runia, D.T., Radice, R., and Satran. D. "Philo of Alexandria: An Annotated Bibliography 1986-87". *The Studia Philonica Annual: Studies in Hellenistic Judaism*, vol. 2, 1990. Atlanta: Scholars Press, 1990, p. 141-169. "Supplement: A Provisional Bibliography 1988-89", p. 170-175.
Runia, D.T., Radice, R., and Cathey, P.A. "Philo of Alexandria: An Annotated Bibliography 1987-88". *The Studia Philonica Annual: Studies in Hellenistic Judaism*, vol. 3, 1991. Atlanta: Scholars Press, 1991, p. 347-68. "Supplement: A Provisional Bibliography 1989-91", p. 369-374.
Runia, D.T., Radice, R., and Satran, D. "Philo of Alexandria: An Annotated Bibliography 1988-89". *The Studia Philonica Annual: Studies in Hellenistic Judaism*, vol. 4, 1992. Atlanta: Scholars Press, 1992, p. 97-116. "Supplement: A Provisional Bibliography 1990-92", p. 117-124.
Runia, D.T., and Radice, R. "Philo of Alexandria: An Annotated Bibliography 1990. *The Studia Philonica Annual: Studies in Hellenistic Judaism*, vol. 5, 1993. Atlanta: Scholars Press, 1993, p. 180-197. "Supplement: A Provisional Bibligraphy 1991-93", p. 198-208.
Runia, D.T., Van Den Berg, R.M., Radice, R., Sandelin, K.G., and Satran, D. "Philo of Alexandria: An Annotated Bibliography 1991". *The Studia Philonica Annual: Studies in Hellenistic Judaism*, vol. 6. Atlanta: Scholars Press, 1994, p. 123-159. "Supplement: A Provisional Bibliography, 1992-94", p. 151-159.
Runia, D.T., Van Den Berg, R.M., Martin, J.P., Radice, R., Sandelin, K.G., "Philo of Alexandria: An Annotated Bibliography 1992". *The Studia Philonica Annual: Studies in Hellenistic Judaism*, vol. 7. Atlanta: Scholars Press, 1995, p. 186–212. "Supplement: A Provisional Bibliography, 1993-95", p. 213-212.
Runia, D.T., Geljon, A.C., Martín, J.P., Radice, R., Sandelin, K.G., Satran, D., Zeller, D. "Philo of Alexandria: An Annotated Bibliography 1993". *The Studia Philonica Annual: Studies in Hellenistic Judaism*, vol. 8, 1996, p. 122–154. "Supplement: A Provisional Bibliography, 1994-96", p. 143–154.
Runia, D.T., et al. "Philo of Alexandria: An Annotated Bibliography 1994". *The Studia Philonica Annual*, vol. 9, 1997, p. 332–355. "Supplement: A Provisional Bibliography, 1995-97", p. 356–375.
Saramanch, F.de P. *Filón: Todo Hombre Bueno es Libre*. Translation, prologue and notes by F. de P. Samaranch. Buenos Aires: Aguilar, 1977.
Smallwood, E. M. *Philonis Alexandrini Legatio ad Gaium*. 2nd ed. Leiden: Brill, 1970.
Terian, Abraham. *Philonis Alexandrini "de Animalibus:" The Armenian Text with an Introduction, Translation, and Commentary*. Chico, CA: Scholars Press, 1981.
Triviño, José María. *Obras completas de Filón de Alejandría*, traducción directa del griego, introducción y notas de José María Triviño. 5 vols. Buenos Aires: Acervo Cultural, 1975-1976.
Yonge, C.D. *The Works of Philo. Complete and Unabridged*. New updated edition. Peabody, Massachusetts: Hendrickson, 1993.
Williamson, R. *Jews in the Hellenistic World: Philo*. Cambridge Commentaries on Writings on the Jewish and Christian World 200 BC to AD 200 I.ii. Cambridge: University Press, 1989.
Winston, David. *Philo of Alexandria: "The Contemplative Life," "Giants," and Selections*. New York: Paulist Press, 1981.

B. Critical Studies

Adler, Maximilian. "Das Philonische fragment De Deo." *Monatsschrift für die Geschichte und Wissenschaft des Judentums* 80 (1936), p. 163-170.
—— *Studien zu Philon von Alexandreia*. Breslau: Marcus, 1929.
Alexandre, Jr., Manuel. "Argumentação Retórica no Comentário de Fílon de Alexandria ao Pentateuco", *Euphrosyne* 13 (1985), p. 9-26.
—— *Argumentação Retórica em Fílon de Alexandria*, Biblioteca Euphrosyne 4. Lisboa: Instituto Nacional de Investigação Científica, 1990.
—— "The Art of Periodic Composition in Philo of Alexandria", in *Earle Hilgert Festschrift, Studia Philonica Annual* 3 (1991), p. 135-150.
—— "Um Caso Típico de Encómio como Técnica de Amplificação em Fílon de Alexandria", *Euphrosyne* 16 (1988), p. 281-288.
—— "A Elaboração de uma Cria no Código Hermenêutico de Fílon de Alexandria", *Euphrosyne* 15 (1986), p. 77-87.
—— "Some Reflections on Philo's Concept and Use of Rhetoric", *Euphrosyne*, 19 (1991), p. 281-290.
—— "A Rhetorical Analysis of Philo's *De uirtutibus*", *Euphrosyne* 21 (1993), p. 9-28.
—— "Rhetorical Argumentation as an Exegetical Technique in Philo of Alexandria", in *Hellenica et Judaica: hommage à Valentin Nikiprowetzky*. Leuven, Paris: Peeters, 1986.
Alexandre, Monique. *De Congressu eruditionis gratia*. "Les oeuvres de Philon d'Alexandrie." Vol. 16; Paris: Cerf, 1961.
—— "La culture profane chez Philon." *Actes de Colloque National sur Philon d'Alexandrie*, Lyon, Septembre 1966; Paris: CNRS, 1967.
Altaner, Berthold. "Augustinus und Philo von Alexandrein. Eine quellenkritische Untersuchungen." *Zeitscrift für katholische Theologie* 65 (1941), p. 81-90.
Amir, Yehoshua. "The Transference of Greek Allegories to Biblical Motifs in Philo," *Nourished with Peace. Studies in Hellenistic Judaism in Memory of Samuel Sandmel*. Chico, CA: Scholars Press, 1984, p. 15-26.
—— "Philo Judaeus." *Encyclopaedia Judaica*. Jerusalem: Keter Publishing House, 1971, vol. 13, p. 410-415.
—— "Philo and the Bible." *Studia Philonica* 2 (1973), p. 1-8.
—— "Sur l'exégèse des noms propres hébraïques chez Philon" (in Hebrew). *Tarbiz* 31 (1962), p. 297.
Argyle, A. W. "The Ancient University of Alexandria." *Classical Journal* 69 (1973-1974), p. 348-350.
—— "The Logos of Philo: Personal or Impersonal?" *Expository Times* 66, p. 13-14.
—— "Philo, the Man and his Work." *Expository Times* 85 (1974), p. 115-117.
Arnaldez, Roger. "Introduction." *Actes du Colloque National sur Philon d'Alexandrie*. Also, "La dialectique des sentiments chez Philon." Paris: CNRS, 1967, p. 299-330.
—— "Les images du sceau et de la lumière dans la pensée de Philon d'Alexandrie." *L'information littéraire* 15 (1963), p. 62-72.
—— "L'oeuvre de l'École d'Alexandrie." *Les Mardis de Dar el-Salam* (Le Caire, 1952), p. 25-121.
—— "Philon d'Alexandrie." *Dictionnaire de la Bible*, Supplement VII. Paris: Letouzey & Ané, Éditeurs, 1966, p. 1305-1348.
—— "Philo Judaeus." *New Catholic Encyclopedia*. 15 vols. New York: McGraw-Hill, 1967, p. 287-291.
Arnim, H. von. *Quellenstudien zu Philo von Alexandria*. Philologische Untersuchungen 11; Berlin, 1888.

Baer, D. "Incompréhensibilité de Dieu et théologie négative chez Philon d'Alexandrie." *Présence Orthodoxe* 8 (Paris, 1969), p. 38-46; 11 (1970), p. 143-153.
Baer, Richard A. *Philo's Use of the Categories Male and Female.* Leiden: Brill, 1970.
Bamberger, Bernard J. "Philo and the Aggadah." *Hebrew Union College Annual* 48 (Cincinnati, 1977), p. 152-185.
Barnes, E. J. "Petronius, Philo and Stoic Rhetoric." *Latomus* 32 (1973), p. 787-798.
Barraclough, R. "Philo's Politics. Roman Rule and Hellenistic Judaism." ANRW II, 21.1. Berlin: W. de Gruyter, 1984, p. 417-553.
Bauer, Bruno. *Philo, Strauss und Renan und das Urchristentum.* Berlin: Neudr d. Ausg., 1874; Aalen: Scientia-Verlag, 1972.
Beauchamp, P. "La cosmologie religieuse de Philon et la lecture de l'Exode par le livre de la Sagesse: le thème de la manne." PAL. Paris: CNRS, 1967.
Beckaert, A. *Dieu et la connaissance de Dieu dans la philosophie de Philon d'Alexandrie.* Typewritten thesis; Paris, 1943.
Belkin, Samuel. *Philo and the Oral Law – The Philonic Interpretation of Biblical Law in Relation to the Palestinian Halakah.* Harvard Semitic Series XI; Cambridge, MA: Harvard University Press, 1940; reprinted 1970.
—— "Some Obscure Traditions Mutually Clarified in Philo and Rabbinic Literature." *Studies in Judaism in Honor of Dr. Samuel Belkin as Scholar and Educator.* New York: Ktav Publishing House, 1974.
—— "The Interpretation of Names in Philo." *Horeb* 12 (1956), p. 3-61.
—— "Philo and the Midrashic Tradition of Palestine." *Horeb* 13 (1958), p. 1-60.
Bentwich, N. de M. *Philo Judaeus of Alexandria.* Philadelphia: Westminster, 1910.
Berchman, Robert M. *From Philo to Origen. Middle Platonism in Transition;* Brown Judaic Studies 69. Chico, CA: Scholars Press, 1984.
—— "The Categories of Being in Middle Platonism: Philo, Clement and Origen of Alexandria", in *The School of Moses*, ed. by J. P. Kenney. Brown Judaic Studies 304. Atlanta: Scholars Press, 1995, p. 98-140.
Bertram, Georg. "Philo und die jüdische Propaganda in der antiken Welt." In: *Christentum und Judentum.* Ed. W. Grundmann; Leipzig: Teubner, 1940, p. 79-105.
—— "Philo als politisch-theologischer Propagandist des spätantiken Judentums." *Theologisches Literaturblatt* 64 (1939), p. 193-199.
Bieler, Ludwig. Θεῖος ἀνήρ. *Das Bild des "Göttlichen Menschen" in Spätantike und Frühchristentum.* 1935 (Bd. 1); 1936 (Bd. 2); reprinted Darmstadt: Wissenschaftliche Buchgesellschaft, 1967, 2 vols.
Bigg, Charles. *The Christian Platonists of Alexandria.* Oxford: Clarendon Press, 1913.
Billings, Thomas H. *The Platonism of Philo Judaeus.* Ed. Leonardo Taran. Ancient Philosophy Series 3; New York: Garland Pub., Inc., 1979.
Birnbaum, Ellen, "What does Philo Mean by 'Seing God'? Some Methodological Considerations", *Society of Biblical Literature Seminar Papers* 34 (1995), p. 535-552.
Borgen, Peder. *Bread from Heaven. An Exegetical Study of the Concept of Manna in the Gospel of John and the Writings of Philo.* Novum Testamentum Supplements X; Leiden: Brill, 1965.
—— "Philo of Alexandria. A Critical and Synthetical Survey of Research since World War II." *ANRW* II, 21.1. Berlin, New York: W. de Gruyter, 1984, p. 98-154.
—— "Philo and the Jews of Alexandria", in P. Bilde *et al.* (eds.), *Ethnicity in Hellenistic Egypt.* Aarthus, 1992, p. 122-138.
Borgen, P. and Skarsten, R. "Quaestiones et Solutiones: Some Observations on the Form of Philo's Exegesis." *Studia Philonica* 4 (1976-1977), p. 1-15.
Botte, B. "La vie de Moise par Philon." *Cahiers Sioniens* 8 (1954), p. 173-181.
—— "Philon d'Alexandrie selon le P. Daniélou." *Revue des études grecques* 72 (1959), p. 377-384.

Bousset, Wilhelm. *Jüdische-christlicher Schulbetrieb in Alexandria und Rom. Literarische Untersuchungen zu Philo und Clemens von Alexandria, Justin und Irenäus.* Göttingen: Vandenhoek und Ruprecht, 1915.
—— *Die Religion des Judentums in späthellenistischen Zeitalter.* Ed. Hugo Gressman. Handbuch zum Neuen Testament 21; Tübingen: Mohr, Siebeck, 4th ed., 1966.
Boyancé, Pierre. "Le Dieu très haut chez Philon." In *Mélanges d'histoire des religions offerts à Henri-Charles Puech.* Ed. P. Leuy et E. Wolff. Paris: Presses Universitaires de France, 1974, p. 139-149.
—— "Études philoniennes." *Revue des études grecques* 76 (1963), p. 64-110.
—— "Écho des exégèses de la mythologie grecque chez Philon." PAL. Paris: CNRS, 1967, p. 169-188.
Braun, Herbert. "Das himmlische Vaterland bei Philo und im Hebräerbrief". *Verborum veritas, Festschrift für Gustav Stählin zum 70.* Ed. Otto Böcher, Klaus Haacker. Wuppertal: Theologische Verlag Rolf Brockhaus, 1970, p. 319-327.
—— *Wie man über Gott nicht denken soll, dargelegt an Gedankengängen Philos von Alexandria.* Tübingen: Mohr, 1971.
Bréhier, Émile. *Les idées philosophiques et religieuses de Philon d'Alexandrie.* 3rd ed.; Paris: Librairie philosophique J. Vrin, 1950.
Brewer, D.I., *Techniques and Assumptions in Jewish Exegesis before 70 CE,* Texte und Studien zum Antike Judentum 30. Tübingen, 1992, p. 198-213.
Bruns, J. E. "Philo Christianus: The Debris of a Legend." *Harvard Theological Review* 66 (1973), p. 141-145.
—— "Philo Judaeus." In *Études de philosophie antique.* Paris: Publications de la Faculté des Lettres de Paris, 1955, p. 207-214.
Bultmann, Rudolph. *Der Still der paulinischen Predigt und die kynisch-stoische Diatribe.* Forschungen zur Religion und Literatur des Alten und Neuen Testaments 13; Göttingen: Vanderhoeck und Ruprecht, 1910.
Burke, J. B. *Philo and Alexandrian Judaism.* Dissertation (microfilm); Syracuse, 1963.
Burkhardt, H. *Die Inspiration heiliger Schriften bei Philo von Alexandrien.* Giessen-Basel, 1988.
Burnet, Fred W. "Philo on Immortality: A Thematic Study of Philo's Concept of παλιγγενεσία." *The Catholic Biblical Quarterly* 46 (1984), p. 447-470.
Burtness, J. H. "Plato, Philo, and the Author of Hebrews." *Lutheran Quarterly* 10 (1958), p. 54-64.
Cadiou, R. "Philon d'Alexandrie: La Bible de Philon." *Dictionnaire de la Bible,* Supplement 7. Paris: Letouzey & Ané Éditeurs, 1966, p. 1290-1299.
Canevet, M. "Remarques sur l'utilisation du genre littéraire historique par Philon d' Alexandrie dans la *Vita Mosis,* ou Moise général en chef-prophète", *Revue des Sciences Religieuses* 60 (1986), p. 189.206.
Carlier, C. *La* μητρόπολις *chez Philon d'Alexandrie: le concept de colonisation appliqué à la Diaspora juive.* Mémoire pour l'Académie des Inscriptions et Belles-Lettres, Ecole Biblique et Archéologique Française de Jerusalem; Jerusalem, 1991.
Carson, D. A. "Divine Sovereignty and Human Responsibility in Philo." *Novum Testamentum* 23 (1981), p. 148-164.
Cazeaux, Jacques. *De la grammaire à la sagesse: Le traité "De Cherubim."* Lyon: Centre National de Recherche Scientifique, Institut F. Courby, 1978 (photocopied study).
—— *Filón de Alejandría. De la gramática a la mística;* documentos en torno de la Biblia 9. Estella, Navarra: Verbo Divino, 1984.
—— *Notes sur le "De Abrahamo."* Lyon: CNRS, Institut F. Courby, no date (photocopied study).

—— "Philon d'Alexandrie, exégète." *Aufstieg und Niedergang der römischen Welt* II, 21.1. Ed. H. Temporini and W. Haase; Berlin: de Gruyter, 1984, p.156-226.
—— *Philon: "De Congressu Eruditionis Gratia" – Les ressorts de l'exésèse.* Lyon: CNRS, no date (photocopied study).
—— "Philon, l'allégorie et l'obsession de la totalité", in *Études sur le Judaisme hellénistique. Congrès de Strasbourg (1983), Lectio Divina* 119 (1984), p. 267-320.
—— *La trame et la chaîne: Structures littéraires et exégèse dans cinq traités de Philon d'Alexandrie.* Arbeiten zur Literatur und Geschichte des hellenistischen Judentums, vol. 15; Leiden: Brill, 1983.
—— *La trame et la chaîne: II le cycle de Noe dans Philon d'Alexandrie*, ALGHJ 20. Leiden: Brill, 1989.
—— "Aspects de l'exégèse philonienne." *Revue de Sciences Religieuses* 47 (1973), p. 262-269. Reprinted in *Exégèse biblique et Judaïsme*. Ed. Jacques-É. Ménard. Strasbourg, Leiden, 1973, p. 108-115.
—— "Interpréter Philon d'Alexandrie." *Revue des Études Grecques* 84 (1972), p. 345-352.
—— "Literature ancienne et recherche des 'structures.'" *Revue des Études Augustiniennes* 18 (1972), p. 287-292.
—— "Système implicite dans l'exégèse de Philon. Un exemple: le *De Praemiis*." *Studia Philonica* 6 (1979-1980), p. 3-36.
Chadwick, Henry. "Philo and the Beginnings of Christian Thought." In *The Cambridge History of Later Greek and Early Medieval Philosophy*. Ed. A. H. Armstrong. Cambridge: Cambridge University Press, 1967, p. 137-157.
—— "St. Paul and Philo of Alexandria." *Bulletin of the John Rylands Library* 48 (Manchester, 1965-1966), p. 286-307.
Christiansen, I. *Die Technik der allegorischen Auslegungswissenschaft bei Philon von Alexandrien.* Beiträge zur Geschichte der biblischen Hermeneutik 7; Tübingen: Mohr, 1969.
Chroust, Anton-Hermann. "Some Comments on Philo of Alexandria, *De Aeternitate Mundi*." *Laval Théologique et Philosophique* 31:2 (1975), p. 135-145.
Cohen, Naomi G., *Philo Judaeus: His Universe of Discourse.* Beiträge zur Erforschung des Alten Testaments und Antiken Judentums 24. Frankfurt: Peter Lang, 1995.
Cohn, L. "Kritisch exegetische Beiträge zu Philo." *Hermes* 31 (Berlin, 1896).
—— "Beiträge zur Textgeschichte und Kritik der philonischen Schriften." *Hermes* 38 (Berlin, 1903), p. 498-545.
Colson, F. H. "Philo on Education." *Journal of Theological Studies* (1917), p. 151-162.
Conley, Thomas. *"General Education" in Philo of Alexandria.* PCCHS 15. Berkeley: The Graduate Theological Union & The University of California (includes response by J. Dillon, A. Mendelson, D. Winston and discussion by a group of participants), 1975.
—— "Philo of Alexandria". In *Handbook of Classical Rhetoric in the Hellenistic Period 330 B.C. – A.D. 400*. Edited by Stanley E. Porter. Leiden: Brill, 1997, p. 695–713.
—— "Philo's Rhetoric: Argumentation and Style." *Aufstieg und Niedergang der römischen Welt* II, 21.1. Berlin: de Gruyter, 1984, 343-71.
—— "Philo's Use of *Topoi* In *Two Treatises of Philo of Alexandria. A Commentary on the "De Gigantibus" and "Quod Deus Sit Immutabilis."*" Ed. John Dillon and David Winston. Chico, CA: Scholars Press, 1983, p. 181-188.
Conybeare, F. C. "The Lost Works of Philo." *The Academy* 38 (1890), p. 32ff.
Colpe, Carsten. "Philo." *Religion in Geschichte und Gegenwart*. Ed. K. Galling, 3rd ed., 7 vols.; Tübingen: Mohr, 1957-1965, vol. 5, p. 341-346.
Coppens, J. "Philon et l'exégèse targumique." *Ephemerides theologicae lovanienses* 24 (1948), p. 430-431.

Culpepper, R. A. "Philo's School." In *The Johannine School.* Missoula, MT: Scholars Press, 1979, p. 197-214.
Daniélou, Jean. *Philon d'Alexandrie.* Paris: Librairie Arthème Fayard, 1958.
—— "Die Entmythologisierung in der alexandrinischen Schule." *Kerigma und Mythos* 6:1. *Theologische Forschung* 30 (Hamburg, 1963), p. 38-43.
—— "The Philosophy of Philo. The Significance of Professor Harry Wolfson's New Study." *Theological Studies* 9 (1948), p. 578-589.
Daube, David. "Alexandrian Methods of Interpretation and the Rabbis." *Festschrift Hans Lewald.* Basel: Helbing und Lichtenhahn, 1953, p. 27-44.
—— "Rabbinic Methods of Interpretation and Hellenistic Rhetoric." HUCA 22 (1949), p. 239-264.
Dawson, J.D. *Allegorical Readers and Cultural Revision in Ancient Alexandria.* Berkeley, 1992, p. 73-126.
Delcuve G. *L'exégèse de Philon étudiée dans le commentaire allégorique.* Mémoire dactylographié présenté à l'École Pratique des Hautes Études, section des Sciences Religieuses; Paris, 1945.
Delling, Gerhard. "Wunder – Allegorie – Mythus bei Philon von Alexandreia." *Studien zum Neuen Testament und zum hellenistischen Judentum.* Göttingen: Vandenhoeck und Ruprecht, 1970, p. 72-129.
—— "Philons Enkomion auf Augustus." *Klio* 54 (1972), p. 171-192.
Dey, Lala Kalyan Kumar. *The Intermediary World and Patterns of Perfection in Philo and Hebrews.* SBL Dissertation Series 25; Missoula, MT: Scholars Press, 1975.
Dillon, John. "Philo Judaeus and the Cratylus." *Liverpool Classical Monthly* 3 (1978), p. 37-42.
—— "The Formal Structure of Philo's Allegorical Exegesis." In *Two Treatises of Philo of Alexandria,* by D. Winston and J. Dillon. Chico, CA: Scholars Press, 1983, p. 77-87.
—— "Philo and the Greek Tradition of Allegorical Exegesis", *Society of Biblical Lierature Seminar Papers* 33 (1994), p. 69-80.
—— "The Theory of three classes of men in Plotinus and Philo", in R. Link-Salinger (ed.), *Of Scholars, Savants, and their Texts: Studies in Philosophy and Religious Thought; Essays in Honor of Arthur Hyman.* New York-Bern, 1989, p. 69-76.
—— *The Transcendence of God in Philo: Some Possible Sources.* PCCHS 16. Berkeley: Center for Hermeneutical Studies, 1975, p. 1-44.
Dreyer, Oskar. *Untersuchungen zum Begriff des Gottgeziemenden in der Antike, mit besonderer Berücksichtigung Philons von Alexandrien.* Hildesheim: Olms, 1970.
Drummond, J. *Philo Judaeus, or the Jewish-Alexandrian Philosophy in its Development and Completion.* 2 vols. London and Edinburg: T. & T. Clark, 1888; reprinted Amsterdam, 1969.
Farandos, Georgias D. *Kosmos und Logos nach Philon von Alexandria.* Amsterdam: Rodopi, 1976.
Feldman, Louis H. "Philo of Alexandria." *Encyclopaedia Britannica*, vol. 14, 15th ed. (1978), p. 245-247.
—— *Studies in Judaica: Scholarship on Philo and Josephus* (1937-1977). New York: Yeshiva University, no date.
Festugière, A. J. "Philon." In *La Révélation d'Hermès Trismégiste.* 4 vols. Paris: Lecoffre, 1949-1963, vol. II, p. 519-573.
Fischel, H. A. *Rabbinic Literature and Greco-Roman Philosophy. A Study of Epicurea and Rhetoric in Early Midrashic Writings.* Studia Post-Biblica 21; Leiden: Brill, 1973.
Foakes Jackson, F. J. "Philo and Alexandrian Judaism." In *A History of Church History: Studies of Some Historians of the Christian Church.* Cambridge: Cambridge University Press, 1939, p. 39-55.

Foster, S. S. *The Alexandrian Situation and Philo's Use of "Δίκη" (Personified Justice)*. Dissertation Northwestern University, 1975.
Frankel, Z. *Über den Einfluss der palästinischen Exegese auf die alexandrinischen Hermeneutik*. Leipzig: Barth, 1851.
Fraser, P. M. *Ptolemaic Alexandria*. 3 vols. Oxford: Clarendon Press, 1972.
Friedlander, M. *Geschichte der jüdischen Apologetik als Vorgeschichte des Christentums. Eine historisch-kritische Darstellung der Propaganda und Apologie im Alten Testament und in der hellenistischen Diaspora*. Amsterdam: Philo Press, 1973.
—— *Die religiösen Bewegungen innerhalb des Judentums im Zeitalter Jesu. Eine Untersuchung über Entwicklung und Einfluss der apokaliptischen, essenischen, mindäitischen und am-haarez Bewegungen im palästinenischen Judentum und der Sibyllistick und des jüdischen Hellenismus in der Diaspora*. Amsterdam: Philo Press, 1974.
Früchtel, Ursula. *Die kosmologischen Vorstellungen bei Philo von Alexandrien: Ein Beitrag zur Geschichte der Genesisexegese*. Arbeiten zur Literatur und Geschichte des hellenistischen Judentums 2; Leiden: Brill, 1968.
Gazzoni, Laura. "L''erede' nel Quis rerum divinarum heres sit di Filone Alessandrino." *Rivista di filologia e di istruzione classica* 102 (1974), p. 387-397.
Geiger, F. *Philon von Alexandreia als sozialer Denker*. Stuttgart, 1932.
Giusta, M. "'Ανευπροφάσιστος: un probabile ἅπαξ εἰρημένον in Filone, De aeternitate mundi §75." *Rivista di filologia e di istruzione classica* 100 (Torino, 1972), p. 131-136.
Goodenough, Erwin R. *Jewish Symbols in the Graeco-Roman Period*. Edited and abridged by Jacob Neusner; Bollingen Series; Princeton: Princeton University Press, 1992.
—— "New Light on Hellenistic Judaism." *Journal of Bible and Religion* 5 (1937), p. 18-28.
—— "Philo Judaeus." *Interpreter's Dictionary of the Bible*. Ed. G. A. Buttrick, 4 vols.; New York: Abingdon, 1962, III, p. 796-799.
—— "Philo's Exposition of the Law and his De Vita Mosis." *Harvard Theological Review* 26 (1933), p. 109-125.
—— "Philo of Alexandria." *Jewish Heritage* 1:4 (1959), p. 19-22.
—— "Philo and Public Life." *Journal of Egyptian Archeology* 12 (1926), p. 77-79.
—— "Problems of Method in Studying Philo Judaeus." *Journal of Biblical Literature* 58 (1939), p. 51-58 (review of Völker, W., *Fortschritt und Vollendung*).
—— "Wolfson's Philo." *JBL* 67 (1948), p. 87-109.
—— *The Jurisprudence of the Jewish Courts in Egypt. Legal Administration by the Jews under the Early Roman Empire as Described by Philo Judaeus*. New Haven: Yale University Press, 1929; reprinted Amsterdam, 1968.
—— *By Light, Light. The Mystic Gospel of Hellenistic Judaism*. New Haven: Yale University Press, 1935.
—— "Literal Mystery in Hellenistic Judaism." In *Quantulacumque: Studies Presented to Kirsopp Lake*. Ed. R. P. Casey et al.; London, 1937, p. 227-241.
—— *An Introduction to Philo Judaeus*. 1st ed. New Haven: Yale University Press, 1940; 2nd ed. Oxford: Basil Blackwell, 1962.
—— *Jewish Symbols in the Greco-Roman Period*. 13 vols. New York: Pantheon, 1935-1965.
—— "Philo of Alexandria." In *Great Jewish Personalities in Ancient and Medieval Times*. Ed. Simon Noveck (B'nai B'rith Great Books Series). New York: Farrar & Cudahy, 1959, p. 98-119.
—— *The Politics of Philo Judaeus, Practice and Theory*. New Haven: Yale University Press; London: Oxford University Press, 1938 (with a general bibliography of Philo by Howard L. Goodhart and E. R. Goodenough).

Goppelt, Leonhard. *Typos. The Typological Interpretation of the Old Testament in the New.* Grand Rapids: Eerdmans, 1982 (Philo, p. 42-58).
Gretchen J. Reydams-Schils, "Stoicized Readings of Plato's *Timaeus* in Philo of Alexandria, *Society of Biblical Literature Seminar Papers* 33 (1994), p. 450-462.
Greenspoon, Leonard. "The Pronouncement Story in Philo and Josephus." *Semeia* 20 (1981), p. 73-80.
Grossman, G. L. *Quaestionum Philonearum primae particula prima: de theologiae Philonis fontibus et auctoritate.* Lipsiae, 1829.
Guastalla, R. M. "Judaisme et hellénisme. Le leçon de Philon d'Alexandrie." *Revue des Études Juives* 7 (1946-1947), p. 3-38.
Haas, Jacob de. "Philo Judaeus." *The Encyclopedia of Jewish Knowledge.* New York: Behrman's Jewish Book House, 1946.
Haase, W. (ed.). *Hellenistisches Judentum in romischer Zeit: Philon und Josephus,* ANRW, II.21; Berlin-New York: De Gruyter, 1984.
Hamerton-Kelly, Robert G. "Sources and Traditions in Philo Judaeus: Prolegomena to an Analysis of his Writings." *Studia Philonica* 1 (1972), p. 3-26.
—— "Some Techniques of Composition in Philo's Allegorical Commentary." In *Jews, Greeks and Christians. Religious Cultures in Late Antiquity. Essays in Honor of William David Davies.* Ed. by Hamerton-Kelly and R. Scroggs. Leiden: Brill, 1976, p. 45-56.
Hanson, A. T. "Philo's Etymologies." *Journal of Theological Studies* 18 (1967), p. 128-139.
Harl, Marguerite. "Adam et les deux arbres du Paradis (Gen. II-III) ou l'Homme milieu entre deux termes (μέσος-μεθόριος) chez Philon d'Alexandrie." *Revue de Science Religieuse* (Paris, 1962), p. 321-388.
—— "Cosmologie grecque et représentations juives dans l'oeuvre de Philon d'Alexandrie." PAL. Paris: CNRS, 1967, p. 189-205.
Hartwig, H. *Der Stil der jüdisch-hellenistischen Homilie.* Göttingen: Vandenhoeck und Ruprecht, 1955.
Hay, David M. (ed.). *Both Literal and Allegorical: Studies in Philo of Alexandria's Questions and Answers on Genesis and Exodus.* Brown Judaic Series 232; Atlanta: Scholars Press, 1991.
—— "Defining Allegory in Philo's Exegetical World", *SBL Seminar Papers* 33 (1994), p. 55-68.
—— "Philo's View of Himself as an Exegete: Inspired, but not Authoritative", *SPhA* 3 (1991), p. 41-53.
—— "*Pistis* as 'Ground for Faith' in Hellenized Judaism and Paul", *JBL* 108 (1989), p. 461-476.
—— "What is Proof? – Rhetorical Verification in Philo, Josephus, and Quintilian." *SBL Seminar Papers* 17 (1979), p. 87-100.
Hecht, Richard D. "The Exegetical Contexts of Philo's Interpretation of Circumcision." *Nourished with Peace. Studies in Hellenistic Judaism in Memory of Samuel Sandmel.* Chico, CA: Scholars Press, 1984, p. 51-80.
—— "Patterns of Exegesis in Philo's Interpretation of Leviticus." *SPhA* 6 (1979-1980), p. 77-155.
—— "Scriptures and Commentary in Philo." *SBL Seminar Papers* 20 (Chico, CA: Scholars Press, 1981), p. 129-164.
Hegermann, Harald. "Griechisch-jüdisches Schrifttum." In *Literatur und Religion des Frühjudentums: eine Einführung.* Ed. Johann Maier, Josef Schreiner. Würzburg: Echter Verlag; Gütersloh: Mohn, 1973, p. 163-180.
—— "Das griechischsprechende Judentum." In *Literatur und Religion des Frühjudentums: eine Einführung.* Ed. Johann Maier, Josef Schreiner. Würzburg: Echter Verlag; Gütersloh: Mohn, 1973, p. 328-352.

—— "Philon von Alexandria." In *Literatur und Religion des Frühjudentums: eine Einführung.* Ed. Johann Maier, Josef Schreiner. Würzburg: Echter Verlag; Gütersloh: Mohn, 1973, p. 353-369.
—— "Philon von Alexandria." In *Umvelt des Urchristentums.* Ed. Johannes Leipoldt, Walter Grundmann. Berlin: Evangelische Verlagsantalt, 1966, 4th ed., 1975, I, p. 326-342.
—— "Philo und seine Kreis." In *Die Vorstellung vom Schöpfungsmittler im hellenistischen Judentum und Urchristentum.* TU 82; Berlin: Akademie Verlag, 1961, p. 6-82.
Heinemann, I. "Die Allegoristik der hellenistischen Juden ausser Philo." *Mnemosyne* 4/5 (1952), p. 130-138.
—— "Philo." *Universal Jewish Encyclopedia,* 10 vols. New York: Universal Jewish Encyclopedia, Inc., 1939-1943, vol. 8, p. 495-496.
—— "Philo als vater der mittelalterlichen Philosophie?" *Theologische Zeitschrift* 6 (1950), p. 99-116.
—— *Philos griechische und jüdische Bildung.* Hildesheim: Georg Olms, 1962.
Heinisch, P. *Der Einfluss Philos auf die älteste christliche Exegese.* Alttestamentliche Abhandlungen I, 2; Münster, 1908.
Heldermann, Jan. "Anachorese zum Heil. Das Bedeutungsfeld der Anachorese bei Philo und in einigen gnostischen Traktaten von Nag Hammadi." In *Essays on the Nag Hammadi Texts in Honour of Pahor Labib.* Ed. Martin Krause. Leiden: Brill, 1975, p. 42-55.
Hengel, Martin. *Der Sohn Gottes. Die Entstehung der Christologie und die jüdisch-hellenistische Religionsgeschichte.* Tübingen: Mohr, 1975. English: *The Son of God. The Origin of Christology and the History of Jewish-Hellenistic Religion.* Philadelphia: Fortress Press, 1976, p. 51-56.
Henrichs, A. "Philosophy, the Handmaiden of Theology." *Greek, Roman and Byzantine Studies* 9 (1968), p. 437-450.
Héring, J. "Eschatologie biblique et idéalisme platonicien." In *The Background of the New Testament and its Eschatology . . . in Honour of Charles Harold Dodd.* Cambridge, 1954, p. 444-463.
Hilgert, Earle. "Bibliographia Philoniana 1935-1981." ANRW, II, 21.1. Berlin: W. de Gruyter, 1984, p. 47-97.
—— "Central Issues in Contemporary Philo Studies." *Biblical Research* 23 (Chicago, 1978).
—— "Philo Judaeus et Alexandrinus: The State of the Problem", in *The School of Moses.* Brown Judaic Studies 304. Ed By J. P. Kenney. Atlanta: Scholars Press, 1995, p. 1-15.
Holladay, Carl H. Θεὸς Ἀνήρ *in Hellenistic Judaism. A Critique of the Use of this Category in New Testament Christology.* SBL Dissertation Series 40. Missoula, MT: Scholars Press, 1977.
Horovitz, J. *Untersuchungen über Philons und Platons Lehre von Weltschöpfung.* Marburg: Elwert Verlag, 1900.
Horowitz, M.J. "La Philosophie judéo-hellénistique de Philon d'Alexandrie", *Nouvelle Revue Théologique* 110 (1988), p. 220-244.
Horsley, Richard A. "The Law of Nature in Philo and Cicero." *Harvard Theological Review* 71:1-2 (1978), p. 35-79.
—— "Wisdom of Word and Words of Wisdom in Corinth." *The Catholic Biblical Quarterly,* Vol. 39 (1977), p. 224-239.
Howard, G. E. "'Aberrant' Text of Philo's Quotations Reconsidered." *Hebrew Union College Annual* 44 (1973), p. 197-207.
Janacek, K. "Philon von Alexandreia und skeptische Tropen." *Eirene* 19 (1982), p. 83-97.

Janowitz, N. "The Rhetoric of Translation : Three Early Perspectives on Translating Torah", *Harvard Theological Review* 84 (1991), p. 129-140.
Jaubert, Annie. "Philon d'Alexandrie." *Encyclopedia Universalis*, Vol. 12, p. 969-970.
Jonas, H. "The Problem of the Knowledge of God in the Teaching of Philo of Alexandria." In *Commentationes Judaico-Hellenisticae in Memorian Johannes Lewy.* Eds. M. Schwabe et I. Gutman. Jerusalem, 1949, p. 75-84.
—— *The Gnostic Religion.* In particular "Virtue in Philo Judaeus." Boston: Beacon Press, 1958, p. 278-281.
Juster, J. *Les juifs dans l'empire romain.* 2 vols. Paris, 1914; reprod. New York, 1970.
Kahn, J. G. "Connais-toi même, à la manière de Philon." *Revue d'Histoire et de Philosophie Religieuse* 53 (1973), p. 293-306.
—— "Philo on Secular Education", *Tarbiz* 54 (1985), p. 306-314.
—— "Philo savait-il l'hébreu? Le témoignage des Etymologies" (in Hebrew). *Tarbiz* 34:4 (1965).
Kannengiesser, C. "Philon et les Pères sur la double création de l'homme." PAL. Paris: CNRS, 1967, p. 277-296.
Karavidopoulos, Ioannes D. "Φίλων. Ὁ Ἀλεξανδρεύς' (Philo Alexandrinus)." Θρησκευτικὴ καὶ Ἠθικὴ Ἐγκυκλοπαιδεία (*Religious Ethical Encyclopedia*) 11 (Athens, 1967), p. 1157-1162.
—— Ἡ περὶ ἑοῦ καὶ ἀωθρώπου διδασκαλία φίλωνος τοῦ Ἀλεξανδέως (The Teachings of Philo Alexandrinus Regarding God and Man). *Theologia* 37 (1966), p. 72-86, 244-261, 372-389.
Kasher, Aryeh. *The Jews in Hellenistic and Roman Egypt.* Tel Aviv University, 1978.
Katz, P. *Philo's Bible. The Aberrant Text of the Bible Quotations in some Philonic Writings and its Place in the Textual History of the Greek Bible.* Cambridge: Cambridge University Press, 1950.
Kaufmann, P. "Don, distance et passivité chez Philon d'Alexandrie." *Revue de Métaphysique et de Morale* 62 (1957), p. 37-56.
Kennedy, H. A. A. *Philo's Contribution to Religion.* London, New York, 1919.
Kenney, John Peter (ed.), *The School of Moses. Studies in Philo and Hellenistic Religion.* Brown Judaic Series 304; Atlanta: Scholars Press, 1995.
Kieseweiter, K. "Philon d'Alexandrie." *Rencontre orient-occident* 10 (1973), p. 10-15.
Kilaniotis, A.L. *Philo of Alexandria,* De Agricultura: *an Analytical Commentary.* Dissertation Trinity College, Dublin, 1989.
Klein, F. N. *Die Lichtterminologie bei Philon von Alexandrien und in den hermetischen Schriften. Untersuchungen zur Struktur der religiösen Sprache der hellenistischen Mystik.* Leiden: Brill, 1862.
Knox, W. L. "A Note on Philo's Use of the Old Testament." *Journal of Theological Studies* 41 (1940), p. 30-34.
Koester, Helmut. "*NOMOS PHYSEOS.* The Concept of Natural Law in Greek Thought." In *Religions in Antiquity. Essays in Memory of E. R. Goodenough.* Ed. Jacob Neusner, Studies in the History of Religions, Supplement to *Numen;* Leiden: Brill, 1968, p. 521-541.
Kohnke, F. W. "Das Bild der echten Münze bei Philo von Alexandria." *Hermes* 96 (1968), p. 583-590.
Kraft, Robert A. "The Multiform Jewish Heritage of Early Christianity." In *Christianity, Judaism and other Greco-Roman Cults. Studies for Morton Smith at Sixty.* Studies in Judaism and Late Antiquity 12. Leiden: Brill, 1975, p. 174-199.
—— "Philo and the Sabbath Crisis: Alexandrian Jewish Politics and the Dating of Philo's Works", in B.A. Pearson *et al.* (eds.), *The Future of Early Christianity: Essays in Honor of Helmut Koester.* Minneapolis, 1991, p. 131-141.

Kraus, R. Clara. *Filone Alessandrino e un'ora tragiça della storia ebraica*. Napoli: Morano, 1967.
—— "I rapporti tra l'impero romano e il mondo ebraico al tempo di Caligola secondo la 'Legatio ad Gaium' di Filone Alessandrino." ANRW II, 21.1. Berlin, New York: W. de Gruyter, 1984, p. 554-586.
Kraus, Mathew A., "Philosophical History in Philo's *In Flaccum, Society of Biblical Literature Seminar Papers* 33 (1994), p. 477-495.
Krüger, P. *Philo und Josephus als Apologeten des Judentums*. Leipzig, 1906.
Kuhr, F. *Die Gottesprädikationen bei Philo von Alexandrien*. Diss. theol. (handschriftlich). Marburg, 1944. Theologische Literaturzeitung 74, 1949.
Kümmel, Werner Georg. *Jüdische Schriften aus Hellenistisch-römischer Zeit*. Gütersloh: Gütersloher Verlagshaus Gerd Mohn, 1973-1976.
Kweta, G. *Sprache, Erkennen und Schweigen in der Gedankenwelt des Philo von Alexandrien*, 2 vols. Dissertation, München, 1988.
Laporte, J. *La doctrine eucharistique chez Philon d'Alexandrie*. Paris: Ed. Beauchesne, 1972.
—— "Philo in the Tradition of Biblical Wisdom Literature." In *Aspects of Wisdom in Judaism and Early Christianity*. Ed. Robert L. Wilken (University of Notre Dame Center for the Study of Judaism and Christianity in Antiquity 1). Notre Dame, IN: University of Notre Dame Press, 1975, p. 103-141.
Larson, C. W. "Prayer of Petition in Philo." *Journal of Biblical Literature and Exegesis* 65 (1946), p. 185-203.
Lauer, S. "Philon von Alexandrien. Sein Leben und seine Welt, sein Werk und seine Wirkung." *Israelitischen Wochenblatt* 69/37 (1969), p. 88-90.
—— "Philo's Concept of Time." *Journal of Jewish Studies* 91:1-2 (1958), p. 39-46.
Laurentin, A. "Le pneuma dans la doctrine de Philon." *Ephemerides Theologicae Lovanienses* 27 (1951), p. 390-437.
Lebram, Jürgen C. H. "Eine stoische Auslegung von Ex. 3,2 bei Philo." In *Das Institutum Judaicum der Universität Tübingen in den Jahren 1971-1972*. Tübingen, 1972, p. 30-34.
Leisegang, Hans. "Philo aus Alexandreia." *Paulus Real-Encyclopaedie der classischen Altertumswissenschaft* XX, 1. Stuttgart: Metzlersche Verlagsbuchhandlung, 1941, p. 1-50.
—— "La connaissance de Dieu au miroir de l'âme et de nature." *Revue d'Histoire et de Philosophie Religieuses* (1937), p. 145-171.
—— "Philons Schrift über die Ewigkeit der Welt." *Philologue* 46 (1937), p. 156-176.
—— "Philons Schrift über die Gesandtschaft der alexandrinischen Juden an den Kaiser Gaius Caligula." *Journal of Biblical Literature* 57 (1938), p. 377-405.
Leopold, J. "Philo's Style and Diction." In *Two Treatises of Philo of Alexandria*, by D. Winston and J. Dillon. Chico, CA: Scholars Press, 1983, p. 129-170.
Levine, Israel. "Philo and Maimonides." In *Faithful Rebels: A Study in Jewish Speculative Thought*. London, 1936; reprinted New York, 1971, p. 43-56.
Lewis, J. P. *A Study of the Interpretation of Noah and the Flood in Jewish and Christian Literature*. Leiden: Brill, 1978, p. 42-74.
Lewy, H. *Sobria Ebrietas*. Giessen, 1929.
Lieberman, S. *Hellenism in Jewish Palestine*. New York: Jewish Theological Seminary of America, 1950.
Llamas, J. "Reseña del estado de las cuestiones: Filón de Alejandría." *Sefarad* 2 (1942), p. 437-447.
Loewe, Raphael. "Philo and Judaism in Alexandria." In *Jewish Philosophy and Philosophers*. Ed. R. Goldwater. London, 1962, p. 20-24.

Longenecker, Richard. *Biblical Exegesis in the Apostolic Period.* Grand Rapids: Eerdmans, 1975, p. 45-50.
Lord, James Raymond. *Abraham: A Study in Ancient Jewish and Christian Interpretation.* Dissertation, Duke University, 1968.
Lovis, M. *Philon le Juif.* Paris, 1911.
Mack, Burton L. "Decoding the Scripture: Philo and the Rules of Rhetoric." In *Nourished with Peace. Studies in Hellenistic Judaism in Memory of Samuel Sandmel.* Chico, CA: Scholars Press, 1984.
—— *Logos and Sophia. Untersuchungen zur Weisheitstheologie im hellenistischen Judentum.* Göttingen: Vandenhoeck und Ruprecht, 1973.
—— "Philo Judaeus and Exegetical Traditions in Alexandria." ANRW II, 21.1. Berlin: W. de Gruyter, 1984, p. 227-271.
—— "Exegetical Traditions in Alexandrian Judaism: A Program for the Analysis of the Philonic Corpus." *Studia Philonica* 3 (1974-1975), p. 71-112.
—— "Imitatio Mosis. Patterns of Cosmology and Soteriology in the Hellenistic Synagogue." *Studia Philonica* 1 (1977), p. 27-55.
—— "Under the Shadow of Moses: Authorship and Authority in Hellenistic Judaism." *SBL Seminar Papers Series* 21 (1982), p. 299-318.
—— "Weisheit und Allegorie bei Philo von Alexandrien." *Studia Philonia* 5 (1979), p. 57-105.
Maddalena, Antonio. "L'ἔννοια e ἐπιστήμη in Filone Ebreo." *Rivista di filologia e d'istruzione classica* 3:96 (1968), p. 5-27.
—— *Filone Alessandrino.* Milano: U. Mursia & C., 1970.
—— "Filone Alessandrino." *Revue d'histoire des religions* 187 (1975), p. 204-215.
Marcus, Ralph. "A 16th Century Hebrew Critique of Philo." *HUCA* 21 (1948), p. 29-71.
—— "A Textual-Exegetical Note on Philo's Bible." *Journal of Biblical Literature* 69 (1950), p. 363-365.
—— "Wolfson's Reevaluation of Philo: A Review Article." *Review of Religion* 13 (1949), p. 368-381.
—— "The Hellenistic Age." In *Great Ages and Ideas of the Jewish People.* Ed. L. W. Schwarz. New York, 1956, p. 95-139.
—— "Hellenistic Jewish Literature." In *The Jews, their History, Culture and Religion.* Ed. Louis Finkelstein. New York, 1960, p. 1017-1141.
Martín, J.P. "El encuentro de exégesis y filosofia en Filón Alexandrino", *Revista Biblica* 46 (1984), p. 199-211.
—— *Filón de Alejandría y la Génesis de la Cultura Occidental.* Buenos Aires: Depalma, 1986.
—— "El platonismo medio y Filón según un estudio de David Runia", *Methexis* 5 (1992), p. 135-144.
—— "El *Sofista* de Platón y el platonismo de Filón de Alexandría", *Methexis* 4 (1991), p. 81-99.
Massebieau, L. "Le classement des oeuvres de Philon." *Bibliothéque de l'École des hautes Études, Sciences Religieuses.* Paris, 1889, p. 1-91.
Massebieau, L. et Bréhier, É. "Essai sur la chronologie de la view et des oeuvres de Philo." *Revue de l'Histoire des Religions* 53 (1906), p. 25-64; 164-185; 267-289.
Matuszewsky, S. *Filozofia Filona z Aleksandrii i jej wplyw na chze_cija_stwo.* Warschau, 1962 (*Die Philosophie Philons von Alexandrien und ihr Einfluss auf das Christentum;* especially p. 36-40).
Mayer, Günter. "Aspekte des Abrahambildes in der Hellenistisch-Jüdischen Literatur." *Evangelische Theologie* 32 (1972), p. 118-127.
Mayer, Reinhold. "Geschichtserfahrung und Schriftauslegung. Zur Hermeneutik

des frühen Judentums." In *Die hermeneutische Frage in der Theologie*. Ed. O. Loretz, W. Strolz. Schriften zum Weltgespräch 3; Freiburg: Herder, 1968, p. 290-355.
Mciver, R.K. "'Cosmology' as a Key to the Thought of Philo of Alexandria", *Andrews University Seminary Studies* 25 (1988), p. 267-279.
Méasson, A. "Le De Sacrificiis Abelis et Caini de Philon d'Alexandrie." *Bulletin de l'Association Guillaume Budé* (1966), p. 309-316.
Méasson, A., and Cazeaux, J. "From Grammar to Discourse: a Study of the *Quaestiones in Genesim* in Relation to the Treatises", in D.M. Hay (ed.), *Both Literal and Allegorical: Studies in Philo of Alexandria's Questions and Answers on Genesis and Exodus*. Brown Judaic Series 232 (1991), p. 125-225.
Melnick, R. "On the Philonic Conception of the Whole Man." *JSJ* 11 (1980), p. 1-32.
Ménard, Jacques É. "Philon d'Alexandrie et le Judaism Palestinien." *Dictionnaire de la Bible*, Supplement VII. Paris: Letouzey & Ané, Éditeurs, 1966, p. 1299-1304.
Mendelson, Alan. *Encyclical Education in Philo of Alexandria*. Dissertation, University of Chicago, 1971.
—— *Philo's Jewish Identity*, Brown Judaic Studies 161. Atlanta: Scholars Press, 1988.
—— *Secular Education in Philo of Alexandria*. Cincinnati: Hebrew Union College, Ktav, 1982.
Meyer, Albrecht. *Vorschungsglaube und Schichsalsidee in ihrem Verhältnis bei Philon von Alexandria*. Dissertation, Tübingen, 1976.
Michel, A. "Quelques aspects de la rhétorique chez Philon." PAL. Paris: CNRS, 1967, p. 81-103.
Milgrom, J. "On the Origins of Philo's Doctrine of Conscience." *Studia Philonica* 3 (1974-1975), p. 41-45.
Moehring, Horst R., "Arithmology as an Exegetical Tool in the Writings of Philo of Alexandria", in *The School of Moses*. Brown Judaic Studies 304. Ed. by J. P. Kenney. Atlanta: Scholars Press, 1995, p. 141-176.
Moeller, Christa. *Die Biblische Tradition als Weg zur Gottesschau. Eine Hermeneutik des Judentums bei Philon von Alexandria*. Dissertation, Tübingen, 1976.
Mondésert, Claude *et alii*. "Philon d'Alexandrie ou Philon le Juif." *Dictionnaire de la Bible*, Supplement VII. Paris: Letouzey (1966), p. 1288-1351.
Mondin, Battista. "Esistenza, natura, inconoscibilità di Dio nel pensiero di Filone Alessandrino." *La Scuola Cattolica* 95 (1967), p. 423-447.
—— "Il problema dei rapporti tra fede e ragione in Platone e in Filone Alessandrino." *Le Parole e la Idee* 9 (1967), p. 9-15.
—— "L'Universo filosofico di Filone Alessandrino." *La Scuola Cattolica* 96/5 (1968), p. 371-394.
Muehl, M. "Zu Poseidonios und Philon." *Wiener Studien* 60 (1942), p. 28-36.
Mühlengerg, Ekkard. "Das Problem der Offenbarung in Philo von Alexandria." *Zeitschrift für Katholische Theologie* 64/1-2 (1973), p. 1-18.
Myre, A. "La loi dans l'ordre moral selon Philon d'Alexandrie." *Science et Esprit* 24 (1972), p. 93-113.
—— "La loi dans l'ordre cosmique et politique selon Philon d'Alexandrie." *Science et Esprit* 24 (1972), p. 217-247.
—— "La loi et le Pentateuque selon Philon d'Alexandrie." *Science et Esprit* 25 (1973), p. 209-225.
—— "Les caracteristiques de la loi mosaique selon Philon d'Alexandrie." *Science et Esprit* 27 (1975), p. 35-69.
Nazzaro, Antonio V. "Il γνῶθι σαυτόν nel'espistemologia filoniana." *Annali della Fac. di Lettere e Filosofia dell'Univ. di Napoli* 12 (1969), p. 49-86.

—— "Filone Alessandrino e l'ebraico." *Rendiconti della R. Accademia de archeologia, lettere e belle arti di Napoli* 42 (1968), p. 61-79.

—— "Il problema cronologico della nascita di Filone Alessandrino." *Rendiconti della R. Accademia de archeologia, lettere e belle arti di Napoli* 38 (1964), p. 129-138.

—— "Realtà e linguaggio in Filone d'Alessandria." *Le Parole e le Idee* 11 (1969), p. 339-346.

Nearly, M. "Philo of Alexandria: Alexandrian Judaism", *Irish Theological Quarterly* 54 (1988), p. 41-49.

Neel, J. E. "Le philonisme avant Philon." *Revue de Théologie et de Philosophie* 25 (1892), p. 417-433.

Neumark, H. *Die Verwendung griechischer und jüdischer Motive in den Gedanken Philons über die Stellung Gottes zu seinen Freunden.* Dissertation, University of Würzburg, 1937.

Nicolas, M. "Études sur Philon d'Alexandrie." *Revue de l'Histoire des Religions* 5 (1882), p. 318-339; 7 (1883), p. 145-164; 8 (1893), p. 468-488, 582-602, 756-772.

Nikiprowetzky, Valentin. "L'Exégèse de Philon d'Alexandrie." *Revue d'Histoire et de Philosophie Religieuses* (1973), p. 309-329.

—— "Note sur l'interprétation littérale de la loi et sur l'angélologie chez Philon d'Alexandrie." *Mélanges André Neher* (1975), p. 181-190.

—— "Problèmes du 'Récit de la Création' chez Philon d'Alexandrie." *Revue des Études Juives* 124 (1965), p. 271-306.

—— "La spiritualisation des sacrifices et le culte sacrificiel au Temple de Jérusalem chez Philon d'Alexandrie." *Semitica* 17 (1967), p. 97-116.

—— "Les suppliants chez Philon d'Alexandrie." *Revue des Études Juives* 122 (1963), p. 241-278.

—— *Le commentaire de l'écriture chez Philon d'Alexandrie.* Leiden: Brill, 1977.

—— "La doctrine de l'"elenchos' chez Philon, ses résonances philosophiques et sa portée religieuse." *PAL.* Paris: CNRS, 1967, p. 255-273.

—— "L'exégèse de Philon d'Alexandrie dans le *De Gigantibus* et le *Quod Deus.*" In *Two Treatises of Philo of Alexandria.* Chico, CA: Scholars Press, 1983, p. 5-75.

—— "Sur une lecture démonologique de Philon d'Alexandrie, *De Gigantibus,* 6-18." In *Hommage à Georges Vajda, études d'histoire et la pensée juives.* Ed. G. Nahon et C. Touati. Louvain, 1980, p. 43-71.

—— "texte et discours dans l'interpretation de Philon d'Alexandrie", *Sileno* 11 *[Studi in onore di A. Barigazzi]* (1985), p. 2.105-128.

Nock, Arthur D. "Philo and Hellenistic Philosophy." *Classical Review* 57 (1943), p. 77-81.

Oesterly, W. O. E. *The Jews and Judaism during the Greek Period. The Background of Christianity.* London, 1941.

Otte, K. *Das Sprachverständnis bei Philo von Alexandrien. Sprache als Mittel der Hermeneutik.* Beiträge zur Geschichte der biblischen Exegese 7; Tübingen: Mohr, 1968.

Paglialunga de Tuma, M. "Filón de Alejandría en la temática calderoniana." *Cuadernos del Sur* (1969), p. 90-105.

Parente, F. "La Lettera di Aristea come fonte per la storia del giudaismo alessandrino durante la prima metà del I secolo A.C." *Annale della Scuola Normal Superiore di Pisa* 2. 1972, p. 177-237; 517-567.

Paruzel, H. "Filono el Aleksandrio." *Biblia Revuo* 11 (1975), p. 81-114.

Pascher, Joseph. Ἡ Βασιλικὴ Ὁδός. *Der Königsweg zu wiedergeburt und Vergottung bei Philon von Alexandreia.* Studien zur Geschichte und Kultur des Altertums 17, 3-4; New York: Johnson Reprint Corp., 1971.

Pearson, Birger A. "Hellenistic-Jewish Wisdom Speculation and Paul." In *Aspects of Wisdom in Judaism and Early Christianity.* Ed. Robert L. Wilken (University of

Notre Dame Center for the Study of Judaism and Christianity in Antiquity 1). Notre Dame, IN: University of Notre Dame Press, 1975, p. 43-66.
—— "Philo and the Gnostics on Man and Salvation." PCCHS, Ed. W. Wellner. Berkeley: The Center for Hermeneutical Studies, 1977.
—— "Philo and Gnosticism." ANRW II 21.1. Berlin: W. de Gruyter, 1984, p. 295-342.
Peisker, Martin. *Der Glaubensbegriff bei Philon, hauptsächlich dargstellt an Moses und Abraham.* Dissertation, Breslau, 1936.
Pelletier, A. "Les passions à l'assaut del'âme d'aprés Philon." *Revue des Études Grecques* 78 (1965), p. 52-60.
Pépin, Jean. *Mythe et allégorie. Les origines grecques et les contestations judéo-chrétiennes.* Paris: Aubier, 1958.
—— "Remarques sur la théorie de l'exégèse allégorique chez Philon." PAL, Paris: CNRS, 1967, p. 138-168.
Perrot, C. "La lecture de la Bible dans le Diaspora hellénistique", in *Études sur le Judaisme hellénistique. Congrès de Strasbourg (1983). Lectio Divina* 119 (Paris, 1984), p. 125-132.
Petit, Françoise. *L'ancienne version latine des questions sur la Genèse de Philon d'Alexandrie.* Berlin: Akademie Verlag, 1973.
Petit, Madeleine. "Les songes dans l'oeuvre de Philon d'Alexandrie." *Mélanges d'histoire des religions offerts à Henri-Charles Puech.* Paris: Presses Universitaires, 1974, p. 151-159.
Pfeifer, G. "Mitteilungen zur Beurteilung Philons." *Zeitschrift für die alttestamentliche Wissenschaft* 77 (1965), p. 212-214.
Philon d'Alexandrie. *Actes du Colloque National. Lyon 11-15 septembre 1966.* PAL, Paris: Édition du Centre National de la Recherche Scientifique, 1967.
Planck, H. *Commentatio de principiis et causis interpretationis philonianae allegoricae.* Göttingen: Vandenhoeck und Ruprecht, 1806.
Pohlenz, Max. "Philon von Alexandria." *Nachrichten von der Akademie der Wissenschaft in Göttingen.* Göttingen: Vandenhoeck und Ruprecht, 1942, p. 409-487; in M. Pohlenz: *Kleinere Schriften* I. Hildesheim: Olms, 1965, p. 305-383.
—— *Die Stoa. Geschichte einer geistigen Bewegung.* 2 vols. Göttingen: Vandenhoeck und Ruprecht, 3rd ed., 1964 (esp. I, p. 369-378; II, 180-184).
Pouilloux, J. "Philon d'Alexandrie. Recherches et points de vue nouveaux." *Revue de l'Histoire des Religions* 161 (1962), p. 135-137.
Priessnig, Anton. "Die literarische Form der Patriarchenbiographien des Philon von Alexandrien." *Monatsschrift für die Geschichte und Wissenschaft des Judentums* 73 (1929), p. 143-155.
Quispel, Gilles. "Jewish Gnosis and Mandaean Gnosticism." In *Les textes de Nag Hammadi. Colloque du Centre d'histoire des religions* (Strasbourg, 23-25 octobre 1974), p. 82-122. Ed. Jacques-É. Ménard. Leiden: Brill, 1975 (esp. p. 93-94).
Rabinowitz, H. R. "Philo, the First Jewish Preacher of the Dispersion." *Nib Hamidrashah* (1971), p. 192-199.
Radice, R. "Filone di Alessandria nella interpretazione di V. Nikiprowetzky e della sua scuola", *Rivista de Filosofia Neoscolastica* 74 (1984), p. 15-41.
—— *Platonismo e creazionismo in Filone di Alessandria.* Studi e testi 7; Milan: Rusconi, 1989.
Reale, Giovani. "Filoni di Alessandria e la prima elaborazione filosofica della dottrina della creazione." *Paradoxos Politeia, Vita e Pensiero* (1979), p. 247-287.
Reister, Wolfgang. "Die Sophia im Denken Philons." In *Lang, Bernhard. Frau Weisheit. Deutung einer biblischen Gestalt.* Düsseldorf: Patmos Verlag, 1975, p. 161-164.
Renan, E. "Philon d'Alexandrie et son oeuvre." *La Revue de Paris* 1 (1894), p. 37-55.

Richardson, W. "Philo and his Significance for Christian Theology." *Modern Churchman* 30 (1940), p. 15-25.
—— "The Philonic Patriarchs as Νόμος "Εμψυχος." *Studia Patristica* 1 (1957), p. 515-525.
Rist, John M. "The Use of Stoic Terminology in Philo's Quod Deus Immutabilis Sit 33-50." *PCCHS* 23. Berkeley, 1976 (includes responses from T. Conley, J. Dillon, V. Nikiprowetzky, David Winston).
Robbins, William J. *A Study in Jewish and Hellenistic Legend with Special Reference to Philo's "Life of Moses."* Dissertation, Brown University, 1948.
Rokeah, D. "A New Onomasticon Fragment from Oxyrrhynchus and Philo's Etymologies." *Journal of Theological Studies* 19 (1968), p. 70-82.
Royse, James R. "Further Greek Fragments of Philo's Quaestiones." In *Nourished with Peace. Studies in Hellenistic Judaism in Memory of Samuel Sandmel*. Chico, CA: Scholars Press, 1984, p. 143-154.
—— "Philo and the Immortality of the Race." *JSJ* 11 (1980), p. 33-37.
—— *The Spurious Texts of Philo of Alexandria: a Study of Textual Transmission and Corruption with indexes to the Major Collections of Greek Fragments*, ALGHJ 22; Leiden: Brill, 1991.
Rudolph, Kurt. *Die Gnosis: Wesen und Geschichte einer Spätantiken Religion*. Göttingen: Vandenhoeck und Ruprecht, 1977.
Runia, David T. *Exegesis and Philosophy: Studies on Philo of Alexandria*. Variorum Collected Studies Series; London, 1990.
—— "How to Search Philo", *Studia Philonica Annual* 2 (1990), p. 106-139.
—— "Mosaic and Platonic Exegesis: Philo on 'Finding' and 'Refinding'", *Vigiliae Christianae* 40 (1986). p. 209-217.
—— *Philo of Alexandria and the "Timaeus" of Plato*. Leiden: Brill, 1986.
—— "Philo's De Aeternitate Mundi. The Problem of its Interpretation." *Vigiliae Christianae* 35 (1981), p. 105-151.
—— *Philo in Early Christian Literature: a Survey*. Compendia Rerum Iudaicarum ad Novum Testamentum III 3; Assen-Minneapolis, 1993.
—— "Polis and Megalopolis: Philo and the Founding of Alexandria", *Mnemosyne* 42 (1989), p. 398-412.
—— "Some Statistical Observations on Fifty Years of Philonic Scholarship", *Studia Philonica Annual* 1 (1989), p. 74-81.
—— "The Structure of Philo's Allegorical Treatises: a Review of two Recent Studies and some Additional Comments." *Vigiliae Christianae* 38 (1984), p. 209-256.
—— "Was Philo a Middle Platonist? a Difficult Question Revisited", *The Studia Philonica Annual* 5 (1993), p. 180-208.
—— "Why does Clement of Alexandria call Philo 'the Pythagorean'?", *Vigiliae Christianae* 49 (1995), p. 1-22.
Ryle, H. E. *Philo and Holy Scripture or the Quotations of Philo from the Books of the Old Testament with an Introduction and Notes*. London, 1895.
Safrai, S. *et alii* (ed.). *Jewish People in the First Century, Historical Geography, Political History, Social, Cultural and Religious Life and Institutions*. Compendia Rerum Iudaicarum ad Novum Testamentum. Philadelphia: Fortress Press, 1974-1976.
Sandmel, S. "Philo Judaeus: An Introduction to the Man, his Writings, and his Significance." ANRW II, 21.1. Berlin: W. de Gruyter, 1984, p. 3-46.
—— *Philo of Alexandria. An Introduction*. New York, Oxford: Oxford University Press, 1979.
—— "Philo's Place in Judaism: A Study of Conceptions of Abraham in Jewish Literature." *HUCA* 25 (1954), p. 209-237; 26 (1955), p. 151-332. Reprinted

Cincinnati, 1956; with new introduction by the author. New York: Ktav Publishing House, Inc., 1972.
—— "Virtue and Reward in Philo." In *Essays in Old Testament Ethics. In Memoriam J. Philip Hyatt.* Eds. James L. Crenshaw, John T. Willis. New York: Ktav, 1974.
—— "The Confrontation of the Greek and Jewish Ethics: Philo, De Decalogo." *The Central Conference of American Rabbis Journal* 15 (1968), p. 54-63, 96.
—— "Philo's Environment and Philo's Exegesis." *Journal of Bible and Religion* 22 (1954), p. 248-253.
—— "Philo's Knowledge of Hebrew." *Studia Philonica* 5 (1978), p. 107-112.
Savon, Hervé. "Saint Ambroise devant l'exégèse de Philon le Juif." 2 vols. Paris: *Études Augustiniennes*, 1977.
Scarpat, G. "Cultura ebreo-ellenistica e Seneca." *Rivista Biblica* 13 (1965), p. 3-30.
Schmidt, Helmut. *Die Anthropologie Philons von Alexandreia.* Würzburg: Triltsch, 1933.
Schmitt, Armin. "Interpretation der Genesis aus hellenistischen Geist." *Zeitschrift für die alttestamentliche Wissenschaft* 86 (1974), p. 137-163.
Schneider, Carl. *Kulturgeschichte des Hellenismus.* 2 vols. München: C. H. Beck, 1967, 1969 (esp. I, p. 876-881, 891-900; II, p. 558-559, 620, 840).
Schoeps, Hans-Joachim and Heinemann, Isaak. "Rund um Philo." *Monatsschrift für die Geschichte und Wissenschaft des Judentums* 82 (1938), p. 269-280.
Schürer, Emil. *The History of the Jewish People in the Age of Jesus Christ (175 B.C. - A.D. 135).* 2 vols. Revised and edited by Géza Vermès and Fergus Millar. Edinburgh: T. and T. Clark. 1973-1979. Spanish version: *Historia del Pueblo Judío en Tiempo de Jesús 175 A.C. - 135 D.C.,* 2 vols. Madrid: Ediciones Cristiandad, 1985.
Schwarz, Jacques. "L'Égypt de Philon." PAL, Paris: CNRS, 1967, p. 34-44.
Schwarz, W. "A Study in Pre-Christian Symbolism. Philo *De Somniis* 1. 216-218, and Plutarch, *De Iside et Osiride* 4 and 77." Institute of Classical Studies Bulletin 20, 1973, p. 104-117.
Segalla, G. "Il problema della volontà libera in Filone Alessandrino." *Studia Filonica* 12 (1965), p. 3-31.
Shroyer, Montgomery J. *Alexandrian Jewish Literalists.* Dissertation, Yale University Press, 1935. Condensed in Journal of Biblical Literature 55, 1936, p. 261-284.
Siciliano, Francisco. *Alla luce del "Logos": Filone d'Alessandria.* Cosenza: Pellegrini, 1975.
Siegfried, Carl G. A. *Philo von Alexandria als Ausleger des Alten Testaments . . . an sich selbst und nach seinem geschichtlichen Einfluss betrachtet.* Jena: Hermann Dufft, 1875. Reprinted Amsterdam: Philo Press, 1970.
Simom, Marcel. "Éléments gnostiques chez Philon." In *Le origini dello gnosticismo.* Ed. Ugo Bianchi. Studies in the History of Religions (Supplement to *Numen*) 12, 1967, p. 359-376.
—— "Situation du Judaïsme alexandrin dans la Diaspora." PAL. Paris: CNRS, 1967, p. 17-31.
Sly, Dorothy I. *Philo's Alexandria.* London and New York: Routledge, 1996.
—— *Philo's Perception of Women.* Brown Judaic Series 209; Atlanta: Scholars Press, 1990.
Smallwood, E. M. "The Chronology of Gaius' Attempt to Desecrate the Temple." *Latomus* 16 (1957), p. 3-17.
Sowers, Sidney G. *The Hermeneutics of Philo and Hebrews.* A comparison of the interpretation of the Old Testament in Philo Judaeus and the Epistle to the Hebrews. Zürich: EVZ – Verlag; Richmond: John Knox Press, 1965.
Spicq, Ceslaus. "Le philonisme de l'Épître aux Hébreus." *Revue Biblique* 56 (1949), p. 542-572.
Staehle, Karl. *Die Zehlenmystik bei Philon von Alexandreia.* Berlin: Teubner, 1931.

Starobinski-Safran, Esther. "Signification des noms divins – d'après Exode 3 – dans la tradition rabbinique et chez Philon d'Alexandrie." *Revue de Théologie et de Philosophie* 3rd series 23 (1973), p. 426-435.
—— "La communauté juive d'Alexandrie à l'époque de Philon", in *ΑΛΕΞΑΝΔΡΙΝΑ: hellénisme, judaisme et christianisme à Alexandrie; mélanges offerts à Claude Mondésert S.J.*. Paris: Éditions du Cerf, 1987, p. 45-75.
Stein, E. *Die Allegorische Exegese des Philo aus Alexandria*. Beihefte zur Zeitschrift für die neutestamentliche Wissenschaft 51; Giessen: Töpelmann, 1929.
—— *Philo und der Midrasch*. Giessen: Töpelmann, 1931.
—— *Philo Alexandrinus. The Writer, his Writings and his Philosophical Teachings*. Warsaw, 1935.
Sterling, G.E. "*Creatio Temporalis, Aeterna, vel Continua?* an Analysis of the Thought of Philo of Alexandria", *Studia Philonica Annual* 4 (1992), p. 15-41.
—— "Philo and the Logic of Apologetics: an Analysis of the *Hypothetica*", *SBL. Seminar Papers Series* 29 (1990), p. 412-430.
—— "Platonizing Moses: Philo and Middle Platonism", *The Studia Philonica Annual* 5 (1993), p. 96-111.
—— "Recluse or Representative? Philo and Greek-Speaking Judaism Beyond Alexandria", *Society of Biblical Literature Seminar Papers* 34 (1995), p. 595-616.
Tcherikover, Victor A., *Hellenistic Civilization and the Jews*. New York: Atheneum, 1979.
—— *The Jews in Egypt in the Hellenistic-Roman Age in the Light of the Papyri*. Jerusalem: Magnes Press, 2nd ed., 1963.
—— ed., et al. *Corpus Papyrorum Judaicarum*. 3 vols. Cambridge: Harvard University Press, 1957.
Terian, A. "A Critical Introduction to Philo's Dialogues." ANRW II, 21.1. Berlin: W. de Gruyter, 1984, p. 272-294.
—— "Some Stock Arguments for the Magnanimity of the Law in Hellenistic Jewish Apologetics", in B. S. Jackson (ed.), *Jewish Law Association Studies* I (Chico, CA 1985), p. 141-149.
Ternus, J. "Die Anthropologie Philons." *Scholastik* 11 (1936), p. 82-98.
Theiler, Willy. *Forschungen zum Neuplatonismus*. Berlin: W. de Gruyter, 1966.
—— "Philo von Alexandria und der Beginn des kaiserzeitlichen Platonismus." In *Untersuchungen zur antiken Literatur*. Berlin: W. de Gruyter, 1970, p. 485-501.
—— "Philo von Alexandria und der hellenisierte Timaeus." In *Philomathes: Studies and Essays in the Humanities in Memory of Philip Merlan*. Ed. Robert B. Palmer and Robert Hamerton-Kelly. The Hague: Martinus Nijhoff, 1971, p. 25-35.
Thiselton, A. C. "The 'Interpretation' of Tongues: A New Suggeston in the Light of Greek Usage in Philo and Josephus." *Journal of Theological Studies* 30 (1979), p. 15-35.
Thoma, Clemens. "Judentum und Hellenismus im Zeitalter Jesu." *Bibel und Leben* 11 (1970), p. 151-159.
Thorne, G.W.A. "The Structure of Philo's Commentary on the Pentateuch", *Dionysius* 13 (1989), p. 17-50.
Thyen, H. *Der Stil der jüdisch-hellenistischen Homilie*. Göttingen: Vandenhoeck und Ruprecht, 1955.
—— "Philo von Alexandria." *Lexikon der Alten Welt* (1965), p. 2301-2302.
Tobin, Thomas Herbert. *The Creation of Man: Philo and the History of Interpretation*. Dissertation, Cambridge, MA: Harvard University, 1980.
—— "Tradition and Interpretation in Philo's Portrait of the Pariarch Joseph", *SBL. Seminar Papers Series* 25 (1986), p. 271-277.

—— "Was Philo a Middle Platonist? Some Suggestions", *The Studia Philonica Annual* 5 (1993), p. 147-150.
Towner, Wayne Sibley. *The Rabbinic "Enumeration of Scriptural Examples." A Study of a Rabbinic Pattern of Discourse with Special References to Mekhilta d'R. Ishmael.* Studia Post Biblica 22; Leiden: Brill, 1973, p. 109-116.
Treitel, L. *Gesamte Theologie und Philosophie Philos von Alexandria.* Berlin, 1929.
Trevers, Piero. "Philon." *Oxford Classical Dictionary* (1949), p. 684.
Trisoglio, E. F. "Apostrofi parenesi e preghiere in Filone d'Alessandria." *Rivista Lasalliana* 31 (1964), p. 357-410; 32 (1965), p. 39-79.
Vanderlinden, E. "Les divers modes de connaissance de Dieu selon Philon d'Alexandrie." *Mélanges de Science Religieuse* 4 (1947), p. 285-304.
Verhnes, J. V. "Philon d'Alexandrie. De sacrificiis Abelis et Caini." *Revue de Philologie* 94 (1968), p. 298-305.
Vian, G.M., "Les Quaestiones di Filone", *Annali di Storia dell'Esegesi* 9 (1992), p. 365-388.
Völker, Walther. *Fortschritt und Vollendung bei Philo von Alexandrien.* TU 49.1; Leipzig: J. C. Heinrichs, 1938.
—— "Neue Wege der Philoforschung?" *Theologische Blaetter* 16 (1937), p. 297-301.
Wagner, Walter Hermann. "Philo and Paideia." *Cithara* 10 (1971), p. 53-64.
Wallis, Richard T. "The Idea of Conscience in Philo of Alexandria." *Studia Philonica* 3 (1974-1975), p. 24-40.
—— "The idea of Conscience in Philo of Alexandria." PCCHS 13. Ed. Wilhelm Wüllner, Berkeley, 1975. (With response by John M. Dillon, William S. Anderson, Jacob Milgrom, Samuel Sandmel, David Winston, Wilhelm Wüllner, discussion by a group of participants, and author's reply).
Walter, Nikolaus. *Der Thoraausleger Aristobulos. Untersuchungen zu seinen Fragmenten und zu pseudepigraphischen Resten der Jüdisch-hellenistischen Literatur.* TU 26; Berlin: Akademie Verlag, 1964.
Warnach, Walter. "Selbstliebe und Gottesliebe im Denken Philons von Alexandrien." In *Wort Gottes in der Zeit.* Festschrift K. H. Schelkle; Düsseldorf: Patmos, 1973, p. 198-214.
Watkin, E. I. "New Light on Philo." *Downside Review* 86 (1968), p. 287-297.
Weaver, M. J. *"Pneuma" in Philo of Alexandria.* Dissertation, University of Notre Dame; Notre Dame, IN, 1973 (microfilm).
Weddenburn, A. J. M. "Philo's Heavenly Man." In *Novum Testamentum, Monograph Series* 15, 1973, p. 301-326.
Wegner, Judith Romney. "The Image of Woman in Philo." *SBL Seminar Papers* 21 (Chico, CA: Scholars Press, 1982), p. 551-563.
Weiss, Hans-Friedrich. *Untersuchungen zur Kosmologie des hellenistischen und palästinischen Judentums.* TU 97; Berlin: Akademie Verlag, 1966 (esp. p. 18-74).
Wendland, Paul. *Die hellenistisch-römische Kultur in ihren Bezeihungen zum Judentum und Christentum.* Tübingen: Mohr (Siebeck), 1972, p. 203-211.
—— *Philo und die Kynisch-stoische Diatribe* (Beiträge zur Geschichte der griechischen. Philosophie und Religion. Von P. Wendland und O. Kern); Berlin: Töpelmann, 1895, p. 1-75.
—— "Philo und Clemens Alexandrinus." *Hermes* 31 (1896), p. 435-456.
Wilken, Robert L. ed. *Aspects of Wisdom in Judaism & Early Christianity.* Notre Dame, IN: University of Notre Dame Press, 1975.
Williamson, Ronald. *Philo and the Epistle to the Hebrews.* Leiden: E. J. Brill, 1970.
—— *Jews in the Hellenistic World: Philo.* Cambridge Commentaries on the Writings of the Jewish and Christian World 200 B.C. to A.D. 200, vol. I,ii; Cambridge: Cambridge University Press, 1989.

Willms, Hans. Εἰκών. *Eine Begriffsgeschichtliche Untersuchung zum Platonismus. I. Teil: Philon von Alexandreia.* Münster: Aschendorff, 1935.

Wilson, R. M. "Philo of Alexandria and Gnosticism." *Kairos, Zeitschrift für Religionswissenschaft und Theologie* 14 N:3 (1972), p. 213-219.

Winden, J. C. M. von. "The World of Ideas in Philo of Alexandria. An Interpretation of *De Opificio Mundo* 24-25." *Vigiliae Christianae* 37 (1983), p. 209-217.

Windisch, H. *Die Frömmigkeit Philos Und ihre Bedeutung für das Christentum.* Leipzig, 1909.

Winston, David. "Freedom and Determinism in Philo of Alexandria." *Studia Philonica* 3 (1974-1975), p. 47-70.

—— "Judaism and Hellenism: Hidden Tensions in Philo's Thought", *Studia Philonica Annual* 2 (1990), p. 1-19.

—— "Philo and Middle Platonism: Response to Runia and Sterling", *The Studia Philonica Annual* 5 (1993), p. 141-146.

—— "Philo's Ethical Theory." *Aufstieg und Niedergang der römischen Welt,* II, 21.1; Berlin: W. de Gruyter, 1984.

—— "Philo's Theory of Cosmogony." In *Religious Syncretism in Antiquity. Essays in Conversation with Geo Widengren.* Ed. Birger A. Pearson. Series on Formative Contemporary Thinkers 1; Missoula: Scholars Press, 1975, p. 157-171.

—— "Theodicy and the Creation of Man in Philo of Alexandria", in *Hellenica et Judaica: hommage à Valentin Nikiprowetzky.* Leuven-Paris: Peeters, p. 105-111.

—— "Was Philo a Mystic?" In *Studies in Jewish Mysticism.* Ed. by Joseph Dan and Frank Talmage. Cambridge, MA: Association for Jewish Studies, 1982, p. 15-39.

Winston, David S. and Dillon, John. *Two Treatises of Philo of Alexandria. A Commentary on De Gigantibus and Quod Deus Sit Immutabilis.* Brown Judaica Studies; Chico, CA: Scholars Press, 1983.

Winter, Bruce W. *Philo and Paul among the Sophists.* Cambridge: University Press, 1997.

Whittaker, John. "God and Time in Philo of Alexandria." In *God, Time, Being. Two Studies in the Transcendental Tradition in Greek Philosophy* (symbolae osloenses, fasc. suppl. 23). Oslo: Universitetsforlaget, 1971, p. 33-57.

Wolfson, Harry A. "Philo on Free Will." *Harvard Theological Review* 35 (1942), p. 131-169.

—— "The Philonic God of Revelation and His Latter-Day Deniers." *Harvard Theological Review* 53 (1960), p. 101-124. Previously in *The Jewish Expression.* Ed. Judah Goldin. New York: Bantam Books, 1970, p. 87-108.

—— "Philo on Jewish Citizenship in Alexandria." *Journal of Biblical Literature* 63 (1944), p. 165-168.

—— "Philo Judaeus." *The Encyclopedia of Philosophy* vol. 6. Ed. Paul Edwards. New York: MacMillan, 1967, p. 151-155. Reprinted Wolfson, H. A., *Studies in the History of Philosophy and Religion.* Ed. Isadore Twersky, George H. Williams. Cambridge, MA: Harvard University Press, 1973, p. 60-70.

—— *Philo. Foundations of Religious Philosophy in Judaism and Islam.* 2 vols. Cambridge: Harvard University Press, 1947; 1962.

—— "What is New in Philo?" In *From Philo to Spinosa: Two Studies in Religious Philosophy.* New York: Behrman House, 1977, p. 17-38.

—— "Greek Philosophy in Philo and the Church Fathers." In *Studies in the History of Philosophy and Religion.* Ed. Isadore Twersky and George H. Williams. Cambridge, MA: Harvard University Press, 1973, p. 71-97.

—— "The Veracity of Scripture from Philo to Spinosa." In *Religious Philosophy. A Group of Essays.* Cambridge, MA: Harvard University Press, 1961, p. 217-245.

Zandee, J. "Les enseignements de Silvanos et Philon d'Alexandrie." In *Mélanges d'histoire des religions offerts à Henri-Charles Puech*. Paris: Presses Uni-versitaires de France, 1974, p. 337-345.
Zeitlin, Solomon. "Did Agrippa Write a Letter to Gaius Caligula?" *Jewish Quarterly Review* 56 (1965), p. 22-31.

II. ON RHETORIC: THEORY OF ARGUMENTATION

A. *Primary Sources*

Aristotle. *The Art of Rhetoric*. Trans. J. H. Freese. LCL; Cambridge, MA: Harvard University Press, 1975.
—— *Rhétorique*. Trans. M. Dufour (vol. III by M. Dufour and A. Wartelle). Paris: Les Belles Lettres, 1960 (vols. I and II), 1973 (vol. III).
—— *Categories, on Interpretation, Prior Analytics*. Trans. H. P. Cooke and H. Treddenick. LCL; Cambridge, MA: Harvard University Press, 1967.
—— *Posterior Analytics, Topica*. Trans. H. Tredennick and E. S. Forster. LCL; Cambridge, MA: Harvard University Press, 1976.
—— *On Sophistical Refutations*, etc. Trans. E. S. Forster. LCL; Cambridge, MA: Harvard University Press, 1965.
—— *Topiques*. Trans. J. Brunschwig. Paris: Les Belles Lettres, 1967.
(Aristotle). *Rhetorica ad Alexandrum*. Trans. H. Rackham. LCL; Cambridge, MA: Harvard University Press, 1965.
Arnim, H. von (ed.). *Stoicorum Veterum Fragmenta*. 4 vols. Leipzig: Teubner, 1905-1924.
Cicero. *Academicorum Reliquiae Cum Lucullo*. Ed. O. Plasberg. Stuttgart: Teubner, 1961.
—— *De Natura Deorum and Academica*. Trans. H. Rackham. LCL; London: Heinemann, 1933.
—— *Brutus*. Ed. H. Malcovati. Leipzig: Teubner, 1965.
—— *Brutus*. Trans. G. H. Hendrickson. LCL; Cambridge, MA: Harvard University Press, 1939.
—— *De Finibus Bonorum et Malorum*. Ed. T. Schiche. Stuttgart: Teubner, 1966.
—— *De Finibus Bonorum et Malorum*. Trans. H. Rackham. LCL; London: Heinemann, 1914.
(Cicero). *Ad C. Herennium* (Rhetorica ad Herennium). Trans. H. Caplan. LCL; Cambridge, MA: Harvard University Press, 1977.
Cicero. *De Inuentione, De Optimo Genere Oratorum, Topica*. Trans. H. M. Hubbel. LCL; Cambridge, MA: Harvard University Press, 1976.
—— *De Natura Deorum*. Ed. O. Plasberg. Leipzig: Teubner, 1911.
—— *Orator*. Ed. P. Reis. Stuttgart: Teubner, 1963.
—— *Orator*. Trans. H. M. Hubbell. LCL; Cambridge, MA: Harvard University Press, 1939.
—— *De Oratore*. Ed. K. Kumaniecki. Leipzig: Teubner, 1969.
—— *De Oratore*, 2 vols. Vol. I: *De Oratore I e II* (trans. E. W. Sutton and H. Rackham); Vol. II: *De Oratore III, De Fato, Paradoxa Stoicorum, De Partitione Oratoria* (trans. H. Rackham). LCL; Cambridge, MA: Harvard University Press, 1942.
—— *Tusculanae Disputationes*. Ed. M. Pohlenz. Stuttgart: Teubner, 1965.
—— *Tusculanae Diputationes*. Trans. J. E. King. LCL; Cambridge, MA: Harvard University Press, 1945.

Demetrius. *Demetrius on Style*. Ed. W. Rhys Roberts. Hildesheim: Georg Olms Verlag, 1969. Also Aristotle. *Poetics and Longinus* (trans. W. Hamilton Fyfe), *Demetrius on Style* (trans. W. Rhys Roberts). LCL; Cambridge, MA: Harvard University Press, 1973.
Dionysius of Halicarnassus. *Critical Essays*. Trans. S. Usher. LCL, 2 vols.; Cambridge, MA: Harvard University Press, 1974.
Hermogène. *L'art rhétorique*. Trad. by Michel Patillon. Paris: L'Age d'Homme, 1997.
Hock, R. F. and O'Neil, Edward N. *The Chreia in Ancient Rhetoric. Volume I: The Progymnasmata*. Philadelphia: Scholars Press, 1985.
Plato. *Oeuvres Complètes*. 14 vols.; Paris: Les Belles Lettres, 1953-1964.
—— *Opera*. Ed. John Burnet. 6 vols.; Oxford: Clarendon Press, 1900-1913.
—— *Cratylus*, etc. Trans. H. N. Fowler. LCL; Cambridge, MA: Harvard University Press, 1970.
—— *Charmides*, . . . *Epinomis*. Trans. W. R. M. Lamb. LCL; Cambridge, MA: Harvard University Press, 1964.
—— *Eutrypho, Apology, Crito, Phaedo, Phaedrus*. Trans. H. N. Fowler. LCL; Cambridge, MA: Harvard University Press, 1971.
—— *Lysis, Symposium, Gorgias*. Trans. W. R. M. Lamb. LCL; Cambridge, MA: Harvard University Press, 1967.
Quintilian. *Institutio Oratoria*. Trans. H. E. Butler. LCL; Cambridge, MA: Harvard University Press, 1969.
—— *Institutionis Oratoriae*, Libri duodecim. Oxford: Oxford University Press, 1970.
—— *Institutionis Oratoriae*, Libri XII. Ed. L. Radermacher. Leipzig: Teubner, 1959.
Rabe, H. *Hermogenis Opera*. Stuttgart: Teubner, 1969.
Ross, W. D. *Aristotle's Prior and Posterior Analytics*. Oxford: Oxford University Press, 1949.
Spengel, L. (ed.). *Rhetores Graeci*. 3 vols.; Leipzig: Teubner, 1853-1856.
Walz, C. (ed.). *Rhetores Graeci*. 9 vols.; Stuttgart: Cottage, 1832-1836.

B. *Secondary sources*

Achard, Guy. *Practique rhétorique et idéologique dans les discours "Optimates" de Cicéron*. Mnem. Suppl. 68; Leiden: Brill, 1981.
Adamik, Tomás. "Aristotle's Theory of the Period," *Philologus* 128:2 (1984), p. 184-201.
Alexandre Jr., Manuel, *Argumentação Retórica em Fílon de Alexandria*. Lisboa: Instituto Nacional de Investigação Científica, 1990.
—— «Rhetorical Argumentation as an Exegetical Technique in Philo of Alexandria». *Hellenica et Judaica. Hommage à Valentin Nikiprowetzky*. Leuven-Paris: Éditions Peeters, 1986, p. 13-27.
—— «Some Reflections on Philo's Concept and Use of Rhetoric». *Euphrosyne* XIX (1991), p. 281-290.
—— «A Rhetorical Analysis of Philo's *De Virtutibus*». *Euphrosyne* XXI (1993), p. 9-28.
—— «The Chreia in Greco-Roman Education». *Grammaire et Rhetorique: Notion de Romanité*. Actes du colloque de Strasbourg (novembre 1990), édités par Jacqueline Dangel. Strasbourg: AECR, 1994, p. 85-92.
Anderson, Graham. *The Seconq Sophistic: A Cultural Phenomenon in the Roman Empire*. London & New York: Routledge, 1993.
Arnhart, Larry. *Aristotle on Political Reasoning. A Commentary on the "Rhetoric."* DeKalb, IL: Northern Illinois University Press, 1981.

Auerbach, E. *Literary Language and its Public in Late Antiquity and in the Middle Ages.* Princeton: Princeton University Press, 1993.
Baird, A. Craig. *Argumentation, Discussion, and Debate.* McGraw-Hill, Series in Speech, Clarence T. Simon, consulting editor. New York: McGraw-Hill Book Company, 1950.
Balthrop, V. Williams. "Argument as Linguistic Opportunity: A Search for Form and Function." PSCA. Ed. J. Rhodes and S. Newell. Alta: University of Utah, 1980.
Barker, Evelyn M. "A New Aristotelian Approach to Dialectical Reasoning." RIP (1980), p. 133-134.
Barthes, R. "L'ancienne rhétorique," *Communications* 16 (1970), p. 172-233.
Bellanger, R. *Techniques et practique de l'argumentation.* Paris: Dunod, 1971.
Benoit, William. "Analogical Reasoning in Legal Argumentation." PSCA. Ed. Jack Rhodes and Sara Newell. Falls Church, VA: SCA, 1980, p. 49-61.
Betz, Hans Dieter. *Der Apostel Paulus und die sokratische Tradition.* BHT 45; Tübingen: Mohr, Siebeck, 1972.
—— "The Literary Composition and Function of Paul's Letter to the Galatians." NTS 21 (1975), p. 353-379.
Bitzer, Lloyd. "Aristotle's Enthymeme Revisited." QJS 45 (1959), p. 399-408.
Bitzer, Lloyd and Black, Edwin (ed.). *The Prospect of Rhetoric.* Englewood Cliffs, NJ: Prentice-Hall, Inc., 1971.
Black, E. B. *Rhetorical Criticism: A Study in Method.* New York: MacMillan, 1978.
Bonnellus, Eduardus. *Lexicon Quintilianeum.* Hildesheim: Georg Olms, 1962.
Bonitz, H. *Index Aristotelicus.* 2nd ed. Granz: Akademische Druck-u. Verlagsanstalt, 1955.
Bornecque, H. *Les clausules métriques latines.* Travaux et mémoires de l'Université de Lille, nouvelle série I.6. Lille: Au Siège de l'Université, 1907.
Botha, Jan. *Subject to whose Authority? Multiple Readings of Romans 13.* Atlanta: Scholars Press, 1994.
Bouchard, Guy. "Rhétorique des mots, rhétorique des idées." LTP 35:3 (1979), p. 301-313.
Brandt, William J. *The Rhetoric of Argumentation.* New York: Bobbs-Merrill, 1970.
Braulik, Georg. *Der Mittel deuteronomischer Rhetorik.* Anal. Bibl. 68, Rome, 1978.
Brockriede, Wayne. "Rhetorical Criticism as Argument." QJS 50 (1974), p. 165-174.
Brownstein, Oscar L. "Plato's Phaedrus: Dialectic as the Genuine Art of Speaking." QJS 51 (1965), p. 392-398.
Bryant, D. C. (ed.). *Ancient Greek and Roman Rhetoricians. A Biographical Dictionary.* New York, 1968.
—— *Rhetorical Dimensions in Criticism.* Baton Rouge, LA: Louisiana State University, 1973.
Burger, Ronna. *Plato's Phaedrus: A Defense of a Philosophic Art of Writing.* University, AL: University of Alabama Press, 1980.
Burke, Kenneth. *The Philosophy of Literary Form.* Baton Rouge, LA: Louisiana State University Press, 1941.
—— *A Rhetoric of Motives.* Englewood Cliffs, NJ: Prentice-Hall, Inc., 1950.
Calboli, Gualtiero (ed.). *Cornifici Rhetorica ad C. Herennium: Introduzione, testo critico, commento.* Bologna: Ricardo Patron, 1969.
—— "La retorica preciceroniana e la politica a Roma." *Eloquence et rhétorique chez Cicéron.* Vol. XXVIII de entretiene sur l'antiquité classique. Genève: Vandoeuvres, 1981, p. 41-107.
Calboli Montefusco, L. "Exordium narratio epilogus". *Studi sulla teoria retorica greca e romana delle parti del discorso.* Bologne: Pubblicazzioni del Dipartimento di filologia classica e medioevale, 1, 1988.

Campbell, George. *The Philosophy of Rhetoric.* Ed. Lloyd F. Bitzer. Carbondale: Southern Illinois University Press, 1963.
Caplan, Harry. *Of Eloquence. Studies in Ancient and Medieval Rhetoric.* Ithaca: Cornell University Press, 1970.
Carter, M.F. "The Ritual Functions of Epideictic Rhetoric: The Case of Socrates' Funeral Oration", *Rhetorica*, 9 (1991), p. 209-232.
Charles, Michel. *Rhétorique de la lecture.* Paris: Éditions du Seuil, 1977.
Clark, Donald Lemen. *Rhetoric in Greco-Roman Education.* New York: Columbia University Press, 1957.
Clark, Ruth A. and Delia, Jesse G. "Topoi and Rhetorical Competence." QJS 65 (1979), p. 203ff.
Clarke, M. L. "The Thesis in the Roman Rhetorical Schools of the Republic." CQ 45 (1951), p. 159-166.
Classen, C. Joachim. "Poetry and Rhetoric in Lucretius." *American Philological Association* 99 (1968).
Coenen, Hans Georg. "Rhetorische Argumentation bei Pascal." Essay presented at the *Quarto Congresso Bienal da International Society for the History of Rhetoric.* Florence, 13-17 June, 1983.
Conley, Thomas M. "Πάθη and πίστεις": Aristotle 'Rhetoric' II, 2-11." *Hermes.* ZKP 110:3 (1982), p. 300-315.
—— "Logical Hylomorphism and Aristotle's κοινοὶ τόποι." CSSJ 29 (1978), p. 92-97.
—— *Philo's Rhetoric: Studies in Style, Composition and Exegesis.* Center for Hermeneutical Studies, Monograph 1; Berkeley: Center for Hermeneutical Studies, 1987.
Consigny, S. "Gorgias' Use of the Epideictic", *Philosophy and Rhetoric*, 25 (1992) p. 281-297.
Convegno Italo-Tedesco. 1; Bressanone, 1973. *Attualità della retorica. Atti del I Convegno Italo-tedesco.* Saggi di R. Baehr, R. Barilli, G. P. Brunetta., A. Daniele *et alii.* Padova: Liviana, 1975.
Corbett, Edward P. J. *Rhetorical Analysis of Literary Works.* New York: Oxford University Press, 1969.
—— *Classical Rhetoric for the Modern Student.* 3rd ed.; New York: Oxford University Press, 1990.
Côté, Marcel. "La philosophie du raisonable de Chaïm Perelman." *Laval théologique et philosophique* 41:2 (1985).
Cousin, Jean. *Études sur Quintilien.* Tome I: Contribution à la recherche des sources de l'Institution Oratoire. Amsterdam: Verlag P. Schippers, 1967.
Crable, Richard E. *Argumentation as Communication: Reasoning with Receivers.* Columbus, OH: Charles Merrill Pub. Co., 1976.
Daube, David. "Rabbinic Methods of Interpretation and Hellenistic Rhetoric." *Hebrew Union College Annual* 22 (1949), p. 239-264.
Dorolle, Maurice. *Le raisonnement par analogie.* Paris: Presses Universitaires de France, 1949.
Douglas, Alan E. "The Intellectual Background of Cicero's Rhetoric: A Study in Method." ANRW I, 3. Berlin: W. de Gruyter, 1973, p. 95-137.
Dubois, J. *et al. Rhétorique générale.* Paris: Larousse, 1970.
Ducrot, et Todorov, "Rhétorique et stylistique." *Dictionnaire Encyclopédique des Sciences du Langage.* Paris: Seuil, 1972, p. 99-105.
Eden, K. "Hermeneutics and the Ancient Rhetorical Tradition", *Rhetorica* 5 (1987), p. 59-86.
—— *Hermeneutics and the Rhetorical Tradition: Chapters in the Ancient Legacy and its Humanist Reception.* New Haven and London: Yale University Press, 1997.

Engel, E. S. *Plato on Rhetoric and Writing.* Unpublished doctoral dissertation; Yale University, 1973.
Enos, Theresa (ed.). *Encyclopedia of Rhetoric and Composition. Communication from Ancient Times to the Information Age.* New York & London: Garland Publishing, Inc., 1996.
Erickson, Keith V. (ed.). *Aristotle: The Classical Heritage of Rhetoric.* Metuchen, NJ: Scarecrow Press, 1974.
—— "Plato's Theory of Rhetoric: A Research Guide." *Rhetoric Society Quarterly* 7 (1977), p. 78-90.
—— *Plato: True and Sophistic Rhetoric.* Amsterdam: Rodopi, 1979.
Ernesti, I. C. T. *Lexicon Technologiae Graecorum Rhetoricae.* Leipzig: C. Fritsch, 1795.
—— *Lexicon Technologiae Latinorum Rhetoricae.* Leipzig: C. Fritsch, 1797. Hildesheim: G. O. Verlagsbuchhandlung, 1962.
Fischel, Henry. "The Usage of Sorites (Climax, *Gradatio*) in the Tannaitic Period." *Hebrew Union College Annual* 44 (1973), p. 119-151.
Fleshler, Helen. "Plato and Aristotle on Rhetoric and Dialectic." *Pennsylvania Speech Annual* 20 (1963), p. 11-17.
Fortenbaugh, W.W. "Aristotle on Persuasion through Character, *Rhetorica* 10 (1992), p. 207-244.
Fortenbaugh, W.W., and Mirhady, D.C. (eds.). *Peripatetic Rhetoric after Aristotle.* New Brunswick, NJ and London: Transaction Publishers, 1994.
Freely, Austin J. *Argumentation and Debate.* 3rd ed.; Belmont, CA: Wadsworth Publishing Co., 1971.
Fumaroli, Marc. *L'age de l'eloquence.* Paris: Droz, 1980.
Gallardo, Miguel Ángel Garrido. *La Musa de la Retórica. Problemas y Métodos de la Ciencia de la Literatura.* Madrid: Consejo Superior de Investigaciones Cientificas, 1994.
Garavelli, Bice Mortara. *Manual de Retórica.* Madrid: Catedra, 1991.
Genette, Gérard. "La rhétorique des figures." *Les figures du discours.* Paris: Flammarion, 1968, p. 5-17.
—— "La rhétorique restreinte." In *Communications* 16 (1970).
Girandin, Benoit. *Rhétorique et Théologique: Calvin, Le commentaire de l'épitre aux Romains.* Paris: Édition Beauchesne, 1979.
Gitay, Yehoshua. *Rhetorical Analysis of Isaiah 40-48: A Study of the Art of Prophetic Persuasion.* Ann Arbor, MI: Xerox University Microfilms, 1978.
Goldschmitt, Victor. *Essai sur le "Cratyle."* Paris: Vrin, 1982.
González, Antonio A. "Cicerón y Quintiliano ante la retórica." *Helmántica. Revista de Filología Clásica y Hebrea* 34 (1983), p. 249-266.
Gotoff, Harold. *Cicero's Elegant Style.* Urbana, Chicago, London: University of Illinois Press, 1979.
Göttert, Karl-Heinz. *Argumentation: Grundzüge ihrer Theorie in Bereich theoretischen Wissens und praktischen Handelns.* Tübingen: Niemeyer, 1978.
Gommel, J. "Rhetorisches Argumentieren bei Thukydides." *Spudasmata* 10. Hildesheim: Olms, 1966.
Grassi, Ernesto. *Rhetoric as Philosophy.* University Park, PA and London: The Pennsylvania State University Press, 1980.
Grenet, Paul. *Les origines de l'analogie philosophique dans les dialogues de Platon.* Paris: Éditions Contemporaines, 1948.
Grimaldi, W. M. A. "Σημεῖον, τεκμήριον, εἰκός in Aristotle's *Rhetoric.*" *American Journal of Philology* 101:4, 1980.
—— "Studies in the Philosophy of Aristotle's Rhetoric." *Hermes, Zeitschrift für Klassische Philologie* 25. Wiesbaden: Franz Steiner, 1972.

Grize, J. B. et al. "Recherches sur le discours et l'argumentation." *Travaux du Centre de Recherches Sémiologiques de l'Université de Neuchâtel. Revue Européene des Sciences Sociales* 32. Genève: Droz, 1974.
Gronbeck, Bruce E. "From Argument to Argumentation: Fifteen Years of Identity Crisis." In *Proceedings of the Summer Conference on Argumentation.* Alta: University of Utah, 1980.
Grube, G. M. A. "Educational Rhetorical and Literary Theory in Cicero." *Phoenix* 11 (1962), p. 234-257.
Gwynn, Aubrey Osborn. *Roman Education from Cicero to Quintilian.* Oxford: Oxford University Press, 1926.
Harper, Nancy. "An Analytical Description of Aristotle's Enthymeme." *The Central States Speech Journal* 24:4 (1973), p. 304-309.
Havet, Ernest. *Étude sur la rhétorique d'Aristote.* Paris: Vrin, 1983.
Havelock, Eric A. and Hershbell, Jackson. *Communication Arts in the Ancient World.* New York: Hastings House, 1978.
Hill, F. I. "The Rhetoric of Aristotle." In *A Synoptic History of Classical Rhetoric.* New York: Random House, 1972.
Horner, W.B. *The Present State of Scholarship in Historical and Contemporary Rhetoric.* Columbia, MO and London: University of Missouri Press, 1990.
Hunt, Everett Lee. "Plato and Aristotle on Rhetoric and Rhetoricians." *Studies in Rhetoric and Public Speaking in Honor of James Albert Winans.* New York, 1962, p. 3-60.
—— "Plato on Rhetoric and Rhetoricians." *Quarterly Journal of Speech* 6 (1920), p. 35-56.
Jackson, J. J. (ed.). *Rhetorical Criticism.* Pittsburg: Pickwick, 1974.
Janson, Tore. "The Problems of Measuring Sentence-Length in Classical Texts." *Studia Linguistica* 18 (1964), p. 26-36.
Johnson, W. R. *Luxuriance and Economy: Cicero and the Alien Style.* University of California Publications Classical Studies 6. Berkeley: University of California Press, 1971.
Johnstone, Christopher Lyle. "An Aristotelian Trilogy: Ethics, Rhetoric, Politics, and the Search of Moral Truth." *Philosophy and Rhetoric* 13:1 (1980), p. 1-24.
Johnstone, H. W., Jr. "A New Theory of Philosophical Argumentation." In *Philosophy, Rhetoric and Argumentation.* University Park: The Pennsylvania State University Press, 1965, p. 126-137.
—— *Philosophy and Argument.* University Park: The Pennsylvania State University Press, 1959.
Jost, Walter and Hyde, Michael J. *Rhetoric and Hermeneutics in our Time.* New Haven and London: Yale University Press, 1997.
Kalinowski, Georges. "Le rationnel et l'argumentation. A propos du 'traité de l'argumentation' de Chaïm Perelman et Lucie Olbrechts-Tyteca." *Revue Philosophique de Louvain* 70:7, 4th series, 1972.
Kennedy, George Alexander. *Aristotle On Rhetoric: A Theory of Civic Discourse.* New York & Oxford: Oxford University Press, 1991.
—— *The Art of Persuasion in Greece.* Princeton: Princeton University Press, 1963.
—— *The Art of Rhetoric in the Roman World.* Princeton: Princeton University Press, 1972.
—— (ed.). *The Cambridge History of Literary Criticism: Vol I. Classical Criticism.* Cambridge: Cambridge University Press, 1989.
—— *Classical Rhetoric and its Christian and Secular Tradition from Ancient to Modern Times.* Chapel Hill, NC: The University of North Carolina Press, 1980.

—— *Classical Rhetoric under Christian Emperors*. Princeton: Princeton University Press, 1983.
—— *Comparative Rhetoric: An Historical and Cross-cultural Introduction*. New York: Oxford University Press, 1998.
—— *New Testament Interpretation through Rhetorical Criticism*. Chapel Hill, NC: The University of North Carolina Press, 1984.
—— *Quintilian*. New York: Twayne Publishers, Inc., 1969.
Kinneavy, James L. *A Theory of Discourse: The Aims of Discourse*. London & New York: Northon & Company, 1980.
Kneale, William & Martha. *The Development of Logic*. Oxford: Clarendon Press, 1965.
Koller, H. "Die dihäretische Methode." *Glotta* 39 (1960), p. 6-24.
Kroll, W. "Rhetorik." *Realencyclopaedie der klassischen Altertumswissenschaft*. Supplementband VII. Stuttgart: Metzlersche Verlagsbuchhandlung, 1940, p. 1039-1138.
Kucharski, P. "La rhétorique dans le *Gorgias* et le *Phèdre*." *Revue des Études Grecques* 74 (1961), p. 371-406.
Kustas, George L. "Diatribe in Ancient Rhetorical Theory." *Center for Hermeneutical Studies in Hellenistic and Modern Culture, Colloquy* 22. Berkeley, 1976, p. 1-33.
Lana, I. *Quintiliano, il "Sublime" e gli "Esercizi Preparatori" de Elio Teone*. Turin, 1951.
Lausberg, Heinrich. *Elemente der literarischen Rhetorik*. 9th. ed.; Munich: Max Heuber, 1987.
—— *Handbuch der literarischen Rhetorik: Eine Grundlegung der Literaturwissenschaft*. 3rd ed., 2 vols.; Stuttgart: Franz Steiner, 1973, 1990. Spanish translation: *Manual de Retórica Literaria*. 3 vols. Madrid: Editorial Gredos, 1975.
Leeman, A. D. *Orationis Ratio. The Stylistic Theories and Practice of the Roman Orators, Historians and Philosophers*. 2 vols. Amsterdam: Hakkert, 1963.
Lundeen, L. T. *Risk and Rhetoric in Religion. Whitehead's Theory of Language and Discourse of Faith*. Philadelphia: Fortress, 1972.
Lynch, John Patrick. *Aristotle's School. A Study of a Greek Educational Institution*. Berkeley: University of California Press, 1972.
Mack, B.L. *Rhetoric and the New Testament*. Minneapolis: Fortress Press, 1990.
Madden, E. H. "The Enthymeme. Crossroads of Logic, Rhetoric and Metaphysics." *Philosophical Review* (1952), p. 368-376.
Malherbe, Abraham J. "Μὴ γένοιτο in the Diatribe and in Paul." *Harvard Theological Review* 73:1-2 (1980), p. 231-240.
Martin, H. C., Ohmann, R. M. and Wheatley, J. H. *The Logic and Rhetoric of Exposition*. 3rd ed. New York: Holt Rinehart and Winston, Inc., 1969.
Martin, Josef. *Antike Rhetorik: Technik und Methode*. Handbuch der Altertumswissenschaft 2, no. 3. München: Beck, 1974.
McBurney, James H. "The Place of the Enthymeme in Rhetorical Theory." *Speech Monographs* 3 (1936), p. 49-74.
McCall, Marsh H., Jr. *Ancient Rhetorical Theories of Simile and Comparison*. Cambridge, MA: Harvard University Press, 1969.
Merguet, H. *Lexikon zu den philosophischen Schriften Ciceros*. Hildesheim: Olms, 1961.
Meyer, Michel et Lempereur, Alain. *Figures et confits rhetoriques*. Bruxelles: Editions de l'Université de Bruxelles, 1990.
Michel, Alain. "L'eloquenza romana." REA 61 (1959).
—— *Rhétorique et philosophie chez Cicéron*. Paris: Presses Universitaires de France, 1960.
—— "Rhétorique et philosophie dans les traités de Cicéron." ANRW I, 3. Berlin: W. de Gruyter, 1973, p. 139-208.
—— "Rhétorique, philosophie et esthétique générale." *Revue d'Études Latines* (1973), p. 302-326.

―― "Rhétorique et philosophie dans le *Tusculanes*." REL, 1961.
―― "A propos du *Pro Quinctio:* les aspects philosophiques de l'argumentation cicéronienne." *Revue des Études Latines* 34 (1956), p. 34-35.
―― "La théorie de la rhétorique chez Cicéron: Éloquence et philosophie." *Le Classicisme à Rome.* Vol. XXV de *Entretiene sur l'Antiquité Classique.* Genève: Vandoeuvres, 1978, p. 109-147.
―― "Un type d'argumentation philosophique (l'epicheirema) dans les discours de Cicéron." *Revue des Études Latines* 35 (1957), p. 46-47.
Morier, Henry. *Dictionnaire de Poétique et de Rhétorique.* Paris: Presses Universitaires de France, 1981.
Morton, Andrew Q. and McLeman James. *Paul the Man and the Myth. A Study in the Authorship of Greek Prose.* New York: Harper and Row, 1966.
Mudd, Charles S. "The Enthymeme and Logical Validity." *Quarterly Journal of Speech* 45 (1959), p. 409-414.
Muilenburg, James. "Form Criticism and Beyond." *Journal of Biblical Literature* 88 (1969), p. 1-18.
Murphy, James J. (ed.). *A Synoptic History of Classical Rhetoric.* New York: Random House, 1972.
―― *Rhetoric in the Middle Ages: A History of Rhetorical Theory from Saint Augustine to the Renaissance.* Berkeley: University of California, 1974.
Naidoff, Bruce D. "The Rhetoric of Encouragement in Isaiah 40:12-31." *Zeitschrift für die Alttestamentliche Wissenschaft* 93:1. Berlin: W. de Gruyter, 1981, p. 62-76.
Natanson, Maurice (ed.). *Philosophy, Rhetoric and Argumentation.* University Park, PA: The Pennsylvania University Press, 1965.
Nobles, W. Scott. "The Paradox of Plato's Attitude Toward Rhetoric." *Western Speech* 21 (1957), p. 206-210.
Norden, Eduard. *Die antike Kuntsprosa vom VI. Jahrhunderts vor Christus bis in die Zeit der Renaissance.* 2 vols. Leipzig: Teubner, 1958. Vol. II, p. 451-479.
Ochs, Donovan J. "Cicero's Rhetorical Theory." In *A Synoptic History of Classical Rhetoric.* Ed. James J. Murphy. New York: Random House, 1972.
Oliver, Robert T. "Philosophy, Rhetoric, and Argumentation: Congenial or Conjunctive?" In *Philosophy, Rhetoric and Argumentation.* Ed. M. Natanson and H. W. Johnstone, Jr. University Park: Pennsylvania State University Press, 1965.
Oltramare, André. *Les origines de la diatribe romaine.* Lausanne: Payot, 1926.
Ortega, Alfonso. *Retorica: El Arte de Hablar en Publico. Historia-Metodo y Tecnicas Oratorias.* Madrid: Grupo Editorial Industrial, 1989.
Paci, E. "Dialettica, metodo diairetico e rettòrica nel *Fedro* di Platone." *Archivio di Storia della Filosofia Italiana* 4 (1935), p. 145-158.
Patillon, M. *Le corpus d'Hermogène. Essais critiques sur les structures linguistiques de la rhétorique ancienne, accompagnés d'une traduction du corpus,* 3 vols., thèse, Paris, 1985.
―― *La théorie du discours chez Hermogène le Rhéteur. Essai sur les structures linguistiques de la rhétorique ancienne* (Collection d'études anciennes, 117), Paris, 1988.
Paulhan, Jean. *La preuve par l'étymologie, métrique collection.* Paris: Les Éditions de Minuit, 1953.
Pelletier, A. "Les passions à l'assaut de l'âme d'après Philon." *Revue d'Études Grecques* 78 (1965), p. 52-60.
Pelletier, Yvan. "Aristote et la découverte oratoire." *Laval Théologique et Philosophique* (I) 35:1 (1979), p. 3-20; (II) 36:1 (1980), p. 29-46; (III) 37:1 (1981), p. 45-67.
Perelman, Chaïm. *Le champ de l'argumentation.* Bruxelles: Presses Universitaires, 1970.

—— "Éducation et rhétorique." *Revue Belge de Psychologie et de Pédagogie* XIV: 60 (1952), p. 129-138.
—— *Élements d'une théorie de l'argumentation.* Bruxelles: Presses Universitaires, 1968.
—— *L'empire rhétorique. Rhétorique et argumentation.* Paris: Vrin, 1977.
—— *The Idea of Justice and the Problem of Argument.* London: Routledge and Kegan Paul, 1963.
—— *The New Rhetoric and the Humanities.* Boston: Reidel Publishing Company, 1979.
Perelman, Chaïm and Olbrechts-Tyteca, L. "Logique et rhétorique." *Revue Philosophique,* 1950.
—— *La Nouvelle Rhétorique: Traité de l'Argumentation.* Paris: Presses Universitaires de France, 1958.
—— *Rhétorique et philosophie. Pour une théorie de l'argumentation de philosophie.* Paris: Presses Universitaires de France, 1952.
Pernot, Laurent. *La Rhétorique de l'Éloge dans le Monde Gréco-Romain.* 2 vols. Paris: Institut d'Études Augustiniennes, 1993.
Pfeiffer, W. M. "True and False Speech in Plato's Cratylus 385b-c." *Canadian Journal of Philosophy* 2 (1972), p. 87-104.
Reichel, G. *Quaestiones Progymnasmaticae.* Dissertation. Leipzig, 1909.
Richards, I. A. *The Philosophy of Rhetoric.* New York: Oxford University Press, 1936.
Ricoeur, P. *La métaphore vive.* Paris: Seuil, 1975.
Riposati, Benedetto. "Problemi di retorica antica." In *Introduzione alla filologia classica.* Milan: C. Marzorati, 1951, p. 657-787.
Robbins, Charles J. "Rhetorical Structure of Phil. 2:6-11." *The Catholic Biblical Quarterly* 42:1 (1980), p. 73-82.
Robbins, Vernon K. "Pronouncement Stories and Jesus' Blessing of Children: A Rhetorical Approach." *SBL Seminar Papers* 21. Chico, CA: Scholars Press, 1982, p. 407-430. *Semeia* 29 (1983), p. 43-74.
—— *Exploring the Texture of Texts: A Guide to Socio-Rhetorical Interpretation.* Valley Forge, Penn.: Trinity Press International, 1996.
Roberts, William Rhys. *Greek Rhetoric and Literary Criticism.* New York: Cooper Square, 1963.
—— "References to Plato in Aristotle's *Rhetoric.*" *Classical Philology* 19 (1924), p. 324-346.
Romilly, Jacqueline de. *Les grands sophistes dans l'Athènes de Périclès.* Paris: Fallois, 1988.
Romilly, Jacqueline de. *Magic and Rhetoric in Ancient Greece.* Cambridge: Harvard University Press, 1975.
Rommetveit, R. and Blakar, R. M. (ed.). *Studies of Language, Thought and Verbal Communication.* London: Academic Press, 1979.
Ross, W. D. (ed.). *Aristoteles. Fragmenta Selecta.* Oxonii: Clarendoniano, 1955.
Rowell, Edward Z. "Prolegomena to Argumentation." *Quarterly Journal of Speech* 18 (1932), p. 1-13, 224-248, 381-405, 585-606.
Rutherford, I. "Inverting the Canon: Hermogenes on Literature", *Harvard Studies in Classical Philology,* 94 (1992), p. 355-378.
Ryan, E.E. *Aristotle,s Theory of Rhetorical Argumentation.* Montreal: Bellarmin, 1984.
Schmid, W. *Über die klassische Theorie und Praxis des antiken Prosarhythmus.* Wiesbaden, 1959.
Schoenfeld, M. "Argumentation et présentation des faits chez Démosthène." *L'Antiquité Classique* (1959), p. 201ff.
Sesonske, Alexander. "To Make the Weaker Argument Defeat the Stronger." *Journal of the History of Philosophy* 6 (1968), p. 217-231.

Scroggs, Robin. "Paul as Rhetorician: Two Homilies in Romans 1-11." In *Jews, Greeks and Christians*. Leiden: Brill, 1976, p. 271-297.
Smith, Robert W. *The Art of Rhetoric in Alexandria*. The Hague: Mouton, 1974.
Solmsen, F. "Aristotle and Cicero on the Orator's Playing upon the Feelings." *Classical Philology* 33 (1938), p. 390-404.
────── "The Aristotelian Tradition in Ancient Rhetoric." *American Journal of Philology* 62 (1941), p. 35-50, 169-180.
Stowers, Stanley Kent. *The Diatribe and Paul's Letter to the Romans*. SBL Dissertation Series 57. Chico, CA: Scholars Press, 1981.
Süss, Wilhelm. *Ethos, Studien zur älteren griechischen Rhetorik*. Leipzig: Teubner, 1910.
Thionville. E. *La théorie des lieux communs dans les topiques d'Aristote et des principales modifications*. Paris: Vrin, 1983.
Throm, H. *Die Thesis. Ein Beitrag zu ihrer Entsthehung und Geschichte. Rhetorische Studien XVII*. Paderborn, 1932.
Todorov, Tzvetan, PEPIN, J. et al. *Rhétorique et Hermeneutique*. Paris: Seuil, 1975.
Toulmin, Stephen Edelston. *The Uses of Argument*. Cambridge: Cambridge University Press, 1958.
Varga, A. Kibedi. *Rhétorique et littérature, études de structures classiques*. Paris: Didier, 1970.
Vignaux, Georges. *L'argumentation*. Genève: Libraire Droz, 1976.
────── *La nouvelle rhétorique* (a critical analysis of *Traité de l'argumentation*). Université de Neuchâtel, Travaux du Centre de Recherches Sémiologique, no. 1, 1969-1970.
Volkmann, Richard. *Die Rhetorik der Griechen und Römer*, 2nd ed.; Leipzig: Teubner, 1885; 3rd ed.; Munich: Beck, 1901. Reprinted; Hildesheim: Olms, 1963.
Wallach, Barbara P. "Lucretius and the Diatribe, *De Rerum Natura* II, 1-61." In *Festschrift für Luitpold Wallach, Gesellschaft, Kultur, Literatur: Rezeption und Originalität im Wachsen einer europäischen Literatur und Geistigkeit*. Ed. Karl Bosl. Stuttgart: 1975, p. 49-77.
────── "Lucretius and the Diatribe against the Fear of Death, *De Rerum Natura* III, 830-1094." *Mnemosyne, Supplement* 40. Leiden: Brill, 1976.
────── *A History of the Diatribe from its Origin up to the First Century B.C*. Dissertation, Urbana: University of Illinois Press, 1974.
Welch, J. W. (ed.). *Chiasmus in Christianity. Structures, Analysis, Exegesis*. Hildesheim: Gerstenberg, 1981.
Welch, K.E. *The Contemporary Reception of Classical Rhetoric: Appropriations of Ancient Discourse*. Hillsdale, NJ: Lawrence Erlbaum, 1990.
Wenzel, Joseph W. "Perspectives on Argument." *Proceedings of the Summer Conference on Argumentation*. Ed., J. Rhodes and S. Newell. Alta: University of Utah, 1980.
────── "Toward a Rationale for Value-Centered Argument." *Journal of the American Forensic Association* 13 (1977), p. 150-158.
White, Eugene Edward (ed.). *Rhetoric in Transition: Studies in the Nature and Uses of Rhetoric*. University Park and London: The Pennsylvania State University Press, 1980.
Wilamowitz-Moellendorf, U. von. *Rhetorica: Schriften zur aristotelischen und hellenistischen Rhetorik*. Hildesheim: Olms, 1968.
Wilder, Amos Niven. *Early Christian Rhetoric: The Language of the Gospel*. New York: Harper and Row, 1964; Cambridge: Harvard University Press, 1971.
Wörner, Markus Hilmar. "Enthymeme als Argumentationshandlungen." In *Kongressbericht der Jahrestagung der Gesellschaft für Angewandt Linguistik (GAL)* 9, Bd. 4, Heidelberg, 1979.

Worthington, Ian (ed.). *Persuasion: Greek Rhetoric in Action*. London and New York: Routledge, 1994.
Wuellner, Wilhelm (ed.). *Diatribe in Ancient Rhetorical Theory: Protocol of the 22 Colloquy of the Center for Hermeneutical Studies*. Berkeley: The Center for Hermeneutical Studies, 1976.

III. MISCELLANEOUS

Arnim, H. von (ed.). *Stoicorum Veterum Fragmenta*. 4 vols. Leipzig: Teubner, 1905-1924.
Bonner, Stanley F. *Education in Ancient Rome*. Berkeley and Los Angeles: University of California Press, 1977.
Bousset, Wilhelm. Κύριος Χριστός: *A History of the Belief in Christ from the Beginning of Christianity to Irenaus* (Trans. J. E. Steely). Nashville and New York: Abingdom, 1970.
Boyancé, P. "Etymologie et Théologie chez Varron." *Revue des Études Latines* 51 (1975), p. 99-115.
Clarke M. L. *Higher Education in the Ancient World*. London: Routledge and Kegan Paul, 1971.
Daube, David. "Alexandrian Methods of Interpretation and the Rabbis." *Festschrift Hans Lewald*. Basel: Helbing & Lichtenbahn, 1953, p. 27-44.
Dillon, John M. "The Academy in the Middle Platonic Period." *Dionysius* 3 (1979), p. 63-77.
—— *The Middle Platonists: 80 B.C. to A.D. 220*. Ithaca, NY: Cornell University Press, 1977.
Doty, William G. *Letters in Primitive Christianity*. Philadelphia: Fortress Press, 1979.
Farrar, F. W. *History of Interpretation*. 1st ed., 1886. Reprinted; Grand Rapids: Baker Book House, 1979.
Funk, Robert W. *Language, Hermeneutic, and the Word of God*. New York: Harper and Row, 1966.
Gadamer, Hanz-Georg. *Philosophical Hermeneutics*. Berkeley: University of California Press, 1976.
—— *Wahrheit und Method: Grundzüge einer philosophischen Hermeneutik*. 3rd ed.; Tübingen: J. C. B. Mohr, 1975.
Guthrie, W. K. C. *A History of Greek Philosophy*. 5 vols.; Cambridge: Cambridge University Press, vols. III and IV, 1975; vol. V, 1978.
Hengel, M. *Juden, Griechen und Barbaren. Aspeckte der Hellenisierung des Judentums in worchristlicher Zeit*. Stuttgart: Verlag Katholisches Bibelwerk, 1976. English version: *Jews, Greeks and Barbarians*. Philadelphia: Fortress Press, 1980.
—— *Judaism and Hellenism. Studies in the Encounter in Palestine During the Early Hellenistic Period*. 2 vols.; Philadelphia: Fortress Press, 1974.
Hester, James D. *Epistolography in Antiquity and Early Christianity. A Proposal for a Pacific Coast Region, SBL Seminar*. Redlands: Jameson Center for the Study of Religion and Ethics, University of Redlands, CA, 1975.
Hoy, David Couzens. *The Critical Circle. Literature, History, and Philosophical Hermeneutics*. Berkeley: University of California Press, 1978.
Onvernizzi, G. *Il Didaskalikos di Albino e il Medioplatonismo*. 2 vols.; Roma, 1976.
Koester, Helmut. *Introduction to the New Testament*. Vol. I: *History, Culture, and Religion of the Hellenistic Age*. Philadelphia: Fortress Press, 1982. Translated from the German: *Einführung in das Neue Testament*. Chaps. I-VI; Berlin: W. de Gruyter, 1980.

Kraemer, Hans Joachim. *Platonismus und hellenistische Philosophie.* Berlin: W. de Gruyter, 1971.
Longenecker, R. N. *Biblical Exegesis in the Apostolic Period.* Grand Rapids: W. B. Eerdmans, 1977. Especially chap. I: "Jewish Hermeneutics in the First Century," p. 19-50.
Marrou, Henri I. *Histoire de l'éducation dans l'antiquité.* Paris: Seuil, 1981.
McKnight, Edgar V. *Meaning in Texts: The Historical Shaping of Narrative Hermeneutics.* Philadelphia: Fortress Press, 1978.
Mette, H. J. "Enkyklios Paideia." *Gymnasium* 67 (1960), p. 304ff.
Momigliano, Arnaldo. *The Development of Greek Biography.* Cambridge: Harvard University Press, 1971.
Palmer, Richard E. *Hermeneutics. Interpretation Theory in Schleiermacher, Dilthey, Heidegger, and Gadamer.* Evanston: Northwestern University Press, 1969.
Pepin, Jean. "Herméneutique ancienne." *Poétique* 6 (1975), p. 289-300.
Ricoeur, Paul. "Biblical Hermeneutics." *Semeia* 4 (1975), p. 130ff.
—— *Interpretation Theory: Discourse and the Surplus of Meaning.* Fort Worth: The Texas Christian University Press, 1976.
—— "La métaphore et le problème central de l'herméneutique." *Revue Philosophique de Louvaine* 70:50 (1972), p. 93-112.
Rijk, L. M. de. "Enkyklios Paideia. A Study of its Original Meaning." *Vivarium* 3 (1965), p. 24-93.
Sanders, E. P. (ed.). *Jewish and Christian Self-Definition.* 2 vols.; Vol. II: *Aspects of Judaism in the Graeco-Roman Period.* Philadelphia: Fortress Press, 1981.
Schürer, Emil. *The Literature of the Jewish People in the Time of Jesus.* New York: Schochen Books, Inc., 1972.
Seltzer, Robert M. *Jewish People, Jewish Thought: The Jewish Experience in History.* New York: McMillan Publishing Co., Inc., 1980.
Stucki, Pierre-André. *Herméneutique et dialectique.* Genève: Éditions Labor et Fides, 1970.
Tarrant, Harold. "Agreement and the Self-Evident in Philo of Larissa." *Dionysius* 5 (1981), p. 67-97.
Walter, N. "Frühe Begegnung zwischen jüdischen Glauben u. hellenistischer Bildung in Alexandrien." In *Neue Beiträge zur Geschichte der alten Welt.* 1, ed. C. Weiskopf; 1964, p. 367-378.

INDICES

I. INDEX OF PASSAGES FROM PHILO

De Abrahamo

52	153
53	143
54	136
61-84	8
83	212
103	220

De Agricultura

9	88
18	88, 122, 152
42	219
97-98	144
118	99
159-165	100

De Cherubim

1-10	213-215
3,6,8,10	88
11-20	215
21-39	215
40-52	213, 215, 216
42	217
43	103
45	195
52b	219
65-83	213-218
65a	219
67-71	219
74	220
93,102,105	88
113	103
121	195

De Confusione Linguarum

34-39	100
129	100

De Congressu Eruditionis Gratia

2,9,10,14,19,20,23,24,35, 72,74,121,145	88
10,18,19,20	177
17	103, 205, 225
19	122
22-23	88, 177
33	225
35	232
71-72	88, 178

73,79	88, 89
74	88, 99
74-76	1
79	89, 91, 122
121	88
148	88
154	122

De Vita Contemplatiua

75	103

Quod Deterius Potiori Insidiari Soleat

1-2	205
12	103
18,24	217
34-45	204-209
35-45	100
37-45	107
38	103, 189
38-40	100
40	103
41	205
43	101
126	195
126,127	103, 199
126-128	100
127-129	225
129,130-131,132-133	100, 101

Quod Deus Sit Immutabilis

26,42,77-79,78,83,86,95, 117-119	99
111	196
159-165	200
173-177	192

De Ebrietate

11-153	246
34-39	145
47-51	177
49	88
154-205	246
157-159	245-248
208	220

In Flaccum

123-124	243-245

De Fuga et Inuentione

44	219
68-70	182, 183
166	152
170	230
183	177
183-188,213	88

De Gigantibus

43	144
60	88
60-61	153
64	200

Quis Rerum Diuinarum Heres Sit

14	128
22	103
52,67,78-79,81	178
108	103
125	100
214	127
230-236	185
242	99
263-265	177
274	88
305	100

De Iosepho

1	186
3-4	186
16	186
17-21	132
23-27	132
28-31	186, 187
29-31	102
38	186
42-48	132
54-58	186
64-66	132
67-68	132
103-106	189
125-143	186-192
165	186
166	186
222-231	132-136
226-230	133-134
240	186
246-250	186
267,269	186

Legatio ad Gaium

1-7	135
53-56	238
166,168	88
236-329	158-177

276-279a	160-162
279b-280	162-163
279b-320	162-170
281-289	163-164
290-320	164-170
309-318	168
321-329	170-175

Legum Allegoriae I

36-37a	178
63	148
64	136
105-108	185

Legum Allegoriae II

1-3	178
73-75	148
85	1
185	195

Legum Allegoriae III

15-22	219
36	212
129	186
162-168	228
167,244	88
185	114
212	220
231-233	145
236-237	144
233	100

De Migratione Abrahami

13,14,71-73,78	103
34,35	1
70-82	209-213
71-78	100
72	88, 205
73	225
76	114
78	100, 212
82	101
82-85	212
146	200
158-163	196
168-170	128

De Vita Mosis I

1-4	110
5-333	110
23	88
34	135
92	189
157	114
162	111

De Vita Mosis II

1-287	109-112
2	111
3-15	111
8-65	110
12-41	187
35,44	107, 109
45-52	223
46-47	2
48	187
51	98
66	107
66-186	110
187	113
187-287	110
188	107
216	229
253-255	240-243
288-291	110

De Mutatione Nominum

19,23,88	152
137-140	217
229	88
252-263	223-233

De Opificio Mundi

1	209
7-12	180
8-9	102
45	145, 209
53	148
75-76	183
134-135	182, 184
143	123, 187
160-162	144

De Plantatione

128	98
130-131	98
140-177	153-158
140-149	154
150-155	155
154-155	99
156-164	156
165	99
165-171	156
172-174	98
175-177	155

De Posteritate Caini

22	177
100-111	197-204
101-102	91
137	88

124-125	177

De Praemiis et Poenis

1-2	2
24-51	136-143
40	217

Quod Omnis Probus Liber Sit

1-15	119-120
16-20	123-125
21-151	123-133
26-27,141	1
32-40	125
40	99
41-47	126
48-57	126
58-61	127
62-135	128-130
136-143	130-131
144-151	131
152-160	119-123
160	88

De Prouidentia II

103,107	1

Quaestiones et Solutiones in Genesim III

20	99

De Sacrificiis Abelis et Caini

11-13,21,81,136	145
21	144
21-44	143-153
38,43,44,192	88
45	143
82-83,85	101

De Sobrietate

2-16	193-197
9	88

De Somniis I

89	189
170	152
205	98
240	88

De Somniis II

1-3	189
134	99

De Specialibus Legibus I

336	88

De Specialibus Legibus II

229-230	90

De Specialibus Legibus III

1-6	1
1-7	88

De Specialibus Legibus IV

147	217

De Virtutibus

64	145
178	217
195	186

II. INDICES OF AUTHORS

1. INDEX OF ANCIENT AUTHORS

Anaximenes 54, 55, 56, 57, 75, 210
Antiochus of Ascalon 68, 69, 79, 81, 82, 101, 102
Antonius 70
Aphthonius 59, 69, 219
Aristotle 17, 19, 23, 24, 32, 33, 35-58, 61-63, 66, 68, 70, 74, 75, 80, 81, 101, 116, 137, 145, 165, 235, 236, 273
Arius Didymus 102

Bias of Priene 120
Bion 116

Callimachus 80
Cicero 18, 19, 38, 58, 60-75, 81-83, 101-103, 117, 127, 137, 139, 147, 154, 178, 187, 213, 234, 236, 237, 242, 243, 249, 250, 261, 273, 276, 277, 278, 279, 280, 282
Crassus 70

Demetrius of Phalerum 80, 235, 236, 237, 242
Demosthenes 234, 235
Dio Chrysostomus 187
Diogenes Laertius 121, 130

Epictetus 116
Eudorus of Alexandria 81, 82, 102
Euripedes 120, 130
Eusebius 5

Hermagoras 68
Hermogenes 59, 74, 115, 116, 223, 224, 225, 226, 281
Herodotus 158
Hieronymus 5

Homer 120

Isocrates 33, 60, 61, 81, 109, 142, 224, 234, 235, 237

Josephus 158, 251, 258, 260, 263, 270

Libanius 219
Lucretius 116

Musonius 116

Nicolaus 59

Philo of Larissa 62, 68, 81, 82, 101, 284
Plato 3, 5, 7, 9, 19, 24, 31-38, 45, 61, 63, 67, 79, 91, 120, 137, 152, 169, 182, 198, 199, 277, 278, 281
Plutarch 81, 82, 110, 269

Quintilian 19, 42, 58, 60, 64, 70, 71-73, 83, 133, 137, 145, 160, 169, 173, 233, 236, 237, 260, 274, 275, 277, 278, 279

Seneca 89, 102, 154, 269
Sophocles 124

Teles 116
Theognis 120
Theon of Alexandria 55, 59, 69, 74, 81, 83, 192, 218, 221, 223, 224, 226, 227
Theophrastus 80, 199
Thucydides 158, 234

Xenophon 110, 144, 158

Zeno 102, 129

2. INDEX OF MODERN AUTHORS

Adamik, T. - 236-238
Adler, M. - 13, 14, 251, 154
Aichele, G. - 14
Alexandre, M. - 16, 74, 79, 88, 89, 90, 91, 122, 205, 225, 254
Alexandre, Jr., M. - 74, 79, 176, 234, 254
Anderson, R.D. - 16, 56
Anderson, R. and Douglas, F. - 34, 35
Arnaldez, R. - 26, 6, 8, 18, 79, 82, 87, 91, 93, 103, 109, 112, 114, 132, 148, 152, 187, 198, 200, 203, 209, 230, 251, 254
Arnhard, L. - 45, 49, 50, 51, 52
Attridge, H. - 159
Ausfeld, R. - 114

Baer, R. A. - 4, 94, 255
Baron, S. W. - 118
Barthes, R. - 18, 23, 39, 42, 275
Barwick, K. - 63
Beckaert, A. - 136, 141
Belkin, S. - 14, 15, 78, 96, 255
Bentwick, N. - 255
Berchman, R. M. - 101
Bitzer, L. - 42, 43
Black, E. - 17, 32, 275
Bonner, S. F. - 68, 219, 223, 283
Booth, W. C. - 17
Borel, M-J. - 26, 27
Borgen, P. - 6, 9, 228, 229, 230, 232, 255
Botha, J. - 16, 30
Botte, B. - 109
Bouchard, G. - 23, 34, 275
Bousset, W. - 6, 12, 13, 78, 82, 96, 256, 283
Boyancé, P. - 102
Brandt, W. J. - 17, 24, 26, 53, 75, 121, 126, 136, 137, 138, 146, 174, 175, 191, 275
Bréhier, É. - 2, 77, 78, 90, 92, 93, 98, 114, 146, 151, 152, 182, 189, 201, 204, 205, 256, 264
Brochard, V. - 81, 82
Brownstein, O. L. - 35
Burke, K. - 39
Butts, J. R. - 224

Cadiou, R. - 198
Capelle, W. - 152
Caplan, H. - 60, 142
Cassin, B. - 31, 39
Cazeaux, J. - 8, 11, 12, 17, 92, 96, 98, 107, 213, 138, 172, 197, 215, 220, 221, 222, 256, 265
Christiansen, I. - 8, 11, 93
Clark, D. L. - 42, 70, 89, 276

Clarke, M. L. - 68, 69, 89, 276, 283
Cohn, L. - 2, 6, 114, 251, 257
Colson, F. H. - 23, 92, 109, 112, 120, 121, 122, 127, 132, 142, 146, 148, 153, 154-157, 186, 203, 219, 228, 230, 246, 251, 257
Conley, T. - 16, 17, 28, 87, 88, 89, 90, 97, 98, 101, 103, 141, 154, 155, 157, 204, 234, 243, 257, 268, 276
Corbett, E. P. J. - 17, 39, 40, 42, 276
Cousin, J. - 72, 73, 74, 276
Crable, R. E. - 28

Dähne, A. F. - 78
Daniélou, J. - 4, 91, 93, 255, 258
Daube, D. - 15, 86, 97, 143, 258, 276, 283
Davies, Stevan L. - 159
Davies, W. - 82, 260
DeGroot, A. W. - 234
Dillon, J. - 7, 9, 16, 62, 82, 87, 90, 92, 94, 95, 257, 258, 263, 268, 271, 272, 283
Drummond, J. - 78
Dubois, J. - 23

Earp, J. W. - 196, 219
Edeline, F. - 23
Ehninger, D. - 28
Erickson, K. V. - 31, 32, 33, 34, 199
Ernesti, C. T. - 27, 116, 277

Feldman, L. H. - 6, 86
Festugière, A. J. - 4, 6, 191, 258
Fischel, H. - 86, 258, 277
Fohlen, C. - 117
Folena, G. - 39
Fortenbaugh, W. - 44, 45, 47, 277
Fraenkel, Z. - 114
Fuks, A. - 90

Galay, J. L. - 42
Genette, G. - 18
Gochet, P. - 28
Gonzalez, A. - 71
Goodenough, E. R. - 6, 7, 8, 10, 84, 94, 96, 109, 111, 186, 228, 251, 259, 262
Goppelt, L. - 13, 260
Gorez, J. - 193
Gotoff, H. - 243, 277
Graetz, H. - 114
Grassi, E. - 61
Grenet, P. - 35
Grimaldi, W. M. A. - 43, 45, 46, 49, 50, 52, 54, 277

Grize, J. B. - 24, 26
Grube, G. M. A. - 235
Guthrie, W. K. C. - 35, 37, 38, 283

Hamerton-Kelly, R. G. - 7, 8, 10, 13, 15, 16, 260, 270
Hanson, A. - 198
Harl, R. M. - 67, 95, 260
Hay, D.M. - 98, 260, 265
Hegermann, H. - 232, 260
Heinemann, I. - 6, 13, 78, 96, 153, 251, 261, 269, 273
Heinze, M. - 78
Hengel, M. - 84, 85, 86, 261, 283
Hercher, R. - 159
Herriet, E. - 92
Hilgenfeld, A. - 114
Hilgert, E. - 3, 6, 77, 251, 254, 261
Hill, F. I. - 53
Horsley, R. - 102, 187, 261
Hunt, E. L. - 33

Jens, W. - 18
Johnson, W. R. - 247, 278
Johnstone, H. W. Jr. - 24, 29, 278
Jonas, H. - 228

Kahn, J. - 198
Kalinowski, G. - 26, 27, 278
Kennedy, G. A. - 10, 14, 35, 38-42, 47, 52, 54, 58-61, 71, 73, 81, 89, 236, 262, 278
Kinneavy, J. L. - 39, 45, 47, 52
Kopperschmidt, J. - 24
Krell, E. - 124
Kustas, G. L. - 115, 116, 279

LaLande, A. - 26
LaPorte, J. - 111, 135, 186, 187, 188, 189, 192
Lausberg, H. - 64, 68, 72, 110, 112, 113, 118, 122, 123, 128, 129, 133, 135, 137, 142, 143, 144, 145, 150, 156, 174, 194, 203, 237, 240, 279
LeBlond, J. M. - 36
Leeman, A. D. - 247
Leisegang, H. - 78, 228, 252, 263
Leopold, J. - 16, 92, 98, 99, 102, 213
Lesky, A. - 83
Licitra, A. - 28
Lienhard, J. T. - 46

Mack, B. L. - 5, 7, 8, 9, 10, 11, 13, 14, 29, 56, 59, 74, 194, 195, 223, 224, 225, 227, 264
Madden, E. H. - 42
Mangey, T. - 2, 230, 252
Martin, J. - 182

Marrou, H. - 17, 61, 79, 83, 88, 89, 152, 284
Massebieau, M. L. - 2, 90, 92, 114, 124, 264
McBurney, J. H. - 43
McHeman, J. - 234
Méasson, A. - 143, 144, 146, 148, 151, 152, 153, 265
Melnick, R. - 185
Ménard, J. E. - 12
Mendelson, A. - 206, 212, 225, 257, 265
Michel, A. - 1, 16, 17, 61, 62, 63, 65-70, 75, 81, 82, 99, 101, 116, 118, 212, 265, 279
Miller, M. - 15
Mirhady, D.C. - 47, 55
Molanger, J. - 117
Momigliano, A. - 158, 284
Mondésert, A. - 18, 109
Montefusco, L.C. - 61
Morrow, G. R. - 33
Mosès, A. - 200
Motzo, B. - 124
Mudd, C. S. - 43
Murphy, J. E. - 60, 61, 70, 80

Natanson, M. -6, 103
Nazzaro, A. V. - 6, 103
Nicol, E. - 25
Nikiprowetzky, V. - 3-8, 10, 11, 12, 16, 78, 91-96, 118, 187, 197, 198, 229, 234, 249, 254, 266, 267, 268, 272, 274
Norden, E. - 116
Norton, A. Q. - 234

Ochs, D. J. - 61
Olbrechts-Tyteca, L. - 17, 23, 24, 29, 75, 122, 123, 131, 278, 281
Oliver, R. T. - 24
Oltramare, A. - 152
Ophuijsen, J.M. van - 47
Otte, K. - 204

Pascher, J. - 78, 228, 266
Patillon, M. - 68, 240
Pearson, B. - 182
Pernot, L. - 110, 118, 281
Pfeiffer, R. - 80
Pellegrin, P. - 36
Pelletier, A. - 158, 159, 161, 163, 166, 168, 238, 240, 244, 267, 280
Pelletier, Y. - 47, 48, 49, 50
Perelman, C. - 23-25, 27-29, 31, 41, 53, 74, 75, 113, 118, 121-124, 131, 155, 276, 278, 280, 281
Petit, M. - 114, 115, 117-120, 123, 125, 126, 127, 128, 129, 170
Pöhlmann, W. - 11
Porter, S.E. - 97, 257

Pouilloux, J. - 18, 140, 153, 156, 157

Quimby, R. W. - 31, 32

Rabe, H. - 316-318
Radice, R. - 2, 6, 77, 252, 253, 267
Reale, G. - 95, 124, 180, 252, 267
Reitzenstein, R. - 6, 78
Reuters, F. H. - 159
Richards, I. A. - 39
Ricoeur, P. - 1, 60
Riposati, B. - 39, 47, 54, 68, 281
Ritter, A. H. - 6, 78
Roberts, W. R. - 80, 235, 274, 281
Robin, L. - 31
Robbins, C. J. - 237
Robbins, V. K. - 17, 74, 223, 224, 225
Runia, D. T. - 2, 3, 5, 6, 7, 9, 10, 69, 77, 79, 96, 182, 252, 253, 264, 268, 272

Sanders, E. P. - 86
Sandmel, S. - 87, 91, 93, 96, 109, 112, 158, 177, 179, 186, 198, 223, 225, 254, 260, 264, 268, 271
Sandys, J. E. - 80
Scroggs, R. - 83
Schürer, E. - 2, 114, 269
Seltzer, R. M. - 1, 86
Siegfried, C. - 1, 7, 93
Simon, M. - 86
Sloan, T. O. - 17
Sly, D. - 87, 269
Smallwood, E. M. - 135, 159, 165, 253, 269
Smith, R. M. - 80, 81, 83, 102, 282
Solmsen, F. - 37, 39, 41, 43, 44, 55, 60, 65, 282
Sonkowsky, R. - 199
Stegemann, W. - 83
Stein, E. M. - 8, 13, 93

Stowers, S. K. - 115, 116, 117, 282
Strugnell, J. - 159

Tcherikover, V. - 90
Terian, A. - 1, 10, 253, 270
Theiler, W. - 5, 9, 93, 95
Thiselton, A. C. - 103, 202, 204
Thompson, W. N. - 32, 33, 35
Throm, H. - 69, 116
Tobin, T. - 5, 10, 11, 12, 13, 182
Todorov, T. - 103
Toulmin, S. E. - 26, 27, 53, 282
Trotti, G. - 92

Vasoli, C. - 24
Vignaux, G. - 24, 25, 26, 28, 282
Völker, W. - 2, 6, 7, 8, 78, 92, 93, 94
Von Arnim, H. - 13

Wagner, W. H. - 176
Wallach, B. P. - 116, 117, 282
Walz, E. C. F. - 55, 192, 218, 221, 223, 224, 227
Wendland, P. - 2, 3, 54, 116, 230, 252
Whitaker, G. H. - 92, 153, 157, 186, 246, 251
White, E. E. - 28
White, J. L. - 159
Wikramanayke, G. H. - 46
Williamson, A.D.R. - 1, 77, 253, 271
Windisch, H. - 228
Winston, D. - 3, 7, 9, 16, 28, 79, 89, 91, 92, 95, 96, 204, 253, 257, 258, 263, 268, 271, 272
Wolfson, H. A. - 4, 6, 13, 78, 84, 88, 89, 90, 93, 96, 122, 180, 228, 258, 259, 264, 272
Wuellner, W. - 122

Zeller, E. - 6, 78

III - INDICES OF RHETORICAL TERMS

1. INDEX OF GREEK RHETORICAL TERMS

ἀδύνατον - 55
αἰτία - 51, 59, 67, 77, 223, 224
ἀληθές - 55, 145, 201, 227
ἀναγκαῖον - 55
ἀπόδειξις - 55, 98, 123, 157, 146
    ἄτεχνος ἀπόδειξις - 98, 153, 157
    ἔντεχνος ἀπόδειξις - 98, 153, 157
ἀπόφθεγμα - 121
ἀρετή - 38, 40, 218, 228, 232
ἀσυμφέρον - 55
ἄχρηστον - 55

γνώμη - 57
γραμματικός - 90

διαίρεσις - 11, 15, 36, 37, 67
διατριβή - 116
διήγησις - 98
δίκαιον - 55
δόξα - 57, 121, 145, 192
δυνατόν - 55

ἐγκύκλιος παιδεία - 88, 90, 91, 152, 214, 224, 228, 232
ἐγκώμιον - 59. 224
εἶδος (τὰ εἴδη) - 44, 48, 54, 70, 246
εἰκός - 45, 46, 47, 54, 98, 145, 193
ἔλεγχος - 57, 59
ἐναντίον - 56, 59, 170, 225, 247
ἐνθύμημα - 41, 43, 51, 54, 57, 72, 77, 101, 184
ἔπαινος - 59
ἐπαγωγή - 51
ἐπίλογος - 58, 77, 98, 246
ἐπιχείρημα - 64, 66, 72
ἐργασία - 5;9, 223, 224
ἔργον - 37, 38
εὔνοια - 40
εὕρεσις - 58, 98, 103

ἡδύ - 55
ἦθος - 39, 40, 41, 43, 44, 45, 50, 51, 53, 58, 121, 145, 174, 227, 228

θέσις - 68, 69, 116

ἴδια εἴδη - 49, 50
ἴδιος τόπος - 47

καλόν (τὸ) - 55, 227
κεκριμένα (τὰ) - 56
κοινός - 48
    κοινὰ εἴδη - 40
    κοινὸς τόπος - 47, 49, 50
κόμμα - 237
κρίσις - 59, 77, 195, 225
κῶλον - 226, 227, 229, 240, 242, 243

λέξις - 58
λόγος - 225, 37, 40, 41, 43, 44, 45, 50, 53, 58, 99, 100, 101, 123, 136, 144, 145, 153, 174, 182, 185, 187, 188, 197, 199, 201, 203, 205, 209, 210, 213, 214, 215, 225, 240, 246
    λόγος ἐνδιάθετος - 100, 201, 212, 249
    λόγος προφορικός - 100, 210, 212, 249

μαρτυρία - 55, 77, 153, 195, 225
μνήμη - 52, 98

νόμιμον - 55

οἰκονομία - 98
ὅμοιον (τὸ) - 56

πάθος - 37-39, 40, 41, 43, 44, 45, 50, 51, 53, 58, 121, 123, 145, 170, 174, 175, 227
παραβολή - 51, 59, 77, 78, 150, 225
παράδειγμα - 41, 44, 46, 51, 52, 54, 57, 59, 64, 72, 77, 78, 121, 194, 225
παράκλησις - 59, 225
πίστις - 35, 39, 41, 43, 44, 45, 46, 47, 50, 53, 56, 57, 58, 77, 78, 98, 112, 153, 155
    πίστεις ἄτεχνοι - 39, 57, 98
    πίστεις ἔντεχνοι - 39, 43, 57, 98
πρᾶγμα - 44, 58
προγύμνασμα - 55, 59, 69, 83, 90, 150
πρόθεσις - 58, 77, 155
προοίμιον - 58, 77, 98, 246
πρότασις - 48

ῥάδιον - 55
ῥητορική - 58
ῥήτωρ - 90

σημεῖον - 44, 46, 57, 71
   σημεῖα ἀναγκαῖα - 46
   σημεῖα ἀνώνυμα - 46
σόφισμα - 205
στοιχεῖον - 49
συλλογισμός - 64, 66, 72
συμφέρον - 55, 227
σοφιστής - 212

τάξις - 58, 98
τεκμήριον - 45, 46, 71, 98
τελικὰ κεφάλαια - 55
τέχνη - 42, 58, 61, 68, 70, 99, 103, 104, 193, 105, 223
   τέχνη ῥητορική - 39, 58

τόπος - 47, 49, 50, 70, 98
   τόποι ἐκ τοῦ ἐναντίου - 56, 77
   τόποι ἐκ τῶν ἐναντίων - 50
   τόποι περὶ ἀδίκου - 50
   τόποι περὶ δυνάτου καὶ ἀδυνάτου - 50

ὑπόθεσις - 68
ὑπόκρισις - 58, 98

φράσις - 98
φρόνησις - 40, 148

χαρακτήρ - 76
χρεία - 55, 59, 74, 76, 90, 121, 150, 218, 219, 223, 224, 225, 226, 227, 248
   παράφρασις τῆς χρείας - 59

ψυχαγωγία - 37

2. INDEX OF LATIN RHETORICAL TERMS

amplificatio - 59, 121, 141, 148, 163, 170, 171, 191, 192, 203, 238
   amplificatio per ratiocinationem - 324
approbatio - 64, 126, 127, 139, 163, 181, 183, 199, 213, 214
argumentatio - 28, 39, 63, 75, 72, 111, 112, 123, 125, 138, 139, 160, 165, 187, 190, 193, 194, 201, 204, 207
   argumentatio per ratiocinationem - 125
argumentum - 72, 144
assumptio - 64, 126, 127, 139, 165, 179, 181, 183, 199, 214
   assumptionis approbatio - 64, 127, 139, 163, 183, 214
auctoritas - 72, 124

beneuolentia - 160
breuitas - 174, 124

causa - 68, 110, 131, 160
clementia - 135
commemoratio - 116, 240
commiseratio - 134, 170
comparatio - 156
complexio - 59, 63, 64, 125, 126, 127, 139, 140, 142, 149, 156, 179, 181, 184, 188, 192, 197, 204, 214
conclusio - 58, 60, 63, 110, 151, 205, 216, 218, 221
confirmatio - 26, 53, 58, 59, 110, 112, 113, 125, 133, 140, 145, 148, 156, 166, 162, 190, 201
confutatio - 58
conquestio - 121, 135, 152, 170, 171, 192
contrarium - 60, 72, 126, 150, 156, 195, 202, 205, 216, 217, 220

delectare - 110, 144, 145
deprecatio - 134
descriptio - 67, 137, 143
digressio - 72, 100, 110, 113, 128, 143, 165, 246
dispositio - 32, 34, 35, 221
dissimile - 72
distributio - 137, 220
diuisio - 58, 66, 136
docere - 110, 145

enumeratio - 63, 120, 152, 170
excursio - 116
exemplum - 59, 60, 72, 75, 113, 119, 125, 128, 150, 163, 191, 205, 216, 217, 219, 260

exordium - 58, 110, 119, 123, 135, 136, 138, 160, 237
exornatio - 59, 125, 141, 148, 156, 163, 187, 190, 191, 195, 201, 203
expeditio - 215
expolitio - 215, 219
expositio - 116

genus - 37, 156
   genera amplificationis - 141
   genus demonstratiuum - 68, 137
   genus uniuersum - 69
gradatio - 127, 129, 134, 153, 169-173, 201, 238

honestas - 160

inclusio - 120, 123, 138, 169, 197, 204, 209, 214, 246
incrementum - 141
indignatio - 170
inductio - 63, 64
interrogatio - 125, 134, 135, 146, 156, 163, 169, 173, 191, 193, 212, 220, 240
inuentio - 221, 233
iudicatio - 59

locus - 72, 73, 178
   loci a persona - 73, 203
   loci a re - 73, 203
   loci communes - 173
   locus a contrario - 120, 124, 125, 126, 127, 156, 157, 163, 171, 178, 189, 191, 193, 210, 228
   locus a minore ad maius - 125, 126, 145, 152, 156, 193, 201, 206, 228, 229
   locus honestatis - 162

maximae propositiones - 70
mouere - 110, 144, 145

narratio - 58, 72, 110, 111, 112, 113, 128, 133, 136, 143, 144, 145, 160, 165, 180, 195
   narratio continua - 110
notatio - 66

oratio - 75
orator - 69, 101
   orator excellens - 69, 101
ornatus - 114, 174

partitio - 58, 66

peroratio - 58, 110, 135, 136, 142, 151, 160, 170, 174
poetica fabula, fabellae - 72
praeteritio - 113, 123, 146, 171
principium - 160
probatio - 111, 112, 119, 123-125, 127, 136, 138
proemium - 69
pronuntiatio - 60, 150, 205, 206, 210, 216
propositio - 59, 64, 75, 119, 125, 126, 127, 138, 139, 140, 147, 160, 162, 163, 178, 180, 188, 189, 193, 213
propositionis approbatio - 64, 125, 126, 213
propositum - 68, 69

quaestio finita, infinita - 68

ratio - 59, 60, 125, 134, 140, 148, 150, 156, 163, 187, 189, 193, 201, 205, 206, 210, 216, 219, 242
   ratio posita in affectibus - 170
ratiocinatio - 63-66, 69, 71, 72, 125, 126, 127, 139, 145, 147, 173, 178, 180, 193, 199, 204, 213, 238
recapitulatio - 170
repetitio - 170

reprehensio - 58
res - 60, 150, 205, 206, 216, 219
   res iudicata - 125, 195

sedes argumentorum - 70, 73
sententia - 141, 150, 191
signum necessarium, non necessarium - 71
simile - 59, 60, 72, 125, 141, 148, 150, 163, 191, 195, 202, 205, 216, 217, 220
   similitudo - 72, 126, 150, 156, 217, 229, 242
   similitudo per conlationem - 126
   similitudo per contrarium - 126, 195, 202
status causae - 122, 131
   status finitionis - 137, 143
   status qualitatis - 137, 143
   status quantitatis - 137
subiectione rationes - 150

testimonium - 119, 220
tractatio - 59, 60, 149, 205, 210, 216
transitio - 110, 111, 123, 145, 164, 226
transitus - 138

uestigia - 71
utilitas - 160

INDICES 299

3. INDEX OF ENGLISH RHETORICAL TERMS

accusation - 55, 56
alliteration - 141, 240
amplification - 35, 56, 57, 74, 97, 115, 116, 141, 142, 148, 156, 159, 163, 196, 221, 237
analogy - 34-36, 56, 60, 64, 67, 120, 121, 125, 126, 147, 150, 151, 164, 177, 181, 193, 202, 208, 220, 224, 225, 229, 231, 238, 240,
antithesis - 35, 137, 218, 220, 242, 243, 245, 247
appeal - 40, 44, 45, 70, 119, 121, 122, 132, 133, 134, 145, 147, 159, 160, 166, 170, 171, 172, 173, 191, 212, 240, 248
   emotional - 44, 122
   ethical - 145
   logical - 240
   pathetic - 121, 173
   psychological - 119, 147, 191, 212
argument - 4, 9, 11, 15, 18, 26, 27, 28, 33, 37, 39, 40, 42, 45, 51-54, 56, 58-60, 62, 64-66, 71-73, 75, 119, 124-126, 130133-136, 139-141, 146, 147, 155-157, 161, 163, 164, 166, 167, 171, 176, 178-181, 185, 187, 188, 190, 191, 196, 198-200, 206, 208, 212-214, 217, 220, 221, 224, 225, 231, 232, 238, 240, 248
   a fortiori - 135, 138, 146
   by analogy - 208, 224, 225, 238
   by authority - 119, 155
   complete - 18, 35, 56, 58-60, 74, 75, 125, 147, 176
   ethical - 40, 51, 146, 154
   etymological - 139, 141
   intrinsic - 66
   logical - 40, 43, 44, 46, 65, 120, 126, 176, 239, 249
   necessary - 63
   pathetic - 40
   psychological - 43
   rational - 71
   supporting - 56, 59, 74, 156, 205, 225
argumentation - 14-19, 23-29, 31, 34-41, 43-60, 62, 71, 73-75, 77, 79, 83, 91, 92, 96, 98-102, 104, 105, 108, 112, 124, 128, 131, 139, 140, 157, 160, 162, 164, 165, 171, 174, 176, 177, 178, 182, 184, 185, 187, 191, 193, 194, 197, 199, 201, 203, 208, 211, 212, 223, 227, 233, 248-250
   apodeictic - 124
   enthymematic - 50, 52, 165
   line of - 39, 57, 60, 73, 124, 162, 194, 211, 233

   logical - 40, 43, 44, 46, 65, 176, 203, 249
   paradigmatic - 52, 53, 165, 167, 196, 217
   philosophical - 53, 67, 89
   psychological - 43
   rhetorical - 14, 21, 28, 39, 41, 43, 45, 50, 53, 66, 75, 79, 92, 96, 104, 108, 185, 208, 250
   scheme, schema of - 53, 67, 104, 108, 174, 180, 182, 199
   strategy of - 18, 35, 49
   structure of - 23, 34, 39, 53, 56, 74
   technique of - 16, 17, 18, 37, 212
   theory of - 24, 30, 31, 38, 41, 50, 60, 63, 70, 71, 79, 83, 102, 104, 128, 223, 248
art, rhetorical - 32, 33, 38, 42, 86, 205, 206
audience - 25, 26, 28, 29, 39, 40, 41, 43, 48, 104, 117, 118, 121, 123, 124, 128, 131, 132, 137, 154, 158, 160, 189, 198, 208, 233
authority - 40, 61, 110, 119, 155, 182, 186, 191, 195, 200, 214, 225, 239, 240

cause - 36, 37, 38, 40, 46, 49, 51, 55, 59, 72, 73, 121, 132, 137, 144, 147, 161, 162, 165, 170, 173, 180, 188, 203, 213, 214, 218, 222
   accessible - 55
   agreeable - 55, 57
   convenient - 55
   just - 55-57, 173, 192
   legitimate - 55, 57
   necessary - 55
   noble - 55, 57
   possible - 55
chiasm - 123, 150, 199, 243, 260
climax - 14, 114, 127, 145, 159, 169, 191, 201
code, rhetorical - 16, 17
commentary - 5, 7, 9, 12-18, 38, 55, 93, 94, 95, 98, 100, 104, 132, 143, 151, 158, 176, 184, 187, 197, 215, 216, 226, 227, 249
comparison - 10, 14, 35, 51, 63, 72, 149, 191, 195, 211, 214, 217, 228, 230
conclusion - 15, 26, 32, 33, 38, 41, 42, 48-53, 57, 63-65, 67, 72-74, 93, 104, 114, 117, 120, 127, 131, 136, 140, 149, 164, 170, 175, 179, 200, 204, 208, 211, 214, 222, 225, 231, 243, 248, 250
confirmation - 55, 57, 64, 88, 111, 112, 131, 248

contrary - 34, 36, 56, 73, 90, 92, 95, 110, 154, 157, 158, 205, 220, 221, 228

deduction - 27, 52, 62, 63, 71, 75, 179, 185
defense - 14, 55, 56, 67, 82, 100, 107, 111, 132, 152, 174, 176, 212, 217
definition - 13, 25, 29, 30, 35-39, 42, 45, 62, 66-68, 101, 110, 112, 115, 119, 136, 137, 143, 158, 163, 171, 178, 216, 238
   Ciceronian - 67
   descriptive - 37, 67
   dieretic - 37, 45, 67, 177
   epideictic - 137
   etymological - 38, 67, 177, 209
   periphrastic - 67
   persuasive - 37
   teleological - 37
demonstration - 25, 27, 36, 37, 42, 43, 54, 101, 104, 157, 163, 175, 179, 190, 194, 199, 205, 222, 224
   of a thesis - 157, 205, 222
   rhetorical - 43, 54, 194
description - 37, 62, 110, 112, 144, 240, 241
diatribe - 115-119
digression - 98, 124, 125, 130, 140
dilemma - 63, 172
discourse - 4, 12, 24-26, 28, 29, 32, 34, 37-41, 43, 44, 47, 49, 52, 53, 55, 56, 57, 68, 73, 75, 81, 83, 90, 92, 93, 96, 97, 98, 100, 101, 103, 104, 107, 109, 110, 112, 114, 123, 131-133, 136, 142, 143, 145, 146, 149, 150-154, 158, 160, 164, 165, 170, 174-176, 197, 198, 201, 202, 210, 212, 219, 223, 225, 227, 233, 235, 236, 237, 239, 248, 250
   argumentative - 28, 34, 40, 53
   deliberative - 52-54, 55, 57, 159, 165, 170
   epideictic - 32, 55, 110, 117, 118, 131, 136, 143, 152, 153, 237
   forensic/judicial - 53, 55, 57, 160
   oratorical/rhetorical - 39, 41, 47, 49, 55, 68, 98, 239, 248
   symbouleutic - 136
   true - 101, 109
dissuasion - 55, 168
division - 31, 36, 38, 39, 47, 64, 72, 92, 98, 112, 113, 114, 212, 237

eloquence - 61, 73, 80, 100, 101, 103, 107, 132, 169, 186, 208, 209
emotions - 40, 45, 116, 121, 139, 160, 173
encomium - 9, 33, 55, 56
enthymeme - 26, 32, 35, 41-43, 45-54, 57, 58, 64, 66, 120, 124, 126, 127, 130, 131, 136, 140, 163, 167, 174, 189, 193, 199, 200, 204, 222, 223
   structural - 26, 124, 126, 127, 131, 136, 189, 222
enumeration - 63, 137, 143
epichirema - 63-66, 69, 72, 147, 161
epilogue - 44, 114, 142, 212, 231, 232
erotema - 138, 168
etymology - 9, 37, 38, 66, 67, 68, 156, 158, 187, 198
example - 4, 6, 14, 15, 32, 35, 37, 40, 41, 43, 45, 50, 51-60, 62, 64, 67, 71, 72, 75, 80, 90, 99, 111-113, 115, 116, 121, 124, 125, 128, 129, 131, 133, 143, 148, 152, 158, 165, 166, 168, 169, 170, 177-179, 191, 193, 197, 205, 209-211, 217, 219, 221, 223-225, 231, 235, 238, 242
   historical - 52, 112
exercises
   preparatory - 55, 90
   rhetorical - 82
exhortation - 55, 56, 115, 131, 149, 150, 151, 152, 171, 197, 212, 217, 221, 225, 230

fable - 51, 52
figure - 1, 3, 4, 25, 27, 65, 74, 75, 77, 87, 91, 97, 116, 119, 134, 137, 141, 143, 144, 146, 150, 165, 166, 172, 173, 176, 178, 193, 197, 208, 210, 215, 216, 218, 224, 238, 240, 245, 248-250
   argumentative - 75, 97, 137, 172, 173, 208, 210
   rhetorical - 24, 27, 240

genre - 5, 10, 38, 47-49, 55, 56, 66, 68, 69, 79, 83, 98, 110, 115-119, 123, 142, 143, 158, 204
   epideictic - 110, 118, 123, 142
   of discourse - 47, 48, 49, 55, 56, 68, 83, 98, 118, 143, 158

induction - 45, 51, 52, 62, 63, 75
inference - 49, 50, 51, 63, 90
investigation - 4, 18, 33, 35, 38, 55

judgments, previous - 56, 57

maxim - 50, 51, 57, 90, 120, 153, 224
minimalization - 56

narration - 113, 133, 144, 166

opinion - 10, 12, 26, 31, 32, 33, 38, 40, 44, 52, 57, 63, 87, 98, 102, 113, 119, 139, 153, 155, 192, 197, 198, 235, 249

orator - 25, 26, 28, 32, 33, 34, 35, 38, 39-41, 43, 45, 48, 50, 51, 53, 60, 62, 65, 69, 74, 75, 80-82, 93, 101, 110, 111, 118, 119, 132, 154, 237
  ideal - 35, 60, 62, 71, 73
  perfect - 32, 153
  true - 38, 145
oratory - 29, 47, 61, 66, 80, 82, 131, 198, 206, 207, 235, 236, 242
order of argument 73
ornamentation - 29

paradigm - 41, 52, 53, 95, 129, 137,155, 166, 182, 194, 224
parallelism - 32, 102, 126, 129, 145, 149, 171, 243, 245
paraphrase - 91, 224
period - 3, 4, 10, 23, 54, 58, 60, 67, 71, 74, 79, 80, 84, 89, 109, 132, 139, 154, 167, 185, 194, 235, 236, 237, 239, 240, 242-248, 250
  oratorical - 235, 236
peroration - 122, 169, 237
persuasion - 28, 29, 33, 34, 39-44, 57, 58, 62, 97, 138, 165, 175, 201, 213, 214, 223
place, common - 48, 50, 70, 155, 188
probability - 46
proem - 133, 137, 138, 143, 145, 155, 160
proof - 12, 16, 27, 38-41, 47, 52, 53, 56, 59, 64, 65, 67, 71, 73, 74, 75, 113, 124, 127, 133, 136, 147, 156, 157, 162, 179, 190, 194, 199, 200, 210, 212, 218, 224, 226, 233
  artificial - 71
  common - 45
  ethical - 71
  pathetic - 71
  primary - 56, 57, 59, 156, 190
  specific - 45
psychology - 31, 34, 44, 199

questions - 75, 92, 113, 173, 197, 203, 211

reason - 14, 25, 27, 28, 40, 43, 45, 50, 51, 59, 60, 65, 70, 72, 91, 100, 101, 102, 113, 117, 119, 126, 127, 132, 135, 137, 139, 141, 144, 145, 148, 153, 162, 178, 181, 183, 187, 189, 191, 201, 206, 210, 215, 220, 224, 225, 227
reasoning - 25-28, 37, 39, 41, 42, 45-47, 49, 50-53, 64, 65, 74, 75, 100, 111, 119, 124, 127, 128, 139, 141, 148, 156, 161, 164, 169, 173, 185, 189, 191, 192, 194, 196, 199, 201, 210, 212, 222, 235
  analogical - 141, 148, 156, 189, 191, 199, 201

analytical - 41
apodeictic - 124, 157
deductive - 42, 46, 51, 55
dialectical - 41
enthymematic - 49, 51, 52, 57, 111
inductive - 41
logical - 119
paradigmatic - 52
probatory - 26, 194
rhetorical - 46, 235
sophistic - 212
syllogistic - 53, 64, 173, 192
rhetoric - 12, 14, 16-19, 23-25, 27, 29, 31-34, 37-39, 41, 44, 45, 56, 61, 66, 68-71, 75, 81-83, 86, 87, 89, 92, 97-104, 107, 109, 132, 158-160, 175-177, 198, 199, 204, 205, 208, 212, 223, 225, 233, 234, 248-250
  art of - 31, 59, 60, 61
  definition of - 29, 39
  false - 32, 100, 109
  Hellenistic - 15, 58, 86, 117, 155, 179, 236, 251
  new - 25, 31
  perfect - 70
  philosophical - 18, 40, 41, 42, 72, 76, 77, 101
  sophistic - 34, 101, 102, 251, 252
  strategy of - 101
  structure of - 19, 28, 41, 42, 109, 111, 159, 162, 178, 190, 215, 216, 221, 225, 236, 251, 252
  theory of - 16, 19, 30, 33-35, 37, 41, 43, 45, 56, 60, 64, 76, 77, 81, 100, 101, 251
  traditional - 19, 28, 46, 70
  true - 33, 35, 47, 63
rhythm - 77, 237, 239, 241, 242, 245

sophism - 16, 33-35, 41, 43, 56, 75, 77, 100-103, 119, 121, 130, 139, 191, 197, 199, 200, 202, 204, 207-209, 212, 214, 216, 224, 251, 252
species - 50, 51, 57, 58, 68, 103, 204, 206, 211, 212, 241
structure - 5, 10-12, 16, 18, 23-28, 30-32, 34-36, 38-40, 45, 50, 53, 54, 56-60, 63, 65, 66, 73-75, 79, 83, 87, 94, 97, 98, 100, 104-105, 107-110, 115, 117, 124, 126-128, 130, 134, 135, 138, 139, 142, 145-147, 152, 154, 155, 157-161, 163, 167, 171, 174-176, 178, 179, 181, 183, 184, 186-191, 193, 194, 197, 199, 201, 203, 204, 210, 212-215, 218, 219, 223-226, 229, 233-235, 238-250
  formal - 16, 18, 30, 34, 35, 38, 39, 50, 57-59, 63, 65, 73, 74, 98, 104, 109, 117, 127, 161, 187, 247, 250

periodic - 108, 234, 238, 240, 244
rhetorical - 19, 28, 41, 42, 109, 111, 159, 162, 178, 190, 215, 216, 221, 225, 236, 251, 252
rhythmic - 108, 240, 241, 242
style - 16, 17, 29, 32, 38, 69, 70, 92, 97, 115-117, 119, 123, 136, 167, 173, 199, 203, 204, 234, 235, 237-240, 242, 243, 245-247, 250
  diatribic - 116, 117
  periodic - 234, 235, 237, 240, 242, 243, 245, 246, 247
syllogism - 36, 37, 41, 42, 43, 45, 46, 64, 66, 67, 69, 72, 75, 121, 126, 136, 146, 174, 178, 239
  rhetorical - 42, 46, 64, 72, 75, 121, 126, 146, 174, 178, 239

testimony - 1, 61, 79, 82, 88, 157, 158, 162, 182, 212, 217, 220, 231
thesis - 7, 10, 25, 27, 31, 33, 34, 35, 55, 59, 60, 62, 68, 69, 70, 75, 86, 90, 102, 104, 110, 113, 114, 116, 120, 125, 128, 151, 152, 154, 155, 157, 176-179, 181, 187, 192, 193, 196, 197, 204, 205, 208, 209, 210, 216, 222-227, 231-233, 235, 240, 248-250
topic - 18, 26, 27, 120, 141, 145, 146, 156, 158, 162, 167, 173, 184, 193, 206, 209
tradition, rhetorical - 30, 33, 39, 50, 58, 63, 70, 79, 83, 104, 221, 225, 234, 249, 250

vituperation - 55, 56

www.ingramcontent.com/pod-product-compliance
Lightning Source LLC
Chambersburg PA
CBHW031706230426
43668CB00006B/127